PASSPORT'S G

ETHNIC

NEW YORK

*A Complete Guide
to the Many Faces
& Cultures of
New York*

SECOND EDITION

MARK LEEDS

Printed on recyclable paper

PASSPORT BOOKS

a division of *NTC Publishing Group*
Lincolnwood, Illinois USA

Library of Congress Cataloging-in-Publication Data

Leeds, Mark.
    Ethnic New York : a complete guide to the many faces & cultures of
New York / Mark Leeds. -- 2nd ed.
        p.   cm.
    Includes index.
    ISBN 0-8442-9633-3 (pbk.)
    1. New York (N.Y.)--Guidebooks. 2. Ethnology--New York (N.Y.)
3. New York (N.Y.)--Social life and customs.   I. Title.
F128.18.L397   1995
917.47'10443--dc20   95-38970
                                                           CIP

Cover Photos
New York Convention and Visitors Bureau
American Egg Board, Government of India Tourist Office,
Greater Milwaukee Convention and Visitors Bureau, Inc.,
Terry Farmer/Illinois Department of Commerce and Community Affairs

Contents

Introduction   ix

Introduction to Second Edition   xi

Chapter One   The Melting Pot   1

   History   1

   Place Marks   8

   Museums and Archives   13

   Organizations   15

   Extras   16

   Celebrations   18

Chapter Two   The Founders   21

   History   21

   Founders' Place Marks   24

   Founders' Organizations and Archives   34

   The British Table   36

   British Style   38

Chapter Three   Mittel Europa — 42

Germans — 42

Hungarians — 59

Czechs — 66

Chapter Four   The Scandinavians — 73

History — 73

Bay Ridge — 80

Manhattan — 85

Finns — 90

Chapter Five   The Irish — 96

History — 96

Manhattan—That Old Gang of Mine — 103

Irish Bronx — 113

Irish Queens—Woodside — 120

Irish Brooklyn—Bay Ridge — 122

Irish Celebrations — 125

Chapter Six   The Italians — 127

History — 127

The Old Neighborhoods — 134

Little Italy Uptown — 151

Neighborhoods at Mid-Passage — 157

The Secular Festa — 177

Chapter Seven   The Jews   179

History   179

The Lower East Side   186

I'll Take Manhattan   199

Jewish Brooklyn   207

Chapter Eight   The Greeks   234

History   234

Astoria—Little Athens   237

Manhattan   246

Celebrations   250

Chapter Nine   The Slavs   253

Poles   253

Ukrainians   273

Russians   281

Chapter Ten   The Arabs   286

History   286

Atlantic Avenue Neighborhood   292

Little Lebanon in Bay Ridge   301

Manhattan Arabs   304

Celebrations and Solemn Occasions   307

Chapter Eleven   The African Americans   308

History   308

Harlem   315

Bedford-Stuyvesant—Brooklyn Revival   329

West Indians   334

Haitians   348

Chapter Twelve   The Hispanics   **356**

Puerto Ricans   356

Dominicans   368

Cubans   375

The Other Cubans   379

Mexicans   380

Sunset Park—Latino Renewal   385

The Americas of Jackson Heights   390

Brazilians   397

Little Spain in Chelsea   400

Hispanic-American Day   404

Chapter Thirteen   The Far East Asians   **405**

Chinese   405

Koreans   444

Japanese Manhattan   456

Filipinos   462

Chapter Fourteen   The East Indians   **469**

History   469

Little India on Lexington Avenue   471

Little India in the East Village   476

Festivals   477

Little India in Flushing   479

Little India on 74th Street   481

Index   **487**

Maps

Historic Flushing   31

Ridgewood   55

Sunset Park   93

Bainbridge Avenue   114

Woodside   121

Mulberry Street   135

Court Street to Carroll Street   176

Kings Highway   231

Atlantic Avenue   293

Bedford-Stuyvesant   330

West Indian Crown Heights   338

Sunset Park   387

Chinatown   410

Sunset Park/Chinatown   435

Manhattan/Little Manila   467

Jackson Heights/Little India   483

Introduction

New York is an ethnic city with different nations in different territories. The cityscape changes and so do the faces, customs, and languages. It's around the world from barrio to Chinatown to *shtetl*. All any explorer needs is a subway token to cross the Alps and Andes.

Passport's Guide to Ethnic New York is a passport to foreign places right in the city, to Little Odessa and Aleppo in Flatbush. It is an introduction to and an appreciation of the nations of New York, from Chinese at the tip of Manhattan to Italians in the northern Bronx. It is a cultural itinerary of ethnic restaurants, stores, galleries, museums, and festivals.

The city doesn't stand still; restaurants come and go, ethnics pick up stakes, galleries go broke, and people are always changing the hours. The no-frills store or restaurant of yesteryear is the expensive trend-setting place of tomorrow. In New York, ethnic or not, things are liable to change; the city is always running ahead of itself.

Passport's Guide to Ethnic New York doesn't try to be comprehensive. The foreign nations of New York are endless and the ethnic scene is constantly shifting. The ethnic selections for this book, which span from New Amsterdam to the Haitian and Vietnamese boat people, are based on numbers, influence, history, and present-day visibility. No doubt, some groups that seem insignificant today will be the power brokers of the future.

New York is a subway city. Parking is a problem and taxis can be prohibitively expensive; buses are too slow, especially during the day. The subway is no beauty to behold; it is New York true grit and part of the texture of the city. It is used by millions of commuters and its dangers during daylight hours can be overstated.

Traveling in the city and trekking to and through ethnic neighborhoods is not shopping-mall antiseptic. New York, high rent or transitional, requires a heads-up attitude and a certain amount of caution. It's best to visit any unfamiliar area during the day. At the same time, minority neighborhoods shouldn't be considered forbidden zones.

New York is a city of regions; in the English tradition they are called boroughs. The boroughs, five in all, are the principalities of the ethnics. Manhattan has the reputation and the skyscrapers while the other boroughs are sometimes belittled as the outer boroughs of bridge and tunnel people. Yet the images and the reality are different. Brooklyn, the Bronx, Staten Island, and Queens are not burnt-out districts or bland suburbias. Like Manhattan, they have their cultures and people from many other countries; they are places to discover.

Don't try to be inconspicuous when exploring ethnic New York. It is obvious in most places, as in an actual foreign country, that you are a stranger. Ask questions and look (don't gawk) and listen. If you are genuinely enthusiastic the local residents will appreciate the interest and open up, although some people inevitably will turn off. Don't be disappointed.

The transportation directions for ethnic New York are the most convenient, direct, and accessible routes. There are no milk-train locals or roundabout buses. The jumping-off points are the midtown stations between 42nd Street and 59th Street. Most of Manhattan is easy to get around in, with avenues running east and west and the streets running north and south. The older Manhattan neighborhoods like Chinatown and the Lower East Side are exceptions.

Passport's Guide to Ethnic New York doesn't give the admission charges for places of interest or the prices for restaurants because they often change. It does indicate whether there is an admission or contribution, and in New York a contribution is anything above a penny. In ethnic areas restaurants tend to be reasonably priced or inexpensive—very inexpensive—and the exceptions are clearly mentioned.

Passport's Guide to Ethnic New York is not a guide to New York City, it is a guide to New York City's ethnics. The Empire State Building and the Metropolitan Museum of Art are mentioned as footnotes to ethnic experiences. The nuts and bolts of New York touring and lodging sights are left to other books.

This round-the-world tour of New York covers a lot of territory, and I would like to take this opportunity to thank my guides in the neighborhoods and ethnic communities for their extraordinary assistance. Most of all I would like to thank my wife, Dee, without whom this book would never have been written.

Introduction to Second Edition

Since the publication of the first edition of *Passport's Guide to Ethnic New York* in 1989, the ethnic map of the city has radically realigned its borders and contours. Ethnics from the East and West, from the Pacific rim to the Sierra Madre, have arrived in record numbers. The brand new following on the heels of the most recent, has lead to further internal urban emigrations.

Ethnic populations from places like The People's Republic of China, Pakistan, Lebanon, The Dominican Republic, Yemen, Turkey, and the Philippines have expanded their enclaves and gained even greater visibility. They are now familiar enough to be taken for granted by the ever impervious New Yorkers. Meanwhile, the younger generation of ethnics is dressed in baggies and listening to rap and hip-hop.

A vaunted new world order and revamped immigration laws have encouraged fresh ethnic waves from western, southern, and eastern Europe. The new old immigrants from Poland, Ireland, and other nations across the Atlantic are reuniting with their established compatriots and are already on the road to assimilation.

In the 1990s the city continues to be renewed and revitalized by new immigrant populations, inspired and motivated by the American dream. One day they're cab drivers, short-order cooks, sewing machine operators, or retail clerks and the next they are opening stores and restaurants or even marketing new products and services. The latest New Yorkers are reclaiming crumbling neighborhoods and reinventing music and art forms through the force of their cultural identity.

As I re-explored the nations of New York to revise *Passport's Guide to Ethnic New York,* I was amazed by the rapid pace and extent of the city's ethnic transformations. In five years and less, I have seen scattered residences, stores, and restaurants become real ethnic communities with their own distinctive character and institutions. I have watched these communities prosper, become ethnic cosmopolitan and Gotham glossy. The new nations of New York have even multiplied, following subway and bus lines into other neighborhoods and boroughs.

The sheer magnitude of contemporary ethnic New York and its susceptibility to quicksilver change make it difficult to pin down on paper. Despite the best intentions, it is not possible (or even productive) to aim to be comprehensive and inclusive. Tough choices had to be made. The ethnic groups, neighborhoods, associations, museums, landmarks, restaurants, businesses, traditions, and festivals included here can only be a representative sample. I have tried to make selections that are compelling, distinctive, and accessible, and that both provide pleasure and convey the essence of a particular ethnic experience.

In this edition of *Passport's Guide to Ethnic New York,* I continue to provide the days open along with opening and closing hours, where possible, for my ethnic New York neighborhood destinations. Reader feedback suggests that posted days and hours may sometimes prove unreliable and are subject to change on short notice. The only foolproof method when planning an outing (and also to learn the prices) is to call in advance and ask.

Since writing this book, incidents have marred the tranquillity of a few of the city's most fascinating ethnic enclaves. The streets of Bensonhurst rang with gunfire and there were three days of looting and rioting in Crown Heights. These summer eruptions reveal the tensions and misconceptions that sometimes underlie the relations between ethnics in New York. Though the city is still feeling the repercussions of these events, I would not in any case issue a "travel advisory" for any community covered in this book. I do recommend daylight touring in the city's more marginal areas and an approach that is alert and cautious.

As with the original edition of the book, I owe a special debt to the ethnics themselves who patiently helped me view their communities from an "insider's" vantage point. They were gracious guides, generous with both their time and insights. I would again like to thank my wife, Dee, for her ungrudging support in this demanding and difficult undertaking. Her clear understanding of the book's overall purpose helped to keep me on track. Special thanks also go to my editor, Dan Spinella, for his encouragement and astute advice.

The Melting Pot

History

From the days when New York was New Amsterdam the city has been a melting pot. Whether by design or accident, New York has attracted a polyglot pluralistic population. Father Jogues, a French Jesuit missionary to the Mohawk Indians, was the first to comment; he was amazed to find eighteen nationalities in a colony of less than a thousand inhabitants.

Some Dutch authorities, like the terrible-tempered Peter Stuyvesant, were alarmed by all the foreigners with their "heretical" religious practices and questionable morality, but personal preferences took second place to populating the colony. In 1664 New Amsterdam became British property, but a policy of open immigration continued. Queen Anne, putting the good of New York above any other considerations, encouraged the emigration of thousands of Palantine Germans to New York, and the city entered the eighteenth century with the British representing less than half of an ethnically and racially diverse population.

While the American Revolution attracted freedom fighters from France to Eastern Europe, it generally slowed the flow of new New Yorkers. The pace of immigration picked up again in 1790 with the announcement of the new Republic's two-year (for whites only) waiting period for naturalization. America was the hothouse for democracy and all European comers were welcome. Michael de Crevecoeur, a French ethnic New Yorker, said it all, originating the melting-pot imagery: "There individuals of all na-

1

tions are melted into a new race of men, whose labors and posterity will one day cause great changes in the world."

The Louisiana Purchase of 1803 opened up the West to more land-hungry immigrants. The majority had first landed in New York and some, who ran out of money or ran into opportunity, stayed. The War of 1812, with its naval blockade, briefly held back the immigration tide, and then it hit its stride again in the Port of New York in the 1820s.

The Erie Canal, which began construction in 1817, brought immigrant laborers to New York for pick-and-shovel jobs. Once completed this upstate waterway gave the city access to the resources of the northwest frontier, and a clear advantage as a port over its Boston and Philadelphia rivals.

The immigrants who rushed to this city of promise were mainly Germans, English, and Protestant Irish. They were motivated by economic hardship, religious persecution, political tyranny, or sometimes just a sense of adventure. In the heyday of clipper ships they disembarked at the calm and protected East River ports at the Battery or South Street. They didn't have to face Hudson River ice floes, but the immigrants had to be on the lookout for con men who steered them to crooked carters and thieving boarding houses and when all else failed, picked their pockets.

Between 1840 and 1860 immigration to and through New York took off. The first western European arrivals were artisans and craftsman forced out of work by the Industrial Revolution; they were yeoman farmers who lost their land to large-scale livestock breeding; they were farm tenants surviving on their kitchen gardens which were suddenly devastated by a common mold.

The potato famine was a disaster of twentieth-century proportions, with slow painful deaths and mass graves. It struck the hardest in Ireland in the 1840s, but it also battered the German farmers of Bavaria and Hanover. The ensuing mass emigration took place in an atmosphere of panic, as people desperately tried to escape starvation and disease. Tragically, these emigrants sometimes encountered these twin demons in the steerage of immigrant ships. In the 1850s forty ships never even reached their New York destination.

New Yorkers responded to the problems of the Old World with typical open-hearted generosity. There were public subscriptions to aid the victims and immigration assistance for the survivors. Ethnic immigration societies sprang up to finance the unprecedented movement of peoples. The Irish had the greatest need and the largest organization, the Irish Emigrant Society, which worked closely with the influential German Emigration Society.

In 1849 the New York government went into action establishing a commission to deal with the emigration emergency. Its first steps were to provide medical and quarantine facilities on Staten Island and Roosevelt Island. In 1855 the commission, at the urging of emigrant groups, inaugurated the Castle Garden Landing Depot as an official disembarkation point for the mass of emigrants in steerage.

It was a closed-off processing area on an island fort off the Battery. Names were recorded, people examined, money changed, and food purchased. Emigration society representatives offered counsel and advice and even lent money. There were employment agencies and company representatives. The grifters and steerers were kept away from the green immigrants.

The Civil War temporarily interrupted immigration but the industrial boom of the 1880s coincided with New York's biggest wave of immigration between 1880 and 1914. The Germans, British, and Irish populations predominated in New York in the 1880s and 1890s, but were eventually superseded in numbers by southern and eastern Europeans. Southern Italians, Greeks, Czechs, Slavs, Hungarians, Poles, and Jews (from Imperial Russia and Austria–Hungary) were the new immigrants of this era.

Some of these new immigrants had suffered because of their religion or for a political cause, but in most cases they were peasants living on the edge of subsistence looking for their place in the sun, or at least the money to help their struggling families overseas. Steamships had cut the crossing time from two months to two weeks and the companies had halved the price of steerage. For the first time mass emigration was a reality and even a temporary stay was economically feasible.

The overwhelming majority came just in time to be welcomed by Lady Liberty, her torch held high in New York Harbor. Although some New York natives found the new immigrants a bit exotic and even claimed to be shocked by their customs and traditions, these awkward neophytes soon began to build their own bastions in the city.

Castle Garden didn't have the capacity or facilities to handle the vast number of newcomers. The situation was further exacerbated by a Supreme Court decision that eliminated the city's right to collect fees from the immigrants or shipping companies to defray the costs of running Castle Garden. Fortunately, the Federal Government stepped in to relieve the city's burden with a federally financed and operated immigrant reception center on Ellis Island.

The Ellis Island Immigration Station was all prize-winning architecture and state-of-the-art plumbing but it was built in 1900 to handle only 1,400 immigrants at a time. It definitely didn't have the capacity to process the

2,000 to 7,000 arrivals who daily passed through its portals before World War I made European emigration dangerous if not impossible.

Even before the "war to end all wars," anti-Catholic and antiforeign groups in New York, like the Know-Nothings and the American Protective Association, were agitating for immigration restrictions, equating Anglo-Saxon blood with American institutions. There were no cries of outrage from New York legislators when Congress passed a law in 1882 excluding Chinese laborers from coming to America. America's list of immigration "undesirables" also included idiots, lunatics, and convicts.

Antiforeign feeling was further inflamed by disillusionment with World War I and its diplomatic aftermath. All the lobbying of New York immigrant groups and their government representatives could not buck the trend toward immigration restriction. Congress started the ball rolling in 1917 by forbidding the entry of illiterate foreigners.

In 1921 the Origins Quota Act was passed and what had started as grass-roots isolationism became the law of the land. The act was based on the 1911 Dillingham report, which positively proved that recent southern and eastern European emigrants were difficult to assimilate and were bringing down the American standard of living by accepting "slave wages."

New national quotas were to be based on three percent of the individual nationalities in the country at the time of the 1910 census. The Johnson-Reed Act of 1924, which went into effect in 1927, was even more exclusionary, with quotas predicated on two percent of the national groups residing in the country in 1890. It was weighted heavily in favor of the British, with relatively large quotas for the Germans, Irish, and Scandinavians.

Black migration from the South in part replaced foreign-born immigrants, while some of the immigration slack was taken up by nationalities in the Western Hemisphere who were not included in the overall quotas. The first significant numbers of Puerto Ricans emigrated to the city after the Jones Act granted them most of the privileges of citizens. People living in British colonial possessions like Jamaica, Trinidad, and Barbados were able to take advantage of the high British quota. West Indians, who were the largest new immigrant group from the Western Hemisphere, usually set their sights on New York, which had a reputation for racial tolerance.

While the depression of the 1930s further decreased immigration to New York even from the Western Hemisphere, German Jews and their Christian compatriots fleeing Nazi persecution flocked to the city. Though many were ordinary people, German and Austrian refugees also represented an intellectual elite of writers, artists, and scientists.

During World War II public opinion about restrictive immigration began to slowly shift. In 1943 America recognized the struggle of its Chinese allies by repealing the Chinese Exclusion Act. Following the Allies' victory the Displaced Person's Act of 1948 opened America's doors to four hundred thousand refugees from Germany and points east, outside of the official quotas. They were the survivors of the concentration camps, veterans of partisan bands, and cold-war casualties of the new map of Europe. Meanwhile, the city was the main destination for the airborne migration of hundreds of thousands of non-quota Puerto Ricans.

Quotas were loosened by the McCarran-Walter Act of 1952 and based on more objective criteria. Immigration eligibility was related to the country's occupational needs and familial and blood ties. But the law still discriminated against national groups, who were part of the latest big wave of immigrants. Immigration from the Western Hemisphere was now restricted, with West Indian countries like Jamaica limited to a mere hundred immigrants a year. It had to be amended three times to allow for the entry of European political refugees, Hungarian freedom fighters, and Cuban exiles.

The 1965 Hart-Celler Act attempted to do away with the inequities of the immigration system while retaining immigration ceilings. Emphasis was placed on reuniting families, while there were still large quotas for individuals with scarce job skills and for political refugees.

After a brief flurry of applications the rapid recovery of Europe and Iron Curtain country restrictions interfered with the Act's original intent. Asians, Caribbeans, and Latin Americans provided almost half of the new Americans in the 1960s and eighty percent two decades later. Again the character of the new emigrants to New York changed radically. Besides differences in racial composition and religious background, they were better educated and occupationally prepared than earlier immigrants. They were trained professionals who didn't have to assimilate culturally to enjoy the city's economic benefits.

New York City was being transformed. The Chinatown of elderly bachelors became a borough-wide community of ninety thousand in the space of two decades. The Jamaican population mushroomed from 11,000 to 93,000 from 1960 to 1980. From a small circle of Jewish anti-Soviet activists in 1973, New York's disaffected Soviet Jews were 75,000 strong seven years later. In the 1970s and 1980s the city's political refugees also included thousands of boat people from Haiti, Cuba, and Vietnam.

Since 1976 the Hart-Celler Act has been extended and amended, and ceilings and limits have been raised. In 1980 refugees were removed from the overall quotas and were defined to include people fleeing from non-communist countries like Haiti or Honduras. In the same year steps were taken to provide benefits for Haitian and Cuban boat people whose status was in doubt.

The 1986 Immigration Reform and Control Act again attempted to revamp the whole system to make it more equitable for immigration groups past and present. Illegal aliens residing in the United States since at least 1982 could now apply for legal residence and there was a special amnesty. At the same time the government provided stricter penalties for employing illegal aliens. It was now possible for immigrants to enter the country who did not fall within one of the preferential quotas involving work skills or a blood relationship with an American resident.

Immigration to New York really mushroomed in the 1980s. Between 1982 and 1989 685,000 immigrants became permanent residents of New York City. The majority, over sixty-three percent, opted to settle in Queens and Brooklyn. More than a third of two of the largest groups of recent immigrants, the Chinese and Dominicans, made their American homes in Manhattan. The Chinese gravitated to Chinatown and lower Manhattan, while the Dominicans headed for Hamilton Heights, Washington Heights, and Inwood.

In the election year of 1990, the government went back to the immigration drawing board and started rethinking the terms of the Act. President Bush signed the Immigration Act of 1990 into law on November 29, 1990. It had something for everybody in the American melting pot. The new ethnics were issued more visas for family reunification, while the traditional western European "white ethnics" had a "diversity" pool earmarked for their entry, with forty percent of the visas reserved for new Irish immigrants. Religious workers were allotted their own preference categories, and the rich earned their visas by investing at least a million dollars into America to create at least ten jobs.

Today one of every three New Yorkers is foreign born and ninety thousand documented immigrants enter the city each year. Whether they come from Odessa, Seoul, Beirut, or Port-au-Prince, they dream the American dream and the sheer vitality of their hopes and ambitions fuels the irrepressible energy of the city. They are the fascinating face of New York: energetic Italians discarding cards in an Bronx social club, Russian Jews exuberantly toasting the bride and groom in a Brighton Beach night club, Indian women scrutinizing fabrics in a Lexington Avenue sari shop, and Senegalese street vendors with studied nonchalance selling watches on the Upper East Side. They are Cypriots practicing soccer in Flushing Meadows Park next to Jamaicans scoring runs in a leisurely game of cricket.

New York's remarkable new immigrants cluster around occupations and businesses almost to the point of stereotype. Korean greengrocers, Indian newsdealers, Israeli boutique owners, and Hasidic camera and electronics discounters have changed the retail face of the city. New York's famous garment industry now depends on Chinese, Cuban, and Dominican subcontractors, with cutters, sewing machine operators, and porters courtesy of the Caribbean, Hong Kong, and Latin America. Gotham's health services are in the capable hands of Korean, Indian, and Middle Eastern physicians with many nurses from the West Indies, Korea, and the Philippines. Even the hospital staff supplying support and maintenance services is likely to be Latin American, Caribbean, or West Indian. Korean and Indian pharmacists have filled an important health gap. The legendary New York cabby is likely today to be a Soviet refusenik, a Sikh in a turban, or a Haitian refugee, while the limousine service and the movers are provided by Israelis. The cuisines of the Near East, the Far East, Latin America, and the Caribbean have changed the eating habits of the city from fast food to high-price trendy. Immigrant retailers from the Near East and the Far East have reinvented the retail business and in the process changed the face of Main Street. The new ethnics, like the old ones, are reshaping the city in their own image and changing themselves in the process.

Lately, with the heavy influx of new immigrants, legal and undocumented, and the economically upward thrust of earlier arrivals, immigrants of even one or two decades standing are beginning to employ and form alliances with the newest New Yorkers. Korean greengrocers are hiring rural Mexicans to cut, spray, and package fruits, vegetables, and flowers. Latino garment subcontractors are signing on sure-handed Chinese as sewing machine operators. Greek restaurant owners are hiring industrious Indians and Ecuadorians to work as waiters, busboys, cooks, and dishwashers. Arabs are hiring determined Central Americans (even if their English needs work) to handle orders in their sandwich shops and delicatessens. Through these symbiotic relationships, different cultures and peoples are drawn together and bonds of friendship are forged.

In 1994 the State Department launched a new "immigrant lottery" with the USA Green Card as the prize for fifty-five thousand lucky winners. The lottery was aimed at citizens of countries with low immigration rates as well as countries with high rates, such as China, Taiwan, India, the Philippines, the Dominican Republic, and the United Kingdom. Immigrants from Hong Kong, Northern Ireland, Jamaica, Canada, Mexico, South Korea, and El Salvador were ineligible. Between June 1 and June 30, millions applied to be a part of this precious lottery. The winners were chosen by computer.

Place Marks

Castle Clinton, *Battery Park (212-344-7220). Free.*

Directions: Subway 4 or 5 to Bowling Green.

Castle Clinton, built in 1807, appears properly fortress-like and martial, although it never actually engaged in combat. During the War of 1812 Castle Clinton, then known as the West Battery, guarded the city from a rocky shelf two hundred feet off the shore, but it only fired its twenty-eight cannons for target practice.

Directly after the War of 1812 this dubious fortification was presented to the city and named in honor of Governor De Witt Clinton. The enterprising city fathers added some flowers and shrubbery, turned the officers' quarters into a bar, and called this exhibition and amusement center Castle Garden. Foreign dignitaries from Lafayette to Edward VII were feted here. It was the scene of the first demonstration of the telegraph and the debut of the Swedish Nightingale, Jenny Lind.

In 1855 it was converted into the country's largest immigration station. Immigrants entered Castle Garden through a great door built through eight-foot-thick walls facing the sea. The reception area was massive but it was difficult to be awed in the crowded atmosphere of money changers, food concessions, and ticket sellers. It usually took six hours for official processing and a cursory medical examination, then a long wooden gangplank led directly to the Manhattan shore.

During the Civil War it was used as a recruiting center for immigrants straight off the boat, but at this time Castle Garden and its emigrant society representatives mainly aided the immigrants with information about jobs and housing and, if necessary, helped them contact family members or friends in the country. Between 1855 and 1890 7,690,606 immigrants passed through Castle Garden.

In 1896 Castle Garden went through another major change, becoming the New York Aquarium. By all accounts it was one of the city's most spectacular tourist attractions, with two rings of giant tanks circulating three hundred thousand gallons of water and every variety of aquatic creature. Unfortunately, city politics intervened and the Parks Department closed it down. In 1946 Congress declared it a national monument and it now contains an interesting exhibit of its many transformations.

Off a circular path to the right of Castle Clinton there is a plaque commemorating Emma Lazarus, who wrote the poem that is inscribed on the Statue of Liberty. Emma Lazarus was the daughter of a prominent Jewish family whose ancestors landed in New Amsterdam in 1649. Her most famous poem, "The New Colossus," was her response to seeing the survivors of the first Russian pogrom, who were detained on Wards Island. Two days later the work was auctioned off at a literary gala to raise money for a base for the Statue of Liberty.

Statue of Liberty, *Departure slip: Battery Park (212-269-5755). Daily, April–October: first ferry 9:15 A.M., then every half hour on the hour from 10 A.M. to 5 P.M.; November–March: every hour on the hour from 10 A.M. to 5 P.M. Ferry charge includes admission and Ellis Island visit.*

The ferry for this American symbol, actually titled *Liberty Enlightens the World,* departs from a slip at the foot of the battery. Though its image is on everything from paperweights to towels, looming over the sea on Bedloes Island, it still has the capacity to thrill.

The Statue of Liberty was the brainchild of Eduard-Rene Lefebvre de Laboulaye, a staunch French republican, member of the French senate, and author of a history of America. He wanted to seal French–American friendship with a monument to liberty. Frederic Auguste Bartholdi was the artist who breathed life into the project, which he conceived on a vast seven-wonders-of-the ancient-world scale. He adapted the design of an earlier planned work, *Egypt Carrying Light to Asia,* and selected the site of Bedloes Island.

Alexandre Gustave Eiffel, who would engineer the Eiffel Tower, devised the revolutionary design of iron pylons that would frame the 151-foot figure. His pioneering work later influenced the construction of New York's first skyscrapers. Although New York's big money scoffed at the idea of Lady Liberty and the respected *New York Times* thought it was a waste of money, Joseph Pulitzer and his crusading *New York World* turned it into a circulation campaign and helped raise the money to put up the magnificent pedestal designed by Richard M. Hunt.

In 1874 the Union Franco–Americaine was formed in Paris to promote the Statue of Liberty. Laboulaye wanted it to be ready by July 4, 1876, in time for America's centennial. He underestimated the enormity of the undertaking, as it took five years just to raise the funds—a million francs—to begin work on the monument and another five years for Bartholdi to complete his task, using all the best artisans in Paris.

The statue was cast in sections and carried aboard the French ship Isere in 214 boxes. On October 28, 1886, President Grover Cleveland dedicated the statue. New York City took the day off to celebrate. Everywhere American flags and Tricolors were flying as thousands from France and America marched down Fifth Avenue to the Battery. There was a huge naval procession in the harbor with bands playing and cannons firing in salute. The crowning moment of the day came when Cleveland pulled the cord, unveiling the statue.

History repeated itself in 1986 when a completely refurbished *Liberty Enlightening the World* was feted again on her centennial. Lady Liberty was completely cleaned for her party and her interior swabbed out with liquid nitrogen. She was covered with strips of copper and her ninety-eight-year-old torch was replaced with a new streamlined one from California.

Her birthday on July 4, 1986, featured a parade of tall clipper ships and the city's biggest display of fireworks ever. When her new torch was hoisted into place, in attendance were presidents and captains of industry and crowds of the descendants of immigrants she once welcomed.

The **American Museum of Immigration** is located in the base of the Statue of Liberty, up a single flight of stairs. It recounts the history of immigration starting from the migrations of the Native Americans. Each immigrant group is treated separately with displays of memorabilia and photographs. Dioramas bring to life the immigrant experience.

The climb to the pedestal of this American symbol is 161 steps, with another 171 steps to Liberty's crown. The views at each level are spectacular but the challenge of the spiral staircase is not for everybody. On the grounds of Bedloes Island, now renamed Liberty Island, there is a group of five lifelike statues by Philip Ratner sensitively depicting the statue's midwives: Laboulaye, Bartholdi, Eiffel, Pulitzer, and Lazarus.

For those who don't want to make a voyage to the Statue of Liberty there's an iron replica weighing a modest ton standing on a scaffolding at 219 West Broadway, lighting people's way to the rather mundane building below.

Ellis Island, *Departure slip: Battery Park (212-269-5755). Daily, April–October: first ferry 9:15 A.M., then every half hour on the hour from 10 A.M. to 5 P.M.; November–March: every hour on the hour from 10 A.M. to 5 P.M. Ferry charge includes admission and Ellis Island visit.*

Ellis Island holds the place of honor in America's immigration saga. It is estimated that eighty-five percent of all Americans are descended from people who came through its reception center.

Before Ellis Island became a landmark it had quite a checkered history. The Native Americans called it Kioshik Island for its sea gull population, then the British dubbed it "Gibbet Island" for the gallows where a bloodthirsty pirate breathed his last.

Samuel Ellis, for whom the island was named, took title around the time of the Revolution, but he preferred to stay on his farm in New Jersey and rented it to a tavern keeper. The government purchased it in 1808 to build a fort to protect the harbor. Since the fort turned out to be a strategic fiasco, it was converted into an ammunition dump. Despite the complaints of neighboring residents on the mainland of New Jersey, it fulfilled this function until 1890.

In 1890, when the federal government took control of immigration, Ellis Island by default became the country's main immigration station. Bedloes Island, the home of Lady Liberty, may have been a more appropriate site, but patriots in France and America thought that the presence of real refugees would somehow demean this national monument. Ellis Island was enlarged with a landfill and its pine administration buildings were completed in a hurry in 1892 to handle the hordes of new arrivals. Five years later it burned down, along with voluminous immigration records dating from 1855 to 1890.

The new station, which opened in 1900, was a sturdy fireproof structure, but solid construction did not provide any protection for the immigrants from the thievery and abuse of greedy concessionaires. It was also overcrowded. President Theodore Roosevelt put an end to intentional mistreatment, but the endemic overcrowding continued.

World War I immigration quotas, with a ceiling of 164,000 and a new policy of processing immigrants in their own countries, ended the Ellis Island era. After serving as a detention center for enemy aliens during World War II and a screening center for suspected alien subversives in the early 1950s, it finally shut down in 1954. In 1965, at the same time that the Congress was passing a liberalized immigration law, Ellis Island was declared a national monument. A decade later it was open to the public.

New-found feelings of pride in our immigrant heritage have led to the restoration of the Ellis Island Immigrant Station and the preservation of our whole immigrant experience in the form of fascinating and evocative exhibitions and displays. Through the efforts of public figures like Chrysler's miracle man Lee Iacocca and New York civic leader Bill Fugazy, 156 million dollars were raised to restore and open to the public this national monument in 1990.

The actual buildings of the immigration station are to the right of the ferry slip where the visitors disembark. The tall towers of the reception hall dominate the horizon. The reception station is not a typical institutional complex; the Great Hall has high arched windows, brass chandeliers, and a ceiling of Gustavino tile. In the dining hall the Works Progress Administration (WPA) created a mural dedicated to immigrant achievements.

In this landmark of American immigration visitors relive the immigrant rite of passage from the Baggage Room through the Registry to endure the cursory medical examination and finally, by way of the Staircase of Separation, to the ferryboats and freedom. The "Treasures from Home" exhibit poignantly presents individual immigrant sagas using personal artifacts and photos, while "Silent Voices" documents the decay and restoration of Ellis Island itself. There is an oral history archive open to the public and a modern interactive exhibit that enables visitors to trace their own immigrant ancestry. The "Immigrant Wall of Honor," which runs along the sea wall, contains the names of two hundred thousand individuals who were processed at Ellis Island.

South Street Seaport, *South Street and Fulton Streets (212-748-8600). The hours for the South Street Seaport exhibits and attractions (though not all the stores and restaurants) are generally from 10 A.M. to 5 P.M. but subject to seasonal changes.*

Directions: Bus M15 on Second Avenue to Fulton Street; Subway 4 or 5 to Fulton Street; or Subway A to Broadway and Nassau Street. Walk east to the river.

In its prime the South Street Seaport was the seat of the city's international trade. Clipper ships flying the flags of sixty nations filled its harbor. It was a cosmopolitan hubbub of longshoremen, seamen, and traders, a Tower of Babel costume ball, with people from everywhere speaking every language. As a counterpoint to the relentless activity there was the on-again off-again hum of the Fulton Farmer's Market and the Fulton Fish Market.

The opening of the Erie Canal, linking New York to the Northwest Frontier, only made the Seaport bigger and more frenetic. In one year over five hundred new shipping companies opened offices here. The firms of South Street built big business New York, opening the lucrative Far Eastern trade and following the Gold Rush out to California. But then the South Street Seaport glory days were over with the development of the steamship and the Hudson River waterfront.

Nowadays the South Street Seaport still attracts people from around the world, but they are sightseers rather than mariners or merchants. In an eleven-block historic district encompassing Piers 15, 16, and 17, along South Street from Peck Slip to Burlingham Slip, the Seaport offers up a fascinating collection of galleries, historic houses, and restored clipper ships. The emphasis is on historic New York and its connection with the sea.

Before making the Seaport rounds check in at the Visitors Center near the Titanic Memorial Lighthouse at 14 Fulton Street and find out about special programs, museum exhibits, or free concerts. Tickets are available here for all or part of the South Street Seaport scene. Do not miss the multimedia *Seaport Experience* on Pier 17 depicting its multiethnic past

The Seaport is a melting pot of restaurants whose variety of cuisines adds flavor to the harborside doings. Along with formal dining there are fast food and take-out, but even the informal food has formal prices. This around-the-world tour in restaurants and food shops is located in the Cannon's Walk Building, the Fulton Market Building, Pier 17, along Schermerhorn Row, and the 1 Seaport Plaza skyscraper. It includes Italian gourmet at Gianni's and take-out Chinese at Kam Wan, an authentic British Pub (the North Star Pub), and a tourist Irish pub (MacMeanin's). The Seaport contains outlets of old New York standbys like Italian Zaro's in the restored Fulton Fish Market, as well as ethnic originals like the New York-style Jewish deli, the Pastrami Factory. For coffee and cakes, very sweet and Viennese, the Cafe Fledermaus elegantly occupies a corner of 1 Seaport Plaza.

Visitors also come to the Seaport for the pleasures of shopping. Parts of the Fulton Market building and Pier 17 resemble suburban malls. Many of the stores, such as the United Kingdom's Laura Ashley, The Body Shop, and Williamson's Irish Imports, bear foreign labels.

Immigration and Naturalization Service, *26 Federal Plaza (212-206-6500).*

Directions: Subway 4, 5, or 6 to Brooklyn Bridge.

This tall contemporary government building with its spacious plaza stands out among other civic structures from an earlier era. It is also identifiable by the endless snaking lines of multiethnic new Americans waiting to become "legal." The offices contain everything you need to know in order to live, work, go to school, and travel in America.

══════════ Museums and Archives ══════════

New York City is a living immigrant museum, but for those who are also interested in a less immediate immigrant experience and the history of the city's ethnics, there are museums and libraries that provide the fascinating details and background.

New-York Historical Society, *170 Central Park West at 77th Street (212-873-3400). Tuesday–Friday 10 A.M.–5 P.M.; Saturday 1 P.M.–5 P.M. Admission charge.*

Directions: Subway A, B, C, D, or K to 81st Street.

The New-York Historical Society is a stickler for tradition even in the way it spells its name. (There was a hyphen in old New York.) The building only looks like a mausoleum from the outside; inside it has the warmth and intimacy of an old country home, very refined.

In its library the New-York Historical Society has all you want to know about early New York and its immigrant population in books, original manuscripts, periodicals, and prints. There are also exhibits, permanent and otherwise, with paintings by old American masters including Stuart and Copley, pre-Revolutionary and early American glassware and silver, and coaches of every size, age, and purpose in the Fahnestock Collection. Styles of furniture from the seventeenth to the nineteenth century are elegantly on display.

Museum of the City of New York, *Fifth Avenue between 103rd and 104th streets (212-534-1672). Tuesday–Friday 10:30 A.M.–4:30 P.M.; Saturday and Sunday 1 P.M.–4 P.M. Admission charge.*

Directions: Bus Ml, M2, M3, or M4 to Madison/103rd, Subway 6 to 103rd Street.

The Museum of the City of New York, housed in a handsome rambling neo-Georgian building on Fifth Avenue, makes the essentials of New York's muticultural history come to life. The Dutch Gallery on the first floor charts the Dutch colonial adventure from Henry Hudson and the *Half Moon* through the Indian War—started over a peach—to the Dutch surrender to England. The early history of New York comes to life with fascinating dioramas and authentic-looking scale models. The British colonization of America is given equal time on the same floor, with a whole series of maps and pictures detailing their progress after 1664.

The second floor features rooms with period furnishings. There is a portrait gallery including famous New Yorkers from the past and a treasure house called the Silver Gallery with the art of early American silversides. The multimedia show tracing the city's story from the Indians to the present is more fun than the usual information-packed seminar and should not be missed.

The city's multicultural neighborhoods past and present are on regular display in special exhibits. Photographs and modern artifacts reveal the high points and the hardships of the city's Latino, Asian, African-American, southern European, eastern European, northern European, and Jewish populations. Whether the exhibition is the Puerto Rican elderly in East Harlem, the Harlem Renaissance of 1920s, or the German-Jewish experience in Harlem, the subject matter is treated with sensitivity and understanding and the exhibits are imaginatively mounted.

The Bronx County Historical Society, *3309 Bainbridge Avenue (718-881-8900). Monday–Friday, 9:00* A.M.*–5:00* P.M. *Admission charge.*

Directions: Subway 4 to Mosholu Parkway.

A comfortable but unassuming Bronx residence is the depository of 350 years of Bronx history, from Native American encampments to Puerto Rican casitas. This local institution is totally committed to the preservation of the Bronx historical record, whether it is in the form of artifact, document, oral history, or landmark. It accomplishes its objectives by producing books and other publications, mounting exhibits, and conducting cultural and multicultural projects.

The Brooklyn Historical Society, *128 Pierpont Street (718-624-0890). Monday–Friday 9:00* A.M.*–5:00* P.M. *Admission charge.*

Directions: Subway N or R to Court Street. Walk one block up Clinton Street.

The Brooklyn Historical Society is an intimate museum that in permanent and temporary exhibits examines the ethnic evolution of the borough from the Dutch landholders of Vlacke Bos to the Jamaican homeowners of Flatbush. The Society, while maintaining a vast archive of Brooklyn documents and memorabilia, continues to actively research the most recent immigrant arrivals.

═══════════ Organizations ═══════════

City Lore: The New York Center For Urban Folk Culture, *72 East First Street (212-529-1955).*

City Lore is committed to the preservation of New York's multicultural mosaic, from local landmarks to metropolitan street scenes. Throughout the year it sponsors festivals, exhibitions, radio programs, films, and research projects. In 1993 the organization initiated the "People's Hall of Fame" to honor grass-roots contributions to New York's cultural life.

The Ethnic Folk Arts Center, *131 Varick Street (212-691-9510).*
The Center encourages the performance and appreciation of ethnic music and dance and documents the culture of New York's living ethnic communities. It collaborates with immigrant artists from a wide range of musical traditions to produce records, concerts, and music festivals.

Extras

The melting-pot ethos that enables a city to function effectively with a population as varied as the planet does not rule out ethnic individuality and cultural pluralism. Mutual understanding between groups has been enhanced by self-understanding within groups and a stronger sense of ethnic identity. Newspapers, radio, and now television are the community resources that have enabled new immigrants from the Irish to the boat people to relate to one another and to their own cultural heritage.

The first immigrant-oriented paper in New York was *The Shamrock* (Irish), which went to press in 1810. The first foreign-language newspaper goes back to 1827, to the intellectual exiles who started the French-language paper now called *France Amerique.* The German *New Yorker Staats-Zeitung und Herrold* started soon after in 1834. It would eventually be owned by the Ridders of Knight-Ridder fame who would build it into a communications empire. The first Italian journal, *L'Eco d'Italia,* was published in 1849, before there was any significant Italian population, and *Il Progresso,* which came out in 1890, was the first successful Italian daily. The Yiddish paper that won the circulation wars in the early years of the twentieth century was the *Jewish Daily Forward.* It emphasized social consciousness as much as Judaism.

Before free immigration was blocked in 1924 it seemed like every foreign-speaking group had its own publication. Between 1898 and 1907 the small Syrian community of New York put out six newspapers to represent all points of view. At that time ethnic papers were similar to the popular press, very partisan and opinionated. Objectivity was secondary to political ideology or religious affiliation and press wars were routine.

The resurgence in New York's ethnic press mirrors the new waves of immigration. The Hispanic newspaper *El Diario La Prensa* has the largest circulation of 250,000. This Spanish-language tabloid has transcended its original Puerto Rican readership to appeal to other Latinos from the Caribbean and South America. It is now going head-to-head with *Noticias*

Del Mundo, which has emphasized the coverage of South American nationalities.

The exploding Chinese community currently boasts eight dailies, representing the whole Chinese political spectrum from People's Republic left to Nationalist right. The *World Journal* is winning the circulation wars by breaking the one hundred thousand mark. The Korean presence in New York, which seems to have grown overnight, already supports six dailies.

New York's ethnic papers, including dailies and weeklies, as of 1986, numbered sixty-eight. They are a new breed of publication less parochial and more professional than earlier ethnic publications. Editor Chin-Fu Woo of *The United Journal,* New York's oldest Chinese daily, is proud to say: "We cover news fairly." Malgorazata Cwiklnska, editor of the Polish-language *Nowy Dziennik,* insists on professionalism in serving the non–English-speaking Polish community.

While New York's regular newspapers have decreased in number since World War I the ethnic press is breaking sales records. Yet the success of the local ethnic press has not interrupted the flow of foreign dailies to these shores. For instance, Colombians and Dominicans both buy native newspapers on the newsstands of Jackson Heights and Corona; New York now imports five Colombian and seven Dominican papers.

New York's radio has for decades made immigrants feel more at home. Again it has changed with the times and the immigration patterns. WEVD-FM started out in 1927 as the voice of the *Jewish Daily Forward* but gradually its voice went from Yiddish to Italian to Chinese. While WEVD still has eighty hours a week of Jewish programming in Yiddish, Hebrew, Russian, and English, it also broadcasts Italian, Portuguese, Albanian, Greek, Irish, and Turkish programs.

Most Italian radio—forty-four hours a week—in the metropolitan area is heard on WNWK-FM. There is also a cable radio service offering round-the-clock Italian programming.

The largest non–English-speaking radio audience is Hispanic. There are four full-time Hispanic AM stations: WSKQ, WKDM, WADO, and WJIT. WNWK also has plenty of air time for Spanish-speaking Argentines, Dominicans, Peruvians, and Ecuadorians.

Cable television is starting to supersede radio for the larger and more prosperous ethnics. WXTV has twenty-four-hour a day Spanish language programming, with Spanish-language films and variety shows from all over Latin America, while WNJJ has a full lineup of Hispanic programs alternating with paid programming. WNYC has programs in Italian, Polish, Japanese, and Chinese, with every type of program from game shows to the news in foreign-language equivalents.

Celebrations

The American Ethnic Parade

Directions: Subway N or R to 57th Street/Seventh Avenue.

The American Ethnic Parade is an April-in-New-York international entertainment. All the nations of the city dress in native costume and sing and dance their way along the Avenue of Americas from 56th Street to 37th Street. There are also antique cars, floats with plenty of national character, an angry papier-mâché dragon or two, and the world's largest American flag. In this salute to ethnicity even the smallest group from Malta or Mali has a chance to strut their stuff and show their colors.

The marchers and performers along the route mostly represent the city's recent immigrants. They still have their roots and the freshness and spontaneity of the first glow of the New York experience. This parade is not an exercise in nostalgia, however. Peruvian Indians draped with colorful blankets blow on Pan's pipes while sedate Portuguese serenade on a float resembling the deck of an explorer's ship. People's Republic Chinese in Mao red do a dragon dance followed by a troop of Taiwanese maidens taking delicate steps in embroidered kimonos. There's an all-Arab float with the children of twenty-two Arab nations and an all–Native American float representing ten local tribes. The small community of Kurds has an enthusiastic contingent of ten and the populous Dominicans have a long line of marchers, including their own folklorica ballet.

Foreign dignitaries in the reviewing stands solemnly wave to their own national groups, while the local elected officials in the same stands keep trying to smile sincerely. Most of the spectators, who represent a fair cross section of the world, enthusiastically enjoy the whole show. It is definitely their day.

Ninth Avenue Fair

Directions: Crosstown bus on 42nd Street, 51st Street, or 57th Street.

In the days when the El cast a shadow over Ninth Avenue and Hell's Kitchen's fires were still burning, pushcarts lined Ninth Avenue from 36th Street to 44th Street. New Yorkers called the multiethnic pushcart brigade Paddy's Market. It was the place to go for rare and unusual international food products. When Major La Guardia removed the pushcart from the city thoroughfares (along with the trolley car) the international markets went indoors.

Peep shows, porn shops, and traffic in drugs and human bodies turned this working class neighborhood into a tenderloin and led to the decline of this urban bazaar. By the 1980s only a remnant of Paddy's Market remained on Ninth Avenue, which included Italian salumerias and sausage makers, Greek food and spice shops, and the odd ethnic restaurant.

In the 1990s Paddy's market has made a real comeback. The old Hell's Kitchen ethnic food fair has been reclaimed by multicultural merchants, attracted by relatively low rent and a burgeoning loft and luxury high-rise community. While the old reliables like Esposito's Pork Store and the Poseidon Bakery remain, the lackluster hardware or plumbing supply stores and the seedy beer-and-a-shot joints have given way to an array of honest ethnic food shops and restaurants. By the latest count, thirty new ethnic locations have opened for business. The new Ninth Avenue restaurant row includes Turkish food from Turkish Cuisine, Arab mazza from the Lemon Tree Cafe, curry-in-a-hurry from the Bengal Express Indian Restaurant, and even genuine English fish and chips via The English Harbor.

The multiethnic spirit of this unusual neighborhood, where Paddy's Market once flourished, comes alive every year in the larger-than-life Ninth Avenue Street Festival. It happens in mid-May when the city closes off Ninth Avenue from 37th to 57th Streets for the weekend. Half a million people jam the streets and sidewalks, sampling food and purchasing crafts and products from around the world. Ninth Avenue ethnic old stand-bys, with sons, grandsons, and granddaughters of the original owners now in charge, take to the streets.

The food is all freshly prepared on open barbecues and grills and even in Chinese woks. There are stir-fried dishes from the Far East and kebabs and *köfte* from the Near East; there are Mexican burritos and Puerto Rican cuchifritos and Jamaican jerk chicken; there are Italian sausage heroes and Greek gyros. Occasionally, a made-in-New-York hot dog makes an appearance along with king-size, very salty pretzels. Though American beer is the beverage of choice, there are also Mexican margaritas and Jamaican ginger beer to wash all the goodness down.

Dancers, bands, and singers from the neighborhoods or aspiring semi-professionals sponsored by some soft drink or beer company appear on portable stages, while jugglers, mimes in whiteface, and street musicians perform their routines among the crowd. The salsa bands, uptown jazz combos, and Harlem marching bands are usually standouts.

Brooklyn Ethnic Music and Dance Folk Festival, *Prospect Park Picnic House Long Meadow, Prospect Park West Entrance between Fourth and Fifth Streets (718-788-0055).*

Directions: Subway 2 or 5 to Grand Army Plaza.

In the last week in September Prospect Park in Brooklyn becomes the site for an all-out ethnic happening. The musical and dance traditions of many continents and nations combine for a day of melodic and rhythmic epiphanies. The concert is free flowing and freewheeling; the players and dancers are truly enjoying themselves and the performances are effortless and spontaneous. The music is true to its roots, down to earth, and close to the people. For one day at least, cultures are bridged, and there is one world of music and dance.

This festival celebrates the ethnic diversity of the city's music and dance and thrives on contrasting cultural styles and approaches. Nine or ten ethnic dance troops and musical groups perform inside and outside of a spacious tent located on the Prospect Park Picnic House parking lot. There are no spectators in this special festival: in between acts there are workshops to teach everyone—beginners and advanced—all the intricacies of different folk dances, and musicians take time to share the secrets of their instruments with festival participants. Foods and beverages that fall into the exotic category keep ethnic appetites fully satisfied.

It's a kaleidoscope of ethnic culture. A Haitian big band may be succeeded by a serene Irishman on the melodeon or exuberant clog dancers. Plaintive Yemeni voices precede the gospel shout of an elderly church woman only to be followed by a high-pitched Chinese voice accompanied by a four-string lute. Pontic Greek dancers, who skip and jump to the spirited note of the clarina, are followed by rollicking Balkan brass and equally high-spirited "peasant" dancers. For a finale there is a hot salsa ensemble that cannot stand still.

The Founders

The Dutch and the British were the city's originators, founding colonies that set the cosmopolitan and mercantile tone of New York City. Although they were soon superseded by other ethnics with different styles, their influence endures.

History

The Dutch

The Dutch were the first ethnics to take Manhattan. Henry Hudson, the intrepid English captain of the *Half Moon,* claimed it for the Netherlands in 1609. At the time the friendly locals called it Manna-Hata, the Island of Hills; Hudson and his crew were more dazzled by the Indian women smoking pipes than they were by the landscape. Four years later Adriaen Block returned to the island and took a look at some of the outlying boroughs, including Staten Island. After losing his ship, the *Tiger,* to fire, the Indians helped him build another, the *Onrust* (restless), and he continued his voyage, collecting valued beaver pelts and their precious oil, considered a cure for dizziness, rheumatism, and trembling.

Watching the Spanish and Portuguese get rich on their empires, the Dutch decided to make a profit on their more northerly possessions. The economic future of the island, renamed New Amsterdam, and the whole of New Netherlands became the responsibility of the Dutch West India Company and the Heeren XIX (19 Lord Directors). Like some future rulers of the Big Apple, greed affected their judgment.

At first New Amsterdam was a stopover on the way to fur trading settlements up the Hudson River. In 1625 William Verhulst laid the foundations for a permanent settlement with six farms and the site for a fort. In no time bark houses gave way to stone and the outlines of modern Pearl Street, Beaver Street, and Whitehall Street began to take shape. As an afterthought, Peter Minuit purchased the Big Apple for sixty guilders' (twenty-four dollars') worth of goods. He was more generous in apportioning land to the colony's privileged elite, the patroons, and was eventually recalled for favoritism.

Wouter Van Twiller was the next governor to gain notoriety. He was a callow and inexperienced twenty-seven year old with a weakness for the bottle. When he took office in 1633 New Amsterdam was prospering. Before long he and his corrupt cronies were squandering the company's surplus on private revels and claiming the choice real estate for themselves. At loggerheads with New Amsterdam's pastor, Everardus Bogardus, and the sheriff, Lubbertus van Dincklage, his recall was inevitable.

Van Twiller's replacement was a very different personality, incompetent in his own inimitable way. Governor Willem Kieft, who took office in 1638, was a high-handed autocrat with little use for moderation or basic honesty. His attempts to ride roughshod over the Native Americans, who far outnumbered the Dutch, resulted in bloody Indian wars that depopulated parts of the Dutch possession and turned New Amsterdam into an armed camp. Kieft crushed the colonists with taxes yet emptied the treasury by fighting senseless wars. Petitions to the Company and a remonstrance to the Hague resulted in yet another governor's recall.

Peter Stuyvesant was the last of this rogues' gallery of Dutch governors. He took charge of the Dutch Colony in 1647 and stayed on to the bitter end. Although his personality was no more attractive than any of his predecessors, old "Wooden Leg" had a certain stiff-necked honesty, martial skills, and administrative ability. He ruled for seventeen years, longer than anyone in the history of colonial New Amsterdam and New York.

During his term of office he worked hard to overcome the effects of mismanagement and restore order and prosperity. He organized a primitive police force, appointed fire marshals, and established strict laws against fighting and reckless carriage driving. He captured the Swedish colony in present-day Delaware and negotiated a lasting peace with the Native Americans and a fair treaty with British settlers in New England.

Stuyvesant was quick to anger and had a penchant for feuds. At different times he had disputes with the colony's Jews, Quakers, his own Dutch Reformed Church, the business community, and even the administration of the Dutch West India Company itself. His general intolerance and high-handed approach to government led to company restrictions on his power and the appointment of an advisory council in New Amsterdam.

Finally, in 1664 all his efforts and outbursts came to naught when Colonel Richard Nicolls handed him an ultimatum from the British Crown. Stuyvesant would have defended New Amsterdam against the British, but he had no backing from Dutch settlers, who welcomed the liberal British peace terms.

The British

Nicolls' lenient peace terms made surrender very easy for the Dutch. In essence, the Dutch were promised the rights of free Englishmen and, at least for a time, could still ship their tobacco and furs back to Holland. Governor Nicolls was a tolerant man with his own coterie of Dutch advisers, but he had no problem expropriating the Dutch West India Company.

His successor, Colonel Francis Lovelace, was impressed with a city comprised of ethnics that had the "breeding of courts." He saw possibilities everywhere and worked to expand the colony. Lovelace improved transportation and communications, opening a road between New York and Harlem and improving ferry service from Spuyten Duyvil on the Harlem River. This dynamo even attempted to rebuild the colony's defenses, but it was too little too late.

The Netherlands retook New York in 1673 and the local Dutch threw up their hands and declared their neutrality. The new Dutch authorities didn't have time to do more than rename the city New Orange and blow up Fort Amsterdam before their government gave New Orange back to the English in the Treaty of Westminster.

Tensions continued in the city between the Dutch and British; there were problems in the courts and friction on the city watch. Governor Thomas Dongan, New York's first Catholic governor, took a conciliatory approach, and with the approval of King James II, issued the Dongan Charter of Liberties in 1686, which guaranteed certain rights and provided for greater self-government. The city was divided into six wards, with a mayor, an alderman, and a city recorder.

Most of the British governors who succeeded Dongan thought that public office was an easy way to line their own pockets. Governor Montgomery took big bribes from members of the city council seeking to enlarge their powers, and Cosby, who followed him, extorted extra income from his predecessor and suspended the judiciary. Their actions led to the kind of conflict and protest that triggered the American Revolution.

Even in colonial days New York was a "business first" kind of place. During the French and Indian War, from 1756 to 1763, New York became America's second largest city, trading furs and guns with the enemy. Before the Revolution New York's main disagreements with Britain involved commercial interference as well as abstract issues like freedom and the rights of man. It was an import duty on tea that led to New York's own "tea party" on April 22, 1774, in which twenty-two crates of tea were dumped into Manhattan Bay by New Yorkers masquerading as Mohawks.

While Manhattan radicals were holding congresses to form a militia and defend the city against the British in 1775, the British governor, Tryon, was organizing sympathetic loyalists in Queens. When the revolutionaries stopped talking and started shooting and the statue of George III in Bowling Green was converted into 42,088 bullets, thousands of New Yorkers sought the protection of the British army. New York Tories were everywhere; England was their motherland and New York in most of its essentials was an English city.

Founders' Place Marks

Philip Hone, a social commentator of the early nineteenth century, put it very succinctly: "The whole of New York is rebuilt about once every ten years." Yet while New York can be very cavalier with its artifacts and relics, the founders have managed to leave behind some curious footprints in the city sands. The landmarks and monuments to New York's Dutch and English colonial founders start at the tip of Manhattan Island, make their way north through Harlem, and are scattered throughout the outer boroughs.

Most of colonial New Amsterdam's or New York's history happened in lower Manhattan. The Colonial adventure began at the Battery in 1625 with thirty Dutch families and slowly insinuated itself northward. At the time Peter Stuyvesant paved the streets of New Amsterdam, its northern border was the Wall Street Stockade, and even the English waited until

1699 to cross over that line. In 1771 English New York City had expanded to Grand Street and boasted a population of twenty-two thousand.

Lower Manhattan

Directions: Subway 4 or 5 to Bowling Green; Subway 1 to South Ferry; Bus MI, M6, or M15 to South Ferry.

The Netherlands Memorial Monument

The founders' New York starts at the entrance to Battery Park. The Netherlands Memorial Monument is a flagpole for the ages, standing on a granite flagstaff which was donated by the Dutch people in 1926. The history lesson on the base shows a map of Dutch Manhattan and Peter Minuit and the Manhattan Native American tribe closing their twenty-four-dollar deal for the island.

The U.S. Custom House

The former U.S. Custom House is beyond the Battery between State and Whitehall Streets on Bowling Green. It's located in the area where the first white settlers built their basic shelters and erected a fort. The British maintained the structure, renaming it Fort George in 1664, but victorious New York revolutionaries razed it along with other reminders of this unpopular monarch in 1789.

In 1907 the current U.S. Custom House building, designed by Cass Gilbert, was completed. Its elegant neoclassical facade depicts with four heroic sculptures an ascendant and confident America beside a backward and benighted Asia, Africa, and Europe. In 1994 a newly restored Custom House became the home of the National Museum of the American Indian.

National Museum of the American Indian, *1 Bowling Green (212-668-6624). Open daily; no admission fee.*

This museum is dedicated to the city's original New Yorkers. It contains a superb collection of Native American art, artifacts, and crafts, imaginatively displayed.

Bowling Green

The Bowling Green, just north of the Battery dividing Broadway, is a vest-pocket park with plenty of history. The Dutch originally used it as a cattle market, but later it became a place for the game bowls and, under the British, a parade ground. In 1771 officials put a fence around it to protect a statue of a very regal George III dressed up to look like a Roman emperor. But nothing could stop American patriots in 1776 from tearing it down and melting it into bullets for the Revolution.

Fraunces Tavern, *54 Pearl Street (212-425-1778). Monday–Friday 10 A.M.–5 P.M. Gratis from 10 A.M. until noon, otherwise there's an admission charge.*

Fraunces Tavern is on the corner of Pearl and Broad Streets between the present financial district and Battery Park. It's a reconstruction and a replica of the old DeLancey Mansion, which was built in 1719; only the west wall contains the original Holland brick. The loyalist DeLanceys made their mansion a Georgian classic, all order and symmetry, with high chimneys and an ornamental balustrade on a hipped roof. In 1763 the DeLancey house became the premises of Samuel Fraunces's Queen's Head Tavern. George Washington made his famous farewell address in the Tavern's second-floor dining room in 1783. Nowadays Fraunces Tavern does double duty as a museum of early Americana and as an old-fashioned Yankee restaurant. The exhibitions in the upstairs rooms are all about Washington, the American Revolution, and the curious history of Fraunces Tavern.

Trinity Church and Churchyard, *74 Trinity Place (212-602-0800).*

The original Trinity Church was constructed in 1697 at Wall Street and Broadway. It was the main house of worship of the established Anglican Church and was built with city taxes. In 1776, while New York was occupied by the British, it was destroyed in a suspicious fire. The current church was erected in 1846 in the Gothic revival style.

The Trinity churchyard is two and a quarter tranquil acres in the fast-paced world of Wall Street. There are magnolias that bloom in the spring and tombstones from the seventeenth and eighteenth century.

St. Paul's Chapel, *Broadway Avenue between Vesey and Fulton Streets (212-602-0874).*

St. Paul's was built in what were the hinterlands of New York in 1766 and is the oldest building in Manhattan. The church is modeled after London's St. Martin's-in-the-Fields, with a portico more like a Greek temple than an Episcopalian church porch. The interior of St. Paul's has diamond-faceted Waterford crystal chandeliers and a magnificent carved pulpit that predate the Revolution. In 1794 a spire and clock tower was added, duplicating the one at St. Martin's.

St. Mark's-in-the-Bouwerie, *131 East 10th Street (212-674-6377).*

St. Mark's started out in 1660 as Peter Stuyvesant's private chapel on his *bouwerie* (Dutch for farm), where in his declining years he entertained the British governor. When Stuyvesant died at the age of 80, he was buried near the chapel door. The church was entirely rebuilt in 1799 in the then-popular Georgian style, and a steeple and portico were added in the nineteenth century. In 1915 Queen Wilhelmina of the Netherlands presented the church with a statue of Stuyvesant, which now occupies a place near his grave.

Harlem and Washington Heights

In simpler colonial times Harlem was a village governed by loose committees and magistrates selected in an open meeting. The people in Harlem all knew one another, and represented the best families in the Dutch and later the British communities. Harlem and Harlem Heights were estate areas, a sort of colonial Greenwich or Westport. There were DeLanceys, Beekmans, Rikers, and Coldens. As late as the 1880s families like the Bensons, Hoppers, and Raubs lived on lands with titles granted in the seventeenth century. It was inevitable that at least part of this legacy would survive.

Call ahead before visiting these uptown treasures, and tread lightly in surrounding marginal areas.

Morris-Jumel Mansion, *corner of Edgecombe Avenue and 161st Street (212-923-8008). Tuesday–Sunday 10 A.M.–4 P.M. Admission charge.*

Directions: Subway A or B to 163rd Street; Bus M2 or M3.

This elegant Georgian mansion, built circa 1765, stands serenely in an area between Harlem and Washington Heights. It originally belonged to a Tory named Colonel Roger Morris, who backed the wrong side in the Revolution and left for England on very short notice.

In 1810 the house became the property of a wealthy merchant named Stephen Jumel. It was a present for his ambitious bride and former mistress, Betsy Bowen. She was rumored to have been a lady of easy virtue, and she was eager to gain respectability. In between trying to crash polite society, she had the front of the Morris-Jumel Mansion redone several times until it resembled a plantation portico. Years after her husband died, leaving her millions, she married the seventy-seven-year-old Aaron Burr and attained, at least in her own mind, the position she craved.

The mansion is open to the public and displays Madame Jumel's most prized pieces, with English Chippendales in the front parlor and a complete Empire bedroom set on the second floor. There is a study with pre-Revolutionary War American furniture and a room for dipping candles.

Dyckman House, *204th Street and Broadway Avenue (212-304-9422). Tuesday–Sunday 11 A.M.–4 P.M. Admission charge.*

Directions: Subway A to 207th Street.

When the Dyckman House was built in 1783, it was a typical Dutch homestead composed of fieldstone, brick, and wood on a very untypical farm covering three hundred acres. The Dyckman farm, which was acquired in stages beginning in 1677, remained the biggest farm in Manhattan for two hundred years.

In 1917, when developers were about to destroy Dyckman House, the Dyckman family restored the old place and rearranged its rooms with Dutch and English period furniture and pre-Revolutionary War toys, clothing, and curios. Behind the building there is a traditional smokehouse and a storage shed. Everyday eighteenth-century life is mirrored in this simple dwelling.

The Bronx

The Bronx was one of the earliest parts of the city to be settled. In 1641 a Scandinavian named Jonas Bronck crossed the Harlem River and bought five hundred acres from the Indians and started clearing and cultivating the land. The Bronx that was born in that bygone era was a dangerous place, vulnerable to the attacks of Indians and fraught with disputes between the Dutch burgers and English dissenters. The Bronx grew slowly and wasn't really developed until the twentieth century; however, some very early Dutch houses have been preserved in the Bronx backwater.

Van Cortlandt Mansion, *Van Cortlandt Park near 242nd Street and Broadway Avenue (212-546-3323). Tuesday–Saturday 10 A.M.–4:45 P.M.; Sunday 2 P.M.–4:45 P.M. Admission charge.*

Directions: Subway 1 or 9 to 242nd Street/Van Cortlandt Park.

The Van Cortlandt Mansion is an evocative return to colonial times, set among broad shade trees and bushes on a bluff in Van Courtland Park. The Dutch Van Cortlandt clan owned this section of the Bronx from the late seventeenth century to the late nineteenth century. An accomplished family, it boasted the first native-born mayor of New York (1677) and a general in the Continental Army.

Frederick Van Cortlandt built the mansion in 1748 in a four-square sturdy version of Georgian architecture. This manor house alternates brick and rough fieldstone, the natural materials blending with the natural setting. It has interesting touches like the comic masks in the keystones above the double-hung multipaned windows.

The rooms of the house are stuffed with Van Courtlandt family memorabilia and furniture from the Dutch and British colonial eras. The east parlor features a portrait of Augustus Van Cortlandt. There is a Dutch bedroom on the second floor with a Dutch cupboard bed, and the kitchen has an actual Dutch oven. George Washington slept in the Munro room.

Valentine-Varian House, *3266 Bainbridge Avenue (212-881-8900). Saturday and Sunday 10 A.M.–5 P.M. Admission charge.*

Directions: Subway D to 205th Street/Bainbridge Avenue or Subway 4 to Mosholu Parkway.

The Valentine-Varian House is a simple, unpretentious Dutch farmhouse, compact and rough-hewn, vintage 1758. It is located in the North Bronx in a neighborhood called Norwood near the entrance of Williamsbridge Oval Park.

The Valentine-Varian House was built by Isaac Valentine in 1748 on land he had purchased from the Dutch Reformed Church. He was a farmer and a blacksmith and a man of action who sided with the Sons of Liberty. He and his family were forced to flee their farmstead during the Revolution, as it was the scene of violent skirmishes and was even occupied by Hessian troops. The Varians took title to the land along with the house in 1791. There was a Varian mayor and a Varian alderman among the generations of prosperous Varian farmers.

Blocking the demolition ball of developers, the Bronx Historical Society preserved the house and filled it with an interesting selection of old pictures, photos, documents, maps, and memorabilia that tell the whole story of the Bronx.

Flushing

Directions: Subway 7 to Roosevelt Avenue/Main Street.

Vlissingen, now called Flushing, was named for a Dutch town and chartered in 1645. This outlying area of New Netherlands found few Dutch takers and was soon settled by English dissenters. The Quakers who came in the 1640s and 1650s were Vlissingen's leading "heretics," and the established Dutch Calvinist Church and its official defenders wanted to close it down.

In 1657 Governor Peter Stuyvesant issued an edict affirming the special status of the Dutch Reformed Church; it was a clear warning to "abominable sects" like the Quakers. In the fall Robert Hodgson, a newly arrived English Quaker, was arrested for preaching the Quaker doctrine, whipped by the public executioner, and imprisoned. Despite the threats of Governor Stuyvesant and inquisition-like torture, he refused to submit to forced labor and was banished before the end of the year.

The people of early Flushing took up his cause and made their famous remonstrance to the governor on December 27, 1657. They would not "persecute" the Quakers and could not "in conscience lay violent hands on them." Hodgson's stand and the courageous actions of the people of Flushing were a milestone in the fight for religious freedom.

Over the years Flushing's Quaker farmers were replaced by wealthy Manhattan merchants who used it as a vacation hideaway. Flushing became famous again in 1939 when new highways, designed by Robert Moses, led to a science-fantasy World's Fair. These same roads were then used by commuters, who flocked to this newly accessible suburb. Still, the Quaker tradition of tolerance persists in modern Flushing, a community that accepts people of all races and religious backgrounds.

A Stroll Through Historic Flushing

St. George's Episcopal Church

Just across from the subway stop near the junction of Main Street and Roosevelt Avenue stands St. George's, built in 1854. The church is all brownstone respectability with a quaint white wooden steeple. Francis Lewis, a Declaration of Independence signer, was vestryman at the first church on this site in 1761.

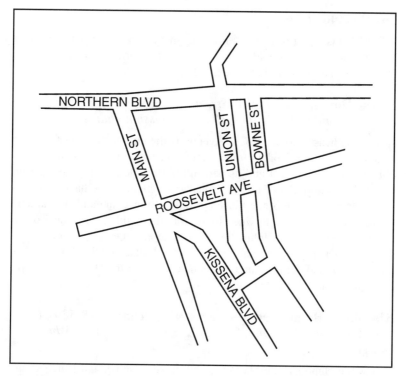

Historic Flushing

Friend's Meeting House, *137-16 Northern Boulevard.*

Walking north toward Northern Boulevard, make a right turn between Main Street and Union and stop at the site of the historic Friend's (Quakers) Meeting House, dating from 1694 and restored between 1716 and 1719. The back of the frame building is on the boulevard while the front faces a tiny cemetery with Quaker headstones without any names. Quakers have been meeting here nonstop since the American Revolution.

Flushing Town Hall, *137-35 Northern Boulevard.*

On the opposite side of the boulevard, the Town Hall dates from 1862. It is all Victorian extravagance with ornamental cornices, decorative turrets, and giant gables. This impressive brick structure keeps changing identity: it has been a courthouse, opera house, bank, library, and jail. Its halls, which once rang with the voices of Theodore Roosevelt, Ulysses Grant, and P. T. Barnum, are today vacant.

Fox Oaks Rock

A block up is a part of colonial Flushing that really deserves to be called a milestone. This big boulder, on 37th Avenue, marks the spot where the famous Quaker, George Fox, preached in 1672.

Bowne House, *37-01 Bowne Street (212-359-0528). Friday, Saturday, and Sunday 2:30 P.M.–4:30 P.M. Admission charge.*

At the southeast corner of 37th Avenue is the site of the oldest historic structure in Queens. Today Bowne House is a small museum dedicated to Flushing's colonial past and its part in the struggle for religious liberty. The house is a model of low-key Quaker simplicity. The backyard contains a bronze plaque of the Flushing Remonstrance and an herb garden.

From 1661 to 1945 Bowne House was the residence of the Bowne family. Their ancestor, John Bowne, was another Quaker who dared to stand up to Peter Stuyvesant. Banished to Holland for holding Quaker meetings, he had the last laugh when he convinced the Dutch West India Company to accept the Quakers.

Kingsland Homestead, *143-35 37th Avenue (718-520-7049). Tuesday, Saturday, and Sunday 2:30 P.M.–4:30 P.M. Admission charge.*

This white clapboard farmhouse, which mixes English and Dutch architectural styles, would fit right into an old New England village. Queens preservationists saved this circa 1674 house and opened it as a museum in 1968. It has a small intimate collection of photos, maps, and other memorabilia of local history.

The house was built by a Quaker named Doughty, who was the first person to free a slave in New York. His son-in-law, Joseph King, who nearly lost his head in the French Revolution, retired here after all the excitement. Kingsland House stayed in the socially prominent Murray family (for whom Murray Hill was named) for more than a century.

Staten Island

The Dutch named it Staten Island and the English named it Richmond. The city fathers officially call it Richmond, but mostly everybody else, including mapmakers, call it Staten Island. For a lot of its history it was so underpopulated that no one cared what it was called.

In 1639 the Dutch opened the island to colonization, but each time they thought they had something going, the Native Americans chased out the settlers. There were a number of Indian wars with peculiar-sounding names like the Pig War in 1641, the Whiskey War in 1643, and the Peach War in 1655. Every time they made peace with the Native Americans, the colonists would negotiate another deal to buy the island. They wound up buying it five times.

The original capital of English Richmond was called Cocles Town, but when the name became corrupted to Cuckold's Town the people in charge moved that it be changed to Richmond. People were always doing things like that to neglected Staten Island.

For the first two centuries of its life it was a fishing and farming backwater. Later the rich discovered the backwater and made it a luxury resort and literary colony. Inevitably, the rich started looking for new places to summer and, although Staten Island would have gladly returned to its semirural isolation, industry had different ideas; pollution soon followed the oil refineries. Finally, it took the Verrazano Bridge to bring Staten Island into the New York mainstream and make it another bedroom suburb. Still, the borough's gradual development helped preserve its past, which is alive and well in the Richmond Restoration.

The Richmond Restoration, *intersection of Richmond Road, Clarke Avenue, and Arthur Kill Road adjoining La Tourette Park (718-351-1617). Wednesday–Friday 10* A.M.*–5* P.M.*; Saturday– Monday and holidays 1* P.M.*–5* P.M. *Admission charge.*

Directions: Subway 4 or 5 train to Bowling Green or Subway 1 to South Ferry, then Staten Island Ferry. S74 bus to Richmond Hill Road near St. Patrick's Place.

The Richmond Restoration has more of the founders' New York than the other four boroughs put together, so it is definitely worth the bother of getting there. The first leg of the Staten Island journey is the ferry. It's transportation if you live in Staten Island, but for anyone else it's a bargain at 25 cents for a half-hour excursion, with spectacular views of the Statue of Liberty, Ellis Island, and the Verrazano Bridge. The ferry lands in St. George, the capital of the borough, in the vicinity of the bus terminal, where a bus leaves regularly for the Restoration. It's just a short walk after getting off the bus to the information office, a converted courthouse from 1837, for brochures and tickets.

The Richmond Restoration is a thirty-acre village of twenty-five representative houses (soon to be more) from early America. Ten are in their original Richmond Town sites; the others were retrieved from all over the Island through the untiring efforts of the Staten Island Historical Society. Each building reflects a way of life. There's a print shop, a carpenter's shop, a combination bakery–post office, a saddler and harness maker's shop, and homes of assorted people from physician to shipping magnate.

The Restoration is a living museum where guides in period costume explain the intricacies of cooking in a beehive oven or setting type in the nineteenth century. In one house there is a woman in a bonnet turning a potter's wheel; in the next a tall man in hayseed overalls plaits a straw basket. It contains the oldest elementary school in the United States, dating from 1695. The Guyon-Lake-Tysen house is the best example of Dutch colonial architecture in the city. Even the humble snack bar with homemade brownies (not prepared in the beehive oven) and cider is in the Greek revival Bennett house, completed in the middle of the last century.

═Founders' Organizations and Archives═

The Dutch Inheritance

The Dutch colony of the seventeenth century set the mold for modern New York. The city is still all about dealing and deal makers, though it is no longer officially run by a single company and a coterie of merchants. Like seventeenth-century patroons, the city's contemporary power brokers still make fortunes from real estate. The colonial smugglers who raked in the guilders on bootlegged pelts also have their twentieth-century equivalents who deal in less benign forms of contraband.

The drinking and roughhousing that characterized New Amsterdam have not disappeared despite periodic public crusades in the spirit of Peter Stuyvesant. New York is not effete. It is a convivial town that can sometimes get contentious; the wild good times are in its blood. Cultural pluralism is another part of New York's Dutch inheritance. Even in the days when the population numbered in the hundreds, there were eighteen languages being spoken and there were almost as many religious sects. Welcoming foreigners started as a necessity in underpopulated New Amsterdam and quickly became a New York tradition.

The Dutch left a legacy in the New York vocabulary with words like boss (*baas*), scow (*schouw*), and snoop (*snoepen*). Some of New York's favorite treats like the waffle (*wafle*) and the cookie (*koekje*) are of Dutch origin. Dutch place names can still be found from the Bowery (*bouwerie* means farm) to Brooklyn (*Breukelen*). Though the Dutch didn't invent the yule log or the Christmas tree, Santa Claus is derived from the Dutch *Sinter Klass*. Even the word "Yankee" comes from the name of a New

Netherlands freebooter, Jan Keese. The typical New York stoop is a Dutch architectural convention, which in old Amsterdam protected living spaces from floods.

In a footnote to the Dutch founders, there was a small spurt of Dutch immigration to New York in 1953 via a special act of Congress which granted seventeen thousand visas to Dutch emigrants. In 1955 there was a special quota for Dutch citizens leaving their newly liberated colony of Indonesia. Altogether, eighty thousand Dutch left the Netherlands between 1945 and 1965, with the majority settling in Los Angeles and New York. They eagerly assimilated and were diffused throughout the metropolitan area.

The last Dutch vestiges are preserved in some very special and exclusive organizations.

Holland Society of New York, *122 East 58th Street (212-758-1675).*

All members are direct descendants of the Dutch who settled New York prior to 1675. They meet to discuss their pedigrees and compare genealogies. The Society has a six-thousand-volume library containing many rare documents and heirloom books dealing with Dutch history and culture and their presence in New York. The organization's Burgher Guards dress up in seventeenth-century costume and participate in patriotic events and parades.

Netherlands-America Community Association, *One Rockefeller Plaza (212-246-1429).*

The group is a partnership of the Netherlands Benevolent Society (founded in 1905) and the Netherlands-America Foundation (founded in 1921). Its activities are split between community service and promoting Dutch education, literature, and art.

The English Inheritance

The English are New York's nonethnics, the ideal that future ethnics envied and emulated. New York's English imprint has never been lost. It is in the spoken and written language of the city, though slightly obscured by New York's dialects. It is in the courts and the common law and the office of mayor.

New York's buildings imitated English architectural styles from Georgian to Gothic revival. Chippendale furniture adorned New York drawing rooms along with made-in-England Mappin and Webb silver and Royal

Worcester porcelain. Manhattan enjoyed English drama and English acting companies like the Hallam. English higher education set the standard
for New York with the establishment of Kings College, today Columbia
University. New Yorkers kept hounds and hunted like English squires, or
were Sunday sailors, like good descendants of a seafaring nation.

Englishmen founded many of the city's most important private institutions from banks to libraries and went on to become the city's unofficial
aristocracy in the New York Social Register.

The English tradition continues in a number of organizations with links
to the "mother country."

St. George's Society of New York, *71 West 23rd Street (212-924-1434).*

This is the granddaddy of all New York "charitable" organizations, having
begun life in 1691. It's been a long time since the Society helped immigrant Brits find jobs or shelter. These days it's primarily a social organization for people of British or Commonwealth birth or descent.

English-Speaking Union of the United States, *16 East 69th Street (212-879-6860).*

The organization awards scholarships and travel grants in the process of
promoting English-language culture. It has a very British library with the
latest English papers and tweedy English types.

Pilgrims of the United States, *74 Trinity Place (212-943-0635).*

Pilgrims is the elite of English overseas organizations. In between toasts
for Queen and country the Old Boys promote Anglo-American relations.
The British Ambassador comes here to make his inaugural address.

The British Table

Though the combination of *English* and *cuisine* is seen in some quarters
as a contradiction in terms, in another era the English chop house was a
hallowed New York institution. The combination of prime meat, potatoes,
fireplaces, wainscoting, and bronze antiques caught New Yorkers' fancy.
In the past, the New York version of the English pub was usually just a
gimmick with a Union Jack and Hogarth prints for atmosphere. Lately
new arrivals from Britain who have taken prominent places in the worlds

of advertising, publishing, and retailing have created a more authentic scene.

Manchester New York, *920 Second Avenue at 48th Street (212-223-7484). Monday noon–1 A.M.; Tuesday–Friday noon–2 or 3 A.M.; Saturday and Sunday 2 P.M.–3 or 4 A.M.*

The big wraparound bar with the overhead telly (for the rugby and soccer matches from Old Blighty) dominates this bit of Manchester in New York, and the emphasis is on the brew. Besides the forty-two bottled beers on sale, which include Samuel Smith's Oatmeal Stout and Old Peculiar, classics like Double Diamond Ale are on tap. The pub food is a perfect match for the drink.

North Star Pub, *93 South Street (212-509-6757). Monday–Saturday 11:30 A.M. to whenever it cools down (1 or 2 A.M.); Sunday noon–midnight.*

The North Star attracts the Wall Street Brits and local Anglophiles. Designed by Welshman John Belle (the architect who directed the restoration of Ellis Island), it is an exact replica of the real thing. The menu with its many varieties of pasty, single malt bread pudding, Scotch egg, and mushy peas also gets the details right.

English Harbor Fish & Chips, *246 East 14th Street (212-777-5420). Monday–Saturday 11 A.M.–11 P.M.; Sunday 2 P.M.–10 P.M.*

The fish is authentic English, crisply battered with just the right crunch and deep-sea flavor. The master British fry cook keeps the fish moist and the oil fresh. Just add a jolt of vinegar and salt to taste. The look is fast-food immaculate, with a clipper ship and lighthouse mural.

Guv'nors, *443 East 6th Street (212-614-3260). Tuesday–Sunday noon–8 P.M.*

Guv'nors is a cozy corner of England with ploughman's lunches, crumpets, and Victoriana on the walls that attracts the trend-setting Bohemian Brits of the East Village.

NW3, *242 East 10th Street (212-260-0891). Daily 9 P.M.–3 A.M.*

NW3 is a well-known British postal code and a popular hangout for British expatriates. It's a contemporary pub with a downtown New York feeling.

Tea and Sympathy, *108 Greenwich Ave between 12th and 13th streets (212-807-8329). Monday–Friday 11:30 A.M.–10 P.M.; Saturday and Sunday 10 A.M.–10 P.M.*

This is the home of the authentic British tea, with fabulous scones, clotted cream, strawberry and raspberry preserves, and finger sandwiches. It has the sedate charming flower-print and chintz style that goes with this afternoon ritual. Come lunch and dinner, Tea and Sympathy caters more to full-blooded shepherd's pie and banger-and-mash appetites.

British Open, *320 East 59th Street (212-355-8467). Monday–Saturday 11 A.M.–11 P.M.; Sunday noon–10 P.M.*

The British Open is a pub with a golf theme, balls and clubs for decoration and golf magazines providing the clutter. The crowd at this nineteenth hole is English ex-pat and golf enthusiast.

At the bar there are British brews like Double Diamond and John Courage, and in the attractive dining room in the back there's an all English menu.

British Gourmet

Homesick English expats and fanatical New York Anglophiles have been known to get yens for such epicurean English fare as Bisto instant gravy and tinned plum pudding. New York's last English food shop meets that need.

Myers of Keswick, *634 Hudson Street (212-691-4194). Monday–Friday 10 A.M.–7 P.M.; Saturday 10 A.M.–6 P.M.; Sunday noon–5 P.M.*

Peter Myers is an artist if your taste in food includes English savouries, sausage rolls, and pork pies. It's all the best ingredients and family recipes from Keswick in the Lake District.

British Style

While the populations of Anglo-Saxons, Scots, and Welsh who reside in New York are consistently on the rise, they do not make up a numerically significant portion of Gotham's new immigrants. Still, the latest Brits to conquer the island of Manhattan are a high-impact, high-profile segment that caters to the City's rampant Anglophilia. Hard-edged New Yorkers love the sound of an English accent (high or low), and cannot resist the soft rustle of English quaint. Things and customs English are the New York vogue from afternoon tea to Aquascutum raincoats.

Clothing

Aquascutum, *680 Fifth Avenue at 54th Street (212-975-0250). Monday–Wednesday, Friday, and Saturday 10 A.M.–6 P.M.; Thursday 10 A.M.–7 P.M.*

It is the old English class act applied to ready-to-wear. There are the internationally known raincoats and much more. The styles are conservative, very careful solids and plaids, simple and functional. The prices are straightforwardly expensive and the service is respectful.

Berk of Burlington Arcade, *781 Madison Avenue between 66th and 67th streets (212-570-0285). Monday–Saturday 10 A.M.–6 P.M.*

This shop appeals to the snob in every New Yorker, as if clothes make the class and the title comes with the cashmere. The saleswomen believe in the Berk myth and cater to it.

Burberrys, Ltd., *9 East 57th Street (212-371-5010). Monday–Wednesday and Friday 9:30 A.M.–6 P.M.; Thursday 9:30–7 P.M.; Saturday 10 A.M.–6 P.M.*

No surprises here, just four floors of Burberrys' popular English styles for men and women and all the required plaid linings. The famous raincoat takes center stage with plenty of accessories to go with it, many of which have never been seen in London.

Jaeger, *818 Madison Avenue between 67th and 68th streets (212-628-3350). Monday–Saturday 10 A.M.–6 P.M.*

Jaeger is the Regent Street look of conservative style for men and women, though in New York only women's clothes are on offer. Since the 1920s it has been the place for camel's hair coats, sweaters, and color-coordinated sportswear. Although spruced up, it is still very set in its ways.

Laura Ashley, *21 East 57th Street (212-752-7300). Monday–Friday 10 A.M.–7 P.M.; Saturday 10 A.M.–6 P.M. 398 Columbus Ave. at 79th Street (212-496-5110). Monday–Wednesday, Friday, and Saturday 11 A.M–7 P.M.; Thursday 11 A.M–8 P.M.; Sunday noon–6 P.M. 4 Fulton Street (South Street Seaport) (212-809-3555). Monday–Saturday 10 A.M.–9 P.M.; Sunday noon–8 P.M.*

Laura Ashley has soft and flowered fabrics in gentle English colors. She represents pastoral England with prints and delicate patterns and the return of the romantic.

N. Peal, *118 East 57th Street (212-826-3350). Monday–Saturday 10 A.M.–6 P.M.*

The English keep promoting cashmere to compete with the Far-East imports. The designs here are so original, who can tell they are sweaters? Shoppers don't have much room to explore the merchandise.

Asprey and Company, *Trump Tower, 725 Fifth Avenue at 56th Street (212-688-1811). Monday–Saturday 10 A.M.–5:30 P.M.*

Elegant jewels, fine silver, and splendid accessories are the order of the day. The air is as rarefied as the merchandise, but now and again it is possible to find a small enamel box at less than a king's ransom.

Home Furnishings and Accessories

Floris, *703 Madison Avenue (212-935-9100). Monday–Wednesday and Friday 10 A.M.–6 P.M.; Thursday 10 A.M.–7 P.M.; Sunday noon–6 P.M.*

The original in England is on Jermyn Street at the better end of Piccadilly. There are scented soaps, shaving toiletries, sachets, and natural flower fragrances all wrapped in the store colors of blue and gold.

Laura Ashley Home, *714 Madison Avenue (212-735-5000). Monday–Wednesday, Friday, and Saturday 10 A.M.–6 P.M.; Thursday 10 A.M.–7 P.M.*

Everything in this store looks like it came out of English *Country Life* magazine. The same motifs of flower patterns are on the bed linens, towels, fabrics, tea sets, and lampshades. It can get monotonous.

Antiques

Hyde Park, *836 Broadway between 12th and 13th streets (212-477-0033). Monday–Friday 9:00 A.M.–5:00 P.M.; Saturday 10:00 A.M.–2:30 P.M.*

The gallery caters to the carriage trade with thoroughly researched and authenticated English pieces from the eighteenth and nineteenth century, and the largest inventory in the country. It takes pride in its especially fine examples of eighteenth-century Queen Ann and nineteenth-century Regency furniture.

Phillip Colleck of London Ltd., *830 Broadway between 12th and 13th streets (212-505-2500). Monday–Friday 9:00 A.M.–5:00 P.M.*

Since 1938 Colleck has provided high-quality pieces and gracious service. The patient and knowledgeable staff takes time to inform the customer about their Queen Ann, William and Mary, Georgian, and Regency furniture.

Kentshire, *37 East 12th Street between Broadway and University (212-673-6644). Monday–Friday 9:00 A.M.–5:00 P.M.; Saturday 10:00 A.M.–3:00 P.M.*

Kentshire is eight floors of eighteenth-, nineteenth-, and twentieth-century antiques, with the heaviest concentration on prime Georgian and Regency items. The antiques on each floor are artfully arranged, creating the feeling of a museum collection.

S. J. Shrubsole, *104 East 57th Street (212-753-8920). Monday–Saturday 9:30 A.M.–5 P.M.*

The silver items sold here are practically museum pieces. There are finely etched tea sets and trays as well as finely crafted Georgian serving pieces.

Mittel Europa

Mittel Europa is the European heartland, Germanic, Slav, and Magyar. It's Hapsburg and Hohenzollern Europe, a hierarchy of autocrats, artisans, and peasants. Though their languages, customs, and traditions differ, they share the same geography and climate, and perhaps even the same aspirations. When the Mittel Europeans came to New York they were drawn to the same neighborhoods and re-created their own central Europe in New York. Though they were different and had different loyalties, they had common memories and a common history, which was reassuring in a strange and unfamiliar land.

Germans

History

Germans are America's largest ethnic group. Before the twentieth century they were consistently New York's second ethnic group. Two world wars with Germany destroyed the community's identity, and today the Germans are the city's invisible ethnics.

German refugees from the Thirty Years' War were among the first settlers of New Amsterdam. Hans Kierstede, a native of Saxony, was New Amsterdam's first physician, and Ulrich Lupolt was sheriff of New Amsterdam during the early Indian wars. Even after the British took over in 1664, Jacob Leisler of Frankfort Am Main was a spokesman for the interests of the Dutch minority and led a New York revolution.

In the eighteenth century German immigrants from the Palatinate entered New York as "redemptionists"; they were sold to the highest bidder in a market near City Hall to pay the cost of their passage. They were in great demand for their industry, honesty, and skills. Unlike the English, they rarely ran away.

Peter Zenger was one Palatine immigrant who distinguished himself in eighteenth-century New York. Starting as a printer's apprentice, he was soon publishing his own newspaper. In 1734 he had the temerity to attack in print the high-handed and dishonest British governor Cosby. Four editions of his paper were consigned to the public hangman and he was sent to jail. His legal vindication set the precedent for press freedom in the city.

The British recruited Germans to put down the American rebellion of 1776. These Hessians, who were dragooned into service, didn't have any real loyalties, and in areas with large German populations, the unwilling soldiers defected to the enemy. Many of the Hessians who occupied New York during the war stayed on to become citizens of the Republic.

The dedicated Germans fighting on the Revolutionary side included a genuine military genius from Prussia, Baron Von Steuben. The Baron's claims to rank and privilege may have been exaggerated, but he knew how to train and organize an army and win battles. Von Steuben continued to take an active part in American public life after the Revolution and was a prominent figure in New York German organizations and society.

In the early years of the Republic a German named John Jacob Astor from Waldorf became the city's first millionaire. He started out as a butcher's assistant, but quickly learned there was more money in fur than in meat. His trading posts extended to the Oregon territory. Like Donald Trump, another fabulously wealthy New Yorker of German ancestry, he made his fortune investing in New York real estate and the city's first luxury hotels were Astor's.

The defeat of a German revolution in 1848 led to an influx of German political refugees. They were intellectuals and free thinkers who contributed to the overall intellectual life of the city. Franz Lieber taught international law at Columbia University and Carl Schurz championed reform as editor of the very liberal *New York Evening Post*.

German intellectuals were intent on preserving German culture in America's largest city. By the end of the 1850s they had established fifty German schools, ten book stores, four daily newspapers, and a German theater. They had also formed local *turnerverein* (gymnastic societies), which combined physical education with progressive politics.

But the "Forty-eighters" were more than thinkers; they were also men of action. They took their abolition seriously and six thousand German political exiles were among the first to volunteer for the city's militias to fight in the War Between the States. Germans filled the ranks of ten New York regiments. The versatile Carl Schurz led German-American armies along with that other outstanding German, Franz Lieber. Both were generals.

The immigrants of Forty-eight were followed by emigrants from Germany's own potato famine. This emigration wave also included rural Germans dispossessed from large estates and urban Germans who were casualties of the Industrial Revolution. The new Germans were more expansive than the political refugees. They enjoyed the camaraderie of the volunteer fire house and the culture of the German beer garden. They preferred marching bands to concert halls.

The established German community organized the German-American Society to aid new German arrivals, and joined forces with the Irish to create the Board of Commissioners to oversee emigration. Frederich Kapp was the leading German spokesman on the board and helped found the Castle Garden Emigration Station to safeguard German emigrants from fraud and exploitation. By 1860 New York's German-born community numbered over one hundred thousand.

In the boom following the Civil War, New York industry beat the bushes for talented German craftsmen and artisans. Germans went to work making elegant furniture and cabinets and fine musical instruments. They rolled cigars, baked bread, and brewed beer. When they got tired of working for someone else, Germans started their own factories, workshops, and retail businesses.

There are many German success stories, such as Heinrich Engelhard Steinweg, who came to New York from Brunswick with his four sons. He was an Old World master who crafted concert pianos with the quality of a Stradivarius violin. In New York Steinweg became Steinway and concert pianos became big business. In 1872 William Steinway and his workers left the piano workshop in Manhattan for a four-hundred-acre company town on Bowery Bay near Astoria. The Steinway industrial community had its own park, library, ball field, schools, and row housing.

In the Gilded Age New York had more German-American breweries than St. Louis and Milwaukee combined. The Rupperts were the leading brewing family and the first to promote sports with their beer. In 1923 Jacob Ruppert built Yankee Stadium in the Bronx with a short right wall so another German by the name of Babe Ruth could hit more home runs. George Steinbrenner is the latest German American to own the Yankees.

New York's Germans were great music lovers and many joined glee clubs and choirs. They belonged to classical music singing groups like the Liederkranz, which was started in 1847, and the Arion, which was formed after the Liederkranz first admitted women. The Liederkranz choral was world renowned and even commissioned a work by Richard Wagner for the 1876 presidential inauguration. German singing groups periodically gathered to entertain one another and compete for prizes. One *sangerfeste* in 1900 in Brooklyn involved six thousand singers and 774 groups.

Germans were great joiners. German New Yorkers enjoyed one another's company in every kind of group, from shooting clubs to church sodalities to amateur drama societies. Holidays, profane and religious, were a time when the ordinarily restrained Germans could let go. They observed the Sabbath with lighthearted picnics and outings, shocking some of their prim Protestant neighbors.

German immigrants originally resided in the Lower East Side's *Kleine Deutschland,* but there were also pockets of Germans on Dutch Hill on 40th Street and First Avenue and in Hell's Kitchen. German society, families like the Rhinelanders and Schermerhorns, had staked out Yorkville as early as the 1830s and by the 1890s wealthy German brewers built mansions in this German reserve. Brooklyn also had a substantial German community in Williamsburg and Bushwick. It was a typical German mix of tobacconists, tailors, lithographers, and brewers. After the tragic sinking of the excursion ship the *General Slocum* in 1904, when over one thousand residents of Kleine Deutschland drowned, the ethnic map of the city changed; thousands of inconsolable working-class Germans deserted Kleine Deutschland for Yorkville.

No one doubted the loyalty and patriotism of German New Yorkers in 1901—more than ninety percent had their first citizenship papers—but European power politics and propaganda changed that positive image. The industrious Teuton became the bestial Hun overnight, as Germany invaded neutral countries and German U-boats threatened shipping at the start of World War I.

Even before America entered the war, a German newspaper publisher was ordered by the New York mayor to remove the German flag from outside his office. In Brooklyn government authorities decreed that the name of Hamburg Avenue be changed to Wilson Avenue. German schools and cultural organizations were vandalized and members were harassed. In July of 1916 the whole German community became suspect when a ship carrying British war munitions blew up in New York Harbor.

After war was declared German participation in Liberty Bond drives and even service in the trenches in France didn't change the anti-German attitude on the home front. Germans were practically forced to deny their heritage. Some Germans anglicized their names and in self-defense started their own Americanization programs.

German Americans withstood this period of prejudice to become trend setters in the Roaring Twenties. They were the showmen, the creators of glamour and glitter. The great Florenz Ziegfield was the toast of Broadway and cafe society. His Ziegfield Follies was the musical event of the season and his showgirls were the Twenties ideal.

In the years of the Great Depression, New York became a center for Nazi propaganda and German New Yorkers were prime targets. Fritz Kuhn and his Nazi Bund recruited in the streets of Yorkville. Although claiming to have a following of 250,000 German Americans, the FBI estimated it was closer to 6,500. Most German New Yorkers weren't interested in Hitler's message of hate and some German groups like the German Workers Club demonstrated against these Nazi bigots.

While a small minority of German-American extremists were making a lot of noise in Yorkville, a German New Yorker was making history in the U.S. Senate. Born in Germany, Robert Wagner made his way from the state assembly to the U.S. Senate to become one of the key legislators of Franklin D. Roosevelt's New Deal. The Act, which bears his name, finally gave the working man the right to organize and bargain collectively without fear of retaliation.

German New Yorkers didn't wait to be drafted after the sneak attack on Pearl Harbor. They served in both theaters of the war and a disproportionate number were commissioned officers. German Americans like Donald Roebling, the great-grandson of Brooklyn Bridge builder John Roebling, used their scientific ability to devise "miracle weapons" such as the amphibious tank.

In the postwar prosperity a second-generation Wagner, Robert F. Wagner, Jr., became mayor of New York. Calm and low key, Wagner went about thoroughly rebuilding the city. He knocked down the Third Avenue El, redeveloped the West Side around Columbus Circle, and built over a hundred thousand units of medium-income housing. New York's master builder and reform mayor also went about dismantling Tammany's political machine.

In the 1950s a new breed of German emigrated to New York seeking opportunity. Thousands of technicians and scientists came to the city in the first stages of a postwar "brain drain." As the German economy improved in the 1960s and even began to outperform the U.S. economy in the 1970s, the only Germans who came to New York were employed by German banks and international corporations.

Deutschland on the Lower East Side

Before Germans staked out Yorkville they lived on the Lower East Side. Turn-of-the-century Germans, first and second generation, were concentrated in Kleine Deutschland from 12th Street to Houston and the Bowery east to the river. The neighborhood was completely German speaking, with big signs in German Gothic letters. The population was mainly from the German south—Baden, Bavaria, Wertenberger and Rhineland—and had a reputation for being more "Latin" and light hearted than northern Germans.

The streets surrounding German Tompkins Square Park were filled with German groceries, delicatessens, *konditorei,* and rathskellers. The beer gardens that lined the Bowery were spirited scenes of polkas and accordion playing. The waitresses were beer hall Brunhildes who had no problem hefting the liter steins. Kleine Deutschland was also very keen on sports from soccer to shooting to gymnastics.

The intellectual elite of the German neighborhood provided German lending libraries and a *volkstheater* with German productions of Hauptmann, Shakespeare, and Ibsen. There were competitions between German singing societies and classical concerts and band concerts in the park.

In 1904 a tragic accident ended the era of Kleine Deutschland. It was a fine June morning when two thousand neighborhood people, mostly women and children, boarded the paddle-steamer the *General Slocum* for a picnic on the Long Island Sound. The ship was too old and overcrowded; she had a reputation as a bad luck ship and a history of accidents. A fire started from a careless match and a carelessly cleaned boiler. When the *General Slocum* began burning out of control, instead of tacking to shore, the captain panicked and sailed straight into the wind, fanning the flames. Over one thousand died, and Kleine Deutschland never recovered.

Kleine Deutschland

Directions: Subway 6 to Astor Place/Fourth Avenue or Bus M15 to East Seventh Street.

Five remnants of Kleine Deutschland are still visible in the East Village of Slavs and the avant-garde.

The headquarters of the Deutsch-Amerikanische Scheuetzen Gesellschaft was located at 12 St. Mark's Place. It is one of the few remaining buildings where German clubs, in this case a shooting club, flourished.

The Freie Bibliotek und Lesehalle lends dignity to an East Village avenue that has seen better days. Anna and Oswald Ottendorfer, the proprietors of the New York *Staats Zeitung,* donated this attractive red brick building on 135 Second Avenue to the community for a library.

The German Dispensary on 137 Second Avenue was also a gift of the Ottendorfers to Kleine Deutschland. Built to house a medical clinic, it was adorned with the terra cotta busts of renowned doctors and scientists from Hippocrates to Humboldt. World War I anti-German hysteria forced the occupants to change the building's name from the German Polyklinik to the Stuyvesant Clinic.

Off Avenue A on the 10th Street side of Tompkins Park, there is a monument to the *General Slocum* disaster. It is a simple statue of a girl and boy gazing at a steamboat, which expresses both loss and hope. The park, which was once a pleasant village green for the Slav and Hispanic ethnics, has been "rehabilitated" to keep out a population that turned the park into an open-air crash pad.

The Most Holy Redeemer Church, located on 173 East 10th Street, was the "mother" Catholic church for German Americans arriving in the nineteenth century, and was informally known as the German Cathedral. The architecture of this church is Rococo, but it has the vastness of a Gothic house of worship. The church was consecrated in 1852 by the revered Archbishop and later Cardinal John Hughes. In 1994 New York's Cardinal O'Connor celebrated a mass commemorating its 150th anniversary.

Yorkville

Directions: Subway 4, 5, or 6 to 86th Street; or Bus MI, M2, M3, or M4 to Madison Avenue/86th Street.

In the eighteenth century Yorkville was made up of country estates separating commercial New York from the wide-open spaces of Harlem. At first it attracted old German class, like the Schermerhorns and Rhinelanders. When the New York and Harlem Railroad made Yorkville more accessible, the new German money, the brewers and the sausage kings, came in droves. Solid townhouses kept the upper classes coming for over a century.

After the *General Slocum* disaster, these buildings were broken up into apartments to handle the influx of German families eager to forget the tragedy of Kleine Deutschland. Yorkville, or at least a substantial part of it, became the new German colony in the process.

German Yorkville extended north from 84th Street to 89th Street and west from the East River to Central Park. The thriving German colony was reinforced by German immigration in the 1920s. Germans took advantage of their relatively high quota under the new restrictive immigration code to escape the unstable political and economic conditions of Weimar Germany.

These post-World War I German immigrants had a deep nostalgia for a mythic Germany of country maidens and romantic waterfalls. They sang sentimental songs about the "Fatherland" in their clubs and societies. Some members of the German Yorkville community accused them of being cut off from American society.

Yorkville's Broadway was 86th Street. It had loud wild Bavarian beer halls with singing waiters and oompah bands. Barkers in *liederhosen* and alpine hats stood in front of the all-night German clubs buttonholing the browsers. There were elegant Viennese cafes with candlelight and rich pastry and hunting lodge *hofbraus* with fireplaces and wild boar.

The Yorkville Casino, at 210 East 86th Street, was one of several theaters showing German movies. There were theaters with German actors and actresses and cabarets with German entertainers. In the neighborhood cafes people played cards and talked politics or read one of a large selection of German newspapers from a rack.

In the thirties Yorkville was a hotbed of politics. In and out of the cafes and bars an army of true believers, from anarchists to Nazis, handed out pamphlets and got into brawls. At 178 East 85th Street Fritz Kuhn established the offices of the German American Bund and its mouthpiece, the *Deutscher und Beobachter*. Occasionally he'd parade his bully boys down 86th Street in regulation-issue Storm Trooper uniforms. Once at the Yorkville Casino some American Legion Germans had enough and there was a bloody free-for-all.

The Nazi episode and World War II changed Yorkville. After the war the German displaced persons who landed in the German East Side community didn't identify with the romantic, nostalgic Old World culture. They wanted to start careers as quickly as possible and assimilate into mainstream America.

Gradually German Yorkville moved to the suburbs and the neighborhood lost its German character. First, the big beer halls and dance halls closed and the theaters stopped showing German movies. Restaurants that depended on the German family trade folded and traditional German bakeries started baking strawberry shortcake. Finally, landmarks like Jaeger's and the Yorkville Casino closed. Suddenly there were more fast-food franchises than German delis and cafes on 86th Street, and it got harder to find a German language newspaper.

A kernel of the old Yorkville remains, along with the old German holdouts who haven't been gentrified out of their walk-ups. They still fondly remember a Yorkville of closeness and caring, when being German was more than wurst and lager and the Von Steuben Day Parade.

Yorkville Place Marks

Directions: Bus M86 to York Avenue.

Carl Schurz Park

Carl Schurz was the most influential German-born American of the nineteenth century. He was an Illinois senator, a New York newspaper editor, and a general in the Union army. He was an intimate of President Lincoln and served in another president's cabinet in 1877. He retired to Yorkville and was active in German community affairs.

The park that bears his illustrious name is a green belt and concrete promenade (Finley Walk) overlooking the East River and running from 84th Street to 90th Street and Gracie Square. It is the place to watch the barges and the joggers pass, and to survey the smokestacks in Queens and the currents of Hell Gate. New Yorkers who can't get to the Hamptons lie down on the grass or across a bench and bake in the sun here.

Henderson Place

In the early part of the nineteenth century, when Yorkville was estate territory occupied by first German families like the Rhinelanders and the Schermerhorns, John Jacob Astor purchased a country seat that included the present-day Henderson Place. When the estates were broken up and developed, other notable German families like the Ehrets and Rupperts of brewery fame lived here. In 1881 John C. Henderson built a picturesque series of houses on the street that now bears his name. Twenty of the original thirty-two have survived in all their extravagant Queen Anne glory, with turrets, gables, and paired entrance ways with sweeping staircases.

German Classics

German political exiles were catalysts for concert music in the city. Twenty-three revolutionary refugees started the Germania Orchestra in 1848. The group performed 829 concerts in six years. It introduced German classics like Beethoven's Ninth Symphony to New York and the American classical repertoire. After the orchestra disbanded, individual members helped form classical ensembles throughout the nation.

Carl Bergmann became the director of the New York Philharmonic, and later, Theodore Thomas of Essen became the orchestra's conductor. Leopold Damrosch made the big transition from leading the German Liederkranz Society Orchestra to founding the New York Symphony and directing the Metropolitan Opera. His son, Walter, followed in his foot-steps, promoting German composers like Richard Straus and refining the symphony to meet exacting European standards. The German connection with the symphony continued with immigrant German conductors like Otto Klemperer and Bruno Walter, who were refugees from Nazi Germany.

Avery Fisher Hall, *Lincoln Center, Broadway at 65th Street (212-874-2424).*

German classical music excellence is alive and well at Avery Fisher Hall, which is named for the building's donor, a hi-fi component manufacturer of German descent. The hall's acoustics have been a source of problems in the past but the symphony has maintained Damrosch standards. Behind the Lincoln Center glitz is Damrosch Park, offering free concerts, which the father and son would have enjoyed.

German Exhibits and Archives

Goethe House, *1014 Fifth Avenue (212-972-3960). Tuesday and Thursday 11 A.M.–7 P.M.; Wednesday, Friday, and Saturday noon–5 P.M.*

The cultural outlet of the Federal Republic of Germany has a sixteen-thousand-volume library, mostly in German, and the latest German newspapers. There are exhibits, lectures, and films of German or German-American cultural interest.

Deutsches Haus, *42 Washington Mews (212-998-8660).*

Deutsches Haus is an outlet of Goethe House at New York University. It's hidden away in a brick mews conversion from Henry James's era Washington Square. German language classes are offered throughout the year. Deutsches Haus has sponsored cultural events such as a series of German auteur films.

Austrian Cultural Institute, *950 Third Avenue, at 57th Street (212-759-5165). Monday–Friday 10 A.M.–5 P.M.*

The Austrian Cultural Institute is an unheralded outpost of modern Germanic culture. On the twentieth floor of an office tower, it houses a small library filled with German and Austrian books and publications and recent

Austrian newspapers. The institute is a resource for official and unofficial Austrian cultural happenings throughout the city.

The German Table

German cooking has no pretensions to haute cuisine; it doesn't mind being obvious. The tastes are satisfying and full-bodied, the seasoning doesn't strain for effect. It's simple meat-and-dumplings kind of food: roasted meats and brown gravies, with maybe a pickled vegetable, some sauer-kraut, or red cabbage on the side. Some basics are *wiener schnitzel* (golden fried veal cutlet), *sauerbraten* (sweet and sour pot roast), and the *kassler ripchen* (smoked loin of pork swimming in dark gravy). All these foods stick to the ribs and are to be energetically enjoyed.

For a quick bite, New York's Germans popularized the ubiquitous frankfurter. Their endless varieties of wurst made the delicatessen a New York institution before the Jewish deli came on the scene. German pastry can compete with the French for sheer richness and whipped cream, but there is also the simpler strudel and coffee ring side with an emphasis on natural fruit taste.

Kleine Konditorei, *234 East 86th Street (212-737-7130). Daily 10 A.M.–midnight.*

This *konditorei* looks like the real thing, with pastries in the window and at the front counter and an elegantly turned-out dining area full of flowers and polished brass. In the evening it's darkly lit and intimate; couples sip Liebfraumilch and dine on sauerbraten and schnitzel. Midmornings white-haired German regulars sit down for *kaffee mit kuchen* topped up with *schlag* (fresh whipped cream). The new owners, who include Otto Kollar, a former maitre d' at the fine French restaurant Le Metairie, have added style to the surroundings and character to the kitchen without sacrificing the *gemutlikeit.*

Heidelberg Restaurant, *1648 Second Avenue (212-650-1385). Daily 11 A.M.–11 P.M.*

This restaurant is an urban wine garden with blue and white checkered tablecloths and plastic grapes suspended from the ceiling. The waitress wearing a dirndl looks like an extra from the *Student Prince.* She keeps glasses brimming with rare German brews like Spaten or Dinkel Acker, and there's a nice selection of Rhine wines. The German basics are best here, a plate of pigs knuckles and sauerkraut, bratwurst with grainy mustard, or deep-fried schnitzel. Try the *jaeger schnitzel* in a creamy mushroom gravy.

Ideal, *322 East 86th Street between First and Second avenues (212-737-0795). Daily 7 A.M.–10 P.M.*

The Ideal, even in its latest contemporary banquette incarnation, is still a Yorkville institution. The *braten schweine* manages to be both lean and rich. The dumplings and potato pancakes are light and tasty. Come early for a German breakfast with unsurpassable pan fries.

—Restaurant Detours—

Before the world wars a small pocket of Germans, mostly Lutheran, occupied an area on the East Side between Murray Hill and Gramercy Park. A few churches, like the Gustavus Adolphus Lutheran, remain, as do a couple of choice German restaurants.

Silver Swan, *41 East 20th Street (212-254-3611). Daily 11:30 A.M.–11:30 P.M.*

Inside the Silver Swan are comfortable forest green booths, a long friendly bar with stools that swivel, and kitsch German pictures. Come for the game (in season), luscious boar and venison with larger-than-life potato dumplings and tart red cabbage, and wash it down with a tall glass of refreshing Paulaner draught.

Rolf's German-American, *281 Third Avenue at 22nd Street (212-477-4750). Monday–Friday 11:30 A.M.–10:30 P.M.; Saturday and Sunday noon–10:30 P.M.*

Rolf's is as dark as a traditional German wine or beer cellar, and as much fun. The bar is whimsically adorned with hanging plastic grapes and a mannequin with a sweet smile who sits on a stool behind the bartender (her legs crossed). It has a great line-up of German beers, draught and bottled, and exceptional German specialties such as sauerbraten and *kassler ripchen* (pork loin in gravy).

Torte and Strudel

Germans and their Austrian country cousins must plead guilty to a sweet tooth; having cookies or cake between meals and cookies and cake between cookies and cake is a Teutonic habit. Bakeries once lined the streets and avenues of Yorkville to cater to this German addiction and some exceptional ones still remain.

Kramer's Pastries, *1643 Second Avenue between 85th and 86th streets (212-535-5955). Monday–Saturday 7 A.M.–7 P.M.*

German *fraus* with sturdy linebacker figures still wait in line for the *Sacher torte* (chocolate cake layered with apricot preserves) and the *schwartwalder kirsch torte* (chocolate Black Forest cake with cherries and whipped cream). Come Christmas there is a rush on the stollen, crusted with sugar and studded with nuts and raisins.

Glaser's Bakery, *1670 First Avenue between 87th and 88th streets (212-289-2562) Tuesday–Friday 7 A.M.–7 P.M.; Sunday 7 A.M.–4 P.M.*

Glaser's is well worth a long wait but should be avoided on busy Sundays. The fine assortment of cookies, plain and fancy, and *Linzer torte,* with rich raspberry filling, are local favorites.

Cream Puff, *1388 Second Avenue between 71st and 72nd streets (212-517-3920). Monday–Saturday 8:00 A.M.–10 P.M.*

The Cream Puff is slightly off the German Yorkville beaten track in location, but its *Linzer torte* and apple *strudel* are worth the extra steps. The Gattnig family, who started the local landmark bakery G & M (now closed) in 1958 and opened the Cream Puff in the 1990s, are no-nonsense Austrians who refuse to stint on quality. Coffee is also available in a charming Viennese setting.

Yorkville Gourmet

Ever since the first Astor set up shop as a butcher, German New Yorkers have been renowned for their meats. Their smoked meat and sausages, especially the frankfurter, struck the fancy of the city and their delicatessens became an institution.

Schaller & Weber, *1654 Second Avenue between 85th and 86th streets (212-879-3047). Monday–Saturday 9 A.M.–6 P.M.*

Schaller & Weber is a Yorkville institution dating from 1937, offering German delicatessen in all its varieties, with wurst ranging from *brat* to *bauern* to *knock.* The *nuss Schinken* (Westphalian ham) is the filet mignon of ham and their Oldenburger onion liverwurst makes liverwurst into a pate. It has all the right cuts for German cooking, like *kassler ripchen* and old German hands behind the counter to advise the uninitiated.

Ridgewood

Directions: Subway 6 to Canal Street, change to M train to Seneca Avenue; or Subway 6 to 14th Street, change to Subway L to Myrtle Avenue.

Ridgewood was one of the many areas that Peter Stuyvesant opened up for settlement toward the end of the Dutch era of New Amsterdam. In the seventeenth century, this adjunct of the village of Bushwick was all fieldstone Dutch farmsteads. Later English landholders referred to the region, which is now on the Brooklyn–Queens border, as "the Ridge" because of its most obvious physical feature. The terrain, which was supposed to resemble rural Germany, appealed to the Hessian troops who were billeted here during the Revolution. They were the first German ethnics to start living here after the war.

The largest wave of German immigrants settled in Ridgewood before the turn of the century. They found work in the nearby breweries and

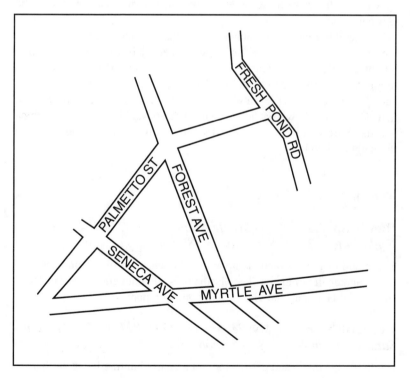

Ridgewood

knitting mills and started their own retail businesses to cater to special German tastes. Many of the new arrivals belonged to the Gottscheers, a pietist religious sect that could trace its roots back to the fifteenth century.

The neighborhood was scrupulously neat and respectable, with *hausfraus* regularly scrubbing down their brownstone stoops. German Ridgewood was a quiet family kind of place, different from the more "strident" immigrant areas that surrounded it.

Times changed in the 1960s and the 1970s as German families completely deserted adjacent Bushwick and started leaving Ridgewood for the picket-fence suburbs of Queens and Long Island. But neighborhood people, third- and fourth-generation German Americans, were determined to preserve and reclaim Ridgewood. Paul Kerzner, president of the Ridgewood Restoration Corporation, and other concerned citizens secured a landmark designation, and the Myrtle Avenue Local Development Corporation was awarded a two-and-a-half-million dollar federal grant to revive Myrtle Avenue. Ridgewood activists lifted local morale in one easy step by winning the right to become part of Queens, but that didn't stop the German exodus.

The neighborhood is no longer predominantly German. In recent years the original German settlers have been joined by other ethnics including Yugoslavs, Romanians, Chinese, Italians, and Arabs. Yet Ridgewood has retained the German ethnic feeling that disappeared from Yorkville years ago. There are flyers in store windows for bierfests and local groups with names like the Edelweiss Club. The mass at St. Mathias is said in German and there are more than a hundred small German knitting companies in the neighborhood.

Ridgewood Highlights

Hans's Gasthaus, *64-04 Myrtle Avenue (718-828-6704). Monday– Friday 4 P.M.–2 A.M.; Saturday and Sunday noon–2 A.M.*

The mood of the Gasthaus is upbeat and open, with rustic pine trim and tables and chairs to match. The Gasthaus is all about good German beers, substantial German sandwiches, and good company.

Gebhardt's, *65-06 Myrtle Avenue (718-821-5567). Tuesday– Saturday noon–9 P.M.; Sunday noon–9 P.M.*

Gebhardt's is rustic and has the look of an early hunting lodge, with leafy drapes and a moose head. The *sauerbraten* cuts with a fork and is sweet and sour delicious. The *schnitzel* is light and grease free.

Aigner's Chocolates of Distinction, *60-41 Myrtle Avenue (718-386-9183). Tuesday–Saturday 10 A.M.–6 P.M.; Sunday 10 A.M.–4 P.M.*

Aigner's makes distinctive chocolates—milk, bittersweet, and white—the old German way. They create imaginative candy packaging and gift baskets with holiday themes.

Rudy's Bakery, *905 Seneca Avenue (718-821-5890). Monday–Thursday 6 A.M.–7 P.M.; Friday 6 A.M.–7:30 P.M.; Saturday 6 A.M.–6 P.M.*

Rudy's is a real German bakery, down to the accents of its salesladies. It makes *stollen* (Christmas fruit cakes) all year round and features *Schillerlocken,* a creamy pastry in honor of the poet's long locks, and *swartzwalder* and *bienenstich.*

Jobst & Ebbinghaus, *676 Seneca Avenue at Gates Avenue (718-821-5747). Monday–Friday 8 A.M.–6 P.M.; Saturday 7 A.M.–5 P.M.*

This German butcher covers all bases: wild game, wurst, and prime cuts of beef, lamb, and pork. Where else is moose and bear for sale? This unusual shop has a Museum of Natural History deer in the window with lifelike game birds. Every variety of wurst dangles from the ceiling over the counter, along with smoked pork ribs. There are herrings, pickled vegetables, and breads imported from Germany.

Karl Ehmer, *63-35 Fresh Pond Road (718-456-8100). Monday–Friday 9 A.M.–6:45 P.M.; Saturday 9 A.M.–6 P.M.*

Karl Ehmer is the flagship of the fifty-four-store butcher and delicatessen chain. There are a hundred varieties of wurst and the freshest cuts of pork, veal, lamb, and beef. Ehmer also carries German smoked fish and herring and German breads from *bauernbrot* to pumpernickel.

Brooklyn Place Mark—the Brooklyn Bridge

Directions: Subway 4, 5, or 6 to Brooklyn Bridge, change to Subway A to Cadman Plaza West.

The Brooklyn Bridge, which spans the East River from the vicinity of City Hall Park to downtown, is one of the city's genuine masterpieces, with its massive pylons linking fine lines of woven cable. The first steel suspension bridge in the world was the brainchild of John A. Roebling, an emigrant from Prussia. It took him years to convince New York politicians of its value.

He died in a freak accident the year that construction started. His son, Washington A. Roebling, followed his father's dream, directly supervising the construction until he was felled by the bends. The crippled Roebling watched the progress of the bridge through a telescope, periodically dispatching his wife with instructions for the builders. The bridge was completed on May 24, 1883, winning the approval of ordinary people as well as artists and writers. One exclaimed that all modern New York started with the Brooklyn Bridge.

In 1973 the city showed its appreciation on the bridge's ninetieth birthday by giving it a fresh coat of paint in silver and two shades of buff chosen by Roebling. For the bridge's centennial, the city held a huge party, while the national media ran cover stories raving about this architectural wonder. Despite all the hoopla, the city forgot to maintain the bridge and rust did the rest. The walkway of the bridge had to be closed for repairs, but happily it has reopened, to the delight of athletic New Yorkers who bicycle, rollerblade, and jog between the boroughs.

German Celebrations

Von Steuben Day Parade

In the third week in September, usually on a Saturday or Sunday, the German community of the metropolitan area unites to honor the German Revolutionary war hero Von Steuben with a parade along upper Fifth Avenue. It's a wholehearted German spectacle that rivals the grand Munich parade for Octoberfest.

The German drum and bugle corps are something special: medieval banners held aloft, brass regally blaring, and drummers stepping lively and raising their arms high in time to the big bass beat. A Steuben society comes dressed for the Revolutionary War in knee britches, ruffled shirts, and three-cornered hats, marching to the strains of "Yankee Doodle Dandy." German folk dancers, men and women in embroidered Bavarian village costumes, dance along the line of the march. The men whirl the women around and perform a humorous slap dance in time with the music. There is a bucolic float with a waterfall and a fetching German beauty queen, followed by a float resembling the bow of a clipper ship from a German shipping line.

Following in the Octoberfest tradition, there are old-fashioned brewery wagons carrying attractive blond women, with the barrels pulled by heavy draft horses. The German marchers are joined by local high school bands, many representing communities in New York, New Jersey, and Pennsylvania founded by Germans. The crowd is lively, often calling out in German to particular marchers from the sidelines. For a change the refreshment stands along the route serve real wurst rather than anemic hot dogs, and the big salty German pretzels aren't stale.

Hungarians

History

The Magyar man on horseback, Colonel Michael Kovat, trained the cavalry force that finally defeated the English. This hero of the American Revolution died while leading a cavalry charge at Charleston. Though he wasn't a New Yorker, the Hungarians of the city have honored him with a statue.

There's also a statue in the city dedicated to Louis Kossuth, the leader of 1848 Magyar revolution, who spent his exile in New York. He was the first Hungarian to attract New York's attention. Between 1851 and 1852 the Hungarian hero was acclaimed and admired and generally treated like a matinee idol. Meanwhile, Kossuth spread the message of a free and democratic Hungary, and tried to drum up donations to continue his fight.

He was feted by the city's commercial establishment and intellectual elite, but later fickle New York attacked him for his liberal views and his refusal to take positions regarding American politics. He left New York confused by the city's "celebrity treatment" and disappointed by its lack of support for continuing his campaign against the Hapsburg Empire.

Many fellow Hungarians, veterans of the 1848 battles, stayed behind in the city, forming New York's first Hungarian community. These men of Forty-eight were writers and thinkers. In 1853 Karoly Kornis started *Magyar Szamuzottek* (Hungarian Exile's News), the first Hungarian-American newspaper. The New York Hungarian Society, which was founded in 1865 after some false starts was more than a mutual benefit society; it offered a platform to Hungarians for the free exchange of ideas.

Hungarian New Yorkers put their revolutionary fervor to work for the Union cause. These fighters of 1848 fought for the Union in 1861. They filled half the places in New York's famed "Garibaldi Guard" and were an important element in the city's "Black Rifles." Hungarians made up a disproportionate share of the Union officer corps, with two major generals and five brigadier generals. Joseph Pulitzer, the future publisher of the *New York Sun,* also was an officer for the Northern side.

While the first wave of Hungarian immigrants, from 1850 to 1870, were political exiles and adventurers, the next wave, from 1880 to 1914, were economic emigrants. They were mostly single men: landless peasants, unskilled industrial workers, and day laborers. They were poor men with simple needs who wanted money to feed their families overseas and to later return and buy land and homes in their native villages.

The Hungarian peasant was not afraid to make sacrifices to save for the future. Hungarians lived collectively, at times twenty to forty-five men in a New York boardinghouse, four to ten to a room. The boardinghouse collective appointed a married man to be their *burdos gazda* and oversee their living arrangements. He had the easy job of purchasing provisions, paying the rent, and handling the accounts, while his wife slaved at the cooking, cleaning, and washing.

New York's Hungarians averaged $8.70 a week for the most hazardous work. They were frequently underpaid even by the standards of the time, but they were in the habit of taking orders from authority. In their closed world the New York pittance was a Hungarian fortune. Even the worst New York workplaces had a freedom and informality that the Hungarian newcomers welcomed.

Despite the difficulties of work and boardinghouse living, Hungarians enjoyed an active community life. In New York City alone there were seventy-eight associations. The Hungarian Sick Benefit Society was started in 1884 to help Hungarian workers in medical emergencies. The First Hungarian Self-Culture Society of New York, started in 1888, offered the Hungarian workingman a program for self-improvement, including lectures, literary readings, and plays. Politically active Hungarian New Yorkers joined the American Hungarian Federation to promote Hungarian freedom.

Hungarian culture flourished in choirs, traveling theaters, and literary societies. While New York and Brooklyn had lodges and associations for Hungarians from different geographical areas, local branches of national groups like the Verhovay and Rakoczi Aid Societies united Hungarians from all around America. Newspapers like New York's *Amerikai Magyar Nepszava* (American Hungarian People's Voice), first published in 1899, also created a sense of group solidarity.

The destiny of New York's Hungarians was also shaped by events across the sea. Patriotic Hungarians supported Hungary in the propaganda battle prior to World War I and backed up their words by enlisting in the Hungarian army in 1914. But America entered the war on the other side, allied with France and England. New York Hungarians did not know how to deal with their divided loyalties.

Hungarians bought American War Bonds and became part of an industrial war effort that shed Hungarian blood. Surrounded by a city in a patriotic all-American war fever, the New York Hungarian community in its Yorkville enclave felt cut off and resentful. In the peace that was supposed to end all wars, their nation lost more than seventy percent of its territory and more than sixty percent of its population.

By the end of the war Hungarian community leaders were preaching the gospel of Americanization. The future was in the United States, they said. Life became more settled for the Hungarians; they opened shops and sent for their wives. The boardinghouse became a thing of the past, and New York's Hungarian neighborhood in Yorkville began to thrive.

Still, Hungarian New Yorkers retained their ethnic pride. In 1928 the community erected a statue of Louis Kossuth to the the applause of five hundred Hungarian dignitaries and officials from Hungary. In 1931 two brave Hungarian-American aviators displayed the Hungarian colors in a Lindbergh-like flight from New York to Budapest in a one-engine plane named *Justice for Hungary*.

Hungarian political refugees who came to New York between the wars were a genuine source of pride. The urbane playwright Ferenc Molnar took literary New York by storm and the innovative composer Bela Bartok was hailed by the city's music critics. Hungarian physicists Leo Sziliard, Eugene Wigner, and Edward Teller were among the great scientific minds of the age; they worked on the Manhattan Project, which produced the atom bomb.

Hungarian New Yorkers had less ambivalent feelings when World War II again put them on the opposite side of America and her allies. They saw Hungary as an unwilling hostage to Hitler, and their loyalty to America was absolute. After the war was won, Hungarian New Yorkers set about helping Hungarian victims of the war and aiding refugees in resettlement.

The first group to enter New York was called the Forty-fivers. They were displaced persons, Hungarian royal soldiers, and politicians fleeing the relentless Soviet army. These men of the old order often had a hard time adjusting to a new land.

The Forty-fivers were soon joined by the Forty-seveners. They were liberals of a Western stripe who were forced out of the Hungarian government by the Stalinist dictator, Matyas Rakosi. They became a significant part of New York's Hungarian community.

In 1956, Hungarians rebelled against authoritarian Stalinist rule and Russian tanks rumbled through the streets of Budapest. Outgunned Hungarians fought valiantly, but the freedom fighters, like earlier Hungarian revolutionaries, were forced into New York exile. The Fifty-sixers joined forces with earlier refugee groups to form a new political organization to represent the Hungarian community, but the real voice of these politically committed exiles was the Hungarian Freedom Fighters Federation, started by General Bela K. Kiraly, a former leader of the Hungarian National Guard.

New York's Hungarians have hopes for Hungary in a new era of Magyar freedom. They have been heartened by Hungary's open society and free enterprise system. With its first free elections in the 1990s, Hungary has become a true parliamentary democracy. Many members of New York's small but culturally active emigre community have even returned to their homeland. Successful Hungarian New Yorkers like financier George Soros and restaurateur George Lang have returned to Hungary to rebuild its institutions and economy.

Hungarian Yorkville

New York's first Hungarian neighborhood was centered in the German area of Kleine Deutschland, around Avenues A and B and Houston Street. In the early 1900s the Hungarians followed their German neighbors to Yorkville. They settled between 78th Street and 84th Street in the vicinity of Second Avenue. The Hungarian neighborhood, like Hungarian history, alternated between passionate romantic outbursts and resignation. It was like the moody music of a gypsy violin or a fist fight in a basement bar followed by a solemn mass at St. Stephen's.

Little Hungary was a land of gray walk-ups and hanging fire escapes, enlivened by a beehive of social clubs. Over cards and cigars, socialists and monarchists fought their political wars. Though Hungarian Yorkville didn't have the Hapsburg grandeur, it had shops as colorful as old Budapest which sold Hungarian wines (*egri-bikavar*), garlicky Hercz, Pick, and Drossy salamis, and *lekvar* (prune butter) from the barrel. The restaurants were appropriately homey in a neighborhood of single men, with curtains and candles and steaming bowls of goulash soup. It took another generation for people to make the move to the suburbs of Brooklyn.

Just when Hungarian Yorkville looked like it was becoming Upper East Side anonymous, the old Hungarian stock was renewed by successive generations of refugees following World War II and the abortive Hungarian uprising. Yorkville Hungarians opened their homes and their pocketbooks, and local organizations provided language classes and vocational training. The city's postwar Hungarians, in return, revitalized the cultural life of the Hungarian community.

They brought books and Hungarian book publishing to Yorkville. Emigre writers formed their own literary circles and even had their own literary controversies. *Free Hungarians,* a monthly with a nationalist stance, was launched in Yorkville in 1956, but its life was cut short by a libel suit from a rival Hungarian publication in 1962. *New Yorki Magyar Elat* (New York Hungarian Life) is the mouthpiece for Yorkville's Hungarian intelligentsia today.

Hungarian Place Mark

St. Stephen's of Hungary, *414 East 82nd Street (212-861-8500).*

This Roman Catholic Franciscan Church, named for Hungary's patron saint, still has an active Hungarian parish, with a mass said in Hungarian on Sundays and holy days and a Hungarian-language church bulletin. The church entrance has a carved likeness of the Magyar king atop the columns at the entrance. The interior of the church is illuminated by beautiful stained-glass windows behind the altar. Behind the church, set in a raised flower garden, is a poignant sculpture tableau of peasants praying to the Virgin Mary.

Hungarian Cultural Highlights

New York's Hungarian quarter may have decreased in numbers since the early part of this century but its cultural community still flourishes.

Puski-Corvin, *217 East 83rd Street (212-879-8893). Monday–Saturday 9 A.M.–6:30 P.M.*

The local Hungarian literary crowd, as well as academic Hungarian specialists, come here for the impossible-to-find Hungarian book. Puski has the largest selection of Hungarian books dealing with literature and sociology in the United States, and also publishes some volumes of its own. Hungarian intellectuals come here to talk, to discuss their works in progress, and make their own prognostications on the current Hungarian regime. Puski is also an informal community bulletin board for upcoming cultural events. Non-Hungarian readers can buy Hungarian cookbooks and more in English.

Hungarian House, *215 East 82nd Street (212-744-5298).*

Boldly painted a deep Hungarian red with the American and Hungarian flags in front, Hungarian House is impossible to miss. A plaque proudly marks Prince Primate Cardinal Midszenty's reception for local community representatives. It is a gathering place for Hungarian organizations and culture clubs and a site for lectures and exhibitions.

American Hungarian Library, *215 East 82nd Street (212-744-5298).*

A small library with a small collection of books, many of them old if not rare, this is a place where people come to read and perhaps share old memories. Call ahead to determine times or make an appointment.

The Hungarian Table

Hungarian cuisine straddles the German West and the Slavic East. It is wurst and stuffed cabbage, kielbasa (*kolbasa*), and sauerkraut. These literary masters of the bittersweet excel in the sweet and sour, which is sometimes overwhelmed by the sour cream. But the hallmark of Hungarian cooking is paprika, the singular spice that adds zest without disguising natural flavors.

Red Tulip, *439 East 75th Street (212-734-4893). Wednesday–Sunday 6 P.M.–midnight.*

The Red Tulip is very rustic, with trestle tables and chairs like gingerbread, but that doesn't seem to bother the East Side types waiting for a table. The food is Hungarian rich, from the sour cherry soup to the veal goulash to the *somloi galuska,* which combines cake, rum chocolate sauce, and whipped cream.

Mocca Restaurant, *1588 Second Avenue at 83rd Street (212-734-6470). Daily 11:30 A.M.–3:45 P.M.; 4 P.M.–10:30 P.M.*

The food is first rate at the Mocca, which features superb roast duck with crisp skin and succulent meat. Gypsy violins add flavor on weekends.

Paprika and Prune Butter

The Hungarian shops have the look of yesteryear, with hanging smoked meats and barrels and bags instead of streamlined packaging. There is something old fashioned about the warm personal service. Hungarian Yorkville once had food shops specializing in everything from soup to nuts and Hungarian shopping was a daily hunt for the freshest foods. Hungarian variety is a thing of the past now though; even the Budapest Bakery is not strictly Hungarian.

Paprika Weiss, Importers, *1572 Second Avenue at 82nd Street (212-288-6117). Monday–Saturday 9 A.M.–7 P.M.; Sunday 11 A.M.– 5 P.M.*

Edward Weiss parlayed ten kilos of paprika from Szeged into a Yorkville tradition one hundred years young. Another Edward Weiss runs the show today, minding the endless varieties of paprika and all the different grains, nuts, and herbs. There are also utensils for every conceivable function for the yuppie homemakers who have taken over the neighborhood. Still, where else in the city can you get *lekvar* (Hungarian prune butter) the old-fashioned way, from the barrel?

Budapest Pastry, *218 East 84th Street (212-628-0721). Monday 8 A.M.–6 P.M.; Tuesday–Friday 7:30 A.M.–7:30 P.M.; Saturday 9 A.M.– 7:30 P.M.; Sunday 10 A.M.–5 P.M.*

The Budapest is no longer strictly Hungarian; the new ethnic management (Syrian) has diversified into Levantine *spanokopita* and *baklava,* but the Hungarian strudel is a pure poppy seed high. The poppy seed is to Hungarian baking what paprika is to the rest of Hungarian cookery.

Rigo Hungarian Viennese Pastry, *318 East 78th Street (212-988-0052). Tuesday–Saturday 8:00 A.M.–6:00 P.M.; Sunday 9:00 A.M.– 4:00 P.M.*

This Hungarian bake shop continues the tradition of Austrian-Hungarian cooperation by preparing *Linzer torte* and *Sacher torte* along with its *lekvar* goodies, *babka,* and poppy seed strudel.

Tibor Meat Specialties, *1508 Second Avenue at 78th Street (212-744-8292). Monday–Saturday 7 A.M.–6 P.M.*

There is an actual Tibor who smokes all the veal and pork sausage the traditional Hungarian way, with plenty of paprika. His wife, Barbara, has a special relationship with her central European clientele, and she's generous with her samples of Hungarian salami and black bread. Homemade soups, noodle dishes, and other Hungarian delicacies are also now on sale. Hungarians from the whole metropolitan area come to Tibor's.

Yorkville Packing House, *1560 Second Avenue at 81st Street (212-628-5147) Monday–Saturday 7* A.M.*–6:30* P.M.

The Yorkville Packing House attracts the best of both Upper East Side worlds, emigre Hungarian and high-rent gourmet. Where else could one find goose liverwurst and smoked goose, or Hungarian potato bread, for that matter? This Hungarian butcher shop has packaged foods that even food halls like Dean and Deluca haven't discovered.

Hungarian Celebrations

St. Stephen's Day is on August 20 and is usually celebrated on the Sunday closest to the saint's day. In an earlier age the whole Hungarian community came out for a patriotic parade, but now it's primarily a religious feast followed by a parish picnic.

Hungarian Independence Day is commemorated on March 15. Patriotic Hungarians used to march from their Yorkville community to the statue of their national hero, Louis Kossuth (by the Hungarian sculptor Horvathy), on 113th Street and Riverside Drive. The Hungarians now drive to the monument from all over the city to hear speeches and celebrate the Hungarian tradition of individual and cultural freedom.

Czechs

History

Augustine Herman, an experienced surveyor and merchant, was the first Czech to make his mark in the New World. He came over to New Amsterdam in 1643 as an agent for Amsterdam's largest commercial organization, Gabry and Company. While taking care of business, Herman served as an adviser of Governor Stuyvesant and was involved in delicate border negotiations with the British colonies. He made his fortune surveying Maryland for Lord Baltimore, for which he received twenty thousand acres of prime land. In honor of his home region he called his estate New Bohemia, which he planted with tobacco.

Frederick Philipse was another talented Czech merchant. He arrived in the colony in 1647. He was enough of a wheeler-dealer in colonial real estate to create the Phillips dynasty. His granddaughter was so grand she refused the proposal of George Washington. Though early Czech New

Yorkers were outstanding successes, by the 1840s there were only five hundred Bohemians in the whole city.

The failure of the 1848 uprising in Bohemia led Czechs to seek freedom in New York. These first political exiles were plodding intellectuals and expert craftsman who shared a fierce belief in something they called "free thought." While they had a tendency to be opinionated, the men and women of 1848 laid the foundations for the New York Czech community's spirited intellectual, social, and cultural life.

In 1848 Czech organizational life got off to a flying start with a group named after the revolutionary society *Slovanska Linda.* This group did not last long, but it did provide a model for future groups with its library and amateur Czech theatricals and choral society. Two years later Czech "Forty-eighters" launched the first mutual aid society, *Ceska Spolecnost.*

Finally, in 1854 the Czech Slavonic Benevolent Society (CSPS) was organized in the city and is still going strong. Many branches of the organization followed and they all embraced such advanced causes as abolition and women's rights, but it wasn't until 1897 that the CSPS actually admitted women as equal members.

In a tradition dating back to religious dissenters like Jan Hus, Czech liberal Forty-eighters dismissed the conventional dogmas of church and state and favored both political and social freedoms. In 1865 Czech New Yorkers with liberated beliefs opened their own free school in New York, called *Svobodna Skola,* with sixty-five pupils. In 1907 these outspoken Czech free thinkers organized *Svaz Svobodomslnych* (Free Thought), a secular equivalent of a church, with humanistic weddings and funerals.

Czech New Yorkers believed in a strong body as well as a sound mind. They formed gymnast societies called *Sokols* where physical training and discipline were combined with a program of character development and Czech nationalism. One Czech American compared the Sokol code with the rigor, honor, and discipline associated with the Japanese samurai. In 1878 the National Sokol Union joined together thirteen groups in New York. That year the first gymnastic festival took place with Sokols from around the country competing. In a 1933 *Sokol Slet* 2,556 gymnasts participated.

In the 1870s the Hapsburg Empire loosened restrictions on Czech travel and this, coupled with a failure of the sugar beet crop, triggered a mass movement of Czech peasants to New York City. They were very different from their sophisticated forebears, and at least at the beginning only identified with their extended families, villages, and Bohemian or Moravian region.

Newly arrived peasant families did piecework in cramped tenement workshops, rolling cigars and sewing garments at breakneck speed for as much as eighteen hours at a clip. The closeness of Czech families and the self-reliance of their children helped them to work as an efficient economic unit. Jacob Riis, in his exposé of immigrant life published in the 1870s, called *How the Other Half Lives,* marveled at the strength and equanimity of these working Czech families.

New York Czechs rivaled the Germans as metal workers and competed with the Jews in the needle trades, but they were most heavily involved in making cigars and manufacturing pearl buttons. By the turn of the century more than ninety percent of Czech New Yorkers were rolling cigars and more than half the pearl buttons in the United States were made by Czechs in the city. The efforts of these indefatigable workers paid off and they were able to leave the deteriorating Lower East Side for model tenements in what would become Czech Yorkville.

Although Czechs never voted as a block, Czech workingmen were socially conscious and politically committed. As early as 1870 the *Delnicky Klub* was established for industrial workers. In 1872 the Czech trade unionists formed a section of the Socialist Labor Party of Now York, and in 1893 Czech labor, which refused to socialize with its class enemies, started its own Sokol, which came to be called the "Red Sokol."

But New York's Czechs were not all high-minded thinking and intellectual controversy. The industrious and thrifty Czechs liked to sing and dance and raise a glass of pilsner even if the city's Puritans upbraided them for doing it on Sunday. The city's Czechs were very musical; one third of Czech professionals in the early 1900s proved the Czech proverb *co cech to muzikant,* if he's Czech he's a musician. All the major conservatories in Manhattan had Czech teachers. Even the famous Czech composer of The New World Symphony, Antonin Dvorak, directed the National Conservatory of Music in New York between 1892 and 1895. The superb musician and composer Rudolph Friml was the toast of New York in the 1920s, acclaimed for his operetta, *The Vagabond King.*

World War I brought Czech New Yorkers together. On May 15, 1916, the Red Sokol and the more conservative Blue Sokol symbolically marched together out of Fort Slocum after eighty-four members of the New York groups enlisted. New York Czechs backed the exiled leader Thomas Masaryk, who was married to a Brooklyn woman and had lectured many times to local Czech audiences. In 1918 Masaryk met with President Wilson and the terms for Czech independence were hammered out before the Versailles Peace Conference.

Immigration restrictions after World War I and a trend toward assimilation had impeded the development of Czech communal life. It became more and more diffuse and less self-aware. The economic depression was another blow, closing the city's most important Czech ethnic institutions. Czechs did not have the resources or organizations in place to help their homeland when the Munich Agreement became a prelude to a full-scale Nazi invasion.

Just when it looked like Czechoslovakia would regain its independence after World War II, Stalinists, with the backing of the USSR, staged a coup. The machinations of Czech communists led to a new generation of Czech Forty-eighters in New York, who were victims of left-wing rather than reactionary tyranny. They were more conservative than other generations of Czech immigrants and stridently anticommunist. While developing their own Czech organizational base, they were able to enter the American occupational mainstream with their skills as professionals and craftsmen. Czech culture flourished again in the city, with groups like the Czechoslovak Society of Arts and Sciences.

Twenty years later the Forty-eighters were joined in New York by the Sixty-eighters, as Alexander Dubcek's democratic reforms and the hopes of the "Prague spring" were crushed by Soviet tanks and armies. The new refugees were more left-wing than their predecessors and less liable to identify with hard-core anticommunist causes.

Many were socialist intellectuals or progressive party *apparatchiks.* They were distrusted by the new conservative Czech establishment, who viewed them as lacking real conviction, or even unreconstructed Communists. Despite the rift in the Czech community, the refugees from 1968 added to Czech cultural renewal. Josef Skvornecky, a leader in the group, started an experimental Czech publishing house in New York.

In 1989 the Marxist Czechoslovakian regime was overthrown by spontaneous demonstrations of the people, the nonviolent "Velvet" Revolution. In a stunning reversal, Vaclav Havel, the nation's leading dissident and a renowned playwright, became president. Local Czechs were thrilled with the turn of events and many returned "home" to provide advice and direction.

Little Bohemia

The Czechs may have started in New Amsterdam, but by the time the Civil War was over they were growing tobacco in the Morrisania section of the Bronx and the Dutch Kill enclave of Queens. The earliest Manhattan Little Bohemia thrived from 1870 to 1905 on the Lower East Side in close proximity to other Slavic immigrants groups and the large German colony.

Its boundaries were Eighth Street on the north, Third Street on the south, and Avenue A east to the river. The blocks between Third and Fifth Streets on Avenue A were known as the Czech Broadway. The most popular saloon in the area, August Hubacek's, was even well known in Prague. The main Czech Hall, the *Narodni Budova,* was located on East Fifth Street and contained a library as well as a saloon; its public rooms were the site of heated political debates.

The neighborhood also had its own Czech-Slavic Benevolent Society, which achieved its moment of glory when Mayor George Updyke unfurled the future national flag (backwards) at a gala reception in City Hall Park. There were also two transplanted Czech villages representing the cigar rollers from Sedlec and the pearl button makers from Zirounice on display.

By the end of the nineteenth century Little Bohemia had followed the Czech cigar stores uptown. It bordered Hungarian and German territory, covering the area between 65th Street, 78th Street, Second Avenue, and the river. Czechs were proud of their new neighborhood, the clean and roomy tenements and the impressive modern buildings housing their organizations.

The showplace of Czech Yorkville was the new *Narodni Budova* (Czech National Hall) on 335-37 73rd Street, which was completed before World War I for the then-grand sum of $250,986. It still stands today, but the old splendor is missing, along with most of the neighborhood's inhabitants.

The Czech community pioneered low-income housing. On 507-523 East 77th Street they built the six-story Cherokee Apartments, which set a new standard with its advanced architectural design. There were balconies, ornamental ironwork, and tiled entryways leading to attractive courtyards. It still retains some of the old charm, though there are very few Czechs living there to appreciate it.

As Czechs turned from ideology to making the American dream happen in New York, the community began losing its identity and the organizations their membership. Affluent Czechs started moving to Queens and Long Island, and though they attempted to re-create Little Bohemia with their own Bohemian Hall in Astoria, it couldn't compete with American social and service organizations.

Czechs also tried to revive Little Bohemia by resettling successive generations of political refugees in Yorkville. But cosmopolitan Czech arrivals looked beyond ethnicity for their personal satisfactions and viewed assimilation as their passport to financial and career success. Even the Czech intellectuals of the sixties who came to

New York to escape literary repression congregated around American universities.

Czechoslovak Place Marks

It is ironic that despite the strenuous Czech and Slovak efforts to make organized free thinking a viable alternative to organized religion, the main reminders of the flourishing Czechoslovak community are churches.

Jan Hus Presbyterian Church, *351 East 74th Street (212-288-6743).*

The Jan Hus Presbyterian Church is named for the Czech martyr of the reformation. It is a real landmark church for the Czech community, with its bell tower modeled on the Powder Tower of old Prague. The church always played an active part in the life of the community. In the days of immigrant Czech Yorkville it acted as a settlement house where people could learn English and become familiar with alien customs and traditions. Jan Hus houses a theater and various community service groups and has a wide choice of self-improvement programs. In 1993 the church building and its replica tower were handsomely restored.

St. John Nepomucene, *411 East 66th Street (212-734-4613).*

In this Roman Catholic church a mass is said every Sunday in Slovak and it is well attended. The outside of the church is brick neo-Romanesque and classical; the inside has the feeling of a village sanctuary, dimly lit with the triptych of St. Cyril and St. Methodius almost floating in the background.

—Czech Place Mark Detour—

Bohemian Hall, *29-12 24th Avenue, Astoria, Queens (718-274-4925).*

Directions: Subway N to Astoria Boulevard/Hoyt Avenue.

Bohemian Hall is a popular meeting place for New York's Czech community. Founded in 1892 in rural Queens by the Bohemian Citizen's Benevolent Society, its tree-lined courtyard has been the venue of ethnic festivals and Sokol gymnastic exhibitions for more than a century. Czech is still spoken in Bohemian Hall's beer hall, though the old crowd is thinning out. There is a campaign to designate Bohemian Hall as a city landmark.

The Czech Table

Czech cuisine has been described as a crossroads cuisine, a mingling of central European influences from the German to the Magyar to the Slav. Czechs eat schnitzel, goulash, and stuffed cabbage and they even eat them at the same time. Like their neighbors in New York, the Hungarians, the Czechs are connoisseurs of goose and duck, which have the place of honor in their restaurants. Lately, with thinning cuisines in style, Czech eating places are disappearing one by one.

Vasata, *339 East 75th Street (212-988-7166). Tuesday–Saturday 5 P.M.–11 P.M.; Sunday noon–10 P.M.*

Vasata is an Old World inn with dark low-beamed ceilings and white stucco walls. Color is provided by fresh flowers on every table and bright Czech ceramics. The roast duck is the house specialty, unless it is October and there is game such as leg of venison, wild goose, or pheasant. The *palacinty,* the Czech dessert version of a bliny filled with apricot jam or crushed walnuts and brown sugar and covered with powdered sugar, is the perfect way to end an evening at Vasata.

Czech Celebration

During the Memorial Day weekend Czech clans gather from the New York metropolitan area for the **Czech Festival.** The courtyard of Bohemian Hall is a scene of Czech brass bands, high-stepping boots, and whirling peasant skirts. People sit at picnic tables drinking Czech pilsner and enjoying breaded mushrooms, stuffed cabbage, and goulash. There are quiet moments when speakers discuss Czech heritage and history and pause to salute heroes like Thomas Masaryk and Vaclav Havel.

The Scandinavians

The Scandinavian nations—Norway, Sweden, Denmark, and Finland—share a culture and history. When the Scandinavians came to New York as immigrants, they gravitated to the same neighborhoods and worked in some of the same trades and professions. The Scandinavians excelled as individuals in science, business, and engineering. They were inventors and master builders. As a group, they made a contribution to the development of New York City's commerce, construction industry, and shipping far out of proportion to their numbers.

History

Danes

Two of the first ships sent by the Dutch to explore the waters around New Amsterdam Harbor and the Hudson River were commanded by Danish captains named Block and Christiansen. Block lost his ship in a fire but built another one with the help of friendly Native Americans and made his own early version of the Circle Line Tour, discovering Block Island in the process. He sailed back to Holland with Christiansen, carrying a cache of valuable beaver pelts. Their voyages encouraged Dutch commercial investment and colonization.

In 1636 the first Danish family went to live in New Amsterdam. Like later generations of Danish New Yorkers, the Jansens quickly assimilated to the dominant culture and took the Dutch name Van Breestede. They were followed by a Thomsen, who became a Van Ripen, and an Andriessen, who switched to Van Buskirk.

The next two Danes to arrive in 1639 did more than change their names. Jonas Bronck became one of the largest landholders, buying five hundred acres from the Native Americans for odds and ends, including two rifles, a barrel of cider, and six gold coins. He was a successful tobacco planter and when duty called, helped Governor Kieft negotiate peace with the Native Americans. At a time when drinking and brawling were favorite pastimes, he collected the colony's largest library. His former lands are now a part of the borough bearing his name, the Bronx.

Bronck's friend and fellow Dane, Jochem Pietersen Kuyter, gained title to four hundred acres in Harlem, but he became famous for his battles with the local Dutch officials. As a member of the Board of Twelve Men, he petitioned the authorities in Holland and was instrumental in the recall of Governor Kieft.

Danes readily adapted to the colony under British rule. They learned English and educated their children in English schools. Unlike their experience under the Dutch, they were free to establish their own Lutheran church, which was built on Broadway and Rector Street in 1704. Life was so comfortable in Anglo-Saxon New York that they gradually discarded their distinct identity.

Danish emigration to the city in the era of the young Republic was a succession of isolated individuals. Danes may have helped found New York's first Scandinavian Society in 1844, but they remained a negligible part of the organization and the community.

In 1863 Prussia's devastating defeat of Denmark resulted in a loss of forty percent of its territory. The war, combined with industrial decline and the rising population on scarce rural lands, led to increased emigration. Between 1867 and 1914 three hundred thousand Danes crossed the ocean.

New York City was primarily a place for Danes to get their bearings and maybe make some money prior to the big push into the Midwest. Only a small group of sailors, artisans, and service workers stayed. Danish female domestics were always in demand and made up a large segment of this ethnic population. The Dania Club, which was organized in Scandinavian Brooklyn in 1886, provided some of these Danes with a social outlet as well as health insurance and other services.

By the turn of the century the Danish influx changed to mainly middle-class professionals and business people. These self-assured Danes did not need the company of their fellow countrymen to ease their transition to an unfamiliar society. They did have a tendency to cluster around other Scandinavian groups, and if possible attended Danish denominational churches in the Bronx and Brooklyn. Their sense of Danish identity came primarily from the Danish newspaper *Nordlyset* and organizations like the Danish American Historical Society, which emphasized their unique heritage.

Though few in numbers, Danes made their mark in the city. Jacob Riis, the muckraking journalist, stirred the social conscience of a nation with his words and pictures. He came to New York in 1870 with only forty dollars in his pocket and a strong sense of justice. By the end of the decade, he was a leading New York journalist and social critic and a spokesman for the settlement-house movement. His series in the *Evening Star,* which graphically detailed the suffering and squalor of the city's immigrant populations, led to the enactment of New York housing laws. Theodore Roosevelt once referred to him as "the best American I have ever known."

Niels Poulson made his reputation as one of Brooklyn's leading businessmen in the early part of this century. As head of the Hecla Iron Works, he was responsible for the ornamental flourishes of such New York landmarks as Grand Central Station and the original Penn Station. This public-spirited Scandinavian left a fortune, which today still funds scholarships and Danish cultural exhibitions.

Swedes

Sweden in the seventeenth century was exhausted by military adventures and on the decline. Gone were Gustavus Adolphus's dreams of a gilded empire. Some Swedes hoped to recoup their fortunes in the New World. A colony was established in Delaware and Swedes even schemed with Peter Minuit to take over Dutch New Amsterdam; there were a few scattered Swedes in the Dutch colony at that time. A party of Swedish pioneers helped clear Harlem for farmland and Mons Pietersen, a Swedish surveyor, laid out the village of Harlem.

There were only one hundred Swedes in New York in the 1830s but twenty-two of them got together in 1836 to found an organization called the Swedish Society. It was the first Scandinavian mutual-aid society in the New World and only the second in the whole world. The members were merchants and manufacturers with a real sense of community spirit. In 1837 Swedish Brooklynites formed the first Swedish congregation, Swedish Immanuel Methodist. In addition, there was already the Bethel

Ship Mission, which ministered to Swedish seamen in the Port of New York.

In the middle of the nineteenth century Swedes were primed for mass emigration. There was a scarcity of fertile arable land and too much political privilege. Swedes doing their military service resented the high-handed treatment they received from young aristocratic officers. Thousands of men, women, and children set off for America, with the first stopover at New York. Swedish emigrants went on the cheap, spending twelve to fifteen dollars on steerage in freighters carrying Swedish iron ore. After docking in New York a few hardy Swedes, usually of the seafaring variety, opted to stay.

In 1850 the Swedish population in the city was only five hundred, but it didn't stop Anders Gustaf Obom from starting the first Swedish newspaper, which ran on and off from 1851 to 1853. Despite their small numbers, Swedish Americans rallied round the Union colors. They held an officers' ball on April 26, 1861, in which Swedish women presented Swedish volunteers with a silk Swedish flag. The Swedish regiment had a full military review on May 25 at Astor House.

Captain John Ericson, a member in good standing of the Swedish Society, made the largest Swedish contribution to the Union effort by developing and building the first ironclad warship to run on steam, the *Monitor*. His state-of-the-art steamships, which were constructed at the Greenpoint docks, gave the Union the edge in the battle at sea.

Sweden was in trouble in the 1890s with labor unrest, declining wages, and rising populations in the cities. Swedish emigrants to America at this juncture were mostly from urban backgrounds. Some had even participated in the mammoth three-hundred-thousand-strong general strike, which nearly crippled Stockholm.

This wave of Swedes headed for New York or one of the big Swedish strongholds, like Chicago or Minneapolis. The Swedish Aid Society of New York was formed in 1891 to help these working-class immigrants. In only fifteen years it placed twenty thousand Swedes in new jobs; only eighty-three returned to Sweden.

Swedish workingmen moved to Hamilton Avenue in South Brooklyn or settled in the Swedish section of Sunset Park, along Buttermilk Channel and Upper Bay behind the Bushwick Terminal. They were initially ships' carpenters, seamen, and longshoreman. Under the supervision of the Swedish engineer Carl J. Mellin, they did pioneering work in the Brooklyn Navy Yard in the early 1900s.

In 1912 Swedish-born New Yorkers numbered over thirty-five thousand. That year the city's biggest parade was held in their honor to celebrate the Swedish victory in the 1912 Stockholm Olympics. It was a time of real ethnic pride as the yellow and blue Swedish flag preceded the victorious Swedish athletes up the avenue. All of Swedish New York turned out, marching with their associations and organizations, wearing blue and yellow sashes or the folk costume of their country. Ernie Hjertberg was the hero of the day; he not only coached the champion Swedish track team, but was a former trainer at the New York Athletic Club.

Swedish professionals were also drawn to this city of opportunity. In 1888 the American Society of Swedish Engineers was established. Its members went on to change the New York skyline. David L. Lindquist was responsible for the new elevators that made the Empire State Building a reality. Gustave A. Sandblom perfected skyscraper steelwork in innovative buildings like New York Life. Werner Nygren made high-rise buildings habitable with heating and ventilation systems for buildings as diverse as the Woolworth Building and Macy's. John A. Johnson cut his teeth as a housing contractor for Swedes in Bay Ridge and went on to be the leading contractor for the 1939 World's Fair.

Public-spirited Swedes got involved in government service. Emil F. Johnson, an analytical chemist from Stockholm, was a city public health inspector from 1895 to 1915 and established a system for ensuring safe milk. Arthur W. Wallander worked his way from being a patrolman on the beat to becoming the first Swedish police commissioner under Mayor La Guardia and a leading fighter against police corruption. Thomas Hoving, a second-generation Swedish American, served as a very popular parks commissioner under the Lindsay administration and created imaginative events that brought the people back to the parks. In 1977 Joanna Lindlof, a devoted teacher of Swedish descent, became the first woman on New York's Board of Education.

Norwegians

Norwegians like to think that they were the first people to visit America, with the Norseman Leif Ericson arriving from Vinland more than a century before that Johnny-come-lately, Columbus. While that is not undisputed fact, it is clear that Norwegians were among the first peoples to settle in the United States. A Norwegian named Sand was even supposed to have been Peter Minuit's interpreter when he negotiated for Manhattan. Early New Amsterdam had its share of Norwegian sailors and carpenters, and a Norseman named Arent Andriessen supervised the Dutch colony's first shipyard.

In 1825 the sloop the *Restauration* was the first Norwegian ship carrying Norwegian passengers to reach New York. The ship was smaller than the Mayflower and not made for transatlantic travel, but the brave Quakers on board risked their lives in their quest for religious freedom. It turned out that their ship violated New York law by carrying too many passengers, but a generous New Yorker came to their rescue by putting up a bond and successfully petitioning President Adams to waive their three-thousand-dollar fine. The landing of the *Restauration* is still commemorated by Norwegian Americans on October 9.

A scattering of Norwegians settled on the New York waterfront in the 1830s and 1840s. Even in that early era it was said that you could draw a crowd of Norwegians by going to the harbor and shouting the Norwegian salutation, "Svedisker Norveisk Mand." It was a seafaring community with many temporary New Yorkers, but people were starting to put down roots. One, Fredrik Wang, ran a popular tavern frequented by the Norwegian community.

The numbers of Norwegians emigrating to New York became significant in the middle of the nineteenth century. In no time they were the largest group of Scandinavians to settle in the city. Many were responding to the unemployment brought about by the change from sailing ships to steam ships. They were hard hit by the cuts in crew size and the closing of shipyards. Many simply jumped ship in the New World for the higher wages and work opportunities.

The Agder region, on the south coast of Norway, lost a large portion of its maritime population during this period. It was commonplace to have American ships entirely manned by Norwegians. These newcomers to the city received practical support and spiritual assistance from Norwegian missions representing a whole variety of Christian denominations.

By the turn of the century, an increasing Norwegian population was putting down roots in Brooklyn, first in Park Slope and later in Bay Ridge. It was the largest urban concentration of Norwegians in the United States. Along its tree-lined streets, there were Scandinavian-style bakeries, groceries, and restaurants. Norwegian was spoken in the bars and boarding-houses, and Norwegian resounded from the church pulpits.

As in the past, these urban Norwegians were primarily involved in maritime employment. They worked the coastal and transatlantic ships, tugs, and barges and even crewed on luxury yachts. They were involved in the construction of docks and ships and provisioned ships as chandlers. Thousands of Norwegians went to work in the new shipyards of Staten Island and eventually called "the Island" home.

These highly skilled Norwegian workers had a strong sense of their own value and were highly independent. They were avid supporters of unions and at one time sixty percent of all Norwegian laborers in the metropolitan area belonged to labor organizations. For many Norwegians the union took the place of the Norwegian church and national fraternal organizations.

New York's Norwegians were enthusiastic joiners. They were members of local churches and missions. They formed village associations called *bygdelags* and Norwegian lodges. In 1905 the *Det Norske Nationalforbund* became the umbrella organization for Norwegian groups in Brooklyn and Manhattan. In less than a decade the Norwegians of greater New York boasted forty separate organizations.

The most successful aggregation was the Norwegian Club, which acted as a forum for important figures from Norway and the Norwegian-American community. The Norwegian newspaper, *Nordisk Tidende,* stood at the center of New York's Little Norway. Editors like Carl Soyland and Andreas Nilssen Rygg emphasized their common cultural and historical ties. The paper promoted community-wide events like the Norwegian May Festival and campaigned for Norwegian charities like the Norwegian Lutheran Home and Hospital.

The city's loyal Norwegians showed the colors in 1917, volunteering for service in World War I with New York's 308th Infantry. The Sons of Norway were at the forefront of Liberty Bond rallies; Norwegian New Yorkers pledged six million dollars in 1918. While fighting for their adopted country, they were avenging the deaths of two thousand Norwegian seamen who perished in the North Atlantic as a result of Germany's unrestricted U-boat warfare.

In New York's postwar building boom, Norwegian workers and businessmen made the transition from shipbuilding to housing and public works construction. Many became successful carpenters and contractors. Seafaring Norwegians worked on skyscrapers as riggers, using their knowledge of rope and tackle to hoist huge steel beams. Norwegian engineers from the country's prestigious technical institutes, innovators like Ole Singstad, Olaf Hoff, and Hans Rude Jacobsen, supervised the construction of the city's most important bridges and tunnels.

In 1925 New York recognized the contributions of the Norwegian community with the dedication of Leif Erikson Square on the centennial celebration of the landing of the first Norwegian immigrant ship, the *Restauration.* Little Norway was coming of age, with a population of 109,000, including 55,000 native born, but its ties to its homeland were still strong.

The Nazi invasion of Norway mobilized the whole Norwegian community. They donated food and clothing and raised funds for the Norwegian Red Cross and provided jobs and shelter for Norwegian refugees. After the Allied victory generous Norwegian New Yorkers aided in the reconstruction of Norway. This total community involvement kept

Norwegian Bay Ridge together long after similar ethnic neighborhoods had disappeared.

Bay Ridge

Directions: Subway R to 77th Street/Fourth Avenue.

Before the Scandinavians came to Brooklyn, Bay Ridge was Dutch territory. The founding families included the wealthy and socially prominent Cortelyous and Barkaloos. They were succeeded by English gentlemen farmers like the Bennets. In that simpler time when agriculture was the main pursuit, Bay Ridge was known as Yellow Hook for the yellow clay in the soil.

Yellow Hook became Bay Ridge in the 1850s, as local boosters endeavored to dispel the memory of a recent yellow fever epidemic. It was named for the physical features that originally attracted the first Scandinavians to the area. This seafaring people favored Bay Ridge for its open spaces and panorama of the ocean. Some said the Narrows separating Brooklyn from Staten Island brought back memories of the fjords.

Scandinavians had a proprietary feeling for this Brooklyn neighborhood spanning Fourth to Eighth Avenues from 54th Street to 90th Street. It was practically a suburb of Oslo or Stockholm or Copenhagen. Between 1900 and 1930 the population grew by leaps and bounds, a phenomenon the Norwegians called *Myostkolonien* (the area was maturing like a sweet Norwegian cheese). In 1930 there were sixty thousand Norwegians in Bay Ridge, with the overwhelming majority Norwegian born, and a third as many Swedes.

In its prime Bay Ridge was a slice of Scandinavian life. The buildings were neat and the streets were tidy. Products from Norway and Sweden were on sale in the stores and the signposts and advertising circulars were in Scandinavian languages. People drank *aquavit* in the bars and ate *lutefisk* at church suppers. They celebrated Scandinavian festivals and civil holidays. In Bay Ridge Christmas was always *Jul*. There were Norwegian and Swedish glee clubs and lodges and charitable organizations. Bay Ridge had its own Scandinavian hospitals, schools, and even an orphan asylum. There was mutual respect between people that sometimes took the form of quiet reserve, and when the occasion demanded it, free-spirited communal celebration.

World War II and the Nazi occupation of Norway brought the Norwegian community of Bay Ridge closer together. Their concern for friends and family overseas inspired a small-scale cultural revival. But the erosion of this Scandinavian neighborhood was inevitable with the outward movement of more affluent Scandinavian families to Long Island and New Jersey, coinciding with the influx of Italians and other ethnics. Ironically, the bridges and expressways that the Scandinavians played such an important part in building spelled the end of their splendid isolation. Though no longer a majority, the Scandinavians are still a presence in Bay Ridge, with their ethnic landmarks and occasional shops.

Scandinavian Organizations and Culture Clubs

Scandinavian clubs no longer blanket the neighborhood, but the ones that remain are energetic boosters of Norway and Norwegian Americans.

Norsemen's Federation, New York Chapter, *358 87th Street (718-680-4530).*

This Norwegian fraternal organization does more than socialize, though it does that very well. It works hard to make the Norwegian young people in and out of the neighborhood aware of their roots.

Sporting Club Gjoa, *850 62nd Street (718-745-9436).*

This Scandinavian sports center and social club sponsors a soccer league for youngsters and adult softball and organizes field-and-stream activities. Every year members get together for an annual hunting and fishing expedition.

Norwegian Extra

Nordisk Tidende, *8104 Fifth Avenue (718-238-1100).*

This Norwegian language newspaper has been publishing since 1891. It has all the news of Norwegian Bay Ridge that is fit to print, plus what is going on in Norway and the latest about Norwegian visitors to the city. The Norwegian paper is a cultural lifeline for older Norwegians. The only concession it has made to the times is a page in English.

The Scandinavian Table

The standing joke about Scandinavian eating is that the "Danes live to eat, the Norwegians eat to live, and the Swedes eat to drink." (The Finns are unaccountably left out.) Actually, they have a lot in common in their approaches to food, which were dictated by the climate and terrain of their native countries and their involvement with the sea.

Throughout Scandinavia smoked and cured fish, from the humble cod to *gravlax* (salmon cured in sugar, salt, white pepper, and dill), are staples. Hearty root vegetables and dried beans are for soups and side dishes. The long winter is the season for pickled vegetables.

The Swedish smorgasbord, with its endless *aquavit* toasts and varieties of herring, smoked meats, cheeses, and hot-course old reliables like Swedish meatballs, has been adopted by all of Scandinavia, with the warmer-weather Danes adding more salads. Sweden's *svart* (black) soup, made with goose and pigs blood, has also caught on, though it is not as popular as Norwegian *spekeskinke,* a Nordic version of prosciutto. The very basic ingredients of Scandinavian food are embellished with sour cream, horseradish, dill, and egg yolks. Yellow pea soup with pork and mustard is Sweden's national dish while the Norwegians are addicted to *fiskepudding.* The Danes are the original herring mavens and the Finns' favorite pudding, *mammia,* is made with rye, malt, molasses, and bitter orange peel.

The days of a Scandinavian restaurant row are long past. There is one Norwegian survivor among the multiethnic restaurants of Bay Ridge.

Lillehammer, *7715 Fifth Avenue between 77th and 78th streets (718-745-9058). Monday–Friday 5 P.M.–10 P.M.; Saturday and Sunday 10 A.M.–10 P.M.*

The pictures on the rustic wood walls of this spacious new restaurant are of snowscapes and Viking ships. Old-time Norwegian and Swedish locals flock here and the background music is Scandinavian. The food is Scandinavian too, with fat Swedish meatballs and substantial Norwegian pancakes featured on the menu, along with Nordic-style fish cakes, fish puddings, and fish soups. The kitchen may be a little slow, but the cooking is worth the wait.

Scandinavian Bakeries

The Scandinavians are inventive when it comes to breads and baked goods. It takes real genius to add raspberry filling to a marzipan cake. Their line-up of breads includes a dark sweet raisin bread, Norwegian rye, Danish pumpernickel, Swedish *limpa* flavored with anise and molasses, and Norwegian *lofse athin,* which is a flat bread made from potatoes. For Christmas they add citrus peel to a raisin loaf and call it *Jul kage.*

Scandinavian bakeries used to be Brooklyn fixtures and gave the city its favorite breakfast pastry, the Danish. Bay Ridge still has a matching set of Scandinavian bakeries.

Olsen's, *5722 Eighth Avenue between 57th and 58th streets (718-439-6673). Monday–Saturday 6 A.M.–6 P.M.*

The bakery may be Norwegian but it has the best buttery fruit Danish, sweeter and less doughy than the commercially produced variety. The king of breads here is *mellambrod,* a sour-rye wheat bread that is both tart and rich as cake. In this changing area Olsen's has added items like cupcakes and brownies, which cannot compete with their Scandinavian treats.

Leske's, *7612 Fifth Avenue between 76th and 77th streets (718-680-2323). Tuesday–Friday 6 A.M.–7 P.M.; Saturday 6 A.M.–6 P.M.; Sunday 6 A.M.–3 P.M.*

The bakery has been serving the Bay Ridge community since 1916. No one remembers if the original owner was Dutch or Swedish, but the latest one is a German with a thorough command of Scandinavian baking. On weekends Norwegians and Swedes come from northern New Jersey and the Island to buy *kneip* (wheat bread), Danish pumpernickel, and sweet Christmas bread, which they make all year round. They make different varieties of Danish including the pretzel-shaped *kringle* and the cruller-shaped *stang,* which is filled with custard.

Scandinavian Gourmet

The neighborhood Scandinavian market with its own smoked sausage called *polse,* Norwegian *spekeskianke,* and *lutefisk* (codfish cured in brine) is now a rarity in Bay Ridge. Lingonberry jam and Swedish rye crisp are no longer on every grocer's shelf. However, there are a couple of Swedish food outposts that cater to the old Scandinavian remnant and the new gourmet trade.

Mike's Delicatessen, *534 86th Street (718-680-2555). 9510 Fifth Avenue (718-238-5200). Monday–Saturday 8 A.M.–10 P.M.; Sunday 9 A.M.–8 P.M.*

These neighborhood delis are down-to-earth and friendly spots for relaxed browsing. There are fresh herring and lingonberries, and in the canned-goods section you can find King Oscar fishballs and Stabburet reindeer meat in gravy.

Mejlander & Mulgannon, *76-15 Fifth Avenue (718-238-6666). Monday–Friday 7 A.M.–9 P.M.; Saturday 8 A.M.–8 P.M.; Sunday 8 A.M.–5 P.M.*

It's a spic-and-span neighborhood deli with friendly service and a Scandinavian twist. In the appetizer area, Swedish meatballs and fish pudding are likely to be on the bill of fare. The frozen-food section includes lingonberries along with the TV dinners. On the shelves at the front, the theme is definitely Scandinavian, with sheets of potato *lefsa* (a type of bread), Kavli crisps, Swedish ginger snaps, Mollers cod-liver oil, and canned fried venison. Mulgannon is the Irish partner.

Nordic Delicacies, *6906 Third Avenue (718-748-1874). Monday– Saturday 9 A.M.–6 P.M.*

Nordic Delicacies is one take-out that delivers home cooking. It was started by two Bay Ridge women in love with authentic Norwegian cooking who decided to share it with the whole neighborhood. Their biggest successes are their daily specials. If it's Monday it must be *kjottkaker* (Norwegian meatballs); Wednesday is *komper* (potato dumpling); and Thursday is *lapkaus* (a beef hash with onions and potatoes). Buy early in the day because they sell out.

Norwegian Gifts

In the long, dark Scandinavian winters when people are housebound, handicrafts like knitting and crewel work flourish.

Signes Imports, *5906 Eighth Avenue between 59th and 60th Streets (718-492-5004). Tuesday–Friday 10 A.M.–5 P.M.; Saturday 10 A.M.– 3 P.M.*

Signes is an ethnic gift shop with everything from "Kiss Me I'm Norwegian" mugs and sweatshirts to fine porcelain plates with Nordic designs. There are even canned Scandinavian foods on sale in this eclectic grab bag of a shop. Handmade sweaters in traditional patterns at reasonable prices are the main feature.

Norwegian Celebrations

On May 17, Norwegians from the metropolitan area make a pilgrimage to the old neighborhood to reaffirm their ethnic identity and explore old associations. It is a patriotic celebration marking the day Norway received its democratic constitution—a Norwegian Fourth of July without fireworks. It started in Brooklyn in response to another Norwegian milestone, when the country declared its independence from Sweden in 1905.

The parade moves down Brooklyn's Fifth Avenue from 90th Street to Leif Ericson Park at 66th Street. The marchers represent a wide array of organizations, from the avuncular Sons of Norway to the dignified Norwegian Society of America. Young and old move along the Avenue in brightly embroidered peasant costumes—vests and knee britches and billowing skirts and aprons. There are floats of Viking ships with bearded men on deck waving cardboard swords and blonde Norwegian beauties throwing flowers to the spectators. A Miss Norway is crowned, getting a far more enthusiastic reception than the speeches made by the Norwegian dignitaries. After the parade Norwegian families can be seen strolling through the neighborhood reminiscing about the old block and visiting the often personal landmarks.

Manhattan

Scandinavian Place Marks

It is not surprising that Scandinavian monuments begin at the Battery where Scandinavian seamen made so much history.

There is a bronze statue of the Swede John Ericson, the designer of the first ironclad man-of-war, the *Monitor,* which helped win the Civil War.

The Customs House on Bowling Green has a fresco on the domed ceiling of another Scandinavian named Ericson, Leif Ericson, who is supposed to have landed in America.

The seafaring tradition combines with the staunch evangelical Scandinavian religious tradition in the seamen's churches in midtown Manhattan, which have become gathering places for the Scandinavian community after the partial disintegration of Scandinavian neighborhoods in New York.

Norwegian Seamen's Church, *317 East 52nd Street (212-319-0370).*

The Norwegian Seamen's Church has moved to larger quarters. There is more space for Norwegian sailors on liberty, and for stray Norwegian tourists to chat with church volunteers, catch up on the latest editions of Norwegian newspapers, drink coffee, and eat Norwegian pancakes. Shelves of books and Norwegian food products and souvenirs line the walls. Models of Norwegian ocean liners and abstract sculptures are the austere decoration. Toward the back there is a magnificent carved crucifix and the church altar.

Swedish Seamen's Church, *5 East 48th Street (212-832-8443).*

The exterior of the building, with its granite stonework and leaded windows, is properly ecclesiastical, and the public rooms are rustically trimmed with wood imprinted with passages from the Bible. The tone of the room is not at all solemn, and above on the mezzanine there is an exhibit of Swedish abstract art. There's a library with up-to-date Swedish newspapers, which are devoured by Swedish tourists along with the waffles that the church ladies serve.

Scandinavian Organizations and Exhibitions

Scandinavian organizations and institutions preserve America's Scandinavian past through art, education, and cultural exchanges.

The American-Scandinavian Foundation, *127 East 73rd Street (212-879-9779). Monday–Friday 10 A.M.–5 P.M.*

The American-Scandinavian Foundation is a truly cross-national group deeply involved in educational exchanges and cultural interchanges both here and in Denmark, Iceland, Sweden, Norway, and Finland. They sponsor scholarships and award literary prizes. Their New York headquarters is not just an office; upstairs there are two large rooms that exhibit Scandinavian art—paintings, sculpture, and whatever else will travel.

The American Scandinavian Society of New York, *245 East 49th Street (212-751-0714).*

The movers and shakers in Scandinavian (mostly Norwegian) New York congregate to celebrate their people's achievements in the United States and in their Scandinavian homelands. They have lectures and meetings and sponsor exhibits. They raise money to preserve the Scandinavian past in New York's present.

Manhattan Smorgasbord

Before New York turned its sophistication on food, Scandinavian food was smorgasbord restaurants, with all-you-can-eat buffets on Manhattan's tourist route. They were fun but no big loss in the taste department. The replacements are superior.

Nyborg and Nelson, *153 East 53rd Street (Citicorp Center) (212-223-0700). Monday–Friday 11:30 A.M.–9 P.M.; Saturday and Sunday noon–6 P.M.*

The restaurant-cum-Scandinavian deli counter is supposed to look functional and high-tech but it just looks bare. The proof is in the eating here. The authentic Scandinavian cuisine attracts Swedes, Danes, and Norwegians from the nearby consulates and information offices. There are open Danish sandwiches, *smorebrod,* and tasty smorgasbord salads supplemented with *polse* and main dishes like loin of pork stuffed with prunes and apples from Denmark.

Aquavit, *13 West 54th Street (212-307-7311). Monday–Friday noon–2 P.M., 5:30 P.M.–10:30 P.M.; Saturday 5:30 P.M.–10:30 P.M.*

Aquavit is expense-account territory, with *prix fixe* luncheons and dinners that are only reasonable if someone else is paying. The restaurant is named for the potent Scandinavian liquor, which is drunk ice cold with lager chasers. Genuine aquavit is on the drink list, but most of the food is only quasi-Scandinavian. The *gravlax* is a stunning exception.

Snaps, *230 Park Avenue at 46th Street (212-949-7878). Monday–Friday 7:30 A.M.–10 A.M., noon–3 P.M., 5:30 P.M.–10:30 P.M.; Saturday 5:30 P.M.–10:30 P.M.*

Snaps is Swedish modern with sleek lines, light woods, and a wraparound banquette. The food is Scandinavian nouvelle, with the emphasis on subtlety, lightness, and presentation. The grilled fish and *gravlax* are memorable.

Scandinavian Style

Clothing

Scandinavian clothes in the past have been mostly reindeer sweaters and hiking boots, but now things are changing.

Marimekko, *698 Madison Avenue, second floor, between 62nd and 63rd streets (212-838-3842). Monday–Wednesday and Saturday 10 A.M.–6:00 P.M.; Thursday 10 A.M.–8 P.M.*

Marimekko has made the leap from designer sheets to designer dresses. The fabrics are still brightly colored and contemporary, while the designs are classical and comfortable. The ready-to-wear is expensive, but there are fabrics on sale for the creative. There are also children's clothes, toys, and accessories.

Furniture

In Scandinavia working in wood is a hallowed tradition and the wood of choice is pine. Almost all houses are made of wood, and even brick dwellings are frame houses with brick skins. In the rural villages of Scandinavia furniture-making was and is a high art. Swedish *allmoge,* or country style, is highly respected in all of Scandinavia. The practical Scandinavians took to modern design, where form follows function, and combined it with their devotion to natural materials. The Swedish modern that lends itself to small city apartments may be Finnish, Danish, or Norwegian.

Wim and Karen's Scandinavian Furniture, *319 East 53rd Street (212-758-4207). Monday–Wednesday and Friday 10* A.M.*–6* P.M.*; Thursday 10* A.M.*–7:30* P.M.*; Saturday 10* A.M.*–5* P.M.

Wim and Karen Samson's collection of Scandinavian furniture is for every room in the house. The furniture, whether of teak, oak, or pine, is made to fit into those small city spaces. They have a complete line of wall units that are refreshingly solid looking. The store has the right accessories, lamps, and ceramic pieces for Scandinavian designs.

The International Home, *460 Park Avenue South (212-684-4414). Daily 10* A.M.*–5* P.M.

The International Home carries a wide range of Scandinavian wall units, bookcases, dining room sets, and bedroom suites in teak and rosewood at affordable prices. Sturdy chairs by the Norwegian manufacturer Ekorness are a best bet.

Scandinavian Design, *127 East 59th Street (212-755-6078). Monday–Friday 9:30* A.M.*–5:30* P.M.

For those with decorators, Scandinavian Design offers a modern environment created with track lighting and economical furniture design. The New York apartment is approached as a whole by the store's knowledgeable staff.

Scandinavian Handmade

Scandinavian crafts are more than the cottage industries of the country-side; they work in sophisticated mediums like porcelain and glass and make fine china and flatware and deep-etched crystal and sculptured glass. Scandinavian companies like Arabia, Orrefors, Kosta Boda, and Royal Copenhagen are world renowned.

Royal Copenhagen Porcelain, *683 Madison Avenue at 61st Street (212-759-6457). Monday–Saturday 9:30 A.M.–5:30 P.M.*

This sleekly elegant showroom has a wide selection of contemporary porcelain, silver, and crystal fit for a Danish queen. Their Danish Georg Jensen silver is a modern classic.

Gallery Nilsson, *138 Wooster Street (212-431-0050). Monday–Saturday noon–7 P.M.; Sunday noon–5 P.M.*

Swedish glass blowers, like Swedish furniture makers, keep things simple. Everything at Nilsson's from bowls to glasses are hand-blown one-of-a-kind or limited editions. They work with one- and two-man companies that are moved more by the creative urge than the bottom line.

Swedish Celebrations

St. Lucia Day

St. Lucia Day is a special feast day that Swedish vikings brought back from Sicily in the Middle Ages. It is dedicated to a young virgin named Lucia who was very virtuous and holy—too virtuous and holy for her pagan suitor, who stabbed her after she refused to marry him and gave her dowry away to the poor. At least that is one version of the story.

St. Lucia Day, which takes place every December 13, is a festival of lights with some resemblance to pagan Scandinavian rites celebrating the end of the dark days of winter and the reemergence of light from the underworld.

In the St. Lucia festivities the youngest girl in the Swedish household dresses as St. Lucia, in white robes and a red sash with a crown of candles adorning her hair. In the middle of the night she wakes the rest of the family singing the hymn of the Queen of Light, and serves them special St. Lucia sweet saffron current buns. There are three toasts with potent Swedish grog before dawn, and then a heavy Swedish breakfast.

The St. Lucia tradition is carried on by New York's Swedish community. Every year the city's Swedish churches rent a hall to accommodate the hundreds of people who want to bring in the St. Lucia year. Recently, over a thousand attended this celebration, which freely mixes Christian solemnity and Norse gaiety. It begins with a stirring procession of young Swedish women dressed like St. Lucia slowly walking up the aisle two by two. They climb the stage and break into the hymn to the Queen of Light of Norse legend. For an hour they intersperse Christmas carols with traditional Scandinavian songs.

This important Swedish holiday rates a formal invitation-only dinner at the residence of the Swedish consul, which includes Nobel Prize winners on its guest list. The Swedish-American Chamber of Commerce holds a December 13 wingding every year at the Waldorf Astoria Hotel, with a special St. Lucia queen chosen from the Swedish community.

Finns

Finns settled in New Amsterdam in the 1630s and 1640s. They were farmers and mechanics, few in number, and hardly distinguishable from their Scandinavian neighbors. Two hundred years later Finnish "true-believers" passed through the city as part of a Protestant revival group formed around Lars Levi Laestadius.

Mostly Finnish seamen populated New York before the mass migrations of the 1890s. They generally jumped Scandinavian ships to draw superior American wages. In the War Between the States Finnish New Yorkers were actively recruited by the Union navy.

The Finns of the "great migration" were reluctant emigrants. Mainly tenant farmers and landless laborers from the agricultural region of Vaasa Oulu, one-third of the males were forced off the land by overpopulation and the expansion of large farms. By 1900 Finnish emigrants were also responding to the increasingly reactionary policies of their Russian sovereigns, who sought to substitute the Russian language for Finnish and who had instituted military conscription.

Determined Finns worked their way from Helsinki to Stockholm and endured the dangers of steerage from Liverpool to New York. At first they didn't have the help of a Finnish colony overseas or the support of their people at home. For their trouble and struggle they were the often the targets of self-righteous clergymen and reporters. They were attacked as traitors and weaklings without scruples or character. The Lutheran Church even refused, at least at first, to accept their overseas marriages as binding.

The Finns of New York were hardly the deserters depicted in the popular Finnish press. They were serious and conscientious. Individually and as a community Finns weighed their every action. They would not abandon one another or their national traditions. Though they had no organizational experience in their native land, they were soon banding together in mutual aid societies and lodges.

From the time the immigrant Finns disembarked at Ellis Island in the early part of the twentieth century, they were met by community representatives. There were Finnish-speaking clergymen who provided spiritual support and assisted Finns in contacting the local Finnish community in Sunset Park. Enterprising Finnish women operated six employment agencies at the immigration station to help newcomers find jobs as domestics. Finnish community representatives also directed emigrants to cooperative boardinghouses where the new immigrants could share cooking, cleaning, and expenses with their compatriots.

In New York Finnish maids were in great demand and women even outnumbered men in the early days of Little Finland. Finnish women were the backbone of Finnish Lutheran and Congregational churches; they formed church societies and played a key part in fund raising. They worked to preserve Finnish culture through their own groups and as auxiliaries of men's organizations like the Knights of Kaleva.

Finnish males followed the example of other Scandinavians and became carpenters and riggers on the city's big construction projects. In the 1890s these Finnish laborers formed socialist societies and workers' leagues like the Imatra Society. The Finns of this time were radical and committed, actively working for left-wing candidates like Eugene Debs, participating in strikes, and demonstrating against antiunion companies and rightist candidates. Later they would be at the forefront of the movement for cooperative stores and housing, which would take the profit away from the middleman capitalist and hand it to the consumer.

Finns from all walks of life joined the Knights of Kaleva, named in honor of the Finnish national epic, the *Kaleva*. As knights, Finns could celebrate their cultural identity and keep up Finnish traditions. The lodge also combined medical assistance and burial insurance with plain old Finnish fellowship. Local Finn halls in Sunset Park and Harlem provided the whole Finnish community with spirited expressions of ethnic pride. There were dramatic readings of the *Kaleva*, folk-song festivals, and regular appearances of Finnish dance companies.

The New York Finnish community was candid about drinking and its problems. They were very active in the Temperance Union movement and there were many separate Finnish temperance organizations throughout the city sponsored by Congregationalist and Lutheran churches and socialist groups. They had a full social program to compete with community-wide events where alcohol was served.

The ties between Finns and their native country remained strong, with almost a third of the community accumulating a nest egg and actually returning home. Some of the socially concerned left New York to participate in experimental socialist communities in Soviet Karelia.

Finnish New York suffered from these defections and was even more hard-hit by immigration quotas that put an end to a vital foreign-language culture. Between 1925 and 1929 only 471 Finns a year could enter the whole country; this figure was only raised to 566 a year until the big changes in the immigration law. Despite this enforced cultural isolation and the pressures of assimilation, Finns had a real bond with the young Finnish republic, which was gamely struggling against the Soviet colossus. Finns were particularly proud of their country's gallant defense against the Soviets in 1939 and the fact that they were the first nation to repay their debt to America after the Marshall Plan ended.

Sunset Park

Directions: Subway N or R to 45th Street/Fourth Avenue.

The Finns who settled in the community of Sunset Park were taken by the park's resemblance to the rich rolling hills of their homeland. It seemed familiar and somehow reassuring to a people confronting a complex urban landscape. The heart of Finntown covered 40th to 45th Streets and Fifth to Ninth Avenues. Skilled in the building trades, the Finns created a charming area of neat frame houses. They also built the first cooperative housing in the city, which Mayor O'Dwyer said was twenty-five years ahead of its time. These neat four-story brick apartment houses are still standing in all their glory.

Before the Gowanus Expressway forced out Finnish homeowners and Robert Moses' idea of progress put an end to a neighborhood, Finntown was a bustling ethnic enclave with cooperative stores selling Finnish foods and handicrafts and a host of Finnish centers and halls. Sunset Park had a half-dozen Finnish saunas where hardworking locals could relax and unwind in the dry heat of this Finnish institution. There were Finnish restaurants which turned meat loaf into a delicacy with sour cream and a pastry shell, and made crayfish something special with dill, vinegar, and beer. Midsummer's eve they lit bonfires in Sunset Park and on *Kaleva Lepos* they celebrated in Imatra Hall by singing ancient songs and reciting from their folk epic, the *Kaleva*.

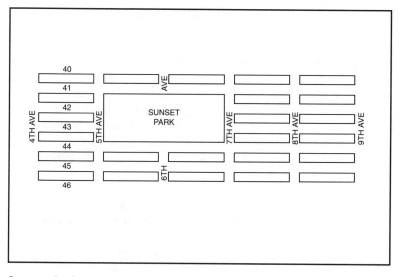

Sunset Park

After World War II, the aging Finnish community could no longer afford to support its network of organizations, and its labor and temperance groups were out of step with the times. Most of the Finns moved out of Finntown, preferring Finnish communities in warmer climes like Lantana and Lake Worth in Florida. But five thousand Finns stayed on, and active second- and third-generation Finnish Americans have continued to maintain the Finnish heritage in a neighborhood where now more Spanish is spoken than any Scandinavian tongue.

In 1990 the remaining Finnish community met with Sunset Park's Community Board Seven to propose that 40th Street (between Seventh and Eighth Avenues) be renamed Finlandia Street in honor of the Finnish community's contribution to this area in Brooklyn and in conjunction with the centennial of Finntown's leading organization, the Imatra Society. In 1991, with the city fathers and Finnish dignitaries looking on, the Finlandia Street sign was unveiled.

Finnish Place Marks

Imatra Hall, *740 40th Street between Seventh and Eighth Avenues (718-438-9426).*

The Imatra Society (named after a legendary Finnish waterfall) was formed in 1891 to defend the interests of Finnish workingmen and support working-class causes. It provided health and death benefits for Finnish laborers along with education and social activities. Culture was also a part of its program; the society had its own library and offered "edifying" lectures, and encouraged Finnish singing and study groups.

In 1902 the Imatra Society of Brooklyn joined with thirty-two other similar groups to establish the American Finnish Workers League to back the labor movement. The Imatra Society also started publishing their own politically slanted paper, *New Yorkin Uutiset,* which was edited by the idealistic Matti Kurikka, who had founded a Utopian community in the British Colombian wilderness. The group was ideologically leftist and a partisan of strong unions.

As time passed, the organization's predominantly working-class character changed and the Finnish newspaper became more mainstream. The organization gradually accepted members representing every class and political view in the Finnish community. Imatra Hall now consisted of friendly Finns gathering in the Imatra Bar or game rooms, or the whole of Finntown coming out for a Finnish holiday celebration.

Most Imatra Hall traditions haven't changed, though the society has had to accept associate members who are not of Finnish descent to keep the organization's Sunset Park identity. The Hall has regular appearances of Finnish singers, bands, and dancers and its own Finnish dance fetes in its social hall or in the Imatra gardens. For the midsummer's eve summer solstice celebration there is traditional Finnish dancing, eating, and drinking, and a giant bonfire in the big backyard.

Imatra Hall has seen better days, but its current leadership keeps this old rambling wooden monument together and is talking about major fund raising and a full-scale rehabilitation. They celebrated this Finnish institution's one-hundred-year anniversary with a big Finnish-style blowout and a gathering of Finnish friends and families. These redoubtables are now working toward their second century.

Alku Toinen Finnish Cooperative Apartments, *816-826 43rd Street.*

Alku Toinen Finnish Cooperative Apartments was the city's first cooperative, built in 1916. The building represented a fresh start for many of its Finnish occupants, who literally built the place. The building's name appropriately means "beginning." In this true cooperative the actual residents of the building shared the costs of construction and maintained the property with no middlemen making a profit. The building still has plenty of Finnish tenants.

Finnish Classics

The sauna is a three-thousand-year-old Finnish tradition connected to pre-Christian religious rites. In Finland it was the custom to build the sauna even before building the house. This ancient heat bath, made by heating rocks to high temperatures, still has an almost mystical significance, part purification rite and part exhilarating penance. More prosaically, it is a way of sweating out a hangover and keeping clean. Finnish sauna enthusiasts rub themselves with steel brushes and whack one another with birch branches as a type of massage. People also socialize in the sauna, solving the world's problems while dousing the rocks with water which rises in burning clouds of steam. It is a place where Finnish businessmen negotiate and politicians make deals. As one Finnish wag insisted, "We just keep on pouring the water on the rocks until they say yes." Sunset Park's last remaining sauna is in Imatra Hall.

chapter five

The Irish

The Irish of New York started out Protestant, but once they were joined by significant numbers of poor uneducated Irish Catholics, they decided it was more "society" to be called Scotch-Irish, and the New York Irish became the Catholic Irish. The Irish are New York's prototypical rags-to-riches story. They came with the clothes on their back and starvation gnawing at their bellies, and in a generation they were running the city. They were the cops, the firemen, and the mayors or the Tammany powers behind the throne. Nowadays the American-born Irish are as likely to be financiers and businessmen as they are policemen and firemen. But the story of Irish immigrants isn't over. There is a whole new group of Irish immigrants as eloquent and independent as the last batch who are fighting different battles and creating their own success stories.

History

The first Irishman to set foot on what would become New York was John Coleman, an able-bodied crewman aboard Henry Hudson's *Half Moon.* Coleman lost his life in a dispute with the Native Americans and became the first Irishman—and white man—to be buried on Coney Island.

The Irish played an important part in New York from the time it became the property of King Charles II in 1664. Governor Thomas Dongan, a

Catholic and Irish nobleman of Limerick, gave New York its first city charter. In his charter, which was later rescinded, he recognized liberties that were later included in the Bill of Rights.

Both Protestant and Catholic Irish gained positions of prominence in commerce and government in colonial New York. Despite their wealth and power, these Irish still welcomed the American Revolution and the opportunity to strike back at unfair British rule. Even Sir Henry Clinton, a loyalist to the core, had to admit that the Irish were the best soldiers on either side. By the beginning of the nineteenth century, the city's Irish were taking sides in the political battles between another Clinton heading the Federalists and a new political organization called Tammany Hall.

The American Revolution inspired another revolution on the Emerald Isle. The British were able to crush this uprising, which created the first generation of Irish political refugees. They were intellectual men of action who brought their knowledge and abilities to the city. Thomas Addis Emmet was one of the leading conspirators in the failed 1798 revolution. He escaped to New York to become a power in city politics and an ardent backer of Jefferson. In 1812 he became the attorney general of New York.

The city's early Celtic population was very lace curtain—merchants and professionals and capable craftsmen. They had a newspaper called *The Shamrock* and their Society of St. Patrick rivaled the English St. Andrew's Society. They were divided by religion and united by their Irish identity. Their charitable organizations benefited both Protestants and Catholics. In 1826 New York's united Irish community was large enough to swing the city to Andrew Jackson in a presidential election.

The city's "carriage-and-four" Irish were soon joined by the Irish poor, who were attracted by stories of full larders and meat every day and fat pay envelopes. These Irish tenants were tired of a homeland where they weren't allowed to hold property or practice their own religion. They were tired of the brutal tax collectors and soldiers and the humiliating privileges of an alien nobility. Rural Ireland was ready to emigrate.

The Irish population rise translated into more political power. They went from being barred from Tammany Hall to nominating the first Irish Catholic, Patrick Mackay, to the state assembly. In 1817 the bias against the Irish continued, and outraged Celts broke into the Tammany wigwam to protest the organization's refusal to support the Irish leader Thomas A. Emmet for Congress. New York's passage of a law guaranteeing universal white suffrage meant that Tammany politicians like the president-to-be Martin Van Buren courted the Irish-Catholic electorate.

These New York Irish built the Erie Canal, which made New York the commercial power it is today and ushered in a golden age. In 1841 Irish-Catholic notables like Bishop John Hughes and Congressman

Thomas McKeon formed the Irish Emigrant Society under the auspices of the Catholic Church. In New York it was official—Irish and Catholic were one and the same. Over the years the Society stopped the abuse of immigrants and provided services for poor Irish New Yorkers.

Before the biggest Irish famine in 1845 (there were five Irish potato famines between between 1817 and 1848), Irish peasants were squatters on their own inheritance. They rented lands that their families had farmed for generations from foreign landlords who extorted large sums for this privilege. The only way the Irish farmers could meet this bill was by planting crops for the British export market and depending on a potato kitchen garden for survival.

The blight that left the potatoes black and rotting in 1845 set in motion a cycle of starvation and death. While freighters were leaving Irish ports for Liverpool packed with produce, human skeletons in the countryside were scavenging for grass and eating dirt. The moderate pace of Irish emigration to New York became a stampede.

Whether Irish emigrants raised the fare from a government anxious to get rid of them or from a New York charity, the ordeal was far from over. Ocean travel was still risky and traveling in "Irish berths" below the freight in steerage had its own dangers.

There was the strain of the endless din in dark cramped spaces. Sudden violence was common under decks and there were cases of unprotected women being attacked. If the weather wasn't right the usual eight-week voyage could become a six-month agony. Sometimes provisions were short or spoiled and there was another famine on board. Disease ran rampant in these airless areas. Many Irish died from cholera or typhus before the "coffin ships" reached shore. For some Irish, steerage turned out to be not so different from a slave ship.

The Irishman from "the old sod" was a familiar figure, with his brimless *caubeen,* knee britches, flowing cape, and big buckled shoes, clattering down the gangplank at New York Harbor. Before local and federal governments overhauled the immigration process, these naive newcomers were fair game for con men called "shoulder hitters," who sold them counterfeit train tickets, overcharged them for storing or carting their luggage, and steered them to crooked boardinghouses. The unwary Irishman often wound up living in a glorified grog shop on Greenwich Street, where the only thing for free was a plate of loose tobacco. Fast-talking landlords stripped them of their savings and possessions in a few days.

Irish immigrants crowded forty to a cellar in decaying Five Points housing and squatted in shanty towns in the wastes of Harlem. They even lived in "dugouts" under the floorboards of cellars, and when they went out to look for work there was the standard "no Irish need apply" in the ads in the newspaper.

Though uneducated, they quickly adapted their rural skills to the urban landscape. They used pure brawn as stevedores and porters, while their knowledge of horses helped them progress from grooms to cabmen and carters. The Irishman who had dug the potato cellars now dug foundations for city buildings. Eventually they proved themselves in the building trades, first as hod carriers, then as bricklayers and masons. Irish women used their domestic skills as housemaids and laundresses and took in sewing.

The Irish-famine immigrants were mistrusted for their Catholicism and disdained for their poverty. The *Herald* political cartoonist, Thomas Nast, caricatured the Irish as apes. The hardworking Irish were lumped together with the violent Irish in the Five Points gangs. The Know-Nothing Party in the 1850s pledged to get rid of the Irish and Catholic menace. The Irish fought back, organizing themselves to disrupt Know-Nothing rallies and defeat them at the polls. Their participation in Democratic politics, like their church, became a way of life.

In 1855 Fernando Wood was elected mayor, with Irish voters deciding the outcome. By 1860 one out of every four New Yorkers was Irish. During Wood's administration the immigration station at Castle Garden was opened, allowing new immigrants from Ireland to enter the country unmolested. Representatives of the Irish Immigration Society helped them contact their families and find employment. Representatives of Tammany did some hiring and led the new immigrants off to be naturalized so they could vote in the next election.

In Wood's era, Irish Catholics received permission to build St. Patrick's Cathedral. This impressive sanctuary made it clear that Catholicism was one of the city's major religions and that the governing Catholic hierarchy was Irish. The ancient Order of Hibernians was formed at this time to defend the Church and keep alive traditions like the St. Patrick's Day Parade.

In New York the Irish, who were basically a rural people, faced choices they never encountered in their villages. Sometimes their passions got out of hand. In July 1863 a group of Irish joined Native Americans in a protest against the Civil War draft that turned into one of New York's worst riots.

In the year of the riots there were tensions between the Irish, who were divided on abolition, and New York's established black community. The Irish had no conception of Southern slavery but cheap black labor was a direct threat. Blacks had recently been used to break a bitter Irish long-shoremen's strike and bad feeling was running high.

The immediate cause for the riot was the injustice of a new law that allowed the rich to be exempted from the Union draft for a three-hundred-dollar fee. It was hot, and perhaps agent provocateurs were at work. For three days the New York mob was out of control. Blacks were lynched and the Colored Orphan's Asylum was gutted. But the Irish also saved the day. Archbishop Hughes calmed the mob with words and Irish policemen enforced the peace with guns and nightsticks.

The Irish were of one mind where the Union was concerned and rallied to the colors. Thousands enrolled in the city's militias when the Civil War broke out. Flamboyant Irish fighters went into battle with shamrocks and harps, lots of bravado, and gaudy uniforms. Irish soldiers wore Turkish fezzes and red firemen's shirts to the battle of Bull Run. The honor roll of New York's daring Irish forces included the sixty-ninth Regiment, the thirty-seventh Regiment, and the Tammany Regiment, led by officers with names like Meagher, Corcoran, and Shields.

After the war Irish immigrants returned to New York as American heroes. They were no longer outsiders; they were the core of the city's uniformed professionals—police and firefighters. Michael Kerwin, who fought for Irish freedom as well as the Union, became police commissioner. The Irish were more than foot soldiers of the Democratic Party; they were also ward leaders and precinct captains. Honest John Kelly represented his Irish neighborhood in Congress.

New York's Irish were organized labor's rank and file and leaders. They used the talent for organization that they revealed in politics to unionize construction workers and stevedores, the skilled and the unskilled. They were past masters of the fine art of negotiation. The Irish labor leader Peter J. McGuire went national, helping to found the American Federation of Labor, and earned the right to be known as the "Father of Labor Day."

In 1871 Boss Tweed, the city's most flagrant grafter, had his comeuppance and Honest John Kelly became the first Irishman to head Tammany. Honest John was a boxer and an actor and a volunteer fireman. He also invented the Tammany machine, the chain of command from block captain to district leader, which won elections. He initiated the Irish political succession, which was only broken by Carmine De Sapio in the 1950s.

Richard Croker was Kelly's political heir and was also a former volunteer fireman and prizefighter. He made a fortune as coroner and parlayed himself into a position as head of a finance committee that didn't keep any books. Croker had champagne tastes and retired to an estate in Ireland to raise racing horses.

Charles Francis Murphy succeeded Boss Croker in 1902. He was a ball player and the proprietor of four taverns that doubled as Tammany political clubs. He ruled Tammany for twenty-two years and kept politics out of the police department, the schools, and the judiciary. When Murphy died city politicians lamented that "the brains of Tammany lie in the Calvary Cemetery."

When William R. Grace, the millionaire founder of Grace Lines, was elected mayor of New York in 1880, the majority of Irish were still struggling to make ends meet as laborers and maids and living in run-down tenements in neighborhoods like Hell's Kitchen. Some of the kids strayed, breaking and entering into the West Side railroad yards and drifting into gangs like the Knuckle Dusters and the Dead Rabbits. While Irish politicians controlled Tammany, Irish thugs controlled the rackets on the West Side.

The Irish were also joining the ranks of the respectable super-rich. Thomas E. Murray was one of the first of the Irish tycoons. He started out as a lamplighter in Albany, but this Irish Edison had a real scientific genius and was soon earning patents for circuits, switches, and dynamos. While garnering wealth for his inventions he managed the Brooklyn Edison Company. Murray died just months before the stock market crash, leaving an estate worth well over ten million.

Murray's daughter Anna married a man with as much energy and wit as her father. James Francis McDonnell was a canny Wall Street trader who had started the high-flying firm of McDonnell & Byrne. He vowed he would make a million before he married and another million for each of his fourteen children. He kept his word. The McDonnells knew they had arrived when they joined dynasties with the Fords and it was Henry II who converted.

Although the Irish are rarely associated with "trade," before Gristede and D'Agostino became household words in New York, a Butler from Kilkenny had a lock on the grocery business. All his stores, which at one point numbered 1,100, were painted green and his fortune in green amounted to thirty million in pre-Depression dollars. Butler loved the racetrack and eventually bought his own in Yonkers. In lieu of allow-ances, the "squire" gave his children tips on the races.

In 1916 New York Irish rich and poor backed the Easter Rebellion in Ireland. When the rebellion failed and the British executed the uprising's gallant leaders, the Irish community held demonstrations and special masses were said in the churches. Despite their feelings against Britain, loyal Irish New Yorkers volunteered for the forces in World War I and the Fighting Sixty-ninth, under the command of "Wild Bill" Donovan, was one of the first units to see action in Europe. In the peace following World War I, Ireland at last became Eire, the Irish Free State.

While New York's personable Roaring Twenties' Irish Mayor Jimmy Walker was making headlines with Broadway showgirls, another Irish New Yorker, Al Smith, fought the good fight for the presidency of the

United States. Eventually both left public life but the New York tradition of Irish officeholders and Irish political kingmakers continued.

The new Irish politicians followed their Irish constituents to suburban Brooklyn, the Bronx, and Queens. The last Irish mayor was a Brooklynite named O'Dwyer. He went from walking a beat in Brooklyn to the Brooklyn District Attorney's office and took off time from city government during World War II to be a general. In 1974 a former Brooklyn congressman named Hugh Carey became the governor of the state. An intelligent and effective negotiator, he was instrumental in saving the state and city from bankruptcy.

Ed Flynn of the Bronx became the city's Democratic political leader after the death of Charles Francis Murphy and he gained national political stature advising Roosevelt in the 1932 presidential election. In 1960 history was repeated when Bronx Democratic leader Charles C. Buckley helped propel John F. Kennedy (for a time a resident of the Bronx) into the presidency.

Patrick Moynihan, a New York Irishman who went from the slums of Hell's Kitchen to a professorship at Harvard, was a member in good standing of Kennedy's inner-circle Camelot. After the assassination of the great Irish hope he divided his time between academia and appointive politics. He ultimately ran for elective office and became New York's Democratic senator through the 1970s, 1980s, and into the 1990s. His rise reflected the success of the New York Irish community, which was now overwhelmingly white collar and professional.

Despite Irish political power the new immigration law of 1965 severely limited Irish access to the country at a time of high unemployment and economic stagnation in Ireland. In the words of one New York Irish immigration activist, it was "immigration or die."

Although the law of the land continued to restrict Irish admittance to the States in the 1970s and 1980s, Irish men and women continued to be drawn to the American dream. The young and adventurous came to New York City in droves, creating new communities and revitalizing old ones.

Many, if not most, lived under the constant strain of being an "illegal," without the proper documents and the rights that come with being a resident or a citizen. They were forced to work "off the books" and were afraid to contact government agencies even in emergencies. In 1986 many Irish became Americans through a special amnesty that was part of the Immigration Reform and Control Act. In 1990 continued Irish-American activism and lobbying resulted in a law sponsored by Senator Edward Kennedy and Brooklyn Congressman Charles Schumer which granted sixteen thousand extra entry visas to Irish applicants through a visa lottery. Four years later, this process was repeated.

With eighteen percent unemployment in Ireland, and with the young being the hardest hit, Irish emigration continues unabated. The best estimates put the number of undocumented Irish entering New York every year at twenty thousand. The new Irish are fresh out of school and single. Though more educated than an earlier generation of immigrants, due to their immigration status, they often must settle for jobs as bartenders, laborers, or nannies.

The new Irish still manage to thrive. They are raising families and building neighborhoods. The latest Irish immigrants are keeping alive old traditions and creating new cultural forms. Irish music, rock and folk, is alive and well in a lively new pub scene from the Bronx to Brooklyn. Irish sports are also on a roll, with Irish football and hurling in venues like Paddy's Field and Gaelic Park.

═ Manhattan—That Old Gang of Mine ═

The Old Neighborhoods

The Irish at one time or another have lived in nearly every neighborhood in the city. They struggled out of a Lower East Side slum called Five Corners in the early years of the nineteenth century only to find later generations living in a truly hellish Hell's Kitchen on the West Side of Manhattan between 30th Street and 57th Street. In both neighborhoods, a century apart, they had gangs that terrorized the city. In the nineteenth century there were poor Irish squatters in Harlem and at the turn of this century there were working-class Irish just north of German Yorkville. The last Little Ireland in the city was near the Bronx divide in Inwood and Marble Hill, the only vestige of Manhattan on the north shore of the Harlem River.

Place Marks—Police, Firemen, and Pols

Directions: Subway 4, 5, or 6 to Brooklyn Bridge. Bus M1, M6, or M15 to City Hall.

The Civic Center

It is officially called the Civic Center, though most New Yorkers refer to it by nearby street names, Foley Square or Center Street. This collection of imposing public buildings that make up the Civic Center is a testament to the Irish who governed the city for more than a century. In their Irish homeland they weren't allowed the most rudimentary legal rights; in New York they built modern temples to administer justice.

North of City Hall, the core of the Civic Center is Foley Square, at the junction of Duane, Lafayette, Pearl, and Center Streets. The area has gone through a number of changes from the time it was sixty feet under water and surrounded by the Lippensard swamp.

The English called it the Collect, and while tanners polluted its waters, the first paddle steamer was tested here. In 1800 it was filled and drained as part of a relief project, and turned into a recreation site. The property was abandoned by the city to the slumlords when it started to sink. The Collect became the squalid habitation of last resort for freed slaves and destitute Irish immigrants. Respectable citizens considered it a den of crime and demanded its demolition. A later generation of Irish turned it into one of the most architecturally impressive parts of the city.

Foley Square

Foley Square was named for an influential Irish politician named Thomas F. Foley. Working behind the scenes from his saloon, he pulled the strings to get Al Smith the nod for governor and stop Hearst from winning a seat in the U.S. Senate. The Square is the location of two Corinthian-columned courthouses of grand dimensions. The U.S. Courthouse, designed by Cass Gilbert, is a thirty-two-story office tower with the classical impact of a Greek temple. It has fifty-foot columns and is topped by a gold pyramid. On the northeast corner of Pearl Street the County Courthouse rises like another Greek epic. The building's finely proportioned portico, three columns deep, holds aloft heroic representations of Truth, Law, and Equity.

Tombs, *100 Center Street.*

The infamous "Tombs," the Criminal Courts Building and Prison, is below the classic courthouses at 100 Center Street. Its morbid nickname relates to an earlier prison on the same site that looked like a pharaoh's tomb. Today the Tombs, despite its associations with crime and punishment, is an impressive art deco structure with towers of Babylon and cast-aluminum detail. Temporary detention has been shifted to Riker's Island.

Police Headquarters, *One Police Plaza.*

New York's Police Headquarters dominates Police Plaza just opposite Foley Square. It's a red brick and cement block with a grid of small windows. This is one of the more recent additions to the Civic Center, circa 1973. On the south side of the plaza is the Rhinelander Sugar House Prison Window Monument, a small bit of history salvaged from a sugar warehouse of the eighteenth century, where Revolutionary War patriots were imprisoned.

Law enforcement in New York owes a large debt to the Irish. Throughout the years the police, the cop on the beat, and later the cop in the patrol car, were practically synonymous with the Irish. As early as 1815 an Irishman named John McManus headed the New York police. By the time of the mass immigrations of the 1850s, the force was solidly Irish born. The highly respected Irish police chief of that time, John A. Kennedy, went on to be the superintendent of the nation's main immigrant station at Castle Garden.

In 1895 a New York Irish police inspector became a national celebrity for his ability to crack difficult cases. He also rose to the rank of police commissioner. A New York Irish woman, Mrs. Ellen O'Grady, became the first female deputy commissioner in 1918. Although the office of police commissioner is no longer an Irish sinecure, the last two were Irish Americans named Kelly and Bratton. The Irish still represent a significant portion of the force, especially at the higher levels of captains and inspectors.

Police Academy Museum, *235 East 20th Street between Second and Third avenues (212-477-9753). Monday–Friday 9 A.M.–3 P.M. Closed on weekends and holidays.*

The museum traces the history of the New York Police Department through police equipment and uniforms. There are early and unusual weapons and modern SWAT team gear and the nuts and bolts of emergency services. The Police Academy itself is on the guided tour.

Firehouses

The firehouse is an important part of the Irish New York experience. In the first half of the nineteenth century the majority of New York's volunteer fire companies were manned by the Irish. In that early era of firefighting, companies raced one another to the scene of a fire and fought to be first at the hydrant. The companies were like fraternities, with whimsical names like Old Maid's Boys, Fly by Nights, and Dock Rats. They were devoted to their horse-drawn engines, which they washed and polished all day and gave pet names to like Hope and Honey Bee. Dousing fires created a big thirst and each company had a steward assigned to keep the drink flowing. The volunteer fire company, with its deeds of daring, was a real source of satisfaction for the city's dispossessed Irish. With a sense of pride, they wore the brilliant uniforms of their companies in citywide parades. When New York's firemen were put on the city payroll, the courageous Irish were the core of this efficient city service.

Firehouse Company No. 31 at 87 Lafayette Street, a block from Center Street, looks like a French Renaissance chateau. It's all towers and turrets and dormers and decorative crests. Now defunct, when it was built in 1895 it was state-of-the-art fire-fighting technology, with automatic latches to release the horses at the sound of the alarm.

Fire Department Museum, *278 Spring Street (212-691-1303). Monday–Friday 10 A.M.–4 P.M. Closed on weekends and holidays.*

There is a whole fleet of fire engines from 1820 to the present along with modern fire equipment. Paintings and drawings illustrate firefighters at work and at home in the firehouse.

St. Patrick's New and Old

New York's Irish had a special regard for their priests, who stood by them in times of persecution and suffering and guarded with their lives Irish national traditions. Priests endured the great potato famine with their parishioners and followed them into exile, sometimes with a price on their own head for refusing to obey the British authorities.

When the British barred Catholic education, Irish parish priests started secret "hedge schools." In New York it was natural for the Irish clergy to lead the Irish community. Their greatest leader was Archbishop John Hughes, who guided the development of New York's Catholic church during the critical years of mass Irish immigration.

John Hughes was already a bishop when he arrived in New York in 1838. He also possessed an indomitable will and the administrative skills that Irish politicians brought to Tammany Hall. From the beginning in 1839 he fought for Irish-Catholic justice, demanding a fair share of the public school society funds controlled by the Protestant establishment. When he was denied what he believed was his community's due, he started his own parochial school system.

In the 1840s, when thousands of Ireland's destitute landed in New York, he worked tirelessly for their welfare. He was a founder of the Irish Emigrant Society and brought over the Sisters of Mercy from Ireland to help immigrant women find employment. In the days when nativist Protestant mobs threatened Catholic churches and even burned down a cathedral in Philadelphia, he pledged in a typical rousing speech that the city would burn like "another Moscow" if anyone touched a single church. In another example of his powerful oratory, he stopped a raging mob in its tracks during the Civil War antidraft riot.

The archbishop's greatest labor of love was St. Patrick's Cathedral, which he considered a monument to the New World's Catholics, "worthy of the Catholic religion and an honor to this great city." Irish Catholics, who were routinely vilified and attacked for their religion, would have the most noble house of worship in the city.

The original St. Patrick's Cathedral still stands at the corner of Prince and Mott Streets. It was an impressive sanctuary when it was completed in 1809. St. Patrick's was only America's second Gothic revival church and was executed by the distinguished architect, Joseph Mangin. A fire in 1866 did substantial damage to its front, which could not be completely rectified by thorough reconstruction.

The Cathedral of St. Patrick's on Fifth Avenue between 50th and 51st Streets was designed by the foremost architect of the day, James Renwick, Jr., who happened to be a Protestant. The dimensions of this house of worship were and are spellbinding. Its twin 330-foot Gothic towers and arched doorways dominate Fifth Avenue like no other building. The church has nineteen bells that still call the faithful to worship. Inside, a brilliant geometric rose window lets in the shimmering light above a great organ with nine thousand pipes. Candles flicker along the north and south aisle in front of the statues of saints and the Holy Mother. Above the altar are the "galeros," the hats of all the Irish Cardinals who have served St. Patrick's.

St. Patrick's Cathedral Rectory, *460 Madison Avenue between 50th and 51st streets (212-753-2661).*

Irish Arts and Archives

The Celtic tradition of the spoken and sung word is also a New York tradition. George M. Cohan applied it to the Broadway musical and Eugene O'Neill in his tragic dramas (often dealing with Irish families) applied it to the Broadway stage. Some of New York's best writers have been Irish journalists. The late Jimmy Cannon, Pete Hammil, and Jimmy Breslin have expressed more with greater subtlety in a column of daily journalism than so-called serious writers who work out of ivory towers. Some important Irish writers like James T. Farrel and Wilfrid Sheed are transplanted New Yorkers by choice. Irish institutions support these artistic endeavors.

Irish Books and Graphics, *90 West Broadway (212-962-4237). Monday–Friday 11 A.M.–5 P.M.; Saturday noon–5 P.M.*

Irish Books and Graphics has all the Irish books that can't be found anywhere else. It has books in Gaelic and rarities that have been translated from Gaelic into English. This bookstore stages an annual Irish-language short-story contest with an award for the winning entry. It also carries Irish prints, engravings, and maps.

The Irish American Cultural Center of New York, *1560 Broadway at 47th Street (212-391-1120).*

This group, made up of influential Irish union leaders, businessmen, and politicians, supports the whole spectrum of Irish-American culture. They are particularly active in fostering Irish-American cultural exchanges and Irish education. In the past they have had scholarship funds.

The Irish Arts Center, *553 West 51st Street (212-757-3318).*

The Irish Arts Center has classes in every aspect of Irish culture: dance, music, the Gaelic language, and Irish history. They are available at a nominal charge for members. The Irish Arts Center has an accomplished acting company, and leading Irish writers and directors have involved themselves in their productions.

The American Irish Historical Society, *991 Fifth Avenue at 80th Street (212-288-2263).*

The American Irish Historic Society has an extensive library of documents, letters, books, and newspapers dealing with the Irish experience in early and present-day America. It is all housed with infinite care in a grand Fifth Avenue mansion. The Society has its own speakers' bureau.

Irish Extras

Irish Voice, *432 Park Avenue South (212-684-3366).*

The *Irish Voice* is the voice of young Irish Americans, the most recent arrivals. It thoroughly covers the Irish domestic scene and the "troubles" in Northern Ireland. The paper deals candidly with the problems of undocumented Irish aliens, and is an advocate for immigration reform. Every week it carries the most comprehensive listing of upcoming cultural events and community happenings with addresses and phone numbers.

Political Saloon to Pubs and Restaurants

The public house of Ireland was transformed into the Irish neighborhood saloon. It was the New York Irishman's private club, a place to enjoy the company of his peers and forget about his problems. Like the leather-armchair clubs of New York society, the Irish saloon was a pathway to political and employment contacts and a source of invaluable advice and information. In the sawdust precincts of some local saloon, the awkward Irishman from the other side learned how to fit in. The Irish saloon was also the home of the free lunch, where for the price of a beer a hungry workingman could feast on meat and potatoes. The Irish saloonkeeper had stature in the community, was frequently politically connected, and in times of difficulty, openhanded. The Irish saloon was a neighborhood institution where people celebrated weddings and birthdays and political questions were settled over the bar.

In the age of standardization the Irish saloon became the chain Irish bar. Hundreds of identical bars bore the names of Grant's, Blarney Stone, Claney's, White Rose, and Smith's. The heir of the Grant fortune even kept the political connection alive when he let Tammany elect him mayor. By then the only thing left of the old free lunch was a table with pickles and onions. The bars' working-class patrons were sold good cheap lunches straight from a steam table. Lines formed for a corned beef, roast beef, fresh ham, or Virginia ham sandwich, with side orders of baked beans, mashed potatoes, home fries, or cabbage. There were long bars with light provided by neon beer signs and Four Roses and Fleischman's bar specials for singles and doubles. The glasses had bottoms as thick as two fingers and the bartenders were brisk and professional and came equipped with brogues. If the talk flagged there was always the juke box and later television. McAnn's is the last of this breed.

The Irish saloon changed with the times in Manhattan and the emphasis in past years has been on food and ambience. The sophisticated city Irish have turned their backs for the most part on traditional Irish fare and have opted for steaks and chops and American ideas of Irish cooking. The Irish food in the typical restaurant/pub is represented by dishes like shepherd's pie (minced lamb in a mashed potato crust), fish and chips, steak and kidney pie, and corned beef and cabbage. Still some Irish pubs offer the real McCoy of boiled Irish bacon (more like smoked ham than American fatty bacon) and cabbage instead of the American Irish equivalent of corned beef and cabbage, but they have had few takers. Only the Irish breakfast, with Irish bacon or Irish sausage, has caught on as a Manhattan brunch.

Irish bar classics like Costello's have gone yuppie for lunch and dinner, and P.J. Clark's, Irish playwright Brendan Behan's favorite, now takes reservations. Despite all the changes, Irish restaurant/pubs are alive and well in Manhattan. Irish pub keepers from the old sod have landed and opened real public houses everywhere on the shores of Manhattan (with authentic Irish music) for their immigrant compatriots. The pub crawl is again in fashion and the best place to begin is in the granddaddy of them all, McSorley's Old Ale House.

McSorley's Old Ale House, *15 East Seventh Street near Third Avenue (212-473-9148). Daily noon–1 A.M.*

Before 1970 the bar was filled with old Irishmen with hacking coughs and big thirsts and young NYU students staring at all the old Collier brothers curios on the walls. Women weren't permitted entry in those days and the onion on the liverwurst burned like jalapeno peppers. Now only the college students are left, along with the sawdust on the floor. The bar is still a wonderful relic and nothing can ruin the Guinness.

Tommy Makem's Irish Pavilion, *130 East 57th Street (212-759-9040). Daily noon–3 A.M.*

The Irish Pavilion is a sanitized Irish pub, where even a temperance society gentlemen would feel comfortable. In the front there is a tiny gift shop, 57th Street sleek, selling Aran sweaters and Waterford crystal. They have fine Irish folk music from Thursday to Sunday and sometimes the Irish virtuoso himself.

Glocca Morra, *304 Third Avenue between 23rd and 24th streets (212-473-9638). Daily 10:30 A.M.– 4:30 A.M.*

The Glocca Morra is nothing fancy—just good Irish fun. Wednesday to Saturday at 10:30 P.M. there's an Irish balladeer on the guitar and everybody joins in a freewheeling Irish singsong. The hamburgers are the best thing to eat here.

Kinsale Tavern, *1672 Third Avenue near 94th Street (212-348-4370). Daily 8 A.M. –4 A.M. Restaurant 11 A.M.–1:30 A.M.*

The Kinsale Tavern is an old fashioned Irish saloon for the 1990s, with Guiness in 20-ounce Gaelic pints. The crowd is young and old immigrant. The brunch is traditional: Irish bacon, sausage, and blood pudding.

Eamon Doran, *998 Second Avenue between 52nd and 53rd streets (212-753-9191). Daily noon– 4 A.M.*

Eamon Doran started out as a typical New York beer-and-shot bar where it was so dark you could barely see the drinks. They added a menu with things like Irish-American corned beef and cabbage and hamburgers. Eventually, they moved across the street to larger quarters, and now with a rise in the prices Doran is a "licensed vintner." The food is still tasty Irish American with dishes like Gaelic steak made with good Irish whiskey. Doran also has steak and kidney pie and boiled bacon and cabbage.

Flannery's, *14th Street and Seventh Avenue (212-929-9589). Monday–Saturday 8 A.M.– 4 A.M.; Sunday noon– 4 A.M.*

Flannery's keeps up the tradition of 14th Street's now defunct Eagle Tavern, with Irish jam sessions called *seisiuns* on Monday, and hard-driving Irish folk music on Wednesday, Friday, and Saturday. The crowd is a mix of Irish "born to be wild" and Village bohemian.

Ryan's Irish Pub, *151 Second Avenue between Ninth and Tenth streets (212-979-9511). Daily noon– 4 A.M.*

Ryan's is part of the New York Irish bar revival. The old and new Irish belly up to the bar for Guinness and Murphy's and are storytellers in the Irish tradition. There is a great Sunday brunch with singing Irish lasses.

Abbey Tavern, *Third Avenue at 26th Street (212-532-1978). Daily noon– 4 A.M.*

The Abbey Tavern is a set designer's idea of a Dublin pub but that doesn't change the fact that it is pleasant, spacious, and attractive. The crowd is young at the bar and in the booths for the weekend Irish brunch, and the waitresses are Irish. The Irish-American specialties like the shepherd's pie and the corned beef and cabbage are anemic.

Irish Pub East, *121 East 58th Street between Second and Third avenues (212-980-4616). Daily 10 A.M.– 4 A.M.*

The Irish Pub East is a popular meeting place for the midtown office Irish. Every Saturday the pub presents Irish folk and ballad music. It telecasts via satellite all the important all-Ireland football and hurling finals.

O'Flanagan's, *1251 First Avenue at 65th Street (212-439-0660). Daily 11 A.M.– 4 A.M.*

O'Flanagan's is a real Irish singles bar, with dancing and Irish groups every night of the week. It is crowded and noisy, but it doesn't have that feeling of New York anonymity. People come here from Bainbridge, Woodside, and Irish Bay Ridge for a night out. The steak is prime and the Irish stew is rich with tender chunks of lamb and vegetables that haven't lost their flavor.

Costello's, *225 East 44th Street (212-599-9614). Monday–Friday 11 A.M.–4 A.M.*

The scene nowadays is more newspapermen than Irish, but the weathered bar still has plenty of old-time atmosphere, and the conversational free-for-all is frequently interesting.

Aran Sweaters and Other Irish Crafts

Manhattan's Irish craft shops prove that skilled Irish craftspeople can compete with the best.

Mattie Haskin's Shamrock Imports, *A & S Plaza, 901 Sixth Avenue at 32nd Street (212-564-7474). Monday, Thursday, and Friday 10:00 A.M.–8:30 P.M.; Tuesday, Wednesday, and Saturday 10:00 A.M.–6:45 P.M.; Sunday 11:00 A.M.–6:00 P.M.*

Mattie Haskin's rich stock of Irish imports has been rearranged and more attractively displayed to fit into its new shopping-center surroundings. It is still a treasure trove of hand-knit turtleneck and crew-neck sweaters, intricately carved Celtic crosses, and Waterford crystal. There are Irish newspapers and books and canned and packaged Irish foods.

Bernadette Ryan's Irish Shop, *630 Fifth Avenue (212-826-6511). Monday–Saturday 10 A.M.–6 P.M.*

Bernadette Ryan's Irish Shop has moved to Rockefeller Center but still retains its Irish warmth and graciousness. The shop is teacup quaint with the prim flower-print look of a Victorian parlor. The Irish sweaters, lace, linen, mugs, and medals are attractively displayed.

The Irish Secret, *155 Spring Street (212-334-6711). Sunday–Wednesday 11 A.M.–7 P.M.; Thursday–Saturday 11 A.M.–8 P.M.*

Decorated in the colors of the Emerald Isle, The Irish Secret has both men's and women's clothes in jewel tones. The service comes with a brogue.

══════════ Irish Bronx ══════════

Bainbridge

Directions: Subway 4 to Mosholu Parkway.

The Irish were among the earliest immigrant groups to cross the Harlem River into the Bronx. They glimpsed this scenic playground for the rich while building High Bridge and the Harlem Railroad. It reminded them of the meadows and bays of another time and place and they became nineteenth-century commuters.

While wealthy neighbors like the Lorillards built bigger mansions and bred horses, the Irish of Morrisania and West Farms agitated for paved streets and adequate drainage. They wouldn't stop at anything, even annexation to the dreaded Manhattan. In 1874 the city absorbed 12,317 Bronx acres and 33,000 people, and in 1895 it took the other 14,500 acres.

The Irish enjoyed their Shangri-La with its thousands of acres of park land (Croton, Claremont, and Van Cortlandt) and convenient industrial zones. The extension of the El to West Farms created a real estate boom that changed the face of the Bronx. Thousands of immigrants—Italian and Jews—moved into the borough's fully equipped modern housing.

The Bronx Irish, like their Manhattan forebearers, had a gift for political organization and in no time they were building a Democratic base second to none. Edward J. Flynn was the leader of the organization built around his Pondiac (an inadvertent misspelling of Chief Pontiac's name) Club. A man of intellect and taste, he was hardly the image of the backslapping pol. He was a political kingmaker, Roosevelt's principal adviser in the rough and tumble of getting elected. He also championed Robert Wagner's first candidacy for mayor.

His chosen successor, Charles A. Buckley, was single-mindedly political. A bricklayer and a boxer in his youth, as Bronx Democratic leader and congressman he was a tough infighter. Like Flynn, Buckley played an important role in national politics. Buckley's well-timed endorsement provided John F. Kennedy with the momentum to win the Democratic presidential nomination. When Buckley lost his seat in Congress in 1962, it was more than a personal defeat; it marked the end of the Irish era in Bronx politics.

Although the Irish are long gone from Mott Haven, Melrose, and Hunt's Point, the latest batch of Irish immigrants are making Bainbridge in the Bronx their home. They have come from Cork, Kerry, Limerick, Dundalk, and Donegal to this corner of the Bronx to find work, and if not a pot of gold, a more secure future.

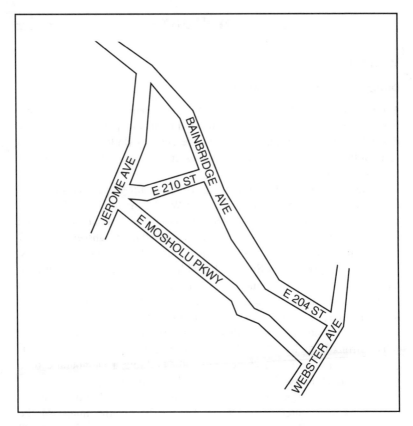

Bainbridge Avenue

The area where they have rented apartments and begun to raise families was once a solidly Jewish part of the largest Jewish neighborhood in the city. After the World War II the majority of these Bronx Jews, like the majority of Bronx Irish, opted for the suburbs of New Jersey and Long Island and exchanged a neat red-brick apartment house for the sanctuary of a one-family framehouse with a patch of lawn.

Bainbridge is north of New York's modern "burnt-out district," the South Bronx, but a sense of community has kept out the drugs and violence. People know one another and look out for their neighbors. Crime is not a runaway problem, though some Irish in Bainbridge, who do not look forward to a visit from Immigration and Naturalization, might hesitate about reporting a burglary.

Many of the one hundred thousand or more Irish born of Bainbridge must struggle with immigration problems. Unlike their ancestors, their only chance to enter the country is "to bend the rules." They come as tourists and later get jobs in the city's "off-the-books" economy. The men find occupational anonymity in construction gangs while the women work informally as waitresses and baby-sitters.

Like the spunky Irish of the past, the Bainbridge immigrants are making real efforts to help themselves. They have formed the Irish Immigration Reform Movement (IIRM) to campaign for changes in the immigration law. The group also provides advice and support, helping local "illegals" deal with problems relating to their status from health care to finances. They meet regularly in the dance hall in Gaelic Park.

The Bainbridge Avenue neighborhood follows Bainbridge Avenue in the northern Bronx from 210th Street near the Montefiore Hospital and makes its way downhill until it turns east on 204th Street and ends at Webster Avenue.

Bainbridge Avenue and 204th Street are the spine of the neighborhood, the place for shopping and socializing. At 3266 Bainbridge Avenue, between Van Cortlandt Avenue and 208th Street, Bainbridge even has its own historical landmark, the Valentine-Varian House, an artifact of earlier ethnics.

The housing in the area ranges from brick mansions with front gardens (on Bainbridge between 210th Street and the Reservoir Oval) to six-story apartment houses with fire escapes to frame houses sided with shingle. Off the Reservoir Oval there is a park and a playground. The neighborhood rubs shoulders with some of New York's worst slums and some of the city's best parkland.

Pubs and Music

The Irish pub of Bainbridge is no throwback to yesteryear, trading on memories of an Ireland that no longer exists. It is not interested in bringing in tourists with sawdust and plaster leprechauns. The pubs are the kind that are currently on the Streets of Kilkenny or Kildare. The jukebox is not all Danny Boy Irish. There is traditional Irish music along with the latest Irish rock from groups like U2 and the Pogues.

The ambience, if you can call it that, is casual and friendly, occasionally wild and rambunctious. The look is traditional. The pubs have a preference for natural wood on the walls and facades. The long wooden bars are works of art, and booths or tables in most cases are merely afterthoughts. One has a street sign from Dublin and another Guinness mirrors. There are team scarves and sometimes snaps of the regulars. The memories of home are in bottles or on tap: Guinness, Harp, Bulmer's, Woodpecker cider, and Jamison Irish whiskey. The conversations with rolling cadences and the ringing laughter are all about the present and tomorrow. On weekends and special occasions there are Irish singers and Irish bands or videos or cable hookups of Emerald Isle sporting events. There are pool tables for cutthroat snooker, and eight-ball and darts, with the loser paying for the drinks.

Irish traditional music isn't "When Irish Eyes Are Smiling," which was actually written by an American named Earnest Ball. There is a whole songbook of Irish classics known as *seisuns* (sessions) that the singers of Ireland have passed on from generation to generation.

In Bainbridge they sing songs about life and death, joy and melancholy. They sing about love's longing and the longing for a drink. They sing about Ireland's tragic history and a punch-up at a country fair. The Bainbridge bands usually include some combination of accordions or melodeons, tin whistles, pipes, flutes, fiddles, guitars, and banjos. Although similar to American folk music, it takes itself less seriously and has a lilt and surer step-dance rhythm.

Irish rock in the sixties was Van Morrison-Boomtown Rats, English rock-and-roll, and American rhythm and blues. The new sound of Irish rock is more experimental; groups like Enya and Hothouse Flowers interweave country, jazz, and Irish traditional with the latest rock sounds.

Bars with music (never any food) are always opening up but the good ones are there forever. Opening time is generally 8 A.M. Monday to Saturday and noon on Sunday, closing at 4 A.M.

Big Paddy's, *3178 Bainbridge Avenue at 207th Street (718-655-2748).*

Light wood finished inside and out, Big Paddy's is favored by the sporting crowd. Often there are videos of the latest Irish hurling and football matches. The weekend means mostly Irish rock music beginning on Friday. The Guinness and Harp are on tap.

Black Thorn, *3117 Bainbridge Avenue (718-652-8501).*

Black Thorn is a handsome traditional pub that appeals to the sporting set. Irish football and hurling are enjoyed on TV with Guinness and Jamison. Weekends it's music and wall-to-wall people.

Roaring Twenties, *366 East 204th Street (718-655-8337).*

The Roaring Twenties cannot be missed with the windmill blades on the front. There are more Irish Americans than recent immigrants. It alternates between Irish rock and traditional *seisun* Sunday and Monday nights.

There are also music and sports videos from Ireland. The pool table gets a lot of attention.

McMahon's, *357 East 204th Street (718-655-6726).*

McMahon's is older and more low key than some of the other Bainbridge pubs. The entertainment at McMahon's is old-fashioned Irish tenors from Thursday to Sunday, with sports videos direct from Ireland on Monday nights. The Guinness and Bulmer are on draught.

The Derby Pub, *3120 Bainbridge Avenue (718-655-9436).*

The Derby is an old fashioned Irish saloon with plenty of banter and laughter. The crowd is mostly male, middle-aged Emerald Isle and everyone seems to know one another.

Irish Gourmet

Ireland is rural and the fare is simple straight-up country table. Irish shoppers in the old country fill their string bags with potatoes, leeks, cabbage, bacon, country sausage, and Irish soda bread. New York Irish have to settle for cooking traditions in cans, with some major exceptions.

The Irish cakes and pastries are not overly sweet or rich, although Irish bakers generally use double cream rather than whipped cream in their fillings. The Irish prefer plain cakes with raisins, nuts, and ginger to seven layers with fruit fillings and thick icing. Even Irish wedding cakes are usually standard fruitcakes with a thin layer of white almond paste icing.

Eddie's Delicatessen, *3165 Bainbridge Avenue (718-655-7784). Monday–Saturday 7 A.M.–11 P.M.; Sunday 7 A.M.–10 P.M.*

Eddie has a shrine in the window surrounded by small American flags. It is dedicated to the Yankees; yellowed newspaper clippings tell the story of a dynasty from the Babe Ruth Yankees to the Casey Stengel Yankees. Eddie has Irish products with brand names like Erin. He has blood pudding (frozen) and genuine Irish bacon and sausage.

Oval Park Delicatessen, *281 East 204th Street (718-881-4146). Daily 7 A.M.–11 P.M.*

The Oval Deli has the most extensive selection of Irish foods in the Irish Bronx. It has McCann's oatmeal and Erin soups and every Irish jam in creation. It has a full line of Irish meat products, including black and white blood pudding, Irish sausage, and Irish bacon. There are fourteen newspapers from the different counties of Ireland to take home with the authentic food.

Traditional Irish Bakery, *3120 Bainbridge Avenue (no telephone). Daily 6:30 A.M.–6:30 P.M.*

The best Irish baking in the city, it has scones, Irish soda bread, porter cake with almond icing, and a carrot cake with the crunch of nuts. The "barm brack," which straddles the line between fruit cake and raisin bread, is very special. The Bainbridge branch of the Traditional has tables to enjoy the baked goods with coffee. The colleens behind the counter are helpful and will take the time to explain the mysteries of Irish baking.

Gifts

The best Irish gift shops are in Manhattan, where they are a novelty, not a part of everyday life. Most shops in Bainbridge are card shops with a few framed mottoes in Gaelic.

The Celtic Connection, *282 East 204th Street (718-231-1210). Monday, Wednesday, and Friday 10:30 A.M.–6:30 P.M.; Sunday noon–5 P.M.*

The Celtic Connection covers Irish culture with books by greats like James Joyce and upcoming writers like poet Eamon Grennan. They have hard-to-find Irish music tapes on cassettes and compact disks. Their gift items include bibs in green imprinted with "Irish Princess," green shamrock coffee mugs, Irish knit ties, and Irish glassware.

Woodlawn

Directions: Subway 4 to Woodlawn, change to bus BX 34 to Katonah Avenue.

Woodlawn is bordered by Woodlawn Cemetery on the south, Van Cortlandt Park on the west, the Bronx River Parkway on the east, and Yonkers to the north. Although it is physically isolated, it is a real extension of the Bainbridge area. The Woodlawn residential area supports the Bainbridge businesses. Woodlawn is the quiet single-family-house suburb of the Bainbridge Broadway.

The Woodlawn neighborhood has had a middle-class character for most of its history, from the time Washington and his army stopped using the

Hyatt Homestead as an ammunition dump. The new Irish immigrants have revitalized the area.

Irish Highlights

Katonah Avenue is Woodlawn's main street. It has its own pubs and shops.

Traditional Irish Bakery, *4268 Katonah Avenue (718-994-0846). Monday–Saturday 5 A.M.–6:30 P.M.; Sunday 6 A.M.–1 P.M.*

Woodlawn has its own outlet of the Traditional. It is smaller than the Bainbridge branch and some of the Irish treats are sold out by noon.

Tri-Eddy's Deli, *4345 Katonah Avenue (718-324-4649). Monday–Saturday 8:30 A.M.–10 P.M.; Sunday 8:30 A.M.–8 P.M.*

Tri-Eddy's is a small deli with a large variety of Irish products that include farm-fresh Galtree cheese, Irish bacon, and black pudding.

Fiona's, *4344 Katonah Avenue (718-324-8263). Daily 8 A.M.–4 A.M.*

Fiona's is a handsome pub with paneled walls and Tiffany-style chandeliers. It is a place where recent immigrants gather for darts and a pint.

Irish Sports

The Irish have a strong sporting tradition. New York's Irish, especially the new immigrants, participate in fast-paced Gaelic games through sports clubs and associations. These amateurs bring a full-tilt enthusiasm to hurling and Irish football that is often missing from big-money professional sports.

Hurling has been played in New York Irish leagues since the middle of the nineteenth century. It's similar to field hockey, except that players can carry the ball downfield balanced on their sticks. Players score by hurling the ball under or over a crossbar. Women's hurling (*comogie*) is also popular in New York.

Gaelic football is similar to soccer and rugby. The ball in this brand of football, besides being kicked, can be dribbled and punched with a fist to get it downfield and into a net smaller than a soccer goal. The punching part can lead to impromptu boxing.

Gaelic Park Sports Center, *240th Street and Broadway (718-548-9568).*

Directions: Subway 1 to 242nd Street/Broadway.

Irish hurling and Gaelic football are regular Sunday events at Gaelic Park. There are leagues for all ages and levels of proficiency. The teams have loyal followings and Cup Matches decide which is number one. The Gaelic Park Center is used for community benefits, and community organizations like the Irish Immigration Reform Movement hold meetings here.

Clan Na Gael

Directions: Subway 4 to Woodlawn.

Before the end of summer, Irish families from the metropolitan area gather on the last Sunday in August for an old-fashioned Celtic reunion and field day. An Irish pipe band opens the festivities with a parade from East 235th Street to Paddy's Field in East Van Cortlandt Park. The contests and competitions include Irish sheaf throwing and a fifty-six-pound weight toss, as well as just-for-fun children's pillow fights and an egg and spoon race. There is a baby show, plenty of food and drink, and bands for dancing.

══════ Irish Queens—Woodside ══════

Directions: Subway 7 to 46th Street.

Woodside is an old Irish working-class community. It was originally named by a newspaperman named John Kelly in the days before marsh and woodlands were replaced by warehouses, light industry, and semi-detached houses. In the 1920s the Irish were just one among German, Jewish, and Italian ethnics following the subway line out of Manhattan into Queens. After World War II, Woodside had a real Irish flavor, with Irish papers on the newsstands and pools for Irish football in the bars. In the heyday of organized labor, the mainly Irish Local 6 of the International Typographical Union built the Big Six Towers in Woodside, a huge cooperative complex which was occupied by predominantly Irish families. Irish affluence and Irish retirement led to a movement out of the neighborhood. Just when it looked like Woodside was becoming completely Asian and Hispanic in the 1970s and 1980s, fresh Irish immigration revived the aging Irish enclave.

Woodside Pubs

The Woodside Irish no longer dominate the blocks but they definitely wear the Green in the bars and clubs scattered throughout the neighborhood.

Opening time is 10:30 or 11 A.M. during the week and noon on Sunday; Closing time is 4 A.M. unless otherwise specified.

Farel O'Toole's, *70th Street and Queens Boulevard (718-478-6655). Restaurant closes at 10:30 P.M. during the week and at 11:30 P.M. on the weekend.*

Farel O'Toole's is big, very big, with five hundred or so turning out for its closed-circuit showings (on four TV screens) of Irish sporting events like the All Ireland Hurling Final. Weekends this pub/restaurant has rock music for its mostly young crowd. There is not much nostalgia for Irish cooking. When O'Toole's tried to serve real traditional boiled bacon with cabbage instead of corned beef and cabbage there were no takers. Sundays there is an Irish brunch with Irish bacon, blood pudding, sausages, and soda bread. Sometimes there's hurling in the back on Sundays starting at 9 A.M.

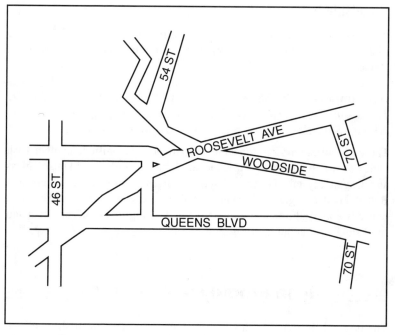

Woodside

Bliss Tavern, *45–50 46th Street (718-729-9749).*

The Bliss accommodates both old-neighborhood Irish and the new immigrants. Their music policy is strictly traditional, Wednesday through Saturday, with a lone singer guitarist or a quartet of two guitars, a piano board, and drums. The drink is also strictly Irish with Guinness, Harp, Bulmer's, Bailey's Irish Cream, and potent Irish coffee. The bar food sticks to hamburgers with an occasional bow to corned beef and cabbage.

Sally O'Brien's, *45–52 46th Street (718-729-9870).*

Sally O'Brien's is a cheerful pub with music every night but Tuesday. Mondays are crowded when the Irish papers arrive and are picked up by the neighborhood people. There are occasional Irish sports videos.

The Starting Gate, *59–10 Woodside Avenue (718-429-9269).*

The Starting Gate is an Irish singles' pub with regular Ladies' Nights. The weekend gets off to a flying start with a Friday Happy Hour that cannot be believed.

Woodside Gifts

If Woodside Irish are looking for Irish crafts and gifts they take a trip to Irish Imports, which has all the world-respected Irish names in crystal and china.

Irish Imports, *54th Street and Roosevelt (718-476-0633). Monday 11 A.M.–midnight; Tuesday–Thursday 11 A.M.–6 P.M.; Friday noon–10 P.M.; Saturday 11 A.M.–6 P.M.; Sunday noon–midnight.*

The Irish ladies who run the shop are patience personified, as other Irish ladies try to choose between Donegal china and Beleek or Duiske glass and Cavan crystal. The merchandise ranges from Aran sweaters and Beleek crystal to green sweatshirts and framed Gaelic mottos. The Irish music is both traditional and modern and the imported foods are Irish and English. They encourage browsing.

===== Irish Brooklyn—Bay Ridge =====

The original Brooklyn Irish were refugees from the 1798 Irish rebellion. They settled in an area near Wallabout Bay in a neighborhood that became known as Vinegar Hill. They lived in a pleasant residential area of small cottages and cobblestone streets. During the nineteenth century this Irish community on a hill overlooking the Navy Yard was called Irishtown. The Irish who lived here were either laborers and longshoremen at the "Yard," hands on the Fulton Ferry, or hired help for the wealthy Anglo-Saxons in Brooklyn Heights.

The area quickly declined with the construction of the Brooklyn Bridge. By the 1890s Irishtown was a slum, a Brooklyn bowery, that catered to seafarers and derelicts. It was all seedy bars and flophouses. It was time for the hardworking and respectable Irish to make the move to Park Slope South, Windsor Terrace, and Sheepshead Bay. A large Irish contingent would eventually make their homes in Bay Ridge.

Before the subway system reached Bay Ridge in 1916, this Brooklyn village was comprised of mansions, summer houses, farms, and estates. Irish were among the original settlers, but they did not come in any numbers until the one- and two-family houses and moderate-size apartments started going up on Shore Road and Fourth Avenue in the building boom of the 1920s and 1930s. As the Scandinavian population that had dominated the neighborhood declined in the years after the war, the Irish population increased and Irish groceries and pubs joined the other ethnic businesses on Main Street. In recent years a new group of Irish born and bred have come to Bay Ridge to live. They have helped to reawaken Irish cultural awareness and instill pride.

Place Marks

Bay Ridge has been connected with famous people from George Washington, who fought a battle in Bay Ridge, to Thomas J. "Stonewall" Jackson, who attended church in Bay Ridge. A couple of prominent Irishmen made their homes here as well.

Owls Head Park, which is located between Colonial Road and Wakeman Place, is a lovely green belt overlooking the sea and a perfect place for quiet strolls and gazing at the gulls and whitecaps. In the nineteenth century this was a part of the extravagant estate of Henry C. Murphy, Brooklyn Democratic Party power broker and founder of the *Brooklyn Eagle* newspaper. He was instrumental in the construction of the Brooklyn Bridge.

At 118 96th Street stands the James F. Farrel residence (circa 1845). It is a typical example of the Greek revival wooden houses occupied by early Irish residents before the Civil War. It has the feel of a weathered clapboard New England snuggery.

Bay Ridge Pubs

Peggy O'Neill, *8121 Fifth Avenue between 81st and 82nd Streets (718-748-1400). Daily 10:00 A.M.–4:00 A.M.*

Peggy O'Neill's is noisy, good natured, and very popular. Uniform Services Irish and Crafts Union Irish mix with new arrivals from Dublin and Donegal. The food is Irish-American stick-to-the-ribs with a very rich Irish stew and a golden baked, mashed potato shepherd's pie. Though every night is Irish night, Wednesday night is Irish night with Irish music.

The Wicked Monk, *8415 Fifth Avenue (718-921-0601). Daily 11 A.M.–4 A.M.*

This is a happening pub with a young singles' crowd. The mood is free spirited and Irish funky, with wild theme nights all year round. The music alternates between Irish hard rock and traditional fiddles and accordions.

Ryan's Ale House, *87th Street and Fourth Avenue (718-836-8524). Daily 11 A.M.– 4 A.M.*

Name an Irish beer and they are sure to serve it at Ryan's. They carry twenty beers on tap and thirty bottled beers. On stage, the cream of Irish rock bands play from Thursday to Sunday. The Irish banter is fast and furious.

Bally Bunion, *9503 Third Avenue at 95th Street (718-833-2801). Monday–Sunday 11:30 A.M.–11:00 P.M.*

Bally Bunion is an exercise in Irish pride, with plenty of green and shamrocks to go around. The bar is monumental in size and buzzing with memories. The people here will try anything (at least once), whether it's fish and chips or shrimp teriyaki.

Bay Ridge Gifts

Village Irish Imports Plus, *83-25 Fifth Avenue (718-238-2582). Monday–Wednesday and Saturday 10 A.M.–6 P.M.; Thursday and Friday 10 A.M.–7 P.M.; Sunday noon–4 P.M.*

"Kiss Me I'm Irish" souvenirs definitely don't set the tone. The shop has an air of delicacy in keeping with the fine Waterford crystal and tasteful Irish jewelry on sale. They also have a splendid selection of religious articles and framed Irish inspirational mottoes.

Bay Ridge St. Patrick's Day

Directions: Subway R to 95th Street/Fourth Avenue.

Though the Irish were among the first groups to live in Bay Ridge, they did not get around to having their own St. Patrick's Day Parade until 1993. The inaugural parade that took place on the first Sunday following St. Patrick's Day was a stirring but happy event and a coming of age for the Irish community. Periodic showers did not dim the enthusiasm of the onlookers or the marchers waving the Irish Tricolor from 95th Street to 67th Street along Brooklyn's Fifth Avenue. These older established Irish were very relaxed and unself-conscious showing the colors on their own territory. With the grand marshall, a retired fireman, in the lead, kilted bagpipers followed cheerleaders with pompons, who were succeeded by a precision drill team. The parade was sponsored by the Fifth Avenue Board of Trade and the Ancient Order of Hibernians.

══════ Irish Celebrations ══════

St. Patrick's Day

The St. Patrick's Day Parade and celebration never had much to do with the city's Friendly Sons of St. Patrick, a Protestant association founded in the eighteenth century. The Ancient Order of Hibernians, a very active fraternal and charitable organization, was the guiding force for this Irish day of recognition.

By the middle of the nineteenth century the Irish had enough political clout to draw a crowd of politicians to this occasion. One mayor, the Honorable Abraham Hewitt, lost an election by refusing to attend the 1880 parade, but most followed the example of the Tammany political hack Mayor A. Oakley Hall, who wore a green tie, coat, and gloves to the reviewing stand.

St. Patrick's Day in Ireland is a solemn commemoration of the saint who brought Christianity to Ireland and a reaffirmation of the faith. In New York it's a no-holds-barred celebration of Irish identity. The parade march starts at noon at Fifth Avenue and 44th Street and continues up Fifth Avenue to 86th Street and over to Third Avenue.

March 17, St. Patrick's Day, is New York's day to be Irish. Everyone wears green, including bald-headed Jewish mayors, and brogues bust out all over. There are green carnations and green buttons hawked on the street and a kelly green stripe runs up Fifth Avenue. Every year there are a couple of clowns waving shillelaghs or puffing on Irish pipes or dressed like an advertiser's idea of a leprechaun. School kids from the whole metropolitan area take the day off and try very hard to have a good time. Like others in the crowd busting to let loose, they are sometimes long on enthusiasm but short on spontaneity.

New York's Tammany Irish enjoy a traditional Irish breakfast with blood sausage and Irish bacon and maybe a drop of Jamison. Many attend a solemn mass at St. Patrick's. Afterwards Irish dignitaries with ceremonial sashes and medals mount a reviewing stand with childlike pleasure. St. Patrick's Day is the city's biggest and brassiest parade, with the most spectators and the most marchers. Marching band after marching band after marching band strides up the avenue: Cardinal Hayes High School follows the Fighting 69th and is succeeded by a group of firefighters in dress blues. Along the way some character, not necessarily Irish, climbs a lamppost for a better view. The beat of the parade goes on: one moment it's traditional "Stars and Stripes Forever" and the next it's jazzy "Blues in the Night"; kilted police pipers precede a boy's club band from Harlem. The crowd pauses to applaud a precision drill team, and then there's the wink and the smile of the real Irish spirit as a group of elderly Hibernian rebels look like they are on a stroll.

The Great Irish Fair

Directions: Subway B or D to Coney Island stop.

The Great Irish Fair is New York's fun-filled meeting of the Irish clans. More than a million head to Coney Island for this Hibernian celebration on the second weekend of September. The site is particularly appropriate, since it was an Irishman named Patrick Boynton who opened the world's first amusement park in this former Brooklyn wilderness.

The legendary Steeple Chase Park looks like new for this yearly event. There are bandstands and spacious food tents and the boardwalk is filled with a lighthearted family crowd. Leading Irish folk singers perform and Irish athletes compete in special Irish sports like Irish hurling, sponsored by the Gaelic Athletic Association. There is also a Colleen Queen with more style and grace than Princess Di. Each year traditional Irish boats race to Sheepshead Bay.

The Fair is organized by the Ancient Order of Hibernians, the same folks that organize the St. Patrick's Day Parade. It is sponsored by private companies like Stroh's Beer and Aer Lingus, and restaurants from Brooklyn like Peggy O'Neill's have food tent concessions.

The Italians

The first Italians to come to New York were educated, politically and culturally aware, and from the North. They included a friend of Jefferson, a collaborator with Mozart, and founders of the Metropolitan Museum of Art and the first New York opera company. They were a cultivated elite who captured the fancy of society New York. Italians came to settle in the city in significant numbers only during the last decades of the nineteenth century and the first decade of the twentieth century. They were poor peasants from the South, who with a pick and shovel built the infrastructure of New York City. Despite adverse conditions, poverty, and illness, they persevered and created safe and secure lives for their families and gained acceptance from their neighbors. Later generations of Italian New Yorkers created close-knit communities that are still true to their roots and traditions. In an era when Italians have gained fame and success in every form of endeavor, new Italian immigrants are arriving to live the American dream. Today, an Italian-American holds the top government office in New York City.

History

Columbus may have discovered America but Giovanni da Verrazano, an aristocratic Tuscan, was the first to land in New York. He admired the natural harbor and appreciated the native hospitality, but he did not claim it for his sponsor, Francis I, King of France.

The real Italian presence in America began with the American Revolution. Filippo Mazzei played an important role in the fight for liberty. He was a friend of Jefferson, and his political thought influenced the Declaration of Independence. The British military authorities in New York jailed this revolutionary firebrand and he was forced to escape to France, where he wrote the first history of the American Republic.

Throughout the nineteenth century New York attracted Italy's own revolutionaries and political liberals. Lorenzo da Ponte was one of the first. He arrived in 1805 to begin a new life at the age of fifty-six. This Renaissance man had already been a priest, a revolutionary conspirator, and had written librettos for Mozart. Da Ponte was appointed as the first professor of Italian at Columbia University and was instrumental in founding the Italian Opera House.

Giuseppe Avezzana was one of the leaders in the failed Piedmontese uprising. This soldier of the Italian Revolution found a safe haven in New York before he joined Mazzini and Garibaldi in an attempt to capture Rome. During his New York exile, he ran a successful wholesale business on Pearl Street.

In 1835 an amnesty released twenty Italian freedom fighters from the dungeons of the Austrian Empire. New Yorkers warmly received the exiles and most decided to stay. Though they were a small group, they gained prominence in the business and cultural life of the city. Felice Forest became a professor at Columbia, a leading cultural commentator, and finally consul to Genoa. His friend, Louis Tinelli, made a fortune as a pioneer in the silk industry and bankrolled Italian freedom.

The year 1848 was a time of promise for the Italian revolution, but by 1849 the forces of reaction had triumphed and another generation of disappointed Italians sought asylum in New York. Giuseppe Garibaldi, the famed man on a white horse and leader of the Red Shirts, was forced to contemplate the defeat of his Roman republic in Rosebank, Staten Island.

Italians living in New York before the Civil War were not all notable men of action but many had talent to spare. Italian musicians and opera singers entertained in society drawing rooms, while the works of Italian painters and fine cabinetmakers filled the best New York salons. The portrait painter Joseph Fagnani, who painted the crown heads of Europe, made a fortune in America doing touched-up likenesses of New York's Four Hundred.

A small population of Italian barbers, bakers, tailors, and organ grinders were also struggling to make a living in the city. They lived in a northern

Italian colony near the notorious Collect. New York's Italian elite provided them with a night school and a library to improve their English and learn about Italian culture.

New York Italians, rich and poor, mainly hailed from the northern region of Liguria. This New York community was large enough to support its own newspaper, *L'Eco d'Italia,* first published by G.P. Secchi de Casali in 1849. They were patriotic enough to form the Italian Guard as part of the New York Militia under the command of that veteran of the Italian revolution, Marquis de Sant'Angelo.

Public-spirited Italian New Yorkers made an impact in the Civil War far out of proportion to their numbers. They formed their own volunteer Italian legion, staffed with crack Italian officers. A second New York Italian regiment, the Garibaldi Guards, was led by the Italian silk industry millionaire Lieutenant Colonel Louis Tinelli, but was not completely manned by Italians.

The city's brashest and most flamboyant Civil War hero was also Italian. Count Luigi Palma di Cesnola was a courageous cavalryman with a hair-trigger temper who was resented by his superiors but commanded the loyalty of the enlisted men. He always led the charges of his unit, the Fourth Cavalry, into battle. In a skirmish at Aldie he was nearly killed and captured, but he lived to fight another day, leading the Fourth in a critical battle near Malverne Hill. Twenty years later he would receive the Congressional Medal of Honor. In the meantime, he made his mark as a diplomat, amateur archaeologist, art collector, and the director of the New York Metropolitan Museum of Art.

In the Gilded Age of the 1870s Italian immigration increased at a rapid rate. Whether from northern or southern Italy, these immigrants were poorer and less educated than earlier arrivals. Artists and artisans were succeeded by pick-and-shovel laborers. Some Italian civic leaders, like the newspaper publisher Secchi de Casoli, actively discouraged these immigrants from coming. They believed that these lower-class Italians would damage the Italian image.

Italians, especially from the poorer south, had no choice but to emigrate. Conditions in Italy were steadily becoming impossible. Both the taxes and the population were rising while the soil eroded and the crops failed. Earthquakes and other natural disasters made things even worse. Southern Italians left their villages unwillingly. Even though they planned to return, leaving was an admission of failure.

New York's streets of gold were sometimes a shock. The urban squalor of Mulberry Bend was very different from the poor Mezzogiorno (south), even if the house in the old country had a dirt floor and no chimney. The decaying buildings of the Bend were damp and airless with forty families packed into five old wood-frame houses. The yards and alleys never saw the sunlight.

Despite the scrub brush and soapsuds, these slums were breeding places for disease. One neighborhood where Italians were dying from tuberculosis was called "lung block." The new arrivals had to deal with this unfamiliar and intimidating urban environment, usually without any English or even basic literacy. Sometimes they were also exploited by a labor boss called a "padrone" who used his superior knowledge of all things American to overwork and underpay them.

These *contadini* (peasants) brought a code and a communal feeling that outweighed their cultural disadvantages. They moved in with family and friends, duplicating supportive village ties in the New World. The streets of New York's Little Italy were reassuringly divided according to extended families, villages, and regions.

Southern Italians had the security of custom and social institutions in this alien city. They helped each other find work and shelter. Their sense of family honor enabled them to sacrifice for others in time of need. In the changing world of New York's urban jungle, Italian family relationships were stable. Divorce was rare and grown children took care of their parents.

A generation of southern Italians built New York's subways and streets and sewer system. They dug the tunnels and ditches, poured the concrete, and laid the pipe. It was backbreaking labor making a modern city. Their children would have the luxury of joining skilled trades or getting an education and becoming professionals. Italian immigrants were workers; they weren't interested in politics that smacked of Old World deceit and intimidation.

The Italians were comfortable in a world of personal face-to-face relationships; mutual aid societies and village associations were usually local groups, an extension of the vertical villages where families and *paesani* lived. The padrone who hired the southern Italian laborer and acted as the go-between with the bosses may have taken a big percentage of the wages, but his face was familiar and he spoke the same dialect.

Southern Italians were handicapped by a lack of English and little education but they weren't the narrow suspicious immigrants of the tabloid stereotypes. They learned quickly to help one another as a group. As early as 1883 Manhattan Italians joined groups from Brooklyn and Hoboken and Newark to raise money for the victims of the earthquake at Ischia. A year later a larger New York–New Jersey confederation raised funds for the city's Italian poor.

The Society of Italian Immigrants was formed in 1901, bringing together American progressives, the Italian community, and the Italian government to deal with the underlying causes of Italian-American poverty. Though Italian welfare groups weren't on the scale of other immigrant nationalities, Italians weren't on the public rolls or dependent on public charities.

Gino C. Speranza, as secretary of the Society for Italian Immigrants, urged the construction of a building to lodge new arrivals. In 1908 the Society's spacious five-story building provided clean rooms and Italian cooking at a fair charge. Dr. Antonio Stella, a pioneer in public health, investigated the health problems of Italian New Yorkers with the aid and support of the Italian government. His findings led to the establishment of a clinic in the city in 1910.

Italian New Yorkers, though more concerned with work than international politics, patriotically supported America and their Italian homeland in World War I. Some Italian reservists even crossed the sea to rejoin their units. New York's Little Italy was the scene of many rallies and parades, American bond drives, and collections for the Italian Red Cross.

Two hundred thousand Italian-born Americans were now settled in the five boroughs of Manhattan. The majority were Manhattanites, while a quarter were Brooklyn *paesani;* the remainder were spread throughout the other three boroughs. Counting second-generation Italian Americans in the city, they were 420,000 strong.

Italians were starting to come of age politically. They lost their distrust of American politics fostered by Old World feudalism. Tammany took note and began to back Italian political leaders and candidates. Michael Rofrano was Tammany's eyes and ears in the Lower East Side's Italian districts. In 1912 sixty thousand Italians in East Harlem elected the first Italian, Salvatore Cotillo, to the state assembly. He would become one of many Italian state supreme court judges.

It was a freewheeling independent Republican at odds with the Tammany machine who finally put Italians on New York's political map. His name was Fiorello La Guardia and though he was not the typical immigrant Italian, he reflected Little Italy's hopes and aspirations.

La Guardia's family came from northern Italy and his mother was a Triestina of Jewish descent. He was born in New York City, brought up in Arizona, and raised in the Episcopalian faith. He developed his strong social conscience while working as an interpreter on Ellis Island. In 1916 he became the first Italian American to be elected to Congress, serving his Italian East Harlem district for a decade, with time off to earn medals in World War I.

In 1933 La Guardia became the ninety-ninth mayor in New York's history. In his twelve years in office he won the support of New Yorkers from every ethnic group interested in good government and reform. The flamboyant "Little Flower" was always in the public eye, whether smashing slot machines with an ax, fighting a tenement fire, or reading the funnies on the radio. He saved the city with a "No more free lunch" philosophy, but by the end of his watch he could take credit for sixty new parks and a vastly expanded public housing system.

While La Guardia was making his name in politics, Generoso Pope was becoming the most powerful Italian businessman in the city. He came to New York with ten dollars in his pocket and in less than twenty years was the city's first Italian millionaire. Pope owned *Il Progresso,* the most popular Italian-American newspaper, and sat on the board of banks, but he made his millions supplying sand and gravel for the city's big construction projects such as the New York subway.

New York's Italians had their own Italian sports heroes. In 1936 Joe DiMaggio took over center field for the New York Yankees. A figure of grace and power, the image of the Yankee Clipper, he won the Most Valuable Player award three times and his record for hitting safely in fifty-six games is still considered unassailable. Having a DiMaggio in the local limelight made Italian immigrants feel less alienated. He was an inspiration for Italians to excel.

Though the city's Italians were making great strides, they were still objects of prejudice, employment discrimination, and immigration restrictions. Italian New Yorkers responded to this bigotry with a renewed sense of pride in their ethnic identity. They proclaimed an Italian identity that transcended their village and region. They joined the Sons of Italy en masse and supported the city's Italian *prominenti* in erecting statues to Italian national heroes like Garibaldi.

Though Mussolini appealed to Italians' pride in their past, he eventually alienated Italian New Yorkers with his foreign adventures; when war came they enthusiastically rallied behind the Stars and Stripes. Former Mussolini supporters like Generoso Pope disavowed the dictator, admitting the error of their ways. The New York Italian community mobilized to buy forty-nine million dollars' worth of war bonds.

World War II disrupted traditional Italian-American life. Italian women left their insulated communities to work in war industries and began to question customary roles and traditions. Italian men came back from the war with new American dreams. For some it was time to move out of the neighborhood and get a white-collar education on the G.I. Bill. Postwar prosperity had its own momentum and Italian New Yorkers became upwardly mobile.

In politics Italian Democrats didn't have to petition Tammany. They were Tammany. Carmine De Sapio became the Manhattan leader in 1949. From the start he cut the Party's connections to organized crime and wiped out obvious patronage abuses. De Sapio had style and intelligence, and

Bronx leader Ed Flynn said he was the "first Tammany man since Murphy I can sit with and not have to talk out of the side of my mouth."

In 1949 there was a three-way race for mayor involving four Italians. There was the Regular Democrat Ferdinand Pecora, the independent renegade Democrat Vincent Impelliteri, the Republican Edward Corsi, and the notorious radical Vito Marcantonio. Impelliteri ran on his record as a crusading prosecutor and as one who refused to take orders from Tammany. "Impy," as he was known, won handily.

Italian communities were closer than other ethnics; transplanted Italian villages shared traditions and a common history. Yet despite a determination to preserve their neighborhoods, the demolition ball and the siren song of the suburbs led to an exodus from the Italian inner-city enclaves.

The sixties were a time of change. Families were smaller and the Italian husband was no longer the unquestioned patriarch. The grandchildren of Italian laborers were moving up. There were Italians in the staid merchant banks of Wall Street and even on the boards of the stock exchange. Ralph De Nunzio was director of Dreyfus Offshore Trust and served as vice-chairman of the board of the New York Stock Exchange.

The world of New York media was their oyster. Grace Mirabella was the New York fashion phenomenon who edited *Vogue,* and Gay Talese was pioneering "new journalism" at the *New York Times.* Jerry Della Femina made people laugh in Madison Avenue's most imaginative ads and founded an agency that would advise presidents.

Though Italians were very visible and in positions of high status and authority, they were routinely categorized as criminals and part of an international Italian crime conspiracy. Exposés about the Mafia sold papers and political crusades against the Mafia got people elected to office. In too many instances Italians were depicted in films and television as gangster heavies or ignorant buffoons.

On June 29, 1970, over fifty thousand Italian Americans came to New York's Columbus Circle to celebrate Italian-American Unity Day. Everywhere there were Italian flags and green, white, and red bunting and big buttons with catchy Italian pride slogans. Italian New Yorkers who had never attended a rally in their lives were here to express pride and anger. Some of the speeches were emotional harangues, but there was a real sense of warm Italian togetherness.

In the era of black power, many thought the time had also come for Italian ethnic affirmation. Italian groups like the Sons of Italy organized letter-writing campaigns and boycotts. In the universities there were calls for Italian studies along with black and Puerto Rican studies. Taking a leaf from other activist ethnics, Italians formed groups like the Americans of Italian Descent (AID) to fight group defamation and the Italian American

Civil Rights League to aggressively pursue "Italian power." A new generation of Italian New York politicians, including future vice-presidential candidate Congresswoman Geraldine Ferraro, made Italian-American rights a national issue.

In the 1990s New York is a city of one million Italian Americans. They can point to Italian-American Senator Alfonse D'Amato and to Peter Vallone, the very influential leader of the city council. Italian-American judges and district attorneys are commonplace. The Italian community knows it has arrived. In 1993 it added Mayor Rudy Giuliani to its list of notables.

══════ The Old Neighborhoods ══════

Mulberry Street

Directions: Subway 6 to Canal Street.

Before the mass Italian migrations to Little Italy in lower Manhattan, the Mulberry Street area was already a byword for urban decay. It was an Irish ghetto ruled by street gangs with housing going back to the Revolutionary War. The Mulberry Bend block was the worst in the area, no more than a series of wood-frame hovels without drainage or sanitation.

The southern Italians who came to Little Italy in the 1880s and 1890s were forced to live in "eight-by-ten rooms" in tall brick tenements in which windows were scarce. These "dumbbell tenements" were built so close to one another that the rear apartments never saw daylight.

The Italians of the Mulberry Street neighborhood were forty thousand strong. They were packed into seventeen short blocks in a neighborhood that had no public baths and no playgrounds and only three public schools. Diseases like tuberculosis ran rampant in these "lung blocks." Fires were a constant hazard.

The Italian immigrants banded together for mutual support and a sense of community in a strange land. The further divided up their small Mulberry Street territory according to the region of Italy that they came from. The Neapolitans occupied Mulberry Street; the Sicilians lived on Elizabeth Street; Mott Street was the New World for the Barese.

Despite the crowds and congestion, Italian neighborhoods were alive with activity. Peddlers in front of ash barrels and carts shouted and touted day-old bread and secondhand clothes, while housewives with lace shawls bargained hard with vendors for meat, fish, or vegetables. Men with handlebar mustaches lounged in front of storefront village associations and social clubs or took careful aim on the *bocce* court in a busy park.

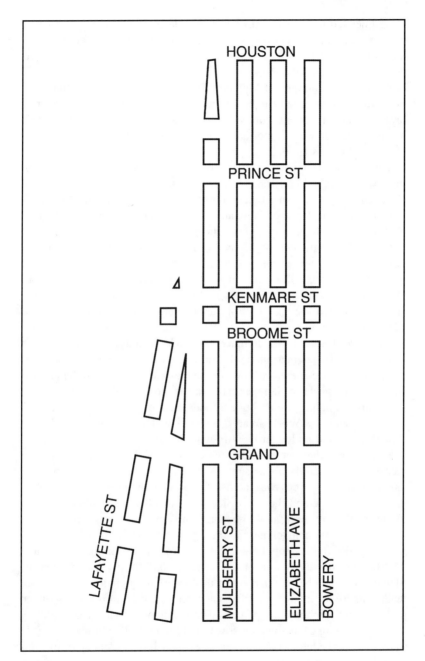

Mulberry Street

Long lines led to Italian banks where people sent remittances to the old country. On saints' days everyone joined the colorful processions with the movable shrines and the uniformed bands. Mulberry Street Italians were developing a sense of community.

While the Italian men of Mulberry Street labored on the city construction projects or worked for Italian building contractors like the Paterno brothers, Italian women worked in the garment industry. The women of Mulberry Street were important supporters of the International Ladies Garment Workers Union.

The unofficial mayor of Little Italy was James March (Antonio Maggio), who recruited construction gangs for the railroad and was the Republican Party's man in the neighborhood. Paul Kelly (Paolo Vaccareli) got out the vote for the Tammany machine and later became a vice-president of the International Longshoreman's Union.

By 1915 the Italians of Mulberry Street started moving out of the neighborhood. They established a large Little Italy in East Harlem and over in the Bronx. They moved to the Brooklyn areas of Red Hook, Williamsburg, and Greenpoint, where they found work on the docks. They soon represented less than half of the population of the Lower East Side neighborhood.

But there was still a vital Italian culture in Little Italy, with Shakespeare in Italian and Italian marionette shows. There was even Italian vaudeville. When movies became the art form of the masses, there were Italian movie theaters. The Festa of San Gennaro was as much a cultural celebration, with music, singing, and traditional foods, as a religious commemoration.

By the end the World War II second- and third-generation Italian Americans could no longer identify with the "old ways"; they looked for the acceptance that comes with Americanization. They longed to live in tree-lined, one-family house suburbs instead of tenement walk-ups. The threat of a new expressway across the neighborhood to unite the Williamsburg Bridge and the West Side highway also contributed to Italian flight. Little Italy was fated to become an ethnic enclave of the old who still had the Italian attachment to their geographical home.

Today the Italian population of Little Italy is declining. The young families are mostly Latino or Chinese. According to the 1990 census, Italians only number ten percent of this traditional Italian neighborhood, with Chinese the majority at fifty-one percent, and Latinos gaining on the Italians with a robust nine percent. The neighborhood itself is shrinking as an expanding Chinatown crosses Canal Street. Still, commercial Little Italy has succeeded in maintaining a sense of Italian identity from Mulberry to Houston Streets.

While a lot of the Italian locals have deserted to suburbia, Italian businesses have stayed behind along with the tourists. Little Italy's restaurants, gift shops, food stores, and cafes exist for the tourist trade. They have in most cases been modified to mainstream American tastes. There aren't enough Mulberry Street *paesani* to keep all the prices moderate and all the food authentic, although the tourists from the outer boroughs and from out of town don't seem to mind. Little Italy is a feeling, a whole-hearted delight in food and wine and friends. The street scene is fun, especially during the summer, when white wrought-iron furniture blocks the sidewalks and diners sigh with satisfaction as if they were seated in an Italian garden instead of breathing in the fumes of Mulberry Street gridlock.

Mulberry Street Place Marks

Church of the Most Precious Blood, *113 Baxter Street (212-226-6427).*

The mass for New York's most spectacular festa, San Gennaro, is held in this simple sanctuary. The shrine of San Gennaro has a place of honor in the front of the church. When the church was consecrated in 1891 the parish was Italian in religious traditions and spirit. Now there is not even a regular mass said in Italian. The Most Precious Blood refers to the blood of Christ but it also has special significance for San Gennaro, whose blood was recovered as a relic and miraculously liquefies on September 19, the date of his martyrdom.

— Place Mark Detour —

Garibaldi-Meucci Museum, *420 Tompkins Avenue at the corner of Chester Street, Rosebank, Staten Island (718-442-1608). Tuesday–Friday 9 A.M.–5 P.M.; Saturday, Sunday, and holidays 1 P.M.– 5 P.M. Free.*

Directions: Subway 5 or 6 to Bowling Green; Staten Island Ferry to St. George Terminal; Bus S52, S78, or S79 to Tompkins Avenue.

After Napolean III destroyed Garibaldi's dream of a united Italy, the exiled warrior mulled over his temporary defeat in the wilds of Rosebank, Staten Island. He stayed a year with an unsung genius named Meucci, making candles in Meucci's workshop.

Antonio Meucci tried to make a living at a variety of businesses, but inventing was his passion. He invented a special glue, a formula for fizzy drinks, and a hygrometer. Twenty years before Alexander Graham Bell he created a crude telephone, which he never had the resources to develop. Today his house stands as a reminder of his own thwarted ambitions and of the liberator of Italy's sojourn in America. The Garibaldi-Meucci Museum contains a wealth of memorabilia dealing with the lives of these two Italians.

Mulberry Street Restaurants

Little Italy's Italian restaurants don't pretend to be gourmet. Their clientele isn't interested in subtlety. The portions are big, the sauces are unadventurous—not too much garlic or seasoning—and the service is warm and obliging. In this Americanized Italian cuisine regional cooking is irrelevant. The pasta sauces of choice are *carbonara* (a white sauce with cream and bacon), *Alfredo* (with heavy cream and cheese), Bolognese or *ragu* (a red sauce with meat), and an all-purpose *marinara* (tomato sauce).

The authentic cuisine of the South, which uses olive oil instead of butter, stints on cream and is lavish with tomatoes, and prefers vegetables like eggplant to T-bone steak, is all the rage outside of Little Italy in this health-conscious city. Mulberry Street has heavier, home-style stuffed pastas like *canneloni,* (a pasta tube filled with ricotta cheese and flavored with meat) and *lasagne* (sheets of pasta layered with meat sauce). The meat, fish, or fowl can be prepared in a number of ways from Milanese to Francese, but there is a preference for *parmagiano* (covered with melted Parmesan cheese) with a thick topping of marinara. Everything is drowned in the sauce as if to give the customers more for their money.

Benito's The Original, *174 Mulberry Street (212-226-9171).*

Benito's II, *163 Mulberry Street (212-226-9012). Daily 12 noon– 11 P.M.*

Benito's The Original was so small—tables on top of one another—they had to open another one. The *mozzarella in carozza* (in carriage), the Italian version of a cheese melt, and the pepper stuffed with vegetables, real tastes of the South, are best.

Da Nico, *164 Mulberry Street between Grand and Broome streets (212-342-1212). Sunday–Thursday 11:30 A.M.–11:00 P.M.; Friday and Saturday 12 noon–midnight.*

The pizza ovens are from Milan and the pizza is Neapolitan with a fine thin crust. It is so delectable with its straight-from-the-garden toppings that it brings in the affluent food lovers from uptown, who feel comfortable in its *Architectural Digest* surroundings. The antipasto bar is not to be missed, and the suckling pig on a spit competes with Caribbean lechon.

Paolucci's, *149 Mulberry Street (212-925-2288). Monday, Tuesday, Thursday, and Friday noon–10:30 P.M.; Saturday and Sunday noon–11 P.M.*

Paolucci's is gaudy chandelier and gold-trim Little Italy. The simple but well-prepared dishes like the manicotti, lasagne, and the veal *pizzaiola* are served in the Federalist splendor of nineteenth-century Van Rensselaer mansion.

SPQR, *133 Mulberry Street (212-925-3120). Daily 11 A.M.–11 P.M.*

Sal Anthony's, the upmarket Gramercy Park restaurant, now has a branch in Little Italy. It tries to be different, more reserved and elegant than the typical Little Italy article. In the food department, it flies on reputation; for sauces and savors it's as obvious as the rest.

Umberto's Clam House, *129 Mulberry Street (212-431-7547). Daily 11 A.M.–6 A.M.*

Umberto's is for late-night hunger pangs. The pictures of the celebrities (Cher, Frankie, and Johnny) on the walls are the restaurant bona fides. The clams are all right and the linguine in hot sauce is not so hot, but the *scungilli* (conch) in the hot sauce calls for a second order.

Il Cortile, *125 Mulberry Street (212-226-6060). Daily noon–1 A.M.*

Il Cortile is northern *prominenti* Italian, a restaurant for unhurried four-course dinners. The interior is formal and the waiters know when to anticipate. The *linguine pescatore* with shrimp, mussels, and clams in the shell is a seafood dinner in itself.

Luna, *112 Mulberry Street (212-226-9683). Tuesday–Saturday noon–2:30 P.M., 5:30 P.M.–8:45 P.M.*

With only twelve booths, Luna is long lines and long waits. The restaurant is from the good old days when New Yorkers never heard of *pesto* and *penne* was something to write with. It is a spaghetti and meatball and sausage kind of place where everything comes *parmigiano.*

Puglia of Little Italy, *189 Hester Street (212-966-6006). Tuesday–Sunday noon–1 A.M.*

Puglia opened in 1919 and it hasn't really changed with the times. It still has long tables for big parties and is family-style fun. The walls are decorated with old-fashioned restaurant art depicting Little Italy in the Roaring Twenties. The menu doesn't take the cholesterol count into account, with special delicacies like steak *contadina,* which combines steak, sausages, potatoes, and chicken! Nightly Neapolitan music completes the bill.

The Original Vincent's, *119 Mott Street between Mulberry and Hester streets (212-226-8133). Sunday–Thursday 11:30 P.M.–1:30 A.M.; Friday and Saturday 11:30 P.M.–3:30 A.M.*

The Original Vincent's (clam bar) is ninety years young with authentic southern Italian seafood flavors and a real neighborhood clientele ensconced at its sweetshop-style counter. Order the *calamari,* scungilli, and mussels in combination with Mama Siano's original sauce: sweet, medium, or hot.

Patrissy's, *98 Kenmare Street (212-226-8509). Monday–Friday noon–11 P.M.; Saturday and Sunday 1 P.M.–11 P.M.*

Patrissy's is Little Italy not too far from the maddening crowds. But the dining room is spacious and formal and the waiters don't have to shout to be heard. Patrissy's features a plate called the "Contadino," an Italian-American invention that is a contadino dream with potatoes, onions, and mushrooms combined with filet mignon, chicken, and sausage.

Cafes and Pasticcerie

The Italian cafe is the right dessert ending to Little Italy dining. Linger over espresso spiked with Sambuca or Amaretto and a custard-rich *sfogliatelle* (thin layers of pastry filled with sweetened cream) and watch the other tourists watching you. The cafes come in all sizes from banquet big to shake-hands-with-the-next-table. Like everything else in Little Italy, the pastries aren't afraid to be obvious; richness and sweetness are in overdrive.

Cafe Biondo, *141 Mulberry Street (212-226-9285). Daily noon–2 A.M.*

Cafe Biondo has cathedral ceilings and high windows which create a feeling of space in this intimate room. The cappuccino comes frothy, with the barest touch of cinnamon, and the espresso is rich enough to be spiked with Sambuca. The *cannoli* with fresh custard and crisp pastry are standard Italian *pasticceria* and are well above standard.

Caffe Roma, *385 Broome Street (212-226-8413). Daily 8 A.M.–midnight.*

Caffe Roma is where the Italians in Little Italy go for their cappuccino and cheesecake. Afternoons, old men in button sweaters and non-power suspenders sit around the ice-cream parlor tables under the big chandelier munching on *pignoli* cookies and nursing their espressos.

Ferrara's, *195-201 Grand Street (212-226-6150). Daily 8 A.M.– midnight.*

Ferrara's is so big that it should be impersonal, but it isn't. Its pastries may be mass produced but they still manage to taste homemade. Ferrara's special coffee roasts and chocolates are available with twenty-one kinds of desserts in its sleek on-the-premises shop.

Pasta Makers and Salumerie

Little Italy before the wars had specialty stores for every variety of Italian food. There were *latticini* for dairy and cheeses, *salumerie* for smoked meat and sausage, and fresh pastas from the pasta maker. Today the food shops in Little Italy are fewer in number and more eclectic. Food shopping has become a one-stop outing.

Alleva Dairy, *188 Mulberry Street (212-226-7990). Monday– Saturday 8:30 A.M.–6 P.M.; Sunday 8:30 A.M.–2 P.M.*

The white tile floor and the provolone hanging from the pressed tin ceiling are reminders that Alleva is almost a century old. Rows of rare and common imported Italian cheeses—delights like smoked mozzarella with pepperoni, fresh mozzarella with prosciutto, and *manteche,* mozzarella wrapped around a ball of butter—line the display cases.

Di Paolo's Dairy, *206 Grand Street (212-226-1033). Monday– Saturday 8:30 A.M.–6:30 P.M.; Sunday 8:30 A.M.–2:30 P.M.*

Di Paolo's is so unassuming, who would know it's bursting with small treasures? Its gorgonzola cheese is so special that it makes you forget rich desserts.

Italian Food Center, *186 Grand Street (212-925-2954). Daily 8 A.M.–7:30 P.M.*

The Italian Food Center is just an old-fashioned Italian grocery with a newfangled name. There's a deli counter where people line up during the lunch hour for hero sandwiches. The shelves are filled with family-size cans of olive oil, boxes of imported pasta, and specialty items like the Motta *panettone* (Italian fruit cake).

Piemonte Homemade Ravioli Company, *190 Grand Street (212-226-1033). Tuesday–Saturday 8:30 A.M.–6 P.M.; Sunday 8:30 A.M.–4 P.M.*

Piemonte has the familiar spinach pasta and lasagne as well as the more novel *calamari* pasta made with squid ink. It has the flat noodles of the North and the hard eggless macaroni of the South. The round and square ravioli come filled with meat and cheese, as do the *tortellini* and the *capelleti.*

Italian T-Shirts and Novelty Spaghetti

Every tourist strip has its souvenirs and Little Italy is no exception. The gift and souvenir shops are mostly of the button and T-shirt variety—it's all for a laugh. There are examples of Italian kitsch that even a mother couldn't love, and not much Italian craftsmanship.

Carosello Pentagramma Italiano, *119 Mulberry Street (212-925-7253). Daily noon–10 P.M.*

Il Pentagramma has statues of Italian heroes, saints, and men playing cards. Some are for a shrine, most are for a rec room. The lamps and ceramic stands are so extreme the tourists can't stop staring.

Forzano Italian Imports, *128 Mulberry Street (212-925-2525). Daily 10 A.M.–midnight.*

Forzano is the source for Italian imports from hardware to cooking utensils. It has the most extensive collection of Italian records and cassettes in the city. The store is large enough to browse around in without being approached by a sales clerk.

E. Rossi & Co., *191 Grand Street at Mulberry Street (212-226-9254). Monday–Thursday 9:30 A.M.–6 P.M.; Friday and Saturday 9:30 A.M.–7 P.M.; Sunday 10 A.M.–5 P.M.*

At first sight it seems like total chaos and disarray, but the silver-haired ladies in charge seem to know the location of everything in the store, whether it's sheet music, Italian cassettes, bowls, religious statues, a macaroni machine, espresso makers, or buttons that say "Kiss Me I'm Italian." Some of the inventory has the charm of yesteryear.

Italian Feste

The Italian *festa* is a set-piece celebration in every Italian village. It is a universal religious rite and the affirmation of a very specific regional heritage. It is the saint's day of a neighborhood. The *feste* in Italy were ancient rituals sanctioned by both civil and spiritual authorities. They were dedicated to a saint or the Virgin Mary, for whom a locality or village was consecrated.

Festa San Gennaro

San Gennaro was the bishop of Benevento when Emperor Diocletian declared war on Christians in 305. He was arrested and tortured but would not recant his faith. The proconsul had him thrown into a burning furnace, but miraculously he came out unscathed. This patron saint of Naples has been called upon to intercede in fires, plagues, droughts, and other natural disasters.

The Feast of San Gennaro is New York's most popular *festa.* Every September the stately bronze and silver bust of the Bishop of Benevento, San Gennaro, passes through the crowded streets of Little Italy to the accompaniment of local bands as theatrical as any New Orleans marching band. The movable shrine is the object of prayers and is showered with bills of all denominations. It's a spiritual homage and a sentimental return to a simpler ethnic past.

For seven days, visitors to Mulberry Street—temporarily renamed Via San Gennaro—gorge themselves on sausage heroes, calzone, *scungilli,* and *calamari* or any of the Chinese, Philippine, or Greek dishes that have been added to the *festa* menu in recent years. There are rides, games of chance, and shooting galleries with stuffed animals for prizes. Every year there are those who say San Gennaro is getting too commercial, but it's only getting bigger and better. Anyone with an aversion for crowds should take a detour.

The Italian Village

Directions: Subway D or F to West Fourth Street.

Little Italy south of Washington Square Park in Greenwich Village was the site of the city's first Italian parish, which was established in 1866. Before immigration was blocked by World War I, it was the third largest Italian neighborhood in Manhattan.

As Italians became Italian Americans, many moved out of the Italian village. But thousands stayed and there was new sense of solidarity based on the neighborhood instead of their Old World connections. They dropped out of *paesani* associations and joined local chapters of the VFW and local social and athletic clubs.

The Italians emulated their fellow Catholics the Irish and built church halls and gyms and started vocational schools. They joined the old Irish political organization and elected their own man, "Bashful Dan" Marinelli, as district leader. He was succeeded in 1943 by Carmine De Sapio, who would become head of the city's Democratic Party.

After the World War II, middle-class Americans and Bohemians started moving into this convenient New York neighborhood. They were outsiders who could not enter into the communal life of the Italian Village, and gradually these American-born interlopers changed the character of the neighborhood. In 1961 an aspiring politician named Ed Koch took the Democratic leadership away from Carmine De Sapio.

The rents in parts of the Italian Village have stayed low and parts of the neighborhood, around Sullivan and Thompson Streets from Bleecker Street to Spring Street, have retained an Italian population. The neighborhood is aging and there are few young families. Italian young bloods no longer hang out on the corners and few Italian housewives hang out of the windows to watch the passing parade of people.

The neighborhood still has a sprinkling of Italian ethnic sights and sounds. On warm nights South Village Italians, including Old World widows in black, sit outside their tenements talking in dialect and watching the SoHo types with their haircuts of the month. There is the pasta maker and the old Italian parish and the Italian bakery with brick ovens. It is also *risorgimento* time in the South Village for commercial Italian ventures. Luncheonettes are being transformed into "Casa di Cafes" and the restaurants are going "al fresco." The Italian Village is going up-market.

South Village Place Marks—The Saints of the South Village

St. Anthony's Church, *163 Sullivan Street (212-777-2755).*

St. Anthony's is the first American Italian parish church, and it has the cornerstone from 1866 to prove it. The church still impresses with its Gothic facade of arches and stained-glass windows, especially at night when it's lit up. The church is losing its predominantly Italian character and no longer has a regular mass in Italian.

Our Lady of Pompeii Church, *25 Carmine Street (212-989-6805).*

When Francesca Cabrini first came to America to serve the Italians of New York, she was assigned to the parish of Our Lady of Pompeii, where she helped parishioners cope with the problems of a strange country. She established hospitals, schools, and orphanages and taught teenage girls embroidery. There is now a shrine in the Church of Our Lady of Pompeii dedicated to the first American saint, St. Francesca Cabrini, who did so much to help Italian Americans.

The church still has Italian masses on Sundays and holidays at 11 A.M. and its own *festa.* It had tried for a number of years to hold a *festa* in honor of their Neapolitan patron, Our Lady of Pompeii, but the inclement October weather eventually put an end to it. Now they hold the *Festa Italiana.*

South Village Cucina

The Italian restaurants in the South Village are in most cases less frantic than the ones in the downtown Little Italy. The restaurants have their share of out-of-towners, but they also have neighborhood followings that keep their food honest. The portions are a proper size and there is enough time between courses to be sociable. The menus have their original touches and gimmicks. The main restaurant drag runs from Thompson Street to Bleecker Street.

Grand Ticino, *228 Thompson Street (212-777-5922). Monday–Saturday noon–11 P.M.*

The Grand Ticino is a South Village original, where the old mustaches and their sons once played *bocce* between *piati.* Today it has a reputation for being too commercial. Although it is on the verge of expense-account prices, Grand Ticino is true to its peasant roots, with hearty and satisfying specials such as the *pasta fagioli,* veal kidney, and polenta with wild mushrooms.

Cucina Regionale, *208 Thompson Street (212-475-9021). Daily 4 P.M.–11 P.M.*

The restaurant is Keith Herring graphics and a young crowd; the bill of fare is a sampler of pastas from the regions of Italy. The exotic pastas like the one from Trentino, *Capellini Bassano del Grappa,* made with apples and *grappa* (a potent grape liquor), usually taste much better than they sound.

Rocco Restaurant, *181 Thompson Street (212-677-0590). Daily noon–11 P.M.*

Rocco doesn't put on any airs. It's an old tile floor, pressed-tin-ceiling type of place. It delivers real southern Italian food. The veal cutlet Siciliana with eggplant and mozzarella is a regular specialty of the house that gets repeat business.

Il Bocconcino, *168 Sullivan Street (212-982-0329). Daily noon–11 P.M.*

The restaurant is plastered with pictures of famous people photographed by the owner, Gilberto Petrucci, whom the press once called the King of the Papparazzi. He runs the restaurant with the same dedication that enabled him to capture celebrities on film in compromising situations. His *rigatoni* in artichoke sauce is light and as refreshing as the Italian Raffo beer.

Trattoria Pesce Pasta, *262 Bleecker Street (212-645-2993). Daily noon–midnight.*

The Trattoria is an unpretentious place with natural brick, globe lighting, and an open kitchen. It creates magical combinations with seafood and risotto or pasta. The *linguine inchiostra* (with squid and ink) is a noteworthy if unusual taste of the sea.

Trattoria Spaghetto, *232 Bleecker Street at Sixth Avenue (212-255-6752). Daily noon–midnight.*

Once upon a time this red-checkered tablecloth trattoria used to be a counter called the Bleecker Luncheonette. It served great minestrone and *pasta fagioli* and heroes. The soups are still superb but now it also has a delicious range of pastas with sauces that have a healthy Sicilian slant.

Cafes with Cannoli

Rocco's, *243 Bleecker Street (212-242-6031). Daily 8 A.M.–midnight.*

Rocco's is the New York source for *panettone,* the Genovese version of fruit cake with a hint of anisette and fennel. The bird's nest here is flaky and light with just a dusting of powdered sugar. Rocco's is less expert when it comes to layer cakes and rich pastries.

Bleecker Street Pastry, *245 Bleecker Street (212-242-4959). 7:30 A.M.–10:30 P.M.; Saturday and Sunday 7:30 A.M.–midnight.*

Bleecker Street tries hard to be a traditional Italian cafe, with a fresh plaster ceiling done up to resemble pressed tin and rotating ceiling fans along with the air conditioning. Still, among other things, it is a contender for the best Italian cheesecake, with or without Amaretto, in the city.

Casa Victoria, *271 Bleecker Street (212-255-3855). Daily 11* A.M.–
1 A.M.

Casa Victoria tries to have the best of both worlds with Italian pastry specials
and American cakes and pies, and falls somewhere in between. It outdoes
itself with the chocolate *cannoli* and lobster tail. Have *orzata* (steamed milk
with almond extract) with one of the the nineteen coffee variations.

The Bleecker Street Market—Italian Gourmet

The food stores in the Italian Village have the necessary ingredients to
gratify an exacting Italian chef. Shoppers come from all over Manhattan
in pursuit of some of their special products. The butchers, bakers, and
pasta makers are mostly on Bleecker Street, where pushcarts once were
the rule.

Ottomanelli's Meat Market, *281 Bleecker Street (212-675-4217).
Monday–Friday 6:30* A.M.–*6:30* P.M.; *Saturday 6* A.M.–*6* P.M.

Success and a chain of unremarkable restaurants haven't taken away the
Ottomanelli edge. It sells the young baby veal that makes for a tender
scaloppine. In October Ottomanelli's features venison and wild boar sausage.

Faicco Pork Stores, *260 Bleecker Street (212-243-1974). Tuesday–Thursday 8* A.M.–*6* P.M.; *Friday and Saturday 8* A.M.–*7* P.M.;
Sunday 9 A.M.–*2* P.M.

Coils of hot pepperoni, fennel, and cheese sausages are displayed like
choice sirloins. In the sausage department there are also dry-cured sweet
Italian sausages (a pepperoni with less bite) suspended from the ceiling.
Center-cut pork chops take center stage, stylishly flecked with fennel.

Zito & Sons, *259 Bleecker Street (212-925-9803). Monday–Friday
6* A.M.–*6* P.M.; *Saturday 6* A.M.–*4* P.M.; *Sunday 6* A.M.–*1* P.M.

The Bleecker Street Zito is a 1925 brick-oven original and it shows it. It is
the yardstick for all other Italian bakeries in the city. The breads, studded with
bits of prosciutto and olives, don't need anything in the sandwich.

Porto Rico Importing Company, *201 Bleeker Street (212-477-
5421). Monday–Saturday 9:30* A.M.–*9:30* P.M.; *Sunday noon–7* P.M.

Shoppers come from all over the city to buy Porto Rico's special blends.
They have two types of espresso roasts: Italian and French, and both are
outstanding. There's a choice of coffee makers and a tea section for the
non-coffee drinkers.

Raffetto Ravioli, *144 West Houston Street (212-777-1261). Tuesday–Saturday 8* A.M.*–6* P.M.

Ravioli—round and square, cheese and meat—is a small part of this pasta storehouse. Besides the standard pastas Raffeto has small squares of *quadrucci* for soup and the tiny *conchigliette* (small shells) that really hold the sauce. They have the right Arborio rice for al dente *risotto.*

Italian Celebrations

St. Anthony's Festa

St. Anthony of Padua is very popular in Italy and a patron saint of many villages. This *festa* commemorates the saint as the patron of the South Village neighborhood where the New York Italians had their first parish. Before Cardinal John McCloskey brought Italian Franciscans over to open St. Anthony's in 1866, Italians held their services in the basements of Irish churches.

The Feast of St. Anthony of Padua is an eleven-day tribute to one of the founders of the Franciscan Order. St. Anthony, like St. Francis, was a gentleman of wealth and position who embraced a life of poverty and service. The image of this saint, associated with good fortune and the recovery of lost objects, is carried in a grand procession from St. Anthony's on Sullivan Street on the last day of the *festa,* June 15.

The *festa* is smaller than the nearby one for San Gennaro, but there are enough sausage and zeppole stands and games of chance to keep the tourists occupied and the church coffers filled.

Festa Italiana

The *Festa Italiana* is a celebration of the Italian religious tradition and Italian customs. It takes place for ten days from July 20 to 30, when Carmine Street is the site of Italian food stands, games of chance, and children's rides. Our Lady of Pompeii Church is opened to the general public with guided tours and special masses. The Our Lady of Pompeii band entertains the crowds.

East Harlem

Directions: Subway 6 to 116th Street/Lexington Avenue, or Bus M15 to 116th Street/First Avenue.

In its prime, Italian East Harlem was one of the largest Italian neighborhoods in America. It went from 100th Street to 116th Street and from

Third Avenue to the East River. The neighborhood had a strong sense of its Italian village past. The streets in Italian Harlem were divided into the regions of Italy. Natives of Piacenza occupied 104th, 105th, and 106th Streets. The Sicilians settled on 107th Street. Naples and Salerno were represented on 109th and 110th Streets. Benevento took over 111th and 112th Streets. The Barese lived on 117th and 118th Streets.

The wide thoroughfare of 116th Street, with its neat row houses, was reserved for the *prominenti* of the neighborhood and was sometimes called Doctor's Row. It was the home of the wealthiest Italian business-men, lawyers, doctors, and pharmacists. The Italian workingman came here for advice in dealing with the city bureaucracy.

The streets of early Italian East Harlem were also divided into villages. The inhabitants of San Fratello in Sicily made 107th Street in East Harlem their destination when they traveled to the New World. The immigrants from Polla in Salerno transplanted their village to 110th Street. They eventually carried over their village *festa* for Our Lady of Mount Carmel in the 1880s. This pattern repeated itself all over East Harlem, which resulted in countless village associations.

First Avenue was the main shopping street and pushcart market. All the foods from home were available here: Italian butchers sold tripe, brains, and tongue; Italian dairy stores, *latticini,* sold fresh mozzarella and ricotta; fresh pasta was offered for sale every day. There were separate restaurants for the different regional cuisines.

The East Harlem neighborhood had a strong sense of independence. It chose and elected its own leaders without the help of Tammany. In 1912 it put Salvatore Cotillo into the state assembly. When La Guardia couldn't get elected as congressman in Democrat-controlled Mulberry Street, he moved up to East Harlem and was elected in 1917. La Guardia was succeeded by Vito Marcantonio, who continued La Guardia's crusade for the poor and even represented East Harlem when it ceased to be Italian.

One of the neighborhood's most active citizens was Leonard Covello. He was a prominent member of political and cultural committees repre-senting the neighborhood. He was the principal of Benjamin Franklin High School from 1937 to 1957 and was instrumental in adding Italian-language subjects and Italian cultural courses to the public school curriculum.

With each new American-born generation Italian East Harlem changed dramatically. The neighborhood became more cohesive and people were more aware of their Italian identity. They dropped the village dialects and mixed Italian with their English and English with their Italian, coining words like *stritto* for street. The old men still played *bocce,* but the kids played stick ball and stoop ball and flew kites from the roofs.

In the 1940s and 1950s affluent Italians deserted the area by the thousands for the detached houses and backyards of the Bronx, Brooklyn, and Queens. They left the increasing crime and the teenage gang violence with little regret. The Italian areas of East Harlem decreased in size and every year more Italian businesses disappeared. By the 1980s Italian East Harlem consisted of a few buildings on Pleasant Avenue and 116th Street and twelve businesses, which included a plumber and an auto repair shop. Yet each year former residents return to the old neighborhood to relive its glory and participate in the Feast of Our Lady of Mount Carmel, although they realize that the day is approaching when it will become only a memory.

Italian Harlem Place Mark—Our Lady of Italian Harlem

Shrine of Our Lady of Mount Carmel, *449 East 115th Street (212-534-0681).*

The Church of Our Lady of Mount Carmel was revered as a religious sanctuary for its replica of the village of Polla's Lady of Mount Carmel and the Christ Child, which became an object of prayers and the medium for miracles. Pope Pius X recognized the value of this statue by donating two emeralds to the crowns of the Virgin and Child. The church had an active rectory and a school that helped the immigrants make the transition to American life.

The Church's days of glory are over now. The Puerto Ricans in the neighborhood go to Spanish parishes and the church ministers to a small aging population. It has many more funerals than first communions.

Italian Harlem's Last Stands

Rao's Restaurant, *455 East 114th Street at Pleasant Avenue (212-534-9625). Monday–Friday 7 P.M.–10 P.M.*

Rao's has the reputation, the limousine clientele, and a three-month wait for reservations. The southern Italian food is better than ordinary and the ambience is a change from the Four Seasons, but is it really worth all the fuss?

Andy's Tavern, *2257 First Avenue at 116th Street (212-410-9175). Monday–Thursday 4:30 P.M.–9 P.M.; Friday and Saturday 4:30 P.M.– 10 P.M.*

Andy's Tavern is not exactly gracious dining; it's a neighborhood bar that looks like a neighborhood bar. But Andy's is all about food and any of the old timers in the neighborhood will back that up. Andy's owner is the chef who made Rao's a restaurant legend. He works magic with any *scaloppine* (veal chop), pasta, or *risotto*.

Patsy's Pizza, *2297 First Avenue between 117th and 118th streets (212-534-9783). Tuesday–Sunday 11:30 A.M.–2 A.M.*

Patsy's is the real-thing pizza. His sauce doesn't come out of a can, his mozzarella is fresh, and his sausage is a special Old World recipe. All the first-rate ingredients are baked in a brick oven.

Festa of Our Lady of Mount Carmel

The Feast of Our Lady of Mount Carmel is celebrated in both Italian East Harlem and Little Italy in the Bronx between July 6 and 17. The East Harlem feast was initiated by immigrants from Polla, a village in the province of Salerno in southern Italy noted for its violin virtuosos.

In New York these natives of Polla started out as pick-and-shovel laborers but were soon proprietors of popular restaurants. They formed a society in 1883 under the auspices of the church, vowing to continue the Polla tradition of the veneration of Our Lady of Mount Carmel. It began with a paper image of Our Lady and a handful of people in a courtyard on 110th Street. By the beginning of the twentieth century it had become a religious event that attracted thousands of pilgrims from around the country.

In its heyday the East Harlem feast attracted half a million people. The streets were practically impassable in the days leading up to and following the July 16th procession of the crowned Virgin. Today only a remnant of this once-proud Italian neighborhood follows the Holy Mother up and down the streets of East Harlem, and the big band that leads the parade has dwindled to less than ten pieces. Most of the celebrants are Haitians, who also venerate Our Lady of Mount Carmel, and they provide their own music, chanting prayers and repeating Mary's name.

Surrounding the church are food stands offering sausages and zeppole, games of chance, and even small amusement park rides. But in this feast the carnival spirit doesn't intrude upon the solemnity of the occasion.

Little Italy Uptown

The Upper East Side of Manhattan is the site of a high-style, high-cachet Little Italy. The Italians who live and work here are prosperous and international. They live in the city but are not necessarily of it. These high-status immigrants came on assignment for Italian corporations and stayed for the financial opportunities. They were slick entrepreneurs eager to profit from the New Yorkers' fascination for things Italian. Their sophisticated boutiques and restaurants are a phenomenon of the 1980s and 1990s.

Uptown Place Marks—Italian Opera in Lincoln Center

The Metropolitan Opera House, *Lincoln Center, Broadway at 65th Street (212-580-9830).*

The Italians gave New York opera. They were the first opera impresarios in the city and the first operas performed—even if the music was by Mozart—were sung in Italian. Lorenzo De Ponte, who was a librettist for Mozart, was involved in the building of New York's Italian Opera House and helped form its opera company. An Italian businessman, Fernando Palmo, lost a fortune trying to attract an American audience to its productions.

For its first season (1883–1884) the Metropolitan Opera chose the Italian conductor Agusto Vianesi, who recruited the best musicians from the opera houses of Venice and Naples for his orchestra. The program of mostly Italian opera was put together by the Metropolitan's director, Cleofante Campinni. Soon its leading singer was the Neapolitan baritone Antonio Scotti. In 1903 another Neapolitan, the tenor Enrico Caruso, took the city by storm and became a national celebrity.

The Metropolitan Opera came of age in 1908, when the demanding and dictatorial Giulio Gatta-Casazza of La Scala became the manager and the legendary Arturo Toscanini wielded the baton. Their spectacular production of *Aida* and dramatic production of *Rigoletto* featuring Caruso are a part of New York's opera lore.

At the same time another Italian impresario, Alfredo Salmaggi, was promoting opera for the masses. He staged productions in Madison Square Garden and in city stadiums with a twenty-five-cent top price for tickets.

Even after Gatti-Cassaza retired in 1935 and impresarios started to have names like Bing, the Italian singers were still the leading performers. There was Giovanni Martinelli, Rosa Ponselle, Enzio Pinza, Franco Corelli, and many more. The operas that were the most popular were also Italian: Puccini's *La Boheme* and Verdi's *Aida.* Today Luciano Pavarotti is opera's heir to Caruso, with a celebrity that transcends opera.

The Metropolitan Opera House is Lincoln Center's ten-story wonder, with high marble arches revealing vivid Chagall murals. In the spirit of opera black-tie, it is very grand in gold, red plush, and marble with endless nineteenth-century staircases. On the concourse there is a gallery of the Metropolitan's greatest singers, many of whom are Italian. Busts of the two men who truly built this house of operatic music, Giulio Gatti-Cassaza in bronze and the great Caruso in marble, have the place of honor.

Preserving the Heritage of Dante and Michelangelo

Italian Historical Society of America, *111 Columbia Heights, Brooklyn (718-852-2929).*

The Italian Historical Society has a complete collection of materials documenting the Italian experience in America. But the Society's main function is to make Italian Americans aware of their contributions to the city, the country, and the world at large. It is responsible for monuments in the city honoring Italian notables from Verrazano to Verdi, and joined the Sons of Italy in the preservation of the Garibaldi-Meucci House.

The Italian Cultural Institute, *686 Park Avenue (212-879-4242). Monday–Friday 9 A.M.–12:30 P.M.*

The Italian Cultural Institute is housed in a Park Avenue mansion along with the Italian Consulate. The library (when it is open) has books both in Italian and English about Italy. It also keeps up-to-date Italian newspapers and periodicals. There are lectures in the upper rooms for those interested in art and culture. The Institute awards prizes to Americans for Italian language writing.

Casa Italiana, *1161 Amsterdam Avenue at 117th Street (212-854-2306).*

Casa Italiana is on the Columbia University campus in an Italian Renaissance piazza created by Italian-American stone cutters. It sponsors art exhibits, concerts, conferences, and lectures.

Call for information about upcoming events, which sometimes don't receive their fair share of publicity.

Italian Monuments

In Italy the people erect statues and monuments to their great men and women in the main public piazza and in this way they are close to their past. Dante, Michelangelo, and Garibaldi are a constant bronze and marble presence. They are the examples for the future. Italian New Yorkers have adopted this tradition and Italian masters and heroes appear in the parks, busy avenues, and streets of Manhattan.

Francisco Verrazano, *Battery Park.*

Verrazano in bronze gazes on the sea. He discovered before Hudson.

Giuseppe Garibaldi, *Washington Square Park, Greenwich Village.*

Giuseppe Garibaldi stands at attention near an arch dedicated to the father of this country. He galvanized the forces that united Italy.

Christopher Columbus, *Columbus Circle, 59th Street and Broadway and Eighth Avenue.*

Columbus is elevated on a seventy-seven-foot granite pedestal. He discovered the New World if not North America.

Dante Alighieri, *Dante Park, Broadway and Columbus Avenues at 63rd Street.*

Dante in bronze is severe and dignified. He made writing in the vernacular respectable and was the author of the *Divine Comedy.*

Giuseppe Verdi, *Verdi Square, Broadway triangle north of 72nd Street.*

Verdi in Carrara marble contemplates his greatest operatic creations: *Aida, Othello, Falstaff,* and *Leonora.* He was the nineteenth century's most popular composer of opera.

Spaghetti Splurges

Before New York put on gourmet airs northern Italian food was *fettucini Alfredo* (in heavy cream and butter via a famous Roman restaurant), but now it goes so far north Scandinavian salmon is a standard dish on the menu.

The up-market restaurants have definitely made New York diners more familiar with Italian geography and the culinary regions of Tuscany, Emilia-Romagna, and Lombardy. They have also reaffirmed Italian eating etiquette. Forget about appetizers and entrees: antipasto hot and cold, shellfish or stuffed vegetables to open the appetite; *primi piati* (first plate), soup or pasta or risotto to alert the taste buds; *secondi piati,* fish or fowl or meat with *contorno* (side dish of vegetables) for the grand climax; and rich desserts or fruit for a rough or smooth landing.

Though some restaurants claim to be strictly Northern, they aren't technical about it and avoid the heavy meat dishes that characterize the North, opting for the trendy light cuisine that a city of joggers craves.

Le Madri, *158 West 18th Street (212-727-8022). Monday–Friday noon–3 P.M., 6 P.M.–10:30 P.M.; Monday–Saturday 10:30 P.M.– 12:30 A.M., special pizza and salad menu.*

Le Madri has earned stars for its consistently original kitchen and advance reservations are still a necessity. The restaurant follows Italian *trattoria* tradition in having a wood-burning pizza oven, while it also provides the latest high-fashion sauces and pastas. For pasta with a difference, try the buckwheat noodles with potatoes, sage, and taleggio cheese.

Il Nido, *251 East 53rd Street (212-758-0226). Monday–Saturday noon–2:30 P.M., 5:30 P.M.–10:30 P.M.*

II Nido is a New York townhouse transformed into a Tuscan farmhouse. The restaurant does magical things to basics like spaghetti Bolognese and *saltimbocca,* which literally means "jump into the mouth," but which is actually veal layered with prosciutto and cheese. The wine list has Italian wines that travel.

Primavera, *1578 First Avenue at 82nd Street (212-861-8608). Daily 5:30 P.M.–midnight.*

Primavera is lace curtains and white linen tablecloths and professional flower arrangements. The staff is black-tie formal. The food would be very good at any price and Primavera's are high. The ingredients are fresh garden, and dishes are prepared to order. There are surprises like baby goat, which is moist and tender without being gamey.

Sette Mezzo, *969 Lexington Avenue between 70th and 71st Streets (212-967-7850). Monday–Friday noon–2:30 P.M., 5 P.M.–midnight; Saturday and Sunday 5 P.M.–midnight.*

Always busy, Sette Mezzo's fare is less interesting than the smart set who hang out there eyeing one another over chilled white wine. They prefer safe food and are comfortable with old reliables like linguine *alle vongole* with white clam sauce and veal Milanese. Call ahead for reservations.

Coco Pazzo, *23 East 74th Street (212-794-0205). Monday–Saturday noon–3 P.M., 6 P.M.–midnight; Sunday 5:30 P.M.–11:30 P.M.*

This is an Italian restaurant for the nineties, with authentic Northern food in family-sized portions. True to its Tuscan roots it has hearty *ribollita* (bean and bread soup). The grills are great, whether it's an Italian-style steak or vegetables, and the pastas are served al dente in imaginative sauces.

Il Vigneto, *1068 First Avenue between 58th and 59th streets (212-755-6875). Tuesday–Friday noon–3 P.M., 5 P.M.–11 P.M.; Saturday 5 P.M.–11 P.M.*

The polite and very accommodating waiters may be from Ecuador, but the owner and the food are all Sicilian. Il Vigneto outdoes itself when it comes to vegetables, whether it's a Portobello mushroom starter, *risotto porcini,* or a *fusilli primavera* with peppers, eggplant, and mushrooms in a light sauce. Although the main room is kind of bare, there is a comfortable sense of space.

Paola's, *347 East 85th Street (212-794-1890). Monday–Saturday 5 P.M.–11 P.M.; Sunday 5 P.M.–10 P.M.*

The restaurant is intimate, with seating for thirty and candlelight. The gracious hostess is Paola Marracino; her taste and the menu are wide-ranging regional. An antipasto from the South such as broccoli rabe and white beans shares the menu with a veal chop Valdostana from the North. The pastas are particularly inventive.

Gourmet Stops

Designer Italian food shopping with all the high prices and pretensions is a city-wide phenomenon. In these emporiums the ingredients of a hearty dinner are elevated into art objects; bottles of olive oil are put on pedestals. Vivaldi is heard in the background as New York's food *cognoscenti* go into raptures over squid ink linguine.

Balducci's, *424 Avenue of the Americas between Eighth and Ninth streets (212-613-2600). Daily 7 A.M.–8:30 P.M.*

Balducci's is a New York Italian success story. Old timers reminisce fondly about the little Italian vegetable market across the street that had the freshest vegetables and hard-to-get herbs. Today, Balducci's is a food spectacular and the source for the best of Italy. They even have a mail-order service.

Todaro Brothers, *555 Second Avenue between 30th and 31st streets (212-532-0633). Monday–Saturday 7:30 A.M.–9 P.M.; Sunday 8 A.M.–8 P.M.*

Todaro's was once a neighborhood grocery with its own rich blends of coffee beans, homemade sauces, and Italian deli counter. The people who owned the store worked there and knew their customers. It's gone gourmet with esoteric oils and flavored vinegars, but Todaro's has kept its Italian identity even if it has lost a bit of its Italian soul.

Manganaro's Groceria, *488 Ninth Avenue between 37th and 38th streets (212-563-5331). Monday–Saturday 8 A.M.–7 P.M.*

Manganaro's is exhaustive when it comes to Italian foods, from pickled *scungilli* to stuffed figs. It covers all the cheeses, table, dessert, and grating, and has more sausages hanging from the ceiling than other places stock in a year. There are breads and fresh pastry and a restaurant in the back. This is one-stop Italian shopping without the piped-in music and the pretenses. Next door they have their Hero Boy stores with six-foot heroes for office parties and the best egg and pepper and sausage heroes in the Big Apple.

===== Neighborhoods at Mid-Passage =====

Belmont

Directions: Subway 2 to White Plains Road, BX12 bus to Arthur Avenue/ Fordham Road; or Subway D to Fordham Road/Grand Concourse.

Italians call this Little Italy in the Bronx, Arthur Avenue, or Belmont. Originally on land that had belonged to the Lorillard estate, it was part of an area called Fordham Manor. The Irish and Germans settled here in the 1890s; the Irish worked for the local millionaires while the Germans farmed small truck gardens. The Italians came to know Belmont firsthand by building its streets and train lines.

The Italians who moved to this practically rural area were natives of Sicily, Calabria, and Campania. Many came by way of East Harlem, lower Manhattan, and south Brooklyn. They eagerly occupied the small frame houses of the Irish and set about planting trees, cultivating flowers, and bringing relatives from overseas. In 1906 a storefront mission became the foundation for the Italian parish of Our Lady of Mount Carmel. In 1930 the census counted 27,500 Italian Americans in Belmont.

Mount Carmelo was a vital community with large families and a warm Mediterranean feeling. Bustling streets were filled with pushcarts and the calls of street peddlers and every block was honeycombed with Italian specialty shops. *Bocce* was played in the park and families had picnics at Orchard Beach. The kids raised pigeons and played American games like Johnny-on-the-pony and ring-a-levio until they joined their hard-working fathers in the serious backbreaking business of making a living. It was a world of mutual respect and personal pride where a man gave his all for his family.

After World War II and the postwar boom upwardly mobile Italians followed the new expressways into Westchester and Long Island. They were tired of apartment living and weren't interested in the neighborhood's aging wooden houses. Although their numbers were bolstered by later immigration from southern Italy, by 1970 over five thousand Puerto Ricans were living in this Bronx Little Italy. In another ten years Belmont was merely an Italian enclave in an area that was mostly black and Hispanic.

Many in this old neighborhood still do business and communicate mainly in Italian. Mass is still said in Italian and there are are Old World processions in honor of Saint Anthony and Our Lady of Mount Carmel. Italians play cards in their own social clubs, read Italian newspapers, and listen to records on the Italian hit parade. An equally large group in this community are more American oriented and mainstream in their tastes and preferences. Both groups celebrate with equal enthusiasm an Italian triumph like Italy's World Cup soccer victory.

Though bordering one of the most dangerous areas in the city, this stable Italian enclave is considered by such authoritative sources as the *New York Times* to be one of the safest sections of the city. It is more than just one neighbor looking out for another; community organizations like the Merchants' Association and the Council of Monte Carmelo provide unity and support. In a changing city this is one neighborhood that seems able to maintain its equilibrium. In the borough where graffiti originated, Belmont's neat houses with their small patches of green and shrines of the Blessed Virgin remain miraculously clean.

Recently, Italy's neighbors on the Adriatic, the southern Slavs of the former People's Republic of Yugoslavia and the Albanians, have joined small groups of emigrant southern Italians from Naples and Sicily to make their homes and raise their families in Belmont. Many had lived in Italy before journeying to the New World and have no difficulty adjusting to Arthur Avenue's customs and traditions. They have helped, despite their differences in culture, to prolong the life of this Old-World community. As the new arrivals become more confident, they are even starting their own businesses, founding clubs and associations, and spreading the news through their own publications.

Arthur Avenue Place Marks

Our Lady of Mount Carmel Church, *627 East 187th Street (718-295-3770).*

The church of Our Lady of Mount Carmel dominates East 187th Street between Hughes and Belmont Avenues. Inside the neo-Gothic structure the Virgin of Mount Carmel, patron saint of the community, benignly watches over her "children." Regular masses are said in Italian and confessions are made in Italian. The church is the focal point of the annual feasts of St. Anthony and Our Lady of Mount Carmel.

The Arthur Avenue Retail Market, *2344 Arthur Avenue (718-367-5686). Monday–Saturday 8 A.M.–5 P.M.*

In 1940 the streets around Arthur Avenue at 186th Street were a pushcart bazaar that sold everything from fresh mozzarella to espresso machines. Mayor La Guardia did not want Italian New York to have an old-fashioned pushcart image and decided pushcarts weren't very sanitary. So he had the Arthur Avenue Retail Market built to house the local vendors.

Forty years later Mayor Koch and a small army of Democratic officeholders rededicated the market after a six-hundred-thousand-dollar facelift. Even the Italian Consul was on hand to make a speech. The market is all brick and as sturdy looking as a small armory. Inside, high-quality meats and cheeses attract the most discriminating Italian shoppers in the city. The produce is plentiful and more economical than in Manhattan markets. The market is at its busiest on weekends, but the trade is very steady since locals keep up the Italian practice of shopping daily.

While the market is mainly a produce market where artichoke hearts, eggplants, and radicchio are staples, it also has delis, groceries, and a cafe in the back. Some of the locals come not to shop but to make a meal of Cafe Al Mercato's indescribably delicious calzone with sausage, eggplant, ricotta, or veal, and their fried zucchini, stromboli, and *foccacia*.

Italian Archives and Culture

Enrico Fermi Cultural Center, *610 East 186th Street (718-933-6410). Monday 10 A.M.–6 P.M.; Tuesday and Wednesday noon–*

8 P.M.; Thursday noon–6 P.M.; Friday 1 P.M.–6 P.M.; Saturday (winter only) 10 A.M.–5 P.M.

Belmont's Italians are extremely proud of their heritage. The Enrico Fermi Cultural Center was established to maintain the cultural tradition of great Italians such as Michelangelo, Verdi, and Fermi. It's one of the city's main resource centers for information about the Italian-American experience and has an extensive library of books in Italian. The Center is dedicated to the Nobel Prize-winning physicist Enrico Fermi, an Italian immigrant, scientific innovator, and humanitarian.

Arthur Avenue Eating

The restaurants in Bronx's Little Italy more than hold their own with the Manhattan originals. Fancier than the tile-on-the-floor, plastic-tablecloth Italian restaurants, they still have the unaffected warmth of the old neighborhood. The service is personal and offhandedly friendly; the food doesn't compromise to mainstream American tastes. Even the humble *calzone,* pizza, or *pasta e fagiole* (pasta and beans) get special treatment. The ingredients are high quality and the preparations imaginative.

Mario's, *2342 Arthur Avenue (718-584-1188). Tuesday–Friday noon–10:30 P.M.; Saturday and Sunday noon–midnight.*

Mario's was a location in *The Godfather* and for a while curious Manhattanites traveled to the Bronx. The food is deftly prepared and draws the neighborhood Neapolitans. The *insalata di mare,* a seafood antipasto of mussels, octopus, squid, and shrimp, is the freshness of the sea.

Emilia's, *2331 Arthur Avenue (718-367-5915). Tuesday–Friday noon–11 P.M.; Saturday and Sunday noon–10:30 P.M.*

Emilia (the restaurant's namesake) and her husband Sal make every stray customer feel like family. Along with the chicken and veal Emilia, Emilia may tell tales about Belmont in its prime and recount stories about celebrity customers like Neil Sedaka and Burt Young.

Dominick's, *2335 Arthur Avenue (718-733-2807). Wednesday– Monday noon–10 P.M.*

Dominick's is no menus and offhanded service and shouting across tables. It's bustling and good natured and the payoff is excellent food. The *putanesca* clings to the fettucine with the sharpness of the anchovies, capers, and olives and the *osso bucco* (veal shank) is a giant knuckle of meat practically falling off the bone in a rich, thick pomodoro (tomato) sauce.

Amici's, *566 187th Street (718-364-8250). Tuesday–Friday 11 A.M.–11 P.M.; Saturday and Sunday 11 A.M.–midnight.*

Amici's is leisurely dining, the relaxed hum of conversation, and a concerned and Old World courteous staff. The cooking is of the classic South with plenty of garlic and no stinting on the olive oil. The meat and fish are first quality from the neighborhood.

Roma Luncheonette, *636 187th Street (unlisted telephone). Monday–Saturday 11 A.M.–9 P.M.*

Walk into Roma's and you are in the middle of a conversation; the TV keeps playing and everybody keeps talking. The soups are the thing here and they have specials every day. The *zuppa fagiola* (bean soup) and *lenticchie* (lentil soup) are thick with the flavors of garlic and *pancetta* (Italian bacon).

Espresso and Sympathy

On Sundays families still observe the traditional promenade, strolling along Arthur Avenue and 187th Street. Some push baby carriages or hold the hands of small children and all wear their Sunday best. After the strolling, there's the cafe sitting, with a *torta* dripping sweetness and a strong espresso or cappuccino sprinkled with chocolate.

Gino's Pastry Shop, *580 East 187th Street (718-584-3558). Daily 7:30 A.M.–7 P.M.*

Gino's Pastry is not only adept when it comes to creating rich multilayered cakes for special occasions, but it also brings out the best in a simple *biscotti* or *pignoli* cookie that goes so well with cappuccino and espresso.

De Lillo Pastries, *606 East 187th Street (718-367-8198). Daily 8 A.M.–7 P.M.*

De Lillo is friends and neighbors greeting one another and getting down to the serious business of *cafe panna* (with homemade whipped cream) and a large slice of Italian cheesecake. The homemade *gelato* and *spumoni* are very suitable for this ice-cream parlor setting.

Egidio, *622 East 187th Street (718-295-6077). Daily 7 A.M.–8 P.M.*

During the day the line forms at the bakery counter in front. The mini pastries (bite-sized *cannoli* and *amaretti*) are a favorite to bring when visiting the relatives in Canarsie. Kids in their neat parochial school uniforms line up for *gelato* cones.

Pizza Margherita, *673 East 187th Street (718-364-8910). Daily 8 A.M.–8 P.M.*

Caffe Margherita has recently become Pizza Margherita, and pizza and sandwiches have been added to the old cafe menu. The coffee, whether it's *freddo* (iced), cappuccino, or espresso, can be enjoyed al fresco in the summer. There is a mural inside of Neptune cavorting with the Nereids that is pure cafe primitive.

Artuso's, *670–678 East 187th Street (718-367-2515). Daily 7 A.M.– 9:30 P.M.*

Artuso's is located in a big contoured building that from the outside looks like a modern banquet hall. Rich layer cakes revolve in vertical glass cases and long display counters show off the bird's nests, *cannoli,* and *sfogliatelle* (pastry leaves layered with rich custard). Despite their size and on-the-premises wholesale bakery, Artuso's has not lost the personal touch.

Arthur Avenue Gourmet

In Belmont shopping is no one-stop experience; it is a round of specialty shops: butcher, baker (one for bread and one for pastry), fishmonger, deli, dairy, and pasta maker. For some unexplained reason, the gift shops also sell fresh roasted Italian-style coffee.

—Bread and Cookie Bakers—

Terranova Bakery, *691 East 187th Street (718-733-3827). Daily 6 A.M.–7 P.M.*

The Terranova family brings the same expertise to baking bread as they do to making pasta at the Pasta Factory. They make prosciutto bread and olive bread—winter breads in Italy—year round.

Madonia Bakery, *2348 Arthur Avenue (718-295-5573). Saturday 7 A.M.–6:30 P.M.*

Madonia's cookies are plain and buttery good and their breads are crusty enough for the neighborhood's best restaurants. The semolina bread, which comes in small, medium, and large, is perfect for heroes.

—Pasta Makers—

Borgatti's Ravioli & Noodle Company, *632 East 187th Street (718-367-3799). Monday–Saturday 9 A.M.–6 P.M.; Sunday 8 A.M.–1 P.M.*

Borgatti's deals in the obscure and the hard to find, like *macherroni alla chitara,* a cross between dense dry and light fresh pasta cut on a device that resembles a frame with *chitara* (guitar) strings. It also sells carrot, spinach, and tomato noodles.

The Pasta Factory, *686 East 187th Street (718-295-4857). Daily 9 A.M.–6 P.M.*

The Pasta Factory (formerly Terranova Pasta) prides itself on using extra-fancy durum wheat-enriched flour, whole-milk ricotta, and first-quality Romano cheese in its pastas, plain and stuffed. The round cheese ravioli is so good it doesn't need sauce.

—The Italian Groceria—

Tino's Salumeria, *609 East 187th Street (718-733-9879). Monday–Friday 7:30 A.M.–6 P.M.; 7 A.M.–6 P.M.; Sunday 7:30 A.M.–1 P.M.*

The only problem with Tino's is that they are always so busy. The Italian cold cuts include the fine Bolognese *mortadella* and the *cotechine* (a three-inch sausage) made with pancetta.

Joe's Italian Deli, *685-B 187th Street (718-367-7979). Monday–Saturday 8 A.M.–6:30 P.M.; Sunday 8 A.M.–1:30 P.M.*

Walk through the door and the aroma of hanging cheeses and specially cured meats is intoxicating. The immaculate display cases are filled with tray after tray of olives, peppers, and mushrooms prepared in different ways.

Marchese Grocery, *Arthur Avenue Market (718-933-2295).* *Monday–Saturday 7* A.M.*–6* P.M.

Past the produce to the left Marchese's grocery offers real buys for the experienced shopper. Many items like the extra-virgin Apulia olive oil (equal to the best Tuscan) are half the price of Manhattan's Italian food emporiums.

Calandra Cheese Shop, *2314 Arthur Avenue (718-365-7572).* *Monday–Saturday 9* A.M.*–6* P.M.

Calandra is always looking for new cheeses, imported and domestic, to satisfy their demanding customers. Samples are given out to help the customers decide. They carry all the well-known imports as well.

—Italian Meat and Fish—

Vincent's Meat Market, *2374 Arthur Avenue (718-295-9048).* *Monday–Saturday 7* A.M.*–5:30* P.M.

Vincent's specializes in sausages in all their variety: fennel, cheese, parsley, *cervellata,* and even one made with broccoli rabe. The women in the neighborhood also swear by his tripe.

Arthur Avenue Poultry Market, *2356 Arthur Avenue (718-733-4006). Tuesday–Thursday 9* A.M.*–5* P.M.*; Friday and Saturday 8* A.M.*–5* P.M.

The market is barnyard noisy with cage upon cage of chickens, pigeons, and rabbits. Shoppers pick and choose like they are at an ASPCA kennel, and their dinner comes fresh killed.

Biancardi's, *2340 Arthur Avenue (718-733-4058). Monday–Saturday 8* A.M.*–6* P.M.

Biancardi's is an Old World butcher shop selling whole baby lamb, goat, and rabbit to exacting Old World customers. They stock unusual cuts like heads, hoofs, and intestines, as well as fine-aged steak. On weekends there are long lines and a good deal of "back and forth" between butcher and customer.

Calabria Pork Store, *2338 Arthur Avenue (718-367-5145). Saturday 7* A.M.*–7* P.M.

The Calabria looks like a smokehouse with all the meats hanging from the ceiling. It packs country-thick Calabrese sausages that come studded with peppercorns and bits of garlic.

Frank Randazzo's Sons Fish Market, *2327 Arthur Avenue (718-367-4139). Monday–Thursday 7 A.M.–6 P.M.; Friday 5 A.M.–7 P.M.; Saturday 7 A.M.–6 P.M.*

Randazzo's curbside stand-up clam and oyster bar catches the eye. Nearby there are mountains of ice and nests of seaweed for crab, squid, eel, and swordfish.

—Italian Gifts—

Cerini Coffee & Gifts, *660 East 187th Street (718-584-3449). Monday–Saturday 9 A.M.–6 P.M.*

Among the aromatic mounds of Italian roast coffee waiting to be ground, there's an odd collection of gaudy statues, crystal chandeliers, silver trays, and espresso machines. In the middle of this wild assortment, a line of wedding favors pops out. It's fun rummaging through Franco Cerini's attic.

Costanza's Gifts, *624 East 187th Street (718-364-8510). Monday–Friday 7:30 A.M.–6 P.M.; Saturday 7:30 A.M.–5 P.M.*

The coffee is the main attraction. The lamps, china, crystal, and statues look like they are laid out for a jumble sale. It has everything a new bride needs—if she can find it.

Celebrations

Feast of Our Lady of Mount Carmel

The Belmont Feast of Our Lady of Mount Carmel started in 1906. It was block after block of decorations, bands playing dramatic Italian music, and climactic fireworks.

The procession starts at 5:30 P.M. on the Sunday after the July 16 saint's day. Members of the parish surround the statue of Our Lady of Mount Carmel and adorn it with flowers and scapulas. Male members of the church carry the Madonna on her altar. The women's sodality leads the procession, followed by a small band, who in turn are followed by the priests and church officials. Some women and older men crowd around the statue, at times touching it and crossing themselves. Most walk beside and behind it for the two hours it takes to traverse the whole neighborhood.

Meanwhile the younger people crowd around the stands, which sell all kinds of Italian delicacies, or try their luck on the wheels of fortune. It is more animated than the Manhattan *festa* but it's sometimes tough to navigate the narrow streets and impossible to park.

Festa of St. Anthony

St. Anthony of Padua is honored in the Bronx as well as in Manhattan. The celebration of the Feast of St. Anthony lights up East 187th Street from June 5 to 15. The street carnival of food stands, music, souvenirs, and rides starts every night at 6 P.M.

Bensonhurst and Italian Brooklyn

Directions: Subway N to 18th Avenue/64th Street.

Cornelius van Werkhoven, a functionary for the Dutch West India Company, got this future part of Brooklyn in a Minuit-type swap with the Native Americans. He called it New Utrecht in honor of the old Dutch city. In 1783 this area stood four-square behind the American Revolution, erecting a liberty pole on what is today 83rd Street and Cristoforo Colombo Avenue (18th Avenue).

The neighborhood retained its Dutch character into the nineteenth century and there is still a Dutch Reformed church dating from 1828 in a bucolic churchyard on 18th Avenue. Some of the most prestigious Dutch families in Brooklyn were members of the congregation.

Bensonhurst took its name in 1887 from a family called Benson who owned a square mile of farmland in New Utrecht. Shortly afterward they subdivided their holdings, opening them up for settlement. By the turn of the century Bensonhurst was a thriving resort.

The construction of the BMT subway line brought a new population of Jews and Italians making their way out of Little Italy and the Lower East Side. They moved out of the tenements into sturdy brick and stucco two-family houses, but they still carried the closeness and warmth of the old community. Life was the extended family and local institutions like the house of worship, associations and social clubs, the candy store and the corner grocery.

The old second- and third-generation Jewish-American portion of Bensonhurst has declined, with a remnant concentrated around Bay Parkway, but the Italian presence remains strong. They make up the majority of what the city planning department calls Bensonhurst, an area bounded by 14th Avenue in the northwest, 61st Street and McDonald Avenue on the northeast, 26th Avenue to the southeast, and Gravesend Bay to the southwest.

Bensonhurst still has the flavor of a New York Italian neighborhood circa the 1930s and 1940s. Italians fresh off the boat from Sicily or Argentina mingle with first- and second-generation Italian Americans.

Newcomers nostalgically cling to the stand-up espresso bar and the sit-down card-playing social club, while the old guard belongs to the Rotary and enjoys a sirloin with a side order of pasta.

The neighborhood is close and cooperative; people know the names and faces on their own block and even on the block over. A safe and secure Bensonhurst is everyone's business, and everyone watches out for one another. The *paesan* tradition continues, and urban Bensonhurst has become a village with a tendency to look more inward than outward.

Although the neighborhood is very stable, in the nineties times are changing. Russian Jews from Brighton Beach and Chinese from Sunset Park are moving beyond their urban boundaries to the crime-free promised land of Bensonhurst. Signs have already appeared in Cyrillic, and there are markets selling *mei fun* noodles and bamboo shoots. The local Italians wonder about these "strangers" who sometimes can't speak either of their languages, don't worship in their church, and seem to hold themselves aloof.

Bensonhurst's main drag, 18th Avenue, has a split personality. There are bakeries, cafes, and restaurants that are Old World authentic alongside made-in-New York Italianate pizza parlors and restaurants. Tastes and ingredients change with time in Brooklyn, but the feeling of the grand Italian opera, dramatic and joyful, stays the same. The tenors strut and the sopranos preen.

In honor of Bensonurst's Italian population and their contribution to the neighborhood, 18th Avenue from 64th Street to 86th Street has been dubbed Cristoforo Colombo Boulevard.

Bensonhurst Nights Out

Bensonhurst is still a believer in home cooking; the eating ritual keeps families together, and besides, the food is better. On the cook's night off (and that may mean Father) it's out to Bensonhurst restaurants. The home cooks must be getting more nights off these days because new restaurants keep opening up and they keep getting better.

Il Colloseo, *7704 18th Avenue (718-234-3663). Monday–Friday noon–1 A.M.; Saturday and Sunday 1 P.M.–1 A.M.*

The pizza is real Old World Neapolitan. Every day the best and the freshest become specials on Il Colloseo's board. Look for the stuffed veal chop, the combination swordfish and red snapper, and the penne "Frank Sinatra." The kitchen has real style.

Milano, *7514 18th Avenue (718-259-4300). Tuesday–Thursday noon–11:00 P.M.; Friday noon–midnight; Saturday 3:00 P.M.– midnight.*

Milano is white-tablecloth Bensonhurst, with a vintage wine list and waiters who serve from the correct side. They have an exceptional antipasti table, and the main courses are gourmet. Some of the parties arrive in chauffeur-driven limousines.

Randazzo's Steak House and Restaurant, *7222 18th Avenue (718-234-9125). Sunday–Thursday 11:30 A.M.–11:30 P.M.; Friday and Saturday 11:30 A.M.–1 A.M.*

Randazzo's serves choice New York sirloins and *Mezzogiorno* (Southern) pastas with rich back-to-basics *putanesca* (anchovies, capers, garlic, black olives, tomatoes) and *amatricana* (bacon, hot peppers, tomatoes) sauces. The chicken *scarpiello,* thick with garlic bits in olive oil, and the veal *rollatine picante* are Italian alternatives to the sixteen-ounce steaks.

Gino's Foccaceria, *7118 18th Avenue (718-232-9073). Daily noon–midnight.*

Gino's is pizza-parlor casual and serves pretty fair pizza, but the *foccacia* and Sicilian specialties prepared fresh daily are the draw. People drop in throughout the evening for a plate of broccoli rabe, a rice ball stuffed with meat, or a spinach calzone and to gossip with the boss.

Gambero & Rosso, *7016 18th Avenue (718-259-1858). Tuesday– Sunday noon–11 P.M.*

Gambero & Rosso are the surf part of the Bensonhurst turf. The devil gets his due with their house special, lobster *fra diavalo.* Stick to seafood when it comes to the pastas, white or red *alle vongole* (clam sauce) and the mixed seafood.

Danza's, *6205 18th Avenue (718-232-0271). Monday–Wednesday 11 A.M.–10:30 P.M.; Friday and Saturday 11 A.M.–11 P.M.; Sunday noon–8 P.M.*

At first, Danza's appears to be just a great Italian take-out. The food is fresh and attractively displayed in its endless variety. It includes such Sicilian specialties as rice balls, potato croquettes, and *foccacia,* and authentic Italian heroes made with high-grade olive oil, balsamic vinegar, arugula, and plum tomatoes. Behind Danza's heaping trays of food and cold cuts counter there is a big surprise: a pleasant pastel dining area.

Tommaso's, *1464 86th Street between 15th and 14th avenues (718-236-9883). Daily noon–11* P.M.

Tommaso's is a night out for a full-course dinner from antipasti to dessert and Italian grand opera for entertainment. Even Tommaso gets into the act with an aria or two. New Orleans and Rio have their carnival and so does Tommaso's, with a feast accompanied by traditional music.

Espresso With and Without Music

The cafe/espresso bars of Bensonhurst are out of the Italian immigrant past or Italian modern. They are definitely not Italian local color for the tourists.

Some tables are filled with young Italian men at their ease, making their points in musical Italian and punctuating their speech with an Italian semaphore of the hands. Others are filled with older men—more excitable, splitting their infinitives in Italian and English; most are retired from the construction trades and small businesses. The espresso has a strength only found in Italy, like the bonds between the friends who meet in the cafes regularly.

On weekends the cafes become a family affair, and there is music and Sambuca or Amaretto or a scotch on the rocks to toast the weekend. Italian pastry is consumed and enjoyed with thorough gusto. There is an illusion of being in Italy which is not at all self-conscious or sentimental.

The cafes have conventional groups that play rock with Italian and American lyrics, but there are also traditional musicians and singers playing slow serenades, frantic tarantellas, and whispered lullabies on a concertina, *chitarra battente* (small guitar), shepherd's flute, and tambourine. The music is so infectious you don't have to know the steps to stand up and dance.

Cafe Giardino, *7403 18th Avenue (718-256-5611). Daily 8* A.M.*– midnight.*

The charming young woman behind the espresso bar doesn't know a word of English, but somehow she makes herself understood to the occasional non-Italian speaker. She has no problem either making a foamy cappuccino or filling a cannoli on the spot, so the shell doesn't get soggy. On weekends when there is music, a back room is opened up.

Caffe Mille Luci, *7123 18th Avenue (718-837-7017). Saturday 5 A.M.–midnight.*

The cafe sparkles with its mirrors, pale stucco, and smart chandeliers. This is urban Italian that never hits a false note. The crowd is young and more Italian than American, taking their espresso in the morning with a sweet roll. A sunken floor separates the elegant Il Grattino restaurant from the Caffe itself. Weekends there is music, and though jackets and ties are in order, the mood is relaxed.

Gran Cafe Italia, *6917–6921 18th Avenue (718-232-9759). Daily 24 hours.*

The Gran Cafe is a New York Italian social club without any membership cards. Everyone knows everybody else, and this cross section of older Italians feels at home. The decor is a mixture of prints of saints with soulful eyes and hunting-trophy antlers. The sign behind the bar advertises their homemade *granita di caffe* and *granita di limone* (coffee ice and lemon ice).

The Bensonhurst Bazaar

Shopping for Italian food in Bensonhurst is not strictly a matter of running down to the right store. Specialty stores abound but the all-Italian influence means that any grocery or food store, even if it's a chain supermarket, is going to sell Italian products that are usually reserved for a Manhattan gourmet shop. The Italian-born citizens of Bensonhurst are familiar with made-in-Italy products and they keep the local merchants up to the mark.

—Cheese, Bread, and Italian Cheesecake—

18th Avenue Bakery, *6016 18th Avenue (718-256-2441). Daily 8 A.M.–7 P.M.*

The rolls and loaves here provide the taste and satisfaction of cake. The semolina, twisted and braided and sprinkled with sesame, and the wide rings of prosciutto and cheese bread are Italian treats, not just the staff of life.

Cristoforo Colombo Bakery, *6916 18th Avenue (718-256-3973). Daily 7 A.M.–7 P.M.*

Cristoforo Colombo does it the traditional way, whether it's a simple crusty bread for heroes or a multilayered wedding cake. Old standards like *baba a rhum, sfogliatella,* and *cannoli* are adult sweet with a little spice.

Alba, *7001 18th Avenue (718-232-2122). Monday 8:30 A.M.–5 P.M.; Tuesday–Saturday 8:30 A.M.–9 P.M.; Sunday 8:30 A.M.–7 P.M.*

Alba is four generations of expert pastry chefs. They fill the *cannoli* while you wait (for maximum freshness) and sell rich Sicilian *cassava* and *zuppa Inglese.* Sometimes they serve coffee to their regular customers.

Villabate Bakery, *7117 18th Avenue (718-331-8430). Daily 7 A.M.– 9 P.M.*

Angelo is in charge of the *panetteria* and Emanuele is in charge of the *pasticceria.* Angelo is a master of semolina breads, long and crusty and soft, and high and round with sesame seeds. Emanuele is a master of *tartufo,* the chocolate truffle cake.

Belvedere, *7304 20th Avenue (718-232-1814). Daily 7 A.M.– 7:30 P.M.*

The Belvedere is slightly off the Bensonhurst track but it deserves mention for its extraordinary *prosciutto* bread, with nuggets of peppery *prosciutto,* and its *friselle,* with slivers of almonds.

—Bensonhurst Salumerie—

Sbarro's, *1705 65th Street (718-331-8808). Monday–Friday 8 A.M.–7 P.M.; Saturday and Sunday 8:30 A.M.–8 P.M.*

This is the original location that launched the Sbarro pizza and restaurant empire. It's a neighborhood salumeria brought up to date with modern refrigerated display cases in the trademark Italian tricolor. The cheeses, sausages, salamis, and *prosciutto di Parma* still hang from the ceiling Italian style. If you are interested, there are press clips about Sbarro's in the windows.

Bari Pork Store, *7119 18th Avenue (718-837-1257). 2351 86th Street (718-449-5763). Monday–Saturday 8 A.M.–7 P.M.; Sunday 8 A.M.–2 P.M.*

Bari leads with its pork sausage, mild, hot, fennel, and cheese, and follows up with some fine dairy, fresh ricotta and fresh and smoked mozzarella, and a good assortment of grating cheeses.

Trunzo Brothers Meat Market, *6802 18th Avenue (718-331-2111). Daily 8 A.M.–7 P.M.*

Trunzo's was once a meat market but now it is an Italian supermarket. There are floor-to-ceiling multiliter cans of imported olive oil and box upon box of pastas in every shape and size. There's a butcher counter with

Italian scaloppine cuts, *braciole* (chops), and *rollatine* (veal rolls) ready for the saucepan, and a counter with nothing but sausages.

Piccolo Mondelo Pescheria, *6205 18th Avenue (718-236-3930). Monday–Saturday 6:30 A.M.–6:30 P.M.*

This fish market has *bacalau* (dried cod) for the Christmas, Easter, and everyday table. Plump shrimp and conch sit on mountains of ice and the lobsters tread water in tanks. The *calamari* comes with the ink.

— Pasta Stops —

Bensonhurst is fresh pasta country and the two storefronts that make it for the neighborhood are as busy as bakeries.

Queen Ann Ravioli & Macaroni Inc., *7205-7207 18th Avenue (718-256-1061). Tuesday–Saturday 9 A.M.–6 P.M.; Sunday 8 A.M.– 2 P.M.*

The new expanded Queen Ann has every conceivable configuration of pasta, fresh, dry, and in between, and in back Renato Anticone and his crew make it happen in a giant steel pasta machine. The stuffed shells with spinach and ricotta are in a case along with the ravioli and manicotti.

Pasta Fresca, *6518 11th Avenue (718-680-7193). Monday–Saturday 8 A.M.–7 P.M.; Sunday 8 A.M.–5 P.M.*

The city's finest pasta maker has a small closet of a store practically in Borough Park. Celebrities like Dom De Luise and Sophia Loren have been known to take the long trek for his secret-recipe ravioli and tortellini and special smoked mozzarella.

Bensonhurst Gifts

Bensonhurst is a young immigrant Italian neighborhood. It is a neighborhood where weddings are more important than VCRs. The 18th Avenue main street has more bridal shops, with names like the Wedding Coach and European Bridal Favors, than restaurants. Gift shops that have disappeared from other areas thrive here. They peddle everything for a wedding and all the accessories for the first apartment.

The stock runs the gamut from bud vases to meat grinders and there are displays of fine china that rival Bloomingdale's. Up-to-the-minute Italian top-ten hits are available on records, cassettes, and CDs.

Dalmazio Imports, *7116 18th Avenue (718-232-1332). Monday–Saturday 10 A.M.–6:30 P.M.*

Dalmazio has a rich assortment of supplies for a first apartment or home. The shop's profusion of stock covers the gamut of taste from exquisite crystal to crude copies of classical sculpture. If you need an espresso machine or a macaroni maker go no further.

S.A.S. Italian Records, *7113 18th Avenue (718-331-0539). Monday–Saturday 10 A.M.–9 P.M.; Sunday 10 A.M.–8 P.M.*

S.A.S has all the top tunes on the Italian hit parade, along with the great voices doing Puccini and Verdi. It also has information about Italian artists performing in clubs, cafes, and concerts in the area.

Bensonhurst Celebrations

Festa of St. Rosalia

Santa Rosalia was the fourteen-year-old daughter of a prince. A devout young woman with special powers, she dedicated her life to God and helping the poor. Despite her vows, her father insisted that she marry into another princely family. When the day was set she went to a grotto to pray; a miracle happened, and her soul was lifted to heaven.

The Feast of Santa Rosalia, which begins on August 30th, is an annual week-long event. Arthur Avenue from 67th Street to 75th Street on 18th Avenue is strung with colored lights. Ladies from the church auxiliaries and local merchants serve delicious Italian specialties to neighborhood celebrants and visitors. The *festa* is sponsored by the St. Rosalia Society.

Court Street Nostalgia

Directions: Subway F to Carroll Street.

When the Italians began vacating the Little Italys in Manhattan, south Brooklyn was a convenient destination. The area was called Red Hook in the early 1900s, an anglicization of the Dutch *Roode Hoek,* which referred to seventeenth-century cranberry bogs. Today the neighborhood is comprised of Red Hook and two gentrifying historic districts, Carroll Gardens and Cobble Hill.

In colonial New York a small part of the vast Remsen estate was sold to a shipbuilder named Jackson and converted into a dry dock. In 1801 the Navy bought the dock and it became the Navy Yard, which employed thousands of people. In the Civil War it was the major supply base and debarkation point for the Union forces.

By the time the Italians started coming, Red Hook was the site of huge grain-storage facilities and one of the country's main transshipment points. It provided them with thousands of jobs, on the docks as longshoreman and in the Navy Yard plants. World War II brought the Navy Yard and Red Hook its boom years.

The trend toward containerization meant a loss of jobs for the Italians of this neighborhood. The Queens-Manhattan Expressway, which cut a swath through the area, meant the loss of homes. The city planners renamed portions of Red Hook Carroll Gardens and Cobble Hill to get rid of the waterfront roughneck stigma, and started the process of gentrification.

Italian holdouts have seen all the changes and they just shake their heads. Some Italian commercial outposts have held their ground on Court Street. Other Italian come-latelies are moving in to open businesses and take advantage of the new, more lucrative market for Italian products. The old neighborhood is starting to become expensive.

Bohemians with bankrolls and yuppies looking for charm have moved in and seem to value the neighborhood's ethnic inheritance. They support the local merchants and even join them on the folding chairs come summer. They maintain the area's traditional brick-and-wood low-rise building look that seems to let in the sky and the natural elements.

Court Street Table

Local restaurants are making a comeback, though their clientele tend to be from Park Slope or Brooklyn Heights rather than the old neighborhood of retired longshoremen and sewing machine operators.

Casa Rosa, *384 Court Street between Carroll and President streets (718-787-1907). Tuesday–Saturday 11:30 A.M.–midnight; Sunday 1 P.M.–10 P.M.*

Casa Rosa is imitation Tiffany lamps, exposed brick, an antique wooden bar, and hand-painted carafes for the house wine. Its strong suit is the seafood, like the swordfish *marechinara* and *zuppe de pesce.*

Marco Polo Restaurant, *345 Court Street at Union Street (718-852-5015). Monday–Friday 11:30 A.M.–11:00 P.M.; Saturday 3 P.M.–midnight; Sunday 1 P.M.–10 P.M.*

Marco Polo's is a state of mind, gracious dining that is warm and friendly. The restaurant is handsomely appointed with a pleasant glassed-in dining area. The food is prepared from prime ingredients with no pretensions and the menu is extensive. Every night the piano man keeps the good vibrations flowing.

Caffe Carciofo, *248 Court Street (718-624-7551). Monday–Saturday 5:30 P.M.–10 P.M.; Sunday 11 A.M.–3 P.M., 5:30 P.M.–10 P.M.*

Caffe Carciolo has the look of a Little Italy caffe with natural brick, rotating ceiling fans, and old-fashioned floor tile. The mood is relaxed, with cool jazz in the background, and a friendly waiter who is up on all the flicks at the Cobble Hill multiplex. The menu, which changes daily, is small and manageable, and the food is prepared with great care, whether it's an eggplant *rollatini* starter or the special pork scallopini.

Sam's Restaurant, *238 Court Street between Kane and Baltic streets (718-596-3458). Wednesday–Monday noon–10:30 P.M.*

Sam's is an old-style Italian restaurant with big leather booths, tables with checkered tablecloths, and plenty of room to stretch out and be yourself. The sauce has a certain sameness, but there is plenty to go around on spaghetti with the steaks, chops, veal, or chicken. Or just have a brick-oven pizza.

Court Street Gourmet

Mastellone's Market, *299 Court Street (718-522-6700). Monday–Thursday 8 A.M.–7:30 P.M.; Friday and Saturday 8 A.M.–8 P.M.; Sunday 8 A.M.–6 P.M.*

There are workman-like fresh sausages and pork rinds for cooking, and the best extra-virgin cold-pressed olive oil in the neighborhood.

D'Amico Foods, *309 Court Street between Court and Sackett streets (718-875-5403). Monday–Saturday 9 A.M.–7 P.M.*

D'Amico is authentic Italian, with the pick of olives, mushrooms, and peppers and a tasty *caponata*. The Brooklyn Heights fans swear by D'Amico's espresso roast coffee and grating cheeses.

Esposito Pork Store, *357 Court Street near President Street (718-875-6863). Monday–Saturday 7 A.M.–6:00 P.M.*

Esposito's is more than a pork store with imaginative variations on Jersey Pork sausages. It has the thinnest *scallopini* of milk-fed veal, rice

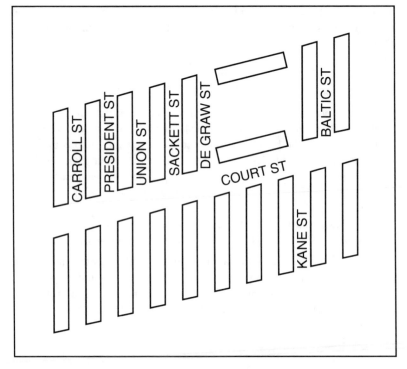

Court Street to Carroll Street

balls punctuated with *prosciutto,* and a turkey sausage that actually tastes Italian.

Monte Leone's, *355 Court Street (718-624-9253). Monday–Friday 9 A.M.–8 P.M.; Saturday 8 A.M.–8 P.M.; Sunday 8 A.M.–7:30 P.M.*

Monte Leone's is a Brooklyn bakery institution going back to 1902. Longevity is no guarantee of goodness, but this *pasticceria* has the touch. The pastries are rich without being overly sweet and the homemade gelato is as light and natural as a fine sorbet.

Caputo's Bakery, *329 Court Street (718-875-6871). Monday–Saturday 6 A.M.–7 P.M.; Sunday 8 A.M.–6 P.M.*

The breads that run out the quickest are the crusty semolina and the grainy wheat bread. The cheese horn pastries filled with ricotta and grated citrus rinds have won the new neighbors over to Italian *pasticceria.*

Court Pastry, *298 Court Street (718-875-4820). Daily 8 A.M.– 8:30 P.M.*

Court Pastry is a local landmark with a sense of humor, where the daughters of Italian immigrants take the quality of the cakes and cookies seriously. The neighborhood really enjoys its almond, hazelnut, and Regina *biscotti.*

Pastosa Ravioli Company, *370 Court Street (718-635-0482). Monday–Wednesday, Friday, and Saturday 9 A.M.–6:45 P.M.; Thursday 9 A.M.–7:45 P.M.; Sunday 9 A.M.–1 P.M.*

Ray Vivola is a newcomer to the block; he has only been here eleven years. His strong suit is his stuffed pastas: cheese tortellini, ravioli, and manicotti stuffed with both mozzarella and ricotta.

Fratelli Raviolli, *200 Court Street (718-330-1183). Monday 11 A.M.–7:30 P.M.; Saturday 10 A.M.–6 P.M.; Sunday noon–6 P.M.*

Fratelli Ravioli is aromatic coffee and the pungent smell of Italian cheeses. The ravioli in the refrigerated cases are stuffed with many things besides meat. Every Wednesday buy one portion of ricotta or cavatelli and get another one free.

The Secular Festa

Columbus Day Parade

On October 12, 1492, a seaman on the *Pinta* sighted one of the islands in the Bahamas and Cristoforo Columbo gained immortality as the discoverer of America. Before World War I Italian community leaders made Columbus Day a celebration of Italian accomplishment. Later, after they won a long campaign to make Columbus Day a legal holiday, it became a way of identifying with America. It was their ethnic rite of passage, a secular *festa.*

New York's Columbus Day Parade follows Fifth Avenue from 44th Street to 86th Street. The crowds along the line of the march are large, almost as large as on St. Patrick's Day. There are school children with Italian Power buttons, union members with signs from their locals, and recent Italian immigrants who wear their accents as badges of pride.

The parade begins with the politicians, a contingent that gets bigger and bigger as the Italian population of New York increases. Every year there are floats of the *Nina,* the *Pinta,* and the *Santa Maria* with a beautiful Italian Isobella or a member of the Sons of Italy in tights and a false beard on board. Marconi has a float and so does Alitalia, complete with a smiling stewardess. There are marchers from the Italian VFW trying to keep in step with a military band and high school kids from an inner-city band doing complicated dance steps. The marching bands from all the city's Italian festivals participate. Members of the Dante Alligheri Society sedately walk down the Avenue, while the Knights of Columbus move with real conviction. The Italian police and firemen are represented, and no parade is complete without the Police Department's Emerald Society bagpipers.

The Jews

The Jews have played an important part in the city from the days when it was called New Amsterdam. The earliest arrivals were refugees from the Brazilian Inquisition. Throughout the eighteenth century New York Jews were primarily Sephardic and descended from the Jews of Spain and Portugal. They were succeeded by German Jews, who became the affluent and culturally sophisticated "Our Crowd." The largest group came from Eastern Europe, escaping pogroms and poverty at the end of the nineteenth century. Today, there is a new generation of Russian Jews making New York their home side by side with their Jewish counterparts from the volatile Middle East.

History

In September of 1654 the *St. Charles* landed in New Amsterdam with twenty-three Jewish passengers who had been rescued from Spanish pirates. The Jews were Sephardic, of Spanish and Portuguese descent. They could trace their ancestry back to Jewish nobility of the "golden age" before the Inquisition.

These grandees of Iberia were an elite, leaders in the arts, sciences, and finance. Again they were fleeing the *auto-da-fé,* this time from Brazil, which the Portuguese had recaptured from the tolerant Dutch. New York's first Jews arrived with little more than the clothes on their backs. In retrospect these refugees would have the stature of Jewish pilgrims.

Governor Peter Stuyvesant was eager to rid the Dutch colony of these heretics, who he feared would "infect and trouble this new colony." Stuyvesant requested the support of his superiors at the Dutch West India Company, but Dutch tolerance and the influence of Jewish stockholders in the Company saved the day. The Jews would stay. They had the Company's protection.

The Jews were granted a charter of settlement by the Dutch West India Company in April 1655, recognizing their loyalty to the Netherlands and upholding their basic rights. Stuyvesant was forced to yield, but he continued to attempt to restrict their participation in the life of the Dutch colony.

Stuyvesant tried to bar Jewish religious worship, but the Company took the Jews' side and backed their right to have services in their own homes. In 1655 New Amsterdam's twenty-three Jews founded a congregation they called *Shearith Israel,* the Remnant of Israel. Shortly afterwards they were permitted to have their own Jewish cemetery just outside the city walls.

Individual Jews tried to secure the full privileges of citizenship. Asser Levy, the proprietor of a popular tavern, refused to pay the "Jewish tax" which exempted him from guard duty. He recognized his duty to protect his community and challenged the governor and the Dutch West India Company to revoke the tax and the exemption.

Another Levy named Moses became the first Jew to hold public office after the colony came under British rule. This wealthy merchant was well known for his philanthropies and was one of seven Jews to contribute to the construction of the Trinity Church steeple.

New York's Jews played a prominent part in the life of British New York. They were leading shopkeepers and major traders who financed their own merchant fleet. They contributed to public subscriptions and joined philanthropic campaigns. Jewish businessmen even had their own "great country seats." Yet the Jews didn't feel fully accepted until they were allowed their own public house of worship. They built Temple Shearith Israel in 1728 on the site of an old mill in the heart of what today is the financial district.

In the era of the American Revolution Jewish New Yorkers had an almost religious regard for freedom. They associated it with their own celebration of the Passover and liberation from the Egyptian Pharaoh. When the Redcoat armies occupied New York, Rabbi Gershom Mendez Seixas, the spiritual leader of Shearith Israel and an American patriot, escaped with most of his congregation to free Philadelphia.

Haym Solomon was a member in good standing of Shearith Israel and the "Banker of the Revolution." He helped provision the New York militia under the command of Philip Schuyler. Later he became involved in a plot to burn British ships in New York Harbor and was imprisoned as an American spy. After his release by the British, Solomon arranged the financing that enabled the Revolutionary Army to continue its fight.

At the time of George Washington's presidential inauguration, the Jews of New York and their fellow Jews in other communities took the opportunity to declare their loyalty to the new government in an open letter. Washington replied with a ringing defense of religious freedom and a pledge to the "stock of Abraham."

In the New York of the new Republic Jews were contributing members of society. Mordechai Manuel Noah was a successful playwright and journalist, a prominent Mason, and a major in the state militia. Noah was not afraid to run for office and at various times served as sheriff and judge of the New York Court of Sessions. He was appointed to such important offices as surveyor of the Port of New York and consul of Tunis.

Uriah Phillips Levy made millions in New York real estate, but that was secondary to his commitment to the U.S. Navy. Despite the anti-Semitism of ranking officers, he rose from cabin boy to commodore and saw combat in the War of 1812. This Jewish New Yorker is credited with abolishing corporal punishment in the Navy. At the end of his career he used his vast wealth to renew a run-down Monticello, creating a national shrine for his hero, Thomas Jefferson.

By the time the first Ashkenazi (German) Jews came to New York in the 1830s Sephardic Jews could count themselves among the city's banking and business establishment. Socially they held themselves aloof in a small aristocratic circle of Baruchs, Lazaruses, Nathans, Hendrickses, and Cardozos. They valued reserve and thought of themselves as high minded and cultivated. The German Jews, with their queer accents and aggressive manners, were definitely not their crowd.

Judge Albert Cardozo disappointed this exclusive Sephardic set when he resigned from the New York Supreme Court bench after rumors of playing favorites. He awarded the majority of lucrative refereeships to members of Boss Tweed's family. His son, Benjamin Nathan Cardozo, was shocked by the loss of family honor. He dedicated his life to regaining that honor and in the process became a respected legal scholar and a U.S. Supreme Court justice.

The German Jews were too busy creating dynasties to be overly concerned by the chilly Sephardic welcome. The Seligmans started out as peddlers in cotton country, but soon opened a string of dry-goods stores from New Orleans to New York. The headquarters of their small retail empire in 1846 was 5 Williams Street, very near the stock exchange, where these future merchant bankers would make history.

Joseph Seligman, the oldest of seven brothers and three sisters, was the patriarch of the clan that would earn the title of the "American Rothschilds." His first speculations were in the gold market and he got out fast enough to make a fortune and avoid the panic of 1857. Seligman liked the company of men in power and was an intimate of President Lincoln. He got into international finance by bankrolling the Union cause with bond sales in Europe.

Three thousand New York Jews joined New York regiments to fight for the Union. The Jews had their own Brigadier General Philip Jochimsen, who led the Fifty-ninth New York Volunteers, and a Jewish enlisted man, Benjamin Levy, received the Congressional Medal of Honor. A Jewish Brooklynite, Colonel Leopold Levy, died a hero's death at Chancellorsville.

The Lehman brothers, unlike the Seligmans, did their peddling from a horse and wagon. They opened a dry-goods store in Mobile, Alabama, which became the center of their cotton empire. After the Civil War they set themselves up in New York, trading in commodities and becoming the biggest cotton brokers in the country. By the turn of the century they were branching out into investment banking.

The Seligmans were the first of the German-Jewish merchant bankers to recognize the profits in railroad investment, but they were soon upstaged by Kuhn, Loeb, and Company, and their rising star, Jacob Schiff. This imperious German, with a streak of old-fashioned Jewish piety, held his own with J. P. Morgan and robber barons like Hill and Harriman. He was on the board of directors of some of the nation's most important railroads.

Some German Jews stuck to retailing. Lazarus and Isidore Straus started in glassware and crockery at R. H. Macy & Company and quickly became the proprietors of the two biggest department stores (Macy's and Abraham & Strauss) in the city. New York's Jewish-owned department stores also included Gimbel's, Altman's, and Bloomingdale's.

Despite their accomplishments and their devotion to charitable causes, the German Jews were victims of social discrimination. Joseph Seligman, himself a member of the prestigious Union League Club, was refused accommodation in the fashionable Grand Hotel in Saratoga. By the end of the nineteenth century, this form of social restriction had spread. Jews were excluded from fashionable Coney Island and Manhattan Beach and were forbidden to ride the Long Island Railroad.

"Our Crowd" retreated into itself. It became more insular and laid more emphasis on its German heritage. They spoke German among themselves and sent their children to a New York school modeled on a German "gymnasium." They embraced German Reform Judaism and worshiped at Temple Emanu-El, the image of a progressive German synagogue.

New York's German Jews socialized with New York's German Jews. They were members of the Harmonie Club and their children prepped at Sachs Collegiate. They occupied mansions on Fifth Avenue and competed for the services of the same French chefs. Though as rich as the robber barons, the German-Jewish style was effortlessly sophisticated and calculatedly low key.

As the first Russian-Jewish waves crowded into Grand Street, the last of the great German-Jewish dynasties made their fortunes. Adolph Lewinsohn and his brothers used a loophole in the law to import cheap copper and profitably export low-grade copper ore. By the 1890s they controlled most of the country's copper and merged with the Rockefeller interests.

In 1881 German Jews spoke out against the persecution of their fellow Jews in Russia after the assassination of Tsar Alexander II. They hated the pogroms but they also believed that the Russian Jews were backward "Orientals."

Though they were ambivalent about the Russian newcomers, Jewish New York mobilized to help them. They formed the Hebrew Emigrant Aid Society to help them find shelter and jobs. They established an employment office in the Castle Garden immigrant station, and a restaurant and boarding house in Greenwich Village. There was also a temporary shelter in Greenpoint, Brooklyn.

The Russian-Jewish emigrants settled at first on the Lower East Side. They were peddlers, did piecework on sewing machines, and rolled cigars. There were Russian-Jewish furriers and Jews who only studied the Torah, the sacred books. They all endured together the damp disintegrating tenements, the dirt and disease, and the rotting garbage on the street.

Jewish uptown met Jewish downtown in the Lower East Side Settlement Houses. Social work pioneers like Lillian Wald helped immigrants adapt to this strange new world with health and educational programs. Often the German or Sephardic Jews who worked with the Russian immigrants (like Emma Lazarus of Statue of Liberty fame) came away from the experience with a strengthened sense of Jewish identity.

In 1896 Jews joined the ranks of the city's most important opinion makers when Adolph Ochs bought the bankrupt *New York Times*. He was interested in objectivity where the news was concerned and keeping personal views to the editorial page. Dorothy Schiff, the granddaughter of the investment banker, was the next Jew to publish a New York newspaper, the *New York Post*. Her unspoken policy was to combine liberal politics and Broadway gossip.

By 1905 studies showed the Jewish "greenhorns" were moving out of the sweatshops and wearing white collars. Jewish children were reared to strive and surpass their parents. They became professionals, retailers, salespersons, and clerical workers. They were also improving themselves by moving out of lower Manhattan and Brownsville into Yorkville, Harlem, and Williamsburg.

Russian Jews were still the backbone of union militants in the city. From 1909 to 1914 garment-worker unions organized waves of strikes, including the first general strike in the needle trades. Uptown Jews led by the millionaire investment banker Jacob Schiff intervened. Sweatshops were eliminated and labor leaders like Sidney Hillman and David Dubinsky won the right to collective bargaining.

The political activist Jews of New York elected the socialist Meyer London to Congress in 1910, 1916, and 1920. Morris Hillquit, the militant socialists' antiwar candidate for mayor, ran a remarkably close race in 1917. At the same time Jewish party regulars like Belle Moskowitz and Joseph Proskauer were advising the future presidential candidate, Governor Al Smith.

New York Jews from the Fifth Avenue and Delancey Street ghettos were singing Irving Berlin's "Oh How I Hate to Get Up in the Morning" when they went off to war in 1917. Their fighting force was the Seventy-seventh Division, which held the line at Meuse-Argonne. A Jewish Gumpertz and Kaufman were Medal of Honor winners.

While the war took many Jews out of the ghetto, others used their special talents to take Broadway and Madison Square Garden by storm. The Marx Brothers, Al Jolson, Fanny Brice, George Burns, and Eddie Cantor were headliners in vaudeville and in Broadway reviews. Benny Leonard and Barney Ross became world boxing champions.

When private colleges had restrictive quotas, City College became the New York Jews' stepping stone for success. The financier and adviser of presidents, Bernard Baruch, was a City College graduate, and the discoverer of the polio vaccine, Dr. Jonas Salk, also received his first degree from City. Supreme Court Justice Felix Frankfurter went to City College and the literary critic Alfred Kazin did his earliest writing for the college literary magazine.

In the years following World War I New York's older Jewish families were heavily involved in public service. Herbert H. Lehman deserted his family's Wall Street offices for the political hustings. He became the governor of New York, a U.S. senator, and a member of the War Refugee Board. Another member of the German-Jewish elite, Henry Morgenthau, Jr., was secretary of the treasury for Franklin Roosevelt.

The lives of Russian Jews continued to improve as they moved out in greater numbers to the suburban Bronx and Brooklyn. Their modern housing came equipped with refrigerators and gas ranges! The Chanins, Brickens, and Backers who cut their teeth on this residential construction eventually changed the skyline of Manhattan with structures like the Chrysler and Woolworth Buildings and the Waldorf-Astoria Hotel.

In the depression, New York Jews struggled like other New Yorkers just to find a job. College graduates took whatever they could get even if it was blue-collar work. Despite their personal concerns, Jewish New Yorkers followed the rise of Nazism in Europe, and through organizations like the American Jewish Committee and American Jewish Congress they tried to help their threatened co-religionists.

Though restrictive immigration laws worked against them, some Jewish refugees from Nazism landed safely in Manhattan. They were mostly intellectuals and artists who settled in the city's Upper West Side and Greenwich Village. They included the writer Isaac Bashevis Singer and the social critic Hannah Arendt. In the 1930s the New School of Social Research was transformed into the University in Exile with a faculty of German political refugees.

Jewish New Yorkers campaigned to aid Britain and enter the war against the Axis powers. They joined the armed forces in record numbers once war was declared. A West Point graduate from Brooklyn, Colonel Mickey Marcus, served on the American general staff and was in the thick of it on D-Day. America won the war, but in the midst of the euphoria of victory Jews came face to face with the horror of the Holocaust.

Jewish soldiers came back to the city to resume their lives with new hopes and expectations. They took advantage of the GI Bill to complete their education and train for new careers. They came prepared for the postwar boom. At the same time the Hebrew Immigration Aid Society (HIAS) and the Federation of Jewish Philanthropies helped Jewish displaced persons from Europe settle in New York, as they would later help Jewish refugees from the Soviet Union.

In this new era of affluence Jews voted for more mainstream candidates. A liberal Jewish Republican, Jacob Javits, succeeded Herbert Lehman as senator. In the 1970s the first Jewish mayor to govern New York was the decidedly middle-of-the-road Democrat Abe Beam. The controversies over Jewish teachers in Ocean-Hill, Brownsville, and the friction between Jews and minorities in Canarsie changed the nature of the Jewish electorate.

Ed Koch was good enough to be the Jewish mayor of the city for twelve years. He seemed to delight in his Jewish identity and was an outspoken supporter of Zionist causes. He was the city's chief administrative officer during the austerity of the budget crunch and also led New York in a time of physical growth and expansion.

While a Jew no longer holds the office of mayor in the nineties, David Garth, a Jewish political consultant, was instrumental in mayor Giuliani's election, and a young Jewish woman, a power in the liberal party named Fran Reiter, became his deputy mayor. A traditional consumer-conscious Jewish liberal named Mark Green became the City's public advocate, while Alan Havesi, a progressive, became city controller.

══════════ The Lower East Side ══════════

Directions: Subway F to Essex Street or Bus M15 bus to Delancey Street.

The eighteenth-century Lower East Side was bucolic country; the Rutger and De Lancey estates shared the geography. As New York grew commercially, Federal-style residences and row houses appeared on the new street grid and rich merchants and shipping magnates took title to the Lower East Side. The neighborhood became fashionable.

In the 1850s and 1860s Irish and German immigrants made the Lower East Side their own. The townhouses were subdivided and in some cases more than one family occupied a room. Although poor, the neighborhood produced its Irish political leaders and German manufacturers. Tammany had its wigwam on Chatham and Frankfort Streets.

Many of the Lower East Side Germans were Jews and they had their own Jewish fraternal groups and newspapers. Starting out working class, they became professionals, garment manufacturers, and jewelers. In 1880 the German-Jewish colony numbered eighty thousand.

The Lower East Side had another radical change in 1881, when pogroms ignited by the assassination of Tsar Alexander II led to a mass Jewish exodus. The Jews, who came in family groups for permanent settlement, were running for their lives. They were very different from their German predecessors.

The men had long beards and fur hats and shabby gabardine coats and the married women shaved their heads and wore wigs. In Russia and Poland they were restricted to Jewish areas. They were second-class citizens with limited job and educational opportunities.

The new Lower East Side arrivals became peddlers and graduated to pushcarts or joined the mass production clothing industry, otherwise known as sweatshops. Peddling was often long frustrating hours with little reward; the sweatshops were low wages and brutal working conditions.

The Lower East Side was more densely populated than London's notorious East End. Over three hundred thousand people occupied a square mile bound by Allen Street, Essex Street, Canal Street, and Broome Street. Russian Jews moved into run-down, fire-escape tenements where tuberculosis and typhus ran rampant. The rooms had little ventilation and light and were divided among families. Privacy was nonexistent.

The Russian immigrants found no relief on the Lower East Side's streets. They were crowded and unclean and reeked of garbage. Street gangs waylaid the "greenhorns" to extort money or for the fun of pulling their beards. Some young Russian Jews were themselves corrupted by the streets and became criminals and prostitutes.

But the Jews of the Lower East Side were more than equal to the hardships and temptations. They persevered from morning to night, working sixteen- and eighteen-hour days. They learned English and made sure their children were educated. They sent them to the Educational Alliance and to the settlement houses.

They counted their pennies and did a good deal of their shopping in the cheapest of the cheap, the *Khazermark* (pig market) on Hester Street. Bargain days were Thursdays and Friday mornings right before the Sabbath; everything was bought and sold, new and used, and in the final stages of decay. It was a colorful shouting and pushing bazaar where the bargaining was always hot and heavy.

The Lower East Side could be crude but it had a rich cultural life. The writer Hutchins Hapgood proclaimed that "no part of New York has a more intense and varied life than the colony of Russian and Galician Jews who live on the East Side who form the largest Jewish city in the world."

The neighborhood was the scene of heated political debates, head-to-head chess matches, literary lectures, and a slew of self-help programs. There were technical schools, business schools, and language classes sponsored by uptown philanthropists. The German Jewish Educational Alliance taught David Sarnoff, the founder of RCA, to speak English and gave Sir Jacob Epstein—when he was still Jake—his first art lessons.

The Yiddish theater was one of the centerpieces of the Lower East Side, with its Jewish King Lears and Hamlets. On benefit nights it was pure audience participation, when families came complete with bawling babies to cheer the heroes and hiss the villains. At the end of a Gordin tragedy there wasn't a dry eye in the house. It was a training ground for Paul Muni, Edward G. Robinson, and a young Walter Matthau.

For the price of a cup of coffee or a strong glass of Russian tea, poetry cliques and political factions whiled away the evenings. In Levine's on

East Broadway or Schreiber's on Canal Street, Jewish intellectuals and sweatshop Lenins argued women's rights, free love, the merits of the latest production at the opera, or the future of socialism. They took on the issues that were discussed in the neighborhood's five Yiddish papers.

The Jews of the Lower East Side refused to depend on German-Jewish charity. They formed *Landsmanschaften* (mutual aid societies) from their Old World villages and towns. These societies provided a place to socialize with friends and reminisce, kept local religious traditions alive, and built synagogues. In time there were *Landsmanschaften* hospitals and convalescent homes.

In 1903 and 1906 the brutal Russian bloodletting and Jew baiting brought another wave of refugees to the Lower East Side. The Balkan Wars from 1908 to 1914 added Sephardic Greeks, Turks, and Syrians to the melting pot. By the time World War I exposed European Jewry to further suffering there were six hundred thousand strong in the neighborhood.

In America the values of Bialystok or Vilna were turned upside down; prayer and religious study suddenly took second place in the race for survival. Jews moved from the synagogue to the secular and aggressively pursued the American identity. They became true believers in the American dream or ideologues of New World utopias. Unions or Zionism or a home in Riverdale were the answers for a new age in a new country.

The success of Lower East Side social programs, educational programs, organizations, and protests eventually led to the end of a solidly Jewish neighborhood. By the 1920s stridently American Lower East Siders were relocating to Riverside Drive and Central Park West and the Bronx. The next influx of Jewish refugees would ignore the crumbling Lower East Side. The German Jews fleeing from Nazism planted their enclave in Washington Heights.

The Jewish Lower East Side is still more than memories. Jews cling to the neighborhood, too poor or too stubborn to retire to the suburbs or Miami Beach. They walk with slow half steps or the spring of an active old age to the Jewish shops and restaurants that survive mostly on the tourist trade. But increasingly, they are joined by younger Jews with families who follow Jewish traditions that go back to eighteenth-century Hungary and Poland.

The Lower East Side's Jewish bazaar is intact, with blocks of stores selling off-price clothes, linens, electronic goods, and china. But the times are changing. Bargaining is common, but by no means across-the-board, and some of the people minding the stores these days are Indian or Chinese.

Though the number of Lower East Side Jews keeps declining and the population, with the exception of some Yeshiva students, is mostly senior citizen, these Jewish survivors still have some political clout. Sheldon Silver, their intelligent and eloquent state assemblyman, has recently assumed the very powerful position of speaker of the state assembly. He will be responsible for the passage of laws in the state house.

Lower East Side Place Marks

While other Manhattan neighborhoods have been gentrified out of existence, the Lower East Side has changed its population but kept a lot of its Jewish character. The story of the Eastern European Jewish immigrants is still revealed in brick-and-mortar Lower East Side survivors.

Bintel Briefs and Brotherly Aid

Jewish Daily Forward, *175 East Broadway.*

In its prime, when Abraham Cahan was editor, the *Jewish Daily Forward* building stood ten stories tall with the largest electric Yiddish sign in creation. It was the eyes and ears and heart of the Jewish Lower East Side, telling it like it was, whether about garment industry goons or Allen Street prostitutes. The paper gave the uninitiated advice along with left-of-center politics and balanced tabloid sensationalism, literary essays, and high-quality fiction. Now the signs on 175 are in Chinese.

Independent Kletzker Brotherly Aid Society, *5 Ludlow Street.*

Just off Canal Street are the former premises, not a little worse for wear, of the Independent Kletzker Brotherly Aid Society. At one time there were six thousand of these *Landsmanschaften* representing villages in Eastern Europe. They provided health and burial benefits and a replica of *shtetl* fellowship for poor Jews.

Yarmulowsky's Bank, *corner Orchard and Canal Streets.*

Yarmulowsky's was tall for its time, with a big clock and the name Yarmulowsky carved above the entrance. It once contained the savings of the Lower East Side, but it failed in 1914 before the days of federally insured bank accounts. Two thousand outraged customers picketed the bank and another five hundred stormed Yarmulowsky's house.

Synagogues

The children of the book took religion very seriously on the Lower East Side and the synagogue was at the center of the community. Since the Jews left the neighborhood some of their houses of worship were converted to churches or public buildings, while others have been deserted and vandalized.

A choice few still have active congregations. East Broadway is still the domain of Jewish Orthodoxy; storefront synagogues proliferate between Jefferson and Montgomery Streets. But in an earlier era Lower East Side Jewish houses of worship were among the most impressive in the city.

Shaarey Shimoyim, *The First American Rumanian Congregation, 89 Rivington Street (212-673-2835).*

Shaarey Shimoyim means the Gates of Heaven. It was the pride of the Lower East Side with seating for 1,600. Lately there aren't enough communicants to keep the Gates of Heaven open.

Beth Hamedrash Hagodol Synagogue, *60-64 Norfolk Street (212-674-3330).*

The Beth Hamedrash Hagodol Synagogue is designated a landmark. Its attractive Gothic revival exterior and the evocative biblical murals and carved pews are kept in good repair. It is difficult to believe that it was a Baptist church in 1852.

Bialystoker Synagogue, *7-13 Wilett Avenue (212-475-0165).*

The Bialystoker Synagogue has seen better days, but it is still admired by for its fieldstone finish and Federalist details from 1826.

Living Museums and Exhibits

The Educational Alliance, *197 East Broadway (212-475-6200).*

German-Jewish millionaires established the Alliance to Americanize their "less-civilized" co-religionists. Besides language lessons, it offered technical training, cultural programs, and business courses. Children could attend Alliance camps or use the gym and take advantage of the showers. Legal aid and pasteurized milk were both available through the wide array of Alliance services.

The Federation of Jewish Philanthropies still runs the Alliance for the benefit of poor Jews, Puerto Ricans, African Americans, and Chinese. Its Hall of Fame on the main floor contains the photographs of such notable Lower East Side alumni as David Sarnoff, the radio and television magnate, Eddie Cantor, the entertainer, and the sculptor Louise Nevelson.

The Henry Street Settlement, *263-267 Henry Street (212-766-9200).*

While its fine Federalist buildings have been designated landmarks, the settlement house organization is still working to improve the lives of the people in the neighborhood. It continues the programs of its founder, Lillian Wald, a German-Jewish nurse who pioneered social work and preventive medicine at the beginning of the century.

Henry Street has a day-care center, a credit union, home care for the elderly, employment training, educational programs, and even an art gallery. The exhibits feature the East Village avant-garde and indigenous Rembrandts.

Lower East Side Tenement Museum, *97 Orchard Street (212-431-0233). Tuesday–Friday 11 A.M.–4 P.M.; Sunday, call for times for special programs. Admission charge.*

This museum preserves the authentic tenement, the log cabin of urban life, along with the artifacts of the Jewish families who occupied them. Sunday afternoons there are plays and slide shows dramatizing the immigrant tenement experience. The Lower East Side Conservancy, the group behind the museum, strives to make it a "truly living experience."

Lower East Side Nosh

Jewish ethnic cooking is as varied as the lands of the Jewish diaspora, but mainstream Eastern European cuisine characterizes the Jews of New York. It is forthright *shtetl* (village) food heavy on the garlic, onions, and *shmaltz* (rendered chicken fat). Following Jewish dietary laws, meat and dairy are separate and there are always two sets of dishes in strictly kosher homes. Kosher meat is always ritually killed and pork and shellfish are forbidden.

The Jews of New York take a special delight in their *vorspiese* (appetizers) such as chopped chicken liver, *shmaltz* providing the extra kick, and *gefullte* fish, chopped pike, carp, and whitefish, with carrot adding sweetness. Jewish chicken soup is legendary with noodles, *kreplach* (a noodle stuffed with meat), or matzo balls (dumplings made of unleavened bread meal). Roast chicken, chicken fricassee with meat balls, boiled beef, potted brisket, and stuffed cabbage are popular main courses while noodle pudding, potato pudding, and potato *knishes* (in a dough shell) are on the side.

The absence of refrigerators in nineteenth-century Eastern Europe made pickled vegetables and smoked meats and fish a necessity. Today pickles, pastrami, and smoked salmon are enjoyed by Jews and their fellow New Yorkers just for their taste. The bagel, a ring-shaped roll that is baked in water, is another Jewish staple that has become mainstream New York.

The Lower East Side's Jewish restaurants are in the tradition of the Jewish mother's refrain *ess ess* (eat, eat). The portions are over the top. Like the Jewish mother, the restaurants are still objects of sentiment to which errant Jewish sons and daughters return regularly. Some of the restaurants still have a built-in floor show—the Jewish waiter. He is the master of the semi-insulting quip and the rude aside. Don't expect bowing and scraping service on the egalitarian Lower East Side.

Sammy's Rumanian Jewish Restaurant, *157 Christie Street (718-673-0330). Daily from 4 P.M. till very late.*

Sammy's is garlic and onions, Jewish heavy and spicy, and please pass the chicken fat. The two cents plain is on the house, but after the *griebenes* (chicken skin and onions fried in rendered chicken fat), the stuffed derma, and a big rib steak, Alka Seltzer is more to the point.

Ratner's Dairy Restaurant and Bakery, *138 Delancey Street (212-674-9406). Sunday–Thursday 11 A.M.–11 P.M.; Friday and Saturday 11 A.M.–midnight.*

When the Jewish Upper East Side shops for bargains on the Lower East Side, it breaks for brunch at Ratner's. The mushroom-barley soup, *kashe varnishkes* (wheat groats with noodles), and lox and eggs are what Jewish memories are made of. Ratner's has its own parking lot for the convenience of its customers running the Delancey Street gauntlet.

Katz's Delicatessen, *205 East Houston Street (212-254-2246). Sunday–Thursday 7:30 A.M.–11 P.M.; Friday and Saturday 7:30 A.M.– 1 A.M.*

The name is Katz's, but that's about the only thing that is strictly kosher. It's an old-style cafeteria where a ticket greets you at the door to be punched as you order. The cold cuts from this landmark deli are not exactly prime and the Coney Island fries are cooked in yesterday's oil.

Jewish Food Markets

The Lower East Side may no longer be a big city *shtetl,* but it still has all the makings for a traditional Jewish meal; it just takes more time to gather them together.

Miller's Cheese, *13 Essex Street (212-496-8855). Sunday 9 A.M.– 6 P.M.; Monday–Wednesday 9:15 A.M.–6:45 P.M.; Thursday 9 A.M.– 9 P.M.; Friday 9 A.M.–two hours before sunset.*

Miller's is fresh farmer cheese with the creamiest curds and special kosher *Mehadrin* milk. Miller's, if given a chance, will introduce the uninitiated to kosher creamy dessert cheeses.

Guss's Pickles, *35 Essex Street (212-254-4477). Sunday–Thursday 9 A.M.–6 P.M.; Friday 9 A.M.–4 P.M.*

Sour pickles or half sours from the barrel are part of the romance of the Lower East Side. Guss's Pickles has not gone Hollywood since appearing in *Crossing Delancey;* the wry quips still come free with the pickles.

Leibel Bistritzky's, *39 Essex Street (212-254-0335).*

Mrs. Leibel, the "Jewish mother" of Essex Street, handles her customers, new and loyal, with real care. She knows her kosher cheeses, American and imported, and slices them to order. The Miller Swiss and the Haolam Edam are favorites with her following.

G & M Kosher Caterers, *41 Essex Street (212-254-5370).*

G & M cooks up Hungarian-Jewish appetizers and entrees for the very demanding Lower East Side trade. During the holidays the customers are four deep waiting for the tender brisket, the sweet and tart stuffed cabbage, the peppery potato knishes and *kugel,* and other delicacies too numerous to mention.

Gertel's Bakery, *53 Hester Street near Essex Street (212-982- 3250). Sunday–Thursday 7 A.M.–5 P.M.; Friday 6:30 A.M.–sundown.*

The bakery abounds with many delights: rich raspberry jelly donuts, coffee cakes with delectable honey and pecan toppings, and pies with melt-in-the-mouth crusts and fillings that aren't canned. Old timers return to the neighborhood for their special treats.

Moishe's Homemade Kosher Bakery, *181 East Houston Street (212-475-9624). Sunday–Friday 7 A.M.–6 P.M.*

Moishe's is *challah* (braided Sabbath bread) warm from the oven and sticky (with honey) *teiglach* made from unleavened dough for Passover. On Sunday take a number and wait.

Russ & Daughters, *179 East Houston Street (212-475-4880). Tuesday–Sunday 9 A.M.–6:30 P.M.*

Russ's daughter Ann is still minding the whitefish, pickled herring, and belly lox. Keeping up with the uptown Joneses, there's also beluga caviar and pâté de foie gras at Lower East Side prices.

Yonah Schimmel Knishes Bakery, *137 East Houston Street (212-477-2858). Daily 8 A.M.–6 P.M.*

The knishes come fresh and hot and heavy from the dumbwaiter. Yonah Schimmel's knishes cannot be compared with the article sold at hot dog stands. The crust melts in the mouth and the stuffing, whether potato, kasha, or cabbage, is nicely seasoned with white pepper and garlic.

Kossar's Bialystoker Kuchen Bakery, *367 Grand Street (212-473-4810). Daily 24 hours.*

People cross the river and double park for these bagels and bialys. They are harder, more chewy, and less doughy than the supermarket varieties.

The Grand Deli, *399 Grand Street (212-477-5200). Sunday–Thursday 11:30 A.M.–midnight; Friday 9 A.M.–2 hours before Sabbath.*

The Grand Deli still sells overstuffed brisket and corned beef sandwiches that put better known delis to shame, but the kosher Chinese is the main event here. Any Chinese dish with veal is a winner. The meaty beef ribs are very special.

Schapiro's House of Kosher & Sacramental Wines, *126 Rivington Street (212-475-7383). Sunday–Thursday 10 A.M.–5 P.M.; Friday 10 A.M.–3 P.M.*

Schapiro's Wines is a city landmark. For generations New York Jews have visited Schapiro's cellars to get a real kosher Malaga with that kiss of sweetness.

Jewish Bargains

Shopping on the Lower East Side is a New York Sunday ritual. It goes back to the days before the uptown stores could open on Sunday and the

Lower East Side, with its Saturday Sabbath, was the only shopping game in town. But the Lower East Side was more than a way of getting around the blue laws; it offered discounts on brand names that New Yorkers and out-of-towners couldn't refuse.

The Lower East Side was a Sunday spectacular that attracted Upper East Side mink and uptown flash. It was a good-natured, multiethnic, and multiracial crowd scene where bargain hunting was the common denominator. The Jewish sellers with Old World accents were more than willing to *hondl* (bargain) even as they insisted they weren't making a profit.

The Sunday ritual is also a weekday ritual and is still going strong on Orchard Street, the Lower East Side's Fifth Avenue, from Houston to Division Streets. It still draws the crowds but there is a feeling that something is missing. The shopping area is now designated with street signs that proclaim it the "Bargain District," and Lower East Side bargain hunting has become more self-conscious. The appeal is to the tourists from Europe and Dubuque, and the streetwise New York shopper is left out in the cold.

The bargains aren't what they used to be years ago. The uptown department stores have their own Sunday openings and constant sales, cutting into the Orchard Street advantage. Top designers like Calvin Klein and Bill Blass no longer manufacture in large quantities; the rising costs and shrinking inventories that provided the source of the Orchard Street bargains are no longer common on Seventh Avenue. These days it's easier to find names in the mid-price range like Liz Claiborne, Evan Picone, and Jones New York with large manufacturing runs.

It's best to get an early start to get the best buys. The stores close early in the afternoon as the shoppers disperse. Be prepared to do a lot of walking and stalking. The action around the racks and shelves requires true grit and determination. Most items have a marked price, sometimes open to bargain, but be ready to pay what the ticket says.

Store hours are set, but more often than not, disregarded. Early closing on Friday and closed on Saturday is a must. Otherwise, Sunday to Thursday 9 A.M.–10 A.M. opening and 5 P.M.–6 P.M. closing is the rule, not always followed.

Women's Clothing

Fishkin's, *63 Orchard Street and 314-318 Grand Street (212-226-6538).*

It's always worth a few minutes at Fishkin's to check out the sportswear and separates. The Grand Street store specializes in more casual styles.

Forman's, *82 Orchard Street, 94 Orchard Street, and 78 Orchard Street (212-228-2500).*

On Sundays they sometimes have to lock the door to keep the crowd manageable. Forman's usually has a lot of Liz Claiborne and Evan Picone, as well as an ample selection of high-quality, discount-priced coats and suits. Petites should look in at the 94 Orchard Street store and large sizes at 78 Orchard.

Klein's of Monticello, *105 Orchard Street (212-966-1453).*

Klein's is not your usual dowdy Lower East Side "shlock" emporium; it's done up to look Madison Avenue trendy with designer mannequins and art photos of anorexic models. The knits, suits, and scarves are as stylish as the store's *haute* decor.

M. Friedlich, *196 Orchard Street (212-254-8899).*

Friedlich's is the store to spy out Italian and French imports, but they don't neglect American sportswear either. It's also possible to find some great buys in coats.

Shulie's, *175 Orchard Street (212-473-2480).*

You go to Shulie's for Tahari's designs. The selection is not quite as up to date as in the Madison Avenue store, but the prices are better.

Women's Lingerie

Well-known brand lingerie and underwear are easy to find in one or the other of the Orchard Street shops specializing in these items. Some shops have a no-try-on, no-return policy, so it's best to know exactly the brand, style, and size before starting out. The discounts on sleepwear can be large—up to seventy percent—but twenty percent seems to be the rule on undergarments. If one shop is out of stock, another or another might just have what you're looking for.

D & A Merchandise, *22 Orchard Street (212-925-4766).*

A. W. Kaufman, *73 Orchard Street (212-226-1629).*

Lolita, *70 Orchard Street (212-982-9560).*

Charles Weiss, *331 Grand Street between Orchard and Ludlow streets (212-966-1143).*

Men's Clothing

G & G Projections, *53 Orchard Street (212-431-4530).*

Shirts and sweaters are the reason for shopping at G & G. The discounts on Hathaway and Christian Dior shirts run about thirty percent.

Jodamo International, *321 Grand Street at Orchard Street (212-219-0552).*

The styles are a little slicker and high fashion. Most come from Italy and are usually a year ahead. The store is spacious enough for easy looking.

Pan Am Men's Wear, *50 Orchard Street (212-925-7032).*

Pan Am's has a fine selection of American designers with more conservative styles. The discounts are excellent.

Men's Underwear

Louis Chock, *74 Orchard Street (212-473-1929).*

You can find most of the well-known brands at Chock's; Calvin Klein, Hanes, Jockey, and BVD are available on the premises and also by mail at discount prices.

Leather Goods—Shoes and Bags

Lace-Up Shoe Shop, *110 Orchard Street (212-475-8040).*

The Sunday lines are an indication that there are good buys to be found in Lace-Up. Heavily discounted prices on top designer, high-style women's shoes—better for looking at than wearing—are the main attractions.

Leslie Bootery, *36 Orchard Street (212-431-9196).*

Women's shoes are on the main and second floors; men's are downstairs. Top designer brands like Cole-Hahn and Bally sometimes appear on the shelves, but you're more likely to find Reebok's and Clark's sportier models.

Fine & Klein, *119 Orchard Street (212-674-6720).*

There's a vast selection of designer handbags at bargain prices, as well as small leather goods. The wallets, belts, and briefcases are a whole lot less than in the uptown department stores.

Linens

One of the best reasons to shop on the Lower East Side is the selection of linens for bedroom and bath. Shops line Grand Street from Forsyth Street to Orchard Street, filled with Fieldcrest and Martex towels, Wamsutta sheets, duvets, and bedspreads, plus all the accessories a well-dressed bathroom needs. The prices are well below the uptown stores; now and then you can come across a buy that is exceptional.

Eldridge Jobbing House, *90-88 Eldridge Street (212-226-5136).*

Ezra Cohen, *307 Grand Street at Allen Street (212-925-7800).*

Harris Levy, *278 Grand Street (212-226-3102).*

Judaica

The Lower East Side maintains its Orthodox religious and cultural traditions; the People of the Word preserve the word. Jewish artists express their devotion in both sacred and secular objects. The storehouses for the Lower East Side's Judaica are usually small and sometimes dark, and inevitably sign-posted in Hebrew letters—a glimpse of the Lower East Side at the turn of the century. There are prayer books and books of Torah commentary and ritual phylacteries (*tfillim*) and prayer shawls (*tallises*). In a place of honor are the sacred scrolls themselves, with silver pointers and velvet covers and shields with the Lion of Judah. This Judaica, which also includes rare and antique items like plates and glasses and decorations with Jewish themes, is found mainly on Essex Street between Canal and Grand Streets.

Rabbi Eisenbach, *41 Essex Street (212-982-4217).*

The Rabbi has an eye for interesting and esoteric Judaiaca, antique and modern, from fine silver replicas of the Holy Ark to electric Menorahs. The Rabbi also carries rabbinical court papers and documents in Hebrew and English, including marriage agreements and divorce papers.

Israel Gift Center, *23 Essex Street (212-475-6035).*

Everything on sale from the Israeli Gift Center is imported from the Holy Land. It has an especially fine selection of tallises and skullcaps embroidered in rich fabrics. The jewelry on display elegantly conveys Jewish identity and expresses Jewish themes. Hebrew is spoken here and there are even Hebrew letters instead of numbers on the electric clocks.

Weinfeld's Skull Caps, *19 Essex Street (212-254-9260).*

Weinfeld's is the house of skullcaps, an item of clothing which is always worn by most observant Jews, even under their hats. They come in a wide variety of sizes, materials, and designs, and can be a form of self-expression as well as part of a sacred duty. Handsome *Bar Mitzvah* sets, which include skullcaps, *tallises,* and phylacteries, are for the buying.

Zelig Blumenthal, *13 Essex Street (212-267-8370).*

Zelig's has beautiful unusual hand-painted porcelain ritual wine goblets and Sabbath and Passover plates for traditional blessings and serving. The candelabrums for the Sabbath candles and the Hanukkah Menorahs are works of art.

Lower East Side Jewish Festival

The Lower East Side Festival takes place on the third Sunday in June. Jews and others with a nostalgia for the old neighborhood come down to glimpse the local color and eat a knish. The local Jewish merchants and restaurant owners roll out the red carpet and share their memories. There are kosher food stalls and stands selling Judaica. The East Broadway Educational Alliance sponsors this exercise in reawakening Jewish identity

I'll Take Manhattan

Manhattan Place Marks

The Jews are now spread throughout the whole borough of Manhattan from the Jewish intellectual Upper West Side to the Jewish artist SoHo to the Jewish businessman Upper East Side. Though they are no longer a people apart, they try to hold onto their Jewish identity. There are neighborhoods in the city where this identity stands out and places of interest where Jews can renew their sense of ethnic awareness. At the same time the Jewish New York experience has influenced the rest of the city in everything from its taste in food to its approach to art. And the Jew has become so much a part of the city that it is difficult to know where New York starts and Jewish ends.

There's No Business Like Business

The Garment Center

The garment center once spanned 25th to 41st Streets between Sixth (Avenue of the Americas) and Ninth Avenues and included the fur district, children's clothes, and men's cloaks and suits, besides women's ready-to-wear. But foreign imports have taken a big bite out of the business and the center, which is not sanforized, is shrinking. The companies with designer names are moving uptown and the small operators are going out of business.

The garment center, from 36th Street to 41st Street between Avenue of the Americas and Eighth Avenue, is still typical New York chaos. While car horns blow and the occasional irate driver vents his frustrations, lines of trucks double park for pickups and deliveries. The sidewalks are clogged with Dominican and Puerto Rican workers and the occasional Hasid dragging racks of coats or skirts or balancing boxes on a hand truck.

In between time they check out the the smartly dressed action on the street. Upstairs in the showrooms of skyscrapers, the companies hold court for out-of-town buyers. The dynamic manufacturer and his protégé on the sales floor are the white-collar offspring of the Lower East Side sewing machine operator and cutter.

Eastern European Jewish characters have left the center with old Jewish hang-outs like the kosher-style cafeteria Dubrow's, to be replaced by Jews with business degrees and pasta joints. But Seventh Avenue (now re-named Fashion Avenue between 36th and 38th Streets) still has the high-rise showroom landmarks at 498, 500, and 512, built before the depression.

The Diamond District

The diamond district used to be between the Bowery and Canal Streets; a conventional row of jewelry stores was the backdrop to bearded and side-locked Hasids dealing in diamonds. Millions of dollars in gems were traded on the sidewalks with a handshake. The jewelers and the merchants and the cutters eventually followed the well-heeled clientele uptown to its current location on 47th Street between Fifth and Sixth Avenues.

While jewelry stores and jewelry exchanges with individual stalls line both sides of the street offering gold, pearls, and gems in different settings, the diamond dealers in the black suits and wide-brimmed hats conduct their trade in lofts equipped with state-of-the-art alarms and video cameras. Most of the stores offer tourist prices, but perseverance and old-fashioned bargaining can work wonders in the exchanges.

In recent years some diamond district locations have gone Fifth Avenue, with fancy facades and lush displays. But the diamond district shopping adventure is all about unset stones produced from folds of white paper and the drawn-out process of making a choice, weighing the stones, and agreeing on a price. It is a jewelry bazaar in the middle of modern Manhattan. The Jeweler's National Exchange on 4 West 47th Street is as good of a place as any to play let's make a deal.

Synagogues

Central Synagogue, *Lexington Avenue and 55th Street (212-744-1400).*

The building, from 1872, has been formally designated a landmark. It is a Moorish revival structure with bulbous domes rising to a height of 122 feet. The architect, Henry Fernbach, was the first Jew to practice architecture in the city. The original synagogue was on Ludlow Street in the Lower East Side.

Temple Emanuel-El, *Fifth Avenue and 65th Street (212-744-1400).*

Temple Emanuel-El is the seat for Reform Judaism in the city; it is thoroughly German Jewish and "progressive." This Romanesque/Byzantine structure seats 2,500 amid the splendor of its bronze ark, Stars of David, and Lions of Judah.

Congregation Shearith-Israel, *Central Park West and 70th Street (212-873-0300).*

Though this Sephardic Jewish sanctuary only goes back to 1897, the congregation has been in existence since 1654. No one can say New York's Jewish grandees don't do things right—the stained-glass windows are by Tiffany. The congregation still preserves a cemetery in Chatham Square, with headstones from the seventeenth century.

Jewish Culture—Manhattan Museums and Archives

The Jewish Museum, *1109 Fifth Avenue at 92nd Street (212-860-1688). Sunday 11* A.M.*–6* P.M.*; Monday–Thursday noon–8* P.M. *Admission charge, except Tuesday evening.*

The Jewish Museum has recently been completely revamped. It took three years and thirty-six million dollars to create a museum space that attempts to define the Jewish experience and identity and trace the history of this special people. The museum is a work of art and of scholarship, creatively mounted and ingeniously conceived. The artifacts and ritual objects of Jews from the East and West are displayed in a way that evoke different cultures and eras. New acquisitions include some amazing Chagalls and haunting Soyers.

Yivo Institute for Jewish Study, *555 West 57th Street, Suite 1100 (212-246-6080) Monday–Thursday 9:30* A.M.*–5:30* P.M.

The Yivo Jewish Institute originated in Vilna in 1925, but was moved to New York during the war to protect its precious manuscripts and books. This library, which is open to the public, contains three million photographs, letters, and documents. There are secret Nazi memoranda in their files and material on the Jewish presence in the Far East.

Yeshiva University Museum, *2520 Amsterdam Avenue (212-960-5390). Tuesday–Thursday 10:30* A.M.*–5* P.M. *Admission charge.*

The Jewish historical experience is depicted through photos, paintings, and Jewish folk art and religious articles. There are ten scale models of the world's most famous synagogues.

The Jewish Theological Seminary, *122nd Street and Broadway.*

The Jewish Theological Seminary is more than a training ground for American rabbis. It is a repository for some of the rarest Jewish books in the world. It has 250,000 volumes, including special finds from the old Cairo synagogue.

Jewish Stages

Folksbeine Theater, *123 East 55th Street (212-755-2231).*

The heritage of the Yiddish theater is still alive in the Folksbeine Theater. They have kept the tradition for seventy-four years, putting on dramas and musicals in Yiddish. The younger actors sometimes need a bit of coaching, but the words of Sholem Aleichem haven't lost their impact. The season runs from October to April, but not continually. Check the box office for the complete schedule.

The Jewish Repertory Theater, *at Playhouse 91, 316 East 91st Street (212-831-2000).*

The Jewish Rep is a contemporary take on the Jewish experience. It is a post-Holocaust world of angst and alienation with a dollop of post–Cold War social consciousness. The performers and playwrights are free to develop in their own directions.

From Deli to Haute Cuisine

Jewish food is alive and well throughout Manhattan. Jewish deli is New York deli and the bagel is the New York equivalent of the French croissant. While New York's nonreligious Jews have become partisans of French and Italian gourmet cuisines, the city's religious Jews have insisted that haute cuisine go kosher.

Lou S. Siegel's, *209 West 38th Street (212-921-4433). Sunday– Thursday 11:45 A.M.–10 P.M.; Friday 11:45 A.M.–2:45 P.M.*

Lou Siegel's is no longer diamond pinky-ring garment district and beef flanken with a teaspoon of horseradish. The kosher designer suit crowd is more comfortable with the Cajun fish.

Glatt Dynasty, *1049 Second Avenue (212-888-9119).*

The host of this kosher Chinese restaurant carries himself with the dignity and authority of a miracle-working rebbe. Unfortunately, there are no miracles in the kitchen. There are diet and low-calorie meals for the weight conscious.

Levana, *141 West 69th Street (212-877-8457). Monday–Thursday 5 P.M.–11 P.M.; Saturday (winter only) 8 P.M.–11 P.M.; Sunday 3 P.M.–11 P.M.*

Levana has the fancy presentation of nouvelle cuisine in kosher continental. It even serves kosher venison in a formal dining room with pastel tablecloths.

La Kasbah, *70 West 71st Street, off Columbus Avenue (212-769-1690). Monday–Thursday 5 P.M.—11 P.M.; Saturday sunset–1 A.M.; Sunday 1 P.M.–11 P.M.*

La Kasbah is North African Glatt kosher cuisine in an exotic Sephardic setting. The couscous and the tajines may be a little heavy-handed, but they seem to go down fine with Carmel sweet and dry reds.

Fine & Schapiro, *138 West 72nd Street (212-877-2874). Saturday–Thursday 8:30 A.M.–11 P.M.; Friday 8:30 A.M.–9 P.M. Restaurant opens at 11 A.M.*

The West Side's "between the wars" Jewish refugees were Fine & Schapiro regulars. The stuffed cabbage is just the right blend of sweet and sour and the boiled beef is better than a French *pot de feu.*

Medici 56, *25 West 56th Street, between Fifth and Sixth avenues (212-767-1234). Monday–Thursday 11:45 A.M.–11 P.M.; Friday 11:45 A.M.–4 P.M.; Saturday sunset–12:30 A.M.; Sunday 11 A.M.–10 P.M.*

Medici is swank, just-off-Fifth-Avenue kosher dining, complete with gallery paintings, piano music to set the atmosphere, gourmet Italian dairy cooking, and book-in-advance reservations.

Trastevere, *155 East 84th Street (212-744-0210). Daily 5:30 P.M.–11 P.M.*

Some recipes are from the ancient Roman ghetto and the food is kosher. It sounds like a gimmick, putting the pasta side by side with the salad, but it works. The restaurant is dark and the seating is tight, but the customers are treated like family and don't seem to mind.

Jewish Appetizers Go Gourmet

The appetizer shops uptown are all gourmet flourishes and snob appeal. Everything must be lark's tongue rare and caviar expensive. The trend started when the dull old neighborhood stores started importing the lox from Nova Scotia and calling it nova. The humble bagel was followed by the baguette and the rest is history. Before you know it they were branching out into walnut oil and balsamic vinegar and selling espresso machines.

Zabar's, *2245 Broadway at 80th Street (212-787-2000). Sunday–Friday 9 A.M.–6 P.M.; Saturday 9 A.M.–midnight.*

Zabar's is where Barbra Streisand goes when she's looking for a bagel and smoked salmon or a can of caviar. It has four hundred kinds of cheese and twenty-two varieties of coffee. It sells more whitefish than all of the stores on the Lower East Side combined. From its upstairs kitchen appliances section it introduced the Cuisinart to New York.

Orwasher's, *308 East 78th Street (212-288-6569). Monday–Saturday 7 A.M.–7 P.M.*

Orwasher's has been creating Jewish designer bread on the Upper East Side since 1916. Their raisin pumpernickel in rolls or bread is particularly delicious.

The Deli Winner's Circle

New York's Jewish deli mavens have long argued the merits of their own favorite deli hangouts over the competition. Articles in New York newspapers and magazines have explored the intricacies of fatty versus lean pastrami and the vagaries of different smoked corned beefs. The delis, besides blowing their own horns with battling publicists, encourage the celebrity trade (which always brings in lots of ordinary people) by honoring them with triple-decker sandwiches. The four winners, in any order, of this ongoing deli competition are listed below.

Barney Greengrass, *541 Amsterdam Avenue between 856th and 87th streets (212-724-4707). Tuesday–Thursday, Saturday, and Sunday 8:30 A.M.–5:45 P.M.; Friday 8:30 A.M.–6:30 P.M.*

Barney Greengrass is what Zabar's used to be before it got pretentious. Greengrass is truly the sturgeon king as it bills itself, and the smoked salmon and whitefish king as well.

Carnegie Deli, *854 Seventh Avenue at 55th Street (212-757-2245). Daily 6:30 A.M.–3:30 A.M.*

Leo Steiner made this place, with all green bagels for St. Patrick's Day and Guinness Book of Records frank-eating contests. The deli is the most ecumenical of the bunch, getting most of the out-of-town orders for pastrami on white with mayonnaise.

Second Avenue Deli, *156 Second Avenue at 10th Street (212-677-0606). Daily 7 A.M.–2 A.M.*

In front there is the Yiddish theater equivalent of Hollywood's Grauman's Chinese with dedications on the sidewalk to Muni, Robinson, the Adlers, and many others. The deli is as authentically Jewish as these stars of the Yiddish theater.

Stage Deli, *834 Seventh Avenue between 53rd and 54th streets (212-245-7850). Daily 6:30 A.M.–2 A.M.*

Max Asnas, the original owner, was funnier than most of the Jewish comedians who did their acts at his tables. He sold out in the 1950s and flopped with a new place called the Star. The Stage today, with its high-and-wide deli on rye sandwiches, are re-creating the days of the old master.

L'Chaim/Celebrations

Salute to Israel Parade

The Jews of New York use the occasion of the Salute to Israel Parade, which marks Israeli independence, to proclaim their support for the Jewish state and celebrate their Jewish identity. It usually takes place on the first Sunday in June.

The parade was kicked off in 1965 with a short line of march from 72nd Street and Third Avenue to Fifth Avenue. Two years later, in the critical days preceding the Six Day War, the parade proved itself by drawing over a million spectators registering support for Israel. Today the Salute to Israel Parade route follows Fifth Avenue from 57th Street to 86th Street with thousands of marchers and professionally mounted floats.

Jewish youth representing Zionist organizations and religious schools (*Yeshivas*) in the metropolitan area make up the majority of marchers. They come in costume representing Jewish pioneers, carry colorful banners, and wear the severe garments of Orthodoxy. These youngsters run the gamut from joyously enthusiastic to solemn.

They are joined by their elders from the Jewish War Veterans, Worlds Zionist Congress, and other Jewish organizations. The ecumenical touch is provided by assorted marching bands from public high schools and groups like the New York Emerald Society bagpipe band.

Though the paraders smile and wildly wave to the crowd in the time-tested fashion, the Salute to Israel Parade is basically a serious affair. The wearing of the six-pointed Jewish star (*Mogen David*) and the showing of the blue and white Israeli flag are testaments to survival in the midst of persecution.

In conjunction with the Salute to Israel Parade there is an Israel Folk Dance Festival and Festival of the Arts. The Israel Folk Dance Institute puts on performances of the vibrant Jewish circle dances like the *hora,* which capture the energy of this young nation. Dramatic presentations from the Israeli stage in both Hebrew and English are featured. They usually deal with themes involving the heroic struggles of this new state.

In 1994, to avoid the same kind of sexual orientation controversies that turned the St. Patrick's Day Parade planning into legal strategy sessions, the parade committee made the Salute to Israel mainly a youth salute, and youngsters became the leading players and participants in the event.

═══════════ Jewish Brooklyn ═══════════

Borough Park

Directions: Subway B to New Utrecht Avenue/55th Street.

Borough Park is the Hasidic capital of Brooklyn, but it was once the Dutch village of New Utrecht with nineteen Dutch families instead of thousands of ultra-Orthodox Jews. The Jews and the Italians came to Borough Park in the twenties, following the subway lines and responding to ads to "Build Your House in God's Country."

The neighborhood was a neat collection of single-family frame houses and six-story apartment buildings. By the next decade it had a settled-in look with some very impressive religious structures and public buildings. By the end of World War II Borough Park was a white middle-class enclave equally split between Italians and assimilated Jews.

New highways and a building boom in the 1950s and 1960s accelerated the move out of Borough Park to the Long Island and New Jersey suburbs. The suburban bound were soon replaced by Orthodox and Hasidic Jews leaving deteriorating areas of Williamsburg and Crown Heights.

Many of these observant Jews were displaced persons from World War II and the concentration camps. They were apprehensive of big-city crime and racial conflicts, but they were more afraid of the assimilating suburbs and stayed in Brooklyn. Borough Park would become a gathering of the Hasidic clans: Vishnitzer, Pupper, Szigeder, and Krasner. The whole Bobover court made the move from the neighborhood of Crown Heights.

The Hasidic and Orthodox communities and their religious institutions rapidly dominated Borough Park. These Jews established a Council of Jewish Organizations in 1975, which helped organize local employment, health, and social service programs. By 1979 there were an estimated three hundred synagogues and fifty or more religious schools. The new Jewish population numbered seventy-three thousand and represented eighty-five percent of the population in the early years of the eighties.

The Jews of Borough Park have the same side curls, called *payoth,* and the same beards and wear the same uniform of dark suit, dark coat, white shirt, and dark broad-brimmed hat as Orthodox or Hasids in other communities. But the fabric of the suits is more expensive and the jackets hang better; closer inspection reveals cufflinks and Rolex watches. These men have a sleek substantial look, the confidence of the things of the flesh. They are students of the Torah, but they are also businessmen who travel to Manhattan to work in the diamond district and the garment center. The women are Orthodox enough to wear wigs and dress modestly, but they haven't lost a feeling for fashion and color.

The character of Jewish Borough Park is casual. Nobody has to be self-consciously Jewish in an area where gentiles are the minority. The bearded Jewish mechanic in greasy coveralls or the youth in *payoth* riding a bicycle are completely at ease. The women wheel their baby carriages along 13th Avenue, speaking Yiddish so quickly they hardly seem to take a breath, and only stop to window shop. Old men in dignified Homburgs embrace one another near the benches in front of the bank where the elderly take the sun. In a shoe-repair shop a woman waits for heels reading from a prayer book. Borough Park is a big Jewish neighborhood; it is a Jewish village in the middle of New York's largest borough.

The main shopping area of Borough Park along 13th Avenue is not *Fiddler on the Roof shtetl.* Aside from touches like the sinks showing in restaurants, this could be main street in any middle-class neighborhood. The window displays—even if they are merchandising Jewish ritual objects—are modern and the store fixtures are glossy and new. Most of the restaurants and food shops have a mainstream American look, whether the bill of fare is kosher chow mein or blintzes. There is even Jewish fast-food with the neat functional style of a McDonald's.

Place Marks—The Domes of Borough Park

Young Israel Beth El, *4802 15th Avenue (718-435-9020).*

This synagogue was built according to a Moorish design and actually, at least in outline, resembles the massive Dome of the Rock Mosque in Jerusalem. Inside this 1920 structure 120 light bulbs illuminate a large Star of David in the center of the dome. You don't have to be Jewish to be moved by the feeling of this vast house of worship.

Bobover Hasidic Synagogue, *15th Avenue and 48th Street (718-438-9791).*

This house of worship, for one of the principal sects of Hasidim in New York city and the world, is truly awe inspiring. It is a veritable cathedral of Hasidism, with a lofty ceiling forty-five feet from the ground and two layers of balconies for the women to worship in their separateness and purity. Like the original Jerusalem temple, it is done in marble and has an Old Testament feeling. A Mexican millionaire named Marcos Katz paid for the building and hired the architects and designers from his own country.

Borough Park Essing

The Jewish restaurants in Borough Park take pleasure in converting other cuisines to Orthodox Jewish. Eastern European Jewish is old hat. Jewish pizza, chow mein, and yakitori are the wave of the future.

Kosher Castle, *5006 13th Avenue (718-436-7474). Sunday–Thursday 7 A.M.–11 P.M.; Friday 7 A.M.–two hours before sunset.*

The Kosher Castle is a cavernous fast food restaurant that manages to be crowded and noisy for a good part of the day. The menu is strictly kosher and dairy with blintzes and vegetable cutlets and a rabinically approved ice cream sundae.

Crown Deli, *4909 13th Avenue (718-853-9000). Sunday–Thursday 7 A.M.–9 P.M.; Friday 7 A.M.–sundown.*

The Crown Deli does a booming take-out business in thick deli sandwiches and hot delicacies like stuffed cabbage and stuffed derma. Those in the know eat in and enjoy their prime Rumanian and rib steaks.

La Nosheria, *4813 13th Avenue (718-436-0400). Sunday–Thursday 11 A.M.–11 P.M.; Friday 11 A.M.–3 P.M.*

The Chinese menu is endless with chow meins, lo meins, and moo goo gai pans galore. It is kosher and heavy on the cornstarch and MSG. The self-service is not at self-service prices.

Kosher Delight, *4600 13th Avenue (718-435-8500). Sunday–Thursday 7 A.M.–9 P.M.; Friday 7 A.M.–two hours before sunset.*

This kosher version of McDonald's, with its French fries, nuggets of chicken, and double burgers is three times the size of the usual Borough Park restaurant and is also three times as loud.

China Glatt, *4413 13th Avenue (718-438-2576). Monday–Thursday 11 A.M.–11 P.M.; Saturday one hour after the Sabbath–1 A.M.; Sunday 12:30 P.M.–11 P.M.*

China Glatt is glatt kosher with barbecued beef spareribs instead of pork and no dairy dishes on the varied bill of fare. The delicious tastes and flavors are authentic Cantonese, Szechuan, and Hunan, with the occasional Jewish spin such as matzo balls in the broth.

Ach Tov, *4403 13th Avenue (718-438-8494). Sunday–Thursday 11 A.M.–9:30 P.M.*

Almost everyone in the restaurant is a Hasidim in a long black coat. They are all eating the soup of the day, which might be a rich mushroom and barley, followed up by side dishes of noodles and cabbage and herring or whitefish salad. Beware of the halibut teriyaki and the sweet-and-sour whitefish.

Mazel Pizza, *4807 New Utrecht Avenue (718-854-3753). Sunday–Thursday 9:30 A.M.–8 P.M.; Friday 9:30 A.M.–3 P.M.; Saturday 8:15 P.M.– midnight.*

The small Yemeni Jewish gentleman at the pizza oven tries very hard to please, but it is clear he doesn't understand a word that doesn't appear on the menu. The *felafel* is better than the pizza.

Ossie's Table, *1314 50th Street at 13th Avenue (718-435-0635). Sunday–Thursday 11 A.M.–10:30 P.M.; Saturday 8:30 P.M.–midnight.*

Ossie's Table is the ultimate night out in Borough Park. The dining area is *Better Homes and Gardens* modern, and the rabbi and the *Rabbitzin* (rabbi's wife) are dressed in their *Shabbos* (Sabbath) best. The seafood fare is also well "dressed" and is served with Soho panache.

Kosher to Go

When it comes to eating, Borough Park prefers to eat at home, even if the wife doesn't feel like doing the cooking. The traditional Jewish food is sold in nontraditional take-out. Some of the customers drive in from Jersey and Westchester.

Meisner's Glatt Kosher, *1312 55th Street (718-436-5529). Sunday–Wednesday noon–7 P.M.; Thursday 11 A.M.–8 P.M.; Friday 8 A.M.–1 P.M.*

At Meisner's they never stop slaving over a hot stove, and the cooking aromas are total temptation. They make everything Hungarian Jewish, from a simple knish to a cauliflower souffle.

Guttman's, *5120 13th Avenue (718-436-4830). Sunday noon–9 P.M.; Monday–Thursday 2 P.M.–9 P.M.; Friday 8 A.M.–4 P.M.*

The food here is made for the meat-and-potatoes man by a friendly and forceful meat-and-potatoes woman. The Guttman's larder includes sides of pot roast, stuffed veal, mountains of mashed potatoes, and oceans of thick gravy.

Mehadrin Supermarket, *5124 12th Avenue (718-435-2678). Sunday–Thursday 7 A.M.–6 P.M.; Friday 7 A.M.–4 P.M.*

Mehadrin is an all-around market, from fresh vegetables to smoked appetizers to dried beans, dried fruit, and nuts. The take-out emphasizes salads of cucumber, eggplant, and salmon.

Jewish Sweets and Desserts

When Borough Park is invited to dinner they are more likely to bring a pecan coffee ring or a box of sweets than a bottle of wine.

Weiss Bakery, *5011 13th Avenue (718-438-0407). Sunday–Thursday 6 A.M.–9 P.M.; Friday 6 A.M.–one hour before sunset.*

Even on an ordinary weekday it is wall-to-wall Jewish housewives. They wait on line for the *rugele* (small cakes made with cream cheese dough), *babka* (sponge cake), and chocolate layer cakes.

Strauss Bakery, *5209 13th Avenue at 52nd Street (718-851-7728). Sunday–Thursday 6 A.M.–7 P.M.; Friday 6 A.M.–sundown.*

Strauss prides itself on having the right stuff for those all-important holidays. It seems to really rise to the occasion with its *Purim Haman-*

taschen (a cookie turnover stuffed with prunes), *Chanukah* jelly donuts, and Passover honey cake.

The Ice Cream Center, *4511 13th Avenue (718-438-0018). Sunday–Thursday 11 A.M.–midnight; Friday 11 A.M.–two hours before* Shabbos.

Little boys with long side curls and little girls in heavy stockings and long dresses line up for larger-than-life dairy and nondairy ice cream cones, with and without sprinkles. The Ice Cream Center competes with Baskin and Robbins when it comes to fabulous fruit flavors.

Candy Man, *4702 13th Avenue (718-438-5419). Sunday–Thursday 9 A.M.–7:30 P.M.; Friday 9 A.M.–4 P.M.*

The Candy Man is easily recognizable because it is usually surrounded by children. They eye sweets very seriously, trying to decide between licorice whips or candy buttons or an all-day sucker. For adults there are hand-dipped chocolates from Israel.

The Real Jewish Article

In a neighborhood identified by its dedication to Orthodox Judaism, stores selling articles connected to worship and Jewish ritual are more common than video stores in other areas. The stores are merchandised with imagination and style.

Kodesh Religious Articles, *5205 13th Avenue (718-633-8080). Monday–Thursday 10 A.M.–10 P.M.; Friday 11 A.M.–3 P.M.; Sunday 10 A.M.–7 P.M.*

Rabbis browse through the aisles looking for the right titles in Hebrew, tugging their beards thoughtfully. The silver *Kiddush* cups (silver cup for prayers over the wine) and candelabrums are works of the silversmith's art. Besides the serious religious articles, there are snappy framed mottoes like, "Stop. It's Shabbos."

Eichler's, *5004 13th Avenue (718-633-1505). Sunday–Thursday 9:30 A.M.–8 P.M.; Friday 9:30 A.M.–4 P.M.*

The clerks are a little shy if you're not from the neighborhood but very obliging. There are pictures of Hasidic leaders for framing and pictures of the Wailing Wall. The *yarmulkes* are embroidered and the prayer books are leather bound.

H & M Simcha Center, *4914 13th Avenue (718-972-0080). Sunday–Thursday noon–6 P.M.; Friday noon–2 P.M.*

The Simcha Center specializes in gifts for Jewish rites of passage, from the *brith* (circumcision) to the *Bar Mitzvah* through marriage. On any given day proud fathers can be seen buying *Bar Mitzvah* sets for their sons and Sabbath candelabrums for their daughters.

Crown Heights

Directions: Subway 3 or 4 to Kingston Avenue/Eastern Parkway.

In the seventeenth century Crown Heights was Dutch farmsteads; later it was a part of the vast Lefferts estate. In the nineteenth century the high ground was settled by free blacks and it came to be called Crow Hill. In 1883 the Brooklyn Bridge was built and the area became more developed. On the edge of Crow Hill near Bedford, high-hat Manhattanites occupied plush apartments and even had a branch of the exclusive Union League Club. Frederick Law Olmstead and Charles Vaux, the designers of Central Park, put the finishing touches on the area, with the imposing tree-lined Eastern Parkway.

Even before Crow Hill became Crown Heights in 1916 Charles Ebbets and the McKeever brothers built Ebbets Field. It became the home of the Brooklyn Dodgers and the hub of the neighborhood until the Dodgers went west and it became a Brooklyn project. Four years later the IRT connected Crown Heights with the rest of the city and the neighborhood developed quickly. It became mostly middle-class ethnics with a professional uppercrust on Eastern Parkway.

In the 1960s, when panic selling and blockbusting were pushing the white nonreligious Jewish population out of Crown Heights, the leader of the Lubavitcher Hasidic community advised his followers to stay. The Lubavitchers, despite the warnings, prospered and thrived in a new Crown Heights side by side with West Indians and Haitians. They had the faith of their leader in the future, and the large Lubavitcher family spread through the neighborhood.

In Crown Heights the leader of the Lubavitcher, Menachem M. Shneerson, was simply called the "Rebbe." For seven generations his family, from father to son, passed down this grand Hasidic title. Though a member of a kind of religious royalty, the Rebbe was far from forbidding; he had the innocence of the elect. His pale blue eyes were clear and very striking and his lips were firmly set. His full white beard in his later years was the image of benign old age. Many in this committed community of twenty thousand believe that he was the potential *moshiach,* the coming messiah.

The streets of Jewish Crown Heights have the glow of commitment. There are many young men and women in this community of large families. They carry themselves with a sense of purpose. If they are not in Manhattan trying to reclaim nonreligious Jews, they are following the Rebbe's dictums about charity. Their elders also have the words of the Rebbe on their lips; they mill around the Lubavitcher's headquarters as if it were the Temple in Jerusalem.

In the 1980s this Hasidic community continued to expand to meet the housing needs of a new generation who wanted to be close to their families, Lubavitcher religious institutions, and the Hasidic holy man. Their efforts to purchase homes from the nearby Caribbean community resulted in occasional friction. This situation was further exacerbated by Hasidic and West Indian competition for scarce government funds.

On August 19, 1991, a traffic accident that involved a Lubavitcher driver, resulted in the death of a young Guyanese, Gavin Cato, and the injury of his cousin, Angela Cato. This unfortunate incident and a spate of unfounded rumors led to three days of rioting, looting, and mutual recriminations between Hasidic and West Indian leaders. In this explosive atmosphere a young Hasidic scholar from Australia, Yankel Rosenbaum, was stabbed.

To forestall further violence and misunderstandings, Lubavitcher Rabbi Jacob Goldstein, who headed the local Community Board, organized the Committee for Racial and Religious Harmony. Crown Heights' Lubavitcher and local black residents met at the Brooklyn Museum to bridge the rift between the two groups, while Lubavitcher and black youths came together to communicate on the basketball court of Medgar Evers College. The peace process culminated in an appearance by Lubavitcher leaders at the West Indian Carnival on Eastern Parkway.

The Seventh Lubavitcher Rebbe Menachem Shneerson died in a New York City Hospital surrounded by his adoring flock shortly after his ninety-second birthday. He had been the heart and soul of the community, but his followers would not mourn forever. For many of them their leader's death was the prelude to a new age.

There is an extraordinary sense of expectation among the Lubavitcher faithful. The bereft "children" of the Rebbe have drawn even closer together to await the Messiah. The new millennium "is on its way," and the prophecy is everywhere. Bannered across Kingston Avenue (the Lubavitchers' main street) in shimmering silver letters and posted and pasted inside and outside every Lubavitcher home and retail store are the words "The Moshiach [Messiah] is coming!"

Despite past events the streets of Jewish Crown Heights have an unexpected air of tranquillity. After all, this is big-city Brooklyn, not a *shtetl* in eighteenth-century Eastern Europe. Everyone seems to recognize one another and there is an unspoken consideration. The face of Jewish Crown Heights is open. The shopkeepers don't know how to stock their shelves or arrange a window, but they know people by name and always ask about their families. In every store there is a picture of the late Rebbe. And the life of the community follows the rhythm of the Jewish calendar, from the penance of Yom Kippur to the joy of Purim.

Lubavitcher Landmarks

The Rebbe's House, *770 Eastern Parkway.*

The Lubavitchers are a world movement. In Israel they have a group that subscribes to the wisdom of the Rebbe and even keeps a model of the Rebbe's Brooklyn house on 770 Eastern Parkway in a place of honor. The house is from the days Eastern Parkway was doctor's row. It's a big brick building with gables and hedges. On Sunday mornings Rabbi Schneerson used to stand in front of his house and distribute one-dollar bills as a gesture to promote *tzadek* (charity).

Lubavitcher Headquarters, *784-788 Eastern Parkway.*

The Lubavitcher Headquarters is the nerve center of the Lubavitcher organization. It plans and administers the group's outreach and charitable programs and day-to-day operations. It has its own communications center with a radio transmitter and video facilities. The Hasidim in the neighborhood spontaneously gather around the building during a crisis or a time of special celebration. The building is now in the process of becoming a twenty-million-dollar shrine.

The Crown Palace Hotel, *570-600 Crown Street (718-604-1777).*

The Crown Palace is a solid brick edifice with classical columns. This hotel and hall for the Hasids looks a little institutional, like a school or courthouse, and in its last incarnation it was actually a hospital. Now it is the home away from home for visiting Lubavitchers from around the world, with free parking, glatt kosher catering, and Jewish entertainment. Next door is a new modern school building for grammar, high school, and religious training, built with the support of affluent followers of the Rebbe, whose names are prominently displayed on the structure.

Chassidic Art Institute, *375 Kingston Avenue (718-774-9149). Sunday–Thursday noon–7 P.M.; Friday noon–three hours before sundown.*

Chassidic art is representational and inspirational. There are paintings of the Rebbe and scenes from the Bible; the Lubavitcher commandments are represented in oils.

Lubavitcher Tastes

The restaurants in Jewish Crown Heights are furnished like someone's kitchen; the food doesn't try to rise above hearty and the food shops seem to take more pains over dietary laws than taste. Jewish Crown Heights is not really about food.

Kingston Pizza, *395 Kingston Avenue (718-773-7154). Sunday– Thursday 11 A.M.–midnight; Friday 11 A.M.–4 P.M.*

Kingston Pizza has replaced "Ess and Bench" as the community's favorite eatery. The pizza may be on the dry side and French fries may be slightly cold but no one seems to notice. Young and old, carrying prayer books and pushing strollers, all wait their turn for bourek, stuffed pepper, lasagna, calzone, felafel, and other Jewish versions of Italian and Middle Eastern dishes in this not-so-fast-food, self-service restaurant.

Mermelstein's, *351 Kingston Avenue (718-778-3100). Sunday– Thursday 9 A.M.–9:30 P.M.; Friday 9 A.M.–4 P.M.*

The Orthodox diners eat with the intensity they bring to their *brucha's* (blessings). The stuffed pepper and stuffed cabbage are heavy on the sweet with currants and raisins. The Southern fried chicken is the south of Hungary.

Crown Bagel, *333A Kingston Avenue (718-493-4270). Sunday– Thursday 8:30 A.M.–10 P.M.; Friday 8:30–two hours before sunset.*

The men enter in twos and threes, wash their hands, and say a prayer. The next stop is the urn in front for tea or coffee and bagels baked the old-fashioned way (very hard), which are layered with lox, whitefish, tuna salad, or egg salad—the best food in the neighborhood.

Albany Bake Shop, *425 Kingston Avenue (718-493-2697). Sunday–Wednesday 7 A.M.–7 P.M.; Thursday 7 A.M.–8 P.M.; Friday 7 A.M.–4 P.M.*

The Jewish mother who presides over Oneg has wide smiles for strangers as well as regular customers. She is particularly proud of the *challah* (a braided egg bread) Oneg bakes for the Sabbath, and the holiday honey and sponge cakes. The more mainstream apple and cherry pies and turnovers are surprisingly good.

Kosher Candy, *419 Kingston Avenue (718-778-6037). Sunday–Thursday 7:30 A.M.–6:30 P.M.; Friday 7:30 A.M.–3:30 P.M.*

This is a vintage Brooklyn sweet shop, only all the candy is made under strict rabbinical supervision with no animal fat or animal enzymes or "milky product." It's a lot of trouble over jelly beans, popcorn, and *parve* tofutti. Lately, dairy sandwiches on bagels have been added. The owner, who one neighbor described as a *mensch* (a man of character), will patiently explain the Lubavitcher way of life.

Nosh World Ice Cream, *386 Kingston Avenue (718-363-1920). Sunday–Thursday noon–1 A.M.; Friday noon–half hour before sunset.*

This ice-cream store, sort of a glatt kosher Carvel, is squeaky clean and the kosher pints and half gallons are neatly displayed in refrigerated cases. At the counter good-natured Hasids serve up soft ice cream, slush, and malts to very demanding tots and teens.

Shabbos Fish Market, *417 Kingston Avenue (718-774-1659). Sunday–Thursday 8:30 A.M.–6:30 P.M.; Friday 8:30 A.M.–2 P.M.*

The fish is so fresh it's still swimming in the tank. The fishmonger wears a rubber apron and hip boots.

A Gift for Religion

Outside the Lubavitchers' main offices there is a banner in Hebrew proclaiming "The *Moshiach* Is Coming." The Lubavitchers follow the millennial tradition; they pray for a messiah and more than half expect it. But while they wait, they endeavor to live worthy lives and follow Jewish traditions. The traditions are reflected in some of the more interesting stores in the neighborhood.

Hamafitz Stam, *361 Kingston Avenue (718-744-0900). Sunday–Thursday 11 A.M.–7:30 P.M.; Friday 11 A.M.–3 P.M.*

Hamafitz Stam supplies Crown Heights with every variety of religious article. The prayer shawls, *yarmulkes,* and Sabbath candelabrums are imports from Israel. There are full-color pictures of the Rebbe appropriate for framing.

International *Moshiach* **Center,** *355 Kingston Avenue (718-604-2000). Sunday–Thursday noon–6 P.M.; Friday noon–3 P.M.*

The *Moshiach* Center is not exactly a store and not exactly a religious educational institution. It does provide T-shirts, bumper stickers, and posters announcing the imminent arrival of the Messiah. Books and pamphlets line its shelves recounting the holy life of the Rebbe and of the miraculous things to come.

Tzivos Hashem, *332 Kingston Friday Avenue (718-467-6630). Sunday–Thursday 11:30 A.M.–7 P.M.; Friday 10:30 A.M.–2 P.M.*

Tzivos Hashem means the Army of God. This army of God is comprised of the children of Jewish Crown Heights. Tzivos Hashem is a toy store with a message. The jigsaw puzzles, board games, and Hebrew letter blocks are Lubavitcher lessons.

Merkaz Stam, *309 Kingston Avenue (718-773-1120). Sunday–Thursday 11 A.M.–7 P.M.; Friday 11 A.M.–2 P.M.*

The silk Sabbath cloths (for the blessing of the bread), silver *Kiddush* cups (for the blessing of the wine), prayer shawls, and velvet Torah covers are works of art at Merkaz. Reverent images of the Rebbe are found on everything from oil paintings to key chains.

Williamsburg

Directions: Subway 3, 4, or 5 to Fulton Street. Change to M or J to Marcy Avenue. Take B24 (free transfer) to Lee/Division Street.

Williamsburg fans out from the bridge bearing its name to Flushing and Bushwick Avenues. It was part of the original Dutch farm settlement of Bushwick, but didn't have a life of its own until it was surveyed by a Colonel Williams in 1810. By the middle of the nineteenth century it was a luxurious resort attracting high society and the latest robber barons from Commodore Vanderbilt to William C. Whitney. In 1903 the Williamsburg Bridge made this attractive corner of Brooklyn accessible to the immigrant masses. Hotels were replaced by congested tenements.

Jews, Poles, and Italians poured out of the Lower East Side to cross the bridge and populate Williamsburg. People marveled at the Williamsburg Houses and favorably compared them with housing on Park Avenue. But it turned out that they exchanged one set of slums for another. The city tried to redevelop the area by building costly public housing. Still, the neighborhood decline continued and the old ethnics deserted Williamsburg for the suburbs after World War II. The Satmar, a sect of Hasidic Jews from Hungary, stepped into the breach.

The Satmar, whose name derives from the Hungarian village of Satu Mare (St. Mary), are the Orthodox of the Orthodox, strict constructionists of an exacting Torah. Their food is under the strict supervision of Hasidic rabbis and must be glatt kosher; their clothes, when not manufactured by one of their own, are taken apart and tested for *shatness* (impurities), and even corpses are given a ritual bath before burial. They do not practice any form of birth control. Unlike other Orthodox Jews they have a deep antipathy toward Israel, a secular state which they believe has interfered with the spiritual plan of the redemptive Messiah.

The Williamsburg Jews live like their Old World ancestors. They have their own theocracy with the Rebbe, the holy man and ultimate authority. There are rabbinical courts that mediate disputes and enact punishments. Many in the community devote their lives to prayer and study, while radio, television, and even some Yiddish newspapers are forbidden. Their spirituality is reflected in their dark austere coats and jackets and the black Homburgs they favor. In the middle of Brooklyn these remarkable people live a slow otherworldly existence out of another century.

The original Rebbe of the Satmar was Rabbi Joel Teitelbaum, a survivor of the Holocaust, who settled in Williamsburg in 1947 and soon attracted followers from Hungary. He was a strong leader who insisted on strict adherence to the "law," while revealing great warmth and compassion in his relations with others. After a stroke in 1968, the Satmar Rebbe reduced his taxing schedule and shared his leadership responsibilities with an assistant, Yosef Ashkenazi. Teitelbaum died in 1979 at the age of ninety-three and was succeeded by his nephew, Rabbi Moshe Teitelbaum, who moderated the sect's attitude on Zionism and the State of Israel.

The main street of the Satmar village is Lee Avenue. It is where mothers wheel baby carriages and communal buses leave for the diamond district. The stores, like everything else in the neighborhood, are stripped of any frivolous decoration. Signs are in Yiddish and English and very direct. Nineteenth-century touches like little girls wearing long dresses with high collars and woolen stockings and bearded men in top hats and Chesterfield coats make this avenue seem like anachronism.

The Satmar, who number more than thirty-five thousand, live primarily on the streets that intersect Lee Avenue between Roebling and Heywood. They live in close proximity to the large Latino community, even in some of the same buildings. Though they employ Latinos in their businesses, they have little real personal contact with this group. While there have been a few incidents involving both groups, there is a constant competition for precious space and housing.

On the surface the Jews of Williamsburg are solemn and severe, a sort of Brooklyn Jewish puritan in black gabardine, the image of formal rectitude. But the men and women of Williamsburg can unbend, especially in the company of playful children. There is a real capacity for joy that comes out in their holiday celebrations, a smile under the dignified display. It is a place of paradoxes: young men with side locks and old faces and old men with beards and young faces.

Place Mark—The Rebbe's House

Congregation Yetev Lev D'Satmar, *554 Bedford Avenue.*

This synagogue is not only a place of prayer, it is a Torah (the first five books of the Old Testament sacred to the Jews) study house and a social center. The Satmar pray with a fervor that can only be compared with Pentecostal Christians. It is pure exaltation, bending backwards and forwards as they pray, almost shouting to the Creator. The stiffness that the Satmar sometimes show totally disappears in Torah worship.

The Way of the Satmar

The Satmar are forbidden to read worldly books, newspapers, or magazines or attend movies. They are permitted the serious pleasures of the Torah, Torah commentary, and the works of their own leaders.

Lee Avenue Sforim, *114 Lee Avenue (718-782-7782). Sunday–Thursday 11 A.M.–9 P.M.; Friday 11 A.M.–3 P.M.*

Lee Avenue Sforim has prayer books, religious commentaries, and Satmar teachings on tape. There are books of instruction for youngsters and very sober children's coloring books.

Strictly, Strictly Kosher

The Satmar are finicky when it comes to judging whether a place serving food conforms to dietary laws, but when it comes to eating their tastes are simple. The rabbinical seal of approval has a more prominent place in restaurant windows than the daily specials.

Itzu's, *45 Lee Avenue (718-384-8631). Sunday–Thursday 5* A.M.*–6* P.M.*; Friday 5* A.M.*–1* P.M.

This is a genuine Satmar hang-out, with Yiddish banter and table-hopping. There is the smell of cheese and potato blintzes frying in butter, and when these beauties come to the table they get a dollop or two of sour cream or applesauce.

Lee Avenue Kosher Pizza, *108 Lee Avenue (718-384-2191). Sunday–Thursday 10* A.M.*–9* P.M.*; Friday 10* A.M.*–2* P.M.

A man in a Homburg with the brim turned up caresses his whiskers and closes in on a large wedge of moist pizza. His smile—and the Satmars don't smile often—says "indescribably good." The *felafel,* which is also recommended, comes lightly fried with a huge portion of salad on a glatt kosher pita.

The food shops are pure pandemonium on Friday morning before the sundown Sabbath and on the eve of a holiday. Satmar men and women compete for a sales clerk's attention to get the best for the family table. At other times the shops are forlornly empty.

Lee Avenue Kosher Bakery, *73 Lee Avenue (718-387-4736). Sunday–Thursday 6:00* A.M.*–9:00* P.M.*; Friday 6:30–before sundown.*

The Lee Avenue Kosher Bakery is not just traditional Jewish *babka, challah,* and *rugelach;* the eclairs, Linzer torte, and cherry pie are equally delicious.

Sander's Kosher Bakery Shop, *159 Lee Avenue (718-387-7411). Sunday– Thursday 6:30* A.M.*–9* P.M.*; Friday 6:30* A.M.*–4* P.M.

Sander's takes a special delight in the large twisted fragrant Sabbath *challahs* (egg bread) and holiday baked goods like the *hamantaschen* (three-cornered cookies for *Purim* filled with prune preserves).

Flaum Appetizers, *40 Lee Avenue (718-387-7934). Sunday–Thursday 8:30* A.M.*–6* P.M.*; Friday 8:30* A.M.*–2* P.M.

The people at Flaum run their business like a public trust, warning you off one item and urging another. The smoked salmon can compete with the yuppie appetizer shops on the Upper West Side of Manhattan at a fraction of the price.

Landau's Glatt Kosher Deli, *65 Lee Avenue (718-782-3700).*
Sunday–Thursday noon–10 P.M.; Friday noon–one hour before sundown.

This Jewish deli may never make a list of New York's ten best, but its thick-cut brisket sandwich on fresh seeded rye cannot be equaled for twice the price in Manhattan.

Dressed for Shabbos

Appearances are important to the Satmar. They have elaborate dress codes and dress taboos that distinguish them from society at large, and even other Hasidic groups. They know one another by their clothing and their place in the group's religious hierarchy. Women are required to wear high collars, long sleeves, low hems, and heavy-gauge stockings. The men wear a wide velvety brimmed hat similar to a Homburg and dark suits and kaftans with a special arrangement of the buttons. Woolen and linen fibers cannot be mixed in any garment. The women wear wigs or turbans on their heads and the men have full beards and side curls.

Waldman's Dry Goods, *156 Lee Avenue (718-522-2003). Sunday–Thursday 10:30 A.M.—6:30 P.M.; Friday 10:30 A.M.–2 P.M.*

Women shop here for turbans, snoods, blouses, and aprons. White is the color of choice for these simple Satmar fashions in linen and organza. Many are imported and embroidered in Europe.

Barbisio & Cellini, *185 Hewes Street at the corner of Lee Avenue (718-782-0700). Sunday–Thursday 10:30 A.M.–6:30 P.M.; Friday 10:30 A.M.–2 P.M.*

The very expensive headgear worn by the Satmar Hasids comes from a manufacturer in Italy. The correct models are on display in this curious shop.

The Festival of Simchas Torah

Satmar has its schools and synagogues on Bedford Street; it is the center of the community's spiritual existence. On joyous Simchas Torah the holy scrolls of Torah are celebrated as the cycle of the Torah readings begins all over again. Bedford Street is closed off on Simchas Torah night and there is a *Hakafos* (a religious procession). All night long the Satmar dance and chant and clap and sway, transported by the wonder of it all.

Simchas Torah usually takes place in October but it is a movable feast. For exact times contact the synagogue.

Brighton Beach

Directions: Subway D to Ocean Parkway/Brighton Beach Avenue.

Brighton Beach in the seventeenth century was just a scrubby section of sand on *Konijn Eisland* (Rabitt Island) with more long-eared rodents than human inhabitants. In the early part of the nineteenth century it was a popular destination for paddle steamers from Manhattan carrying day-trippers out for the sea, the sun, and a picnic. In the 1870s John Y. McKane, a Brooklyn political boss, made some land grants that included Brooklyn's Brighton Beach and it began to be developed as a resort.

A decade later Brighton Beach had a race track, a hotel, and a music hall that attracted big spenders like "Diamond Jim" Brady. It was the Atlantic City of its day, with the glamour and the gamblers but also the prostitution and crime. The resort went respectable in 1909 when racing was banned. The new summer residents were Eastern European Jewish immigrants who stayed in baseboard bungalows.

When the subway expanded to Coney Island in 1920 the summer renters became full-time residents. Suddenly there were thirty six-story apartment houses where there once was sand. There were many synagogues, some with *mikvahs* (ritual baths), and Jewish social and charitable organizations. During the depression and war years, this religious and politically conscious Jewish neighborhood was overcrowded.

After World War II Jewish refugees from the Holocaust settled in Brighton Beach. Older Jews from Brownsville and Williamsburg came to the community in the 1960s and early 1970s, refugees from crime and decay. But Brighton Beach was still aging and moving south for retirement. There was an epidemic of housing vacancies, some of which were filled by unsupervised mental patients. The neighborhood was poised on the edge of decline when emigrants from the Soviet Union saved the day.

These Soviet Jews were part of a protest movement that started in the 1960s and mushroomed after the Israeli Six Day War. They were tired of the restrictions and discrimination that Jews faced in the USSR and they wanted to reassert their own Jewish identities. They risked everything to apply for emigration to Israel. The Jews of Silence became Refusniks.

In 1976 the Hebrew Immigration Aid Society (HIAS) began channeling some of the Soviet emigrants into America. These later refugees were not the committed Zionists of the first waves of Soviet emigration. They were refugees of opportunity who resented the Jewish quotas in the universities and the shortages of food, clothing, and shelter. The majority of these emigrant families were from the seaside city of Odessa, and Brighton Beach had the charm of the familiar, with a long boardwalk and three miles of beach.

Brighton Beach also had cheap and spacious apartments and plenty of commercial vacancies for aspiring Russian entrepreneurs. The Soviet emigres went about remaking the neighborhood in their own image, with Russian-style stores and signs using Cyrillic letters, and the streets came back to life. Most immigrants thrived in the freer, make-your-own-choices environment. While some engineers, doctors, and lawyers wound up driving cabs, there were Odessa cab drivers who became business successes.

The streets of Brighton Beach have lost the old Jewish neighborhood calm. There is a youthful volatility that is pure Russian. The Russian conversation is excited and the pedestrian traffic is impatient. Younger men and women of the newest immigration outwardly enjoy the materialism of the West with smart clothes and fashionable hairdos. Their unsophisticated elders wear Russian suspenders and straw hats and brightly printed scarves and shapeless smocks. They are full-figured and have not discovered the American fad for dieting. When they smile in their sheepish way, bits of gold gleam from their mouths.

As Russia experiences the birth pangs of a new democratic and capitalist regime, the people of Brighton Beach watch intently. They are concerned for the fate of their co-religionists and also swept up by the cultural ferment caused by the new freedom. Newsstands, bookstores, and video shops are filled with Russia's new, experimental works of art and uninhibited samples of its mass popular culture. They are even doing business: importing, exporting, and consulting. This new Russian prosperity is evident on the streets of Brighton Beach.

Borscht Without Tears

Russian-Jewish cuisine à la Brighton Beach is not quite Russian—at least don't expect the "Russian Tea Room"—nor is it brisket and chicken-fat Jewish. The food is southern Ukraine, a hybrid of the cuisines of Mother Russia and the Central Asian Steppe, maybe kosher but not kosher style.

The local cuisine, like Brighton Beach itself, is short on subtlety and very obvious—heavy on the onions, garlic, dill, and lemon juice. The food is to be flat-out enjoyed, not mulled over and appreciated. And drink, preferably chilled vodka with orange peel or buffalo grass, is the necessary complement for this Russian-Jewish eating experience. Brighton Beach Avenue is where most of the good eating starts.

Primorski, *282 Brighton Beach Avenue (718-891-3111). Daily 11 A.M.–2 A.M.*

Primorski cooks with a touch of the Caucauses of Soviet Georgia. Circassian chicken in walnut sauce is served Georgian style as a main course. The *shashlik* (skewered lamb) is moist and tender and the *soylanka* (lamb stew) has the delightful tartness of Central Asia. There is a very reasonable three-course dinner.

Cafe Cappuccino, *290 Brighton Beach Avenue (718-646-6297). Monday–Friday 10 A.M.–8 P.M.*

Despite its name, Cappuccino serves more tea—Russian style in a glass—than coffee. It has ceiling fans for atmosphere and three TV monitors (attached to the ceiling) showing made-in-Russia rock videos. On the tables under the plastic covers, there are ads for local capitalist enterprises from beauticians to travel agents. Russians and others in the neighborhood come here for the prize-winning blinis.

Kavkaz, *405 Brighton Beach Avenue (718-891-5400). Daily 11 A.M.–midnight.*

Kavkaz is glitter on the ceiling, more mirrors than a locker room, and an open kitchen. Still the food is above average and sometimes original. Lamb chops on a skewer are a real improvement over ordinary *shashlik*. The hot borscht is perked up with bits of beef and vegetables. Stolichnaya vodka comes in carafes.

Mrs. Stahl's Delicious Knishes, *1001 Brighton Beach Avenue (718-648-0210). Daily 8 A.M.–6:45 P.M. Manhattan branch on 146 West 72nd Street (212-580-7019). Monday–Friday 8 A.M.–9 P.M.; Saturday and Sunday 10 A.M.–9 P.M.*

The knishes are even better than Yonnah Schimmel's, with tasty and unusual fillings like sweet potato and spinach in a pastry crust.

The Balalaika Plays On

When the Jews of Brighton Beach celebrate, which is practically every weekend, they celebrate Russian style. The music is fast dance or slow sad, the vodka toasts are nonstop, and the eating is total excess. Nobody is taking a cholesterol count or counting the drinks or even noticing how loud the music is playing. While people are enjoying the pleasures of Mother Russia, they are forgetting themselves.

When Russian-Jewish night clubs first opened in Brighton Beach, the people dressed like caricatures of Las Vegas chic, and the clubs themselves had crystal chandeliers and cupid fountains. The balalaikas were electric guitars and the sounds were Russian, Yiddish, and American disco. Though the dance floor was hardly the size of the Rainbow Room, spontaneity ruled and at the right moment everyone got up, formed a circle or threw arms over one another's shoulders, and whirled around the floor till the room started listing.

As Russian Jews entered the American middle and upper-middle class the decor tended to tone down and the dancing wasn't as passionate as it used to be. A lot of the Russians dressed for success rather than *Guys and Dolls*. Still, all-Russian affairs retained an openness and warmth that was truly exhilarating. At the end of an evening, when the lights dimmed and the band played Brighton Beach's unofficial anthem "Oy Odess," there was a true physical sense of closeness.

Since the change from the Union of Soviet Socialist Republics to capitalist Russia, the climate of Brighton Beach is less staid, culturally puritanical, and peasant earthy. Russian rock and rap and counterculture chic are all the rage. The family-style catering hall evening is out and is being replaced by a sophisticated and self-consciously decadent night club scene. One new club—with a touch of true gallows humor—is called Seberny (Siberia) and welcomes customers to the Gulag!

Odessa, *1113 Brighton Beach Avenue (718-332-3223). Daily 8 P.M.–until you can't dance anymore.*

The appointments are streamlined and modern and the dancing is more couples than circles but Brighton Beach obviously approves of the changes, since you still have to wait a month for a reservation. There is one charge for all you can eat and a bottle of vodka for a party of four. The Caucasian chicken, chicken Kiev, and shish kebab just keeps on coming and you haven't even put a dent in the chilled Stolichnaya.

Cafe Arbat, *306 Brighton Beach (718-332-5050). Daily 11 A.M.– 2 A.M.*

The cafe attracts the flash overnight money to its idea of class: forest-green walls and phony impressionist paintings. The chanteuses and accordion players are properly melancholy in that time-honored Russian fashion. The food is lavish, whether it's a capitalist filet mignon or a peasant *vereniki* with potatoes and cheese.

The National, *273 Brighton Beach Avenue (718-646-1225). Friday–Sunday 8:30 P.M.–3 A.M.*

The National is as big as a wedding hall and it gets a lot of the Brighton Beach wedding parties. It also gets most of the rubberneckers from Manhattan. The buffet starts slowly with pickled mushrooms and tongue and works its way through the *pirogen* (small turnovers) and Caucasian chicken to a grand kebab climax. The band is relentless, with more special effects than a Spielberg movie, and the dancers hardly ever sit down.

Rasputin, *2670 Coney Island Avenue (718-332-8111). Daily 2 P.M.–midnight.*

Named after a infamous character in Russian history and a famous emigre club in Paris, Rasputin tries to be Russian wild with a French accent. The entertainment is early Follies Bergere and the French/Russian menu is gourmet and expensive. Hold on to your wallets!

From Kvas to Kaviar

Brighton Beach Avenue's food shops are at a fever pitch on weekends. Russian Jews put the same energy into shopping that they put into having a party. The broad-shouldered *babushkas* (grandmothers) are terrors at the food counters as they maneuver for first place. Though most of the clerks in the stores speak only Russian, it doesn't matter since no one can hear anyone anyway. The big food markets have a range of Russian and Eastern European products that impresses; well worth the crowds.

The Southern Deli, *239 Brighton Beach Avenue (718-891-6569). Daily 8 A.M.–9 P.M.*

The Southern (as in the Ukraine) Deli is a modern, immaculate, split-level supermarket with the best southern Russian salads in Brighton Beach. The first floor is devoted to a vast selection of smoked fish, smoked meats, salads, and pickled appetizers, while the second floor has cakes and breads galore.

M & I International Foods, *249 Brighton Beach Avenue (718-615-1011). Daily 8 A.M.–9 P.M.*

M & I International Food is Brighton Beach's answer to Dean & De Luca. But instead of having shelves of extra-virgin olive oil and balsamic vinegar, it has miles of garlicky Russian sausage and bottle after bottle of sour pickles. M & I needs two floors and an army of thick-skinned clerks to sell all its prepared foods, such as cold-smoked fish, fresh produce, sweets and cakes, net bags of garlic, and caviar.

Mos Deli, *411 Brighton Beach Avenue (718-769-2466). Tuesday– Sunday 8* A.M.*–8* P.M.

In front they sell *kvas* from the barrel, the mildly alcoholic drink of choice for peasants in Dostoevsky novels. It should be avoided, but the cold-smoked chubb (herring) is something special, and so are the pickled vegetables.

Sea Lane Bakery, *615 Brighton Beach Avenue (718-934-8877). Daily 6* A.M.*–9* P.M.

The bakery sells Russian-style cakes and pastries—stuffed and sticky with cherries, cheese, and poppy seeds—from a table in front of the store. Whether it's cookies the size of saucers or butter cream cakes, the goods tend to be slightly heavy and very sweet.

The Golden Key (*Zolotoy Kluchnik*), *1067 Brighton Beach Avenue (718-743-5841). Daily 8* A.M.*–9* P.M.

The Golden Key is a daily no-holds-barred crowd scene with Russian shoppers vying for the bargains. There is a bakery and they sell smoked fish, sausages, and salads. It has a wide range of discounted canned and bottled food products, mostly from former Iron Curtain countries. Their specialty is Russian-style chocolate and sweets.

Brighton Beach Culture

The Black Sea Bookstore, *3175 Coney Island Avenue (718-769- 2878). Daily 11* A.M.*–6* P.M.

The young woman at the front desk is either reading a book or matching wits with the local intelligentsia, all of course in Russian. The Russian readers thumb through Russian books from Paris and Moscow like the place is a library. They have the latest cassettes of Russian rock groups and the most avant-garde literary magazines. As an added service to its customers, the bookstore takes ads for the popular New York Russian newspaper, *Novoye Slovo*.

Aleppo in Flatbush

Directions: Subway F to Kings Highway/McDonald Avenue.

The El station at McDonald Avenue and Kings Highway divides a modest mainstream Italian neighborhood from one of Brooklyn's most fascinating Jewish quarters. It is Oriental Jewish territory, comprised of old-guard Syrian families and Israeli newcomers.

The Brooklyn Jewish Levant is in the southern section of Flatbush, originally called Midwout by the Dutch and anglicized to Midwood. In the seventeenth century it remained a Dutch-speaking enclave even after the British began to rule. For fifty years after the American Revolution the coat or arms of King George II hung in the town hall.

In 1894 Midwood became a part or Brooklyn and by the time the subway linked it to Manhattan in 1920, Horatio Alger ethnics occupied its sturdy brick buildings. It became the preserve of Syrian Jews in the 1940s.

The area's Syrian Jews are proud of their noble pedigree, tracing their ancestors back to the Babylonian captivity and the destruction of the Temple in 586 b.c. They are mainly of the exclusive Jewish clan of Aleppo (H'alab), the ancestral city of Abraham.

For centuries they were intermediaries between the East and the West on the caravan routes to the Orient. Their peaceful and prosperous world came crashing down amid the conflicts and political changes of the Ottoman Empire. This ancient people of the East were forced to leave Syria for the Lower East Side.

The America of streetcars and sweatshops and tenements was a shock. They were outsiders in this alien city and had nothing in common with their Eastern European Jewish neighbors. They banded together in Sephardic boardinghouses, making the most of their limited resources.

Eventually the community managed to make its way to Williamsburg, where scattered Sephardim were reunited with their families. In the 1920s and 1930s the Syrian-Jewish community settled in Bensonhurst. They built a synagogue and a religious school and opened a dozen Oriental food stores on 20th Avenue. By the 1940s the upwardly mobile Syrian Jews had discovered the new promised land in the area of Midwood in Flatbush.

The Syrian Jews have not been spoiled by success. While making money in imports and exports, especially electronics and clothing, they have not deserted their neighborhood or broken the continuity of their centuries-old community. They are a rarity, a Jewish community without identifiable clothing or physical attributes that has maintained its customs and traditions.

Brooklyn Jewish Arabs have reached out to help the surviving Jewish communities of Aleppo and Damascus. After the creation of the State of

Israel, Syrian Jews who were under threat were aided by Aleppo-in-Brooklyn, and this Syrian-Jewish remnant was able to escape or bribe their way to safety. These refugees—and later Oriental arrivals—have injected new life into the Midwood community.

Aleppo in Flatbush looks substantial—large landmark one- and two-family brick houses, tall hedges, and broad shade trees. It extends from Avenue I to Avenue Y, intersected by Ocean Parkway. It is comfortably suburban, a place for close Sephardic families to stroll along tree-lined streets "to temple." There are houses of worship, community centers, and religious schools representing the Syrian-Jewish communities of Aleppo, Damascus, Egypt, and Lebanon.

Today, the Syrian Jews of Brooklyn are being joined by the latest Jewish immigrants from the Mideast. These new arrivals are from Israel and represent both Syrian or other Arab Jews of Sephardic descent and German and Eastern European Jews of Ashkenazi origin.

Israeli emigrants, or *Yoridim,* are sometimes considered to be turncoats by the people they left behind. Still, they continue to come in large numbers, creating long lines for visas in front of the American Embassy in Tel Aviv.

The numbers of Israelis entering New York and the Midwood neighborhood increased after the Yom Kippur War in 1973. They were looking for economic and employment opportunities and for peace. They represent all layers of Israeli society from manual laborers to big business.

Midwood's *Yoridim* say "they will always be Israelis," and the Kings Highway neighborhood displays a direct and matter-of-fact Israeli character and culture. In Midwood Hebrew is sometimes the spoken language, but it is also clear that these Israelis are opening up businesses and putting down roots.

Jewish Near-East Eating

The Midwood Levant is easy to recognize, with signs in Hebrew and Arabic and the aroma of Eastern spices and Israeli *felafel* in the air. The restaurants and food are more blunt Israeli than subtle Sephardic. The Mideastern *meze* (appetizers) like *baba ghanouj* and *hommus* are blander with less lemon and garlic, and the meat dishes like the lamb with okra and the *kebbe* (ground lamb with pinenuts) do not have the cinnamon and rose water delicacy. While the Oriental Jews have adopted a more low-key American style, the vibrant Israelis retain their unwavering directness and dry humor. The "People of the Book" are nonstop talkers, and restaurants and snack shops are scenes of uninhibited Hebrew conversation.

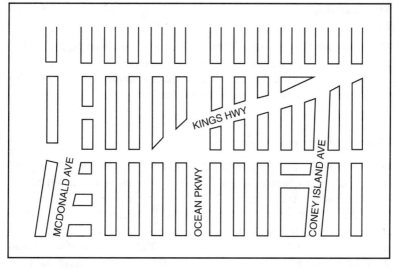

Kings Highway

In recent years restaurants have become more cosmopolitan, mirroring the tastes of a maturing community. There is more emphasis on ambience and service, and though the food may never be gourmet, more attention is paid to preparation. Kings Highway's new Jewish restaurants put their own spin on other ethnic cuisines and polish up their own Mideastern and Israeli cooking.

David's, *539 Kings Highway (718-998-8600). Sunday–Thursday 11 A.M.–11:30 P.M.; Friday 11 A.M.–3:30 P.M.*

The restaurant is small, neat, and functional with an Israeli-style salad bar that includes pickled veggies and sauerkraut. Food is the thing here and it is Middle Eastern and exotic. David is versatile and cooks up delicious Yemenite breads like *melawach* and *jachun,* a spicy Syrian sausage called *sartichitcha,* and the savory Egyptian national dish, *foul medammes.*

McDaniels, *555 Kings Highway (718-627-9668). Sunday–Thursday 10 A.M.–10 P.M.; Friday 10 A.M.–5 P.M.; Saturday 7:30 P.M–11 P.M.*

McDaniels is the kosher McDonald's of Kings Highway. The recent Sephardic arrivals who opened McDaniels add Oriental spice to their fast food. They serve pizza that could pass for *lamajhan* (flatbread with minced meat) and Middle Eastern *bourek* (cheese pie) under the name calzone.

Mon Jardin, *811 Kings Highway (718-339-9733). Daily 11 A.M.–11 P.M.*

This is a small bright dairy restaurant with an artificial hanging Mon Jardin. The red snapper and tuna steaks are prepared with French style, and there is a good selection of Italian pastas and sauces, including a dairy bolognese made with eggplant and feta cheese.

Dates and Spices

On King's Highway between 4th Street and 6th Street there are a host of stores catering to Sephardic and Israeli Jewish tastes which sell bulgar (cracked wheat), Arab yogurt called *leban,* and produce like eggplant and artichokes. The stores have not put on the American gloss; they have a homey look with handwritten signs, uncategorizable shelves, and improvised fixtures. On Avenue M and Avenue U there are assimilated Syrian small businesses from butchers to jewelers that are indistinguishable from American shops.

Kosher Korner, *492 Kings Highway (718-645-2466). Sunday–Thursday 8 A.M.–8 P.M.; Friday 8 A.M.–6:30 P.M.*

The Kosher Korner is a Middle Eastern supermarket. It has everything the atmospheric Arab-Jewish groceries have up the street plus convenient self-service shopping. In the back there is fresh-ground Turkish roast coffee and in the front a comprehensive assortment of dried fruits, grains, and nuts. Syrian foods have joined the twentieth century with frozen *bourek* and *lamajhan.*

Mansoura Pastry, *515 Kings Highway (718-645-7977). Sunday–Thursday 9 A.M.–6 P.M.; Friday 9 A.M.–5 P.M.*

The pastry from *baklawa* to the *knifeh* is Arabic Aleppo. There are Arabic flatbreads to be complemented by Mansoura's full line of *mezes,* which are prepared fresh and are the best in the neighborhood. The courteous owner looks Levantine but there is Brooklyn in his voice.

Beirut Makolate, *515 Kings Highway (718-645-2466). Sunday–Thursday 7:30 A.M.–8 P.M.; Friday 7:30 A.M.–6 P.M.*

Beirut's venerable Jewish community was a casualty of factional strife in Lebanon. Besides shelves of canned goods from Israel and local Arab wholesalers, zip-lock bags of spices, dried fruit, seeds, and nuts, and open containers of olives and pickled vegetables, they have filled the frozen-food case with Beirut culinary classics.

Rafi, *581 Kings Highway (718-998-8870). Sunday–Thursday 8:15 A.M.–8 P.M.; Friday 8:15 A.M–3 P.M.*

Rafi is an Arab-Jewish grocery with a special relationship to Egypt. It sells the okra, broad beans, lentils, and bulgar so essential to the Egyptian table, along with canned versions of national dishes like *foul meddames* and *melankhia,* made with beans and greens. There are also seeds, aromatic spices, pitas, olives, pickled spices, and preserved fruit arranged in no particular order.

The Midwood Legacy

The spiritual traditions of the Middle Eastern Jews predate the Diaspora and the destruction of the Temple in Jerusalem. Some of them are preserved in a small but precious store on Kings Highway.

Sisu, *632 Kings Highway (718-645-8185). Sunday–Thursday 10 A.M.–7 P.M.; Friday 10 A.M.–3 P.M.*

Sisu is the old and new curio shop for Sephardic Judaica, the legacy of Jewish Spain transformed by contact with Arab and Islamic cultures. The store is filled ceiling to floor with ritual objects, prayer books, and Jewish artifacts.

The Greeks

The Greeks came to the New World with Columbus, but they didn't begin their mass migration to New York City until the famines and political upheavals of the last part of the nineteenth century. The Greeks became an integral part of New York without discarding their cultural identity. They built individual businesses and created the city's bustling flower market. In times of crisis, they welcomed their fellow Greeks from the Islands, the mainland, and most recently from partitioned Cyprus. On the streets of Astoria, their Little Athens, Greek is spoken and Greek traditions come alive.

History

New York's first Greek consul general, John Botassi, claimed Columbus was a Byzantine nobleman named Dispatsos. Although this was never substantiated, there is documentation that at least one sailor in Columbus's crew, John Griego, was Greek. The consul general, when not creating history or moonlighting as the representative for the Ralli Brothers Import and Export Company, did his best to discourage fellow countrymen from settling in already overcrowded New York in the early part of the nineteenth century.

Despite official warnings, Chriastos Tsakonas came to New York in 1873. Convinced that New York was the land of opportunity, he went back to Greece two years later with the purpose of bringing out five compatriots. For his efforts this first Greek immigrant to New York has been called the "Columbus of Sparta" in local annals.

But Greek immigration to New York and the whole United States grew slowly, despite the pressure in Greece of an increasing population dependent on a relatively small amount of cultivatable land. Immigration finally took off when Greek agriculture was devastated by the decline of its chief cash crop, the humble currant. In twenty years one-fifth to one-quarter of the Greek labor force emigrated. This large-scale flight began in Sparta and swept through neighboring Arcadia and the whole Peloponnese before becoming a mass movement in central Greece, Crete, and the islands.

Fighting in the Balkans and the revolutionary activity in the Ottoman Empire spurred Greek-speaking populations in Constantinople and Anatolia to follow. Greek emigration was also encouraged by the exertions of enterprising Greek steamship agents who canvassed customers from Alexandria to Constantinople.

The majority of Greek arrivals to America, who came from rural areas, gravitated to the cities. They preferred the urban feeling of being close to people. The farms in America were too spread out from one another for the gregarious Greeks. Most of these Greek immigrants were male—ninety-five percent were men in the peak years between 1899 and 1910—but they quickly returned to bring back other members of their family and get married. The first Greek New Yorkers settled in the south Bronx between 14th and 15th Streets; later they went to live in lower Manhattan, Hell's Kitchen, and Washington Heights.

The earliest generation of Greek New Yorkers came as *padrone* labor; they were indentured for an indefinite period, usually three or four months, to a boss from the old country who provided the passage and show money to meet immigration requirements. The boss, with his knowledge of English and American ways, had a good deal of control over the new immigrant. In Greece, land was mortgaged as a guarantee that the new New Yorker would not renege on this debt. There were many abuses under this system, with some very young or very naive immigrants working years for a *padrone* for practically nothing.

Greeks fresh off the boat usually found work as dishwashers, flower sellers, or bootblacks. Dishwashing was dirty, low-paying, backbreaking work, but it was the first rung on the ladder to owning your own restaurant. In New York Greek involvement in the restaurant business led to the saying, "If two Greeks meet, they start a restaurant." Greeks were also active in the wholesale and retail flower business, and the new immigrant often wound up peddling flowers on the street that were not good enough to be sold in stores. Shining shoes was considered by Greeks to be demeaning work even if the owner of the shoe stand was a fellow countryman, and it was very hard work with a fifteen-hour day.

In 1894 the first daily newspaper in Greek, the *Atlantis,* was started in New York by Solon Vlastos. Although it defended the interests of the Greek-American workingman and fought the abuses of the *padrone* system, it was Royalist and conservative in its outlook toward Greek national politics. *Alantis* didn't have any competition until 1915, when Demetrios Callimachos launched *Ethnikos Kiryx* (National Herald), a newspaper that was anti-Royalist and which supported the pan-Hellenic policies of the Greek Republic leader, Venizelos. Now the political debates that raged in New York's *kafeneia* (Greek coffee houses) were out on the newsstands.

The rivalry between the Royalists and the Republicans reflected regional differences between Greeks, which eventually split the local community. There were separate social organizations and even separate churches representing the two points of view. World War I made this separation even more volatile, with Venizelos backing the Allies and King Constantine calling for neutrality.

Ultimately Greek Americans laid aside past political affiliations to pull together for their adopted country. The Greek community sold over ten million dollars in U.S. War Bonds and over sixty thousand Greeks served in the American army in World War I. Greek New Yorkers faced another sort of political problem after the war, resulting from a wave of antiforeign sentiment. Greek Americans were the victims of unprovoked attacks and calculated business boycotts. In 1921 the Johnson Act was passed, which reduced Greek immigration to one hundred a year.

Greeks responded to this bigotry by strengthening both their American and Greek identities. They formed the American Hellenic Educational Progressive Association (AHEPA) in New York in 1922. Its purpose was to promote Americanization, English language education, and American values. The American Progressive Association (APA), which was established in New York the next year, took the opposite tack, preserving the Greek language and Greek customs among first- and second-generation Greek Americans.

Both of these approaches proved successful. Greek New Yorkers made the leap from blue collar to white collar in one generation. Greeks now have one of the highest percentages of professionals, which includes doctors, lawyers, and engineers, of any immigrant group, and while they have acquired affluence and social prestige, they have kept their ties with their ethnic past. In New York alone there are sixty associations dedicated to the traditions of particular Greek villages, islands, or regions. New York's eleven Greek day schools make sure that the special Greek identity continues into the future.

In 1965 a new immigration act was passed, altering the restrictive ethnic quotas. At the forefront of the movement to change the old law were old-line Greek organizations like AHEPA and APA, Greek-American politicians like Paul Sarbanes and John Brademas, and successful businessmen like Tom Pappas and Spyros Skouras. The new law ushered in a new wave of Greek immigration, which is still continuing. The new immigrants, whether Athenian professionals or dispossessed Cypriots, have revitalized New York's established Greek community. It has created a new sense of national pride in second- and third-generation Greek New Yorkers.

In 1974 conflicts in Cyprus and the de facto partition of the island led to a Greek Cypriot exodus. One of their prime destinations was New York. Many left with just the clothes on their backs and required special social services. Groups like the Hellenic American Neighborhood Action Committee were formed to cope with the immigrants' problems. They were instrumental in implementing bilingual education programs and speeding up the delivery of conventional aid and supplementary benefits. They acted as a liaison between the non–English-speaking immigrants and the city government.

In the nineties the tide of Greek immigration continues. Economic hardship and a lack of vocational and professional opportunities led to a new generation of Greeks crossing the sea to New York. They come from half-empty villages in the North and South, and from overcrowded Athens. They are the dispossessed of Cyprus and the recently liberated Greek minority population of Albania. Like the archetypal Homeric Greek Ulysses, most intend to return to their own Ithaca which gave them life.

Astoria—Little Athens

Directions: Subway N to Ditmars Boulevard.

Astoria is Old World Greece in Queens. Called Little Athens, it is across the East River from Manhattan and north of Long Island City. The faces are Mediterranean, the gestures are expansive, and the accents are rapid-fire Greek. The aroma of dark Greek coffee drifts through the streets along with the wail of tape-deck *bouzouki*. Young couples cafe-sit over rich Greek pastry, and family groups promenade till after midnight. In a night club the size of a small stadium members of the Association of Samos get up to do the *zeibekiko.*

These fifteen hundred acres in northeast Queens weren't always an ethnic enclave. When William Hallett first took title in 1654, it was a beech forest on a riverbank without even a Native American. Governor Peter Stuyvesant didn't need much persuading to sign the land over. For the next 175 years it remained undeveloped, a sleepy summer resort for rich Manhattanites, named Hallett's Cove in honor of its founder.

In 1839 New York's richest man, John Jacob Astor, overpowered local opposition to have Hallett's Cove incorporated as a town under his own name, Astoria. He went on to transform it into a prosperous ferry port doing a thriving trade with Manhattan. In no time the picturesque forest became lumber and the fragile summer houses substantial mansions. Remnants of its opulent past still remain on 27th Avenue. The frame of the Greek revival Remsen House stands on 90-26 27th Avenue, while across the street at 90-29 27th Avenue is Renaissance revival Wayt House.

By the turn of the century the area had lost its cachet and Italian and Irish immigrant families from Little Italy and Hell's Kitchen began to move in. With its rustic village green and attractive detached houses, it was a real contrast to the tenements and teeming streets of Manhattan. In 1927 the first Greek families came to live in Astoria. They declared their intentions to stay and build a community by laying the foundation for the Greek Orthodox Church, St. Demetrios. This magnificent domed Byzantine edifice is still standing on 31st Street and boasts the largest Greek Orthodox congregation outside of Greece.

After World War II returning veterans from Astoria were looking for a change and bypassed the old neighborhood to move further out into Queens and east to rural Long Island. Astoria seemed secondhand and faded. Local industries were leaving and stores stayed vacant. The old ethnic communities had lost their verve.

Astoria was a working-class area on its way to becoming a slum, but in 1965 new life was breathed into the neighborhood with the passage of an amended immigration act that enabled thousands of Greek immigrants to enter the country. The new Greeks were drawn to Astoria by the already existing Greek community and by its relatively suburban atmosphere—at least it was free of high-rises. In a flurry of activity, old buildings were renovated and new buildings were constructed. New businesses catering to the special needs of the community opened up one after another.

The new immigrants were primarily professionals from Athens whose skills were needed in the United States; the relatives of the old immigrants from the villages in the Peloponnese, central Greece, and the islands, and war refugees from Cyprus. Whether the arrivals were middle class and modern, working class and traditional, or Cypriots speaking a strange dialect, they were welcomed with open arms by Astoria's Greeks.

Little Athens is always growing, but at the present time its borders are Ditmars Boulevard to the north, Broadway to the south, 31st Street to the west, and Steinway Street to the east. The Greek population within this rectangle is estimated at eighty thousand. It also contains eleven Greek Orthodox churches, countless two-family brick houses, and an assortment of restaurants, *tavernas,* Greek night clubs, coffee houses, and exotic groceries.

Astoria's Times Square and crossroads is the intersection of Ditmars Boulevard and 31st Street, steps away from the Ditmars Boulevard subway stop, twenty minutes from Manhattan. To get a feel for Little Athens, promenade 31st Street, which is just under the elevated train track. Afterwards, walk up Ditmars Boulevard left of the subway station to Steinway Street and follow 23rd Avenue, making a complete rectangle by turning back up to 31st Street.

Place Marks of Astoria

The Greeks have a strong and enduring Orthodox Christian faith. The New Testament was written in Greek, and many of the first converts were made in Greece. Their form of worship and ritual is different from Western churches, with important parts of the ceremony occurring behind the altar screen. The icon is a figurative expression of their belief, and the faithful pray to icons in times of sickness and trouble. Greek Orthodox churches are an essential element in the life of the community.

St. Demetrios Church, *31st Street and 31st Drive (718-728-1712).*

St. Demetrios is the Greek Orthodox cathedral and houses the largest congregation outside of Athens. The building is impressive, with a large dome toward the back and narrow stained-glass windows on each side. Inside, just above an intricate altar screen in the center of the dome, there is a powerful image of Christ as the severe Pantocrator surrounded by his apostles. Striking icon-like images adorn the church. Near the door there are actual icons on stands where the worshipers kneel and pray.

St. Irene of Chrysovalantou, *36-07 23rd Avenue (718-626-6225).*

The outside of the twin-towered church is white stucco, covered with a veneer of marble and adorned in places with the Greek double eagle. Inside is the ever-present odor of incense, and the whole interior is done in marble. Perhaps you will encounter a Greek Orthodox nun who will point out some of the church's treasures, from its massive chandelier to its ornate altar screen. Many of the priceless icons are encased in silver. During Desert Storm, one is supposed to have shed tears.

From Aeschylus to Theodorakis

CYPRECO, *23-50 27th Street (718-618-9696).*

Through education, research, and performances, the Cypriot Emigrant Cultural Organization endeavors to promote and preserve the Greek-Cypriot cultural heritage. It produces plays both in Greek and in English and sponsors "The Vraka," a Greek folk dance company.

Psitarias and *Tavernas*

The terms *restaurant* and *taverna* have virtually lost their meaning in Astoria and are used interchangeably. A *taverna* in Astoria is just as likely to be an expensive restaurant with music as a standard, reasonably priced eating place with barrel wine and simple village fare. The distinction in Astoria's restaurants are more about the owner or the cook's place of origin in Greece or Cyprus than words like *psitaria* (grill) and *taverna.*

Since Astoria's restaurants basically cater to a Greek population, the Greek food is unequaled in authenticity by restaurants found in other parts of the city. The food is basic and hearty, depending on olive oil, oregano, garlic, and lemon for it singular flavor. Lamb is the meat of choice, whether in a stew or mixed in a layered *moussaka* (the Greek lasagna) or stuffed with cheese Corfu style.

The Greeks are purists where meat is concerned and have a preference for grills, *souvlaki* on a spit, or *brizoli* (chops). The cheese of choice for the Greeks is sharp, pungent feta, which is enjoyed in *horiatiki* or village salad. The Cypriots like *haloumi,* which is often served fried as an appetizer, or *meze.* The *mezedakia* is a collection of small dishes like *taramosalata* (a spread of fish eggs), *tzatziki* (yogurt mixed with garlic and cucumber), *keftedes* (grilled meatballs), and delicacies like lamb brains. Drink always accompanies *meze,* whether wine or ouzo.

Eating out in Astoria is a social occasion. People take their time over food and the conversation is nonstop. Between courses parents and grandparents dandle children, and if there is music and the mood strikes, people get up and dance. Dining, as in Greece, starts late, around 9 P.M., and the restaurant closes when everyone finishes. To find out specific opening and closing times—which are always changing—call in advance.

Telly's Taverna, *28-13 23rd Avenue (718-728-9194).*

Telly's is white stucco walls with pictures of Greek resorts and a glassed-in kitchen. A real neighborhood place, people come to talk as well as eat and drink. Start with an Ouzo (anise-flavored liquor), grilled *oktopodi* (octopus), or *loukanika* (lamb sausage), and complete the meal with a salad and grilled porgies and a bottle of Demestica wine. Then sit back and watch the Greeks being their exuberant selves.

Elias Corner, *24-01 31st Street (718-932-1510).*

This corner has a shark on the wall for decor and fluorescent lighting for atmosphere. Don't ask for a menu, they don't have one. And it is very small. Still, the fish on display are uniformly clear eyed and supple, fresh as the fish in the fabled seafood restaurants of Pireaus. Try the red snapper but remember you pay by the weight.

Zygos Taverna, *22-55 31st Street (718-728-7070).*

Zygos entices almost at the door with a display of rich taverna food featuring lamb with *youvetsi* (small oval-shaped pasta), *moussaka,* and stuffed tomatoes. Walk further in and there's a whole lamb and coils of *kokoretsi* (tripe) rotating over a blazing fire. The open kitchen encourages hearty eating.

Dionysos Taverna, *22-73 31st Street (718-721-3007).*

You will really make the owner of Dionysos happy if you order the fish, preferably a red snapper, or the shrimp. Most things come grilled in this *psitaria.* The *calamari* (squid) is fried in good Greek olive oil and is fresh and delicious.

Roumeli Taverna, *33-04 Broadway (718-278-7533).*

Roumeli's is done up like an outdoor Greek *taverna* with links of lights and artificial vines concealing the white stucco walls. It draws convivial locals who are as interested in the art of conversation as in the traditional Greek dishes like *spanakopita* (spinach pie), *dolmades* (grape leaves), and fried *calamari.*

Uncle George's, *33-19 Broadway (718-626-0593).*

George's is an outsized, twenty-four-hour-a-day Greek diner that actually serves Greek food along with the roast suckling pig and barbecued chicken. The seating is family style at long tables, and you very well may wind up eating with someone else's Greek family. Their rabbit stews and spit-turned lamb are the real thing and very good.

Zacharoplasteia

A *zacharoplasteion* is a cafe cum pastry shop. The *zacharo,* in *zacharoplasteion* refers to sugar, and the pastries are extremely sweet. Two of the most popular, *baklava* (phyllo pastry filled with pistachios) and *loukamades* (a donut variation), are served swimming in honey. The *floghera* is rich with egg custard. The Greek version of espresso also comes *gliko* (very sweet), *metrio* (moderately sweet), and *sketo* (unsweetened). The *zacharoplasteion* is a place to make an art out of doing nothing. It's a place to talk and let the world go by.

Cafe Edelweiss, *31-29 Ditmars Boulevard (718-728-9568). Daily 9 A.M.–midnight or the last customer.*

Cafe Edelweiss is two stories high and modern, like something from fashionable Kolonaki in Athens. The crowd is very lively, sometimes noisy. During the summer it sometimes doesn't close until 4 A.M. Besides a full selection of Greek and French pastries, it has light snacks and the best Greek coffee in Astoria. The upstairs room, which includes a bar, sometimes has popular Greek singers in concert.

The Galaxy, *37-22 Ditmars Boulevard (718-721-1121). Daily 8 A.M.–2 A.M.*

The Galaxy is chrome and mirrors modern with traditional Greek *baklava* that tastes of honey and pistachio nuts. Even better, they serve giant *spanakopita* and *tyropita* (cheese pie) that are a meal and a half, and twice as good. The crowd is mostly Greek speaking and so is the young woman behind the counter.

Lefkos Pyrgos, *22-85 31st Street (718-932-4423). Daily 9 A.M.–midnight.*

Lefkos Pyrgos is called the White Castle for the famous tower in Salonica, the original home of a past owner. It's open and cheerful, adorned with Greek travel poster art. A big part of the clientele is Old World male. They hang out at the front tables. Lefkos Pyrgos is known in the Astoria community for its *koulourakia,* a kind of Christmas cookie.

Nights Out

The music is hypnotic. Combining the harmonies of bazouki, clarina, and violin against a field of insistent rhythm, slow or fast, mournful or happy, it makes a Greek dance. For Greeks it's *kefi,* that feeling of bubbling joy and high spirits that starts the feet moving. Greek dancing is as old as the pagan rites and is still alive in the night clubs of Astoria.

Greek dances are generally put in two categories: the *pedecto* is quick and involves jumping, hopping, and leaping; the *syrto* is slow and involves pulling and dragging steps. The dances are often done in groups, in lines, or in open circles. Three of the most popular are the *haspaiko, tsamiko,* and *syrtaki.* Both the *haspaiko,* the slow and moody butcher's dance, and the *tsamiko,* the whirling acrobatic handkerchief dance, require practice, but the light and bouncy *syrtaki* can be learned in minutes. In Astoria's nightspots they are all performed every evening, sometimes to the accompaniment of breaking plates.

Grecian Cave, *31-11 Broadway (718-545-7373). Monday–Saturday 10 P.M.–4 A.M.*

Grecian Cave has a pseudo–Las Vegas stage show with whey-faced belly dancers of indeterminate nationality. Many of the drinks come in tall glasses with ornamental umbrellas. The club seems to cater to bachelor parties and visiting fire fighters.

Taverna Vraka, *23-15 31st Street (718-721-3007). Wednesday–Monday 10 P.M.–4 A.M.*

For more than twenty years this Cypriot night club has been drawing New York's Greek notables. It's said that the late Aristotle Onassis came here to listen to the sad songs sung by Lambis Krokydas. John Nikas, former Governor Cuomo's assistant, drops in for the *sheftali* (a highly spiced lamb sausage). Even better are the special "Cypriot Delights" starter and the *arni kleftiko* (a Cypriot baked lamb dish). Every night there is Cypriot music and dancing, and the customers are a regular part of the floor show!

Stani, *290-21 23rd Avenue (718-728-4966). Daily 11 P.M.–4 A.M.*

Stani bills itself as the "family night club." It's a place where people bring the kids and the kids chase one another between the tables. Actually it is really a restaurant with a stage show that begins early. It tries hard to be a *taverna* and a club.

Greeks Bearing Gifts

One of the joys of Astoria is doing a walk-about Greek style. Stop in the stores, look in the old-fashioned barrels and bins. Sample some of the foods, try the Kalamata olives or the sharp *mizithra* cheese from Crete, the *bastirma* (the Greek version of salted beef), or the unusual sweet rose petals in syrup. The proprietors don't really care if you buy, but they do enjoy a lively conversation and love to ask questions. Meanwhile, outside there's a sidewalk show. The barest hint of sun brings the old men out with their folding chairs and newspapers to engage in the ancient Greek art of argument. Soon passersby are joining in and people are treating one another to coffee. It's a slice of Greek life without the village fountain and the plane tree.

Expect the unexpected in Astoria's stores. A fruit store has a full line of Greek cheeses and delicacies; a meat market has vegetables and fruit. Gift shops mix Greek daily newspapers with holy icons and country and western records. Shopping in Astoria is just another way of sightseeing.

Food Shops

Kiryakos Grocery, *29-29 23rd Avenue (718-545-3931). Monday–Saturday 8 A.M.–7:30 P.M.*

Kiryakos has the odd, hard-to-find essences necessary for Greek cookery like almond, roses, and tamarind. Its owner, Kiryakos Moutaphopoulos, is proud of his selection from dried beans and peas to the *gigantes* (giant lima beans). He claims that he has brought some of the spices from the spice market in Istanbul where he still has family.

A & B Trading, *29-08 23rd Avenue (718-728-7600). Daily 7 A.M.–9 P.M.*

Appearances are deceiving. A & B at first looks like your average fruit and vegetable store, but wander into the back and you will find metal trays of the best bought-in-bulk Greek feta. There is also an excellent selection of Greek hard cheeses, olives, and olive oils.

Angelo's Food Emporium, *31-27 Ditmars Boulevard (718-278-0705). Monday–Saturday 9 A.M.–9 P.M.*

The owner isn't Italian, he's Evangelous Barcus, and mostly everything in his food emporium is Greek. It is one of the places to go for the chewy Greek candy *loukoum* and nougat. It has barrels filled with feta and Cypriot sheep cheese. The olives are from Chios and Kalamata. Along with Greek food in cans like stuffed grape leaves and *gigantes,* he has freshly prepared Greek spinach pies, cheese pies, and rice pudding.

George's Kreopoleion, *23-35 31st Street (718-545-7524). Daily 7 A.M.–7 P.M.*

George is a true Greek. Who else would have real ivy trained on a trellis above his meat counter and a Greek flag behind? This butcher caters to Greek tastes with whole baby lambs and goats, sheep brains, and all the right cuts for *kokoretsi.*

Gift Shops

Corfu Center, *22-113 31st Street (718-728-7212). Daily 6 A.M.– midnight.*

The Corfu Center is more than a newsstand. In addition to the Greek porcelain, newspapers, and magazines there are tapes of Greek top-ten hits and better-than-average crafts from Corfu, including jewelry and knits.

Astron, *22-81 31st Street (718-932-7012). Monday–Saturday 9:30 A.M.–8 P.M.; Sunday noon–6 P.M.*

Astron must be doing something right; it has been in this precarious business for thirty-five years. The statues, Greek vases, and icons for the home are slightly sentimental but they appeal to Astoria. They also have the latest videos and tapes from the homeland.

Kentrikon Astorias, *31-12 23rd Avenue (718-721-9190). Monday–Saturday 10 A.M.–8:30 P.M.; Sunday noon–6 P.M.*

Kentrikon is a fancy gift shop specializing in the traditional Greek paraphernalia involved in weddings, christenings, and holidays. Unlike other ethnic shops, it stays away from mass-produced souvenirs in favor of authentic handicrafts like village embroidery. There are tapes of the latest *bouzouki* and video cassettes of small-budget Greek movies.

Celebrations

National Heritage Folklore Festival

During the second weekend in June, local Cypriots and their fellow Greeks gather at 27-09 Crescent Street, the Hellenic Cultural Center, for a celebration of their Cypriot identity, arts, and culture. There are theater pieces in Greek and English, poetry readings and composition, and dancing and singing. Cypriots also explore the recent history of their island, and the conflicts and divisions that have resulted in partition and displaced people.

Manhattan

The Greeks never had an exclusive ethnic colony in Manhattan. During the years of mass immigration between 1890 and 1910, numbers of Greeks set down stakes in the West Village near the Washington and Gansevoort Markets, the meat and produce center of the city. It was just the right location for a people who would become heavily involved in the food-service industry. This area, which was known as New York's Levant, also attracted an interesting mix of Egyptians, Turks, Syrians, and Armenians. The streets that lead down to the waterfront were a casbah of exotic spices and exotic dancers, where bargains were sealed over tiny cups of Turkish coffee. But it all disappeared before World War II, making way for the construction of the West Side Highway.

Gansevoort Street is still the southern border of the frenetic New York wholesale meat market, an area of narrow cobblestone streets, nineteenth-century buildings, and twentieth-century traffic. It's worth a sightsee and can be reached by subway (1, 2, or 3 train), getting out at West Houston Street and walking west.

Many Greeks preferred to settle further north, closer to the excitement and hurly-burly of midtown. They moved into an area straddling Chelsea and Hell's Kitchen between 26th Street and 47th Street and lived side by side with the neighborbood's large Irish population. They labored in the Eleventh Avenue slaughterhouses and the flower market spreading out from 27th Street. Gradually the industrious Greeks took control of New York's wholesale flower industry and, instead of hefting sides of beef, served it in their own restaurants. The Greeks left Manhattan tenements to live in the greener pastures of Queens, Long Island, and New Jersey, but they still make their livelihood in the borough's food and flower businesses.

Since the 1950s Greek Manhattan has gone upscale. A new breed of golden Greeks with names like Onassis, Niarchos, and Livanos took Manhattan by storm with their shipping millions. High spending and high profits, they are the 21 Club Greeks. Olympic Towers, the gaudy Onassis skyscraper and personal monument, epitomizes the lavish side of the city's Greek experience. Completed in 1974, in time to be christened but not occupied by Onassis, this fifty-one-story high rise, tinted like the tycoon's ever-present dark glasses, dominates the northeast corner of 51st Street and Fifth Avenue. It claims to be the first skyscraper in Manhattan to combine chic shopping, office space, and luxury apartments, and the first to have a waterfall, trees, and an open bar in its lobby.

The Flower Market

Since ancient times Greeks have had a special affinity for flowers. Pagan Greeks adorned themselves and their shrines with flowers and they were a staple of architectural decoration; the origin of flowers was the subject of classical myth. In present-day Greece flowers ornament city terraces and rural gardens and it's still a popular pastime to pick wildflowers on weekends. On May Day the Greeks exchange bouquets en masse and attach flowers to their car antennas.

It was natural for this nation of flower lovers to turn to the flower business when they came to New York. They got their start as street sellers, buying from the Long Island flower growers at the foot of East 34th Street, and in one generation had their own shops scattered throughout the city. Eventually, they cornered New York's wholesale flower market.

The wholesale flower market is an assortment of competing businesses between Broadway and Seventh Avenues, on and off 27th and 28th Streets. The area is awash with color from standard American varieties to wild tropical blooms. Giant plants and even trees fill the storefronts and sprawl across the sidewalk. At 7:30 A.M. it's total frenzy with a traffic jam of trucks and vans picking up and dropping off plants. Excitable proprietors, voices raised, bargain with retail florists, gesturing to big bundles of flowers. It is a genuine New York scene and the perfume of so many flowers even overwhelms the fabled Manhattan exhaust fumes. Ultimately things settle down for the afternoon retail business, with browsers buying bonsai trees, rubber plants, and even shrubs for roof-terrace gardens.

Everyone knows one another in the flower market. Along the streets there are spontaneous exchanges in Greek and a feeling of community. Many of the businesses in the area are fixtures, family owned and operated for decades. Bill's Flower Market, Mutual Cut Flowers, and the People's Flower Corp. have been going strong for decades, but things are starting to change. The Greek flower market founders are no longer the majority, but they still have a sense of continuity. Wholesalers like Peter Hadges of American Cut Flowers maintains, "My father Gus was here forty-seven years ago, and my son John will be here forty-seven years from now."

During the Dinkins administration, there was talk (and some negotiating) about moving the flower market to the hinterlands of the South Bronx in exchange for tax credits and grants galore. Greek wholesalers, despite the sweeteners, decided to opt for the Manhattan convenience and the Manhattan chaos.

Bill's Flower Market, *816 Sixth Avenue (212-889-8154). Monday–Saturday 7 A.M.–6:30 P.M.*

Here there's a full array of flowers at prices below most retail florists. Bill's also offers a fine selection of miniature rose plants and hybrid tea roses.

People's Flower Corp., *786 Sixth Avenue (212-686-6291). Monday–Saturday 7 A.M.–6:30 P.M.*

Peoples's makes up special odds-and-ends bouquets for the retail market. It's worth a look for its hot-house tropical plants.

Greeks have used their knowledge of flowers and creative powers to move into the high end of the florist trade, where every arrangement is a work of art.

Christatos & Koster, *201 East 64th Street at the corner of Third Avenue (212-838-0022). Monday–Friday 8 A.M.–6 P.M.; Saturday 8 A.M.–noon.*

Christatos caters to the carriage trade, providing flowers for New York society weddings and coming-out parties. His corporate accounts include more than one *Fortune* 500 client. Robert Christatos' flower arrangements belong in museums.

More Greek Tables

The Greeks, with their rural background, do not claim any native expertise in running restaurants, but the *kafeneion,* which serves snacks as well as coffee, was always a respected village institution where people met to transact personal business and deal with community problems. In the New York environment the *kafeneion* quickly lost its Greek exclusivity, and under the name of "coffee shop" became the New Yorker's favorite spot for eating on the run. Large portions of simple foods like goulash or hamburger "to stay or take away" are the main features.

Today, as in the past, the coffee shop is the Greek path to success. Beginning as dishwashers, busboys, waiters, and hot dog stand operators, through perseverance and hard work, many Greeks now own and manage their own restaurants. Currently, Greeks are the most important force in Manhattan's commercial food business, from street vendors to king-sized midtown luncheonettes.

The number of Greek-owned restaurants in Manhattan are too numerous to mention but a contingent specializes in Greek cuisine.

Periyali, *35 West 20th Street between Fifth and Sixth avenues (212-463-7890). Monday–Saturday noon–3 P.M., 6 P.M.–11 P.M.*

Most Greek restaurants in New York are variations on the humble *taverna.* Periayli is smart, swank, and expensive. The basically simple fare of the Greeks gets the royal treatment here. The fried calamari, which usually gets a squeeze of lemon, is served with vinaigrette over greens and the *meletzanasalata* (eggplant salad) comes with semolina. Interesting, but is it Greek?

Molfetas, *307 West 47th Street (212-840-9537). Monday–Saturday 6 P.M.–11:30 P.M.*

This is the oldest Greek restaurant in Manhattan and considered by many to be the best outside of Astoria. The lamb, whether grilled, minced, or in a stew, attracts Old World Greeks with food fantasies.

New Acropolis, *767 Eighth Avenue at the corner of 47th Street (212-581-2733). Daily 11 A.M.–11:30 P.M.*

New Acropolis gets the overflow from Molfetas. It has the look of a luncheonette straining to be a grown-up restaurant. The *baklava* and other pastries are the standouts on the menu.

Uncle Nick's, *402 West 51st Street off Ninth Avenue (212-245-7992). Monday–Friday 11:30 A.M.–11 P.M.; Saturday noon–11:30 P.M.; Sunday 2:30 P.M.–11 P.M.*

The owner, Antonios Manatakis, acts like a very caring uncle even if the customers are not celebrities like Teresa Stratas or Olympia Dukakis. The seafood is charcoal grilled, whether it is a whole red snapper or a swordfish kebab. Combined with a generous Greek salad with feta it is a perfect repast.

Avegerinos, *153 East 53rd Street, Citicorp Center, Plaza Level (212-688-8828). Monday–Saturday 11:30 A.M.–9:30 P.M.; Sunday noon–9:30 P.M.*

This is an airy restaurant with interior arches giving a feeling of al fresco dining. White walls wonderfully show off an attractive assortment of Greek crafts. The Greek specialties are blander, with less olive oil and herbs than the real thing, an Upper East Side version.

Estia, *308 East 86th Street (212-628-9100). Tuesday–Saturday 5 P.M.–11 P.M.*

From the days when it was almost an all-German enclave, Estia has been a familiar and friendly Greek presence on 86th Street. It has the typical white stucco Greek restaurant look and a menu that emphasizes kebabs. The music is exuberant and the waiters double as dancers.

Food Shops

Although the Greeks on the West Side of Manhattan are a thing of the past, the Greek flavor survives in some choice shops.

Poseidon, *629 Ninth Avenue near 44th Street (212-757-6173). Tuesday–Saturday 9 A.M.–7 P.M.; Sunday 10 A.M.–4 P.M.*

The premier Greek bakery in the city sells to the top restaurants as well as to the public. The bakers are masters of the savory *tiropita, spanakopita,* and *kreatopita* (meat pie), as well as honey-drenched *baklava.* On Greek Easter there are lines for the braided bread with a red egg on top called *Christopsomi.*

International Grocery, *529 Ninth Avenue (212-279-5514). Monday–Saturday 8 A.M.–6 P.M.*

This place has all the spices and herbs needed for Greek cooking. There are strings of red peppers and garlic and bundles of mint and oregano. Freshly made phyllo dough is available for Greek baking. Located near the Port Authority Bus Terminal, avoid browsing during the rush hours.

Celebrations

Greek Independence Day

Ever since the conquest of Constantinople in 1453 by the mighty Ottoman forces, the Greeks have longed for freedom. Some escaped to the mountains of the Mani or Rumeli and carried on a campaign of bandit raids, while others marked time in the employ of the Turks, waiting for the opportunity when they were strong enough to strike.

In 1821 Alexander Ypsilanti turned on his Turkish overlords and led an uprising among Greeks in several Ottoman provinces. Alarmed Turkish authorities sought reassurances of Greek loyalty and summoned the titular heads of the Greek community, the Greek Orthodox primates. Disregarding the summons, the Greek prelates gathered at the Monastery of St. Laura. On March 25, 1821, Archbishop Germanos of Patras blessed the banners of the Greek revolutionaries and proclaimed a free Greece.

In New York on March 25 a parade honors the heroic struggle of the Greek people to regain their freedom. The parade follows New York's most prestigious thoroughfare, Fifth Avenue from 59th Street to 49th Street. The crowds lining the streets are not as large as on St. Patrick's Day or Columbus Day, but there is a warmth and enthusiasm not easily equaled.

The parade marshal may be a George Stephanopoulous, Mike Dukakis, or any other Greek celebrity, but it's still a people's parade; Greeks feeling proud and wearing their colors. Blue and white, the colors of the Greek flag are everywhere. Blue and white bunting adorns lampposts and blue and white buttons say "Kiss Me I'm Greek." The not-very-precise drill teams wear blue and white and so do the Olympic Airlines flight attendants in open cars.

It's a time for fancy dress. Men and women in folk costumes pass in review, in black or brightly colored embroidery, an Evzone kilt or an ankle-length Anatolian dress. Some stop to improvise dance steps. Floats with the acronyms of organizations like the Sons of Pericles or the Daughters of Penelope carry members in classical wardrobes. With unforced smiles they throw flowers to the onlookers. There are also the tailored military-style uniforms that the marchers wear with Greek informality. Striding along they shout remarks to friends and family in the crowd.

The Blessing of the Waters

St. Nicholas Orthodox Church, *155 Cedar Street (212-227-0773). Monday–Friday 9 A.M.–4 P.M.; Sunday 8 A.M.–1 P.M.*

Directions: Subway 4 or 5 to Wall Street, or Subway 1 or 9 to Rector Street and walk west.

St. Nicholas was Manhattan's first Greek Orthodox church. It was consecrated in 1892. Dedicated to the patron saint of seamen, its original congregants were seafarers. Besides offering spiritual solace, it was meeting place for immigrants and a source of job information and news from home. Today, with its glowing brass chandeliers, somber icons, and dark intricately carved iconostasis, St. Nicholas is an oasis of serenity in the high-voltage financial district.

Every year on January 19 St. Nicholas is the starting point for a grand religious procession. Bearded priests in black robes and high cylindrical hats lead hundreds of the faithful carrying holy icons, Orthodox banners, and standards of the cross through the center of high finance to the Hudson River.

The archbishop stands on the pier buffeted by the winds, makes the sign of the cross, and chants in Greek. He is blessing the waters. In honor of St. Helen, mother of the Emperor Constantine, and to commemorate her discovery of the original cross, the archbishop flings a gleaming cross into the dark Hudson. Shivering young men covered with grease leap into the choppy water to retrieve it. A cheer goes up from the watchful crowd as one swimmer suddenly emerges, splashing, sputtering, and clutching the precious cross. He ceremonially hands the cross to the archbishop, kneels, and is blessed. Pictures are snapped and videos roll for the afternoon papers and the evening news.

chapter nine

The Slavs

The Slavs who have settled in New York over the centuries represent different tribes and nations. They span an area of Eastern Europe from the Black Sea to the Baltic Ocean and the Carpathian Mountains to the Urals. The Poles, Ukrainians, and Russians have many similarities in language and culture, but throughout their histories they have determinedly defended their individual identities, even when their countries were overwhelmed and conquered. In whichever era they came to New York, whether the Poles in 1830 or the Russians in 1917, these Slavs shared a desire for freedom and national independence. While they adapted to the city and became American, there is something very personal in their links to their native lands.

Poles

History

Daniel Litscho was the first Pole to gain prominence when New York was still New Amsterdam. During the administration of Dutch Governor Peter Stuyvesant, he attained the rank of lieutenant in the tiny Dutch colonial militia and participated in military expeditions against the Swedes and maverick Patroons. Litscho was also a popular innkeeper with taverns on Pearl Street and Wall Street.

Captain Marcin Krygier also served in the Dutch militia under Peter Stuyvesant. He was elected three times to the prestigious office of deputy burgomaster of New Amsterdam. Krygier commanded the fort that defended the city; it was named in his honor for the great Polish monarch, John Casimir.

Litscho and Marcin Krgyier made such a powerful impression on the stolid Dutch governor that he urged the Dutch West India Company to recruit more Polish colonists. Dr. Alexander Curtius was brought to New Amsterdam to start the first high school. Governor Stuyvesant praised this Polish educator for his skill and diligence until he embarrassed the tight-fisted governor by demanding the agreed-upon salary.

The American Revolution brought Polish freedom fighters to the forefront of the American experience. They had been deprived of their ancestral lands and ancestral rights by the joint action of Prussia, Russia, and Austria in 1795. They believed in the rights of man and were ready to strike a blow for freedom in the New World.

Casimir Pulaski was promoted to brigadier general over four American colonels, even without any knowledge of English. He was admired for his bravery and envied for his command of cavalry tactics. He died courageously in battle, charging the Redcoat cavalry.

Thaddeus Kosciuszko joined the Revolutionary forces as an engineer with the rank of colonel. From the beginning General Washington recognized Kosciuszko's importance and placed him under his direct command. He played a major role in the preparations of military fortifications for West Point and Saratoga. On October 13, 1783, the debt owed by the young Republic was recognized and Congress granted Kosciuszko the rank of brigadier general.

The Pulaski Skyway and the Kosciuszko Bridge are two New York monuments to these Polish heroes. New York's Polish community and organizations revere both of these leaders, and the Pulaski Day Parade is the principal celebration of Polish New Yorkers.

In the 1830s New Yorkers were concerned about Russian and Austrian persecution of Poles. The New York City Council was the first official body in the United States to declare support for the Polish uprising of 1831. Forming a committee in Clinton Hall chaired by Columbia President William A. Duer, New Yorkers pledged to support Polish freedom.

New Yorkers were the first to offer asylum to the outnumbered Polish freedom fighters. In 1834 234 Polish exiles arrived at the Port of New York on Austrian ships. They were welcomed with speeches by city luminaries like the writer James Fenimore Cooper. Albert Gallatin, a former secretary of the treasury, organized a committee to aid the proud refugees, who were soon contributing members of New York society.

Despite their lack of English, these extraordinary Poles gained prominence in many fields. Samuel Brilliantowski and Robert Thomain became successful physicians, and a pioneer woman in medicine, Marie Zakrzewska, founded the New York Infirmary. In the arts Eustachy Wysznski became a leading painter and his compatriot Adam Kurek joined the brass section of the New York Italian Opera and became a recognized composer.

These Polish patriots laid the foundations of Polish communal and cultural life in the city and the country as a whole. In 1842 Ludwik Jezykowicz, a staunch Polish cleric, chaired the Association of Poles in America. In the same year Paul Sobolewski and Eustachy Wysznski founded the first Polish periodical, *Poland, Historical, Literary, Monumental and Picturesque*. The Polish Slavonian Literary Association was established in 1846. The Polish community launched the newspaper *Echoz Polski* at the time of the Civil War.

Politically conscious Poles rallied to the Union cause and eagerly enrolled in the city's Garibaldi Guards and the Fourth Cavalry. The Polish military man Alexander Raszewski organized the Thirty-first New York Infantry; Joseph Smolinski led a cavalry regiment.

Wladimir Kryzanowski was a Civil War hero on the scale of Pulaski. He volunteered only two days after war was declared and in no time made colonel and took over the Fifty-eighth Regiment. He was cited numerous times for bravery and was specially singled out for his exploits during the Battle of Bull Run. President Lincoln nominated him for the rank of brigadier general. After the war he made a career of government service, finally retiring to New York City to use his influence on behalf of a new influx of Polish immigrants.

The immigrant Poles of the late nineteenth century and the first decades of the twentieth were very different from their aristocratic forebears. They were peasants with a reverence for the land and had little understanding of geopolitics. Still, they had the strength of character to stand firm against Russian and German efforts to undermine their Polish language and customs. They guarded their Polish identity, but Polish pride by itself could not deal with the problems of starvation and disease and the threat of military conscription. Poles were forced to leave for America.

Polish peasant life centered around the family, the church, and the ancestral village. In America the Polish community revolved around the family, the church, and the neighborhood. Many Poles came to New York with the firm intention of returning to their ancestral villages after they had earned enough money to buy land and a house. Whether they returned or not, they still passionately believed in the Polish proverb that "a man without land is a man without legs."

The Poles who came to New York in steerage were not accorded the same cordial welcome as the freedom fighters. Like other peasant immigrants, they faced prejudice and discrimination. They had no choice but to accept some of the harshest menial work in the city. The tough Poles cleaned the stills in the Brooklyn refineries, removing solid residues in Sahara-like heat. They labored in Brooklyn's iron foundries, inhaling noxious fumes and handling scalding buckets of molten iron.

Polish labor, despite its Old World conservatism, demanded its rights. Poles were active in the wave of strikes that erupted in Brooklyn plants in 1907, 1910, and 1917. Independent Polish workers picketed a Brooklyn sugar refinery when they were forced to work on Easter Sunday and walked out of a Bayonne factory where a foreman made slurs about their nationality. Some militant Poles joined radical groups and were deported during the "Red Scare" of the twenties.

America's enterprise society inspired Polish Americans. They opened all kinds of businesses, from big-city banks to local dry-goods stores. For these Polish Americans it wasn't "business as usual." Polish merchants cultivated a close, almost paternal, relationship with their customers and community. They performed extra services like translating papers and documents and even helped customers find jobs. Polish businessmen put their profits back into the community.

While the Polish immigrants weathered trials and triumphed through determined effort, they never lost sight of their conquered motherland. In New York and Brooklyn they belonged to patriotic Falcon Societies, where they prepared themselves for the national struggle. They practiced gymnastics and fencing and discussed strategies for independence. Polish New Yorkers representing every strand of opinion from radical to monarchist formed coalitions, calling upon the world to grant Poland self-determination.

At the start of World War I Ignatz Jan Paderewski, one of the world's leading concert pianists, became the spokesman of the Polish freedom movement in an impassioned concert tour that combined Chopin and politics. He galvanized national support and helped convince an undecided President Wilson to embrace Polish freedom.

New York's staunch Polish community went even further, with young men volunteering for action and joining a fighting force under the command of the Polish coalition leader, Jozef Haller. Haller's "Blue Army" even recruited soldiers for the American army in 1917. By the end of the war a higher proportion of Poles died on European battlefields than any other American ethnic group.

Stunned by the horrors of battle and depressed by postwar political wrangling, returning Poles were eager to get back into ordinary American life. Many had given up the idea of returning to settle permanently in Poland. They had become New Yorkers. Later they were disappointed and angry at restrictive immigration laws that barred their families and friends from joining them.

New York's Poles were very conscious of their Polish identity. In their own communities on the Lower East Side, in Williamsburg, and Greenpoint, Poles celebrated their identity and homeland in dance groups, glee clubs, and Polish societies. In their parochial schools overseen by Polish nuns, second- and third-generation Polish Americans learned the rudiments of the Polish language and the basics of Polish culture.

High Polish art from theater to concert music also thrived in the city. Stephen Mizwa, a Polish-born Harvard-educated academic, founded the Kosciuszko Foundation in New York in 1925 to encourage Polish creativity and Polish studies. He hoped that his organization would foster American cultural links with a resurgent Poland. At the local level, first- and second-generation Polish Americans formed fine arts clubs.

New York's Poles needed more than cultural pride to cope with the human tragedies brought on by the economic depression of the 1930s. The closeness of the community and Poles' willingness to help one another, providing credit and even shelter for those in need, kept neighborhoods afloat. In the political arena, they supported Roosevelt's relief and welfare measures and voted the Democratic ticket, though they received little in patronage for their efforts.

As prosperity returned, the concerns of Polish New Yorkers shifted to Eastern Europe, where Nazi threats against Poland were realized in a devastating Panzer invasion. *Nowy Swiat,* New York's leading Polish newspaper, mobilized the metropolitan area's Polish population, who bought bonds, gave blood, and participated in newspaper and scrap-iron drives.

The newspaper's publisher, Maximilian Wegrzynek, organized the National Committee of Americans of Polish Descent (KNAPP) to fight against Soviet involvement and for the liberation of Poland. Later his group joined with others in a united front, the Polish American Congress, to defend Poland from Soviet domination.

World War II and the Yalta Agreement, which gave the USSR de facto control over Poland, increased the number of Poles seeking refuge in New York. There were intellectual émigrés like Oscar Halecki, who established the prestigious Polish Institute of Arts and Sciences in the City in 1941. There were members of Poland's defeated government like the exiled minister of education, Waclaw Jedrzejewicz, who became the executive director for the Josef Pilsudski Institute of America, established in New York in 1943.

The majority of new Polish immigrants were displaced persons or DPs, and veterans of special Polish army units and groups of partisans. They came in family units with the intention of making a new life in America. The lobbying efforts of KNAPP and the passage of legislative acts and presidential directives made their entry possible. They brought new life and flavor to the Polonias of New York.

The *General Black* was the first ship to land in New York with this precious human cargo in 1948. The Polish refugees of World War II called themselves the Black Generals in honor of this special ship. They included such notables as Dr. Zbigniew Brezinski, who went from Columbia's halls of ivy and the chairmanship of the Trilateral Commission to become President Jimmy Carter's chief foreign policy adviser and chairman of the National Security Council.

While Polish New Yorkers went from success to success and made the leap from blue-collar respectability to white-collar affluence, they did not and have not forgotten their homeland. They continually sent food, medicine, and money to help their people struggling under the tyranny and incompetence of a Soviet satellite regime. Polish New Yorkers even provided direct support for the labor and political movement *Solidarnosc* and its charismatic leader Lech Walesa. They also raised money to help maintain Polish Roman Catholic institutions.

Even before the breakup of the Soviet Union, Poland became more democratic and open to free enterprise. The country was buoyed by a new sense of purpose and Polish New Yorkers not only cheered from the sidelines, but also became an important source of investment and economic expertise. As Soviet troops left and the whole Communist state apparatus was dismantled, the former dissident labor leader Lech Walesa, whose picture had a prominent place in many Polish-American homes, became president of a free Poland.

In the wake of economic dislocation and unemployment caused by the transition to capitalism, many Poles have taken advantage of lifted travel restrictions to come to America. Some settled legally and others overstayed their tourist visas to seek out New York economic opportunities. As in the past, Poles elected to take the most hazardous jobs, such as asbestos removal, to make a life for themselves and their families in this fiercely competitive city. This new generation of Polish immigrants is rejuvenating the Polonias of Williamsburg, Greenpoint, Manhattan, and Maspeth.

Little Poland in Greenpoint

Directions: Subway 4, 5, or 6 to Union Square/14th Street. Change to Subway L to Lorimer Street or Subway G to Greenpoint Avenue.

Greenpoint, the city's largest Polonia, is across the East River in Brooklyn. It is so close to Manhattan that it offers some spectacular views of the skyline. The World Trade Center seems only steps away. Still, for many of the Polish people of Greenpoint, Manhattan is simply a place to work. Their hearts are in their own close-knit community.

The Dutch purchased Greenpoint from the Indians in 1630. A fertile forested area with underground springs and a meandering creek, it was earmarked for farmsteads. For centuries Dutch and English families plowed and planted its fields.

In the nineteenth century Greenpoint went industrial. The shipyards came first. It was ideally suited for shipbuilding with its central coastal location. At the foot of Cayler Street, the iron-clad warship the *Monitor* was built for action in the Civil War.

In the Gilded Age following the Civil War, Greenpoint was noted for the "five black arts": printing, pottery, gas, glass, and iron. There were also oil refineries on the waterfront. Despite the black smoke of industrial chimneys, the Irish, German, and old American families who resided here created a small-town community in the middle of Brooklyn.

Greenpoint struck a nice balance; there was no room for run-down slums or opulent mansions. Working- and middle-class Greenpoint residents lived in neat brick row houses and attractive brownstones. These neo-Greek and Italianate structures still line Kent Street off Greenpoint Avenue, which has been described by the *New York Times* as "one of the city's better and more completely preserved nineteenth-century streets."

The most exuberant chapter in Greenpoint's history began in the late nineteenth century, when Poles began streaming in to work in the area's ironworks and oil refineries. Poles who had emigrated to Brooklyn from lands under German, Russian, and Austrian domination banded together to re-create their national institutions in a free America.

They built Roman Catholic churches like St. Kostka's, and in their Polish parish reenacted their age-old Slavic rituals. Our Lady of Czestochowa, the Black Madonna, was a source of spiritual unity. In their parish schools they preserved their Polish language and in their fraternities and social clubs they kept alive Polish music and dance. Polish solidarity revealed itself in mutual benefit societies like the Polish National Alliance of Brooklyn, U.S.A.

Greenpoint was a strong, stable neighborhood with well-maintained houses and a thriving commercial area. It was not politically mobilized and loyally Democratic Polish Greenpoint was bulldozed to make way for the Long Island Expressway. Other ethnic enclaves did not survive the wholesale destruction of parts of their communities in the name of progress, but Polish Greenpoint rallied. New Polish immigrants from overseas were a source of new vitality.

Greenpoint forms a rectangle with Manhattan Avenue and Franklin Avenue bordering east and west and Noble Street and Greenpoint Avenue bordering north and south. It is a neighborhood where landmark row houses alternate with small shingled or aluminum-sided single-family houses. Greenpoint's restaurants and shops have the intimacy of someone's living room, while the neighborhood's churches have the grandeur of Old World Warsaw. Its strong character comes from its people, who have the romantic idealism of their aristocratic antecedents and the forthright honesty of their peasant forebears.

Manhattan Avenue is the main shopping street of Greenpoint and has a large number of Polish businesses and specialty stores among the standard American shops. As it leads into Nassau Avenue the area undergoes a change; a border has been crossed and the street becomes an all-Polish main drag. It's a Polish scene of fair faces and flowered patterns and broad-shouldered men with Lech Walesa mustaches. The people have an earnestness when they speak; they are believers.

Greenpoint Place Marks—The Pope's Church

In times of defeat and tyranny the Church has kept the Polish national identity alive. The Poles have repaid it with a special devotion. Polish faith is an integral part of Polish life; it's fatalistic and still believes in miracles. The church and the parish are the tangible center of that existence. The Poles of Greenpoint in the past called their neighborhood St. Stans.

St. Stanislaus Kostka Church, *607 Humboldt Street (718-388-0170).*

The eminence of St. Stanislaus Kostka stands out among the small neat one-family houses of Greenpoint. Every day there are Polish masses and every day candles are lit in front of the shrine of the Polish national patron, Our Lady of Częstochowa. In 1969 Cardinal Karol Wojtyla visited St. Stanislaus and blessed the congregation. St. Stanislaus has not forgotten that day and the dignity and gentle humanity of the cardinal from Krakow.

They honored the Polish pope by naming a square near their church, between Broome and Humboldt Streets, Pope John Paul II Square.

Poland's Martyr Priest

On a small tranquil island of space between the hubbub of Nassau and Bedford Avenues stands the statue of Jerzy Popieluszko, a priest deemed to be so dangerous to the Polish communists that he was murdered and buried in an unmarked grave. In front of the statue is a modest flower garden. Occasionally, a local Pole will add to their number by placing a bouquet beneath the poignant image of this stalwart defender of the Polish Catholic Church and the workingman. The statue has been fenced in since vandals disfigured the statue and the head had to be replaced.

Polish Exhibits and Cultural Archives

The FFA Gallery, *16 Clifford Place (718-383-8932). Hours vary according to show. Call.*

The FFA exhibits the latest works of the more adventurous Polish and Polish-American artistic spirits. The shows are superbly mounted in an unconventional gallery setting. Don't expect traditional realism. These Polish artists are visionaries in form and content. But even in their neon sculptures and minimalist statements there are images of Mother Poland.

Polish National Alliance of Brooklyn, U.S.A., *155 Noble Street (718-389-4704).*

The PNA started as a fraternal group with a mission to advance Polish culture and the Polish nation. Its members volunteered to fight for a free Poland during World War I and condemned the World War II peace that left Poland in the Soviet orbit. The PNA has provided scholarships for students studying the Polish language and culture and has provided grants for Polish schools.

Polish Musical Exchanges

Poland has a great musical tradition that partakes of both the classics of the court musician and the folk songs of the peasants. The music reflects the visceral spirit and the energetic dances of the Polish people. It is the intensely romantic polonaises and mazurkas of Chopin and the accordion and clarinet accompaniment to polkas. It is the soaring exhilaration of the warrior and the death knell of the defeated. Paderewski, the most complete piano virtuoso of the twentieth century, was able to capture the paradoxical moods of the Polish people. Halka, Poland's national opera, presents it with drama and choruses, ballet, and mazurkas.

The local Polish community maintains a close relationship with the current Polish regime and is an active participant in cultural exchanges. Usually a month doesn't go by without a performance of some first-rate troupe from Poland, like the Silesian Opera Company or the Rzeszowiacy Song and Dance Ensemble. Classical and folk, mazurka and highlander's dances, the entertainment is highbrow and traditional. Announcements of the latest events and tickets are usually available at the Polish Book Center (140 Nassau Avenue). The cultural center of the Polish and Slavic Credit Union (177 Kent Street; 718-937-4356) is also a prime source of information about these events.

Hearty Polish Eating

Polish food is not for the fastidious or fainthearted. It is rich and heavy with heaping portions of sour cream and pork and more than a touch of dill and a hint of garlic. This hearty cooking sticks to the essentials: cabbage and dumplings and a pasty called *pierogen* stuffed with cheese or potatoes or minced meat. A real peasant cuisine, it doesn't have any prejudices against pig knuckles or tripe, and the humble smoked sausage, *kielbasa,* is Poland's national dish.

Polish restaurants with richly satisfying portions, the forthright flavors of Eastern Europe, and modest 1950s prices are the rule in Greenpoint. The eating places are usually no-frills with proverbial "eat off the floor" cleanliness. The service is warm and personal; customers are treated like long-lost relatives. There's not much gloss but a lot of heart. The diners "attack" the food with real Polish gusto; the rapid percussion of knife and fork fill the air.

Rzeszowska Restaurant, *931 Manhattan Avenue (718-349-7501). Daily noon–8 P.M.*

The Rzeszowska is out to be elegant with gray and black minimalist decor, mirrors, and recessed lights. The waiter wears a tux and tries very hard. His impression of professional service is at times ungainly. The restaurant has the same laundry list of Polish foods found in Polish luncheonettes. Ask for the daily specials, like the "little veal bridge" and the Polish Stroganoff.

Christina's, *853 Manhattan Avenue (718-383-4382). Daily 7 A.M.–8 P.M.*

The new Christina's was once an unpretentious Polish coffee shop called Paradise. No one spoke English (including the menus), and the kitchen was pure Polski home cooking with thick-cut pork cutlets smothered in gravy, soups thick with vegetables and bits of meat and bone, and *pierogen* that didn't need sour cream or applesauce. Christina's pledges to stick to the Old World Paradise formula.

Stylowa Restaurant, *694 Manhattan Avenue (718-383-8993). Daily noon–8 P.M.*

Lately, young artists and writers have been deserting high-rent, high-velocity Manhattan for the low-rise serenity of Greenpoint. Attractive and low-key Stylowa appeals to these budding Hemingways and Picassos, who take a break from the creative act with a bowl of the cabbage soup or borscht with dumplings, or just linger over a cappuccino with a Polish pastry baked on the premises.

Jagiellonia Restaurant, *646 Manhattan Avenue (718-389-9493). Daily noon–9 P.M.*

Jagiellonia is like eating in a Greenpoint kitchen with flowered oil-cloth tablecloths and cute puppy vases with artificial flowers. The proprietor peers through the door forlornly; the early evening rush has subsided and he is waiting for the next seating. The locals really appreciate Jagiellonia's rumpsteak, pig's feet, and *bigos* (country strew) with substantial sides of sauerkraut or red cabbage, and a potato pancake for good measure.

Pod Strechna, *119 Nassau Street at Eckert (718-349-3543). Daily 10 A.M.–9 P.M.*

Pod Strechna has a raw and sturdy image, with heavy wooden picnic tables for eating, a functional steam table, and an old-fashioned sideboard with free sauerkraut and slaws. The portions, which are served by a spunky lady with a big ladle, are heaping, whether it's Polish-style pork chops, meat loaf, potato pancakes, stuffed cabbage, or pig's feet with potatoes and a vegetable. The prices are practically of the Depression era.

Old Poland, *192 Nassau Avenue (718-349-7775). Daily 12:30 P.M.–10 P.M.*

The owner of Old Poland is a recent immigrant and born-again New Yorker who has put pictures of the Brooklyn Bridge and Marilyn Monroe on the restaurant walls. When the whistle blows to end the workday, the place is pure pandemonium, with strapping Polish workers lining up for big Polish-style dinners of cutlets, chops, or ground meat slathered with gravy and mountains of mashed potatoes and sauerkraut or spinach.

Polska Restaurant, *136 Greenpoint Avenue (718-389-8368). Daily noon–9 P.M.*

Three strapping customers at the counter knock off plates of cheese *pierogen* and follow up with giant pig's knuckles and mashed potatoes, all washed down with brown beer. At the Polska eating is serious business and there is still room for strawberry and blueberry blintzes before blowing a kiss to the owner Jadwiga on the way out the door.

Polish and Slavic Credit Union, *177 Kent Street (718-937-4356). Tuesday–Thursday and Sunday 9:30 A.M.–5:45 P.M.; Friday and Saturday 9 A.M.–8:45 P.M.*

Senior citizens, the men in caps and the women in kerchiefs, grab their trays and take bowls of thick soups with hunks of black bread and sit down. This is cafeteria eating with the clatter of plates and trays and people trying to shout above the noise in Polish. This is no ordinary *kielbasa* house; the credit union that subsidizes this cafeteria provides financing for a good portion of the housing in Greenpoint.

Continental Restaurant, *11 Nevel Avenue at Driggs Avenue (718-383-2768). Monday–Friday 3:30 P.M.–10 P.M.; Saturday and Sunday 2 P.M.–1:30 A.M.*

The entrance to the Continental, with its anonymous door, looks like a "Joe sent me" speakeasy. The Continental has a busy front bar and a back room with a polka beat on Saturdays and Sundays. The cold Polish vodka with buffalo grass complements the plates of sour tomatoes and pickles and the platters of roast chicken and crispy fried veal cutlet.

Shopping Polonia

Though Polish Greenpoint is more than one generation old, it has kept its Polish character. The neighborhood is Polish tastes and Polish styles. The stores are Polish immaculate with maybe a photograph of the Pope or President Walesa or a picture of the Virgin of Częstochowa hanging on the wall for inspiration. Recent arrivals have reinforced the Polish way and added their own contemporary touches to New York's main Polonia.

The Poles of Greenpoint have happily not quite gotten the knack of Western consumerism. They know their local merchants by name and shopping is personal and social. The stores help people connect with their culture. Brightly colored ceramics, carvings, and flower fabrics are an affirmation of Polish identity. Polish bookstores carry Polish classics and best-sellers, as well as books that will help newcomers improve their English and adjust to a new culture. Polish cosmetics and even traditional herbal folk medicines are for sale.

Kielbasa, the Polish smoked sausage, has pride of place in Greenpoint's small markets; big supermarkets have no place in this Polish village. In groceries and butchers it hangs from long metal rods over the counter to tempt the unwary shopper. There are other surprises in the neighborhood's food stores too. There are Polish hams and every variety of sausage, black peasant breads, and pickled vegetables. The shopkeepers know their customers and inquire about the family before taking an order. No one is in a hurry.

Small bakeries and Polish sweet shops are also a part of this Old World neighborhood. Polish shoppers don't mind making an extra stop for a special bread or cake they really appreciate. Convenience is not everything. The number of specialty shops is now increasing with the population.

— Jelly Donuts to Hand-dipped Chocolates —

Rzeszowska Bakery, *948 Manhattan Avenue (718-383-8142). Monday–Saturday 7 A.M.–9 P.M.; Sunday 7 A.M.–5 P.M.*

The young blond woman with the sparkling eyes really goes out of her way to please. She is proud of her high-rise cheese and cherry *babka* which come fresh from the oven throughout the day, creating an aroma that is almost as good as the eating.

Old Poland Bakery, *926 Manhattan Avenue (718-349-7900). Daily 6:30 A.M.–8 P.M.*

Old Poland bakes big loaves of crusty peasant bread and long cakes filled with poppy seeds that are worth a special trip. The locals snack on their prune and cherry pastries and the fat Polish-style jelly donuts that practically spurt raspberry when bitten into.

Poznanski's Bakery, *688 Manhattan Avenue (718-383-3908). Monday–Saturday 7 A.M.–7:45 P.M.; Sunday 7 A.M.–6:45 P.M.*

Poznanski's is versatile. It makes American-style ice cream cakes and many-layered wedding and birthday cakes to order, as well as Polish traditional *Markowiec* (poppy seed cake) and *Szarlotke* (apple cake). Joseph Szczarapa, the proprietor of this bakery, is also a master maker of *gakaretka* (jelly candies).

White Eagle, *600 Humboldt Avenue (718-389-2214). Monday–Friday 7 A.M.–noon.*

Following the mass at St. Stanislaus, an assortment of nimble elderly communicants cross the street for a Polish cheese or chocolate *babka* (a plain cake a little less sweet than a Danish). White Eagle's major business is wholesale, so they close their doors when they are finished baking. Catch them early.

Stodyce Wedel, *772 Manhattan Avenue (718-349-3933). Monday–Saturday 10 A.M.–8 P.M.; Sunday 10 A.M.–6 P.M.*

The Polish chocolates come hand dipped and loose and packaged. There are blocks of milk chocolate and assortments of chocolates with fruit and nuts in fancy boxes. Gourmet cookies from Eastern Europe and Germany and bags of hard candies fill this candyland's shelves.

— The Polish Smokehouse —

Starpolski Delicatessen, *912 Manhattan Avenue (718-389-0294). 1053 Manhattan Avenue (718-349-1432). Monday–Saturday 8 A.M.–9 P.M.; Sunday 9 A.M.–5 P.M.*

The counterman at Starpolski is surrounded by a curtain of hanging *kielbasa* and Polish charcuterie, and surrounded by customers anxious for their *kielbasa* fix. Late in the afternoon, after the bins of Polish black bread and pumpernickel are sold out, friends drift in like it's an open house. But the break is brief, as the evening rush starts for prepared foods from stuffed cabbage to *pierogen*.

Steve's, *104 Nassau Avenue (718-383-1780). Monday–Saturday 7 A.M.–7 P.M.*

There was no voting but somehow Steve's has won the title of number one in *kielbasa*. Steve's deserves it both for the quality of the products and the patience and good humor of everyone who works there. The *kielbasa* doesn't overdo the garlic or the fat. They have the same goodness in a *kielbasa* cold cut called *krakowska,* which makes a very unusual sandwich.

Nassau Meat Market, *121 Nassau Avenue (718-383-3476). Monday–Saturday 8* A.M.*–8* P.M.

The Nassau Market believes variety is the spice of Polish sausages. In addition to the old reliable *kielbasa,* Nassau has dried *kabanosa* sausage, Polish hot dogs called *mysliwska,* veal sausage, and Polish head cheese.

— Natural Drugs and Natural Beauty —

Panacea, *735 Manhattan Avenue (718-383-8953). Monday–Friday 1* P.M.*–7* P.M.*; Saturday 10* A.M.*–5* P.M.*; Sunday 10* A.M.*–4:00* P.M.

Panacea is serious about the power of herbs to improve the digestion and keep the hair healthy. They have special teas, roots, herbs, and powders that have been traditionally and nontraditionally used in Poland, as well as some esoteric reading matter.

Secrets of Beauty, *119 Nassau Avenue (718-389-5793). Monday–Saturday 1* P.M.*–6* P.M.

The women of Greenpoint come here for advice about beauty and hard-to-find Polish creams, lotions, and cosmetics. The shop also carries more conventional beauty products from Europe.

— Book Shops and Folk Art —

Centrum Ksiask Polskiej, Polish Book Center, *140 Nassau Avenue (718-383-3501). Monday–Friday 11* A.M.*–7* P.M.*; Saturday 10* A.M.*–6* P.M.

This Polish bookstore is more than a bookstore, it's the informal cultural headquarters of a community where people can find out about the latest Polish concert, recital, or exhibition. At the Centrum Polish intellectuals discuss the subtleties of Poland's economy and the infighting in Parliament. The shelves of the Centrum are devoted to Polish classics by Lem and Woldt and the literature of the Polish freedom movement. There is a selection of recorded Polish music.

Polska Ksiegarnia, Polish American Bookstore, *46 Manhattan Avenue (718-389-7790) Monday–Friday 11 A.M.–7 P.M.; Saturday 10 A.M.–6 P.M.; Sunday 11:30 A.M.–4:30 P.M.*

The Polish American Bookstore is a Polish browser's paradise. They come in after work to examine the Polish magazines and best-sellers in Polish and scan the racks of greeting cards with their messages in Polish. Seek and you shall find the odd book about Poland in English. They also carry Polish music on tape and video.

Zakopane, *714 Manhattan Avenue (718-389-3487). Monday–Saturday 10 A.M.–7 P.M.; Sunday noon–5 P.M.*

The wood carvings that line the shelves of Zakopane bear no resemblance to a souvenir shop junk; they are painstaking replicas of man and nature. The subjects such as a mountain stag or a peasant dancer reflect rural life. The shop also has some fine examples of Polish Easter eggs and peasant embroidery. The blue and clear crystal gleams like expensive jewelry. Mr. Strug, who presides over this handicraft kingdom, charges very reasonable prices.

Manhattan Renaissance

Polish Manhattan is more than memories. The old neighborhood on the Lower East Side is clearly on the upswing. Each time the native Poles took to the streets to protest—in Warsaw in 1056, in Poznan in 1968, and Gdansk in 1971—they voted the only way they could—with their feet. After each protest, political refugees have come to New York and settled on the Lower East Side.

Though the renewed Polish presence has been lost to the rest of New York in the general Slavic atmosphere, they have a growing community life that goes beyond the neighborhood. They have their own restaurants, where Polish immigrants casually coexist with East Village eccentrics and artists, and their own churches, where the older generation of the Polish tradition stand side by side with the bright young Poles of possibility.

Like the Poles who first came to New York in the early part of the nineteenth century, these post–World War II political refugees are intellectually sophisticated. Many are writers, historians, and artists. They are not the folk art and polka types; they are into experimental writing and modern art. The new Polish immigrants have their own literary circles and artists' support groups.

Old Neighborhood Place Mark

St. Stanislaus Church, *101 Seventh Street (212-475-4576).*

The congregation of St. Stanislaus is primarily Polish born. There are three Polish masses on Sunday and one daily. The Sunday masses bring together a young, vital Polish community; on weekdays it's mostly older women in black. The church has many statues and paintings, but Our Lady of Czestochowa is the focus of attention. Currently, the church is involved in a big drive to collect money to erect a bronze likeness of Pope John Paul II.

Manhattan's Polish Eagles

The eagle of Polish culture flies all around Manhattan from trendy downtown to the palmy Upper East Side. The cultural institutions are conservative and glossy and avant-garde and struggling. Some have stood the test of time and others are hanging on. Polish audiences vary from mainstream to folk art, elitist to experimental. The more recent arrivals look upon culture as a liberation while the older Polish Americans view it as a tradition. It is the Polish newspaper and church and an artists' support group.

Polish Artists' Gallery, *19 Irving Place (no telephone). Call the Polish Institute for information on current showings.*

The Polish Artists' Gallery has twice-a-month shows of Polish artists who are mainly new to America. It is all modern but the mediums change. There are paintings, sculpture, collage, tapestry, and modern ceramics. The Artists' Support Group is associated with the gallery. It helps Polish artists adjust to the competitive world of American art.

Polish Institute of Arts and Sciences, *208 East 30th Street (212-686-4164). Tuesday–Thursday 10 A.M.–4 P.M.; Saturday 11 A.M.–4 P.M.*

The Institute was started in the dark days of World War II to preserve a Polish culture that seemed threatened by Hitler and his minions. It soon broadened its agenda to include the Polish-American experience. It has its own publications and library.

Kosciuszko Foundation, *15 East 65th Street (212-734-2130). Monday–Friday 9 A.M.–5 P.M.*

The Kosciuszko is Polish America's most important cultural resource center. It has an excellent gallery of paintings, traditional and modern, and a fine collection of Polish photographs. The library of the foundation includes over one hundred thousand documents and thousands of books in Polish and English. The organization has sponsored concert series, such as the Chopin Masters (Witold Malcuzynski and Artur Rubinstein), and commissioned a sixteen-part film series on the Polish contribution to America. It awards scholarships to individuals of Polish descent and has an annual Chopin music scholarship.

Polish Extras

Nowy Dziennik, *21 West 38th Street (212-354-0490).*

In English the name of this paper is the *Daily News,* and it does have that from both the local and national Polish-American communities and from Poland. The paper tries not to be divisively ideological, but it makes no bones about being pro-free enterprise and has even raised funds for Polish charitable organizations. It supports all the community's cultural events involving Polish and Polish-American musical and dance groups. It backs Polish galleries and even local choirs.

The Polish Cafe

They look like unpretentious and informal luncheonettes. When a Polish coffee house tries cosy decorative touches it winds up looking like an older woman with too much makeup. The only decorations that work are an old *Solidarnosc* poster or a picture of the Polish pope. The Polish coffee houses live a double life; they get the local trade of post-hippies, college students, and tourists, and have their regular Polish coteries who treat the coffee houses like a social club.

The food, like all the other Polish restaurants in the city, is rich Polish soups, stuffed cabbage and peppers, and their own versions of Hungarian goulash and Austrian schnitzel. There are blintzes and *pierogen* and potato pancakes for snacks and side dishes.

Christine's, *208 First Avenue between 12th and 13th streets (212-254-2474). Daily 7 A.M.–11 P.M.*

Christine took the exotic out of Polish cooking and made it an everyday thing all around the town. Christine's became a chain without sacrificing quality, but this Lower East Side Christine's is the original, with a fresh paint job in shocking orange and a new purple counter. Fortunately, the blintzes, *pierogen,* and thick *bigos* stew have not had a make-over.

Little Poland, *200 Second Avenue between 12th and 13th streets (212-777-9728). Daily 7 A.M.–11 P.M.*

The waitresses at Little Poland are dressed all in white like nurses and very solicitous, almost maternal. Give them half a chance and they will help you order. If they praise the stuffed pepper or stuffed cabbage, go for it.

K & K Restaurant, *192-194 First Avenue (212-777-4430). Daily 7:00 A.M.–11 P.M.*

K & K is a welcoming restaurant with rec room-like pine trim and stripped brick walls. Come the warm weather, the "garden" opens, with its green picket fence, tall shade trees, and potted plants. Local Poles and others in the know come here to enjoy tranquil afternoons and evenings over fat cheese blintzes steeped in sour cream, and the superb stuffed breast of veal in brown onion gravy.

Polonia, *110 First Avenue between Sixth and Seventh streets (212-777-8842). Daily 6 A.M.–midnight.*

It's two steps down to the spare simplicity of Polonia. The restaurant is small and quiet with bachelors in shirtsleeves at separate tables devouring plates of *kielbasa* and reading the sports pages. The best bets are the combination plates with stuffed cabbage, *kielbasa,* and *pierogen.*

Teresa's, *103 First Avenue between Sixth and Seventh Streets (212-228-0604). Daily 6 A.M.–midnight.*

Teresa's attracts an interesting mix of East Village punk and Polish village seniors. They both keep the food honest. The kitchen doesn't depend on rich gravies and heaping portions to please. Teresa's veal in dill sauce, duck with prunes and apples (after 5:30 P.M.), and boiled beef with horse-radish are the most distinctive Polish tastes.

Polish Purchasing

New York's cosmopolitan Poles have no problems dealing with American supermarkets and American tastes, but sometimes they hanker for *kielbasa* or the full-bodied flavor of a Polish beer.

First Avenue Meat Products, *140 First Avenue at Ninth Street Monday–Thursday 8 A.M.–6:30 P.M.; Friday–Saturday 8 A.M.–7 P.M.; Sunday 9 A.M.–3 P.M.*

You don't have to tell the neighborhood people who crowd the counter that First Avenue has real smokehouse meats. The long links of *kielbasa* and the thinner *kabanosa* and fine-ground *mysilianski* sausage are smoked in the back with just the right bite provided by bits of garlic.

E & S Meat Market, *111 First Avenue at Seventh Street (212-677- 1210). Monday–Saturday 8 A.M.–8 P.M.; Sunday 10 A.M.–5 P.M.*

The E & S has mostly Polish imports, from canned hams to jars of Polish pickled vegetables and Polish imported beer. The Polish *kielbasa* and *kabanosa* that dangle from the ceiling are made locally from one of those secret family recipes. E & S tries to be ecumenical and also carries some Ukrainian products.

Polish Celebrations—Patriots in Red and White

Pulaski Day Parade

On the Sunday closest to October 5 Polish New York comes out to pay tribute to a great Polish-American hero of the American Revolution, General Casimir Pulaski, and their own national identity. It is one of the year's most spectacular parades. A typical Pulaski Day line-up includes forty-five floats and fifty marching bands. The parade follows Fifth Avenue from 26th Street to 52nd Street.

The grand marshal, usually representing some important Polish-American organization, leads the march, smiling and waving to enthusiastic crowds. Polish-American leaders follow on foot and in limousines. Many are dressed to the nines in top hats and morning coats with sashes in red and white, Poland's national colors. The parade pauses on the stairs of St. Patrick's to greet the cardinal. Flowers in the shape of a cross are solemnly placed in front of the Cathedral.

In a moment the mood of the parade is lighthearted. A polka band begins to play on a red-and-white float and soon dancers in high boots and embroidered vests whirl down the avenue. The long line of march picks up the polka beat as Polish cops and fire fighters and choirs and high school students pass along Fifth Avenue. The newly crowned Queen of Polonia on the Royal Polonia float holds her scepter aloft as her subjects clap and whistle. Another band picks up a military beat and the mood changes as old men in old uniforms—the uniforms of World War II partisans—step lively up the avenue. There are Polish-American Legionnaires and Veterans of Foreign Wars and marchers in Revolutionary War uniforms. Even the Polish visionary, Copernicus, in a plumed hat and tights makes an appearance on a float.

Ukrainians

History

Ukrainians are characterized by a deep loyalty to their homeland. Even centuries of foreign domination have not destroyed their sense of national identity. Their forebears brought Christianity to the eastern steppes and governed democratically during Europe's dark ages; the Kievan Republic was a legendary center of culture and learning. For Ukrainian New Yorkers it is still a sacred inheritance.

The first modern Ukrainians to land in New York sailed with the Russian fleet between 1862 and 1863. Some of these anonymous sailors jumped ship, never to return, while others went back to relate the wonders of the city to wide-eyed peasants. New York seemed like a dream to these people who were denied their land, language, and religion.

An adventurous clergyman named Ahapius Honcharenko took an unscheduled sabbatical from his religious studies in Athens and arrived in New York in 1865. After traveling throughout the country, supporting himself by teaching Greek, he settled for a time in lower Manhattan in the heart of what would become the Ukrainian community.

In the 1870s, despite government efforts to prevent them from leaving, Ukrainians crossed a continent and an ocean, settling mainly in the mining and industrial areas of the Northeast and the Midwest and the urban area of Manhattan. The majority—Ruthenians, Carpatho-Russyns, and Galicians—were from the western part of their nation. At the outset, most wanted to return to the Ukraine to buy land and begin a family.

The bribes of steamship agents and rural poverty forced Russian government authorities to open the way to mass emigration. Families mortgaged their lands and pawned their possessions to pay the passage. Young men who were eager to avoid lifetime military service deserted their villages and the women followed. Between 1877 and 1899 hundreds of thousands were America bound.

In New York the mainly male population lived four to six to a room in boardinghouses in the Lower East Side between the German and Jewish enclaves. They energetically set to work to pay their passage and relieve the burdens of the people they left behind. They were barbers, bricklayers, tailors, and day laborers. The women who joined them took jobs as domestics and cleaned offices at night.

Ukrainian New Yorkers established a whole network of organizations in the city. Some were connected to Greek Catholic or Orthodox Ukrainian churches like the St. Raphael Ukrainian Immigration Society, which helped Ukrainian New Yorkers find jobs and shelter. Regional associations like the Lemko Brotherhood Society provided a place where people from the same area could socialize and also offered health and burial insurance. Ukrainians generally refused public relief; the Ukrainian National Association aided the sick and the needy. Women's groups, such as the Ukrainian Women's League, preserved Ukrainian traditions and folk arts.

In 1917 the Tsarist state was overthrown and at last, after centuries, the Ukrainians won independence. They declared a free Ukraine on January 22, 1918, but its existence was brief. Russia and Poland quickly carved it up according to the terms of a 1921 treaty. New York's Ukrainian community followed closely the misfortunes of their country and offered support. Local Ukrainian groups demonstrated for Ukrainian freedom and protested deportations and state-sponsored famine and murder.

By 1919 New York was the site of the largest metropolitan Ukrainian community. It was split between the Lower East Side from Third to Sixth Streets and the Upper East Side in the vicinity of 72nd Street. The Ukrainian community on the Lower East Side even sent one of its own, Stephen Jarema, to the New York State Assembly. There was also a scattering of Ukrainians in Williamsburg, Brooklyn, and the Bronx.

During World War II Ukrainian freedom fighters were the victims of Nazi and Soviet brutality. There were even mass Ukrainian executions after the German surrender. New York's Ukrainian population raised money and mobilized themselves politically to save thousands of Ukrainian displaced persons.

In 1948 the Ukrainian Resettlement Center was established in the city. Ukrainian newcomers who were processed through the center were highly qualified academics, clergy, professionals, and intellectuals. They added new luster to the New York Ukrainian cultural community.

Ukrainian New Yorkers were given official recognition by the state and city government in 1955. The occasion was the anniversary of Ukrainian independence, which had been declared on January 22 in 1918. In his proclamation Governor Averell Harriman commended Ukrainian New Yorkers as being a "proud and freedom-loving people" while Mayor Robert F. Wagner praised "their matchless faith and courage." For the first time in the history of the city, the Ukrainian flag flew above City Hall.

Since the breakup of the Soviet Union and a plebiscite in the Ukraine, that same flag is now flying over their new republic. The people of New York's Little Ukraine are happy about their homeland's new independence, though they may have reservations about some of its current leaders. This change has sparked a cultural renewal in the city and a new wave of Ukrainian patriotic pride.

Little Ukraine

Directions: Subway 6 to Astor Place or Bus M15 to Eighth Street.

Little Ukraine lays claim to a corner of New York generally called the East Village, bounded by Fourth Street and 14th Street, Avenue A and Third Avenue. The Ukrainians don't seem to have too many problems coexisting with the hippie leftovers, working-class Hispanics, and elderly vestiges of other immigrant groups. Although the neighborhood only numbers thirty thousand Ukrainians (a steep decline from seventy-five thousand in less than a decade), it still retains its national character in shops, restaurants, and cultural landmarks.

The history of Ukrainian New York is an account of the rich civic life of the Little Ukraine. In 1905 Peter Jarema ushered in a new dynamic era in Ukrainian New York by organizing the United Ukrainian Organizations of New York City to promote Ukrainian activities. In the same year Ukrainian New Yorkers founded St. George's Ukrainian Catholic Church, the spiritual and social hub of the community. The church's school sustained Ukrainian New York by instructing succeeding generations in the Ukrainian language and traditions.

The Little Ukraine was the culture capital of Ukrainians in America. It was the home of the first Ukrainian theater and music hall, which was launched in the twenties, and the first gymnastic society. In 1932 the Surma Book and Music Company, which is still going strong on Seventh Street, sponsored a program of Ukrainian music that was carried on eighteen radio stations around the country. Ukrainian New York even had its own film company, which released two films in Ukrainian in 1936. In the same year Professor Alexander Koshetz directed the Ukrainian Mixed Choirs of New York in their Carnegie Hall debut.

Ukrainian New Yorkers, while celebrating their own culture, never lost sight of the people back home. There were always new committees and protests in the Little Ukraine to make the world aware of the suffering of the Ukrainian people. In the 1930s Ukrainian groups attacked the Polish pacification of the western Ukraine and the Stalinist famine and genocide. Through the Organization for the Defense of the Four Freedoms, founded in the 1940s, Little Ukraine has continued to fight the Communist exploitation of their homeland up through the present.

After World War II Little Ukraine was inundated with displaced persons from Europe. They were determined survivors, trained professionals, and eager young students, the nucleus of the neighborhood's Ukrainian renewal. In 1946 the Self-Reliance Association of American Ukrainians was formed in New York City. It not only assisted Ukrainian students but also built one of the best Ukrainian libraries in the city.

At the same time the Shevchenko Scientific Institute was established to aid Ukrainian scientists. The arts thrived; the Ukrainian Literary Art Club and the Ukrainian chorus were both organized in 1949. The Ukrainian Academy of Arts and Sciences was the crowning achievement in this era. Organized in New York in 1950 to sponsor the study of Ukrainian subjects, it had a library of twenty thousand books and its own prestigious academic journal dealing with Ukrainian history, literature, and social sciences.

In 1955 the Ukrainian-American community celebrated their golden anniversary. It was a time to take stock and to appreciate the solid accomplishments of Ukrainian New York's organizations and associations. Marking this occasion, Dr. Alexander Sokolyshyn wrote the *Golden Jubilee Book Commemorating Organized Ukrainian Life in New York*. The community looked forward to another fifty years of group solidarity and progress.

In the next decade the Ukrainians struggled to maintain their community as the flower people moved in and the Ukrainian Lower East Side became the East Village. Though the conservative Ukrainians could hardly approve of the new Bohemian "life-styles," their art galleries and dance clubs helped the neighborhood thrive commercially.

While the neighborhood stabilized, the Ukrainians' strong organizational base kept the community active and vital. The area's museum, world-famous choir, Ukrainian shops, and festivals flourished. Ukrainians were able to provide social services for a growing elderly population. Even people who had left the Lower East Side stayed close to and supported the community.

Ukrainian Place Marks

Ukrainian Museum, *203 Second Avenue (212-228-0110). Wednesday–Sunday 1 P.M.–5 P.M. Admission charge.*

The museum is an intimate journey into the folk arts and folk ways of a people. The exhibits of painted Easter eggs, ceramics, and embroidered peasant costumes capture a naive delight in color and a sophisticated sense of form. There are special exhibits dealing with the significant and the rare, from icon covers to illuminated manuscripts. The staff is obviously involved and will gladly answer any questions.

St. George's Ukrainian Catholic Church, *33 East Seventh Street (212-674-1615).*

The sanctuary of St. George's Church is a copy of a Carpathian Uniate church. Though a Catholic house of worship, it has icons like an Orthodox church, a massive dome, and sixteen remarkable stained-glass windows. The church plays an important part in organizing community-wide events like the Ukrainian Festival, while the church school keeps Ukrainian culture alive.

— Ethnic Detour —

Directions: Subway 6 to 77th Street/Lexington Avenue.

Ukrainian Institute of America, *2 East 79th Street (212-288-8660). Call for information on special events.*

Voldymyr Dzus, the inventor of the industrial fastener, founded The Ukrainian Institute of America in 1948. It was to be a repository for Ukrainian artifacts and arts and crafts and a center for the study of Ukrainian culture. In a magnificent Gothic revival mansion it houses Ukrainian religious relics and a gallery of Ukrainian portraits and sculpture. It offers special exhibits of Ukrainian art, past and present. The Institute also sponsors Ukrainian concerts and symposiums. While preserving Ukrainian culture and traditions, it also provides community services for elderly members of the community.

Ukrainian Choral Music

Ukrainians are fanatics when it comes to their choral music. The saying goes that when two Ukrainians meet they start another choir. The Ukrainian choir has the range of a symphony orchestra with intricate and precise harmonies. Sometime the choirs are joined by symphony orchestras but usually the traditional *bandura* (a stringed instrument between a guitar and harp) provides the accompaniment.

The Koshetz choir of the independent Ukraine Republic introduced Ukrainian choruses to a wider American audience in the twenties. The leading members of the choir remained in New York after the Soviet takeover of the Ukraine and became involved in New York choirs, which gained a reputation for being the best in the country.

The Dumka is the leading Ukrainian choir in New York. It has performed at Lincoln Center and given concerts to mark milestones in the Ukrainian community. The choir's repertoire includes Carpathian and Cossack folk music and specially written choral music with Ukrainian lyrics and harmonies. The Dumka considers music their first language.

Ukrainian Bigos *Tastes*

Ukrainian cooking is heavy Slavic from the breadbasket of the former Soviet Union. The potato defers to wheat groats (*kasha*) and wheat flour *verhenyly* dumplings (stuffed with meat or cheese) are the Ukrainian ravioli. The Ukrainians eat plenty of beef, but they have a preference for pork and it sometimes stands alone with rice in stuffed cabbage (*holubsti*) and stuffed peppers. They make a rich meat loaf (*zayac*) out of ground pork with veal for a little spice. They are partial to bacon (*bochok*), which is served marinated as a meaty main dish. Like the Poles, Ukrainians are mad about the smoked sausage *kielbasa* (*kobasa*), which they enjoy coarsely ground. Ukrainians also slice it up and add sauerkraut for a favorite national dish called *bigos*. Ukrainian cuisine is not heavily seasoned; a dollop of sour cream is the favorite condiment.

Ukrainian restaurants are plain and fancy—a simple coffee shop with counters and formica tables or a formal dining room with chandeliers and white tablecloths. Whether the restaurants cater to the original locals or the latest hip group of outlanders, they share the Ukrainian sense of hospitality. They haven't learned to be urban brusque. On Sundays after mass at St. George's and a stroll, Ukrainian families pile into the neighborhood's restaurants for an old-fashioned Sunday dinner.

Veselka, *144 Second Avenue at Tenth Street (212-228-9682). Monday–Friday 7 A.M.–1 A.M.; Saturday and Sunday 7 A.M.–4 A.M.*

Veselka is East Village ambience and Ukrainian food, and is usually crowded with the latest counterculture bunch against a modernist backdrop of whooping Native Americans on the wall. They still sell the Ukrainian newspaper from a stand in front and sell out the meat *pierogen*.

Ukrainian East Village Restaurant, *140 East Second Avenue between Ninth and Tenth Streets (212-529-5024). Daily noon– 11 P.M.*

The Ukrainian is located in the Ukrainian National Home. The restaurant is dimly lit and formal for Ukrainian family evenings out. Broad-shouldered Ukrainians, awkward in their Sunday suits, squire their gray-haired ladies; there are often three generations at a table. Suburban Ukrainians make expeditions here for the lean *krakiewska* sausage and the veal with the special stuffing.

Odessa Coffee Shop, *117 Avenue A (212-473-8916). Daily 7 A.M.– midnight.*

Odessa is where the old Ukrainian chess players—the ones who use to play in Tompkins Square Park—come for coffee. Talking gives people an appetite, and thoughts soon turn from chess to cheese blintzes. Ukrainian school kids drop in for poppy seed pastries.

Kiev Restaurant, *117 Second Avenue at Sixth Street (212-674-4040). Daily 24 hours.*

The Kiev is around-the-clock Ukrainian food. New York University kids economize on thick meal-in-a-bowl mushroom barley soup or borscht with fat slices of egg bread, while at the next table a group of Ukrainians from Jersey City reminisce about the old neighborhood over Ukrainian *kotlets* with *kasha* in onion gravy.

A Kabosy *by any Other Name*

Ukrainians are adamant that their foods are unique in taste and texture, and though outsiders may not be able to tell the difference between a Ukrainian sausage and *kielbasa,* East Village Ukrainians will accept no substitutes. Some local food shops cater to their preferences.

Bella's Mini Market, *109 First Avenue, between Sixth and Seventh avenues (212-982-7893). Daily 7 A.M.–9 P.M.*

The bread covers the Eastern European waterfront with a fine pumpernickel that goes well with a spiced Ukrainian sausage or *kielbasa.* The Ukrainian-style *babka* with cheese and poppy seed cakes are what the local ladies have with their tea. Ukrainian-style products run the gamut from cold cuts to preserves.

Kurowycky Meats, *124 First Avenue between Seventh and Eighth Streets (212-477-0344). Monday–Saturday 8 A.M.–6 P.M.*

Three generations of Ukrainian butchers prepare spiced dried Ukrainian sausage and a sausage heavy on the garlic and caraway seeds. Their smoked meats have a reputation that attracts limousines from out of the neighborhood, but the Kurowyckys like it where they are. Their customers are familiar faces.

Pysansky *and More*

Ukrainians are proud of their handicrafts. They are more than a tradition; these folk arts are a part of the present too. The colorful geometrics of Ukrainian kilims and Easter eggs are the centerpieces of Ukrainian households.

For Ukrainians the egg is the symbol of life and renewal. In pagan times there was a spring festival where Ukrainians danced at first light in honor of the sun and spirits. They painted eggs as offerings with special designs and cosmic patterns of the rooster and the sun. In Christian times these magical eggs became associated with Easter and the resurrection of Christ and were blessed by priests on Easter mornings. The art of the Easter egg, called *pysanksy,* is passed on from generation to generation in the Ukrainian East Village.

Surma "The Ukrainian Shop," *111 East Seventh Street (212-477-0729). Monday–Friday 11 A.M.–6 P.M.; Saturday 11 A.M.–5 P.M.; Sunday 11 A.M.–2 P.M.*

Surma started out in the Ukrainian music business. It still has Ukrainian sheet music and records of the Dumka Choir playing with thirty banduras. Surma now needs the tourist trade and has branched out into embroidered peasant blouses and vests and Ukrainian inlaid boxes and carvings.

Arka, *26 First Avenue between First and Second Streets (212-473-3550). Daily 10 A.M.–6 P.M.*

Arka is a study in red and white in pottery, fabrics, and embroidered blouses. There are assortments of carved wooden plates, Ukrainian greeting cards, and Ukrainian music cassettes.

Ukrainian Celebrations

May 17 is a great day for Ukrainians, marking the conversion of their nation to Christianity. The whole Manhattan Ukrainian community—

probably numbering around thirty thousand—crowds Seventh Street between Second and Third Avenues to enjoy national dishes like stuffed cabbage and borscht and to admire Ukrainian Easter eggs and embroidered peasant blouses. There are many older Ukrainians who return to the neighborhood on this day. Their eyes shine with recognition and memories. Grandchildren and even great-grandchildren are in tow.

In the afternoons limber Ukrainian folk dancers in high boots and embroidered blouses go through their acrobatic paces. A special mass is held on Sunday at St. George's Ukrainian Catholic Church, the sponsor of this festival.

══════════════ Russians ══════════════

History

The Russians who made it to New York City were primarily political refugees. In 1905, when the first workers' revolution failed, a spellbinding orator named Leon Trotsky escaped with his family to Brooklyn. When Trotsky, Lenin, and company defeated the Tsar and sent the provisional government packing in 1917, Alexander Kerensky, the leader of that government, turned up in New York.

Russian writers, artists, and composers also found a refuge in the city. The daring composer Igor Stravinsky, after arriving in New York, was the first to cross the boundaries of melody. The Russian émigré ballet master George Balanchine, who came to New York in 1932, was the first to choreograph ballets to Stravinsky's music, breaking the conventional story format.

After World War II the Russian writer Vladimir Nabokov lived in New York between stints in universities. Using his second language, English, he changed the ground rules of the modern novel.

In the years of the Cold War before détente and *glasnost,* defection or exile were the only ways to emigrate from Russia. New York's ballet benefited from these unconventional arrivals. Rudolph Nureyev was not only the leading dancer with the American Ballet but he was the toast of New York nightlife with frequent appearances at Studio 54. Mikhail Baryshnikov, with his acrobatic leaps, was a New York ballet matinee idol. He was also a serious choreographer who wasn't afraid to experiment at the helm of the American Ballet.

Russian émigrés who settled in New York also included generals and foot soldiers of the White Army, though at times it was hard to tell one from the other. There was a whole raft of Russian aristocrats who formed their own organizations where they could spend their time looking up genealogies. These Romanovs and Obolenskys married into notable New York families and became outstanding members of the city's cafe society.

The Russians who came to New York were not the same kind who labored in the mines of Pennsylvania. They were rich enough not to need a neighborhood or they had the intellectual skills to rapidly assimilate. Russian New York was the Russian Orthodox Church, with masses that lasted longer than a double feature, the odd Russian restaurant, and the curio shops with pawned antiquities.

The White Russians Are Coming

The White Russians are traditionalists. They live in a gossamer memory of vast estates and country houses. It is the Russia of white nights and balalaika music, of bowing peasants and diamond Fabergé Easter eggs. The Tsar is the linchpin of this world and the Russian Orthodox Church is its spiritual center. Contemporary Russia, with its grasping "fast buck" ideology, is as foreign to them as the repressive system of the deposed Soviets.

St. Nicholas Patriarchal Cathedral, *15 East 97th Street (212-289-1915).*

The Russian Orthodox church's giant onion-shaped domes tower over the neighborhood like some Arabian Nights fairy tale. Inside, the icons with their religious figures in stylized poses also seem Oriental. The great chandeliers are simply spectacular. The masses in Russian are long but the ritual is moving. The St. Nicholas boys' choir is special.

Synod of Bishops of the Russian Orthodox Church Outside Russia, *1180 Park Avenue near 93rd Street.*

The Synod is ensconced in a large elegant Georgian revival mansion. The sacred icons that adorn the walls are more than decoration. The former ballroom has been converted into a Russian Orthodox chapel.

Russian Nobility Association in America, *971 First Avenue at 52nd Street (212-755-7528).*

The library is all about genealogy, one thousand volumes in all. It is the place where old Russian aristocrats go to polish their coat of arms. It is also the seat of the Russian Nobility Association of America, which keeps track of old Russian families in the States like a college alumni department.

Borscht or Bust

Russian cuisine is the haute cuisine of the Slavs. It is the same food that the Poles and Ukrainians eat, but with the touch of a French chef. The Russian buckwheat *blini,* which wraps the caviar, is a Russian crepe. The Russian *pierogen* stuffed with meat is a Russian brioche. The chicken Kiev, lightly breaded and fried and wrapped around a cube of butter, delicately brings out the taste of the chicken breast. Beef Stroganoff, made with the tenderest strips of beef flavored with mushrooms and sour cream, is almost tart on its delicate bed of white rice.

Russian Samovar, *256 West 52nd Street (212-757-0168). Tuesday–Saturday noon–3 P.M., 5 P.M.–11 P.M.*

The Russian Samovar draws the cream of the Soviet émigrés, including some crossover stars like Baryshnikov and Brodsky. They come for the rich Russian foods, the chilled vodka with pepper, and a piano player who performed at St. Petersburg's Maly Theater. The not-to-be-missed specialty is the *pojarski* cutlet, ground veal and chicken rolled and sauteed and served with *kasha.*

Uncle Vanya, *315 West 54th Street (212-262-0542). Daily noon– 11 P.M.*

Dining in Uncle Vanya is sometimes like being in a Chekov comedy. Everyone is basically well meaning but there are misunderstandings that can create complications and actions at cross-purposes. It used to be an off-the-beaten track Russian take-out with an undistinguished appearance and excellent food. The same fine food now comes to the table made to order.

The Russian Tea Room, *150 West 57th Street (212-265-0847). Daily 1:30 P.M.–4 P.M., 4:30 P.M.–9:30 P.M.*

The Russian Tea Room once was a Russian restaurant but nowadays it's a theatrical landmark. In the interim, the food hasn't improved but the prices reflect the new clientele. The beef Stroganoff is still the best in the city, but it's not easy to appreciate when you are sitting in your neighbor's lap.

The Pie, *340 East 86th Street (212-517-8717). Daily noon–3 P.M., 5 P.M.–10 P.M.*

Once you get past the balalaikas and the Russian dolls at the front of this storefront restaurant, it is simplicity itself, though a little confining. The food goes a long way to compensate for any discomfort. Sample the Pie's down-to-earth delicious variations on the peasant *pierogen,* blini, and noodle.

Andrusha Cafe, *1742 Second Avenue between 90th and 91st streets (212-360-1128). Monday–Friday noon–3:30 P.M., 4 P.M.– 10 P.M.; Saturday and Sunday noon–3:30 P.M., 4 P.M.–11 P.M.*

The Andrusha is a candlelight-and-flowers kind of place. It doesn't project the robustness connected with Russian food and appetites. The Russian cuisine, whether the entrée is a grilled *shashlik* or a *pelemeni* (dumpling), almost hits the mark, but something is missing.

L'Ermitage, *40 West 56th Street between Fifth and Sixth avenues (212-581-0777). Sunday–Friday noon–11 P.M.; Saturday 5:30 P.M.– midnight.*

L'Ermitage serves continental fare with a Russian accent and Russian fare with a continental accent. Neither is entirely satisfying. The ambience is elegant with a pianist who provides more than just background music.

Memories, *239 East 53rd Street between Second and Third avenues (212-980-5821). Monday–Saturday noon–10 P.M.*

Culinary memories are made of light blinis, thick borscht, and rich stroganoff. Memories is a hidden jewel.

The Glory of Russia Past and Present

A La Vieille Russie, *781 Fifth Avenue at 59th Street (212-752-1727). Monday–Friday 10 A.M.–5 P.M.; Saturday 10 A.M.–4 P.M.*

The show window of this exquisite shop displays some of the jewels that might have belonged to the Russian aristocracy before the Revolution. At Easter they set out some of the fabulously crafted enameled and jeweled eggs made by the Frenchman Fabergé for the Russian nobility, just a hint of the opulence that was.

The Russian House, *253 Fifth Avenue between 28th and 29th streets (212-685-1010). Monday–Saturday 10 A.M.–6 P.M.*

The Russian House is the old Soviet Four Continents Bookstore with a capitalist make-over. The Russian coffee-table books, hand-painted lacquer boxes, Matroysha dolls, Easter eggs, peasant blouses, and icons are handsomely displayed. Russian classics, best-sellers, and dictionaries are all available.

Kismet Records, *227 East 14th Street (212-487-2891). Daily 10 A.M.–8 P.M.*

This old curio shop sells an eccentric mix of items including Red Army uniforms, Red Army greatcoats, Soviet pins, Russian Easter eggs, and rare old records, Russian and American. The owner receives regular shipments from St. Petersburg, which he still calls Leningrad.

Sobor Icons, *230 East 14th Street (212-982-3488). Daily noon– 6:00 P.M.*

This shop has a bare Soviet state store look. The icons run the gamut from rare and beautiful to clumsy copy. Russian dolls, enamel and copper samovars, and some stunning eggs are also on sale. Ordinarily the owner, who doubles as a watch repairman, will give a twenty percent discount. Try for more.

Russian World, *18th West 55th Street (212-399-6500). Daily noon–10 P.M.*

Russian World has an extensive selection of Russian collectibles, including lacquered boxes, nesting dolls, amber jewelry, and Russian Orthodox icons.

The Arabs

New York's Arab community is a rich microcosm of the whole Arab world, representing many nations and religious affiliations united by a common Arab language and culture. Arab New York encompasses the traditions of Muslim and Maronite, Yemenite and Syrian. It is the Lebanese and Palestinian fresh from the barricades and the engineer or doctor from Egypt or Iraq. In New York's most recent American Ethnic Parade the Arab contingent represented twenty-two nations from North Africa to the Near East and from the Atlantic Ocean to the Indian Ocean. While the Syrians and Lebanese have far outnumbered other Arab immigrant groups in the past and are still the most influential segment of the Arab community, the latest Palestinian arrivals have infused the community with a new sense of Arab identity. Recent African arrivals from the Sudan and Somalia have reinforced the Arab and Islamic belief in one god and one human family, providing another occasion for legendary Arab hospitality.

History

The first Arabs to make the long journey to New York had only a vague sense of nationality but if put to it, they considered themselves Syrian, whether they came from the wealthy Melkite quarters of Damascus, the mountain strongholds of the Lebanese Shuf, or holy Jerusalem. The overwhelming majority were Christians, who for more than a millennium of Muslim rule had maintained their religious identity.

They were devoted Eastern Rite Catholics of the Maronite or Melkite Communion or Syrian Orthodox. There were significant minorities of Muslims and the Druse of Lebanon, who subscribed to many Islamic beliefs and had their own esoteric holy books. All of these groups shared a deep loyalty to the family, a feeling of tribe that positively influenced their overall behavior and a strict ethical code.

The situation of Syrian Christians and, to a lesser extent, their Muslim neighbors changed with the fortunes of the Ottoman regime. One moment Christians were the privileged intermediaries of the spice route and the next they were infidels squeezed by a heavy head tax. Rich or poor, they were at times vulnerable to the petty persecution of the authorities, but generally, in line with the prescriptions of the Koran, they were treated with respect as a "protected" people.

In 1860 the competition for scarce land in Lebanon led to the massacre of thousands of Maronites and Melkites by a Druse army. The Western powers reacted immediately to the violence by pressuring the Turkish sultan to institute a more autonomous regime in Lebanon under a Christian administrator. This new government, under the sponsorship of the European powers, ushered in a period of economic growth and the expansion of Western culture from 1861 to 1915.

In some areas of Lebanon and Syria agriculture had become too dependent on cash crops and foreign imports and large landholders were able to enlarge their holdings at the expense of small farmers. In an atmosphere of rising expectations immigration became the solution for economic problems.

Following in the footsteps of their adventurous Phoenician ancestors, Syrian Lebanese set their sights on the New World. An advance group of merchants from Damascus, Beirut, and Jerusalem journeyed to the Philadelphia Centennial Exposition in 1876 and sent back glowing reports of commercial success. The response was immediate and overwhelming; young Arab men, eager to make their fortunes and serve their families, crossed a continent.

This first wave of Arab emigrants were mostly Christian. They were helped at every juncture of their journey from Cyprus to Marseilles to Liverpool by local Syrian-Lebanese communities. In New York at Ellis Island, Najib Arbeely, the Immigration Bureau's Arab interpreter, was a one-man information service. He assisted Arab newcomers in contacting their families or their religious communities and counseled the uninitiated about employment opportunities.

After the Syrian-Lebanese emigrants disembarked at the Battery, it was only a short walk to the Arab hubbub and bazaar on Washington Street. They were warmly welcomed by relatives or friends from their villages. The new arrivals, who often thought their stays would be temporary, were anxious to get started. They intended to work hard, spend little, save some dollars, and return home to buy land or finance a business.

In the formative years of Little Syria the inhabitants were mainly male. They lived together in bachelor boardinghouses, saving on expenses and sharing the cooking and cleaning. They helped one another find jobs or get into business and exchanged precious bits of information about home, family, and friends.

Once they had some scraps of English and a handle on American customs, the majority took up the peddler's pack. Though peddling was the preserve of Greeks, Jews, and Armenians in their homeland, more than ninety percent of these mainly agrarian Arabs were peddlers prior to World War I.

New York was known as the "Mother of Peddling Communities." Local Syrian merchants provided the goods, usually local handicrafts or imports from the Mideast. At first the peddlers sold crosses from the Cedars of Lebanon and rosaries from the Holy Land, but later they advanced to such exotica as silk handkerchiefs, embroidered kimonos, and lace shawls. These Arab peddlers traveled alone or in pairs and scrupulously avoided competing with one another.

For Arab New Yorkers, peddling proved to be the quickest path to cultural assimilation and material success. Peddlers traveling cross-country had a crash course in things American and the American language. They were able to develop their entrepreneurial skills and powers of persuasion on farm people in rural backwaters while earning the necessary money to advance in business.

The gradual collapse of the old Ottoman order and an unending series of brushfire wars put added pressures on the peoples of Syria. There were confiscations of food and supplies, and the burden of taxes became unbearable. In 1908 the government of the Young Turks threatened their subject populations with military conscription.

Many Syrian Lebanese left their ancestral lands for freedom and survival. In the decade preceding World War I almost one-quarter of the population deserted the rugged country of Mount Lebanon. Caring and devoted Arab New Yorkers were not cut off from their homeland and many returned regularly to help build and rebuild churches and hospitals. They supported poor family members and assisted others in emigrating. Many Christian Arab women now joined their husbands and fathers in the city.

New York City became the unofficial capital of the Syrian-Lebanese community. Washington Street was a Levantine market, with animated vendors selling exotic spices, Oriental rugs, and gold bracelets. There were tables gorgeously inlaid with mother-of-pearl and scimitars of Damascus steel. In the cafes men in fezzes drank tiny cups of Turkish coffee and sat on cushions, smoking hookahs and playing backgammon.

Hundreds of Syrian men, women, and children filled apartments between Washington and Greenwich Streets and Rector and Carlisle Streets. Merchants established Middle Eastern import and export houses and entrepreneurs opened small garment factories specializing in silk embroidery. Some of the more successful Arab businessmen like Saleem Malouk were even able to move uptown to Fifth Avenue mansions and become patrons of the arts.

The New York casbah became the model for all Arabic-American communities. It had three churches and six newspapers and organized the first Arabic-American Association in the country, which assisted Arabs in learning English and getting an education.

Arab success was no accident. Syrian Lebanese were impelled to succeed by a need to win honor and status for themselves and their families. The American get-rich-quick ethic agreed with Arab values like generosity, hospitality, and munificence. Coming from a society where people were frequently jockeying for position, the Syrian Lebanese were prepared to compete for the rewards of wealth. They were determined to work hard and sacrifice for the source of their identity, the family.

But the Arab people who kept classical learning alive during the Dark Ages had interests beyond mere money. The earliest leader of the Arab intellectual community was Dr. Joseph Arbeely, who reached New York in 1881. He had been involved in a translation of the Bible into Arabic and recognized the importance of the Arab linguistic heritage.

His sons founded the city's first Arabic newspaper and laid the foundation for the whole Arab press in America. The two most powerful organs in this highly sectarian community were *Al-Hoda,* which represented the Maronite point of view, and *Murrat-ul-Garb,* which was the voice of the Orthodox. In 1910 *Al-Bayan* (The News) began publication; it was concerned with issues involving the Muslim and Druse communities.

New York was the center for an experimental Syrian literary movement, which was creating Arabic equivalents for modern Western forms like free verse. Kahlil Gibran, the renowned author of *The Prophet,* was the leader of *Al-Rabitur al-Qalamiyya* (The Pen League), a circle that included writers like the Arab Walt Whitman, Ameen Rihani, who wrote with Whitmanesque energy and verve. The Pen League attacked the literary status quo and encouraged the publication of new Arabic writing.

Arab men and women increasingly dressed American and their actions were no longer strictly limited by parental authority. Women without scarves (even Christian women wore scarves in their villages as a matter of modesty) were even involved in the world of work outside the home. Syrian Lebanese married Americans and immigrants from European countries and some gradually lost their Arab identity.

In 1905 there was a pitched battle in the narrow streets of Little Syria between traditionalists and the forces of Americanization. Five people were injured in the fifteen-minute "pistol-knife" fray that embarrassed the whole Syrian-Lebanese community. Najeeb Malouf and Syrian Orthodox Bishop Hawaweeny tried unsuccessfully to mediate the dispute.

The New York Arabic community was able to unite in the face of old-fashioned American bigotry. In January of 1909 a Lebanese named Costa George Najour was refused citizenship on the basis of the Asian exclusionary rule and Arabs were officially classified as nonwhite. Arab New Yorkers and the local Arab press went into action, raising over a thousand dollars to appeal the case and Najour was finally vindicated and granted citizenship.

Following World War I and the years of accumulating capital, the Arab peddler was replaced by the Arab store owner. The community gained a new stability, which was not even threatened by the movement of Syrian Lebanese from the old Little Syria near the Battery to a new ethnic enclave in Brooklyn. Arabs increasingly went retail, opening dry-goods stores, grocery stores, and fruit and vegetable stands.

While some Arab New Yorkers eagerly assimilated, there was a re-awakening of cultural identity in the New York Arab community. The Maronite Arabs began to view themselves as a special people, the descendants of Phoenician empire builders. This Lebanese national pride was encouraged by a new political entity in the post–World War I Middle East. The Maronites believed that the Greater Lebanon Mandate, which was controlled by the French, was their own nation.

After another world war the whole map of the Middle East changed again and the city's Arabs could now point with pride to the state of Lebanon. The majority could trace their bloodlines back to the mountaineers of this new land. They also found it easy to identify with such a cosmopolitan country, with its long-standing French-Maronite connection. Soon it became the rule to add the Lebanese national identification to the names of local organizations. The notion of Lebanese nationality was so pervasive that even New Yorkers of Syrian Christian descent referred to themselves as Lebanese.

The Celler-Hart Immigration Act of 1965 opened the doors of New York to Arabs from different geographical areas and segments of society. New immigration quotas based on professional skills instead of race or national origin enabled educated elites throughout the Arab world and many more Muslims to immigrate to the city. Engineers and physicians from Egypt and Iraq found employment and economic opportunity; many had previously studied in the United States. Like the early Syrian-Lebanese peddlers, they also took American brides.

The 1967 Arab-Israeli War increased the flow of Palestinian refugees, who had been emigrating to New York in significant numbers since the end of the Arab-Israeli War in 1948. They were very different from other recent arrivals. The Palestinians were politicized and really committed to their Arab identity.

Many Arab New Yorkers rallied around these refugees, believing the time had come to assert their ethnic pride. Arab-American university graduates convened in 1968 to map a strategy to improve the Arab image. New York's Arab churches and organizations inaugurated classes in Arabic language and culture. The Eastern Federation of American Syrian Lebanese Clubs even sought a voice in American foreign policy. Arabs from Lebanon, Yemen, Egypt, and Palestine were united and committed to a Pan-Arabic identity.

In the 1980s there was an increase of rural emigrants from Yemen, Egypt, the Sudan, and Somalia. They were joined by Palestinian refugees from Lebanon, and later from Kuwait, who were often the victims of events beyond their control. Unfortunately, these new Arab immigrants did not always have access to the community support systems that had aided another generation of Arab emigrants. They were also subject to prejudice and unthinking stereotypes which stamped them as fanatics and terrorists.

Still, these new Americans, through a combination of perseverance, a strong sense of duty, and supportive extended families, are beginning to establish themselves in this competitive metropolis. Many put in long hours as cab or livery drivers, while others operate small businesses such as grocery stores, newsstands, and delicatessens. In Brooklyn alone there are one thousand Arab American store owners.

Although the census declares that there are only 51,770 Arabs living in New York, it is apparent that the real figure is much higher. The Arab presence in New York, as revealed in school enrollments, the increasing number of mosques and Eastern Rite churches, and the rise in Arab business ownership, indicates a population closer to two hundred thousand! Without a doubt the burgeoning Arab community will be playing a more prominent role in New York in years to come.

════ Atlantic Avenue Neighborhood ════

Directions: Subway 2, 3, 4, or 5 to Borough Hall.

Atlantic Avenue between Henry and Clinton Streets is the Main Street of the Arab community, not only of New York but of the whole country. This Brooklyn commercial area is the sentimental home for Arabs; it is the place to find Arab food, Arab music, Arab books and newspapers, and Arab cultural artifacts from rugs to worry beads.

Here the Arab presence that is usually so diffuse becomes an actual part of the city. Among their own people and Atlantic Avenue's spice market and bazaar, Arab Americans can live their identity. Atlantic Avenue is more than a street, it is a state of mind.

In another age Atlantic Avenue, where it today meets with Clinton Street, was the crest of a hill called Cobble Hill. During the American Revolution the British army retook this high ground, which George Washington had used as a vantage point to watch the movements of the Redcoats. For all their trouble, the British eventually used Cobble Hill as an evacuation point.

Atlantic Avenue never reached the elegant heights of its close neighbor, Brooklyn Heights, but it did provide pleasant housing for Irish immigrants on the move. Later it attracted Scandinavian residents who were employed at the Navy Yard at Red Hook. Italians from southern Italy and Spaniards from Galicia in northern Spain were next to occupy Atlantic Avenue.

In 1892, while Washington Street's Arab neighborhood was still growing, Arabs started to leave its dark, poorly ventilated buildings for comparatively spacious Atlantic Avenue housing. It was a convenient area to choose, the first stop on the Fulton Ferry leaving Battery Park.

The numbers of new Arab immigrants quickly increased as married Syrian men began bringing over their wives and children, and young ambitious Arab men were drawn to the city by the constant flow of overseas money orders. Soon there was a need for space to accommodate the increased immigrant masses, but the Washington Street neighborhood was hemmed in by the development of commercial buildings for the financial district. In 1940 work on the Brooklyn Battery Tunnel bulldozed Manhattan's Arab neighborhood out of existence, making Brooklyn's Atlantic Avenue the community's center.

Through the efforts of enterprising Atlantic Avenue merchants like the Sahadis, the Malkos, and Moustaphas, the retail businesses on the block prospered, and Syrians and Lebanese were soon moving out of apartments above the stores and moving into the landmark buildings of Cobble Hill and Brooklyn Heights. There was a solid community life of families, churches, and village associations.

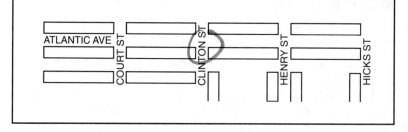

Atlantic Avenue

American politics were foreign to a people who related to others on the basis of blood ties and religion rather than geographical closeness. In 1932 Lebanese and Syrians could not gain the recognition of Tammany, and a local Democratic club voted Republican. Despite the Depression the Arab colony was able to spread out to expensive period houses in Park Slope and nearby Prospect Park.

At the end of World War II Atlantic Avenue was the scene of wild celebrating in honor of V-E Day and the independence of Lebanon. In 1948 another war between the Israelis and the Arabs brought displaced Palestinians to the neighborhood around Atlantic Avenue; the later 1967 Six Day War added West Bank Arabs with Jordanian passports to the influx. Syrian and Lebanese community leaders tried to keep tensions to a minimum with their Jewish neighbors by forming the Salaam (Peace) Club in 1970.

In the late 1960s Yemeni Muslim refugees began leaving their partitioned nation to create their own enclave on Atlantic Avenue. They were welcomed by established Yemeni families like the Almontasers, who have owned a number of popular Atlantic Avenue restaurants.

The civil war in Lebanon was a cause of great concern and renewed Lebanese emigration to Brooklyn between 1975 and 1990. The Atlantic Avenue Lebanese worked hard to integrate these refugees into the community and have continued to send relief to their war-weary homeland. Meanwhile the Arab colony has continued its Brooklyn *hegira* to the more suburban Bay Ridge on Shore Road.

Recent conflicts and famine in Somalia and the Sudan have led to a new Atlantic Avenue presence—black Arabs—and renewed hostilities in Yemen have created another generation of Yemenite war refugees. The cohesive Arabs have readily absorbed these immigrants into the fabric of the community and helped them to find jobs and apply for local services.

Arab Religious Life

Arab Churches

When the Arabs were under the rule of the eight-hundred-year Turkish Ottoman Empire, the Leaders of their churches acted as intermediaries with the Ottoman officials and rulers. The churches were a kind of nation and the church hierarchy had considerable secular power. Even in the twentieth century, Brooklyn Lebanese and Syrian Christian churches are a prime source of individual identity. These churches have an important social role and perform charitable functions that other ethnics have handed over to secular groups.

Our Lady of Lebanon, *13 Remsen Street (718-624-7228).*

This Maronite house of worship is in the landmark church that originally housed the Congregational Church of Pilgrims. An 1845 Gothic Revival structure, it has some unusual details like doors from the luxury liner *Normandie* and a piece of Plymouth Rock in its tower. Father Abdullah is the spiritual leader of this large congregation, which includes many refugees from the civil war in Lebanon. The church helps in any way it can to find jobs and housing for these new Americans and sent aid overseas to their struggling community. On Sundays at 11 A.M. the church holds a mass in Arabic.

The Arab Mosque

The mosque has always been the heart, soul, and even the mind of the Islamic Arab community. This religious sanctuary is a comfortable and comforting refuge for Arab immigrants confronted by unfamiliar customs, life-styles, and unthinking prejudice. It is a source of support, material and spiritual, and an institution that helps to integrate individuals and families into the community. The mosque is also a study house and a place to contemplate the mysteries of life and death.

Masjid Al Farouq, *552-554 Atlantic Avenue between Fourth and Fifth streets.*

There are no minarets in front of Al Farouq. It is in a six-story art deco building. The Muslims who attend the mosque are mainly Arabs from the neighborhood but there are also a large number of African Americans, Pakistanis, and Afghanis. Prayers in the mosque, bowing to Mecca in the East, are not only a vivid act of faith but a demonstration of Muslim brotherhood. Members of the mosque practice charity toward poorer minorities in the community. Since prayers must be spoken in Arabic, instructional classes in the language are given. Members of the mosque also participate in Palestinian relief programs.

Dining

Arab cooking is simple. The ingredients are fresh and natural. Lamb, yogurt, bulgar (cracked wheat), rice, pine nuts, dried apricots, grape leaves, lemons, okra, string beans, chick peas, squash, and eggplant are the essentials of the Arab kitchen. Garlic, lemon, cloves, cinnamon, coriander, cardamom, thyme, mint, and rose water provide the aromatic flavor. The food is hot-weather light and the tastes are subtle.

Among the Arabs, eating is more than satisfying hunger; it is a social occasion and an opportunity for hospitality. The *mazza* is an Arabic selection of appetizer-like dishes shared by a group with pita bread and good conversation. *Hummos* (mashed chick peas with garlic, lemon, and sesame oil) and *baba ghanouj* (broiled eggplant mashed with garlic, lemon, and sesame oil) are typical cold *mazza,* while *felafel* (fried chick pea puree) and *kibee* (fried or broiled lamb mixed with yogurt, bulgar, and pine nuts) are hot *mazza.* Christian Lebanese whet the appetite for more dishes with Arak, an anise-flavored liquor, usually mixed with ice and water.

In the Magreb of North Africa they add a little heat to the food in the form of hot peppers; couscous (semolina grains) replaces cracked wheat as the grain of choice. For the favorite dish of this region the couscous is steamed in a special pot and covered with stewed meats and vegetables served with their juices and *harissa, a hot flavorful sauce.* In Syria and Lebanon stews are made with lamb and a single vegetable, mainly string beans, okra, or squash. The squash is also stuffed with chopped lamb and rice. Touches of rose water, mint, and cinnamon bring out rather than overlay these basic tastes. Broiled meat in the Arab world is the basic lamb kebab cooked on a spit.

Atlantic Avenue's restaurant row offers mostly authentic tastes of the Middle East for an essentially Arab clientele and the yuppies and literary types from Brooklyn Heights. Many of the restaurants represent three generations of Syrians or Lebanese, while others are owned by more recent arrivals.

Fatoosh Barbecue, *1311 Henry Street between Atlantic Avenue and State Street (718-596-0030). Daily 11* A.M.*–10* P.M.

Fatoosh is a small, spotless take-out with the odd table and chairs for eating in. There is a tempting selection of made-that-day *mazza* at the back counter. Besides the extra special *baba ghanouj* and *hummos,* there are standout salads like *fatoosh* (finely chopped lettuce, onion, fried pita, mint, and spices). These fresh and natural flavors attract upscale neighbors from Brooklyn.

Adnan, *129 Atlantic Avenue (718-625-2115). Daily 11* A.M.–*11 P.M.*

Adnan is run by the Yemeni family Almontaster and is a fixture on Atlantic Avenue. It goes back to the days when the only way to woo customers was to modify the native cuisine to Western tastes and call it Continental. Even the ambience, with bare brick walls and Tiffany lamps, owes more to Brooklyn Heights than the Mideast. The staff tries hard, and while the crepes and kebabs don't mix, the Arab dishes from *baba ghanouj* to baked *kibee* are authentic, inexpensive, and delicious. The combination plate lunch is a real bargain.

Tripoli, *156 Atlantic Avenue (718-596-5800). Daily noon– midnight.*

Tripoli is Lebanon before the bombs went off. The restaurant is friendly and free-spirited. It's couples, extended families, and men-only meetings with laughter and banter over *mazza* and Arak and wine from Lebanon. The stuffed zucchini and the Arab lamb stews, *bamia* (okra), and *loubia* (string beans) are satisfying without being at all heavy. The wooden booths carved in arabesques, the ornate balcony off the bar, and the colorful mural of Lebanon keep up the mood of an Arabian Nights party.

Yemeni Cafe, *176 Atlantic Avenue (718-834-9533). Daily 8* A.M.– *10 P.M.*

The Yemeni Cafe is just what the sign says. It is a real old-fashioned Arab cafe where Arab men, mostly new immigrants in ill-fitting suits, while away the hours over thimbles of coffee and Cokes and share true Yemeni-style versions of chicken soup, *hummos, foul* (stewed lima beans), dumplings, and kebabs, which can be very hot or spicy. Even the tea here is an adventure. The occasional interloper is politely ignored. Return a second time and you are a friend of the house.

Fountain Cafe, *183 Atlantic Avenue (718-624-6764). Daily 10:30* A.M.–*10:30 P.M.*

The Fountain Cafe is bright and inviting, with an actual gurgling fountain close to its center. It is a true cafe, a place for casual dining, with daily specials including chicken or lamb kebabs, with *hummos* or *baba ghanouj* or a pita bread sandwich of *kafta* (minced lamb). The desserts, from a rich apricot pudding to a sugary sweet bird's nest filled with pistachios, and the thick Arabic coffee and mint tea are well worth lingering over.

Near East, *193 Atlantic Avenue (718-624-9257). Daily noon–11 P.M.*

The Near East is multinational dining in a spacious traditional Yemeni environment. The cooking covers the waterfront from Moroccan Mahgreb through Beirut French to Yemeni Near East. Ignore the French. Mareb is the land of the Queen of Sheba in Yemen. It is also a dinner special fit for a queen (or king) at the Near East, that includes *hummos,* salad, shish kebab, *kafta,* baked *kibee,* and *tajine* chicken.

Moroccan Star, *205 Atlantic Avenue (718-643-0800). Daily 11 A.M.–3 P.M., 5 P.M.–10 P.M.*

The couscous is chock full of vegetables with a whole soup bowl of juice per portion. The couscous *merguez,* made with the delectable Moroccan lamb sausage, is the star. The waiters try to please while never losing their sense of humor.

Lunch, *145 Court Street (no phone). Daily 11 A.M.–11 P.M.*

The English word "Lunch" in big bold letters identifies this restaurant on 145 Court Street. It's obvious from the outset that the owners are not interested in attracting the tourist trade, but don't let the lack of menus or an inability to communicate in Arabic deter you from authentic Arab eating. Just imagine you are in a foreign country. Come during lunch when the restaurant is crowded and chaotic and trays heaped with lamb shanks and rice flavored with currants are conveyed from table to table. If you want to order, just point.

Arabic Brick Oven

On weekends, returning Arab sons and daughters from Jersey and the Island double-park along Atlantic Avenue to get Syrian bread (they never call it pita) and stock up on spinach and meat pies and maybe sweet syrupy bird's nest or *baklawa.*

The Arabs actually invented bread; their paper-thin bread *macouk* was first prepared over a hot stone. The Arab flat breads come in many varieties: wheat, white *swimson* (sesame), and *zahta* (lightly covered with thyme, sumak, sesame seeds, and olive oil).

Arab pastry has a certain sameness, lots of variations on phyllo sheets and semolina flour, crushed walnuts, and pistachios and honey or a sugary syrup. But nothing is better with strong Turkish coffee. (The Turks named it, but it is another Arab original.) The cookies are simplicity themselves, rings and circles of dough with and without nuts or sesame.

Damascus Bakery, *195 Atlantic Avenue (718-855-1456). Daily 8 A.M.–7 P.M.*

Damascus is the big commercial producer of Syrian flat breads. People come here to buy breads in quantity. The *zahta* is so good it doesn't need any accompaniment. The individual date cakes and the *kanafe* (looking like Shredded Wheat drenched in syrup) are two excellent old standards and the *fatir bil ishta* is the strange thing that happens when phyllo meets custard.

Near East Bakery, *143 Atlantic Avenue (718-875-0016). Tuesday–Saturday 9 A.M.–4:30 P.M.; Sunday 9:30 A.M.–1 P.M.*

This bakery is worth the basement crowds in confined spaces. The three-cornered meat pies made with chopped lamb and onions and the spinach pies made with spinach and onions are nonparallel finger food. The crunchy phyllo bird's nest filled with green pistachios with a hint of rose water and topped with syrup is too rich to be believed.

Fatoosh Pitza, *330 Hicks Street between Atlantic Avenue and State Street (718-243-0500). Daily 10 A.M.–10 P.M.*

Despite the brightly painted Leaning Tower of Pisa on the window, the "pitza" (as opposed to the pizza) at Fatoosh does not try to be Italian. The flavoring is Arab allspice, thyme, and marjoram, and the toppings include *merguez* sausage and sliced lamb. The *la hambajin* is an individual Arab taco with tomato and minced lamb wrapped around a finely diced salad.

Mini-Bazaars

Arab food shops on Atlantic Avenue and its side streets are mini-bazaars. Arab food in cans and packages are a very small part of the show. From seeds to nuts, from olives to coffee, things are sold loose in vats, sacks, or apothecary jars. Arabs like their foods fresh, Shopping Arab-style takes time and a lot of looking and on weekends usually a wait on line.

Like the bazaar, the Atlantic Avenue shops deal in diversity. Even in a small grocery-sized store Middle Eastern coffee makers compete for space with music tapes, canned chick peas, jars of pickled turnips, Turkish camel saddles, Moroccan brass trays, and anything else the proprietor thinks he or she can sell.

El-Asmar International Delights, *197 Atlantic Avenue (718-855-2455). Daily 7:30 A.M.–9 P.M.*

El-Asmar is an old fixture on the Avenue. The owner is not only the congenial man with the sweeping Lebanese mountain man mustache, he is an importer of Middle Eastern food. Among other things, he has the largest and most international selection of dried fruits and nuts for snacking and cooking.

Sahadi Importing Company, *187 Atlantic Avenue (718-624-4550). Monday–Saturday 9 A.M.–7 P.M.*

Sahadi is the longest-running shop on the avenue, having started out in the original Washington Street Arab neighborhood. The inventory of Arab foods, crafts, and manufactured goods is endless. There is more than one kind of anything, whether it is halvah, loose tea, brass coffee grinders, or backgammon boards, and everything an aspiring belly dancer could possibly need. The spice and herb selection is a miniature Mideast spice market. Sahadi even sells canned Arab food under its own label.

Arab Styles

The Arab clothing available on Atlantic Avenue now goes beyond gift shop exotica; there are real Near Eastern styles for the well-dressed Arab woman and her daughter, which are more traditional than fashion conscious.

Alnoor, *199 Atlantic Avenue (718-802-1514). Monday–Saturday 10 A.M.–6:30 P.M.*

They have a full line of embroidered caftans for relaxing in at home or for special occasions. The conservative suits and dresses leave everything to the imagination. The clothes for young women feature ruffles upon ruffles and are very feminine in an old-fashioned way.

Arab Scents

In the East the sense of smell is less taken for granted than in the West. Scents are an integral part of Arab culture and not the result of sophisticated marketing and media images.

Garden of Fragrances and Aromas, *141 Court Street (718-625-6340). Monday–Saturday 10 A.M.–6 P.M.*

The Garden of Fragrances is decorated with Arab calligraphy and hanging giant wooden prayer beads, but the rainbow of colored scents in small transparent bottles put on their own show. The fragrances of rose, sandalwood, musk, and myrrh are practically Biblical.

The Arab Music Connection

Rashid Sales, *191 Atlantic Avenue (718-852-3298). Monday–Saturday 9 A.M.–7 P.M.; Sunday noon–7 P.M.*

There are cassettes and Arab records in other stores but nothing to compare with Rashid's. It covers everything from Egyptian classical to Algerian rock. The people at Rashid's know their stuff and are willing to give the customer the benefit of their knowledge. Rashid's sponsors three and a half hours of Arab music radio every week on WFUV-FM (89.5) and WSOU-FM (90.7). In the past, two generations of Rashids have produced hundreds of records preserving traditional, classical, and Amer-abic sounds.

Al-Sharequi Groceries, *145 B-Court Street (718-855-3337). Daily Monday–Saturday 8 A.M.–9 P.M.; Sunday 8 A.M.–7 P.M.*

Though it claims to be a grocery, a *halal* (the meat is killed according to Islamic ritual law) meat market, and a newsstand, the majority of the store is taken up with thousands of Arab music cassettes. Al-Shasrequi has the latest hits from Egypt, Lebanon, Jordan, and the other nations of the Middle East. It's a hangout for local music lovers.

Celebrations and Solemn Ceremonies

Mahrajan/*The Arab Party*

The first *Mahrajan,* an Arab celebration of self combining both picnic and party, was held in Bridgeport in 1930. This affirmation of identity through food, music, and dancing soon spread to New York and Brooklyn. In the early days it was a fund raiser for churches and groups. The churches are still the main sponsors of these events, but they are all-Arab happenings crossing denominational lines. Families come together and strangers share in this appreciation of the Arab heritage. The music is loud and lively and the dancing is spontaneous, as are the smiles.

Brooklyn's premier *Mahrajan* is held in the churchyard of Our Lady of Lebanon on the first weekend in June. There is an admission charge.

The Atlantic Avenue Antic

The Atlantic Avenue Antic is usually on the third Sunday in September. The Antic block party covers the length and breadth of Atlantic Avenue, spanning ethnics from Gallegos to Belizians, but the real festivities are concentrated on the avenue between Clinton and Court streets. There are portable stages with Arab bands and belly dancers. Arab spectators aren't shy; they hold their hands over their heads, do a few steps, and shake their bodies. The restaurants double as street stands and the smell of barbecuing kebabs fills the air. There is all manner of Arab pastry from *baklawa* to meat pies and all the dishes for a curbside *mazza*. Sahadi even breaks his no-opening-Sunday rule for this special day.

Little Lebanon in Bay Ridge

Directions: Subway R to 77th Street/Fourth Avenue.

The Arabs did not have to leave Brooklyn to relocate in the suburbs; they found them in Bay Ridge. They started coming to live here in the fifties and settled around Shore Road. Originally Christian and Lebanese, the community has broadened its base in more recent years to include Islamic immigrants from Palestine, Jordan, Yemen, and other Middle Eastern nations. The Arabs are an important presence in a changing Bay Ridge. Their foods and flavors add color to the old Scandinavian, Irish, and Italian neighborhood, near the sweeping silhouette of the Verrazano Bridge.

The Bay Ridge Arab community, which shops on Fifth Avenue, is primarily composed of traditional families, extended and nuclear. The father is a figure of authority and deferred to by his wife and children. Women, both married and single, are required to adhere to a high level of modesty. The Arab women of Bay Ridge, who in the past quickly assimilated and became part of the cultural mainstream, can now be identified by their head scarves and long shapeless dresses. Men and women lead very separate lives, at least in public. The Arab restaurants and cafes are primarily male domains.

Bay Ridge Place Mark

The Islamic Society of Bay Ridge, *6807 Fifth Avenue (718-680-0121).*

The Islamic Society of Bay Ridge is housed in a structure of simple white brick, large but not daunting. The building is not identifiable as a mosque or *Masjid,* but it contains an Islamic house of worship and a school for children between three and six and offers religious instruction. It is part of the support system for Arabs of Bay Ridge and is an Arabic cultural oasis.

Restaurants

Merryland, *6824 Fifth Avenue (718-745-7536). Daily 24 hours.*

The name loses something in the translation. Merryland is a morning, noon, and night happening, an Arab coffee house and social club in suburban Brooklyn. It is a primarily male preserve, where young and old pass the time in animated conversation over Lebanese French Napoleons and Arab coffee, a pita sandwich, or a *mazza.* They even have *foul* for breakfast, as well as bagels with cream cheese.

Karam, *8519 Fourth Avenue (718-745-5227). Daily 24 hours.*

Karam has the look and feel of standard fast food. A small arbor of artificial grapes in the corner is a tip-off that this eatery is something completely different. The Arab spinach, meat, and cheese pies are fresh, flaky, and ample. The skewered meats are superbly marinated and seasoned with fresh herbs.

King Felafel, *7408 Third Avenue (718-745-4188). Daily 11 A.M.–midnight.*

King Felafel used to be a take-out and deliver type of place, but it is now an attractive, comfortable restaurant. The fresh vegetarian specialties, felafel, *hummos, baba ghanouj,* and *foul,* are on a par with the succulent kebabs and lean *shawarma* fresh from the spit.

Al-Ghadeer, *7111 Third Avenue (718-680-0505). Monday–Friday 8 A.M.–11 P.M.; Saturday and Sunday 8 A.M.–2 A.M.*

Al-Ghadeer is an Arab hybrid: restaurant, grocery, and take-out. The restaurant is only a table in the corner along with the stand-up counter. Late Saturday or Sunday night it attracts a congenial crowd enjoying the tastes of Beirut. There is buttered lamb liver with herbs and lemon; *kafta* kebab made with fresh parsley, onions, herbs, and spices and sizzling hot *soujouk* (sausage).

Pita and Patisserie

Mideast Bakery, *7808 Third Avenue (718-680-0561). Daily 9:45 A.M.–5 P.M.*

The bakery has great traditional Arab *baklawa* with grade A green pistachios, fine layered phyllo, and the sweetest syrup, but the real specialty, which brings the customers in early, is their tasty Syrian flat bread. By the afternoon the place is cleaned out.

Ayrassi Pastry, *7216 Fifth Avenue (718-745-2115). Daily 8:30 A.M.–8:30 P.M.*

The Ayrassi is sweet memories of old Beirut, the Paris of the Mideast. A sepia photo gallery in front recalls its fountains, neoclassical buildings, and street cars against a backdrop of palms. The spectacularly sweet bird's nest, *kinafe* with cheese and honey, and *Mamoonia* semolina pudding recalls another famous Beirut bakery with the same name.

Arab Groceries Plus

The Family Store, *6905 Third Avenue (718-748-0207). Monday– Saturday 8:30 A.M.–10 P.M.*

The Family Store carries all the staples of the Arab kitchen, from big barrels of bulgar and flat bread in front, to fruits and nuts in the center. But the delicacies at the counter are the real reason for coming here. They even come from Atlantic Avenue for the homemade basket cheese, string cheese, hot and sweet lamb sausage, and stuffed grape leaves.

Al Noor Halal Meat, *4516 Eighth Avenue between 45th and 46th streets (718-435-2781). Daily 7 A.M.–11 P.M.*

Al Noor Halal Meat is more than a *Halal* meat market that provides whole lambs and goats for Islamic feasts. It is a veritable bazaar, with bulging bags of aromatic spices, unusual grains and beans, vats of olives in their own oil, and all sorts of pickled vegetables. Water pipes, Arabic musical instruments, cooking utensils, and images of the pilgrimage to Mecca and the Kabba add to the variety.

Issawi Halal Meat and Groceries, *4824 Eighth Avenue near 49th Street (718-972-0010). Daily 8 A.M.–11:00 P.M.*

Issawi has fine Arab foods, housewares, and religious articles. The shelves are filled with canned and bottled food and other specialties. They have all the Arab brands from Casablanca to Beirut; their own spice market; Mideast olive oil, ghee, tahini, and beans; and grains and seeds galore.

Manhattan Arabs

There are almost no traces of Manhattan's Little Syria left. St. George's (Melkite) and St. Joseph's (Maronite) are gone. Jabbours, the long-standing Lebanese retailer, has moved to Long Island. The Fifth Avenue Arabs, the importer Mallouk, the silk industry Kiamies, and the Persian rug-dealing Tadross have disappeared or assimilated. Even the R. G. Haddad Foundation, which provided scholarships for deserving Arab youngsters, is a part of the past.

The new Arab Manhattan has more to do with multinationals and international diplomacy than merchants and churches. The Manhattan Arabs are highly trained individuals, doctors and engineers, and respected college professors like Edward Said of Columbia University, not a geographical community. Sometimes they are second-generation Arab Americans, like the special prosecutor Maurice Nadjari, who headed the corruption-busting Knapp Commission.

Manhattan Place Marks

Islamic Center, *One Riverside Drive (212-326-6800).*

The Islamic Center is a religious meeting place for Arabs in Manhattan. The center conducts prayers five times a day, offers classes in Arabic, has a religious school for children, and sponsors cultural events.

The Islamic Cultural Center, *1711 Third Avenue at 96th Street.*

This mosque and Muslim cultural center, located in New York's affluent East Side, is a monumental structure in the classic Islamic style. The dome is a mass with authority, while the tall minaret of the Muezzin's call to prayer soars. The lofty interior has the majesty of a medieval cathedral, and the sea of carpets on which the worshipers pray are of precious broadloom. The diversity of people at prayer reflects the universality of Islam. There are Sudanese and Lebanese, Afghanis and Pakistanis, Egyptians and Iranians, and Africans and African Americans.

Manhattan Restaurant Renaissance

Authentic Arab restaurants in the city are no longer a rarity. Eateries serving authentic Arab food in stylish and sophisticated settings are becoming commonplace. A whole range of exciting dishes from the Middle East, cooked to a turn and subtlety seasoned, are now readily available to New Yorkers. This new generation of Arab restaurateurs are mostly Lebanese, sometimes by way of Paris.

Sahara East, *184 First Avenue between 11th and 12th streets (212-353-9000). Daily 11 A.M.–3 A.M.*

This small storefront restaurant has palms painted on the ceiling, a mural of a natural paradise, and a warm Egyptian welcome. The grills may be a little dry for New York tastes, but the *fatoosh, baba ghanouj, hummos,* and felafel are authentic and delectable. Try the surprise specials from Arab stews to lentils.

Byblos Restaurant, *200 East 39th Street and the corner of Third Avenue (212-687-0808). Sunday–Thursday noon–11 P.M.; Friday–Saturday noon–2 A.M.*

Byblos is all about leisurely dining in attractive, spacious surroundings. The restaurant has an extensive list of exotic hot and cold appetizers, including quail, lamb's fries, and lamb's tongue that draws a sophisticated clientele.

Al-Ajami, *246 East 44th Street (212-682-2565). Monday–Saturday noon–10:30 P.M.*

Al-Ajami is the latest "hot spot" for leisurely lunches for the Arab delegations from the nearby U.N. The list of *mazzes* is practically exhaustive, with dishes like lamb brains (delicious with Arak) and lamb tongue. The stuffed squash and the lamb stewed with okra or string beans is lightly seasoned Lebanese style and satisfying.

Felafel 'N' Stuff, *1586 First Avenue between 83rd and 84th streets (212-879-7023). Daily noon–11 P.M.*

The food is Egyptian and there is a mural of pharaohs and Nubian slaves on the wall that also makes the point. The restaurant is modest but good natured. The Egyptian national dish, *foul mudammas* (brown beans with garlic, spices, and oil), is much ado about beans. It is the Egyptian *melokhia* (a leafy green stewed with chicken or lamb) that is the real Egyptian soul food. Fat pita bread sandwiches with *hummos, baba ghanouj,* felafel, and plenty of salad are recommended.

Sido, *1608 Third Avenue between 90th and 91st streets (212-423-0654). Daily 10:30 A.M.–11:30 P.M.*

After a hiatus of two years, Sido is back in a smaller version on the Upper East Side. The food is still exceptional in their new, informal location. The *kibee,* raw or cooked, is perfect and the *mazza* with hot and cold appetizers is a bargain meal.

The Fine Art of Belly Dancing

The musicians do not just play in the background, they are totally involved. The mustachioed man on the *durbek* (Arab bongos) never misses a beat as the *oud* (mandolin-like instrument) player fingers the strings like a Near East Jimmy Hendrix. All the while, the third man on the *kannon* (zither) smiles beatifically.

The music is hot and rhythmically hypnotic. The woman in her harem costume keeps time with her *zills* (finger cymbals) and the movement of a hip and does a counterpoint to the beat with the graceful motion of her hands and arms. Suddenly she's kneeling, and still keeping time, she leans slowly back and her shoulders touch the floor.

In the days before topless bars and X-rated videos there was a strip of Turkish and Greek belly dancing joints with names like the Egyptian Gardens on Eighth Avenue between 28th and 29th Streets. It was the most daring show in a town where La Guardia outlawed burlesque. The clubs today are far more sophisticated and expensive and attract couples.

The Cedars of Lebanon, *39 East 30th Street (212-725-9251). Daily 11:30 A.M.–3 A.M. Belly dancing Wednesday, Friday, Saturday: music starts at 10 P.M.; dancers' first set is at 11:30.*

The Cedars of Lebanon is the oldest restaurant in the city specializing in Lebanese cuisine. A local Arab clientele guarantees that the cuisine is authentic. Nightly belly dancing, with customers occasionally joining in, adds spice to the meals.

Casablanca Ritz Cafe, *170 Thompson Street (212-228-9180). Daily noon–1* A.M. *Belly dancing Wednesday–Sunday at 9* P.M. *and 10:30* P.M.

Casablanca may have been a little like this; the Moroccan decor is straight out of the movies. The couscous, lamb or chicken, is a gargantuan Arab feast with mountains of carrots, turnips, and chick peas for the health conscious. It comes with a *harissa* (condiment) that is really hot. Winter or summer, the exotic belly dancer creates some heat, rhythmically moving her torso to the music with a counterpoint of *zills*.

⸻ Celebrations and Solemn Occasions ⸻

Ramadan

Ramadan is a Muslim observance occurring in the spring at the time of the new moon. It is the holiest month of the Muslim calendar and an occasion for fasting and self-examination. Muslims fast during daylight and at sunset break that fast with dates and water like the Prophet Mohammed. Later they have the *Iftar,* the evening breakfast with thick soups and heavy stews, which will help them endure the long fast.

Toward the end of Ramadan, worshipers sleep in the Atlantic Avenue Mosque. They prepare for the Night of Power, when Mohammed had his revelation and all dreams can come true. Ramadan is ushered out with the *id al fitr,* the festival of fast breaking, feasting and gift giving.

The *Id-al-Adha*

In the summer, Muslims celebrate the Feast of Sacrifice, *Id-al-Adha,* commemorating Abraham's sacrifice of a ram in place of his son Ishmael. It is a time of sharing at the Al-Farouq Mosque, when lambs are slaughtered according to a special ritual (in a slaughterhouse) and the greater part is given to the poor. Some call it the holiday of sharing.

The African Americans

New York's African Americans are Haitian, West Indian, and Southern migrant. There are even vestiges of New Amsterdam free men. They all came to the Western Hemisphere on slave ships and did hard time on the white man's plantations. They exchanged Africa for scraps of French, English, and Southern plantation culture.

New York represented a new start for turn-of-the-century Southern sharecroppers, West Indians who labored on the Panama Canal, and Haitian boat people from the Duvalier seventies. Despite discrimination in the new Jerusalem, they continue to pursue the American dream. In the process, they are also reclaiming their African inheritance.

History

Manhattan's eleven original Africans were carried over as chattels on a Dutch merchant ship in 1626. These "Angolans" had greater freedom than the slaves in British colonies; they were legally entitled to hold property and marry and had the right of free movement. Their children could not be taken from them.

An African slave in early New Amsterdam was not considered very different from a white indentured servant. They were "allowed" to keep their African identity and were not stigmatized by color. In 1644 the original slaves petitioned the Dutch West India Company for their freedom and it was granted. The same year, however, the Dutch legally authorized the slave trade in the colony.

Jansz Van Salee was one black in New Amsterdam who didn't have to petition for his freedom. He was the buccaneering son of a Dutchman who set sail for the Ottoman sultan. He married a Dutch woman named Griet Reyniers and they established a homestead in the present Gravesend. The descendants of their four daughters are in the New York social register.

Most African slaves in New Amsterdam were the property of the Dutch West India Company or belonged to high officials like Governor Peter Stuyvesant, who had forty on his Bouerie estate. The ordinary Dutch citizenry were not generally comfortable with black slavery and often helped runaway slaves. Even slave holders as a rule offered slaves "half freedom." Slaves were released from their bond on the condition that they performed agreed-upon labor at agreed-upon times.

Slavery was far stricter under the British, who took over the colony in 1664. Slaves had neither legal rights nor property. The families of slaves could be broken up with impunity. Slaves who protested or resisted were subject to public whipping and worse. The British viewed slavery as a business; it was a source of high profits and a high priority. The number of African-American slaves more than tripled from 1664 to 1746.

In a city with a limited population, slaves were permitted to develop skills as craftsmen, coopers and carpenters, glaziers, and goldsmiths. They also learned household skills like spinning, weaving, and cooking. They were considered the equal of their white equivalents and hired out in competition with free labor.

Although the slave's movements and rights of assembly were restricted by law, these bondsmen and women routinely disobeyed curfews and socialized in forbidden "tippling houses." There were open gatherings where slaves formed relationships and established a sense of community. The most disaffected joined gangs of runaway slaves that prowled the waterfront.

A slave insurrection, with buildings set afire and ambushed colonists, took place in 1712. The aftermath was white panic and black persecution, complete with public burnings. A botched burglary, accusations of arson, and false confessions led to the public execution of innocent slaves twenty years later. A white woman named Mary Burton was the first false witness to ignite an orgy of false recrimination and brutality on the scale of the Salem witch trial.

The Revolution disrupted the slave system in New York. Redcoats and Revolutionaries urged slaves to join their forces, holding out the promise of freedom. Blacks worked in the British army's arsenal and served with loyalist irregulars. Thousands joined the rebel militias and as a group were specially cited for bravery. Christopher Greene's black regiment fought with great distinction in the bloody battle of Points Bridge.

The New York Assembly freed the city's slave soldiers in 1781. Four years later, the city's leading citizens formed the New York Manumission Society to work for the eradication of slavery. John Jay was the society's first president and his successor, Alexander Hamilton, whose ancestors from Jamaica might have been African, was the leading intellectual light of independence.

Samuel Fraunces was a leading member of the free black community of this era. His tavern on 54 Pearl Street attracted New York's first citizens and was site of George Washington's emotional farewell dinner for his officers. The city's principal businessmen met in the tavern's long room to organize the first chamber of commerce.

In 1799 slavery in New York was on its way to legal extinction; a law was passed freeing all children born to slaves after July 4, 1799. Males were to be freed at age twenty-eight and females at age twenty-five. In 1817 every slave born before July 4, 1799 was technically freed. Nevertheless, many New York City slaves were illegally transferred to Southern slave holders during the time it took for the law to go into effect.

Black liberation did not mean equality in the first half of the nineteenth-century. In 1821, New York's African Americans were the target of a restrictive property requirement that made it almost impossible for them to vote. Black citizens were also denied access to "public transport" and had to pay special licensing fees even for the right to be a carter.

Newly freed blacks were no longer in demand as skilled craftsmen. White workers in the city made certain that they were limited to service and menial jobs. Black men now donned the uniforms of coachmen, porters, barbers, or waiters, while women were cooks, maids, and laundresses.

Often blacks were forced to settle for inferior housing in crime-ridden neighborhoods. They lived in the damp vermin-infested cellars and the leaky garrets of Five Points. White churches restricted them to the galleries or barred them altogether. Public places like the New York Zoological Institute refused to admit blacks. To top it all off, African-American New Yorkers were prey to petty harassment, public humiliation, and assaults.

Blacks vented their anger at these abuses in the pages of the city's first African-American newspaper, *Freedom's Journal*. The city's blacks countered some forms of discrimination by founding their own institutions. They started their own religious denominations, training eloquent clergy and building handsome churches. Thomas Paul in 1809 was the first in a long line of eloquent activist clergymen at the helm of the

Abyssinian Baptist Church. The Reverend Paul Williams, of the pioneering African Methodist Episcopal Zion Church, became one of New York's leading abolitionists.

While black churches were a bulwark for black unity and morale, these activist churches were also a prime target for racist mobs. In July of 1834, in the aftermath of hard-fought city elections, blacks attending an abolitionist meeting at the Chatham Square Chapel were attacked by a proslavery gang. In the course of the next three days, a raging mob of twenty thousand torched black and white churches that vocally supported abolition.

African Americans did not rely completely on religious organizations and churches for social support and stability. They formed their own labor groups and insurance societies. The first mutual aid society was established by black sailors in 1810. Later there was an American League of Black Laborers, and in 1839 a special association for ship's cooks and stewards. The African Dorcas Society was the first black group to help the infirm and indigent.

Deprived of education as slaves, blacks were very aware of the importance of education. They worked closely with socially conscious white New Yorkers to develop black schools through the New York Society for the Promotion of Education and the New York Phoenix Society. They launched successful literacy programs.

Despite economic and social barriers, blacks were able to make their mark in the early New York. James McCune Smith became a respected physician with a prestigious degree from the University of Glasgow. Thomas Downings operated one of the most popular oyster bars catering to the men of the Stock Exchange. In the 1830s Thomas M. Jackson was the caterer to New York high society. Ira Aldredge even became one of the leading actors of this era, learning to perform Shakespeare on the stage of New York's Free African Theater.

New York's African Americans were influential figures in the antislavery movement. Samuel Ringold Ward, known as the "Black Daniel Webster," inspired many to join the cause of abolition with his fiery rhetoric. He became such a threat to the proslavery establishment that he was forced to flee to England. Frederick Douglass conveyed through his own slavery experience the physical brutality, psychic pain, and humiliation of bondage. He was instrumental in building abolitionist sentiment in the North.

New York's entrance into the Civil War on the Northern side did not immediately improve conditions for the city's blacks. Ever the scapegoat, the vulnerable black community of 12,472 became the target for the city's proslavery Democrats and the nation's first disgruntled draftees. In the

1863 Draft Riots, immigrant and native-born Americans lynched blacks, burned down a black orphanage, and chased the whole black population out of their Cherry Street neighborhood.

By the end of the War Between the States, a resurgent black population had gone beyond Lower Manhattan to West Side neighborhoods. They spread out from the twenties to the fifties, in the low-rent Tenderloin, where violence and vice made normal life very difficult. Black New Yorkers, who were city dwellers from colonial times, were able to cope but they were now joined by more impressionable blacks from the rural South.

Eventually the black elite began to relocate to the brownstones of Brooklyn. These successful lawyers, doctors, and businessmen even had their own version of high society. They called themselves the Society of the Sons of New York. Members had to be accomplished and black, and this exclusive group barred Southern blacks and West Indians.

In 1900 black New York was over sixty thousand strong and rapidly growing. Incidents between ethnic whites and blacks were on the rise and a pre–community relations police force added to the friction. On August 15, 1900, a knifing led to black and white mob confrontations with police participating as white partisans. For a month roving bands of white toughs considered blacks fair game.

There were fair-minded white New Yorkers like Mary White Ovington, who worked with the black educator W. E. B. Dubois and others to found the National Association for the Advancement of Colored People. Other interracial groups were formed in the city to help create opportunities for blacks, which were consolidated into the National Urban League in 1911.

In ten years fifty thousand black New Yorkers made the move from the Tenderloin to the wide, tree-lined streets of Harlem. They paid high rents for the privilege of decent housing. Overcrowding was inevitable. By the Depression there were two hundred thousand blacks competing for space in Harlem. Although it was the most deprived section of the city, it received the barest minimum of government services. It had only one playground and new school construction was zero.

Mayor La Guardia's heart was in the right place and he was genuinely disturbed by black poverty and illiteracy, but he did little to improve the black New Yorker's situation. Black areas did not benefit from his major construction programs which changed the face of the city.

He did increase the number of African-American municipal government appointments and raised the status of their positions. In his administration, Hubert Delaney became tax commissioner and Jane Bolin became a judge. He hired Gertrude Ayer to be the first black principal of a city public school.

The Depression devastated African-American New York, resulting in a fifty percent unemployment rate. Black self-help was their only option in an indifferent city. Father Divine's Kingdom provided cheap meals and lodging and opened dry-goods stores and cleaners that employed blacks. Though his divinity was doubtful, he supplied hope. At the same time many conventional black churches followed the example of the Abyssinian Baptist Church in Harlem by offering free meals, shelter, food baskets, and clothes.

Black New York went off to war in 1941 in a segregated force. While their units received commendations, it was clear that they were more isolated and segregated than German prisoners of war. On the homefront in 1943, Harlem was burning. On a hot August night wartime resentments and high rents and employment discrimination led to looting and gunshots. At the end there were five dead and whole city blocks destroyed.

A year later, with the creation of a Harlem congressional district, Adam Clayton Powell, Jr., a young city councilman and minister of the Abyssinian Baptist Church, became Harlem's national representative. The election of Mayor William O'Dwyer in 1946 led to many citywide black political appointments. J. Raymond Jones, the Harlem Democratic leader, became a housing commissioner and Rev. John M. Coleman of Brooklyn became the first black to sit on the board of education. In 1953 blacks had another first, with Hulan Jack elected borough president of Manhattan.

At the same time that blacks were entering New York's political mainstream, they were joining New York's sports teams and becoming genuine sports heroes. Jackie Robinson was the first African-American player to break the "color line" on the Brooklyn Dodger's ball team. Soon the Giant's Willie Mays was competing with a white Mickey Mantle for the title of the best all-around player in baseball.

Between 1940 and 1960 one and a half million white New Yorkers left the city. The black population, which had previously been concentrated in Bedford-Stuyvesant and Harlem, spread out through the other boroughs into Morrisania, the Bronx, central Brooklyn, and southern Queens. Black New Yorkers established new power bases and centers of influence.

In 1963 the civil rights movement in the South was changing attitudes throughout the country. Martin Luther King had made the elimination of Jim Crow a moral crusade. There was an effort to wipe out the effects of bigotry, North and South. In Harlem HARYOU-Act was founded and funded by the federal government to create black pride and break down the cycle of dependency.

Government programs were inadequate to meet the needs of a deprived community. Racial tensions came to a head in the long hot summer of 1964, and there was a repetition of the Harlem riots. Raised black expectations were not being fulfilled and despair was rampant. The assassination of Martin Luther King, Jr., in 1968 led to more riots in Harlem and Bedford-Stuyvesant. A city looking for racial justice elected the fusion candidate John V. Lindsay as mayor. Black New York votes were crucial to his election.

The Lindsay years were a time of racial confrontation. The black community of Ocean Hill-Brownsville in Brooklyn struggled with the white teachers' union for control over their children's future, and white parents in Canarsie blocked African-American children from being bused to their schools. Blacks lobbied for a civilian review board and made continual charges of white police brutality. It was the age of Stokely Carmichael and the Black Panthers.

It was also the age of Shirley Chisolm, a dynamic African-American congresswoman from Brooklyn who was nominated at the Democratic convention for president, and Percy Sutton, an eloquent Harlem politician who many people believed would be the next mayor. In another arena, the writer Claude Browne stirred white consciences with his ghetto memoir, *Manchild in the Promised Land.*

In 1977 the city was racially divided over a scattered-site public housing project in Forest Hills, and Edward Koch beat out Harlem assemblyman Herman Farrel and Mario Cuomo for mayor. Though Koch couldn't win any popularity contests in the African-American community he made some ground-breaking African-American appointments, including Police Commissioner Benjamin Ward and Board of Education Chancellor Richard Green.

David M. Dinkins, who had been a popular Manhattan borough president, brought African Americans to the pinnacle of city power when he was elected mayor in 1990. He continued the tradition of having an African American as police commissioner by appointing Dr. Lee Brown. Though he was a one-term mayor, his reelection was closely contested and he left office with the positive regard of most New Yorkers.

While African Americans gained power and stature on the political front, they also excelled in other callings in a city synonymous with capitalist competition. Reginald Lewis, who died in 1993, was an ambitious African American with the business acumen that enabled him to build the billion-dollar Beatrice Corporation. The late African-American New Yorker, J. Bruce Llewelyn, built a broadcasting, bottling, and retailing empire with annual sales of over 262 million dollars. Young musical entrepreneurs Andre Harrel and Russel Simmons have made fortunes selling rap and hip hop music to mainstream audiences.

African Americans also succeeded in the fast-lane field of communications. Ed Lewis (*Essence*) and Earl Graves (*Black Enterprise*) became publishing tycoons by promoting African-American success. Sam Chisholm (Mingo Group) and Caroline Jones established advertising agencies with annual multimillion dollar billings. Brent Staples and Bob Herbert climbed to the top of the journalistic ladder with by-lines in the *New York Times.* Pierce Sutton founded a broadcasting empire which includes WBLS-FM and WLIB-AM.

In 1990 a forgotten burial ground for African-American slaves was discovered at a government building site between Duane and Elk Streets near the downtown Civic Center. African-American New Yorkers closed ranks to defend this hallowed ground and preserve the remains of their ancestors. Construction was halted. On November 23, 1993, the remains of four hundred victims of oppression, who had died before the century of emancipation, were finally laid to rest. A special ceremony, complete with gospel singers, colonial funeral dirges, funeral orations, and an African libation ritual, paid tribute to the deceased.

═══════════ Harlem ═══════════

Directions: Subway A to 125th Street/Frederick Douglas Avenue or Subway 2 or 3 to 125th Street/Lenox Avenue.

History

Harlem is the heart of African-American New York. Black hip begins here, its styles and trends sweeping through the city and finally capturing a whole nation. From ragtime to rap, Harlem is in a state of perpetual Renaissance.

Harlem's first inhabitants were Native Americans in lean-tos on the banks of the Harlem River. Their reservation would have fit the grid from 110th Street to 125th Street. In 1658 Dutch settlers gave the natives a dispossess and incorporated the village of Nieue Harlem. The soil was rich and the high ground was easy to defend.

A few years later black slaves raised the Nieue Harlem real estate values by constructing ten miles of road from New Amsterdam to Nieue Harlem. In the late eighteenth century New York gentry, whose names are now on street signs—Morris, Hamilton, DeLancey, and Beekman—built their summer houses in the wilds above the present 140th Street.

In 1837 a railroad running down Park Avenue divided East and West Harlem. While West Harlem attracted the "carriage trade," East Harlem became a blighted area of shacks and squatters, with pigs rooting through the garbage. The arrival of the El trains on Second and Third Avenues in 1879 attracted industry and more working-class immigrants to East Harlem. The other Harlem was still reserved for the wealthy: successful German and German-Jewish businessmen and manufacturers bought and built spacious homes in the area.

At the beginning of the twentieth century the IRT line along Lenox Avenue opened Central Harlem to middle-class commuters. The building boom was on. There were luxurious row houses and the most up-to-date apartment units. But when the demand fell short and landlords were caught holding the bag, a smart black realtor, Philip Payton, came to the rescue.

For developers who would rent to his people, he promised top-dollar rents and efficient management. The first blacks to move uptown were relocated from their homes on the site of the future Penn Station. Thousands of African Americans fled the substandard housing of the Tenderloin, Thompson Street, and San Juan Hill for the suburban comfort of Harlem. Rural migrants from the South and West Indian emigrants headed straight for Harlem. Harlem meant unimagined luxury and mystique.

Harlem was the main chance, the new black Jerusalem. Black churches joined their congregations in the exodus. In the 1920s black creative juices produced the Harlem Renaissance and America listened. Claude McKay, Jean Toomer, and Zora Neale Hurston were the literary lions while Duke Ellington, Bessie Smith, and Fletcher Henderson made beautiful music, blue, and red-hot. James Weldon Johnson was the Renaissance man: writer, composer, musician, and philosopher of the black experience. Marcus Garvey preached the new gospel of black self-sufficiency, a world of their own making.

Black capitalism boomed. Lillian Harris started out selling pig's feet out of a baby carriage on 125th Street. She was uneducated, but an astute businesswomen who put her profits in Harlem real estate and retired in luxury to southern California. William Felton made his fortune in Harlem by inventing the automatic car wash. He built a seven-story building to house his enterprise. Madame J. C. Walker devised her own black hair treatment, which earned her millions and an estate in exclusive Irvington-on-the-Hudson.

Meanwhile whites came "slumming" to whites-only clubs like Connie's Inn and the Cotton Club, where they were entertained by black bands and singers and the famous "high yellow" girls of the chorus. The "New Negro" of the black literary set was the weekend adventure of the Roaring Twenties.

There was a burgeoning black bourgeoisie and the sense of a black future when the 1929 Depression postponed the Harlem dream. The glamour and good times gave way to a reality of discrimination and poverty.

During the 1920s black Harlem more than doubled in population from 83,248 to 203,894, with double the density of the rest of the city. Greedy white landlords had subdivided a neighborhood into a slum. Even white businesses that survived on the black trade wouldn't employ blacks.

African-American institutions like the Abyssinian Baptist Church tried to rally the people with their social programs and economic campaigns. Rev. Adam Clayton Powell and his son, the charismatic Rev. Adam Clayton Powell, Jr., offered hope and action and provided crucial leadership. Though riots came with the 1940s, there were also successful black boycotts of white merchants and a black borough president named Hulan Jack.

The Rev. Adam Clayton Powell, Jr., went to Congress in the 1940s and was a powerful congressional committee chairman during much of the 1960s. It was the era of Malcolm and Martin, and Harlem was inspired by the civil rights movement and the drive for black power. Martin Luther King led civil rights marches up 125th Street while Malcolm X spread the message of black pride in the Audubon Ballroom on 166th Street. Both died for their beliefs and Harlem erupted. Hopelessness combined with crime and the epidemic rise in drug use turned Harlem into a Manhattan tragedy.

But Harlem was not about to give up the ghost. A new, more commercial Harlem would stylishly strut its stuff on 125th Street. There would be a skyscraper State Office Building and even that elegant dowager, the Hotel Theresa, would become a gleaming office tower. Percy Sutton would give up his ambitions to become mayor to lead a Harlem economic revival, while another Harlem favorite son, David Dinkins, became New York's first African-American mayor. Charles Rangel, Powell's very competent if less charismatic replacement in Congress, made Harlem renewal a national issue.

During the Dinkins administration Harlem rebuilt with a passion and six thousand housing units were added to Harlem's housing stock. In the four years of his mayorality, Dinkins administered a two-hundred-million-dollar rehabilitation of Harlem's once grand buildings and began to change the face of this former African-American cultural capital.

The artists and writers are returning to their uptown roots from the hot-house world of SoHo and Greenwich Village. Young African-American professionals are restoring Harlem's grand residences or are moving into the old neighborhood's new luxury apartments. Visitors, especially those from Europe, are less fearful about venturing into Harlem and there are even bus tours with predictable guidebook patter. Harlem is working its way back to another Renaissance.

African-American Place Marks

Harlem High Life

Most neighborhoods don't have any historic districts, but the wide open spaces of Harlem have twenty-five, with three nationally known stand-outs: Hamilton Heights, Jumel Terrace, and Audubon Terrace. But they are part of a city history that often excluded African-American people. Harlem has districts where real black history was made, districts that are associated with black leaders, black celebrities, and black milestones.

Sugar Hill

Directions: Subway 1 to 157th Street/Broadway.

These apartments on the bluff overlooking the Hudson were built for Harlem's white superrich, with elevators, maid's rooms, and walk-in pantries. In one of New York's characteristic quick changes, it became the sweetest black neighborhood in Manhattan when black real estate brokers turned the tables on white developers. The Hill may not have an official designation but this neighborhood, between St. Nicholas and Edgecomb Avenues from around 143rd Street to 155th Street, historically housed Harlem's rich and famous. Duke Ellington, Count Basie, Chief Justice Thurgood Marshall, and Sugar Ray Robinson all lived here. More recently it has been home to former mayor David Dinkins' deputy mayor and campaign manager, Bill Lynch.

Striver's Row

Directions: Subway 1 to 137th Street.

In the vicinity of Seventh and Eighth Avenues between West 138th Street and West 139th Street, Harlem goes high-hat. The King Model row houses were designed in 1891 by the city's leading architect, Stanford White, in neo-Italian Renaissance and neo-Georgian styles. These showplaces were custom made for the city's tea-and-cucumber-sandwich set. It was an Equitable Life Insurance Company sure-thing investment.

In 1919, after being lily white for two decades, it became the preserve of the black elite and earned the name of "Striver's Row." W. C. Handy, Eubie Blake, and the bandleader Noble Sissle belonged to the celebrity crowd along the Row. All the Strivers went to the Abyssinian Baptist Church on Sunday after partying on Lenox Avenue Saturday night.

Today, an area near Striver's Row is being revitalized. New housing like the St. Charles Condominiums (sponsored by the St. Charles Borromeo Church) is being designed to blend in with Striver's Row landmarks. Near the Row, the Greater Harlem Chamber of Commerce has completed the first phase of Striver's Center. Both commercial and residential, the center will include office space, a Jazz Hall of Fame, restaurants, and night clubs calculated to bring back some of the glamour of the old Striver's Row.

Harlem Bright Lights—125th Street

Directions: Subway A to 125th Street/Frederick Douglas Avenue or Subway 2 or 3 to 125th Street/Lenox Avenue.

Harlem's main drag hasn't changed, it was always where things were happening and still is. In the 1890s it was the Hammerstein Opera and in the 1990s it's rap and hip hop at the Apollo Theater. The street is the Harlem beat pounding like the A train coming uptown. It's the corner black nationalist handing out the latest ideology and the corner black capitalist playing "Let's Make a Deal." A man in Harlem castoffs pushes a supermarket cart toward the park and a Spike Lee look-alike draped in Armani pushes the gas on his BMW. Tall, lithe African-American women pass the Franco Store gate mural of tall, lithe African-American women. Sharp black shoppers hunker down at Market and Mart 125 to bargain over Yoruba beads or counterfeit Gucci bags. The street market is in full vigorous swing, with vendors selling everything from stylish Afrocentric gear to Hong Kong knockoffs.

Harlem continues to move to the beat of its own funky drummer. Although in November of 1993 the superannuated city fathers thought it was time to relocate Harlem's exciting 125th Street shopping scene to an open air market on 126th Street, Harlem has still not changed.

The Towers of 125th Street

The Harlem State Office Building, *163 West 125th Street.*

Completed in 1973, the State Office Building is the state's recognition of Harlem political clout. The vast plaza opens up the street and provides a place for basking in the Harlem sunshine. The building is Harlem's highest and the design is a variation on Phillip Johnson modern. It adds gloss to Harlem traditional and the offices offer needed employment. Too bad it bumped the Lewis Michaux National Memorial African Bookstore, one of the community's intellectual lifelines.

Theresa Towers, *2090 Adam Clayton Powell, Jr., Boulevard at 125th Street.*

The elegant Hotel Theresa has been transformed into the Theresa Towers. Though some of the 1910 touches were removed in the 1971 renovation, it still lends high style to 125th Street. There are also the memories of a more opulent Harlem when celebrities like Fats Waller called it home. In its refined old age, Fidel Castro and Nikita Kruschev embraced on a Hotel Theresa balcony.

Harlem Houses of Worship

St. Phillips Protestant Episcopal Church, *204 West 134th Street (212-862-4940).*

St. Phillips is the most exclusive and the most sedate church in Harlem. The original congregation was founded in 1809 at Five Points and followed the black population to Mulberry Street and later to the Tenderloin. The church itself sold off its Tenderloin holdings to become one of the largest black property holders in Harlem. It is reputed to be the wealthiest congregation in Harlem.

Abyssinian Baptist Church, *132 West 138th Street (212-286-2626).*

When Striver's Row was high-accomplishment Harlem, the Abyssinian Baptist Church on Sunday was a social as well as a spiritual obligation. The church had a magnificent pulpit in the round and it boasted the city's most spellbinding cleric, Adam Clayton Powell, Sr. His equally charismatic son would succeed him and also become Harlem's representative to Congress. The church now possesses a memorial to Adam Clayton Powell, Jr., with mementos of a life spent defending the cause of human rights. The Reverend Calvin Butts continues the church's committed preaching tradition. The incomparable church choir is a joyful noise unto the Lord every Sunday at 11:30 A.M.

Canaan Baptist Church, *132 West 116th Street (212-866-0301).*

This Baptist celebration is a gospel levitation. The singing and shouting and preaching are ecstatic. The participation is personal and moving. The church is not just sound and fury; it takes charity and social activism seriously.

St. Martin's Episcopal Church, *230 Lenox Avenue near 122nd Street (212-534-4531).*

St. Martin's is where Harlem's West Indians have been praying since 1928. The services are West Indian staid and proper; the sanctuary is Romanesque. The church has a forty-bell carillon that fills Harlem with music.

Masjid Malcolm Shabbazz, *102 West 116th Street (212-662-2200).*

Malcolm X made his reputation preaching here, and this orthodox Sunni mosque continues to bear his name. It's four stories high and topped by a star and crescent. The mosque complex includes a food store and restaurant, with many products from the Muslims' own farms. Mosque leaders are currently making plans to build a bigger mosque with a traditional dome and minaret. They are also joining forces with Harlem community leaders and municipal officials to develop the area around the mosque for new housing, an international business center, and a clinic.

The Second-Time-Around Renaissance

The Harlem art and intellectual scene is a roots and grass-roots kind of thing. It is African *kinte* cloth influences and up-from-the-ghetto grit and reality. It is the Uharu freedom of a reborn continent and the creative freedom of never having done it before. The artifacts and icons of tribe, traditional, and street ritual respond to the hand of the artist. And the chronicler or the scholar records it all.

Museums and Archives

Adam Clayton Powell, Jr., Gallery, *163 West 125th Street (no telephone). Monday–Friday noon–3 P.M.*

On the second floor of the State Office Building a space has been set aside for exhibiting the artwork of the community. The Studio Museum coordinates the shows. Whether it's sculpture or collage or a neorealist painting, the African-American experience is part of the aesthetics.

The Studio Museum in Harlem, *144 West 125th Street between Lenox Avenue and Adam Clayton Powell, Jr., Boulevard (212-865-2420). Wednesday–Friday 10 A.M.–5 P.M.; Saturday and Sunday 1 A.M.–6 P.M. Admission charge.*

The Studio Museum is a showcase for African-American artists; gifted African-American painters, photographers, and sculptors exhibit here. Shows are mounted with African-American cultural and historical themes. The museum is open space and contemporary with baby spots to highlight the art. The museum has cleared and reclaimed an area in the back for an African-American modern sculpture garden and maybe some of the totems of yesteryear.

Black Fashion Museum, *157 West 126th Street (212-666-1320). Monday–Friday noon–8 P.M. By appointment. Contribution.*

Black fashion designers like Patrick Kelly have made it in high fashion and ready-to-wear, and the Black Fashion Museum is all about their fashion heritage. There are pictures and fashion illustrations and actual samples from Yoruba headdresses to the runways of Paris.

Benin Gallery, *240 West 139th Street (212-926-8025). By appointment.*

In the vicinity of Striver's Row aspiring African-American artists exhibit and artifacts of Africa are on display. There are art workshops and audiovisual programs dealing with the African-American artistic experience.

Aunt Len's Doll and Toy Museum, *6 Hamilton Terrace between 141st and 142nd streets (212-926-4172). Tuesday–Sunday by appointment. Admission charge.*

There is an actual Aunt Len, Lenon Holder Hoyte, over eighty years young, who presides over this kingdom of ten thousand dolls. There are life-size Victorian relics and Tom Thumb miniatures, rag dolls, and dolls that cry, wet, and talk. The dolls are a United Nations of nationalities and colors.

Raven Chanticleer's African American Wax Museum of Harlem, *316 West 116th Street (212-678-7818). Tuesday–Sunday 1 P.M.–6 P.M. By appointment only. Admission charge.*

It's not exactly Madame Tussaud's and the famous faces aren't exactly wax. The figures of memorable African Americans from Malcolm to

Magic are the lifelike recreations of Raven Chanticleer, who is also the museum's curator and guide.

The Grinnell Gallery, *800 Riverside Drive at 158th Street (212-927-7941). Six shows a year open to the public. Call for times and by appointment.*

The Grinnell is a multimedia adventure into being African American. It is a platform for African Americans and Caribbeans. Poets and players perform and artists and photographers exhibit.

The Schomburg Center for Research in Black Culture, *515 Lenox Avenue at 135th Street (212-862-4000). Monday–Wednesday noon–8 P.M.; Thursday–Saturday 10 A.M.–6 P.M.*

Arthur Schomburg believed in black culture and black history and wanted to preserve that legacy. His collection first became public in a branch of the New York Public Library. Today it is housed in a modern brick building and a full-time staff of sixty keeps it expanding. There are over three million separate items, including manuscripts of black greats like W.E.B. Dubois and Langston Hughes, and one hundred thousand books about the black experience. The Schomburg is a total media center with paintings, photographs, film, and video. Masterworks by Harlem Renaissance artists Romare Bearden and Jacob Lawrence are on permanent exhibit.

Black Drama, Music, and Dance

In an era when blacks were restricted from attending theater downtown—before 1945 only three Broadway theaters sold seats to blacks—the Harlem stage flourished. Blacks regularly attended the Crescent, the Lafayette, the Lincoln, and the Alhambra. They saw original dramas and musicals by blacks and black variations on Broadway hits. There were black dancers on the Harlem stage, as well as in the Cotton Club floor show. White producers like Florenz Ziegfeld purchased highlights of Harlem shows for their own productions.

Though blacks no longer have any problem attending the legitimate theater or a ballet, African Americans have kept the performing arts in their community. It is a training ground for aspiring dancers, singers, and actors and gives scope to black themes and identity.

Apollo Theater, *253 West 125th Street (212-749-5838).*

The legendary Apollo Theater at 253 West 125th Street between Seventh and Eighth Avenues started out as a "whites-only" burlesque theater in 1913. By 1934, in the competent hands of Leo Brecher and Frank Schiffman, it was presenting first-rate five-shows-a-day black revues. The Apollo audiences were noted for their critical eye and unbridled enthusiasm, and the stellar attractions were a Who's Who of black talent from the era of Bessie to Gladys Knight and the Pips. There was the comedy of "Moms" Mabley, an exuberant pre–Las Vegas Sammy Davis, Jr., and Little Richard with his mile-high hairdo.

In the 1970s the high salaries of stars and flagging box office forced management to switch to movies. In 1980 it was converted by its new owners into a cable TV studio. The Apollo is making a comeback in the 1990s with a stage show policy and even amateur nights.

Dance Theater of Harlem, *466 West 152nd Street (212-690-2880).*

Arthur Mitchell brought ballet to Harlem sixteen years ago, and since then his Dance Theater has become one of the world's cultural treasures. Balanchine ballet standards apply, but there is a fresh approach to ballet classics which takes advantage of Harlem's artistic resources. The Dance Theater of Harlem is also a school. Prima ballerinas in training perform at a monthly open house.

National Black Theater, *2033 Fifth Avenue near 125th Street (212-926-1049).*

National Black Theater is creating a new black aesthetic. The drama is from the black perspective and about the black experience. The accomplished actress and writer Barbara Ann Teer is the theater's creative force.

Soul Food and Soul Singers

Good Eating

The African-American cuisine that came up from the South and flourished in Harlem is soul food. It is food without pretenses, hearty and full-bodied like a blues singer's shout. The ingredients are the staples of sharecropping country: pigs' feet and spare ribs, black-eyed peas, and collard greens. The emphasis is on cooking talent that can turn a scrawny backyard chicken or bony catfish into a delicacy. There is an art to black Southern pan gravies and crusty breading and the barbecue sauces that burn. Even the bread made from corn meal tastes like cake. Good soul food spans the whole of Harlem from Harlem Central to Sugar Hill.

Sylvia's, *328 Lenox Avenue between 126th and 127th streets (212-996-0660). Monday–Saturday 7:30 A.M.–10:15 P.M.; Sunday 1 P.M–7 P.M.*

Sylvia's is South Carolina soul in the cooking and down-home hospitality. The funky be-yourself feeling is a relief after all of New York's restaurant pretenses. It's homey with its winter wonderland mural and pictures on the wall. The jukebox, from rap to synthesizer soul, and the rap humor of the regulars at the counter are the round-the-clock floor show. Sylvia and her kin also have regulars dropping by from Tokyo and Paris for the meaty ribs with pepper and spice and the cinnamon sweet potato pie. The main dishes, fried or barbecued, with the collard greens and yams are almost too ample to finish. Sylvia's keeps expanding in size to meet the soul food demand, and is even taking her show on the road with her own line and label of soul foods.

La Famille, *2017 Fifth Avenue between 124th and 125th streets (212-722-9806). Monday–Friday 11:30 A.M.–11:30 P.M.; Saturday 4 P.M.–11:30 P.M.; Sunday 1 P.M.–9:30 P.M.*

La Famille is dress-up soul with white linen tablecloths and wood paneling. The weekends are to see and be seen at La Famille. But don't try to be continental when it comes to the menu—stick to the Southern-style braised short ribs and black-eyed peas with grainy corn bread.

22 West, *22 West 135th Street between Lenox and Fifth avenues (212-862-7770). Daily 8 A.M.–12:30 A.M.*

22 West has the feeling of an informal Harlem open house. From opening to closing you can choose whatever you want from ham hocks and black-eyed peas for breakfast to grits, ham, and eggs and biscuits for dinner.

Wilson's Bakery & Restaurant, *1980 Amsterdam Avenue at 158th Street (212-923-9821). Daily 6 A.M.–9 P.M.*

Harlem is fried chicken everywhere from fast-food franchises to closet-sized take-outs. Everyone has their unbeatable secret recipe, so why not go into business? Wilson's easily wins any fried chicken competition; the breading is light and slightly spicy and the bird isn't swimming in the shortening. The bakery is conveniently near the entrance for a sweet potato pie or coconut cake on the way out.

Copeland's, *547 West 145th Street between Broadway and Amsterdam Avenue (212-234-2356). Sunday–Friday 1 P.M.–11 P.M.; Saturday 4:30 P.M.–1 A.M.*

Copeland's is formal reservations dining with fresh flowers on the tables and harp music on Sundays. Harlem's high-finance, real estate, and media African Americans break bread here. The menu is mixed from soul to Creole to sixteen-ounce New York-cut steaks. The corn fritters are crunchy and the Southern oxtails are a specialty if you don't mind a lot of bones. There's a Copeland's cafeteria next door, but Copeland's experience is more than food. Copeland's is taking its inimitable soul food formula to Harlem's High Street—125th.

Good Listening

From the blues shout to the jazz saxophone squawk, Harlem is African-American music. It started with Scott Joplin rags and Baptist gospel. Harlem rent parties became the scene of piano battles and horn competitions. James P. Johnson perfected the New York "stride" piano style and Duke Ellington created a jazz band sound with symphony range. Harlem's Cotton Club was king in the twenties. The African-American arranger Fletcher Henderson taught Benny Goodman how to swing.

When jazz became too tight, Charlie Christian and Charlie Parker created a new jazz idiom. Minton's was the place for after-hours jams and bebop. While Harlem went through bop and the birth of the cool, rhythm and blues stole the thunder. The music of the Clovers and Joe Turner was transformed into Motown and a not-so-mad genius named Ornette took jazz beyond tomorrow. Eventually Harlem put it altogether and it spelled fusion, and Miles Davis added a synthesizer.

Harlem is still the place for musical innovation. The players have the room to soar.

Snooky's, *63 West 17th Street between Fifth and Lenox avenues (212-281-3500). Wednesday–Thursday 11 A.M.–10 P.M.; Friday–Saturday 11 A.M.–midnight; Sunday 11 A.M.–6 P.M.*

The jazz comes with a soul food dinner. The jazz brunch with barbecue and waffles is a swinging way to spend Sunday.

Birdland, *2745 Broadway at 105th Street (212-749-2228). Daily 5 P.M.–4 A.M.*

It may be only on the periphery of Harlem, but it showcases some of African America's best jazz. The platters of smothered pork, fried chicken, or barbecued ribs with sides of greens, yams, or potato salad are substantial and soul satisfying.

Cotton Club, *666 West 125th Street (212-663-7980). Closed Tuesday; Monday, Wednesday, and Thursday 6:30 P.M.–midnight; Saturday and Sunday noon–6:30 P.M.*

The flash and glitter are artificial. Sanitized soul and soul food for people who don't know any better.

Showman's Lounge, *2321 Frederick Douglass Boulevard at 126th Street (212-864-8941). Daily noon–4 A.M. Live music Thursday–Sunday.*

The restaurant is of the neighborhood enough to have lobster nights and weekend raffles, but the jazz jams attracts audiences from around the world.

The Lickety Split, *2361 Adam Clayton Powell, Jr., Boulevard near 138th Street (212-283-9093). Monday–Saturday 10 a.m–4 A.M.*

The Lickety Split is happy jazz. The blues on the sunny side matches the good vibes and good talk. It's a place to laugh and drink good bourbon.

Well's, *2247-49 Adam Clayton Powell, Jr., Boulevard at 132nd Street (212-234-0700). Monday–Friday 11 A.M.–1 A.M.; Saturday and Sunday 11 A.M.–4 A.M.*

Monday the big band plays on, and the rest of the time it is a trio or quartet. The place is deservedly famous for its fried chicken and waffles.

Festivals

African-American Day Parade

All Harlem turns out for the the African-American Day Parade on the first Sunday in September. It is one New York parade where the spectators still outnumber the marchers. The line of march is along Adam Clayton Powell, Jr., Boulevard and the reviewing stand is located on the plaza of the Adam Clayton Powell, Jr., Office Building at the corner of 125th Street and the Boulevard. The mood is a kind of good-natured militancy, marching to an African beat.

The grand marshal of the parade is more likely to be wearing a dashiki than a cutaway. This is one event where even the politicians unbend. The marching bands are precision, but the music is wailing Basie saxophones and the steps are Michael Jackson. The bands generally pass on John Philip Sousa for Quincey Jones arrangements. There are drums of Africa played by dignified men in long colorful robes and conga drums played by Dominicans in straw hats. New York's African-American cops of the Guardian Society walk with a military step while some kids from the Police Athletic League do an Ali shuffle. The floats are cultural artifacts of the Yoruba and Timbuktu and the black broadcasters are from KISS or WLIB. The flower of African-American womanhood gaily waves to the crowd from a float decorated in the colors of black liberation.

Harlem Week

Harlem likes to do things in a big way and Harlem Week is actually a two-week event. It is a celebration of Harlem's existence and a reflection on its past and future. All of Harlem's cultural resources get into the act. There are special exhibits of Harlem memorabilia at the Schomburg and a retrospective of great black artists at the Studio Museum. There are symposiums and Harlem symphonies and Harlem's dance theaters keep everyone on their toes. This August bouquet to Harlem is sponsored by the Uptown Chamber of Commerce.

Martin Luther King, Jr., Parade

The Martin Luther King, Jr., Day Parade is on the third Sunday in May, the original Armed Forces Day. The choice of the day may have something to do with the sponsoring organization, the 369th Veterans Association. The 369th, otherwise known as the Harlem Hellfighters, was no ordinary fighting unit. Pershing, the commander of American forces in World War I, went out of his way to commend Harlem's black heroes. In World War II, the 369th saw some of the bloodiest combat in the European Theater. They remained patriots to a cause and died fighting for a country where they were second-class citizens.

Dr. King was the most important leader of the movement that finally brought black people in the United States legal equality. He was the pacifist champion of these African-American fighting men. It is fitting that the 369th leads the commemorative parade.

The line of march follows Fifth Avenue from 44th Street to 86th Street. It is not exactly solemn, but it is more low-key than other African-American parades. There are lots of high school and youth organization bands with energetic musicians and acrobatic baton twirlers. There are unions representing hospital workers and social workers conscientiously trying to keep up with the line of march. The military veterans are spit-polish smart, arms swinging to sharp cadences. The veterans of the alphabet corps (such as SNCC and CORE) of the civil rights wars are relaxed, middle-aged informality, cheerfully acknowledging the clapping and cheers. Leaders of the 1960s boycotts and protests make their eulogies and try to recapture the March on Washington hopefulness.

═ Bedford-Stuyvesant—Brooklyn Revival ═

Directions: Subway A to Nostrand Avenue/Fulton Street.

Among the first inhabitants of what would become Brooklyn and Bedford-Stuyvesant were African-American men and women, slave and free. A free black man named Francisco was one of the original landowners of Boswyk (soon to be Bushwick) in 1660. Throughout the seventeenth and eighteenth centuries, Brooklyn had the highest proportion of slaves in the state.

Fulton's ferry brought Brooklyn closer to Manhattan and it became more prosperous and populous. In the early nineteenth century, blacks were generally scattered throughout New York's second city, with a small colony of free men and women in rural Weeksville-Carrsville, which later came to be included in Bedford-Stuyvesant. Before the Civil War they would actively support the cause of abolition and were station masters on the underground railroad.

In 1863, the New York City draft riots and consequent arson and slaughter led to a mass exodus of blacks to the safety and security of Weeksville-Carrsville. Although the black population steadily increased in this area, by 1870 they were outnumbered by whites escaping from Manhattan overcrowding. Blacks continued to occupy a small corner of Bedford-Stuyvesant, as white and wealthy suburbia grew up around them.

Brooklyn African Americans were socially conscious and community minded. As early as 1817 they established their own churches, and by 1827 they founded an organization to provide support for widows and orphans. Black Brooklynites operated their own school system from 1818 to 1843. By the 1870s, African-American mutual aid societies were commonplace.

In 1890 Brooklyn blacks numbered 10,287 and they considered themselves the cream of African-American society. Their Fifth Avenue ran along Atlantic Avenue and Fulton Street, extending from Fort Greene to Bedford-Stuyvesant. Their roster of distinguished citizens included the physician and pharmacist Peter W. Ray, Alderman Fred R. Moore, suc-

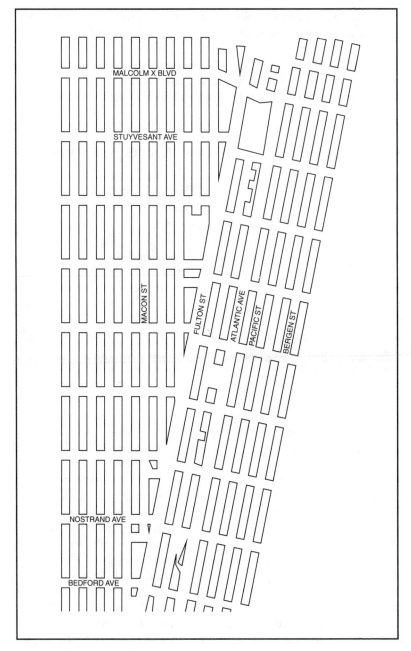

Bedford-Stuyvesant

cessful inventors Lewis Latimer and Samuel R. Scottron, educator William L. Bulkey, and publisher and journalist T. Thomas Fortune.

Southern black migration to Brooklyn escalated in the 1900s, responding both to the boll weevil infestation and the social and economic barriers of Jim Crow. A large and visible influx of African Americans into Bedford-Stuyvesant threatened whites, who reacted with protests and restrictive real estate practices. They even drew up plans to relocate African Americans to other communities!

The African Americans of Brooklyn were determined not to accept unequal treatment and discrimination. Black leaders, like Reverend Thomas S. Harten of Holy Trinity Baptist Church, organized demonstrations against police brutality, Jim Crow education policies, and discriminatory seating in movie theaters. Chapters of the Urban League and the NAACP were organized in Brooklyn to fight for equal rights on the streets and in the courts.

Despite official and unofficial bigotry, black Brooklynites continued to make political gains. Brooklyn African Americans became deputy district attorneys, members of the board of education, and judges. When they were not granted political appointments and earned patronage by the party of Lincoln, they promptly jumped ship and joined the party of FDR.

During the boom years from 1940 to 1950 the black population in Brooklyn increased from 108,263 to 208,468. African Americans became the backbone of Bedford-Stuyvesant. They were the homeowners and the taxpayers. They were the local movers and shakers.

In 1948, Bedford-Stuyvesant elected its first African-American assemblyman, Bertram Baker; in 1953, it elected its first municipal judge, Lewis Flagg. In the sixties Brooklyn blacks continued their rise to power by electing a second assemblymen and a state senator. In 1968 Shirley Chisholm became the first black Brooklynite to represent her community in Congress.

African Americans in Bedford-Stuyvesant also fought for economic equality in the sixties. Grass-roots groups in the community set up picket lines and confronted discriminatory hiring policies. They challenged Sealtest-Sheffield Farms, Ebingers, and Bond Bread. They were not willing to accept flagrant discrimination in their own backyard.

The Bedford-Stuyvesant Restoration Corporation was established in 1967 to promote the development of local businesses and employment. In just one decade it was responsible for financing 125 African-American businesses, negotiating twenty million dollars in black business loans, and salvaging three thousand local jobs.

The concentration of African Americans in Brooklyn led to the development of a black political base. By 1976, African Americans were in control of ten legislative offices in Brooklyn and more were on the horizon. At the same time they held five judicial offices.

Over the years black Bedford Stuyvesant has been the victim of municipal neglect and urban riots, but it has kept its community spirit and weathered many storms. Today it's "a community on the move." Young professionals are putting down roots and crime is on the decline (down nearly ten percent in 1993). There is even a move on to expand its historic district from three hundred to twelve hundred landmark buildings.

Bed-Stuy Place Marks

Brownstone Bed-Stuy is landmark building country bordered by Chauncy and Macon Streets, and Stuyvesant and Tompkins Avenues. It is elegant, high-hat 1890s Brooklyn. The former occupants of these architectural gems were turn-of-the-century rich and famous, like F. W. Woolworth. Inside are handsome wainscotted interiors with magnificent sculpted molding and outside patrician gardens come with flowering rhododendron, juniper shrubs, and blue atlas spruce. Later residents included the great Eubie Blake and other ragtime musicians, who lent their own inimitable class to the venue. In the third week of October local boosters offer tours of the neighborhood's best. Call Brownstoners of Bedford-Stuyvesant House Tours at 718-452-3226 for a full viewing.

The Bedford-Stuyvesant Restoration Center, *1360 Fulton Street (718-636-6900).*

The Bedford-Stuyvesant Restoration took derelict warehouses and factories and turned them into a black enterprise zone. The Kennedy family supplied some of the inspiration and seed money, but black Brooklyn did the building and planning. There's a contemporary complex of stores, offices, and artistic space. The cultural component of the restoration includes The Skylight Art Gallery, a recording studio, and even a theater named for Lady Day.

The **Billie Holiday Theater** (718-636-0918) houses a black theater company that imaginatively mounts musical and dramatic productions that deal with the black experience.

Weeksville Society, *1698 Bergen Street (718-434-7695).*

Weeksville is Bedford-Stuyvesant's answer to Williamsburg. It is a restoration of the old Hunterfly Houses, where free New York blacks lived before the Civil War. Weeksville is named for James Weeks, a proud independent black man who originally farmed this land. The Weeksville Restoration was sponsored by the city's Department of Housing Preservation and Development, but it was built by a new generation of self-sufficient blacks.

Magnolia Tree Earth Center Grandiflora, *679 Lafayette Avenue (718-387-2116). Monday–Friday 9 A.M.–6 P.M. Check for special programs on Saturday and Sunday.*

This environmental learning center contains a magnolia tree that "grows in Brooklyn" with landmark status. The helpful and friendly staff is committed to the greening of Brooklyn and promotes recycling and conservation in the community.

Soul Food in Central Brooklyn

After church on Sundays, when the hymns and the gospel shouts seem to reverberate in the air, men, women, and children in the dignity of their Sunday best sometimes stroll slowly down Fulton for a special eating-out Sunday dinner. It's real down-home molasses and biscuits, with the fried chicken from a pan instead of deep fried, and the black-eyed peas with pork and fat back really slow cooked.

Auggie's Brownstone Inn, *1550 Fulton Street between Albany and Kingston (718-773-8940). Monday–Sunday 4 P.M.–11 P.M.*

Auggie's is a no-frills neighborhood watering hole with soul on the jukebox, the Knicks on TV, and Southern-fried soul food from the kitchen. Fish nights feature crab and whiting.

Pleasant Grove Kitchen, *1927 Fulton Street near Howard Avenue (718-773-0895). Monday–Saturday 7:30 A.M.–7 P.M.*

The real Southern soul home cooking comes by way of the Pleasant Grove Baptist Church. The smothered pork chops and chicken are perfection with sides of greens. The sweet potato pie has a just right hint of spice.

McDonald's Dining Room, *327 Stuyvesant Avenue (718-574-3728). Daily 8 A.M.–10 P.M.*

McDonald's is a big homey counter-and-booths place where the locals shoot the breeze over Southern breakfasts complete with grits and salmon cakes, or Southern suppers with thick center-cut fried pork chops or meaty short ribs as entrees. Clara Walker, the restaurant's proprietor, provides the Southern hospitality. There is a back room for more formal dining.

North Carolina Country Kitchen Restaurant, *1993 Atlantic Avenue at Saratoga Avenue (718-498-8033). Daily 7:30 A.M.–10 P.M.*

This is Bedford-Stuyvesant's re-creation of down-home dining in a rustic North Carolina pine roadhouse. The breakfast is very special with slab bacon, country sausage, eggs, and grits served cafeteria style. Whether it's chicken or chitterlings, the fry cook has a sure hand. The black-eyed peas are pleasantly laced with bits of pork.

The African Street Festival

In a time of national celebration, from June 30 to July 4, Bedford-Stuyvesant's African-American community also celebrates its African heritage in an extended street fair. There is an African market offering traditional jewelry, carvings, and fabrics, along with African music and African delicacies.

West Indians

History

The West Indians of the British Caribbean endured more brutal conditions under slavery than blacks in the American South. For the British planters it was cheaper to replace slaves than treat them humanely. These slaves did not have the benefits of plantation paternalism and were forced to raise their own food and support their own families. Despite crushing demands, they retained their native self-sufficiency. A combination of greater cultural freedom and later contact with compatriots from Africa enabled West Indians to hold onto more of their African heritage than their American counterparts.

West Indians were emancipated earlier than American blacks, with a transitional period to prepare them for a life of freedom. They were still dependent on white plantation owners who controlled the cash-crop economy. Black West Indians learned early that emigration was one of the few alternatives to serfdom. They followed economic opportunity to other islands and South American countries located in or near the Caribbean.

In the late part of the nineteenth century black West Indians began arriving in New York in significant numbers. Many had an introduction to American mores and economic possibilities working on the construction of the Panama Canal. They brought to the city ambition, thrift, and a willingness to make the maximum effort.

First-generation West Indian immigrants were strongly attached to their Caribbean homes and the British culture that nurtured them. Many viewed their stay in America as temporary. They were interested primarily in American economic rewards. They dreamed of returning to their birthplace to buy property or start a business. Though only a few fulfilled this dream, it deterred many from becoming citizens.

Despite this early political non involvement, West Indians had a strong political impact on African-American and New York life. Marcus Garvey, who entered America in 1916, encouraged community unity, black economic independence, and recognition of their African cultural legacy. He was the precursor of leaders as diverse as Father Divine and the Honorable Elijah Muhammad.

Ambitious West Indians became Harlem's leading entrepreneurs. These mainly urban West Indians with a British education had a real advantage over rural African Americans. In 1901 this relatively small minority already controlled twenty percent of Harlem's businesses.

West Indians also contributed to the Harlem literary Renaissance. James Weldon Johnson was the stylist of the Harlem ideal, high black art created from the black experience, while Langston Hughes was the down-to-earth poet of the Harlem everyman. Claude McKay boldly aspired to a more just America.

Occasionally there was friction between the West Indian "interloper" and New York's African Americans. West Indians were sometimes scornful of Southern blacks and Southern blacks in turn resented the highhandedness of West Indians. The Southern blacks were confused by the West Indian social conservatism and radical politics and found their British manners affected.

West Indians in the twenties started the trek out of Harlem via the expanding IRT Line to Brooklyn. They were drawn to the solid one- and two-family houses that had housed elite professionals and members of the financial community in Bedford and Stuyvesant for decades.

Whether from Jamaica, Trinidad, Barbados, the Bahamas, Guyana, Grenada, St. Kitts-Nevis, St. Vincent, or Dominica, their aspirations were mainly middle class and they were intent on "buying house." Many owned businesses, proving the old adage that "as soon as a West Indian gets ten cents above a beggar he buys a business." Whether they were white collar professionals or laborers on construction sites, they were primed for free enterprise and the consumer society.

Through their own independent credit unions and informal rotating credit associations they were able to finance the handsome houses of East Stuyvesant and West Bedford. Between 1930 and 1940 the black proportion of newly united Bedford-Stuyvesant rose from a little more than a tenth to a third.

Some West Indians stayed behind to play politically influential roles in Manhattan. Bertram Baker of Nevis in 1948 became the first black member of the state assembly. Hulan Jack of St. Lucia was elected the first African-American Manhattan borough president in 1953. In 1964 the most successful pol of them all, J. Raymond Jones of Jamaica, became the first black leader of Tammany Hall.

Whites refused to serve blacks in Bedford restaurants, and there were even some attempts to keep them out of the Bed-Stuy real estate market. Whether by unconscious neglect or concerted policy, city services declined over time, affecting the homes that West Indians cherished and maintained with such care.

West Indians did not halt their Brooklyn exodus. They ventured further out along the tree-lined boulevard of Eastern Parkway into Crown Heights and Flatbush. They seeded their new enclave with West Indian businesses, island and hometown associations, and soccer and cricket clubs.

In the 1950s the McCarran-Walter Act closed the doors on mass West Indian emigration. More than a decade later, in a time enlightened by the civil rights movement, the Celler-Hart Act of 1965 resumed West Indian immigration and reunited West Indian families. Between 1965 and 1980 eighty-five thousand Jamaicans, representing the largest group of islanders, settled in the city.

The austerity policies of some West Indian governments, together with island unemployment and political violence, increased the flow of West Indians to New York in the 1970s, 1980s, and 1990s. They came from every level of West Indian society, but all were equally bent on success. While Jamaicans were still the largest West Indian group emigrating to New York in 1990, an increasingly large group from Guyana was running a close second.

Most of these recent arrivals head for the sprawling West Indian neighborhoods in Brooklyn. They may come as domestic house workers or nannies on contract or nurses, but they are soon moving up the success ladder. They may start as low-level clericals, security guards, laborers, and domestics, but a high percentage go on to higher education, professions, and skilled trades. They all keep up the West Indian home-owning tradition.

The new self-confident West Indian population of New York is not interested in returning to the islands in the sun except for a leisurely vacation. They are here to stay and carve out stable and strong communities. They are fiercely proud of their West Indian identities and in this new era are willing to defend West Indian interests.

A new generation of immigrant and first-generation West Indian-American politicians are now being elected to represent the West Indian communities. Jamaican Una Clarke was elected to the city council in 1991, and in 1992 Jamaican Nick Perry became a state assemblyman.

Crown of the Caribbean—Crown Heights

Directions: Subway 3 or 4 to Utica Avenue, or Subway 3 to Nostrand Avenue.

Crown Heights is the largest West Indian neighborhood in the city, and has one of the oldest African-American communities in New York. Two miles square, it is a stretch of land that includes a varied population of West Indians, a much smaller group of African Americans, and a small but very visible population of Hasidic Jews called Lubavitchers, who escaped the Holocaust to settle in Brooklyn.

In the 1830s, when Crown Heights was known as Crow Hill, African Americans were active contributing members of this community and a highly visible population. A hundred years later they represented a tiny proportion of Crown Heights and were hardly noticed. In the 1940s this neighborhood was mainly occupied by Jews, Italians, Irish, Germans, and Scandinavians.

After World War II, the ethnic mix began to change, as returning veterans moved to the suburbs on the GI Bill. This process was further accelerated by illegal "blockbusting," real estate practices that led to panic selling and neighborhood instability in the 1950s and early 1960s. By the end of the 1960s blacks became the predominant group in the neighborhood, representing seventy percent of the population.

West Indians, mainly representing the nations of Jamaica, Guyana, Trinidad, Barbados, and Grenada, poured into Crown Heights with the liberalized immigration laws of 1965. By the 1970s they represented the majority of the Crown Heights' black community. West Indians took the reins of leadership and played important roles in the spiritual and political life of Crown Heights.

Leaders like Reverend Heron Sam, pastor of St. Mark's Church; Clarence Norman, pastor of the First Baptist Church; and Edward S. Hightower, Chairman of Crown Heights Community Board, negotiated with the city's power brokers and helped to ameliorate tensions within the Crown Heights' community. They made an effort to organize West Indians and rebuild neighborhoods.

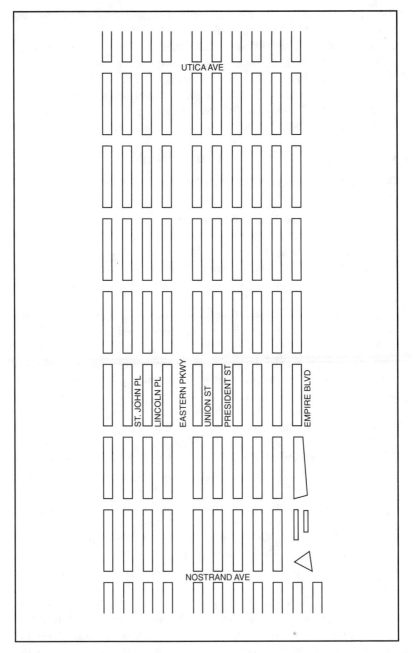

West Indian Crown Heights

In 1982 Clarence Norman, Jr., the son of the popular West Indian spiritual leader Reverend Clarence Norman of the First Baptist Church and a former member of the district attorney's office, was elected to the state assembly. He solidified his leadership by election to both the state assembly and Democratic district leader in 1986.

West Indian Crown Heights joined forces with their Hasidic neighbors in 1989 to successfully support David Dinkins for mayor. In that same year Caribbean blacks exhibited their political muscle by electing two council members, four assembly members, and two state senators.

In 1991, the neighborhood was shaken by a riot that began with the accidental death of a seven-year-old Guyanese and led to the murder of a Hasidic scholar. Both communities worked hard to heal the wounds caused by these tragic happenings. There were community meetings and forums and even a series of museum exhibitions that created understanding and goodwill.

The center of West Indian Brooklyn runs along Eastern Parkway between the Grand Army Plaza and Utica Avenue, following the line of march of the West Indian Day Parade. It is a thoroughfare of Victorian grandeur, venerable brick mansions, and high-towered churches. The best housing—mostly brick and stucco finished with high stoops and porches—are on the south side of the Parkway. The houses are well maintained and the sidewalks are swept clean.

West Indian commerce flourishes on Nostrand Avenue and Utica Avenue. The restaurants and bakeries are West Indian enterprises, while the discount shops, groceries, and fishmongers are shared among Caribbean, Korean, and Arab merchants. On weekends these streets move to a reggae beat as West Indian throngs take their time window shopping along the avenue.

There are bearded Rastas in brightly colored caps and severe church-going women in old-fashioned turbans. The differences don't stop them from gaily greeting one another. The West Indians, man and woman, young and old, are tall and stand ramrod straight. Though they have a fondness for the colors of the tropics, they carry themselves with Quaker-black dignity.

Crown Heights Place Mark

Medgar Evers College, *1650 Bedford Avenue.*

Medgar Evers College is a two-year institution that is part of the city university system of New York. The site of the prestigious Caribbean

Studies Institute, it has an extensive library dealing with the West Indian experience and sponsors West Indian cultural events, exhibitions, and forums.

Rastafarian Corner

The Rastafarian religion is Jamaica's millennial faith. Ethiopia is the New Jerusalem and Emperor Selassie is the Messiah. He is the Christ, the Lion of Judah. *Ganja* is the wine and wafer of the faithful, dreadlocks are the West Indian side curls. They believe in one creator, one aim, and one destiny.

At the corner of Nostrand and Park Avenues, next to a store selling athletic trophies, there is a mural of the Lion of Judah in all his other-worldly glory, along with African-American heroes living and dead. On the southwest corner there is a wall of remembrance for younger members of the community who met untimely ends.

Island Eating

The cuisine of the West Indies borrows from the British colonizers, African slaves, and Indian indentured labor. While it has many ingredients in common with the Hispanic Caribbean, such as breadfruit, yams, plantains, dry cod, and the ever-popular pigeon peas or *goongo,* the black and British islands prefer hot chili pepper to the sweet and make food additionally spicy with allspice, thyme, curry powder, nutmeg, and ginger. Coconut milk and other coconut products are also a regular cooking staple in the West Indies.

Pigeon peas and rice is to the West Indies what beans and rice are to Mexico; when not eaten alone it can accompany almost anything. The combination of coconut milk and hot scotch bonnet peppers in the preparation give it both richness and bite. West Indian meat patties with ground beef set off by Jamaican thyme and hot pepper are ubiquitous in the West Indies. A bland version is even sold along with hot dogs on the streets of New York. Callaloo is a West Indian green that gives its name to a memorable stew that runs the gamut from pork to crab meat and okra to grated coconut. Roti is a West Indian stand-by with an East Indian influence: Asian flat bread is wrapped around the vegetable or meat stew in a piquant take-off of the Cornish pasty.

The West Indian eating place is usually somewhere on the continuum between restaurant and take-out. West Indians are people in a hurry even when they have nowhere to go, and they have taken to the New York practice of eating on the run. But after even a brief wait on line to make their order, which is usually not brief, it turns out that the main dishes from curried goat to callaloo are too heaping to fast-food consume. West Indian service does not stoop to conquer. The proprietor's singsong is peppered with wry humor.

Cheffy's Jamaican, *707 Nostrand Avenue (718-363-9515). Monday–Saturday 11* A.M.*–10* P.M.

Cheffy's is authentic Jamaican, hot and spicy, whether it's the curried goat, codfish cakes, or a rich stew of oxtails. The stew chicken laced with Jamaican Pickapeppa Sauce is not for the faint of heart. The Jamaican soft drinks, including the ginger beer, sorrel, or maubey, also have a hint of spice without the syrupy sweetness common to American beverages.

Dewar's, *807 Nostrand Avenue (718-773-8403). Daily 8:30* A.M.*– 8* P.M.

The Hollis family provides the warmth and the welcome at Dewar's. There are flowers in odd corners and a wall of pictures documenting the family's world travels. There is also warmth in their West Indian cooking, usually verging on the fiery. Curried goat is a taste easily acquired at Dewar's, the gaminess of the goat neutralized by the hot chilies. Breakfast West Indian at Dewar's with akee and saltfish. Akee is a tropical fruit that is transformed by frying it with the fish into an omelet.

Gloria's In and Out, *991 Nostrand Avenue (718-778-4852).*

Gloria's In and Out II, *1148 Nostrand Avenue (718-493-2183). Tuesday–Saturday 11* A.M.*–10* P.M.

Don't mind the bars on the window or the counter enclosed by glass like a teller's window—they do let you out of Gloria's In and Out. It's mostly a lineup for take-out, but stop and set a spell at one of the picnic tables with a bowl of some cow-heel soup with just a hint of scallion, thyme, and pepper. Drink a Jamaican ginger beer, which has the tang of fresh ginger, and watch the world go by.

Ital Delight, *1052 Nostrand Avenue (718-771-3123). Daily 9:00* A.M.*–10:00* P.M.

Although the generous ladles of oxtail stew or the curried goat have put more than a crimp in your appetite, there always seems to be room for Ital's sweet-as-nectar sweet potato pudding or corn meal pudding.

Cock's Bajan Restaurant, *223 Utica Avenue between St. John's and Sterling Place (718-771-8833).*

The Bajan, like other island peoples, are partial to seafood. Flying fish is the Bajan national dish, and Cock's does it right with a touch of heat and a vegetable side of *cou cou.*

Singh's Hot Roti, *387 Utica Avenue (718-363-0198). Daily 7:30 A.M.–8 P.M.*

Singh's Hot shop is the traditional Trinidadian roti that they hawk from carts on the streets of Port of Spain. The chicken, meat, or fish roti is hot as an Indian vindaloo and not for the fainthearted.

Bulla Cake and Spice

West Indian baking crosses the divide between meat and sweet. The West Indians have taken something of India and something of England and the foods of the Caribbean to create their unique style of baking. They start with an English fruitcake and add rum and improvise with Indian breads and spices in their rotis and patties. Bland English-style breads are distinguished by coconut and cassava. Ordinary ginger bread is transformed into a subtly sweet and moist *bulla* cake. Don't be fooled by names—a spice bun is a ginger and spice cake and a bread pudding is a flat cake flavored with rum.

Ronnie's Bakery, *892 Nostrand Avenue (718-756-4435). Monday–Saturday 9 A.M.–8:30 P.M.*

The West Indian rum fruitcake is strong enough to cause a hangover. The currant buns are rich with molasses and the Jamaican patties are very peppery. This Ronnie is a Veronica who learned her trade from mother. She says her baking has a real island taste because she uses island-type flour.

Allan's Quality Bakery, *1109 Nostrand Avenue (718-774-7892). Monday–Friday 7:30 A.M.–9 P.M.; Saturday 7:30 A.M.–8 P.M.; Sunday 7:30 A.M.–6 P.M.*

Like the name says, Allan's uses quality ingredients and sells only freshly baked breads, tarts, and patties. The coconut bread is a unique compromise between cake and bread. The meat patties are authentic island orange with melt-in-the-mouth pastry, and the filling could burn the tongue. The apple turnovers are a pass, too bland and heavy.

Barbados Bakery, *229 Utica Avenue (718-493-5218). Monday–Friday 9 A.M.–8 A.M.; Saturday 8 A.M.–10 P.M.; Sunday 9 A.M.–3 P.M.*

The display case is full of unusual Bajan specialties like Bajan cheesecake with coconut milk and Barbados corn pone and a carrot cake called carrot pudding. The Bajan community from the whole metropolitan area comes here for their favorite sweets.

Tota's West Indian Bakery, *260 Utica Avenue between Lincoln Place and Eastern Parkway (718-773-5503). Daily 8:00 A.M.–8:00 P.M.*

Tota's is West Indian baking with Guyanese flair and imagination. The black pudding is not a pudding at all but a fruit cake marinated in rum. The Guyanese beef (or chicken) patty is lighter and flakier than the Jamaican and more like a pastry. There is seating for those who cannot wait to get home.

Gig Young, *366 Utica Avenue (212-773-9174). Daily 7 A.M.–11 P.M.*

The layer cakes in the window are mostly for display. The spice buns and the *bulla* cake are what sell like bread. Still, pride of place goes to hot Jamaican patties that could remove paint.

West Indian Raps

Calypso, the original West Indian folk music, started out in Trinidad. It's loose and lively and no holding back. The singers like Mighty Sparrow are free spirits ready to rip into politics and personalities. When calypso is played on a variety of oil drums, pots, and biscuit tins, the medium is the steel band message. The bands started in Trinidad in a spontaneous V-E Day celebration. Jamaica took reggae out of Harry Belafonte country and made it an urban Kingston idiom. The beat's insistent and the attitude's radical. Bob Marley was the reggae master, a mixture of prophet and poet and hip studio musician. Dance-hall is the latest West Indian sound, combining rap with an island backbeat.

Straker's Caribbean Record World, *242 Utica Avenue (718-756-0340). Monday–Saturday 10 A.M.–7 P.M.*

Straker's is for Caribbean cult record buyers. It has the impossible to find from Grenada and St. Vincent and the early releases of Bob Marley and Jimmy Cliff. It is a place where people hang out to talk about Caribbean music. Granville Straker, the proprietor of this Caribbean music institution, is both a producer and a promoter of the sounds of the West Indies and the guiding force behind the Caribbean All-Stars Festival, which for some reason takes place on Mother's Day.

Park Heights Records, *317 Utica Avenue (718-773-2891). Monday–Saturday 10 A.M.–10 P.M.; Sunday 10 A.M.–7 P.M.*

The reggae goes round and round and it stops right here, along with calypso and ska and steel bands, and blasts out of the outdoor speaker. Park Heights diversifies with Jamaica T-shirts, Rasta hats, and island carvings.

West Indian Caps

Serengetti, *770 Nostrand Avenue (718-953-8378). Daily 10 A.M.–7 P.M.*

Serengetti is out of Africa by way of Crown Heights and Jamaica. It is authentic African drums and dashikis and leather and knot caps for dreadlocks. It is the flags of many nations, Caribbean and African, and the image of the Lion of Judah. There is nothing more imaginative or better made in the craft shops of Soho.

West Indian Carnival

Carnival is a centuries-old tradition in the Caribbean. The New York version that started in Harlem and moved to Brooklyn in 1960 (with most of Manhattan's West Indian inhabitants) evokes the energy and insistent rhythms of the islands with a flashy big-city quality. Timed to coincide with the Labor Day weekend, it is a frenetic end-of-summer ritual. This New York-style extravaganza runs for five days, and the preparations for next year's dazzling carnival costumes and elaborate carnival routines begin the moment it is over.

Designers create costumes in workshops throughout the city. It may only be silver foil and aluminum tubing, painted cardboard, and cane, but it somehow captures the spirit of myth and legend, outer-space creatures and fairy-tale kings and queens. Meanwhile the dances are choreographed and the dancers go through their paces till the timing is instinctive. It is more than a celebration or putting on a show. For participants like the designer Morris Stewart, it is the supreme form of self-expression.

The parade is the climax of the festival, with carnival groups strutting their stuff to island reggae, calypso, and steel bands. This celebration of West Indian cultural identity is a Crown Heights happening. The bands, the dancers, and the community mingle on and off the wide boulevard of

Eastern Parkway. Beside this grand finale, there are four other days of events featuring West Indian music, culture, and the carnival traditions and competitions. The West Indian-American Carnival is a vast reunion of all the city's hundreds of thousands of West Indian peoples. It is a time for Bajans, Jamaicans, and Trinidadians to get together to dance to the music and eat home-style hot cod cakes and curried goat sold and prepared by the community's best cooks. It is one big West Indian block party.

East Flatbush—Flatbush,
The New Neighborhood

Directions: Subway 2 or 5 to Church Avenue.

As the competition for housing increased in Crown Heights, wealthier West Indians set their sights on East Flatbush, a primarily Jewish area on the border of Crown Heights. Following their home-owning tradition, they were anxious to move into the one- and two-family homes that represent a third of the housing stock in this pleasant tree-lined neighborhood.

In the seventeenth century East Flatbush was Dutch farmland and pasture. The estates of Dutch landowners became family farms in the eighteenth century. Although then called Rugby, this area retained its rural and Dutch character into the early part of the nineteenth century, and even today there is at least one East Flatbush landmark dating from the time New York was New Amsterdam.

The introduction of the Brooklyn, Flatbush, and Coney Island Railroad at the turn of the century resulted in a real estate boom. Rural land was turned into subdivisions, and quaint Queen Anne cottages covered the landscape. Farmers and country gentry of Dutch and English stock were displaced by immigrants from Italy, Ireland, and Germany.

In the real estate boom of the 1920s developers turned East Flatbush truck gardens and vacant lots into row houses and semidetacheds for the masses. This trend continued into the late 1930s when Fred Trump, the father of real estate mogul Donald Trump, built a sprawling development of attached brick row houses.

Jewish families escaping the urban decay of the Lower East Side and nearby Brownsville snapped up these properties. It would be their own neighborhood for the next few decades; the most visible blacks in this neighborhood were the workers who gathered on Rutland Road seeking domestic employment for the day.

In the 1950s this began to change as affluent African Americans, such as the Brooklyn Dodger Jackie Robinson, and West Indians began to buy homes in East Flatbush. By 1970 West Indians made up the majority in East Flatbush and were moving into Flatbush proper.

In the 1970s and 1980s the number of West Indian immigrants was on the rise. More than a third of the Jamaicans who were immigrating to New York made Flatbush their main choice. Between 1983 and 1989 Jamaicans and Guyanese alone accounted for almost a third of the new Americans in Flatbush.

West Indians were drawn to the shady tree-lined streets, big back yards, and sturdy respectable houses. They were looking for more space and comfort, whether it was a rambling wooden Victorian with a porch, a limestone semidetached with a stoop, or a stylish white stucco-and-brick apartment house. They even built their own condos in East Flatbush, the first really substantial new housing in this neck of the woods for three decades.

The main shopping avenues, Church and Flatbush, now had a cinnamon and spice Caribbean flavor. The Jewish delis and bagel shops were replaced by take-outs and bakeries selling Jamaica patties and roti. The record shops dropped mainstream pop for reggae and calypso. Beauty parlors and barber shops became West Indian social clubs, with the latest African cuts and braids.

Flatbush has become synonymous with West Indian. Island energy, openness, and candor characterize the people who live here. They are so hard working and spirited that it has become almost a stereotype. Their strong sense of civic pride and self-respect is evident in the neat houses and well-tended lawns and gardens of Flatbush. A radio soap went on the air in 1990 which deals with the trials and tribulations and hopes and aspirations of this special people; it's called "Flatbush USA" and is set in Brooklyn.

Flatbush Flavors

The tempo seems to slow the further you go from Nostrand and Utica Avenues, and the flavors are the same or even better. Some of the most popular restaurants, take-outs, and bakeries are in this neighborhood.

From Cow's Foot Soup to Goat Curry

Tamarind Tree, *1463 Flatbush Avenue between Glenwood and 28th streets (718-434-9610). Daily 10 A.M.–11 P.M.*

Tamarind is bigger than the usual eat-and-run roti and jerk barbecue joint. The booths are comfortable and an oversized mural of an island paradise is for the looking. There are some unusual tastes for breakfast like fried (corn meal) dumplings and salt cod and callaloo (a green) with banana. Soups have some interesting anatomy–goat's head, cow's foot, and cow's cod—and are to some extent indistinguishable. The stewed red snapper is distinctive.

Guyana Roti House, *3021 Church Avenue (718-940-9413). Daily 10 A.M.–10 P.M.*

The roti itself at Guyana is tasty enough to enhance the fine fillings. The goat and oxtail are best, but the vegetable is still respectable. Take a stool at the counter and catch the beat and rhythms of the voices on the West Indian cassettes. Do not leave without finding out what the Guyanese can do with carrot cake.

Donna's Jerk Chicken, *3125 Church Avenue (718-287-8182). Daily 8:00 A.M.–3:00 A.M.*

Donna's has high-backed chairs straight from a West Indian veranda, perfect for sipping peanut punch. Relax over a plate of red-hot, smokey jerk chicken or pork cooked to falling-off-the-bone tender.

Badoo's International Restaurant, *5422 Church Avenue at 54th Street (718-345-7654). Daily 11 A.M.–11 P.M.*

Badoo's is another contender for the most sizzling, crusty, and peppery jerk chicken cooked Jamaican style in a cut-off oil drum. Don't underestimate the stew chicken; more herbal flavors come through the heat.

— Patty-Cake —

Angel's Flake Patties, *2114 Nostrand Avenue (718-434-0816). Daily 9:30 A.M.–11 P.M.*

Angel's Flake Patties is the patty specialist with light-as-a-feather Jamaica beef patties, chicken patties, jerk chicken patties, and shrimp patties. There's also a comprehensive take-out with codfish cakes to curry.

Nick's, *1744 Flatbush Avenue (718-338-0455). Daily 9 A.M.–10 P.M.*

Nick's is a West Indian staff-of-life bakery. It does the simple things like *hardo* bread, coconut bread, turnovers, tennis rolls, and currant buns well.

Sybil's, *2110 Church Avenue (718-469-0049). Daily 9 A.M.–11 P.M.*

Sybil is a Guyanese phenomenon, a West Indian Sybil who transformed her talent in the kitchen making traditional Guyanese cookies, cakes, and pastries into a chain of successful bakeries. Besides bakery, she has stews, curries, lo mein, and a Guyanese pepper pot. Her *dhall* roti is "bus-up-shut" (made-to-order). Take-out or eat-in, has she spread herself too thin?

Haitians

History

The Haitians are the boat people of the Western Hemisphere—risking it all in a leaky twenty-five-foot craft to escape oppression and want, twenty or thirty people to a boat sharing hunger and thirst under the blazing sun for the seven-hundred-mile trip to Miami. In Haiti they committed the crime of questioning the violence of the Tonton Macoute and their military masters or they merely had something that someone in power desired. Maybe they spoke out for political freedom or human rights and came under the scrutiny of death squads. Like the Vietnamese they chose survival.

Haitians have been coming to New York since the 1790s, when French colonists and Creoles from San Domingue (the original name of Haiti) fled the slave rebellion. James Audubon, the naturalist, was among their number. Creoles in colorful West Indian prints were a familiar sight on the streets of New York in the first decade of the nineteenth century.

Haitian businessmen and professionals came to New York in the early years of the twentieth century to escape the country's political upheavals. Many of the city's five hundred Haitians were supporters of Marcus Garvey's Back to Africa campaign.

Following the American occupation of Haiti in 1934 a number of Haitians followed the American marines back to the States and settled in New York. At the same time Haitians in the Columbia University student-exchange programs decided to remain in the city. After World War II Haitians came to New York as live-in servants.

The mass migration of Haitians began with the election of Francois Duvalier (Papa Doc) in 1958. This supposedly simple country doctor and man of the people spawned a reign of terror in the process of picking clean his country's treasury.

The first to leave were the wealthy mulatto elite, who were against Papa Doc while he still represented himself as a black populist reformer. Trained and well educated, they could fit right into New York while they hatched a succession of unsuccessful coups and invasions. They were followed in the 1960s by a black middle class that couldn't live with the violence and economic insecurity of what one critic called the Duvalier "kleptocracy."

The first documented case of poor refugees fleeing Duvalier's brutality on the high seas occurred in 1963, but the wholesale flight of the boat people didn't commence until the 1970s. Though they landed on the coast of Florida, most continued the journey to New York.

At the beginning this outpouring of people was spontaneous, friends and relatives pooling their resources for a future in the States. By 1980 Haitian fast-buck artists with ties to the regime of Jean-Claude Duvalier were promoting these dangerous boat trips along with promises of employment in America. The kickbacks were supposed to go all the way to the presidential palace.

Between 1977 and 1981 Haiti inundated the coast of Florida with sixty thousand refugees. The Reagan administration reacted by emphasizing the distinction between political and economic refugees, categorizing most Haitians as the latter. Reagan ordered the Coast Guard to intercept the Haitians at sea and send them back to their individual destinies. In the next ten years only twenty-eight of the 22,716 Haitians encountered by the Coast Guard were granted asylum.

While the first emigrants of the Duvalier reign were managerial types, technicians, and professionals, the most recent arrivals are unskilled and semiskilled: laborers, factory workers, and domestics. Some have been forced to accept the jobs of last resort because of their immigration status.

Haitian immigrants in contemporary New York follow many of the same patterns as earlier immigrants from Italy and Eastern Europe. They band together in the same areas of the city with people from the same village or quarter. Despite the availability of city welfare, Haitians help one another through fraternities, associations, and credit groups. Group solidarity is also maintained through the Haitian newspaper *Haiti-Observateur*.

Though the Duvalier regime was finally deposed, conditions in Haiti did not measurably improve. An alliance of military strongmen and the affluent Francophile elite of Petionville ran the show, with police and loose bands of local thugs as their enforcers. Finally, international pressures and a charismatic priest, Jean-Bertand Aristide, forced free elections. Aristide won but was quickly deposed in 1991.

The military took control and there were reprisals against the supporters of Aristide. Death squads came in the night. The regime of Raul Cedras, with his civilian puppets, ruled by fear. A disappointed and desperate people resumed their flight to the United States, with New York or Miami as their ultimate destination. In September of 1994 the America army occupied Haiti without firing a shot, with the intention of eliminating official terror and returning Aristide to the office of president. His regime, for the present, is a source of stability and justice.

Bois Verna

This Haitian colony, which is scattered throughout the Upper West Side from the west eighties to the low hundreds between Broadway and Amsterdam Avenues, is named after Bois Verna, a crowded quarter in Haiti's capital, Port-au-Prince. The men and women of Bois Verna originally lived in the area's SRO hotels until they could find larger accommodations in the outlying boroughs. Since the Upper West Side started to gentrify and the hotels have made way for condominiums, the Haitian population has decreased. But on warm nights groups of Haitians huddle on the side streets and on Amsterdam Avenue, speaking their melodious patois. They have a reserve that is regularly broken by unforced laughter. As Little Haiti in Manhattan has gotten smaller its artifacts have spread throughout the borough.

Haitian Manhattan is intellectually active, with three newspapers, a host of magazines, and Haitian-language radio. Haitians are proud of their culture and history, being descended from the only blacks in the Western Hemisphere who rebelled and claimed their own freedom. They want to preserve their Haitian traditions and French heritage and remain culturally separate from British West Indians and African Americans.

Creole Cooking

Creole cooking combines the French, African, and West Indian. The meat is primarily goat and pork and the potatoes are plantains, breadfruit, and all the root vegetables of the Caribbean. Coconut milk and cassava are the thickener and *piment oiseau* is the spicy hot sauce. The *cabri* and the *lambi* are goat and conch, both in a peppery sauce, and the *griot* is a spicy fried pork. *Poisson* is French for fish, but it's Haitian for a pan-fried snapper with tomato and spice. The Haitians make their own version of chicken fricassee, and instead of French duck there is guinea hen with sour orange sauce.

Le Soleil, *877 Tenth Avenue between 56th and 57th Streets (212-581-6059). Monday–Saturday noon–11 P.M.; Sunday noon–9 P.M.*

In the center of Le Soleil, Madam sits at a counter taking the take-out orders and handing out copies of three Haitian newspapers. She smiles easily, as if she is presiding over a party rather than a frantically busy restaurant that only sounds like a party. The oxtail stew with a big bowl of brown beans and rice is best. The steak is tough and the goat is stringy.

Labelle Capoise Restaurant, *786 Amsterdam Avenue between 98th and 99th Streets (no phone). Daily 7 A.M.–1 A.M.*

The voice on the stereo is singing "Autumn in New York" as a torch song in Creole. The men in the restaurant, sitting alone at separate tables, and the owner in front by the espresso machine sing along to the good parts. A call comes from the kitchen: *poisson.* The owner sidles to the back and returns with a huge red snapper with a plantain on the side.

Haitian Primitives

Haitian painting began to be recognized in 1944 when De Witt Peters, an American artist, opened Le Centre d'Art in Port-au-Prince. Three years later Haitian art was the talk of the Paris ateliers when the UNESCO show introduced Haitian artists to the art world. Later Selden Rodman, an art collector and a Rockefeller, brought Haitian murals to America. By 1949 Haitian paintings were as popular in America as the primitives of Grandma Moses.

The colors of Haitian painting—red, green, orange, and blue—are psychedelic bright. The subjects are of simple rural daily life, a bus ride or a bazaar. Haitian nature is rain-forest luxuriant. The technique ranges from childlike figures with no perspective to a high-fidelity surrealism. There are now Haitian masters like the voodoo priest Hector Hyppolite and Enguerrand Gourgue, who is in the permanent collection of the Museum of Modern Art.

Haiti D'Art Inc., *145 East 92nd Street (212-427-9283). By appointment.*

Haitian art on the East Side is all about established names and the high end of the market. The paintings here set the standard for Haitian primitives. The art is arranged by school or category and carefully mounted. It is museum professional without being museum stuffy.

Mehu Gallery, *West 100th Street (212-222-3334). Tuesday–Friday 11 A.M.–3 P.M., 5 P.M.–7:30 P.M.; Saturday and Sunday noon–6 P.M.*

Mehu shows the new Haitian masters and does retrospectives of the old ones. It also sells a wide selection of Haitian art books including Selden Rodman's tour de force, *Where Art Is Joy: Haitian Art.* Herve Mehu, the owner of the gallery that bears his name, is often on hand to explain the subtleties and intricacies of this not-so-primitive school of art. Haitian music keeps the mood light.

La Saline

Directions: Subway 4 to Sutter Avenue/Rutland Road, or Subway 5 to Church Avenue/Nostrand Avenue, or Subway 5 to Flatbush Avenue/Nostrand Avenue.

Haitians looked for the good life in Brooklyn. They worked their way from Bed-Stuy roosts to sturdy brick houses in Crown Heights and have expanded on the south side of Eastern Parkway to Flatbush. Haitians have banded together with friends and relatives from Port-au-Prince and rural towns like Hinche and Jacmel. Their Brooklyn universe, which they call La Saline after a district in Port-au-Prince, is their separate country.

Brooklyn has the second largest Haitian community in America after Miami. It is a community bound by ties of culture and experience. They are close and supportive of one another, following the spirit of an old Creole adage that says, "If there is enough for two, there's food for three."

Since the establishment of the Haitian Community Center in 1969, they have helped thousands of their fellow refugees to learn English and master new job skills. Through the Haitian Apostolate they have provided the necessary information to cope with the complexities of city living.

Some local Haitians have even entered the political arena and formed the Haitian American Political Action Group. They have gone beyond lobbying for Jean-Bertrand Aristide to organizing campaigns for local Haitian voter registration. They are now aggressively challenging the local power structure to deal with Haitian concerns about jobs, housing, and health care.

Haitian French and Creole Brooklyn mingles with Anglophone West Indian Brooklyn. Though they predominate on some blocks of Crown Heights, East Flatbush, and Flatbush and are rarely in isolation, Haitians are usually in the orbit of the West Indians. They have their own restaurants, barber shops, and bakeries, but they share the main shopping avenues of Nostrand, Sutter, Church, and Flatbush. One Haitian business will frequently attract another.

The faces of La Saline never seem to stand still, one moment resignation and the next determination; the gestures are African and Gallic. The speech on the sidewalk is a molasses patois. This is their world and they express and carry themselves with loose-limbed freedom. They have endured a lot together in a country of Tonton Macoute and a New York of crime and racial politics. There is a closeness, a sense of intimacy, in the ordinary Haitian relations of daily life.

On Church Avenue between Heywood and Rogers the latest Haitians re-create La Saline with an improvised street market. Women hunker down over blankets bargaining over bead necklaces, paintings, bolts of colorful cloth, cloves, dried mushrooms, and whatever else is handy. It's part farmers' market and part yard sale. Though the Haitians are mostly quiet and dignified, these merchants have a tendency to let their emotions run away with them.

La Saline Tastes

The Haitian restaurants in Brooklyn are mostly unsophisticated and family. It's all plastic place mats and familiar faces. In some restaurants they also have Brooklyn security, with the cash box and cashier behind a plexiglass wall. This has a tendency to cramp the friendly Haitian style without affecting the cooking and baking. As Haitians move upscale they try to emulate their French inheritance and strive for elegance in their restaurant ambience and cuisine.

Chez Price & Jean, *1227 Nostrand Avenue (718-756-9653). Daily 9 A.M.–mid-evening.*

Chez Price has a new location and a new TV for entertainment on slow afternoons. The place is cozy in sunny Haitian colors. The chicken stew is a tasty pepperpot with plantain and Irish potato. The *poisson* is their special event.

Rose Restaurant, *1046 Rutland Road (718-774-1635). Daily 9 A.M.–midnight.*

Rose's has a sense of space, with last year's Christmas ornaments for decoration. At lunch there are single men at separate tables; dinner is a full house with animated families. The ragout is a big bowl of soup filled with every Caribbean root vegetable and knobs of bone with more fat than meat. It is enough for four and peppery without being hot. The *lambi* (conch curry) is one dish where the hot peppers complement the natural taste.

Le Rendez-Vous Restaurant, *1438 Flatbush Avenue (718-859-6776). Daily 1 P.M.–midnight.*

Le Rendez-Vous is the restaurant for special occasions. It's formal dining, smart and well-appointed. The service is Petionville. Traditional Haitian dishes like the fried pork and *tassot* (grilled goat) are cooked in sauces with French panache, and even the peas and rice are a delicacy.

Bicentennial Bakery and Restaurant, *1037 Rutland Road (718-773-9772). Daily 8 A.M.–9 A.M.*

Haitian baking has a split personality: part lively Cuban and part staid French. Along with coconut bread, they have Gallic baguettes. The Haitian biscuits are plain to a fault but the Haitian patties filled with fish can compete with the tastiest Jamaican patties.

St. Marc Boulangerie, *1065 Rutland Road (unlisted phone). Daily 7:30 A.M.–9 P.M.*

Mornings on Rutland Road there is the incense of coconut bread and coconut cupcakes coming from the Boulangerie. While the cakes are a match for the heavenly aromas, the St. Marc, with its one glassed-in window, resembles a check-cashing office.

Maxine's Bakery, *1248 Flatbush Avenue near Dorchester (718-856-3702). Daily 8 A.M.–8:30 P.M.*

Along with the Haitian patty with meat or fish and the bread, cake, and scone, there is all the news—Haitian, foreign and domestic—off the rack.

Haitian Sounds

Haitian music is a mixed bag. There are sentimental Creole versions of American pop and hot brass take-offs of Dominican merengue and dance chants powered by a Voudou drum. Haitian political protest is sung to a strummed guitar.

St. Marc Records, *1020 Rutland Road (718-773-9507). Daily 10 A.M.–7 P.M.*

St. Marc's has all the Haitian dance music, including boleros, that has disappeared from everywhere else. There is the latest Haitian-American music, the drums of Africa, and folk music. St. Marc's is bare-looking when it's empty, but at its best it is filled with people enjoying Haitian sounds and occasionally buying a record or a ticket to a local concert.

Manoir Restaurant Banquet, *1744 Nostrand Avenue (718-282-8936). Call for information on special events.*

If it's not booked for a wedding, the mainspring of Haitian music in Brooklyn is the Manoir. There are stars directly from Haiti, like the Super

Stars Music Machine, and Haitian-American groups like Skah Shah. Anything can happen at a Haitian concert; the audiences can't stand still.

Haitian Rites

Haitian Voudou is what remains of African animism. It is a multilevel religion with its own symbols and rituals. Voudou has *houngan* (priests) and *mambu* (priestesses), and the place of worship is the *humfort*. There is a pole in the center of the sanctuary rising up like a steeple. Drums charge the ritual of whirling bodies and Voudou trances. The *loa* (spirits) possess the body and the soul of the *mambu*. The *loa* are intermediaries for the *Gran Mait* (the supreme being). These spirits must be propitiated with lighted candles and libations, or the worshipper prepares a meal, maybe fish or beans and rice, for Ogoun the warrior or the goddess Damballah, who represents fertility and wisdom.

Botanicas

St. Jacques Botanica, *1502 Nostrand Avenue (718-469-0769). Monday–Saturday 11 A.M.–6 P.M.*

St. Jacques has charms and primitive symbols and ceramic and plaster statues of black saints. There are herbal cures and miraculous candles.

Saint Jacques Majeure & Sainte Viergo, *1248 Flatbush Avenue at 26th Street (718-278-5888). Monday–Saturday 10:30 A.M.– 6:30 P.M.*

A heavy-set woman who is central casting for a Voudou priestess minds the store. Maybe to be on the safe side, they have statues of every deity from Jesus to Krishnah. Candles in every size, shape, and form occupy about half of this magical emporium.

chapter twelve

The Hispanics

There are only four cities in the world with more Spanish-speaking people than New York. Hispanic New Yorkers have a rich Hispanic culture. There are Latin-American museums, schools, dance companies, theaters, newspapers, magazines, radio, and television stations The term "New York Hispanic" covers a vast territory, from Spanish diplomats to Dominican bootblacks. Even before the 1960s when the Celler-Hart Act spurred Latin American emigration, there were seventeen Hispanic nationalities in New York, and they have multiplied with the economic dislocations and political upheavals in Latin America. The Latin New York of the 1990s represents racial and cultural diversity, The light-skinned European Argentinian, the Ecuadorian *mestizo,* and the Afro-Caribbean of Puerto Rico or the Dominican Republic all share an Hispanic identity. They are New York's second city.

Puerto Ricans

History

Puerto Ricans may be known as the "airplane immigrants," but they were in New York as early as 1838, forming their own trade associations and social circles. They were merchants and planters in the sugar and coffee trades. These Caribbean islanders were temporary New Yorkers in town to do business and educate their children.

Some Puerto Ricans were political and plotted in New York against their Spanish sovereigns. They spent their time writing manifestos and trying to organize skilled Puerto Rican workers. Dr. Jose Julio Henna, a society doctor, was the spokesman for the *independistas* and twice testified on Puerto Rican affairs before the U.S. Senate and House.

By the time the Spaniards got around to giving Puerto Rico autonomy, the Americans were shopping around for their own territories. In a war trumped up by the Hearst papers, the United States remembered the *Main* and made the hemisphere safe under the Monroe Doctrine. In 1900 Puerto Rico was placed under an American military government.

Puerto Rico was a poor country with a plantation economy. American food companies controlled the islanders' destiny. As the prices of coffee and sugar declined, Puerto Rican laborers lost their jobs. Many *jibaros* (peasants) moved to the cities or hired out as contract labor on other Caribbean islands.

Small-scale local industry could not compete with American imports and Puerto Rican companies went out of business. Even the country's efficient cigar-making industry went into a sharp decline. The Puerto Rican unemployment problem was so desperate that many were ready to leave for the mainland.

While the Puerto Rican economy was depressed, New York was tooling up for the First World War. Puerto Ricans found plenty of work in the city with the war blocking European emigration. They had the additional advantage of the Jones Act of 1917, which gave Puerto Ricans the rights of American citizens and allowed them to settle freely in the United States. Their position in the labor market was further solidified in 1920 by legislation that restricted European immigration.

Puerto Ricans were a mainstay of New York's light and service industries. As Jews and Italians left lower-level garment industry jobs, Puerto Ricans took their places. They were also a mainstay of the hotel and restaurant service sector. On the island Puerto Ricans were recruited by New York City plants producing items from pencils to biscuits.

Spanish-speaking doctors, lawyers, pharmacists, and retailers offered their services to the newcomers, easing the transition to the fast-paced metropolis. The Hispanic professionals provided leadership and advice. Spanish-language newspapers like *La Prensa* carried the news from home and made Puerto Ricans aware of local issues. New York's Puerto Rican entrepreneurs accounted for over 350 businesses in 1920, often providing familiar foods and goods.

Puerto Rican barrios began to honeycomb Brooklyn and Manhattan. There were Puerto Rican cigar makers in Chelsea and the Lower East Side and San Juan stevedores on the Red Hook waterfront. In the 1920s Puerto Ricans moved into the Greenpoint section of Brooklyn to work in the hemp factories and sugar refineries.

In no time neighborhoods had a Puerto Rican flavor, with *bodegas* offering papaya and *chaiote* (a root vegetable) and *botanicas* selling amulets and statues. Puerto Rican restaurants cooked down-home *comidas criollas* (creole food), *mofongo* (mashed plantains), and *gandules* (pigeon peas) with Caribbean root vegetables. The barbershops and boarding-houses had a warm relaxed *Boriqua* feeling.

The majority of New York Puerto Ricans settled in El Barrio itself: East Harlem between 97th Street and 125th Street, an island in Manhattan bound by black Harlem in the north and west and Italian and Jewish Harlem in the east. It was the center of Puerto Rican cultural and community life. When Puerto Ricans thought about coming to New York they dreamed about El Barrio.

In 1930 economic depression interrupted the progress of the thriving Puerto Rican community in New York. The competition for even menial jobs became fierce. It was hard to find work—even washing dishes—and many a regretful Puerto Rican drifted back to the island. Just when things started to get better in the New York job market, World War II put a temporary hold on further Puerto Rican migration to the city.

Peace and the collapse of the sugar economy opened the floodgates of Puerto Rican migration. The airplane provided Puerto Ricans with cheap and easy access to New York. A new life was eight hours and seventy-five dollars away. By the 1950s one out of every six islanders was leaving and the majority were going to New York. Six hundred thousand made the trip in one decade.

These latest Puerto Rican New Yorkers were even less prepared for the city than their predecessors, the so-called *perfumados* (the sweet-smelling ones) who were now starting to enjoy the fruits of the American dream. Most of the newcomers had no work experience and only one in ten had graduated from high school. They were at a disadvantage in an era when jobs for unskilled labor were rapidly disappearing.

While the Puerto Rican mass migration to New York continued, the island was going through its own economic recovery. When Luis Muñoz Marín, leader of the Popular Democratic Party, became the first popularly elected governor of the Puerto Rican Commonwealth, attention shifted from the statehood-independence controversy to the issue of economic development.

The benefits of tax incentives and cheap surplus labor combined with the appeal of a government Marshall Plan called Operation Bootstrap to attract American industry and investment to Puerto Rico. Three hundred new factories meant the country went from creating six hundred new jobs to forty-eight thousand new jobs in a single year; but it couldn't halt the momentum of migration and thousands continued to come to New York.

Soon Puerto Ricans overflowed the borders of the Manhattan and Brooklyn barrios into the Bronx. They crossed the Harlem River to compete with other minorities for scarce housing space in Hunt's Point and Mott Haven. By 1950 sixty thousand Puerto Ricans were creating their own neighborhoods in a Bronx vacated by Jews, Irish, and Italians.

The time had come for Puerto Ricans to fight their own political battles. In 1953 Felipe Torres, a protégé of the regular Democratic organization, was elected to the state assembly. When he became a family court judge in 1961, his son Frank ran against entrenched Irish Democratic power for his seat and won the Fourth District by fifty-two votes.

Puerto Ricans had their biggest political base in the Bronx and in the protest era of the 1960s they found their leader in a self-made man from Caguas. Herman Badillo was an orphan who earned a CPA while setting pins in a bowling alley and put himself through law school washing dishes.

After a stint as the city's first Puerto Rican commissioner, Herman Badillo became the first Puerto Rican borough president in 1965 and went on to capture a congressional seat in 1970, the first Puerto Rican to do so. Badillo aspired to become the first New York City mayor of Puerto Rican descent but was never able to win the Democratic nomination. However, he has not given up his commitment to public service and was an assistant mayor in the Koch administration, and most recently in 1994 became an assistant mayor in the Giuliani administration.

Today, Puerto Ricans make up one of the largest ethnic groups in the city with a population of 897,000. The largest concentration of Puerto Ricans, numbering 350,000, is in the borough of the Bronx.

Their political standard bearer and Bronx borough president is Fernando Ferrer. He has initiated and supported programs that have helped to rebuild the Bronx and is considered a strong potential Puerto Rican mayoral nominee. A former Puerto Rican protégé of his, Ninfa Segara, whom he appointed to the Board of Education, has charted her own political course as an assistant mayor in the Giuliani administration.

Congressman Jose Serrano is another Bronx Puerto Rican politician with clout. As head of the Hispanic caucus in the House of Representatives, he has played a key role in lining up votes for important bills, including those important to his own constituents, like Puerto Rico's "936" tax break for labor-intensive businesses.

El Barrio

Direction: Subway 6 to 116th Street.

East Harlem was always poor Harlem. It was squatter and shack Harlem. It didn't have the estates and mansions of early West Harlem. The best it ever did was the Roosevelt farm at the turn of the nineteenth century, but that soon had to make way for the Harlem railroad.

Irish and German immigrants lived along the train tracks. They did odd jobs and raised a goat or two. They lived in rural squalor in a neighborhood called Goatville. Nineteenth century East Harlem even had its feared youth gangs.

The Irish left the cold-water tenements to the Italians and Jews in the 1890s. It wasn't brownstone Harlem, but it was a step up from Mulberry Street and the Lower East Side. Both communities thrived with churches and synagogues and associations. They went from pushcarts to prosperous stores.

After World War I Puerto Ricans entered East Harlem's ethnic picture. They moved into Jewish East Harlem between 110th and 117th Streets east of Madison Avenue. There were fifty Puerto Rican families there in 1916.

Eventually Puerto Rican New Yorkers concentrated around the open-air market along Park Avenue. The Jewish merchants in the market provided them with Caribbean foods and the housing was cheap. Rapid expansion of Spanish Harlem attracted Puerto Rican professionals.

Spanish Harlem also developed culturally. Pura Belpre, a Puerto Rican librarian, started the first program promoting Spanish writers and the Spanish language. She worked hard to bring Puerto Rican cultural values to the children of the community.

There were political circles around magazines like *Grafico* and literary circles around local Puerto Rican theaters. There was enough of an audience for Puerto Rican music for East Harlem to have its own Puerto Rican record store. Later in the 1940s and 1950s there were barrio theaters showing Spanish-language movies.

In 1926 East Harlem rioted. White ethnics attacked Puerto Ricans without provocation. There were complaints of Puerto Rican business competition and remarks about color led to violence. Fists and bottles were thrown and there were minor injuries. Puerto Rican leaders calmed down tempers and a Puerto Rican power broker from Brooklyn mediated between the communities.

Puerto Ricans were a political power waiting to happen. La Guardia, East Harlem's Italian congressman, realized early on that Puerto Ricans were a potential voting block, though the number of registered voters was relatively low. He actively campaigned for their votes between 1922 and 1933.

Puerto Ricans found a champion in La Guardia's successor, congress-man Vito Marcantonio. He helped his new constituents deal with the problems of housing and unemployment. His office guided Puerto Rican newcomers through the rules and regulations of the city bureaucracy.

In the 1950s El Barrio was inundated with Puerto Rican migrants making the cheap eight-hour flight from Puerto Rico. The Puerto Ricans of the 1950s were mainly unskilled and uneducated. They crowded to-gether in crumbling tenements for their chance at the good life.

The new arrivals found a Puerto Rican glamour and Latino energy on 116th Street. It was Puerto Rican city lights with the raw vitality of immigrant hope. It was San Juan restaurants and casinos with more energy and freedom. *Jibaros* from the farms stared at the street scenes with a feeling of wonder.

Despite the problems of adjustment it was an El Barrio golden age, with Puerto Ricans like José Ferrer and Rita Moreno on the Broadway stage and José Rodriguez crowned middleweight champion. In 1957 Leonard Bernstein's Broadway musical *West Side Story* made Puerto Ricans part of the New York musical idiom.

Spanish Harlem, El Barrio, the city's classic "island in the city," stretches north from 97th Street to Mount Morris Park and 120th Street and from Fifth Avenue to the East River. The spine of this sprawling Puerto Rican neighborhood is still 116th Street.

It's a commercial center where people come to shop or enjoy Latino food or just hang out listening to the salsa big bands from the record-shop speakers. It's surrounded by blocks of tenements ranging from burnt-out to refurbished and high- and low-rise projects. El Barrio has lost some of the gloss from the old days but it's still Puerto Rico's New York capital.

Though the neighborhood still mainly flies the Puerto Rican flag—and there are flags everywhere, laying claim to front windows and fire es-capes—other groups are making their presence known. The Dominicans, the Puerto Ricans' Caribbean neighbor, have had a prominent—though not dominant—place in El Barrio since the 1970s. In the 1990s the Mexicans of Puebla and Chiapas seem to be gaining a foothold in the neighborhood as small-time entrepreneurs with their own restaurants, bakeries, and groceries.

El Barrio Place Marks

La Marquetta, *Park Avenue between 110th and 116th Streets.*

East Harlem was once filled with pushcart markets on a down-to-earth Park Avenue. It was a multiethnic street scene, catering to the neighborhood's established Jews, Italians, Irish, and the emerging Puerto Ricans. After Mayor La Guardia took the pushcarts off the East Harlem avenues, the vendors were relocated to stalls in a market under the Park Avenue railroad viaduct between 110th and 116th Streets. The market took on the character of the neighborhood's new ethnic majority, the Puerto Ricans, and came to be called La Marquetta.

La Marquetta is presupermarket Puerto Rico. Every seller has a specialty: produce, meat, fish, herbs, or folk medicines. Colorful Caribbean yuccas and batatas, and eels and octopus are piled high in profusion. A whole suckling pig hangs above a butcher skillfully cracking bone with a cleaver or fileting a fish with a fishknife. A papaya is poked and sniffed. The sellers shout and the customers shout and the weighing looks like a sleight of hand. The price is scrawled on the bag and paid.

Unfortunately, a steady decline has led to the closure of the arcades and all 450 stalls. La Marquetta has gone from a prosperous cooperative to a weekend farmers' market with produce from the tropics. Community activists have taken steps to reclaim this once bustling market, but negotiations have in the past hit snags and fallen through and the locals are becoming cynical.

Manhattan Boriqua

Boriqua or *Boricua* is the name of Puerto Rico's indigenous people. It is also the term Puerto Ricans use to refer to their own indigenous culture. They are proud of their culture, which, like American culture, partakes of Old World and New World traditions and the European and the African experience. It is a culture that is always searching for its own identity.

—Museums—

El Museo Del Barrio, *1230 Fifth Avenue between 104th and 105th Streets (212-831-7272). Wednesday–Sunday 11 A.M.–5 P.M. Admission charge.*

El Museo is a museum with a human face. The guards actually speak and if someone left a hammer next to a crated painting, big deal. The art covers all the Puerto Rican bases from abstraction to nineteenth-century naturalism to folk art. Recent exhibitions have included the primitive wooden *santos* and modern feminist painters. The gallery has workshops in Puerto Rican culture that involve the community.

Taller Boriqua, *1 East 104th Street (212-831-4333). Tuesday–Sunday 1 P.M.–6 P.M.*

Artists-in-residence put the artistic process in perspective. The artist and his work are side by side; the artist and his Puerto Rican heritage are one. The Taller Boriqua has a community outreach program with films and videos and a graphics show.

— Theater —

Teatro Moderno Puertorriqueño, *250 East 116th Street (212-289-2633).*

The Teatro Moderno Puertorriqueño is reality theater. It deals head on with being poor and Puerto Rican in New York. The plays are usually original or present a new barrio slant to something familiar. The productions can be loose and experimental.

Comidas Criollas

The food of Puerto Rico is *criollo* (creole), combining the influences of the indigenous Taino Indians, the African slaves, and the Spanish conquerors. The taste is robust without being excessively spicy or hot. *Adobo,* a seasoning paste for meat and poultry consisting of salt, garlic, oregano, and oil, and *sofrito,* an all-purpose flavoring and a base for stews of salt pork, oregano, onion, peppers, tomatoes, *cilantro* (coriander), and garlic, set the tone. The most common herbs are fresh *cilantro* and oregano. Lime rind and juice and fresh ginger give the food a characteristically Caribbean flavor as immediate as the sun and the sea. The color of the preparations comes from the *achiote,* or annatto seeds, which are fried in lard or oil, and the *naranja* (orange) of the island sun. *Platanos* (green bananas) are a common side dish and are fried, roasted, boiled, and baked like the American spud. Root vegetables, such as cassava, yams, and pumpkin, beans called *gandules* (pigeon peas), and the starchy breadfruit dominate the Puerto Rican table.

Popular dishes include *guisados* (stews), *rellenos* (stuffed meat and vegetables), and *frituras* (fritters). *Lechonerias* serve the national dish, *lechón asado* (barbecued pig), but seafood from *pulpo* (octopus) to *bacalao* (dried cod) have an equally large following. *Pasteles,* pork or chicken in a paste of plantain and wrapped in plantain leaves, are a Puerto Rican delicacy. For snacking, there are *cuchifritos,* which are variations on the pork rind theme. Desserts run from inventive variations on *flan* (egg custard) to coconut straight and in custards.

On and off 116th Street there are restaurants and snack shops to take the edge off hearty Puerto Rican appetites. Whether in a corner lunch counter with a blaring radio or in a white-tablecloth restaurant with pink lights and autographed pictures of celebrities, don't expect subtlety. The food is direct and unabashedly substantial and the service is straightforward, none of the bowing waiterly rituals.

El Barrio Steak House, *158 East 116th Street (212-987-1442).*

El Barrio is a cafeteria Caribbean style with *rellenos, frituras,* and other *Boricua* snacks sold through an open window in front. The steam table is an endless vista of stews, soups, shellfish, and rice and beans, all doled out with abandon. The steaks are made to order with more than one savory sauce.

Jimmy's Lechonería, *1875 Lexington Avenue (212-369-9613). Tuesday–Sunday 6 A.M.–11 P.M.*

Suckling pig turned slowly on a spit is a Puerto Rican passion. Jimmy's does the best it can but it's just not the same indoors. The *mofongo* (seasoned, mashed plantains) is more like it.

Del Pueblo, *2118 Third Avenue at 116th Street (212-348-9164). Monday–Saturday A.M.–10 P.M.*

It's only a luncheonette but it has the true spirit of El Barrio. People bounce in like something's about to happen. The familiar faces nod and the salsa never stops. The guys behind the counter sing along to the music and do rim shots with the silverware. The *carne guisada* (stewed meat) is tingling with coriander and garlic and is too much to finish.

Sandy's Lechonería, *2261 Second Avenue at 116th Street (212-348-8654). Daily 7 A.M.–10 P.M.*

Sandy's is restaurant renewal in El Barrio, with modern fixtures and furnishings that actually match. The *pollo asado* (roast chicken) and *lechón asado* (roast pork) are slightly tart and very juicy, and not for the faint of heart counting their cholesterol. Go all the way and wash it down with a papaya *batida* (shake). Friends are always dropping in at Sandy's; it's a throwback to the old days when everyone was family.

Puerto Rican Panaderia

The Puerto Rican *panaderia* is much more than a bakery. It begins with *pan de agua* (water-based bread) and sweet rolls, and ends with a Cuban hero packed with ham, roast pork, cheese, and pickles pressed between a hot grill. The layer cakes are mile-high in shocking pink and blue with an icing bride and groom and Batman or Mickey for the kids. There are Puerto Rican patties (*pastelillos*) stuffed with guava, custard cream, and ground meat and cakes soaked with Puerto Rican rum. The coffee comes rich and black or with steamed milk (con leche), and a buttered stump of bread. The barrio *panadería* is big, almost on the scale of the typical Puerto Rican barn and very social.

Valencia Bakery, *1869 Lexington Avenue between 115th and 116th Streets (212-991-6400). Monday–Saturday 9 A.M.–6 P.M.; Sunday 9 A.M.–4 P.M.*

This is the place to prepare for a party. Besides cakes shaped like football fields or baseball diamonds, there are *toda ocasión* (every occasion) and *cumpleaños* (birthdays) and a whole line of party favors. Saturdays and Sundays parents and children pace before the cake displays making their choices.

La Nueva Bakery, *2129 Third Avenue between 116th and 117th Streets (212-876-2990). Monday–Saturday 7 A.M.–9 P.M.; Sunday 9 A.M.–9 P.M.*

La Nueva has the best *pan caliente* (fresh warm bread) in the barrio and the best Cuban sandwiches and everybody knows it. Come in the morning for a *cafe con leche* (coffee with milk) and a *pan dulce* (sweet roll); it beats a continental breakfast.

Capri Bakery, *186 East 116th Street (212–410–1876). Daily 7 A.M.–midnight.*

Capri looks like a Times Square snack shop. Pass on the Cuban sandwiches but take a chance on the *pastelillos* with guava jelly and a black coffee. It's a good place to check out the 116th Street action.

116th Street Snacks

On the streets of the barrio people are always eating and in between bites they are talking. The Puerto Ricans are round-the-clock eaters and talkers; they have a variety of snack food to match their appetites. There are *cuchifritos* (giant pork rinds) that are salty and hard, *alcapurías* (fried mashed plantains with pork), *papas rellenas* (fried mashed potato with pork and chick peas), and *bacalaitos* (croquettes of dried salt cod) that are heavy—and not to put too good a point on it, greasy. The *pasteles,* made with grated yucca, chopped pork, capers, and olives in a folded plantain leaf, can be memorable.

Puerto Rican junk food should be washed down with a *batida,* a tropical fruit shake with flavors like papaya, guava, and orange. (New York Puerto Ricans have started adding milk for more body.)

The best Puerto Rican finger food is usually served in the smallest hole in the wall with the loudest conversation and eardrum-piercing salsa.

Lexington Restaurant, *1869 Lexington Avenue at 116th Street (212-534-4732). Monday–Saturday 5:30 A.M.–7 P.M.*

It has the look of a Times Square luncheonette, but the tastes of a thatched-reed food stand on Luquillo Beach. The fried treats are made with a surprisingly light hand.

Botánica *Magic*

In Puerto Rico the Church was associated with the Spanish white hierarchy. The clergy was alien and the Church was distrusted. Many Puerto Ricans practiced the religion of their African and Indian ancestors, a worship where spirits inhabit everything animate and fate is a potion or charm. *Santería,* with its drums and chants, made the trip to Manhattan and the shamans opened up *botánicas.*

In *botánicas* the herbs and roots of traditional Puerto Rican folk medicine are prescribed. There are also wonder-working images, candles, amulets, and aerosols for sale. The shops are a strange combination of vials and plants, statues of saints and African totems. Some of the supernatural paraphernalia looks like it was lifted from a second-hand store.

Otto Chicas Rendon, *60 East 116th Street (212–289–0378). Monday–Saturday 9:30 A.M.–5:30 P.M.*

This is the oldest *botánica* in the city and it is still going strong with two other branches. Roland, the inheritor of this *botanica* empire, applies modern management principles to the what-dreams-are-made-of elixirs and magic powders.

El Congo, *1789 Lexington Avenue between 110th and 111th streets (212-860-3921). Monday–Saturday 9 A.M.–5:45 P.M.*

This *botánica* is serious *santería,* with books in Spanish and English explaining this mystical religion and its Yoruba roots. There are bamboo fetishes and miracle beads and dried herbs and leaves. The store is in creative disarray, resembling a Puerto Rican rain forest.

Paco's Botánica, *1864 Lexington Avenue at 115th Street (212-427-0820). Monday–Saturday 8 A.M.–6 P.M.*

The music played in Paco's is sentimental serenades for the housewives who come in for an instant miracle. The setup is immaculate, with miracle candles, wonder-working necklaces, and religious prints all in their place. The religious statues that take up most of the shop are shrink-wrapped in plastic.

Saucy Salsa

Puerto Rico's original music was *bomba,* the beat of the bomba drum, fua sticks, and maraca. The bomba dancer duplicated the beat of the drum and the drummer duplicated the dancer in a rhythmic can-you-top-this. The music found words in the city, a guitar was added, and it became *plena.* In the mountains near Bayamon, Spanish musical conventions were transformed into a *jibaro* serenade with guitar and bongo backing. Cuban *Son* came on the scene with its big brass sound driving the African dance of rhumba and mambo. It all came together in New York, as the Puerto Rican sound met black American jazz. Salsa became the up-tempo Latin jazz of the barrio.

East Harlem Music School, *405 East 120th Street (212-876-0136).*

The East Harlem Music School teaches young players the whole Latin music vocabulary from bamba to salsa. There are classes in congas and bongos and marimbas and conventional brass and piano. Aspiring after-school musicians learn to respect themselves as they master the music. The school bands sound very professional and some students turn professional. The recitals have the audience dancing in the aisles.

La Marketa Records, *100 116th Street between Lexington and Park avenues (no telephone). Daily 9 A.M.–10 P.M.*

La Marketa has discount salsa records, compact discs, and cassettes.

El Barrio Center, *2102 Third Avenue at 115th Street (212-876-3402).*

El Barrio makes beautiful salsa through its big powerful speakers pointed toward the avenue; the streets rumble with more than the traffic. They carry the kind of sides that are "hot" on record, cassette, and CD. It also supplies the congas, bongos, and claves to keep the Latin beat.

The Day of the Puertorriqueño

The Puerto Rican parade is on the first Sunday in June. It is a day of cultural pride that spans the eighteen hundred miles that separate Puerto Rico and New York. Puerto Rican politicians and celebrities and ordinary people from the island in the sun and the island in the city march together up Fifth Avenue from 44th Street to 86th Street.

The Puerto Rican Parade has one of the largest turnouts on the city's parade roster. Puerto Ricans are proud about themselves and their homeland, and flag waving has not gone out of fashion. Puerto Rican red, white, and blue flags are everywhere along the line of march.

In the lead is the grand marshal, a celebrity actor like Raul Julia or the leader of a Puerto Rican organization. The crowd, which is always in a state of near hysteria, goes wild for its dignitaries and matinee idols. Even the local politicos who follow get applause and whistles. But the real cheering is reserved for the political delegations from Puerto Rico and the mayors of places like Bayamon and Ponce.

There are floats of Columbus's ships and the Morro Castle in San Juan and a local Puerto Rican radio station. Kids sit on their father's shoulders so they can see the floats and the marchers. Puerto Rican police officers and fire fighters and social workers show their colors and smile broadly to the crowd as a high school band from the Bronx does a medley of salsa hits. Salsa celebrities from Celia Cruz to Willy Colon do their acts on tropical-colored floats and the word passes through the crowd and people stand on tiptoe for a better look. Finally it comes, spread out between twenty-five men and women, a giant Puerto Rican flag, and all the flags among the spectators wave in unison.

Dominicans

History

The first Dominicans landed in New York at the end of the eighteenth century. Both whites and mulattoes, they fled a slave insurrection from what is today the capital, Santo Domingo. The U.S. Congress donated fifteen thousand dollars for their relief.

In the nineteenth century the Dominican Republic was conquered and reconquered by Haiti and Spain. America took its turn in 1916 and ruled the Dominican Republic for eight years in defense of Standard Brands and the American Fruit Company. When the American marines left in 1924 their Dominican dependents joined them in the States. Some Dominicans drifted into the Spanish-speaking neighborhoods of New York City.

Dominican emigration to New York was stopped short when the military strongman Trujillo took over in 1930. The only Dominicans who traveled to New York were polo-playing playboys like Rubirosa or intellectual exiles like Professor Galindez.

Dominicans only started coming to New York in any significant numbers when Trujillo was assassinated in 1961 and exit visas were no longer the privilege of the few. Though a rising population and economic expectations spurred emigration, others were responding to the country's political instability, which led to another American invasion in 1965. Between 1960 and 1980 the numbers of Dominicans coming to New York doubled.

The first-wave Dominicans were mainly people who qualified for occupational immigration quotas. They were high-level professionals—doctors, engineers, and accountants—and skilled labor—tailors and machinists. They moved into neighborhoods like Washington Heights which had Spanish-speaking Cubans with similar backgrounds and apartments with extra-large rooms.

The Dominicans who settled in New York brought over other family members and gradually Dominicans began to form their own colonies on the Lower East Side, in Washington Heights, and in Corona, Queens. Still most Dominicans were barred from emigrating to New York.

The second-wave Dominicans had more determination and will than qualifications, though they were above the Dominican average when it came to education and income. In New York, Dominicans worked as superintendents or did manual work in factories and often held down two jobs at once; they were intent on saving money to open a business or invest in land.

These Dominican pioneers had a solid sense of family and a strong Catholic heritage. Their pride was personal and national. Often they left behind villages populated by the aged and very young. They would not send for their sons and daughters until they were really established.

For poor Dominicans, coming to New York was and still is an obsession. Tourist visas are more valuable than gold. There is a steady traffic of small vessels plying the harbors of Florida and Puerto Rico, which will assist these American dreamers for a price. Sometimes these extralegal emigration routes end in tragedy. On September 5, 1980, twenty-two

Dominicans illegally heading for the "promised land" drowned in the ballast tanks of a Panamanian cargo ship while hiding from port police.

Dominican immigration to New York really took off in the 1980s, reaching a rate of twenty thousand a year. Dominicans followed other Hispanic populations to the Upper West Side, the Lower East Side, Brooklyn's Williamsburg, and Sunset Park, Corona, and Jackson Heights in Queens. The total of Dominicans, documented and undocumented, is estimated to be above four hundred thousand.

The most recent immigrants, men and women, work in the service sector, as custodians, kitchen help, and truck drivers. Others are employed in low-level unskilled factory work. Women often do piece work at home sewing or assembling simple products. The stress of making a living and surviving in this pressure-cooker city has taken its toll on the Dominican family. Parents have separated and children have fallen prey to the streets.

Though Dominicans consider New York their home and most don't seriously think of leaving, they are highly involved in the life of their homeland. They campaign fiercely for their favorite Dominican candidates and vote with absentee ballots in important elections. Dominican candidates or their representatives even make political appearances in Dominican neighborhoods in New York, pressing the flesh like local pols.

The Dominicans who have made it to New York have come of age. In Washington Heights in Manhattan they have their own Broadway, on Broadway from 155th Street to Dyckman Streets. This Dominican scene is too self-confident and bright-lights big-city to be a ghetto. Dominican New York swings to a meringue beat that is more lighthearted than any other *colonia* in the city.

Washington Heights

Directions: Subway A, B, 1, or 9 to 168th Street/Broadway.

The Dutch called it Harlem Heights, the highest elevation in the Harlem wilderness. When the Heights became the private property of an English colonel, Roger Morris, it was called Mount Morris. George Washington retreated to the Morris mansion after the defeat of Long Island. It became for a time his headquarters and the Heights was forever associated with his name.

The Heights remained estate territory for more than a century. It was the home of the naturalist Audubon and the publisher of the *Herald Tribune,* James Gordon Bennett. The Chicago millionaire K.G. Billings had his racing stable in the rolling country of what would become Fort Tryon Park.

The IRT subway made the Heights accessible to working-class and middle-class New Yorkers in 1906. The Irish held the high ground and German Jewish families moved into the valley of Broadway. In 1931 the neighborhood around 179th and 180th Streets was bulldozed for the George Washington Bridge, which linked New Jersey and New York.

German-Jewish refugees resettled in the Heights before and after World War II, and Greek refugees came to the neighborhood to escape the Greek Civil War. In the 1950s the first Hispanics came on the scene from Cuba. They were fleeing a dictator named Batista and they were soon joined in the 1960s by Cubans fleeing Castro.

In the 1960s the Dominicans began coming to Washington Heights after the Trujillo government's travel and emigration restrictions were lifted. The early days were difficult; they had to find work and create a functioning Dominican community. In time, they became the backbone of the garment district downtown and built their own Dominican business district in Washington Heights.

Washington Heights was the destination for many Latino immigrants who settled in Manhattan in the 1980s and 1990s. Dominicans made up a more than eighty percent of this group, with a substantial number coming from Cuba, Ecuador, Colombia, El Salvador, and Mexico. While Washington Heights has more Hispanic variety than in the past, its Dominican identity is still sovereign.

The street beat of Broadway, St. Nicholas, and 181st Street is straight out of Santo Domingo. Young men and their fathers—wearing baggies and bandannas—home from a hard day, slouch on the stoop and hang on the street, all the while speaking rapid-fire Spanish punctuated with ironic laughter. The sidewalk banter continues over dominos, cards, and maybe *cerveza* (beer). The kids never stop running, shouts are hardly heard over the uproar of music, traffic, and discount-store touts. The Dominican woman is Mother Courage wheeling a baby carriage, carrying a bag of groceries, or hawking *empanadas* (meat turnovers) from a pushcart.

Dominican Archives

The Dominican Studies Institute, *CUNY North Academic 6–103, 138th Street and Amsterdam Avenue (212-650-7496). Monday–Friday 9 A.M.–5 P.M.*

Directions: Subway 9 to 137th Street/Broadway or Bus M5 to 137th Street/Broadway.

In Hamilton Heights, another Dominican neighborhood close to Washington Heights, in the halls of the ivy campus of City College, the experience of New York's fastest-growing immigrant population is examined and documented. Particular attention is paid to the formation of ethnic identity, popular culture, and the patterns of everyday life in New York. The institute sponsors seminars, symposiums, and cultural events and publishes the *Dominican Journal.*

Dominican Comidas Criollas

Dominican eating, from a friendly lunch counter to a formal sit-down, is pure *alegría* (joy). It is both the pleasure of the table and the pleasure of the company. Dominican eating is a team sport. Everyone urges everyone else on as they demolish everything from beans and rice to beefsteak. And Dominicans don't mind picking up the check; hospitality and generosity are traditional values.

Dominican cuisine is Hispanic Caribbean with the pork and beef rubbed with *adobo* and everything flavored with *sofrito.* It is rich *guisados* (stews) with peppers and olives and *mondongo* (tripe soup) and *mariscos* (shellfish) with dry rice or wet soupy rice. It has its own version of Puerto Rican *mofongo* called *mangu,* with the mashed plantains mixed with shallots and eaten with cheese, sausage, or ham for breakfast.

Restaurant Caridad, *4311 Broadway at 184th Street (212-928-4645). Daily 6 A.M.–when the last customer leaves.*

The restaurant is spacious and splendid, with a row of hanging plants dividing the dining room from the counter. It shows its Dominican colors with a map of the Dominican Republic on the counter's place mats. The dining area is strictly linen tablecloth. *Mariscos* Dominican style is the thing here. Six waitresses are kept busy ladling big bowls of *calamares* (squid) and *asopado de camarones* (shrimp with soupy rice). There are mountains of rice and *habichuelas* (beans).

Mambi, *558 West 181st Street (212-568-5969). 1446 St. Nicholas Avenue (212-928-2760). 1446 Broadway at 179th Street (212-928-9796). Daily 24 hours.*

Mambi is a triple Dominican treat with three restaurants. The best is the new Broadway location. It's eating to a merengue beat with excellent meat selections. The day's specials are marked up on a blackboard. Look for the *costilla de cerdo con berenjena,* the pork rib with eggplant is Caribbean with a difference. You know it's authentic Dominican because it has *mangu* (boiled mashed plantains with oil and garlic) with cheese, sausage, and ham for breakfast.

La Nueva Cabana Restaurant, *1302 St. Nicholas Avenue at 175th Street (unlisted telephone). Daily 24 hours.*

In the back *mamita* slaves over a hot stove while her two daughters serve up piles of food to stay or to go. The restaurant is a no-frills 24 *horas del dia* operation. It's the food that gets all the superlatives. Leave the greasy *pollo frito* (fried chicken) alone (which is supposedly the specialty of the house), and opt for the daily menu. There are great Dominican *guisados* (stews) with olive and pepper for a change of pace.

El Pollo Dorado, *1497 St. Nicholas Avenue at 185th Street (212-795-2569). Daily 24 hours.*

Just a few stools and a counter for eating in at this awkward Dominican attempt at fast-food ambience. The "chicken al carbon" is too well prepared and cleverly seasoned and spiced to fall into the fast-food category. This El Dorado also offers a real sampler of Dominican snacks from *empanada de yuca* to *cuchifritos* (Dominican style).

Bizcochos *and* Empanadas

The Dominican bakery is a rich rainbow of layer cakes decorated for rite-of-passage events, with everything from plastic cartoon characters to images of affectionate couples. They also have *pan caliente, cubanos, empanadas,* and Caribbean puddings.

Ana's Bakery, *1627 St. Nicholas Avenue between 191st and 192nd streets (212-568-2810). Daily 7 A.M.–9 P.M.*

Ana's is high, wide, and immaculate, even when the customers are three deep pressing against the display cases for specially designed birthday cakes or the very white, soft bread for Caribbean heroes or just a sugary elephant ear for a snack.

Nitin Bakery, *1638 St. Nicholas Avenue at 192nd Street (212-928-2200). Daily 7 A.M.–10 P.M.*

While king-sized cakes in shocking pink and baby blue are on view everywhere, Nitin attracts a snacking crowd on the lookout for a *pernil* (pork) sandwich, an interesting *queso flan* (cheese pudding), or simply an old-fashioned toothsome chocolate eclair.

Dominican Merengue

The merengue—the dance and the music—is the essence of earthy Dominican. In northern Cibao, where most Dominican New Yorkers originate, it was Spanish tinged with more European instrumentation and in the south it was African with hollow-log-drums rhythm. The merengue hollow-log drum and maraca are part of the country's religious mysteries, saints' festivals, and religious brotherhoods. In the 1930s the two merengues came together and the saxophone replaced the tribal drum. It went big band in the 1940s and adopted salsa in the 1960s. The merengue has its own festival every year in the Dominican Republic, when it is celebrated in all its forms and Dominicans from around the world join a pilgrimage to honor their music.

Bahamas, *1490 St. Nicholas Avenue at 185th Street (212-740-6135). Daily 11 A.M.–4 A.M.*

Dominicans say that the merengue is not the same in American dance halls but El Baturro tries to duplicate the true Dominican merengue experience. They don't do it self-consciously, it's simply that the groups and most of the dancers are being themselves. It's a real show with a lot of couples doing a Dominican Ginger and Fred routine.

Sambuca, *4199 Broadway at 178th Street (212-795-4744). Daily 10 A.M.–until the last person leaves.*

During the day it's a bright and neat counter-and-booths place with Latin Caribbean tastes and waitresses with humor and verve. At night, step through a shimmering metallic curtain into a sophisticated supper club with Latin-accented piano runs and riffs and Dominican-style barbecued chicken and all sorts of *mariscos.*

Dominican Record Shop, *3444 Broadway at 140th Street (212-926-9490). Daily 10 A.M.–10 P.M.*

The Dominican Record Shop is more than a place to buy merengue records. It keeps up with the whole Dominican Republic music scene and imports the Dominican top forty. It's a community bulletin board that tells which groups are playing in which places.

Flowers and Sacred Images

Since the Dominican Republic shares an island with Haiti and a sea with Puerto Rico, its folk religion partakes of practices from both regions. The

Dominican *botánica* has a sense of hopefulness and optimism expressed in the flowers it sells along with the standard statuary, prayer beads, chrisms, magical powders, and sprays.

Botánica Reyes, *340 Audubon Avenue between 181st and 182nd streets (212-927-2133). Daily 9 A.M.–7 P.M.*

Beautiful red, long-stemmed gladiolus share the space with queen-sized images of the Holy Mother and sensuous Indian goddesses. Multicolored African beads hang behind the counter near shelves of magical candles. The proprietor of this house of miracles peering over his glasses has a gentle sense of the spiritual.

The Parade with the Merengue Beat

The Dominican Day Parade is merengue bands and dancers on floats. There are a few groups marching and folklorico ballets in ruffled skirts doing twirls and turns. Dominican Day rolls up the Avenue of the Americas from 44th Street to Columbus Circle on the Sunday closest to August 16. It is the day the Dominicans regained their freedom and the dictator Trujillo lost his to a hunting party of twelve.

Most of the floats that move along the line of march to the sounding brass and pounding congas are advertisements for beer companies, radio stations, canned beans, and the "real thing." No one notices or cares; everyone is lost in the music and the perpetual merengue motion. Even the button salespeople are dancing.

The Dominican beauty queens wave as if they really mean it and the Dominican community leaders have patriarchal Eisenhower smiles. The politicians, Dominican and American, look like they are having too good a time to care.

Cubans

History

Cuban political refugees have been coming to New York since the middle of the nineteenth century. Cubans were the largest Latin group in the city before Puerto Rico became an American protectorate. They were intellectuals committed to the American ideal of freedom and a Latin American ideal of culture.

In nineteenth century New York Cubans established a Spanish-language daily and thirty-four different magazines. The great Cuban novelist Cirilo Villaverde edited a newspaper in New York and Jose Marti, the George Washington of Cuba, founded two magazines before his death in 1895.

Most of the Cubans who came to New York were white and well-educated. Many were trained professionals who were quickly absorbed into the life of the city. Their children simply disappeared into mainstream American life.

Between 1867 and 1878 another strata of Cuban immigrants came to New York. These were skilled workers who were making a political statement by boycotting the Spanish-controlled tobacco industry. In New York they found freedom and better wages.

Cuban cigar rollers brought to New York one of their unique Cuban institutions—the factory reader. These highly literate workers paid a trained actor to read plays, novels, and poetry to them while they worked. Some of these factory readers joined the Cuban Theater Company in New York.

When Cuba gained independence in 1898 Cuban immigration to New York slowed, though it did not stop. In the 1950s, during the dictatorship of Fulgencio Batista, Cuban political exiles returned to New York. By 1959 there were fifteen thousand Cubans on the Upper West Side.

In 1960, when it became clear that Castro would remake Cuba in the image of the Soviet East, Cubans left in the thousands. The first Cubans to come to New York in the 1960s were society Cubans, businessmen, and Cubans from the military. They were white and well connected, but between 1960 and 1962, when flights from Cuba were stopped, there was a second wave of lower-middle-class and blue-collar Cubans.

While well-heeled Cubans could live lavishly outside of a Cuban barrio in New York, lower-level Cubans who settled in New York's Upper West Side and Queens sought the support of their fellow countrymen. In Washington Heights and Jackson Heights they established small enclaves. Between 1965 and 1972 the Cuban airlift was renewed and thousands more came to the city.

In 1979 the Mariel boat lift brought more Cubans to the New York metropolitan area. The majority of these Cubans were true political refugees and went to the large Little Havana in New Jersey (Union City, West New York, and Weehawken) rather than New York City. There are still small pockets of Cubans in the city, but their presence is mainly commercial.

It is the Cubans who run Channel 41, New York's Hispanic TV station, the Spanish-language press, and many of the radio stations. Cubans head

Hispanic advertising agencies and Hispanic food companies. They are the entrepreneurs of the Hispanic community.

In 1994, there was a short replay of Mariel, with Cubans landing on these shores by way of an improvised boat and raft lift. The Clinton administration negotiated a new immigration agreement with Castro. While most of these Cuban arrivals headed for the greener pastures of Union City and Miami, some ended up in Washington Heights, Jackson Heights, and Sunset Park. The current government policy is to turn back Cubans attempting to enter the U.S.

Cuban Taste

Cuban restaurants are not bound by the borders of a neighborhood; they are scattered throughout the city. There are country-club Cuban restaurants in the theater district and Cuban luncheonettes on the Upper West Side. The restaurants, high and low, share a pride in their cuisine, which they consider Hispanic haute cuisine and the closest to the original Spanish. And they will prove it to you by having *gazpacho,* the cold, tomato-based Spanish soup, on the menu.

Actually Cuban cuisine has much more in common with other Caribbean cuisines than with Spanish. It marinates meats in an *adobo* paste of garlic, salt, pepper, and lime or vinegar. The food is more aromatic than spicy and vegetables like yucca and chayote and plantains (green bananas) are preferred to Spanish peppers. The Cubans make corn meal tamales and a thick Caribbean soup or stew *ajiaco* with pork, oxtail, or tripe and all the tubers in the subtropical garden. *Ropa vieja,* a stew of shredded beef, is poor man's Cuba but very popular in America. Cuban fast food is a sandwich of roast pork, ham, cheese, and pickle and *chicharrones de pollo,* fried chicken with a hint of coriander.

Eating out is a tradition of these middle-class immigrants. Cuban men in Havana socialized and did business in restaurants and cafes and on Sundays took the whole family out for a walk and dinner. Restaurants are still a big part of the male Cuban world, though Cuban women are no longer necessarily regarded as intruders.

Sabor, *20 Cornelia Street (212-243-9579). Daily 6 P.M.–11 P.M.*

Sabor is New York Cuban before Castro. The restaurant has ceiling fans and folkloric baskets on the walls and tries to look Cuban exotic as if there were never a Cuban airlift or Mariel. It's Cuban rum cocktails with little umbrellas, a watery *gazpacho*, and a *ropa vieja* that tastes like rope.

National Cafe, *210 First Avenue between 12th and 13th streets (212-473-9353). Daily 7* A.M.*–9* P.M.

The restaurant is closet-small with a few afterthought chairs and tables, and a counter with stools that sometimes tilt. The home cooking and friendly service are better than atmosphere. Lunchtime specials usually include the beans and rice of your choice, soup, and entrées like roast pork (*pernil*) and *fricasé de pollo,* and they come at hamburger prices.

Victor's Cafe 54, *236 West 52nd Street (212-586-7714). Sunday– Thursday noon–midnight; Friday and Saturday noon–1* A.M.

When Victor's opened this big glossy restaurant on 52nd Street, leaving behind its more Bohemian Upper West Side location, New York's restaurant snobs scoffed as if this Victor were selling out and going tourist commercial. Actually, this is the restaurant of choice for Cubans in the *colonía* in New Jersey; it is that special restaurant where Cuban families celebrate. Victor's Cafe 54 is Cuba before Castro, with a string orchestra playing *danzón* music. Don't think about the corn tamales or *ropa vieja;* it's a place for lobster in *salsa verde* (a sauce of parsley and herbs).

Floridita, *3451 Broadway at 141st Street (212-281-1500). Daily 6* P.M.*–1* A.M.

The Floridita is an attractive glassed-in version of this Upper West Side Cuban restaurant group. It is a place to relax and listen to Cuban *Son* on the state-of-the-art sound system and eat Cuban simple. It is black beans and rice and fried plantain Cuban. It is a place to order Cuban pot roast or stewed *bacalao* (salt cod).

Liberation Past and Future

On the last Sunday in August Cubans gather their minions from the New York metropolitan area and beyond for an old-fashioned patriotic parade celebrating their past liberation from Spain while looking forward to a free Cuba in the future. Though the numbers of spectators along the parade route on Madison Avenue from 45th Street to 56th Street are not overwhelmingly large, they more than make up for their size with their enthusiasm and conviction.

The parade is led by Cuban dignitaries in exile on foot and in limousines, followed by Cuban cowboys carrying Cuban flags on high-spirited palominos. The floats, in tropical colors with palm trees, Cuban flags, and patriotic sentiments, represent companies like El Pico Coffee, Goya Foods, and Telemundo 47. They carry beauty queens from six to sixty and big bands in straw hats and traditional blouses. There are marching groups from Hispanic societies and dancers from folkloric groups. Everyone is in constant motion, letting the Afro-Cuban rhythm set the pace of the parade.

The Other Cubans

History

During World War I there were one hundred thousand Chinese living in Cuba, mostly working on the sugar plantations. But later immigration restrictions reduced the numbers until there were only twenty-five thousand in 1960. These Chinese had adapted to Cuban culture and in many ways were thoroughly Cuban.

When Castro started to put socialism into practice the Chinese merchants and business people joined the airlift in 1960. Though they only represented a tiny percentage of the Cuban population, they made up two percent of the the first series of airlifts from 1960 to 1962.

Five thousand Cuban Chinese settled in New York. They were spread out from Washington Heights in Manhattan to Jackson Heights in Queens to downtown Brooklyn. The Cuban Chinese in New York are trilingual, speaking Spanish, Chinese, and English with equal fluency. While they have kept their Chinese surnames, they have adopted Spanish first names.

The younger Cuban Chinese identify more with their Hispanic background and many intermarry with Cubans as they did before they left Cuba. There is still an older Cuban Chinese generation that views itself as being more Chinese and identifies with its Buddhist heritage.

Oriente Oriental

Many Cuban Chinese went into the restaurant business when they came to the city, offering a menu that gave equal time to the Cuban and the Cantonese. The restaurants were a fad in the 1960s and became part of the landscape in the 1970s. In the 1980s they have fared best in Hispanic neighborhoods like the Upper West Side and the Bronx Concourse. In gentrifying areas like Chelsea, they have practically disappeared.

Asia de Cuba, *190 Eighth Avenue between 19th and 20th streets (212-243-9322). Daily 11:30 A.M.–midnight.*

Asia de Cuba wasn't the first Cuban Chinese restaurant in New York, but it was the one to introduce Cuban Chinese to trendy eaters in the 1960s.

The restaurant started out small and simple and cheap and wound up taking reservations. It still does special things with sweet and sour pork, and it's fun to end a Chinese meal with a Cuban coconut and cream cheese dessert.

La Victoria China Restaurant, *2532 Broadway at 95th Street (212-865-1810). Daily 11:30 A.M.–11:30 P.M.*

The restaurant has been attracting young people on the West Side for the past thirty years. It is one Cuban Chinese restaurant that gets as big a play for the Cuban food as the Asian. The *chicarron de pollo* is an Hispanic version of chicken McNuggets, with the spice of coriander and garlic.

Mexicans

History

Before the conquistadors Mexico had developed rich Mayan and Aztec civilizations which produced great art and architecture and supported millions in vast cities. In 1519 Cortes introduced the horse and gunpowder to the Americas, and in the process took a king prisoner and defeated a great empire.

The Mexicans were inheritors of both the Empire of the Sun and the Spanish Crown. They were the standard-bearers of Roman Catholicism and the fabled Phoenix. Both conqueror and conquered, they were deeply ambivalent about their *mestizo* inheritance.

Even before America had sought its "Manifest Destiny," Mexicans had explored the great American Southwest and made Texas, New Mexico, and California part of the Spanish Empire. They built great estates on these territories called *haciendas* and farmed these immense lands and raised cattle and horses.

American soldiers invaded Mexico in May of 1846, captured the capital, Mexico City, and dictated the peace terms. By the Treaty of Guadalupe Hidalgo, the Mexicans ceded five hundred thousand square miles of land, which included parts or all of present-day California, Nevada, Utah, Arizona, New Mexico, and Texas.

Eighty thousand former Mexican citizens became aliens in a land that they had discovered and settled. Throughout the Far West, they were forced to defend their land rights. American courts drew out the legal process for Mexican land claims and harassed litigants with contentious appeals. Many were dispossessed and had no choice but to become farm laborers and ranch hands. In 1970 there were land grant cases still being adjudicated before the Supreme Court.

At the same time that they suffered financially, Mexicans became more isolated socially. As white America expanded, whole Mexican-American neighborhoods were displaced. *Chicanos* sometimes came to occupy the most decayed and decrepit areas. They were the victims of restrictive real estate covenants and school segregation. They were denied access to public facilities.

In the years that followed, Mexico was a convenient source of cheap labor. When the western states legislated against the employment of Asian minorities, Mexicans filled low-jevel jobs that came available, and for less money. Five hundred thousand in all emigrated to America to become railroad laborers, miners, agricultural laborers, and cowboys.

Between 1900 and 1930 Mexicans also moved beyond the urban hubs of the West and Southwest to America's industrial heartland. Chicanos rolled up their sleeves and went to work for Detroit automobile makers, in Gary steel mills, and in Chicago meatpacking plants. Mexican-American women joined the work force as domestics, service employees, and sales clerks.

In times of prosperity Americans took advantage of cheap labor from over the border, but Mexican workers lost their usefulness during the economic downturn of the Depression. There were huge programs to repatriate Mexicans. From Los Angeles to Chicago there were indiscriminate roundups of "undocumented aliens." It is estimated that the national hysteria lead to the involuntary deportation of five hundred thousand Mexicans.

Despite discrimination against Mexican Americans, they were patriotic supporters of World War II and three hundred fifty thousand served in the armed forces. Seventeen valiant members of this minority were awarded Congressional Medals of Honor. While Mexicans were earning medals on the battlefield, on June 3, 1943, in Los Angeles, hundreds of unruly soldiers with a grudge against Mexican zoot-suiters rioted in the streets, beating Mexicans with impunity and the active connivance of the police.

After the war the number of Mexicans entering the United States continued to increase. Many were part of a Bracero Program to provide for needed migrant agricultural labor on a seasonal basis, but most were economic refugees who entered the country illegally. Hundreds of thousands took their chances by sneaking over the border with or without a paid guide for their piece of the American dream.

In the turbulent era of the 1960s and 1970s Chicanos became important players in the American system. Cesar Chavez organized the United Farm

Workers Union, and with a nationwide boycott that captured the moral high ground, won rights for migrant farm workers. In the arena of electoral politics in 1974 Mexican-Americans Raul Castro and Jerry Apodaco both became governors of western states. As a group they were influential in the election victory of Jimmy Carter.

For the past two decades Mexicans have been the largest group to enter the United States with or without a visa. Their destinations of choice were usually on the West Coast, in the Southwest, and in the Midwest, where minimum wage (and lower) factory or field hand jobs were readily available and accessible to Mexican-American communities, and where they had support systems. They also began coming to the Big Apple.

The extent of this latest immigration is not revealed in the official statistics. City planning officials believe there are approximately seventy-five thousand Mexicans here legally. Unofficial estimates of both documented and undocumented Mexicans coming out of New York's Latino community run from one hundred thousand to "infinity."

Currently, Mexicans don't even fall in the top twenty of the City Planning Department's latest list of the "Newest New Yorkers," but it is clear from the numbers of businesses and institutions catering to the needs of this community that their presence is substantial. Mexican restaurants, bakeries, and groceries are part of the landscape of Jackson Heights, Washington Heights, El Barrio, and Sunset Park. Mexicans have their own soccer league in the Bronx and an enormous dance hall on the Great White Way. There are twenty tortilla factories in the five boroughs.

The majority of these Mexican-American New Yorkers come from two states in the central part of Mexico: Michoacan and Puebla. They are mainly males who work in the service sector. They wait tables, wash dishes, mop floors, cut, wash, and package produce in vegetable stores, and sell day-old flower bouquets from shopping carts. Like earlier generations of European immigrants, they often live together in dormitory-like arrangements. They share expenses and crucial information that makes survival possible.

These short, broad-shouldered men with tireless energy and an attitude that suggests both resignation and quiet dignity are a familiar sight in every neighborhood in the city. They are slowly making strides, earning their place in the city, and already the women and children in their families have begun to arrive. These urban pioneers are losing their awkwardness and becoming hard-edged urbanites, but at the same time they are adding their influences to the cultural mosaic.

The Mexican Table

Mexican food predates Columbus and Cortes. The indigenous Indians of Mexico created an inventive and versatile cuisine that had far-reaching implications for cooking around the world. Corn is the staple in Mexican food and comes in the form of tortillas, tacos, tamales, and enchiladas. The essential Mexican flavors depend on chili peppers, beans, and tomatoes, with additional accents provided by pineapple, vanilla, and chocolate. The Spanish additions of cinnamon, rice, chicken, pork, and beef put the finishing touches on Latin America's only haute cuisine.

New York Mexican food used to be a parody of the real thing, with canned salsa and corn chips setting the tone. Now, along with the new Mexican arrivals, comes the *típico sabor Mexicano*. The chocolate *mole* sauces are almost black and have real bite and the *posole* is thick with hominy and pork. The range of wrappers for red-hot fillings seems endless with *chimichanga* (fried wheat tortilla), *chilaquiles* (refried tortillas with tomato sauce), *flautas* (fried corn tortilla), and *quesadillas* (folded tortillas with cheese) almost everywhere.

Pedro Paramo, *430 East 14th Street (212-475-4581). Daily Sunday–Thursday noon–11 P.M.; Friday and Saturday noon–11:30 P.M.*

Pedro Paramo is a Mexican hacienda shoehorned into a 14th Street pizza parlor. The kitchen is Mexican authentic with no apologies for the hot chilies. It draws an across-the-board following which includes doctors from nearby hospitals and local Mexican delivery boys. The Puebla-style *mole* (chocolate-based sauce that can be fire-hot) adds distinction to any dish.

Rinconcito Mexicano, *307 West 39th Street (212-268-1704). Monday–Friday 7 A.M.–10 P.M.; Saturday and Sunday 10:30 A.M.–10 P.M.*

Mexican garment center laborers and executives from Time Square renovations rub elbows at Rinconcito Mexicano. Don't mind the long lines for this Mexican-style cafeteria. The flavors are genuine Mexican with the chilies, tomatillo, squash, and cilantro home-grown and the tortillas hand made.

Rosa Mexicano, *1063 First Avenue near 59th Street (212-753-7407). Daily 5 P.M.–midnight.*

Rosa Mexicano has a split personality. The front room is a robust Upper East Side bar scene and Mexican banquet, while the back is a listless no-go area with rose-colored walls and uncomfortable banquettes, The imaginative regional Mexican menu, however, makes up for any short-comings and essentially this upscale Mexican restaurant has no equal in the city. Where else would the *morcilla* (sausage) come wrapped in a tortilla and the grilled trout be served covered by a plantain leaf?

El Ranchito, *1970 Third Avenue between 108th and 109th streets (212-268-1704). Monday–Friday 7 A.M.–10 P.M.; Friday and Satur-day 7 A.M.–midnight; Sunday 10:30 A.M.–10 P.M.*

El Ranchito is the real Mexico in El Barrio. At the entrance there's a haphazard grocery with six varieties of Mexican chilies, Mexican-brand soft drinks, *pan dulce,* brown sugar, and edible cactus. In the back, folding tables and chairs are arranged for the pleasure of the customers, who all seem to know one another; they really enjoy the tacos and more, stuffed with beef tongue, *cecina* (dried beef), or *chorizo.*

The Mexican Bakery

Mexico Lindo Bakery, *2267 Second Avenue between 116th and 117th streets (212-831-2976). Daily 6:30 A.M.–9 P.M.*

The bakery is an outlet for soft corn tortillas and large multicolored breads flavored with cinnamon. It also has fresh-from-the-oven corn cakes, pas-tries, and cookies and provides real Mexican hot chocolate and espresso for sipping. There are layer cakes for parties and even a *piñata* (a fiesta ornament filled with children's toys) or two.

The Mexican Grocery

Azteca Deli Grocery, *698 Amsterdam Avenue at 94th Street (212-749-2380). Daily 7 A.M.–10 P.M.*

One of the first to make real Mexican chilies and chocolate (for mole) available to New Yorkers, Azteca helped change the taste buds of New Yorkers. It carries a host of home-grown Mexican staples, as well as Mexican foods now produced in New York City.

Mariachis and Mexican Rock

Mexicans are musically adventurous and don't mind mixing musical idioms. The music is wide ranging, running the gamut from a strange

German-Mexican hybrid based on the polka (*pokero*) to Mexican salsa, fusing romantic bolero with hard-edged Latin Caribbean jazz. Their signature music is mariachi, melding bold brass and sentimental strings. It has a big sound but can also express tenderness. Most of the recent Mexican immigrants listen and dance to music that is totally eclectic. Contemporary Mexican music has been heavily influenced by American musical trends. The sound is sometimes country western, or transformed into punk by singers like Elsa Garcia. Groups like Cafe Tacuba turned it into funk, while musical heartthrob Luis Miguel makes it sound like a romantic ballad.

Club Broadway, *2551 Broadway at 96th Street (212-864-7600). Daily 11 P.M.–4 A.M.*

Club Broadway is at least a twice-a-week Mexican musical rendezvous. Usually there are two or three bands or singers reflecting the latest fusion sounds. For Mexican New Yorkers, it's all-night Mexican dancing and a chance to meet and socialize with Mexicans from all five boroughs.

═══ Sunset Park—Latino Renewal ═══

Directions: Subway R to 53rd Street and Fourth Avenue

The mainly Latino neighborhood of Sunset Park stretches from 15th Street to 65th Street, from Upper New York Bay and Gowanus Bay to Eighth Avenue. It takes its name from an actual twenty-four-acre park in the heart of the neighborhood, where American rebels defeated the Brits in 1776, and more recently people picnic, sunbathe, play ball, and wheel baby carriages.

Before the first Puerto Ricans settled in, there were succeeding generations of Irish, Scandinavian, German, Italian, and Polish immigrants. They built the streets and the sewer systems and worked in the shipyards, the docks, and nearby Greenwood Cemetery.

The first Puerto Ricans came in the booming 1920s to work on the thriving waterfront of the two-hundred-acre Bush Terminal. This vast commercial center contained an industrial park, nineteen office buildings, and berths for thirty-five ships. These immigrants worked on assembly lines, in shipyards, and as stevedores on the docks.

Though the terminal slumped during the Depression, the war revived the flagging local economy and put the terminal back to work. Sunset Park was at the height of its prosperity and it was hard to believe that it could not go on forever.

Just as a new wave of Puerto Ricans began to occupy the neat two- and three-story row houses of Sunset Park, the local economy crashed. The construction of a new expressway also hurt the community's residential character and contributed to some panic selling. Unethical real estate dealers took advantage of the situation and sowed panic.

The latest Puerto Ricans, from the Lower East Side and El Barrio as well as the island, were soon the majority between Fourth Avenue and the bay, with Spanish the common language. They joined local churches and community groups, and opened their own restaurants and grocery stores.

When the neighborhood was going through hard times in the sixties and properties were abandoned and businesses were bailing out, Puerto Ricans helped form the Sunset Park Redevelopment Committee (SPRC) to save the neighborhood. They joined with aging Scandinavian, Italian, and Irish populations and local institutions like the Lutheran Medical Center to protect and preserve their community.

This grass-roots coalition spurred the rehabilitation of properties, residential and commercial. Vacant buildings were soon repaired and occupied. The whole neighborhood seemed to receive a fresh coat of paint and the community began to take back the streets. Large areas of Sunset Park were granted landmark status. Gentrification and community development were part of the same process. Sunset Park started to stabilize.

In 1979 Puerto Ricans took formal leadership of the Sunset Park revival, as Wilfredo Lugo became director of the Sunset Park Redevelopment Committee (SPRC). The SPRC played a pivotal role in integrating the latest arrivals into the community, who came after 1980, mainly from the Dominican Republic, Mexico, and Central and South America. By 1985 the community, with its burgeoning businesses and increasing sense of optimism, was cashing in on the Reagan boom.

The Latinos of Sunset Park are proud of their most recent Puerto Rican success story. Against overwhelming odds Nydia Velazquez beat out Democratic congressional kingpin Stephen Solarz and captured his seat in the House. As a former director of the Department of Puerto Rican Community Affairs, she is well known in the neighborhood and highly regarded. In her first term, which began in 1992, she worked hard to represent her district and the interests of all Latinos.

On Fifth and Fourth Avenues and the streets in between, from 35th to 65th, the Latin nations, black, white, Indian, and mestizo, are all part of the fascinating passing scene. They New York street strut or do a fresh-off-the-border-bus shamble. There is fear, wonder, self-consciousness, and confidence, and the grace of kings. Unlike their stolid Scandinavian advanced guard, they are quicksilver nations of feeling and sensation. Music—mariachi, salsa, and merengue—is never far from the foreground.

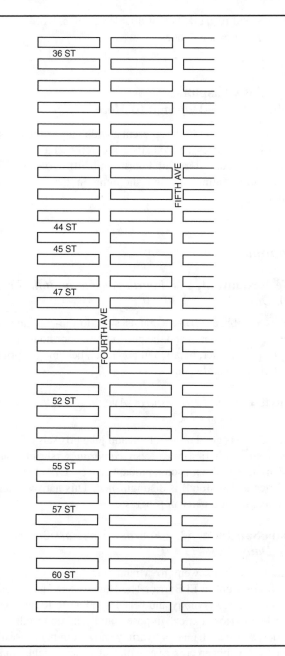

Sunset Park

In the bars and restaurants that double as cafes, words and language are song and gestures are dance.

Sunset Park Hispanic
Combinations—*Mofongo* to *Mole*

The Latinos of Sunset Park represent a wide range of nations and cultures. Their different tastes and cuisines are represented in the restaurants, bakeries, and retail stores of Fourth and Fifth Avenues. This dramatic diversity turns eating out and shopping in the neighborhood into an adventure.

Restaurants

La Fe Restaurant, *941 Fourth Avenue at 36th Street (718-788-0139). Daily 8 A.M.–10:30 P.M.*

La Fe is Caribbean *criollo* that is stick-to-the-ribs unpretentious. The gravies are full flavored and the portions are enormous. Those throwaway parts, the pork trotter, oxtail, and pork ears, become the prime ingredients in a delicious *guisado* (stew).

El Buen Gusto, *5201 Fourth Avenue at 52nd Street (718-492-6001). Daily 9 A.M.–3 A.M.*

El Buen Gusto is good taste in food and juke box salsa. It is the right place for *mariscos* with first-rate, fresh *camorones* (shrimp) and *langostino* (crayfish) accented with some piquant sauces. Even the Caribbean *paella* (baked rice and seafood) is distinguished. This narrow restaurant always has the feeling of a party in progress.

Habana San Juan, *5219 Fourth Avenue at 52nd Street (718-439-9337). Daily 8 A.M.–11 P.M.*

Not all the Cubans went to Miami and Union City, and not all the Puerto Ricos went to El Barrio. The Habana San Juan is home to Sunset Park's small Cuban colony and very large Puerto Rican contingent. In its white-tile interior, exiles, imposed and self-imposed, share poignant memories, while a Channel 47 variety show comments noisily in a corner. The food is Caribbean crossover with Cuban sandwiches and Puerto Rican patties.

Tequalita's, *5253 Fourth Avenue at 52nd Street (718-492-4303). Monday 11 A.M.–11 P.M.; Friday–Sunday 10 A.M.–midnight.*

Tequalita's is a real *pueblo taquería* (village taco cafe) with sombreros, multicolored ponchos, and guitars for decoration. There's a big technicolor jukebox with the tops of the pops Mexican style. The tortillas are handmade corn meal originals that are tasty enough to eat on their own, but who could resist the interesting fillings like *lengua* (tongue), *chorizo* (spicy Spanish sausage), and *barbacoa* (barbecued pork)?

El Conquistador, *5507 Fifth Avenue at 55th Street (718-492-3921). Sunday–Thursday 10 A.M.–11 P.M.; Friday 10 A.M.–1 A.M.; Saturday 10 A.M.–3 A.M.*

El Conquistador is leisurely dining with gracious South American service. This Ecuadorian restaurant draws customers from all over the city. It posts community events and screens soccer games of interest for its Ecuadorian clientele. The *mariscos* (shellfish) in salads, soups, and combined with rice are their claim to fame, but for the really famished, there is the *cabañola a la casa,* which includes steak, half a hen, sausage, onion, and tomato.

International Restaurant, *4408 Fifth Avenue at 44th Street (718-438-2009). Daily 6 A.M.–midnight*

The International Restaurant looks like the local coffee shop that specializes in burgers and BLTs, but looks can be deceiving, and this restaurant has a definite Dominican spin. It opens the day with authentic stick-to-the-ribs Dominican breakfasts like *salchichón* (salami sausage) with eggs and yucca and *longaniza* (pork sausage) Dominican with *mangu* (mashed plantains). For lunch and dinner it serves a savory *mondongo* (tripe soup) Dominican style with rice.

Bakeries

Don Paco Lopez Bakery, *4703 Fourth Avenue at 47th Street (718-492-7443). Daily 7 A.M.–9 P.M.*

Throughout the day carts roll in and out of the front of this *panadería* ferrying fresh pastries, *pan dulce,* tortillas, and colorful breads sweetened with cinnamon. Don Paco's, like other Mexican places of business, has photographic reminders of Mexico on the walls and a sampling of Mexican groceries, from pickled jalapena to *salsa picante* (hot sauce).

La Gran Vía Bakery, *4516 Fifth Avenue at 45th Street (718-853-8021). Daily 8 A.M.–9 P.M.*

La Gran Vía is a pan-Hispanic bakery. It carries very plain *pan Cubano* (soft white bread), Cuban sandwiches, and giant creamy layer cakes with novelty-type decorations. They even sell *piñatas* and helium balloons with Spanish greetings for special occasions. It is modern, neat, and usually crowded.

The Americas of Jackson Heights

Directions: Subway 7 to 82nd Street/Roosevelt Avenue.

A family called Jackson farmed the area that became known as Jackson Heights in the early part of the nineteenth century. In 1859 John C. Jackson chartered a company to develop the terrain lying west of Flushing Creek and built an avenue bearing his family's name.

Jackson Heights, a slow starter at the beginning of the twentieth century, was known as the "corn field of Queens." In 1906 the Queensboro Corporation designated one hundred blocks of Jackson Heights farmland for development. The corporation had the intention of attracting high-income Manhattanites.

The forward-looking project combined architectural styles from English Tudor to neo-Spanish. The large apartment houses had landscaped courtyards and the individual apartments had fireplaces and cathedral ceilings. The Jackson Heights houses were some of the city's first cooperatives.

In 1917 Jackson Heights was no longer a backwater but was connected to Manhattan by the IRT elevated line along Roosevelt Avenue. Five years later it became the first area in Queens to be serviced by Manhattan's Fifth Avenue bus line.

The Queensboro Corporation cashed in on the real estate boom of the 1920s and started to sell off its Jackson Heights acres. Development was no longer tightly controlled and planned parks and open spaces were shelved. In the 1930s it managed to remain a model middle-class garden community with golf courses and tennis courts.

Major changes came to Jackson Heights when the tiny North Beach Airport was converted into a major transcontinental terminal and renamed La Guardia in 1947. By the time the airport grew to 650 acres Jackson Heights gardens were concrete.

The neighborhood was solidly Irish and Italian ethnic in the 1940s and 1950s; it was working class and second generation with middle-class aspirations. As the neighborhood started to lose its glow and bodyshops replaced grocery stores, these ethnics relocated to the Long Island suburbs.

Argentinians were the first to claim Jackson Heights for the Latins in the 1960s. They were refugees of runaway inflation and an unstable government. When Cuban exiles, escaping Castro collectivism, came to New York by the thousands, Jackson Heights was a comfortable Latin option

Though there were older Irish and Italian holdovers, the neighborhood shifted to young-family Hispanic. When the affluent Argentinians dispersed to Forest Hills and Rego Park, Colombians were the next new Latins on the block and the Peruvians and Ecuadorians were waiting in the wings.

In the 1980s, along with continuing South American immigration, a large influx of Mexicans fleeing poverty and Central Americans escaping death squads and revolutionary turmoil arrived in Jackson Heights. They were mostly poor rural exiles in search of survival; men and women with high Indian cheekbones, straight coal black hair, and small sturdy bodies willing to do "hard labor" for less than the minimum wage.

Roosevelt Avenue and Junction Boulevard are the real New York avenues of the Americas. One Latin American nation succeeds another: there is an Argentinian deli, a Colombian night club, a Cuban luncheonette, and a Peruvian take-out. The newsstands carry papers from every nation in South America. The parochial schools are administered by the Spanish Apostolate.

The "*Avenida* of the Americas" is constant movement underneath the rumble of the elevated Number 7 line. Familiar faces meet and speak and shout to one another across the moving traffic and the double-parked cars. Green immigrants, their minds elsewhere, hand out flyers for a Mexican or Colombian night club or a school that teaches *Inglés*. Street sellers stand over pushcarts and folding tables, slicing tropical fruits for snacks and wrapping *arepa* (corn cake). Mexicans prepare the best tacos in the city from the side of an old-fashioned lunch wagon.

Colombians

History

Colombians are among the latest Latin Americans on the New York scene. They came in the hundreds to New York at the end of World War I. They were solid middle-class accountants, technicians, nurses, and pharmacists on the lookout for economic opportunity. Over the years, Colombians created a community in Jackson Heights, an area that offered good middle-income housing and easy access to the Manhattan job market.

The numbers of Colombians coming to New York multiplied in the era of *La Violencia*. From 1945 to 1955 Colombia was a killing field—guerrilla bands ran rampant and government troops were out of control. The peasants took refuge in the towns and when the overcrowding and the unemployment became impossible, they emigrated to Venezuela during the oil boom and ultimately, New York.

The exodus was amazing—three to four percent of the population left annually. The trend continued into the 1970s, with Colombian unemployment sky-high and the cost of air flights to New York relatively low. Many of the emigrants left unwillingly, as a matter of economic necessity, and many who came to the New York were undocumented.

Though Colombians put down roots in the city they kept their attachment to their homeland. The newsstands of Jackson Heights carry five Colombian dailies. Most would like to think they are only temporary New Yorkers. The monotonous factory and warehouse jobs that many Colombians perform are viewed simply as a means to make a new life in Colombia. Unlike other recent immigrants, they are reluctant to become naturalized citizens.

The next generation of Colombians are learning about their heritage in Spanish parochial schools. They speak Spanish with a Colombian accent, which they consider the best in Latin America, and read Colombian books and listen to Colombian music. Colombians are still not ready to assimilate.

New York Colombians have even won the right to vote here in their own national elections. The campaigns are hard fought on the streets of Jackson Heights. In 1975 the president of Colombia, Lopez Michelsen, made a special trip to the United States to speak to his compatriots assembled at the Americana Hotel in Manhattan. He acknowledged a debt to these absentee voters.

Despite decades in the city, the Colombians are socially and culturally self-sufficient. They form their own groups and societies and preserve their country's customs and traditions. Modern communication enables them to watch Colombian television, and even follow the games of their favorite Colombian soccer teams.

In communities like Jackson Heights they have founded large-scale Colombian soccer leagues, and the whole community turns out to watch their games. The Colombian connection is reinforced by the coverage Colombian Americans receive in Colombian newspapers. There are two full-time correspondents for Colombian newspapers who just cover Jackson Heights.

According to the official 1990 American census, the total Colombian population in the United States numbered 378,000. This figure does not take into account the large number of undocumented Colombian aliens. Colombian community leaders estimate that there are at least three hundred thousand Colombians residing in the Queen's neighborhood of Jackson Heights.

They are currently the largest Hispanic group that lives in the "Heights," where sections bear an uncanny resemblance to the Colombian cities of Cali or Medellin. Colombians dominate Jackson Heights commercial areas and own a majority of the local businesses.

The New York experience has helped to change the way Colombians relate to one another. Colombian women are no longer housebound; they often find it easier to secure employment than their husbands, and have become accustomed to bringing home a paycheck. At the same time, Colombian men are beginning to share the female burdens of shopping, cooking, and cleaning. Family decisions are more shared than in the past.

Second-generation Colombian Americans have benefited from American educational opportunities. Many more have opportunities to attend university than they would have in their homeland. Even the children of peasants and laborers are becoming professionals in the New World.

The Colombian neighborhood, which centers around 82nd Street and Roosevelt Avenue, is called Chapinero in honor of a middle-class Bogotá suburb. The Colombians are a gregarious out-of-the-house people. The restaurants, bars, and even the travel agencies along the *Avenida* are informal social clubs. The gestures and rhythms are slightly slower and more reserved than earlier Hispanic arrivals, but the gusto, the pure pleasure in living, is all there.

Colombian Arepa and Crazy Chickens

The Colombians are the largest group in Jackson Heights and most of the restaurants, clubs, and stores reflect their cosmopolitan style. Their operations, whether fast food or formal dining, are polished and self-assured, unlike the more haphazard improvised approaches of some of their Roosevelt Avenue neighbors.

Colombian cooking is hearty eating, part South American Indian and part Spanish conquistador. The *arepas* (corncakes) and *hallacas* (tamales) are pure Indian but enhanced by Spanish fillings like *chorizo* and flavored with garlic, onions, and cilantro. Spanish meal-in-a-dish soups are made even hardier with indigenous vegetables like plantain or yucca and are called *sancocho*. Big Colombian appetites opt for *montañero,* a mountain of food including chuck steak, fried pork, and avocado topped with an egg. From the Colombian coast there are *mariscos* (shellfish) with savory sauces. The Colombian beverages of choice are tropical fruit shakes made with exotica like *guanabana* (sour-sop) and *maracaya* (passion fruit).

Los Arrieros, *76–02 Roosevelt Avenue (718-898-3359). Daily noon–1 A.M.*

Colombian friendliness shines along with the simple dishes served in Las Arrieros. The simple *empanadas* (a turnover stuffed with meat and potatoes) are always good with an interesting *guanabana* shake (it tastes like vanilla). The *picadas* platter (bite-size bits), the Colombian version of Spanish *tapas,* is a great way to sample the cuisine.

Crazy Chicken, *78–09 Roosevelt Avenue (718-565-7389). Daily 24 hours.*

Crazy Chicken is fast-food Colombian. The main taste is charcoal-roasted Colombian chicken with tempting *arepa* and plantain and yucca side dishes. This is a good place for the uninitiated to learn about the Colombian national dish, *arepa,* which comes in many interesting combinations.

La Pequeña Colombia, *83–27 Roosevelt Avenue (718-478-6528). Daily 8 A.M.–midnight.*

The workday over, groups of weary young Colombians unwind around a table with special plates piled high with favorite foods, including eggs, fried banana, fried pork, *arepa,* and more. They have to catch their breath and mop their brows as they devour this monster meal.

Cali Viejo, *84–24 Roosevelt Avenue (718-898-9812).*

Cali Viejo II, *73–10 Roosevelt Avenue (718-424-9812). Daily 11 A.M.–10 P.M.*

Cali Viejo I and II are among the earliest Colombian restaurants in Jackson Heights, and they have a special reputation. Their *arepa* are legendary. Enjoy them with cheese, *chicharrón* (fried pork), or *chorizo* (spicy Spanish sausage). Their top round steak, *bistec alla criolla,* is tops. Wash it all down with a rich sour sop shake.

Casa Del Mar, *85–08 Roosevelt Avenue (718-458-0704). Daily 11 A.M.–10 P.M.*

Casa Del Mar is a small unpretentious spot that serves Pacific Coast Colombian cuisine. The *mariscos* in a variety of sauces or in a hearty *sancocho* are not easily equaled. The restaurant itself has a sunny day on the beach feeling and you can literally smell the sea.

El Meson Colombiano, *82–11 Roosevelt Avenue (718-397-1685).*

El Meson Colombiano resembles a Colombian home in decor and the menu is home style: the *arepas* are just like *mamita* used to make and the *bistec, churrasco,* or *sobre barriga* comes with a terrific *criolla* (tomato onion sauce).

Comestibles

La Colombianita, *84–22 Roosevelt Avenue (718-803-0825). Daily 8 A.M.–10 P.M.*

This grocery cum meat market has all the familiar products from Bogotá to Medellin: the rice, beans, and all the special seasoning. The skirt steaks and spicy sausages are just the kind that Colombians prize. They have more than six kinds of *arepa* on the shelves, along with white and yellow corn meal to make your own.

The Others on Avenida De Las Americas

Colombians dominate Jackson Heights but there is a sampler of other Hispanic nationalities who are growing in size or who have already left the neighborhood. Their restaurants and shops dot Roosevelt Avenue. The Mexicans are among the newest immigrants on the block, and at least from the look of it, they have taken the Avenida by storm.

El Sitio Restaurant, *68–28 Roosevelt Avenue (718-424-2369). Monday–Thursday and Sunday 10 A.M.–1 A.M.; Friday 10 A.M.–3 A.M.; Saturday 10 A.M.–4 A.M.*

The new owner is from Spain, and it is evident in the savory *arroz con pollo* (chicken and rice) and the Spanish-style tortillas (a moist egg and potato omelet). The Cuban traditions of the previous owner continue with dishes like *ropa vieja* (stewed shredded beef).

Viva Mexicano, *81–16 Roosevelt Avenue (718-639-4268). Monday–Friday 11 A.M.–1 A.M.; Saturday and Sunday 11 A.M.–4 A.M.*

Viva Mexicano is authentic Mexicano típico that goes beyond the taco. The service staff is friendly and patient and makes a special effort with newcomers to the cuisine. The *asado mixto fiesta* is a great mixed grill and introduction to a variety of Mexican meats. The Puebla-style stuffed chilies (with chicken, meat, or cheese) are not for the faint of heart.

Portal Norteño, *88–11 Roosevelt Avenue (718-429-9579). Daily 10 A.M.–10 P.M.*

Portal Norteño is a dark restaurant with garish pink neon highlights. The tastes in this Peruvian restaurant are off-beat Inca, and the first choice of Peruvian locals. They have *seco de cordero* (lamb cooked in a sauce laced with coriander) and *ajide gallina* (chicken in a peppery stew).

Tacos Mexico, *88–12 Roosevelt Avenue (718-899-5800). Daily 9:30 A.M.–4 A.M.*

This *taquería* is draped in the Mexican flag with a big painting of Emilio Zapata. It's a place for central Mexican homeboys to chew the fat over bottles of Corona, Dos Equis, or Negra Modela. The enchiladas come dripping cheese and sauce and it's hard not to smack your lips over the herbs, spices, textures, and flavors. The chilies need a warning label.

La Cabana Argentina, *95–51 Roosevelt Avenue (718-429-4388). Daily 3:30 P.M.–11 P.M.*

La Cabana is a typical Argentinian restaurant with the grilling as a floor show. The secret of the mixed grill is the marinade and quality *churasco* (flank steak) and spicy *chorizo*. The chicken and meat *empanadas* are flaky melt-in-the-mouth pastry.

Pan-American Grocery

La Poblanita, *78–03 Roosevelt Avenue (718-672-7114). Daily 7 A.M.–10 P.M.*

La Poblanita started out as an ethnic Mexican emporium, with the usual assortment of sombreros, hot condiments, tropical fruits, dried beef, and cactus for eating. Now, in addition, these enterprising Mexicans have also become a general store for the other Hispanic Central and South Americans in the community, with Peruvian *aji* (pepper), Guatemalan white beans, and Ecuadorian sausages.

Pan-American Music

La Selecta Musical, *88–08 Roosevelt Avenue (718-397-7747). Daily 10:30 A.M.–9 P.M.*

In this era of CDs, cassettes, and digital tapes, this is one music store that is mostly records, imported from all over the Americas in their many musical idioms. They manage to stay current and decorate their shop with posters of the tops-of-the-pop groups from Latin America.

Brazilians

Since the 1960s New York Brazilian has been both multinational big businessman and poor undocumented alien. The extremes of Brazilian society are reflected in the city's Brazilian emigrants. There are the business school graduates and conquistador descendants from Rio de Janeiro and Brasilia and the peasants from Belo Horizonte shining shoes.

When the Brazilian economy went austerity with a multibillion-dollar debt, the poor undocumented Brazilians began to outnumber the affluent. The Regine types are staying home while the men and women of Mineiros are working—in the city's restaurants and on construction projects.

Though the Brazilians' numbers are small, they have a large and influential musical population that keeps New York current with Brazilian jazz and samba. Some of Brazil's top stars, like the jazz singer Flora Purim and the group Airto, are practically permanent Manhattanites.

The more mundane elements of the Brazilian population are widely scattered through the five boroughs. Though they don't have a significant presence, things Brazilian have caught the city's fancy. It is something very basic and very open that strikes the right chord. Brazil is all about desire and the senses and a spirit that is part pagan and pure play. It is life lived as a carnival to the insistent rhythm of the samba, even if tomorrow's an early breakfast and business meeting at the Plaza.

On 46th Street (and a sliver of 45th) between Fifth and Seventh Avenues the Brazilians have staked out several claims to restaurants and retail stores. It is the closest they come to a neighborhood. In 1994, when Brazil won the World Soccer Cup—held for the first time in America—Brazilians from the whole metropolitan area came to their street to hear their language spoken, eat their foods, and feel their music.

Feijoada **Plus**

Brazilian cooking is a combination of Portuguese, African, and Amazonian Indian. The Portuguese brought over the salt cod and took the local shellfish and steeped it in sauces of wine, tomato, and garlic. The Indians and Africans added the subtropical beans, fruits, and vegetables. *Caldo Verde* is Brazil's most popular soup. The chicken stock is green with kale and collard greens and thick with potatoes and sausage.

The national dish is *feijoada,* black beans mixed with rice cooked with various meats, including beef tongue, dried beef, *chorizo* (spicy Spanish sausage), pig's trotters, and slab bacon, and garnished with manioc and orange slices. In the northern region of Bahia there are African flavors of hot peppers and coconut milk with seafood. In cosmopolitan Rio de Janeiro beef and pork are seasoned with onions, garlic, tomato, and coriander.

Most of the area's restaurants have been around a while and have proved themselves to their native clientele. One has to wonder whether they have become complacent or the regulars less demanding. The food's not bad, just not inspired. But whether the food is magnificent or mediocre, Brazilian diners are animated to the point of hyperactive. They like life frenetic.

Brasilia, *7 West 45th Street (212-869-9200). Daily noon–11 P.M.*

Brasilia is handsome white stucco and ceiling beams with oil paintings of its namesake and a corner bar with its own clay tile roof. The bar attracts overseas Brazilians who enjoy the company of their compatriots along with light inexpensive meals from the bar menu and hard-to-find Brazilian beers and liquors.

Cabana Carioca, *123 West 45th Street (212-581-8088). Daily noon–11 P.M.*

Cabana Carioca is a one-flight-up restaurant with gaudy Brazilian paintings and loud Brazilian diners. It's tropical sunshine and a joyful noise, and though the tables are a little close together, it's easy to get used to. The *camarao frito* is delicious and not heavy, with the shrimp deep fried in white wine and garlic sauce. The *bacalhau a braz* is what rich peasant food is made of, with salt cod, black olives, onions, eggs, and potatoes.

Ipanema, *13 West 46th Street (718-730-5048). Daily noon–10 P.M.*

Ipanema is a bright room almost the color of the Ipanema Beach, with paintings of this Brazilian paradise for ambience. In a neighborhood of trustworthy Brazilian restaurants, this one stands out for its food, both Brazilian and Portuguese. The Brazilian *tapas* are a delight and the pork and clam stew must be tasted to be believed.

Via Brazil, *34 East 46th Street (212–997–1158). Daily 11* A.M.–*midnight.*

Via Brazil is Brazilian mahogany trim and watercolors on white walls and samba in the background. The restaurant serves very special African-Brazilian *moquecas* (fish stew with tomatoes and coconut milk). The salt cod *moqueca* is better than the more expensive lobster and shrimp.

Brazilian Shopping

The resident Brazilian population comes to 46th Street to do its shopping, to get the Rio newspapers, to buy manioc to sprinkle over *feijoda,* and to get the latest Baden-Powell guitar album. The stores are Brazilian contemporary and they serve Brazilian food and drink along with the merchandise. Brazilian music is always in the foreground and everybody seems to be enjoying themselves.

Coisa Nossa, *47 West 46th Street (212-719-4779). Monday–Saturday 9* A.M.–*7* P.M.

Brazilians come here for newspapers and magazines and conversation. It also carries a good selection of Brazilian music and videos.

Emporium Brasil, *15 West 46th Street (212-764-4646). Monday–Saturday 8* A.M.–*7* P.M.

Emporium Brazil is a modern Brazilian luncheonette with a small selection of Brazilian food products and the latest Brazilian newspapers, magazines, tapes, and videos. A TV monitor showing a selection of Brazilian music, drama, and news sometimes gets in the way of Brazilian socializing.

Carnival on 46th Street

New York Brazilians celebrate their Independence Day on the first Saturday in September. The city closes 46th Street to traffic and the samba takes over from nine in the morning to nine at night. The Brazilians like to party and they do it full throttle. Man, woman, and child are possessed by the drum and samba. Though the amateur dancers steal the show, there are professional singers and musicians performing Brazilian jazz and bossa nova on a stage at the Avenue of the Americas corner.

It's difficult to move through the dancers and the press of people to get to the stalls and stands lining 46th Street, but what's a little inconvenience in a carnival? The neighborhood's Brazilian restaurants take to the streets, serving heaping portions of *feijoada*. There are also Brazilian carvings and brightly colored papier-mâché figures for sale along with the T-shirts and buttons that inevitably appear at any ethnic event. The carnival closes with the American and Brazilian national anthems.

══════════ Little Spain in Chelsea ══════════

Directions: Subway F to 14th Street/6th Avenue; or Subway A or E to 14th Street/8th Avenue; or Subway 1, 2, 3, or 9 to 14th Street/7th Avenue.

History

In 1750 Captain Thomas Clarke was a merchant seaman who earned enough on the high seas to occupy an estate that covered the present area from 14th Street to 24th Street and Eighth Avenue to the Hudson River. He named it Chelsea in honor of the Soldier's Hospital in London.

His grandson, Clement Moore, who spent his time preparing Greek lexicons and writing verse like the "Night Before Christmas," closely supervised Chelsea's residential development. Every house had a ten-foot setback and stables, and alleys were strictly forbidden.

The Hudson River Railroad shattered Chelsea's suburban calm and soon the neighborhood was made up of glue factories and slaughterhouses. In 1871 the Ninth Avenue El completed the destruction of society Chelsea and Irish immigrants with Tammany connections took over.

Before the turn of the century Spanish seaman from the poor northern province of Galicia settled in New York near the Hudson River waterfront from 14th Street to 23rd Street. In a more carefree age they traveled back and forth between Spain and New York, raising families and operating businesses on shore leave. Though the colony was small in numbers, it had the closeness of a Spanish village and the Spanish formed many organizations, from workingman clubs to merchant's associations.

New York's Spanish population had an active cultural life. The million-aire philanthropist Archer M. Huntington founded the Hispanic Society in 1904, providing Spanish New Yorkers with a first-rate Spanish museum and library. Huntington brought over great figures in Spanish culture, such as the critic Ramon Mendez Pidal and the scholar Federico de Onis.

In the 1920s Spanish political refugees came to New York in increasing numbers. They were democrats and anarchists and socialists who couldn't live under the military dictatorship of Primo Rivera. The new Spanish emigrants had their own theater and magazine; guitarist Segovia gave concerts and the poet Federico Garcia Lorca gave readings.

The Spanish Civil War brought more Spanish refugees to New York and the Spaniards for a brief time were the dominant Hispanic group in the city. Fourteenth Street was their "Great White Way," with twelve Spanish restaurants and numerous Spanish food stores and bookstores. Flamenco guitarists and dancers were a nightly event and Casa Moneo was the city's Spanish supermarket and all-purpose bazaar. Latins from both hemispheres browsed its aisles.

Bohemia in the 1960s tried to turn Chelsea into Greenwich Village, and Little Spain started to look passé. The younger Spanish and Galician generations weren't interested in local color and left for suburban comfort and safety. The rising real estate costs of a gentrifying 1980s completed the change from Little Spain to trendy Chelsea. A small remnant still hangs on in the 1990s, as a new generation of New Yorkers have discovered their traditional restaurants.

Place Marks

Centro Español, *239 West 14th Street (212-929-7873). Call for hours.*

The Centro Español identifies itself culturally with the attractive Spanish tiles on its building's facade and the Spanish classics from Cervantes to Unamuno in its small library. It is a central meeting place where the city's small group of aging Spaniards come together to share memories.

Our Lady of Guadalupe, *229 West 14th Street (212-243-5317).*

This small sanctuary dedicated to Our Lady of Guadalupe was the first New York church to be part of the Spanish Apostolate. The church was the first in New York to offer masses in Spanish for the local Spanish.

Since this church is dedicated to the patron saint of Mexico, it has attracted an increasingly Mexican congregation in recent years.

Spanish Museums, Archives, and Bookstores

Lectorum Libria, *137 West 14th Street (212-928-2833). Monday–Saturday 9:30 A.M.–6:15 P.M.*

Lectorum Libria has a comprehensive collection of Spanish books from around the world. They have dictionaries, children's books, fiction, non-fiction, and the best materials for native Spanish speakers to learn English.

Spanish Institute, *684 Park Avenue at 68th Street (212-628-0420). Gallery hours: Daily 11 A.M.–6 P.M. Call for times of special events.*

The Spanish Institute is housed in a neo-Federalist wonder designed by Stanford White's architectural firm. The elegant building draws the visitor inside to see elegantly mounted exhibits of Spanish painters and sculptors. There are lectures in an upstairs drawing room concerning serious developments in Spanish arts and history. The elegant library could be in a fashionable club. The institute is a private nonprofit organization that offers educational fellowships and prizes.

Americas Society, *680 Park Avenue at 67th Street (212-249-8950). Tuesday–Sunday noon–6 P.M. Contribution.*

The main gallery exhibits the whole range of Latin American art from pre-Colombian to contemporary. Peruvian weaving is side by side with Brazilian photographs. In Latin America folk arts and the fine arts coexist with ease.

Hispanic Society of America Museum, *Audubon Terrace, Broadway and 155th Street (212-690-0743). Tuesday–Saturday 10 A.M.–4:30 P.M.; Sunday 1 A.M.–4 P.M. Free.*
Directions: Subway A to 155th Street/St. Nicholas Avenue.

The Hispanic Society is a testament to Archer M. Huntington and his passion for Hispanic culture. The museum is pure Spanish magnificence, with terra cotta floors and two-story skylights and Valencian tapestries. Its collection of Spanish paintings, which include Goya, El Greco, and Velazquez, is impressive and it also has fine examples of Latin American art. The Hispanic Society has a library dedicated to Hispanic culture with one hundred thousand manuscripts and books.

Spanish Language Theater

Repertorio Español, *138 East 27th Street (212-889-2850).*

Repertorio Español is the theater of Spain and of Latin America, as well as adaptations of other works into Spanish. The company bridges the centuries between Calderon and Garcia Lorca and also does contemporary musical comedies.

Galician Cooking

Manhattan cuisines come and go; one year it's barbecue ribs and the next it's nouvelle cuisine; overnight it changes from chow mein to pasta. While the food fads play musical chairs, Galician/Spanish cooking has held its own on 14th Street. The food is uncomplicated, garlic, oil and *salsa verde* (a piquant sauce with basil and greens) complementing *mariscos* seafood and *paella* (rice with shellfish or chicken and *chorizo*). It is too much back to basics for eaters to ever get jaded. Lately, food snobs from the Upper East Side have been coming down here "slumming" for budget lobster.

Spain Restaurant, *113 West 13th Street (212-929-9580). Monday– Saturday noon–1* A.M.*; Sunday 3* P.M.*–1* A.M.

The restaurant is old Galician. The only thing not casual about the Spain is the red awning. The waiters are absentminded but friendly. The shrimp and the *langostino* (crayfish) in the *salsa verde* are the light at the end of this tunnel.

Riazor, *245 West 16th Street (212-727-2134). Daily noon–1* A.M.

An intimate restaurant with sentimental Spanish appointments and a real Spanish family for atmosphere. The food and drink has solid Spanish standards, with people coming back for the *sangría, paella,* and *arroz con pollo.*

Meson Toledo Restaurant, *318 West 23rd Street (212-691-0529). Daily noon–midnight.*

The Meson Toledo has giant two- to four-pound lobsters at lobster tail prices. Somehow seafood that is a struggle to eat makes people more congenial, and the Meson Toledo is at its best in a big group. The pound and a quarter lobsters in tomato, garlic, or green sauce are one of life's small Spanish pleasures.

Fiesta de Santiago Apostole

For four days at the end of July on West 14th Street Little Spain celebrates the festival of Spain's patron saint, St. James the Apostle. It is a nostalgic return to a Spanish past, with a procession carrying the shrine of St. James and an open-air mass. There are booths with Spanish souvenirs—mostly of bulls and Seville—and food stands with *tapas* (Spanish snacks—bits of Spanish omelet and *chorizo*).

The Church of Our Lady of Guadalupe is the setting for the grand fiesta. The stands, stalls, games of chance, and portable stage with entertainment are outside the church door on 229 West 14th Street between Seventh and Eighth Avenues. The fiesta is sponsored by the Little Spain Merchant's Association, which does nice things for the neighborhood like plant trees. Señor Joe Castro is the president of the organization and the neighborhood's unofficial historian.

Hispanic-American Day

Hispanic-American Day falls on the Sunday closest to Columbus Day, with the Hispanics getting equal time with the Italians, who have their parade on Monday.

The Hispanic parade attracts a cross section, from slight, almond-eyed Hondurans to round-faced copper-skinned Mexicans, to lean, eagle-eyed Argentinians. The new Hispanics come in families with thermoses and sandwiches to stand for hours until their country strides up the avenue. At that moment all shyness disappears and their eyes gaze with recognition and pride as they shout a greeting in Spanish.

Even with such a diversity of groups and affiliations, the organizers of the parade have kept the parade uniquely nonpolitical. The only political statements are unspoken, like the uniformed anti-Castro Cubans marching with Cuban flags.

The parade is a full-scale organization of American states in national dress dancing to their national music down Fifth Avenue from 44th Street to 79th Street. The costumes are theatrical and wildly colorful: Bolivians in turned-up brim hats and striped blankets kick up their heels with bells on their boots; Peruvians in devil masks and clown pants shake their arms like witch doctors; Cubans gallop on horses wearing Stetson hats and chaps. The parade is organized in alphabetical order, beginning with Argentina and ending with Uruguay. It is the longest parade of the year.

The Far East Asians

The Far East Asians have been influenced by the code of Confucius, Buddhism, Catholicism, and American missionaries. A respect for others and a sense of responsibility and commitment is embedded in their culture. In the bad old days before the end of World War II, they were denied the right to become American citizens and their entry into the country was severely restricted. These Asians were represented in New York by an isolated and marginalized Chinatown in lower Manhattan. The Hart-Celler Immigration Act of 1965 at last opened the way for immigrants from China, Korea, Indochina, Japan, and the Philippines to come to America and become full participants in the life of the city. From the Lower East Side to Sunset Park to Flushing they have helped to renew decaying neighborhoods. They have made important contributions to the city's commercial, cultural, and health institutions.

Chinese

History

In the early part of the eighteenth century the Chinese emperor forbid emigration under the penalty of death. Later, in the early part of the nineteenth century, the Imperial government lifted its restrictions in the era of the Chinese "open door" policy, enabling the poor rural populations of South China to cross the Pacific to California in time for the Gold Rush.

Caught between rural poverty and an expanding population, and pressed by the high taxes of an arbitrary imperial government, the southern Chinese were forced to emigrate. They didn't intend to settle in the American West or a northeastern Chinatown; they just wanted to support their families and have enough left over to buy land in their ancestral villages.

During the time the Chinese were building the western section of the transcontinental railroad and working the mines of the Far West, Chinese were a novelty in New York. The Chinese sailor who jumped ship or the Chinese acrobat on the New York stage were objects of wide-eyed wonder. Crowds collected around a Chinese junk that landed in New York harbor. P.T. Barnum literally put Chinese on display in the carnival sideshow he called the American Museum.

Public opinion on the West Coast abruptly changed toward the Chinese in the 1870s. The Chinese, who were viewed as model workers and model citizens, were now the "Yellow Menace." Demagogues East and West called for the abrogation of the Burlingame Act of 1868, which gave Chinese the right to work and live in the America.

Anti-Chinese sentiment in the West led to restrictive local legislation; Chinese were forced out of jobs and off the land. They were physically attacked and their homes and businesses burned. Finally, the federal government responded by passing the Chinese Exclusion Act of 1882, which barred the entry of Chinese laborers.

Chinese went east in search of work (frequently limited to laundries) and the solace of a closed Chinese community. In New York a "China Town" grew up in the garrets and cellars of Lower Manhattan. The neighborhood was self-sufficient; people worked in their own restaurants, curio shops, laundries, and garment workshops. They consciously refused to compete with the white population of the city. They were suspicious of Anglo-Saxon justice and made their own agreements and settled their own disputes.

In 1890 New York's three thousand Chinese existed outside the usual channels of city government and society. They were isolated by their language, an alien culture, and discrimination. The federal government's restrictive immigration and naturalization policies created a mainly male community, where families could never be reunited.

It was an uneventful existence, with many single men crowded into small rooms. The literate read histories and novels and threw the I Ching. Others gambled at *f'an t'an, mah jong,* or *bok-a-bou* in back rooms hidden behind restaurants and stores. Over endless cups of tea, they talked about homes and villages they would never see again. The money they sent overseas kept their families alive and paved the streets and built many schools in Kwangtung and Fukien.

The bachelor society of Chinatown depended on a network of organizations to provide the lost world of family and place for these "birds of passage" who could no longer fly home. Family associations, district associations, and secret societies were the main sources of community.

Family associations like the Lees and Wangs helped the elderly and unemployed and provided credit. District associations were also involved in community welfare, working with people from particular geographical areas of China. They also were the key organizers of traditional Chinese observances like the Moon Festival and Chinese New Year.

The secret societies in China offered some recourse to the all-encompassing state and a position in the world for the dispossessed. In New York the Tongs had an unsavory reputation for criminal activity, but they did supply the isolated people of Chinatown with traditional distractions like gambling, which was legal in their own country. In 1933 they signed a truce in the consul general's office, putting an end to the periodic clashes.

While Chinese laborers were forbidden to enter the United States, merchants were not barred by the Chinese Exclusion Act, and many ordinary Chinese presented themselves as merchants to the immigration authorities in order to enter the country. Chinese also falsely came into the country as the children of Chinese who were conceived during an overseas visit.

Despite stories spread by the tabloid press about Chinese hatchetmen and white slavery, the Chinese community was generally safe and stable by the 1920s. The Chinese Consolidated Benevolent Association (CCBA) in the city brought together many disparate elements in the community and created unity in a hostile world. The Confucian concept of harmony reigned.

Even Tongs that competed for Chinatown spoils now donned the mantle of respectable merchant associations, the On Leung and Hip Sing, and sat on the board of the CCBA together.

The whole complex CCBA organization was reorganized in 1940 to meet the challenges of a wartime situation. The officials of the CCBA represented commercial, family, and governmental Chinese interests. They were mostly from Toishan, one of ninety-eight Kwangtung districts, but they maintained a fair distribution of power by alternating the chairmanship with other groups.

In this same era, other types of organizations were formed to deal directly with the occidental world. The Chinese-American Citizens Alliance took legal action against discriminatory legislation, while the Chinese Laundry Association fought whisper campaigns against Chinese businesses. The National Chinese Welfare Council lobbied against the deportation of Chinese aliens.

Although in 1880 only three percent of Chinese were east of the Rockies, by 1940 it was up to forty percent, and the second largest concentration of Chinese was in New York. There was also a new element in New York's Chinatown, a class of Chinese professionals—engineers and scientists—who were stranded in the country by the surprise Japanese invasion of China in 1937.

They became the foundation for a new Chinese middle class. These high-achieving Chinese first became a statistic in 1940, when it was reported that the Chinese had the highest proportion of high school graduates to go on to college.

Once China and America were allied in World War II, attitudes toward the Chinese changed and bigotry subsided. In 1943 discriminatory laws were lifted and Chinese GI brides were eligible to become naturalized. After the war the eight thousand Chinese who wore the uniform of a country that didn't recognize their right to be citizens were granted permanent citizenship.

The Chinese were no longer regarded by the government as innately alien to American values and were allowed modest immigration quotas between 1945 and 1960. The Chinese who came to New York on these quotas were mainly middle class and professional, and many had close ties to the Nationalist Chinese on Taiwan. While this elite entered New York legally, thousands of undocumented Chinese were smuggled into the city to work in restaurant kitchens and garment sweatshops.

The Hart-Celler Act of 1965 abolished the old national origins quotas and Chinese immigrants for the first time in eighty-five years were put on a par with other groups entering the country. Chinese from all levels of society, rich and poor, skilled and unskilled, flocked to New York.

The new immigrants differed from their Chinatown forbears; they were urban Chinese from Hong Kong and Taiwan, who may have originally come from northern China and Shanghai. The newcomers came with families and were committed to staying in the country. They were Westernized Chinese prepared to follow the American dream.

These Chinese were no longer willing to live passively outside the mainstream. They became involved in the "War on Poverty" and worked with the Chinatown Planning Council to get funds for employment, housing, legal aid, and education programs. They protested against the war in

Vietnam and even staged their own Mao-style cultural revolution to protest the community's conservative leadership.

In 1974 Chinatown activists had their greatest victory. They organized protests against a city building project in their own neighborhood that did not have one Chinese worker on the rolls. They closed down the Confucius Plaza site until the unions promised to hire forty Asian Americans.

Young Chinese immigrants from Hong Kong, who could not cope with the New York educational system and confronted unemployment and dead-end jobs, joined gangs like the Ghost Shadows and Flying Dragons. They became involved in local protection rackets, and Chinese gang violence was again on the front pages of New York's tabloids.

Despite the publicity, gang membership remained minuscule. The real story of Chinese youth in the community has been about merit scholarships and awards for excellence in science and math. It has been about the high number of Chinese students who every year won slots in New York's elite schools like the Bronx High School of Science.

The 1980 census estimated the Chinese population in New York to be just over 150,000. This included eighty thousand Chinese in Chinatown and the rest spread out through downtown Brooklyn and Sunset Park, and the Queens neighborhoods of Jackson Heights, Flushing, and Elmhurst. By 1990 the number of documented Chinese had risen to 250,000, many of the new arrivals coming in response to the Tiananmen Square authoritarian crackdown in 1989. The daunting prospect of a People's Republic of Hong Kong had also fueled emigration.

The official immigration figures do not include a large undocumented population. Many of these FOB (fresh off the boat) Chinese are forced to work off the cost of their illegal passage in Chinatown's restaurants, laundries, and small garment factories. Some of these desperate immigrants are caught in situations not so different from the indentured servitude of their forebearers.

Meanwhile, American-born Chinese (ABCs) are on the ascent. They are entering professions and moving into ethnically mixed middle-class and upper-middle-class neighborhoods. For these suburban Chinese, Chinatown is a place to go on a weekend outing. These new self-confident Chinese Americans are following in the footsteps of award-winning architect I.M. Pei and Wall Street wizard Gerald Tsai. They are writers like Maxine Hong Kingston, film directors like Wayne Wang, and business tycoons like computer pioneer An Wang. New York's Chinese Americans are also aspiring to become multimillionaires, like Sherman Eng, who runs the Chinatown garment district and Harold Ha, whose precious jewelry factories produce glittering profits.

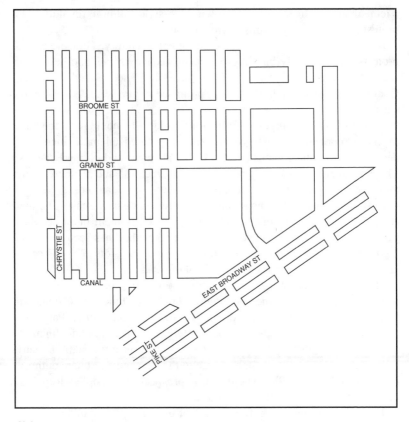

Chinatown

Chinatown

Directions: Subway 6 to Canal Street/Lafayette Street, or Subway N or R to Canal Street/Broadway.

When the area that became Chinatown was still British it was known as the Plow and Harrow district in honor of a seventeenth-century tavern. In American New York it was a neighborhood of contrasts, with Federalist row houses occupied by wealthy merchants and sea captains and hovels filled with the poorest Irish immigrants. By 1858 it had its first Chinese resident, a Kwangtung merchant named Wo Kee, who made his home at 8 Mott Street.

Poor Chinese lived in the cellars and attic rooms of the damp and decaying houses on Baxter and Park (now Moscu) Streets. In 1870 there were twenty-nine Chinese living in the area bounded by Canal, Baxter,

Worth, Park, and Bowery, which would eventually be called Chinatown. In this early era the Chinese sold cigars and papers on the streets, and some even married Irish immigrants from the neighborhood. Twenty years later there were three thousand Chinese in this densely populated Chinese enclave.

The Chinese were "sojourners," isolated from a world that would not accept them. The majority were rural people from Toysan, one of ninety-eight districts in Kwangtung. They were restricted to working in laundries or restaurants or to domestic employment. The only thing that they sold outside of Chinatown were tickets to the Chinatown lottery.

In the popular press Chinatown was portrayed as opium dens and white slavery. Since the ratio of Chinese men to Chinese women was on the order of two thousand to one, the absence of vice would have been surprising. The gambling and other extracurricular activities were controlled by the Tongs, who had one of their bloodiest battles at the "bend" in Doyers Street, which was dubbed the "bloody angle."

The Chinese Consolidated Benevolent Association (CCBA) had its headquarters on Mott Street. It was the law in Chinatown until quite recently. While it was hardly a model of legality, it was the only protection the Chinese had against a hostile outside community. It also provided the credit essential for developing Chinese institutions and businesses.

China's Prince T'sai Chen visited Chinatown in 1902 and made an impassioned speech to his people. He encouraged them to learn to speak English and practice American customs and move out of their segregated community. Despite the Prince's words, New York's Chinatown remained relatively stable.

Though there were screaming headlines about bloody Tong battles with guns and knives in 1912 Chinatown, that did not deter adventurous tourists from visiting. They nervously navigated Chinatown streets, and like present-day tourists, peered into Buddhist temples and shops selling exotic Chinese clothes and curios. They went to American-style Chinese restaurants serving chop suey, a dish of odds and ends invented in Chicago in the 1890s.

Chinatown's community of bachelors may have had a reputation for being passive, but Chinatown had its own civil rights organizations which were not afraid to protest. The Chinese Civil Rights League fought the extension of Chinese exclusion in the Geary Act. Later the Chinese-American Citizens Alliance campaigned in 1915 to eliminate all anti-Chinese restrictions.

In the 1930s, with war breaking out on the Chinese mainland, Chinatown made peace with an invisible line down Mott Street dividing Tong territories. Chinatown's establishment, the CCBA, supported the Chinese

Nationalists, and its local unit, the Chih Tang, which was more active than Chinatown's Democratic Party. There were local Nationalist newspapers like the *Chinese Republic* and the *Nationalist Vanguard,* and Nationalists sat on the board of the CCBA.

The increase in Chinatown's population after World War II revitalized an aging Chinese community. Chinese gift shops and restaurants and markets multiplied. Chinese garment factories became key contractors for New York's garment center. The women employed in these factories joined the International Ladies Garment Workers Union and the Chinese, for the first time, were part of the city's labor movement. Some of the factory owners were recent Hong Kong immigrants who started with nothing and became millionaires.

In the 1960s Chinese youth, who had been characterized as models for being well behaved and industrious, became part of the anti-Vietnam protests. Chinatown organizations used the techniques of student protesters to fight racial discrimination in hiring and forced the construction unions to hire Chinese workers for Chinatown's Confucius Plaza project. Chinatown activism continued into the 1980s, when the community was galvanized to block the building of a corrections facility in their area.

Chinatown had grown from a community of four thousand in the 1930s to a community of eighty thousand in the 1980s. The Chinatown of shabby tourism has given way to a Chinatown of banks and shopping malls and local industry. In the 1990s Chinatown continues to prosper and grow, with 350 restaurants and 600 garment factories. Its flamboyant jewelry district grosses a cool one hundred million dollars annually in gold and diamonds. Chinatown is also booming culturally, with Chinese theater companies and art galleries. Chinatown now publishes many Chinese books and magazines and twelve Chinese newspapers.

The community has organized groups to help new immigrants from Hong Kong, Taiwan, and mainland China to adapt to the city. They have worked with the city through organizations like the Chinatown Planning Association to provide English language programs and vocational training for new immigrants. They have established centers to try and solve the social problems that have led to the Chinese youth gang warfare.

In recent years Chinese big business from Hong Kong has also emigrated to Chinatown. Businessmen are moving their money out of the English colony and investing in New York's Chinese colony. They have brought Hong Kong sophistication to Chinese restaurants and shops, which are now larger and more glossy. While they have expanded Chinatown's horizons to include international finance, they have been buying up the neighborhood. Chinatown's real estate prices have skyrocketed and the old Chinatown image has changed.

The borders of old Chinatown have broken down and the Chinese, in a spirit of manifest destiny, have enlarged their territory. Aging ethnic enclaves and stagnating businesses have been superseded by Chinese enterprise. The Chinese are on the move, traversing Canal Street and crossing into Little Italy; breaching the Bowery and occupying the Lower East Side, from East Broadway to the borders of the East Village and Soho.

Chinese retail businesses, trading companies, banks, restaurants, movie theaters, and Buddhist temples mark the progress of the Chinese population. In their wake, deteriorating communities have been renewed.

Chinese are savers and banks are proliferating to meet their needs. Forty-one branches of American and overseas banks are competing for their money. Along Canal Street banks are replacing Chinese restaurants, and at one crossroads alone the four corners boast Chase, Chemical, Abacus, and United Orient Banks.

The new Chinatown is not only Hong Kong millionaires, garment workers, and restaurant employees, it is also a solid professional class of doctors, dentists, lawyers, and accountants. Creative working artists in dance, music, drama, opera, and the visual arts are an important part of the new Chinatown.

The Chinatown feeling is confident. The Chinese on the streets have dropped their diffidence. They are more New York and more hurried. The new Chinese have helped the old to open up. New York slang and matter-of-fact New York mannerisms are just as common as the musical rise and fall of Cantonese. Young Chinese men and women have taken on American irreverence and dress in the latest fad styles. Chinatown is assimilating as it expands.

Place Marks

While the new neighborhood takes shape, the original preserves its past and builds for the future. Chinatown has weathered the tourist traffic and kept its authenticity. It is a functioning ethnic community along with the convention bureau sights. Today's Chinatown is living contrasts, the sleek and modern side by side with the ornamental and traditional. Everywhere there is the energy of effort and striving, movement with an objective: moving, carrying, cutting, chopping, buying, selling, bargaining, and hurrying, hurrying everywhere.

The Chinese Merchants' Association, *83 Mott Street (212-962-3734).*

The Chinese Merchants' Association has its headquarters near the southwest corner of Canal and Mott Streets. The building is a wild combination of Chinese baroque and Western functional, dating from the first real estate boom in the fifties. It houses the On Leong Tong, which in these sophisticated times takes the trappings of a business group.

The Chinese Consolidated Benevolent Association, *62 Mott Street (212-226-6280).*

Sixty-two Mott Street houses the offices of the unofficial government of Chinatown, the Chinese Consolidated Benevolent Association, and the Chinese Community Center. The aged informally drop in like it's a clubhouse, while younger people take advantage of its employment services. The building also houses the Chinese School, which helps perpetuate the Chinese language and culture and has an enrollment of three thousand.

— Monuments —

Confucius Statue

Where Mott Street meets Chatham Square, a green and black marble statue of Confucius confidently surveys the traffic. This monument to Chinese New Yorkers is an indication that they have truly arrived.

The Kim Lau Memorial

The Kim Lau Memorial, situated on a traffic island in Chatham Square, is dedicated to the Chinese dead of the two world wars. It combines a triumphant arch with a Chinese pagoda. It honors a community that sacrificed for a country that did not recognize their right to be citizens.

Confucius Plaza

Across Chatham Square on Division Street is Confucius Plaza, a public housing development built for the community. Though not notable for its institutional architecture, it is a landmark to Chinese activism. The Confucius Plaza protests mark the first time the Chinese community mobilized to seek redress from an unresponsive city government. They used techniques of civil disobedience to secure jobs for Asian Americans on the Plaza project.

— Houses of Worship —

Eastern States Buddhist Temple of America, *64 Mott Street (212-966-4753). 15 Bowery (212-431-3791).*

The Eastern States Buddhist Temple is just down the block from Cantonese restaurant row. The atmosphere is subdued, the golden Buddha transfixed and aromatic incense rising in the air. Chinese housewives sit in chairs arranged around the wall as the candle flames waver. Behind the altar you can glimpse more golden Buddhas in different poses. It is a place for lighting candles, prayers, and making difficult decisions. The Bowery Temple is almost identical and just as busy.

Church of the Transfiguration, *29 Mott Street (212-962-5157).*

The Church of the Transfiguration was consecrated as an Episcopal church in 1801, but today it has masses in Chinese for the local community. The church is pure Georgian, with a spire as an afterthought. On Saturday, amid the tourist crush, Chinese wedding parties try to pose for pictures.

— Hong Kong Gold —

Before the Hong Kong Chinese came, Canal Street was a place where young couples came to get discounts on wedding rings. The jewelers on Canal Street were the last remnant of the old Jewish diamond district. In the 1980s Chinatown hopped on the conspicuous consumption bandwagon, and shop after shop opened up to mass market gold in the form of chains, bracelets, and medallions. Though the garish gold is gone, in its wake a vast jewelry district was established on the scale of 47th Street. One of the jewelry exchanges occupies the former Golden Pacific National Bank building, a fascinating sight at 241 Canal Street. It was constructed to resemble a gilded pagoda of the Forbidden City of Beijing.

Chinatown's Cultural Umbrella

Chinese-American Arts Council, *456 Broadway (212-431-9740).*

The Chinese-American Arts Council was founded in 1975 to expand and implement the cultural programs that had been initiated by Chinatown's Chinese-American Planning Council. It started as the administrative arm of the Chinatown Summer Outdoor Festival and went on to sponsor Chinese art exhibits, concerts, plays, operas, and dance companies. It presents Chinese art to the Chinese community for little or no payment.

The Chinese-American Arts Council publishes a bimonthly newsletter and books of cultural interest to Chinese New Yorkers.

The Chinatown History Museum, *70 Mulberry Street at the corner of Bayard (212-619-4785). Sunday–Friday noon–5 P.M. Nominal charge.*

The Chinatown History Museum traces the history of Chinatown New York through the individual testimony of its citizens. It is a gallery of photos, illustrations, and even signs that relate to the daily lives of Chinatown's inhabitants. It is an ongoing exhibit of Chinatown artifacts—the objects and implements of everyday life. There are oral histories, Chinese immigration documents, and even antique maps and guide books about Chinatown.

Chinese Art

Calligraphy is the oldest Chinese visual art. This highly disciplined execution of the Chinese character transcends meaning. Originally it was a matter of carving in wood or stone. After the invention of paper in the first century it was inky brush strokes on paper or silk.

Chinese classical painting had its roots in calligraphy. It uses the calligrapher's brush and inkstone. In the spirit of classic calligraphy the representations are simple, idealized, and poetic. The artist is deft and quick; nothing in the painting can be worked over or changed. The moment is captured. The Chinese moderns who studied in Paris built on these traditions.

Chinese art, traditional and modern, is part of the Chinatown Renaissance. Classical painting and calligraphy are promoted alongside abstract sculpture and minimalist watercolors. The Chinese art that developed in Chinatown has also found a following uptown.

Oriental Gallery, *83 Bowery (212-226-8461). Daily 10 A.M.–8 P.M.*

The Oriental Gallery is a place where young Chinese artists can exhibit their work and learn and grow in the process. The emphasis is on painting and sculpture in this Chinatown training ground.

Chinese Performing Arts

The traveling storyteller and the folk traditions of Chinese festivals and religious ritual brought forth Chinese dance, drama, and song. All the forms developed individually in different regions of China and they came together in China's all-encompassing opera.

Chinese Opera, or *Ch'ing Hsi,* is the Chinese national art form. It combines traditional music and song, old-fashioned melodrama, and mime. The costumes, masks, and make-up are elaborate and the gestures and movements highly stylized. Though the sets are bare bones, the graceful, almost balletic, actors provide a grand spectacle.

The plots of the typical Chinese opera include wild coincidences and outrageous changes of fortune. Sometimes the romance verges on American soap opera. The cast of characters is bound to include rulers, scholars, warriors, and even a god or two. Costume color is an indication of character, with red for loyalty and black for integrity.

Chinese operas are updated in the Chinese action movies that play Chinatown. The heroes and villains are pure stereotypes and good always triumphs over evil. The fight scenes in the Hong Kong kung fu epics may not be very realistic but they provide real operatic spectacle.

Though modern American Chinese theater has used the techniques of Chinese opera as a stylistic device, Chinese playwrights in New York work mostly through European dramatic forms, even when they experiment. But their plays are concerned with the Chinese experience in the West, the injustices and the accomplishments of the past, and the problems of identity in the present.

Pan-Asian Repertory Theater, *74A East Fourth Street (212-565-5655).*

The Pan-Asian Repertory Theater is directed by Tisa Chang and is associated with La Ma Ma Experimental Theater Club and shares their facilities. For more than a decade it has encouraged Asian actors and writers in the pursuit of theatrical excellence. It introduced John Lone, the star of the film *The Last Emperor,* and launched the popular play, *Eat a Bowl of Tea.*

Four Seas Players, *Transfiguration Church, 29 Mott Street (212-962-5157).*

This is grass-roots theater at its best, with productions in English, Mandarin, and Cantonese. The members of this community theater go back to the Chinese classics for their sources and sometimes bring them up to date.

Chinese Dance Company of New York, *50 East Broadway (212-966-4747).*

The members of this company chase away the evil spirits in the Lion and Dragon dances. The distaff members perform China's graceful harvest dances.

Asian-American Dance Theater, *26 Bowery (212-233-2154).*

The theater is two flights up to Chinese flights of fancy. There are traditional dances like the sword dance with traditional music and modern dances based on the folk forms or the dances of Chinese opera.

The Chinese Banquet

Confucius said, "Chinese food is the start of Chinese culture." More than mere nourishment, it's the scrupulous arrangement of texture, color, and flavor and the musical counterpoint of courses. It is the painstaking millennial development of the perfectly balanced taste. Chinese chefs are philosophers.

Chinese food is prepared in twenty-two ways, from stir-frying to boiling. There are braised ducks in pieces and whole fried bass. The meat and fowl and fish and vegetables for wok cooking are chopped, diced, and slivered in advance. The vegetables are very different from the Occidental table, with beans sprouts, bamboo shoots, Chinese squash, winter melons, and winter beans taking pride of place. The natural flavors are enhanced by soy, oyster, and plum sauce and accented by fermented black beans, aniseed, and coriander. Ingredients like shark fins, sea slugs, offal, tree fungi, and snake add to the variety of tastes.

Chinatown is populated by over one hundred thousand people and sometimes it seems to have as many restaurants. Chinese restaurants were always an important part of New York Chinese life, a link to the homeland and a link between people. The Chinese, like other immigrant groups, also found American cooking alien and unappetizing. In a time of employment restrictions, the Chinese restaurant also represented one route for economic survival.

Today Chinatown's restaurants range from the cramped and drab to multilevel Las Vegas glitz. A bowdlerized Cantonese concocted for the tourists has been superseded by authentic regional cuisines. Szechwan cooking was the first new arrival, its fiery flavors residing in red chilies. It was soon joined by red-hot Hunan. Later, there was the salty taste of the sea from Shanghai and Peking barbecue. The mountain people called the Hakaa contributed their hearty peasant fare, with meats and fowl baked in salt. Mongolia contributed the hot pot, a cook-your-own meal of broth, meat, vegetables, noodles, and hot chilies in a soup pot served on a hot plate. The Hong Kong Chinese have come up with their own authentic Cantonese, which has lately been superseded by trend-setting *Chaozhou.* And now with the refugees from Fukien on the mainland, comes Foochow cuisine, Chinese comfort food centering on broth, noodles, and the taste of the sea.

Chaozhou (also written *Chao Chow* or *Chiu Chow*) arrived from Guangdong province by way of Hong Kong. *Chaozhou* is Cantonese with a sense of adventure. It is not afraid to be different and borrows freely from Vietnamese and other Indochinese cuisines. Many Chinese cooks of *Chaozhou* cuisine have a Vietnamese or Cambodian connection.

The price range of Chinatown restaurants is very wide. It depends on ambience, the reputation of the cuisine, and the possession of a liquor license. But even the high end is modest by Manhattan's expense-account standards.

Lately, with the rise in Chinatown real estate values and the infusion of Hong Kong money, Chinese restaurants and the best Chinese chefs have been playing musical chairs. Landmark Chinese restaurants are no longer sacred.

Chinatown restaurants, from the banquet hall to the most lowly rice shop, start early and close late. Hours are free-form and don't conform to Occidental conceptions of breakfast, lunch, and dinner. Chinatown restaurants are nonstop and no respite, usually open until the wee small hours of the morning.

— The Banquet Era —

Recently, the Hong Kong Chinese, Taiwanese, and mainland Chinese landed with their celebrity chefs, nouvelle versions of Cantonese, and the capital to bankroll banquet halls as big as cathedrals. In an era characterized by affluence, the Chinese demand an aura of luxury and extravagance to dominate those special occasions in their lives; a banquet is a spectacle.

Larger-than-life banquet houses have been created to provide the rich display to transform the mundane into the magical. Like a church, the halls—or at least their ceilings—reach into infinity. The seating areas are cavernous and can be accessed only by elevator or escalator. These pleasure domes with their rarefied food have captured the big bookings for family societies, business groups, and those special weddings.

Everywhere there is something that glimmers, shimmers, or glows. Wide swathes of mirror and giant chandeliers set the tone with an occasional flash of hot neon. The traditional motifs, perhaps a pastoral scene or the Great Wall or a lion or a dragon, are incorporated into the modernity. Some have criticized the banquet halls for their vulgarity; let's just say they practice the aesthetics of having a good time. Enjoy with the people around you.

The order of a traditional Chinese banquet can be confusing for Westerners. Soup ends rather than begins the meal and a sweet sugared apple slice comes before the two final meat courses. The banquet usually leads off with four cold appetizers, including salted shrimp and sliced kidneys, and has at least eight main courses, with some kind of steamed fish and a whole duck.

When the party is over at these Chinatown banquet halls, they (at least early in the day) acquire a greater sense of intimacy and revert to the rolling cart of *dim sum*. At night they cater to the moneyed conspicuous consumption crowd.

Triple Eight Palace, *78 East Broadway between Division and Market Streets (212-941-8886).*

Triple Eight Palace is unrestrained glitter, all colored lights and luster, golden dragons and teak screens. The Hong Kong cuisine is eclectic, with tastes from Thailand, Korea, and Malaysia. The Honk Kong seafood buffet offers some wonderful variations on clams, oysters, and fat lobsters.

Golden Unicorn, *18 East Broadway near Catherine Street (212-941-0911).*

The Golden Unicorn's sumptuous surroundings excite thoughts of mythological animals and magical meals. During the afternoon it offers an exotic variety of *dim sum* that keeps its flavor and freshness.

Silver Palace, *50 Bowery at Canal Street (212-964-1204).*

The Silver Palace is Chinese swank with lush red decor and golden dragons and a great view of the bridge to Brooklyn. For three terms it was Mayor Koch's favorite Chinese restaurant when the mayor's choices for dinner made the evening news. The food seemed to be on the cutting edge then but now it seems a little tired.

Jing Fong, *20 Elizabeth Street near Canal Street (212-964-5256).*

Jing Fong claims to be the largest banquet hall of them all, with seating for fifteen hundred. During the banquet season in January to February it's hard to impossible to get a table. This masterpiece of golden dragons, massive tasseled chandeliers, and traditional murals was financed by the People's Republic of China.

Oriental Pearl, *103-105 Mott Street near Canal (212-219-8388).*

The Oriental Pearl has an elaborate dining area with colored lights, ceramic mandarins, and Chinese dragons. They also have an equally elaborate buffet (all-you-can-eat) dinner, which includes a hot pot at your table and everything from octopus to roast duck.

— Some *Dim Sum* —

In the Far East (and in Chinatown) steam carts prowl the streets proffering delicious snacks to hungry appetites on the run. The steam carts came indoors and a culinary tradition was born. Every day in Chinatown specialists in *dim sum* provide a meal made up of everyone's favorite delicacies. It is a kind of banquet in miniature. It may begin as early as 8:30 A.M. or start closer to noon, and it usually winds down between 3 P.M. and 4 P.M., but some iconoclasts serve it round the clock.

Waiters or waitresses pass among the diners wheeling carts filled with appetizer-size portions of Chinese delicacies. There are steamed dumplings or baked buns filled with pork or shrimp or bean paste, noodles stuffed with meat and fish, chicken feet, and other dishes too numerous to mention. If you still have an appetite after several rounds of *dim sum,* follow the Chinese example and have a main course.

Hee Seung Fung Teahouse, *46 Bowery between Canal Street and Chatham Square (212-374-1319). Daily.* Dim sum *7:30 A.M.–5 P.M.*

Success has only half spoiled HSF. The ladies pushing the carts usually put out plenty of the steamed *har kow* (shrimp dumpling) and *shiu mai* (pork dumpling), but what about some of the more arcane dishes like pork taro dumpling or the sticky rice *dim sum?* It's the first *dim sum* restaurant to have a Western following.

Harmony Palace, *98 Mott Street near Canal Street (212-226-6603). Daily.* Dim sum *8 A.M.–4 P.M.*

This is *dim sum* for the discerning. Beside the shrimp dumplings, pork buns, and other *dim sum* staples, there are unexpected delicacies like Manila clams that come rolling along.

Tai Hong Lau, *70 Mott Street near Canal Street (212-219-1431). Daily* Dim sum *10 A.M.–4 P.M.*

This example of Chinese chic attracts uptown gourmets hankering for *dim sum* made to order. The menu may be *Chaozhou* imaginative, doing incredible things to oysters, scallops, and a whole carp, but it earns its stars and bars for the afternoon *dim sum.* The little dishes are never gummy or dried out.

Mandarin Court, *61 Mott Street near Canal Street (212-608-3838). Daily.* Dim sum *8 A.M.–3 P.M.*

The Mandarin Court is that rarity, an all-around Chinatown restaurant. It is sleek black on mauve modern and the people are uptown and Hong Kong money. It has excellent *dim sum,* with tastes like turnip cake with Chinese sausage, and fine Hong Kong Cantonese cooking.

— The Venerable Chinese Restaurant —

It used to be that nothing seemed to change in the world of Chinatown. The shops, restaurants, and even the street scenes were caught in a time warp. You could count on your favorite restaurant being there forever. In the current boom atmosphere, with people practically tripping over overseas investment money, restaurants good, bad, and indifferent seem to have a rapid turnover. And now Chinese eating out, which was once just fun, is a pretentious quest.

East Broadway Gourmet Restaurant, *40 East Broadway near Market Street (212-274-0701).*

The East Broadway is a delightfully unpretentious restaurant with both a small Buddhist shrine and a color TV. The Foochow soups with eel, lamb, or sea bass can compete with mother's own chicken. The frog's legs and rabbit with Foochow sauce are delicious, but the jellyfish is an acquired taste.

Canton, *45 Division Street near Bowery (212-226-4441).*

Eileen Leong, Canton's hostess and owner, offers a warm welcome and a short education in Chinese cooking while taking your order. The starters are imaginative, with dishes like clams stuffed with pork and eggplant stuffed with pike mousse. The salt n' pepper loin of pork is inspired. Canton also has a sure hand with familiar favorites like Peking duck.

Peking Duck House, *22 Mott Street (212-962-8208).*

Peking Duck has been around a long time serving up its inimitable namesake. The Peking duck, crisp skin, pancake, and company, is food for the gods, and the Hoisin sauce is Chinese nectar.

Hunan House, *45 Mott Street between Canal and Bayard Streets (212-962-0010).*

Hunan House is the landmark restaurant of hot cuisines, one of the first to move into the Cantonese territory of Mott Street. Concessions are made to American tastes regarding the red pepper. Hunan House does things with snails and black bean sauce that would surprise the French.

Hong Fat, *63 Mott Street between Canal and Bayard Streets (212-962-9588).*

Hong Fat had its day when it was lines and long waits in the wee hours of the morning, when you could count on having strangers join you at your table. The service has the good-guy abrasive quality usually associated with old-fashioned Jewish delis. The Duck or pork *chow fun* (wide stir-fried noodles) and the roast pork are the high points of a Hong Fat pig-out.

New Chao Chow, *111 Mott Street (212-226-2590).*

This outpost for the latest in Chinese eating is short on decoration and dining amenities. Eating family style here means sharing your table with someone else's family. The *congee* (a rice gruel) is worth a try, but you have to ask because it is not on the menu.

Chinese Country Kitchen, *194 Grand Street near Mulberry Street (212-966-8899).*

The country that this refers to is *Chaozhou,* and it is supremely inventive. The Chinese jumbo shrimp salad comes with melon, apple, and pear. There's a rice casserole with sausage and preserved duck that is as satisfying as a French *confite.*

Sun Golden Island, *1-3 Elizabeth Street near Bayard Street (212-274-8787).*

The restaurant is bright and upbeat with golden sun walls and pink tablecloths. The service is friendly and informative and the *Chaozhou* cuisine is filled with surprises. The fried calamari surpasses Spanish and Italian versions. Even lobster purists will be won over by the Sun Golden Island version with ginger and onion.

Oriental Garden Seafood, *14 Elizabeth Street near Canal Street (212-619-0085).*

The Oriental Garden is a Hong Kong-style, aquariums-built-in-the-wall seafood restaurant. Your very fresh dinner, whether fish or shellfish, provides an oddly fascinating floor show. The Dungness crab is a best bet.

Golden Malaysian Restaurant, *95 Chrystie Street near Grand Street (212-966-3663).*

The Golden Malaysian is a snug, off-the-beaten-track, below-street-level, Lower East Side Chinese-Malay restaurant. The triple combination lunch combines curry and coconut with more traditional Chinese tastes at unheard-of prices. Besides the Malay delicacies, there are hard-to-find dishes like pork herbal soup and Hakka chicken (baked in salt).

— Rice Stops —

At the lower end of the Chinese restaurant market there are rice shops featuring very basic meat-and-vegetable mixtures served over heaping portions of rice. The vegetables may be mostly Chinese cabbage and the cuts of meat or fowl aren't exactly choice, but the food is more tasty than the local coffee shop at half the price. In the front of most of the rice shops roast duck, chicken, pork, and spare ribs hang all in a row. It's hard to figure out, but at the rice shops all the Chinese eat with forks and all the Occidentals work the chopsticks. The rice shops are for the quick bite, out-in-a-hurry lunch crowd and may close earlier than some of the other Chinatown eateries.

Tai Tung Rice Shop, *244 Canal Street (212-431-9632). Daily 7 A.M.–9 P.M.*

At the entrance there are two counters, one with a stainless steel coffee urn and *dim sum* and the other with slabs of roast pork and hanging roast ducks and chicken. Take a table in the back and refuse all the tourist exotica in favor of a simple Chinese beef stew on rice.

Sun Say Gay Restaurant, *220 Canal Street (212-964-7256). Daily 7 A.M.–9 P.M.*

This is a basic no-frills rice shop with some specials. The combination of roast meats with rice is a luncheon feast. The Chinese fish cake with pickled vegetables is a taste worth acquiring. The feeling of hurry is catching; don't come here for leisurely dining.

Sunshine Restaurant, *20 East Broadway (212-219-1916). Daily 10 A.M.–10 P.M.*

The rice choices are endless and there are many surprises. The hot squid with black bean sauce is one of them. *Congee* is rice with a difference, a rice gruel with delicious additions, such as preserved egg and pork. The fried rice here is worth a try, especially the chicken fried rice with salted fish.

— Oodles of Chinese Noodles —

Don't confuse Cantonese restaurants with fifty kinds of noodles on the menu with Chinese noodle shops. Chinatown's noodle shops are also the source of good inexpensive meals. Noodles and won tons are served in a broth that has subtlety and body. Greens, scallions, spices, and enough meat to add savor complete this traditional one-dish Hong Kong and Vietnamese Chinese luncheon. The service is very quick and customers don't linger. Even the crowd noise cannot compete with the sound of the customers slurping up the soup.

Chao Fu Lau Restaurant, *89-91 Bayard Street (212-732-5122). Daily 8 A.M.–10:30 P.M.*

The broth is sweet as sugar, with a choice of some of the most interesting combinations in Chinatown. Try curry chicken with flat noodles and the mushroom with duck egg noodles.

Won Ton Garden, *52-56 Mott Street (212-966-4886). Daily 10 A.M.–2:00 A.M.*

The Won Ton Garden caters to tourists having their first fling at noodle-soup dining. The broth with fish balls is their specialty.

Excellent Dumpling, *111 Lafayette Street off Canal Street (212-219-0212). Daily 9 A.M.–10:30 P.M.*

This is a new breed of noodle shop which is functional and contemporary. The noodles—with or without broth—are special. The Singapore rice stick with a curried potpourri of meat and seafood is extra terrific.

N.Y. Noodle Town, *28 Bowery (212-349-2690). Daily 9 A.M.–4:30 A.M.*

The cooks and servers in front laboring beneath the hanging ducks and ribs are in constant motion, a Chinese version of the action at a Sushi bar. Besides the noodles in their excellent broths, there are crunchy pan-fried noodles (Americanized into chow mein) and Cantonese wide noodles with unusual toppings like peppery tripe.

— Chinese Balls and Buns —

Chinese baking—like most things Chinese—always seems to come hot, straight out of the oven. Chinese baking is buns, balls, and tarts, baked and fried. It's made with bean paste, sticky rice, and yeast cake. The fillings don't take sweetness to extremes, whether it's coconut or egg custard or yellow bean. There are pastries with meat centers and cookies that are sculpted to look like fish or birds.

Kwong Wah Company, *242 Canal Street (212-343-2505). Daily 8 A.M.–8 P.M.*

The Chinese pastries packed with chicken or beef curry or pork are flaky melt-in-your mouth delicious, the best of their kind. The bean paste buns and the egg custard tart are sweets with subtlety.

Maria's, *174-176 Canal Street (212-925-3707). Daily 7:30 A.M.– 8 P.M.*

Maria's bakery is Hong Kong buns and pastry, soft sweet rolls sometimes slit like a sandwich filled with tastes that can seem obvious but not overly heavy. It is a multimillion dollar Hong Kong chain that even built its own high-rise hotel in Chinatown, now owned by Holiday Inn. They have many bakeries in all the Chinatowns, but the flagship is on Canal.

Lung Fong Chinese Bakery, *41 Mott Street (212-233-7447). Daily 8 A.M.–9 P.M.*

Lung Fong has an excellent assortment of pastries and cookies, all clearly marked for the non-Chinese customers. The cream sponge and the lotus seed pastry are sweet without being cloying; the big Buddha and fish cookies both look and taste good.

Lucky China Lui Bakery, *280 Grand Street (212-219-8434). Daily 6:30 A.M.–8:30 P.M.*

Lucky China has real versatility and bakes fine almond cookies, marble and sponge cakes with icing, and buns and pastries filled with meat or a sweet. It also has table service (and tea and coffee), which attracts a young amiable local crowd.

— Tea Houses and Tea Ceremonies —

Tea is the favorite beverage in Chinatown. It is aromatic and light, or dark as coffee, and in its own way as rich. There are teas for relaxing and teas that supply energy. Chinese teas are graded in quality and prepared in blends. Tea tasters discriminate the fine shades of difference.

In old China, tea drinking was a stylized ritual and there was a special tea ceremony that is still performed today. Tung Lu, the Chinese philosopher of the Tang Dynasty, devised his own logic of tea drinking and precisely described how it should be consumed. Chinatown is more offhanded in its treatment of tea and unceremoniously chugalugs it from chipped coffee cups and water glasses but it still steeps the leaves in boiling water and hasn't taken the fatal leap to tea bags.

Chinese teahouses take the place of cafes. The teahouse is sipping tea and speaking to friends and unwinding from a long day, and the midmorning or midafternoon break to recharge before going back to business. The tea accompaniment is Chinese pastry and buns and *dim sum.* In the better places they are prepared on the premises. Chinese teahouses are casual and open at all hours.

Ten Ren Tea & Ginseng Company, *176 Canal Street (212-349-2286). Daily 10 A.M.–8 P.M.*

The Ten Ren Tea Company is Taiwan modern with large technicolor photos of waterfalls and gardens. It has thirty different teas, from fermented green Tung Tin to fermented black, which come in bags or fancy gift boxes in 120 grades. Tea sets in clay or celadon porcelain are also on sale. The back area is reserved for tea ceremonies and a videotaped sales pitch about teas.

Nom Wah Tea House, *13 Doyers (212-226-3553). Daily 9 A.M.–8 P.M.*

Nom Wah is a Chinese cafe; older Chinese sit over tea and *dim sum* or a pastry and bat the breeze. The *dim sum* are fresh from the kitchen and go very quickly. The pork dumpling and the shrimp ball and the steamed bun are perfect with chrysanthemum tea. This atmospheric tea house has been used as a movie location.

Sun Hop Shing Tea House, *21 Mott Street (212-962-8650). Daily 7 A.M.–11 P.M.*

Big gleaming urns for tea are against the wall toward the front, situated next to heated display cases filled with dumplings, cakes, rolls, buns, and Chinese pasties. Throughout the morning, afternoon, and evening the mostly Chinese crowd enjoys their tea break as the fresh delicacies keep on coming.

Chinatown Marketing

Chinatown markets are controlled chaos, the battle of the buyers and sellers, Chinese style. Inside and out everyone wants to be next. The clerks are constantly restocking and stacking the shelves, and truckers arrive from the central market with new produce. The noise of cleavers chopping and ice spread out on a jerry-built stall and boxes broken open combine with shouts of prices and shouts of frustration and the never-ending engine of crowd hum. The problem is not enough room along steep Canal Street or along the aisles of a Chinese frozen-food department.

Dairy Farm Food Product, *132 G Lafayette Street (212-966-2020). Tuesday–Friday 8 A.M.–8 P.M.; Saturday–Monday 8 A.M.–10 P.M.*

Dairy Farm is one Chinese supermarket where the clerks are not too busy to smile. The market has shelves of teas, including a special "jasmine slimming tea," and a deep freeze with frozen *moo shu* shells (pancakes to wrap *moo shu* pork) and frozen lotus seed buns. The store's Chinese apothecary has shark's fins and deer's tail extract.

Canal Food Corp, *224 Canal Street (212-966-2524). Daily 9:30 A.M.–8 P.M.*

This busy outdoor fish market stops pedestrian traffic with its red snapper, tile fish, and fluke on ice. The fish are fresh and men in rubber boots and rubber aprons keep replenishing the supply. Inside it's all meat, including *lop chong,* a slightly sweet-dried Chinese sausage.

Lye Yan Inc., *226A Canal (212-966-0237). Daily 9 A.M.–8 P.M.*

Lye Yan is shopping bedlam, but it does have the best and most reasonably priced selection of Chinese vegetables. The only answer you'll get from the harried clerks is the price.

Kam Kuo Food Inc., *7 Mott Street (212-349-3097). Daily 8:30 A.M.–8:45 P.M.*

Off frenetic Canal Street, Kam Kuo feels less crowded than some of the other supermarket-size Chinese markets. It has all the staples from noodles to bean curd and also some surprises, including fresh ginko nuts, black sesame oil from Taiwan, melon juice from Tienjin, and Szechwan spice mix from the Szechwan.

Dynasty Supermarket, *68 Elizabeth Street corner of Hester Street (212-966-4943). Daily 9 A.M.–8 P.M.*

This super supermarket almost takes up a whole block at Elizabeth and Hester. It carries everything but the kitchen sink—a variety of products in small to very, very large quantities. The seafood is noteworthy with giant lobsters and crabs swimming in tanks, and the mussels and clams under a perpetual shower. The supplies of ginseng, dried shark fin, and dried abalone are endless.

Ocean Star Seafood Corp, *250 Grand Street at the corner of Broome Street (212-274-0990). Daily 8 A.M.–8 P.M.*

This fresh-from-the-sea seafood market is the market of choice for Lower East Side mainland Chinese and their Hispanic neighbors. In addition to bargain fish and shellfish, there are Asian and tropical fruits at down-to-earth prices.

Chinese Herbs and Roots

Chinese traditional medicine has been practiced for millenniums. It treats illness—both physical and emotional—with combinations of roots, stems, flowers, leaves, and seeds, and the bones, horn, and internal organs of animals. The Chinese traditional prescription is based on balancing life's organizing principles, the Yin and Yang. Properties such as hot and cold, sweet and sour, and bitter and salty determine treatment. This homeostatic theory resembles early Occidental medicine, which attributed illness to the humors. The traditional physician closely questions a patient about symptoms, examines the patient's tongue, and listens to the patient's voice to determine a diagnosis. Chinatown now has a host of herbal shops with a curious array of medicines to treat every condition and illness under the sun, from fatigue to impotence. A short list of Chinese traditional elixirs and medicines would include red ginseng for energy, Siberian ginseng as a sedative, *Ganme Ching* for fever, loquat for a cough, powdered pearl for cold sores, turtle jelly for dry skin, and powdered seahorse for impotence.

These Old World apothecary shops have a certain sameness. They are usually small and neat, and with the exception of the folk medicine practitioner, nothing breaks the monotony of rank upon rank of teas, herbs, and powders in jars, packages, or boxes. Ginseng roots come wrapped in cellophane or in pill or liquid form. Occasionally, there are folding chairs for waiting patients. A Buddha and electrical candles provide spiritual succor. Don't be surprised if the Chinese apothecary has problems with his or her English; this is a mainly Asian institution.

Guang Ming Herbal Store, *133 B Bowery (212-966-8431). Daily 10 A.M.–8 P.M. Acupuncturist on the premises.*

Wui Chuen Company, *69A Bayard Street (212-227-0194). Daily 10:30 A.M.–8:30 P.M.*

Ho's Ginseng & Company, *88 East Broadway (212-925-5727). Daily 9:30 A.M.–8:30 P.M.*

Chinese Curios and Antiques

Chinatown gift shops run the gamut from souvenirs to genuine antiques. Some look like everything just came off the assembly line and others resemble small museums. They are havens for browsers. The merchandise includes carved ivory and jade, lacquered Chinese screens, framed calligraphy, fine porcelain, and ceramic figures. The better shops are run by venerable Chinese gentlemen with ear-to-ear smiles. They are very knowledgeable about which dynasty produced which objets d'art.

Wardard China and Porcelain, Inc., *130 Lafayette Street (212-219-0240). Daily 8 A.M.–8 P.M.*

Wardard is fine china and porcelain, tea sets and bowls, and delicate figurines. The stock is endless but it rarely descends to the cute or kitsch.

Din Lay Company, *5 Mott Street (212-227-0945). Daily 11 A.M.–8 P.M.*

Din Lay is creative chaos—a profusion of carved ivories, lacquered plates, Chinese scrolls, and painted fans. The Tang horses are not originals, but are wonderful all the same.

Quong Yuen Shin & Company, *32 Mott Street (212-962-6280). Daily 8 A.M.–9 P.M.*

The tea sets are delicate porcelain and mass-produced practical imports from China. The have beautiful bowls for rice and serving and a great selection of plates. This is one place where you can shop without being shadowed by a clerk.

Don Enterprises, *36 Mott Street (212-267-5765). Daily 9 A.M.–10 P.M.*

Don is a curiosity in itself. It is a tiny store that carries the most monumental urns, with designs both tasteful and garish. Each one could fit two of the owner, Mr. Don Cho.

Festivals

New Year

Whether the new lunar year is the year of the ox, snake, or rabbit, Chinatown is bound to have its biggest blowout celebration. Chinese men and women crowd the markets, outdoor and indoor, stocking up on holiday foods for the traditional feast. Golden oranges and fat fish are good luck for the New Year, while lotus seeds ensure fertility for the coming moon year.

Everywhere in stands and stores, symbolic New Year's birds and pagodas are suspended from red streamers, and there are bells to ring in the New Year. *Sui Xien* roots are sold in earthenware bowls, holiday symbols of growth which will sprout into delicate yellow flowers.

In the gift shops of Mott Street, the Chinese buy New Year's cards and batches of red envelopes, *bao,* for gift money for the children and a prosperous New Year. Old men walk with small children to the Buddhist shrine; it is also a time for prayer and reflection.

The giant drums are beaten and the lion goes into its dance at the stroke of midnight. It's a frenetic dance, with one man fiercely tilting the papier-mâché lion's head while a second swings the lion's tail. The third dancer, head bobbing and body bouncing, baits the lion like a toreador without a cape. Total pandemonium reigns on the twists and turns of Mott, Pell, and Bayard Streets. Local Chinese and visiting tourists press forward for the best view as fusillades of firecrackers go off in the night.

Lantern Festival

The fifteenth day after the Chinese New Year the mood becomes more solemn. The Lantern Festival marks the end of the wild celebration. The lanterns, which are carried in processions by the children of Chinatown, represent the torches that people once carried to attract the spirits set loose at the time of the full moon. The Dragon dances in the street with its head and scaly body held aloft by poles. Gongs ring out and firecrackers are thrown in its path.

It's a carnival holiday celebrated with puppet shows and Chinese opera. Children eat the round *yuan hsaio* (sticky rice cake), symbolic of the new moon and perpetual rebirth.

Moon Festival

The Moon Festival occurs in the autumn on the fifteenth day of the eighth lunar month. The moon is supposed to be at its brightest on this day and the god of the earth is thanked for the harvest. In this Chinese thanksgiving, young girls ask Yueh Lao, the man in the moon, for a vision of their future husband and burn incense in the temple. Moon cakes are the traditional food with black bean, lotus seed, egg yolk, and red bean.

The Chinatown Cultural Festival

During the back-to-the-roots cultural explosion of the sixties the Chinese-American Planning Council organized a series of Chinese cultural exhibitions in Columbus Park. In 1970 the exhibitions were broadened to include musical performances and drama with the support of the New York Council on the Arts and the China Institute.

In 1971 these efforts led to the staging of the first Summer Chinatown Cultural Festival. It is now an annual multimedia event from mid-July to mid-September. The Chinese-American Arts Council is the community bulletin board for all the plays, concerts, exhibits, and dance recitals in and out of Chinatown.

The Two Chinese Independence Days

The Chinatown establishment, the leaders of the associations and societies that govern this community, have traditionally had a strong close relationship with the Nationalist Chinese forces of Chiang Kai Shek and the rulers of the Republic of China on Taiwan. The whole community has shown their allegiance by celebrating the National Republic Day on "Double Ten," the tenth of October, with a parade along Mott Street, complete with colorful native costumes, graceful dancers, plenty of flag waving, and a long ferocious dragon making its way to the rumble of drums and clash of symbols.

In 1994 the latest arrivals from the mainland demanded their own parade. They wanted to observe the founding of the People's Republic of China on September 25. The city fathers ruled in their favor, despite the complaints of the Chinatown elite, and they were permitted to have a parade along the more out-of-the-way avenue of East Broadway.

Sunset Park Chinatown

Directions: Subway N to 84th Avenue/62nd Street.

In the 1600s the Canarsee Indians sold a wilderness to the Dutch that became Sunset Park. Most of it became the estate of the Dutch patroon, Michael Hansan Van Berge, who converted it into farmland and grazing areas. Eventually, the English divided up the big Dutch estates and created small villages. As Brooklyn became more urban and then incorporated in 1834, Sunset Park was absorbed, but it did not lose its residential character.

Irish were among the first wave of poorer immigrants to settle there. They were later joined by Norwegians, Finns, and Poles. They all found work at one of the city's largest commercial centers, the two-hundred-acre Bush Market. Bush Terminal included industrial plants, a freight yard, nineteen buildings, and piers for thirty-five commercial and passenger ships.

In 1941 the construction of the Gowanus Expressway resulted in the destruction of attractive residential housing and the shopping area along Third Avenue. This was followed by an economic decline after the war, with the advent of containerized shipping.

The area began to experience the problems of poverty as its population changed. Housing began to decay and commercial businesses moved out. Crime was on the rise. In an attempt to save Sunset Park, public-spirited citizens joined together with The Lutheran Medical Center to form the Sunset Park Redevelopment Committee. With five hundred new housing units, it began the reconstruction of Sunset Park.

At the beginning of the 1980s the Chinese began to buy the homes in Sunset Park, lured by ads in the Chinese papers. It was practically a real estate stampede. Immigrant Chinese felt secure in this new Chinatown because it was directly linked to the old one by the regular N train. In 1980 Brooklyn's Chinese population numbered twelve thousand, but a decade later, in the 1990s, it amounted to over seventy thousand.

The Sunset Park Chinatown is more relaxed and laid back than its Manhattan original. The Chinese produce, fish, and meat markets offer all the fascinating sights and sounds without being frenetic. The restaurants and shops are less crowded and everyone is less rushed.

Eighth Avenue Stops

The best restaurants and food shops, calculated to appeal to discriminating Chinese tastes, are between 50th and 59th Streets all along Eighth Avenue. Though other ethnics may be taken for granted in other Chinatowns, in Sunset Park they get the royal treatment in Chinese restaurant palaces.

— Restaurants—*Dim Sum* to Lobster —

Bay Palace Seafood Restaurant, *5810 Eighth Avenue between 58th and 59th Streets (718-439-0652). Daily 8 A.M.–midnight.* Dim sum *8 A.M.–3 P.M.*

The eels and other big fish in the aquarium up front put on a nice show for the children, as families wait to be seated on a crowded Saturday afternoon. Bay Palace has the taste of the sea, but the *dim sum* is the main event. The fried taro with shrimp, the vegetable dumplings, and the sweet rice with chicken "in a packet" are distinctive.

Oriental Palace Chinese Seafood Restaurant, *5609 Eighth Avenue between 56th and 57th Streets (718-633-6688). Sunday–Thursday 7:30 A.M.–midnight; Friday and Saturday 7:30 A.M.–1 A.M.* Dim sum *7:30 A.M.–4 A.M.*

During the day the Oriental Palace is *dim sum,* inexpensive rice dishes, and a meal in a bowl of noodle soup. At night it becomes seafood gourmet, with fat prawns cooked in spicy salt, lobster with ginger and scallions, and those special dishes that are available by request to its mainly Chinese clientele.

Ocean Palace Seafood Restaurant, *5421 Eighth Avenue near 55th Street (718-871-8080). Daily 7:30 A.M.–11:30 P.M.*

The Ocean Palace is as spacious as a palace, with its own golden dragon and the standard Chinese restaurant aquarium. The *dim sum* cart is a constant source of astonishment and even the humble noodle is set off by things like sea cucumber meat and Kowloon dried squid.

Little Shanghai, *5405 Eighth Avenue (718-438-2000). Daily 8:30 A.M.–11:30 P.M.* Dim sum *8:30 A.M.–3 P.M.*

The restaurant practices Shanghai hospitality. Return twice or thrice and you are a member of the family. The seafood casserole alone is worth more than one trip. The Shanghai *dim sum* has its own unusual twists, with extra spicy scallion pancakes, twisted dough sticks, and cold appetizers including wine chicken and aromatic beef. The red bean and green bean Chinese ice are memorable desserts.

— Bakeries —

Bright Bakery, *5612 Eighth Avenue (718-492-1953). Daily 7 A.M.– 9 P.M.*

The Bright Bakery fills its display cases with thick pastry rolls stuffed with pork, beef curry, chicken curry, and other fillings substantial enough for a lunch, as well as lighter buns with bean paste, lotus, and coconut. There are tables and chairs for friends and neighbors to keep the baker company, and have a cup of oolong tea.

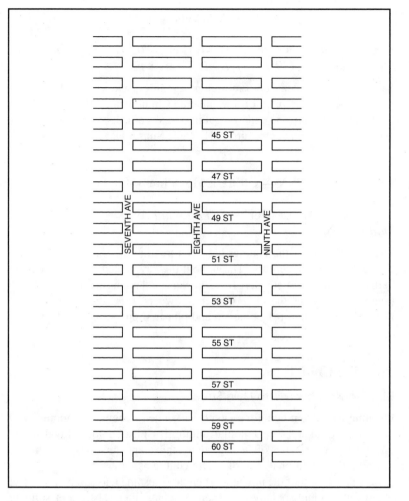

Sunset Park/Chinatown

The Savoy, *5223 Eighth Avenue (718-435-8225). Daily 7 A.M.–8 P.M.*

The Savoy Bakery is for Chinese sweets lovers, with big layer cakes for special occasions, coconut bars and buns, giant almond cookies, almond bean cake pudding, Chinese sponge cake, and water chestnut cake.

— Markets —

Sea King Sea Food & Meat Market, *5802 Eighth Avenue near 58th Street (718-439-1818). Daily 7 A.M.–8 P.M.*

Sea King is crowded come mornings, evenings, and weekends, but not quite at the frenetic pitch of a Manhattan Chinatown market. The fish is fresh out of the tank and expertly cut into steaks or fillets. The high-quality eels, squid, and conch also attract Hispanic Sunset Park.

— Chinese Medicines —

Yah Hong Chinese Herbs, *5317 Eighth Avenue (718-972-3199). Daily 10 A.M.–8 P.M.*

The elderly man at the counter has been treating the ills of the body for over a quarter of a century. Throughout the day he can be seen plucking herbs, measuring out powders from drawers, and preparing folk elixirs and treatments. Besides the pills, plasters, powders, teas, and energy drinks, there are bracelets for rheumatism and rubber slippers for tired feet.

Flushing Chinatown

Directions: Subway 7 to Main Street.

Flushing went from being the Dutch Vlissingen to being a community of dissenting Quakers. The colonial authorities pleased local loyalists by turning it into an area of lush gardens and plant nurseries. In Chinese Flushing this traditional love of nature continues.

In the latter half of the nineteenth century Flushing was a luxury summer resort for rich and socially prominent Manhattanites. The era of summer affluence ended with Flushing's incorporation into New York, which brought sidewalks and eventually the IRT subway. Despite two World Fairs in Flushing Meadow in 1939 and 1964 with the future as the theme, the once-proud Gilded Age Flushing was deteriorating.

When the Chinese and other Asians began opening businesses in the 1970s in downtown Flushing—the sixth largest shopping district in New York City—there were many vacancies and very little hope, but their optimism and energy succeeded in turning Flushing around.

By 1990 the majority of the sixty thousand Chinese who settled this Queens community were mostly from Taiwan and identified less with Manhattan Chinatown than with their own Chinese immigrant group. Their language was Mandarin, traditionally the official language of China, and the language of the cultural elite. They shopped and socialized strictly in the neighborhoods of Queens.

They joined or started up their own cultural organizations and centers. The Taiwanese had no connection with old "bachelor society" Chinatown, Cantonese Chinatown. They had learned from their own national experience to be more involved with their own family unit than with family associations or geographical groupings.

The Chinese are the largest Asian group in Flushing. They are upwardly mobile Chinese and thoroughly middle class. They look at Flushing as a stepping stone to even more affluent suburbs. Many of these Chinese are later arrivals from Hong Kong and Taiwan who never experienced anti-Chinese discrimination and are comfortable with Chinese customs and American culture. Chinese Flushing is confident and on the make, but still values family and duty above everything else.

Flushing Place Marks

China Buddhist Association, *136-12 39th Avenue (718-460-4318).*

The building housing this Buddhist shrine and Buddhist community center is modern and functional. The Buddhist sanctuary on the ground floor is tranquillity itself, with the golden Enlightened One (protected by glass) surrounded by an altar of flowers and oranges. The communicants kneel on low leather squares in the red glow of the temple and gaze up at the Buddha.

The Taiwan Center, *137-44 Northern Boulevard (718-445-7007).*

The Taiwan Center was the first community center for the Chinese in North America. It has a small library with books dealing with Taiwan and regularly receives current Taiwanese newspapers and magazines. The center sponsors the performances of musicians and dancers from Taiwan and provides information regarding immigration questions. Recently it has become the focus of demonstrations concerning the Taiwan government.

The Flushing Chinatown Planning Council, *41-25 Kissena Boulevard (718-358-8981).*

This social service originated in Chinatown but it has branched out to any area where there is a significant Chinese population. It has implemented day care and medical care programs and has helped Chinese in Flushing obtain housing and employment. It has supported Chinese arts in the community and sponsored performances of Chinese musical, dramatic, and dance groups.

Chinese Cultural Organization

Tung Ching Chinese Center for the Arts, *145-17 45th Avenue (718-539-4682).*

Tung Ching endeavors to keep alive the traditional opera of China through education, training, and actual productions. There are workshops on Sundays and regular visits to schools and colleges for lectures and performances.

Flushing Eating

The Chinese of Flushing and its environs keep Flushing's restaurant district thriving. The styles of Chinese cooking are regional with emphasis on Taiwan, the original home of seventy-five percent of the population. The restaurants themselves—with a few exceptions—are high gloss and cosmopolitan. They run at peak efficiency for an ethnic on the move.

East Lake, *42-33 Main Street (718-539-8532). Daily 9 A.M.–2 A.M.*

The East Lake is a vast restaurant on a banquet hall scale with neighborhood Chinese restaurant prices. Barbecued filet mignon vies with preserved duck egg with jelly fish. The fish is fresh from the water; even the shrimp have their own tank prominently on display. There's a separate take-out for *dim sum.*

The Happy Dumpling, *135-29 40th Road (718-445-2163). Monday–Thursday 11 A.M.–10 P.M.; Friday–Sunday 11 A.M.–10:30 P.M.*

The Happy Dumpling has a hostess who makes that extra effort. The food is well prepared and graciously served. The dumplings come fried and boiled and the noodle dishes are the house specialties.

Yao Han, *135-21 40th Road (718-359-2828). Daily 11 A.M.–11 P.M.*

Yao Han's owners are Chinese from Saigon and specialists in Chinese and Vietnamese noodle dishes. The Vietnamese beef noodle soup made with eye of round, flank steak, and brisket is a meat-eater's delight.

Golden Monkey, *133–47 Roosevelt Avenue (718-782-2664). Daily 11 A.M.–11 P.M.*

The Golden Monkey is a no-frills downstairs joint with red-hot Sichuan. Whether it's cold noodles with sesame or a ginger and spice chicken, you'll be reaching for the ice water.

Fang Yang Old House, *135–20 40th Road (718-762-1717). Daily 11 A.M.–11 P.M.*

Fang Yang is a barn of a restaurant done up in the rustic style of old Shanghai. It's just the right setting for the delicious, stick-to-the-ribs earthen pot casserole dishes. Try the assorted seafood or the three-meat casserole.

Jade Palace Sea Food Restaurant, *136-14 38th Avenue (718-353-3366). Daily 8 A.M.–midnight.* Dim sum *8 A.M.–4 P.M.*

Golden dragons adorn the walls along with enormous fish tanks. The maitre d' is dignified and the service is very serious. In the afternoon and evening the Jade Palace attracts the local power brokers. The shark's fin soup, black pepper scallops, and lobster with garlic are highly prized.

Flushing Shopping

The Chinese shops in Flushing attract Chinese from all over the metropolitan area who want to avoid the Chinatown crowd scene. For the Chinese of Flushing the shops of Main Street and 40th Road and Roosevelt Avenue are their neighborhood stores and there is a communal feeling here that doesn't quite break through in anonymous Manhattan.

Taipan Bakery, *135-20 Roosevelt Avenue (718-461-8668). 7:30 A.M.–8 P.M.*

The Taipei Bakery provides Taiwan baked goods that straddle the line between the Occidental sandwich and the traditional Oriental bun. The fillings run from ham and hot dogs to bean paste and taro root. If you decide to eat in, point to your choices and a waitress will carry your tray, along with tea and coffee, to a table.

Yi Mei Fung Bakery, *135-38 Roosevelt Avenue (718-886-6820). Daily 8 A.M.–9 P.M.*

Yi Mei Fung is the most popular bakery in the neighborhood for birthday and wedding cakes, Taiwan raisin bread and cheese bread, the scallion dry pork bun, and red bean and yolk pastry. Expect a wait.

Kam San Food Market, *41-79 Main Street (718-939-2560). Monday–Saturday 8:30 A.M.–8:30 P.M.; Sunday 9:30 A.M.–8:30 P.M.*

There is Chinese muzak in the background as Chinese shoppers push their carts down the aisles. At the door there are roots and herbs to cure what ails you, and Gillette razor blades. There are miles of aisles of soy sauce and noodles (dry, rice, sheet, and instant). The rice is in twenty-five-pound bags and the vegetables run to bok choy and bean sprouts. The market has a prepared food section with hanging barbecued and roasted meats and oodles of cooked noodles, and its own bakery.

Main Street 28 Food, Inc., *40-28 Main Street (718-359-3388). Daily 9* A.M.–*8* P.M.

This is a food market with as much action as a kung fu movie. There is constant movement of customers eyeing the produce bins, fish counters, and meat display cases as truckers offload boxes, and butchers and fish-mongers continue chopping and cutting. The fish restlessly swim in their tanks, while the crabs try to clamber over their bushel baskets.

Take-Out Shop (translated from the Mandarin), *135-02 Roosevelt Avenue (718-321-9070). Daily 8* A.M.–*8* P.M.

This Taiwan home-cooking take-out is barely the size of a phone booth and filled with steam and aromas from the kitchen. The bill of fare includes pancakes, deep-fried fish and fowl, and soups with mushrooms. There are a few stools and a counter against the wall that draw students, office workers, and business people in a hurry.

Chinese Apothecary

Shun An Tong, *132-24 Roosevelt Avenue (718-445-9358). Daily 9* A.M.–*8* P.M.

Shun An Tong is Chinese traditional medicine, keeping the healthful balance of yin and yang through the proper roots, extracts, and herbs. Some of these elixirs claim to cure anything from fallen arches to the common cold. The ginseng here is from northern China and more potent because of its age. There are ginseng teas and ginseng cosmetics and ordinary health supplements like wheat germ.

Indo-Chinatown

In April of 1975 America began its wholesale evacuation of South Vietnam. Many Vietnamese joined the airlift or followed months later using their own resources. By May there were 130,000 Vietnamese refugees in America with sixty thousand in relocation camps outside of the country.

The Vietnamese who came to America were mostly middle class, urban, and Catholic. Many were originally from North Vietnam and had fled an earlier Communist victory. They settled primarily in the warmer climes of California and Texas, but Vietnamese with New York sponsors settled in the City.

By 1979 there was a new Vietnamese mass migration. Life in Vietnam had become so unbearable that Vietnamese crowded leaky boats to make the long and dangerous trip to freedom. A large number of these "boat people" were ethnic Chinese who were in a vulnerable position after the 1979 Chinese invasion of Vietnam.

Though the Vietnamese New York population is small, they are highly visible in Chinatown. It is not just the handful of Vietnamese shops and restaurants; Vietnamese has become a third language in Chinatown. In the markets and stores the signs are increasingly trilingual, and there are products like *nuoc mam,* geared to the Vietnamese.

The majority of New York's Vietnamese are of Chinese extraction and their relationship with ethnic Vietnamese is not always cordial. In Vietnam the Chinese were resented as an old hereditary foe and a wealthy minority. But both groups share a nostalgia for a time and place that in New York increasingly brings them together. Vietnamese of all backgrounds are scattered throughout Chinatown, Flushing, and the University Heights section of the Bronx.

Vietnamese Nouvelle Cuisine

Vietnamese cooking is sometimes called the nouvelle cuisine of the Orient. It is light and subtle and sprightly seasoned with the freshness of mint and coriander. The Vietnamese table is international, combining the sophistication of the French and the technique of the Chinese. It borrows the curry, cocoa, and tamarind from India and lemon grass and hot chilies from Thailand. Vietnam's own unique contribution is *nuoc mam,* the essence of fermented anchovies, which is salty and slightly fishy and does service as an all-purpose condiment.

Vietnam's national dish is the spring roll *cha gio,* which has a thin rice-paper wrapper and a filling combining diced mushrooms, pork, shrimp, crab, and noodles. It is wrapped in fresh lettuce leaves and plunged into *nuoc mam.* The *ga xao xa* (chicken with lemon grass) is the most popular Vietnamese entree. It is chicken at its most succulent, with just a hint of pepper and citrus.

The Vietnamese are soup fanatics and even eat it for breakfast. The Vietnamese breakfast of champions is *pho bo,* thick beef broth poured over rice noodles, raw beef cut thin, scallions, coriander, and *nuoc mam*. The eel with tamarind and pineapple is the soup for the evening and very hot.

— Restaurants —

The first Vietnamese restaurants to set up shop in Chinatown were geared to the mainstream Chinese and American tastes, with fish, chicken, and pork dishes taking the lead and the very popular beef stock soups with noodles and thin rice noodles playing secondary roles. The famous Vietnamese baguettes, borrowed from the French, were practically nonexistent. In the last five years, with the New York rage for all things noodle, Vietnamese restaurants that specialize in *pho* have become the rule rather than the exception.

New Viet Huong, *77 Mulberry Street near Canal Street (212-233-8988). Daily 11:30 A.M.–11 P.M.*

The New Viet Huong is old Vietnam revisited with plenty of coconut, curry, and fish sauce. It makes the everyday dishes, like the rice-paper spring rolls, seem extraordinary. The seafood and shellfish are their strong suit whether in soups, casseroles, warm Vietnamese salads, or with lemon grass. The *banh mi* (baguettes) with Vietnamese paté are different.

Saigon Restaurant, *60 Mulberry Street (212-227-8825). Sunday–Thursday 11:30 A.M.–10:30 P.M.; Friday and Saturday 11:30 A.M.–11 P.M.*

The Saigon is a family-run restaurant with Mom at the cash register and her two daughters patiently explaining the ins and outs of Vietnamese cooking to a mainly Occidental crowd. The food can be good, with high marks going to the lemon grass chicken, Vietnamese pork, and shrimp crepe. There is a tendency for the quality of the kitchen to fluctuate, especially when it becomes busy.

New Vietnam, *11-13 Doyers Street (212-693-0725). Daily 9 A.M.–11 P.M.*

The New Vietnam is a friendly downstairs restaurant where the waiters have a sense of humor. The Vietnamese curries and sweet and sour eel soup are hot stuff.

Pho Bang Restaurant, *117 Mott (212-966-3797). Daily 10 A.M.–10 P.M.*

Pho Bang popularized *pho* in the Big Apple. This perfect cold-weather soup from the hot delta appealed to New Yorkers raised on mother's own chicken soup. Pho Bang has repeated its soup and appetizer formula in two other successful branches.

Pho Tu Do, *119 Bowery near Grand Street (212-966-2666). Daily 9:30 A.M.–10 P.M.*

Pho Tu Do is the real thing. The Vietnamese who work in the wholesale and retail markets and businesses along the Bowery come here for the reassurance of *pho,* their national comfort food. For a *pho* sampler, try the *dac biet xe lua* in an extra big bowl with six popular cuts of beef from brisket to eye of round.

Cong Ly Restaurant, *124 Hester Street at Chrystie Street (212-343-1111). Daily 9:30 A.M.–9:30 P.M.*

Cong Ly is an unpretentious family-run restaurant that doesn't strain for culinary effect. The cooking is uncomplicated Vietnamese without the laundry-list menu. The rice noodles and rice crepes are great accompanied with grilled pork or beef, as is the shrimp paste with sugar cane. Wash it all down with a salt plum soda.

— Markets —

Dai Thanh, *247 Grand Street near Chrystie Street (212-431-3103). Daily 9 A.M.–8:30 P.M.*

Dai Thuan is an everyday Saigon reunion. Vietnamese from around the city come for the just-like-home chilies, lemon grass, and banana leaves. In the meat department they are able to buy the right cuts of beef round, tenderloin, and brisket for an authentic Vietnamese *pho.*

Southeast Asia Food Trading Company, *68A Mott Street (212-431-5012). Daily 9 A.M.–8 P.M.*

Southeast Asia has choice Vietnamese products among its all-Asian assortment. The *nuoc mam* is the authentic article from Phuc Quoc, an island on the south coast of Vietnam.

The Tet New Year

In the Vietnamese communities of Lower Manhattan and University Heights, young and old celebrate the Tet New Year. It is a time for optimism and positive gestures to set the best possible pattern for the upcoming year. Friends and family exchange sweet cakes and candies to herald a "sweet" year. People are painstakingly polite for the first three days of the celebration to propitiate the spirits and ensure good fortune for the coming year. On the fourth day of Tet, the Vietnamese bid good-bye to the spirits of their ancestors and life resumes its normality. Tet has additional significance for the Vietnamese refugees because during the Vietnam War a crucial North Vietnamese offensive was timed for the Tet holiday, which resulted in the fall of the South and their own exile.

Koreans

History

The Koreans are a typical New York phenomenon, the overnight immigrant success story. One day they are selling wigs on street corners and driving taxicabs and the next they own retail businesses in every neighborhood in the city and are moving into real estate and shopping centers.

The city's original Koreans were academics and Christian converts who settled in the Columbia University area. In 1920 there were seventy Koreans in the city and thirty formed their own Christian church on 633 West 115th Street, attracting students and political refugees.

At the conclusion of the Korean War, Korean war brides flocked to the city with their GI husbands. They did not attempt to join the established Korean community or start their own, though they did maintain contact with other war brides. They felt liberated by the freedom America offered women and they took the assimilationist route.

In the era of the cold war, the United States encouraged Korean students to attend American universities and Korean physicians were offered American internships. Some were even able to stay in the country after their schooling and training and chose to live in the City. Korean pharmacists came directly to New York to practice, since they could be licensed in both by passing a single exam.

The 1965 Hart-Celler Immigration Act, with its preferences for skilled occupations and professions, opened up the city to an influx of educated Koreans. Korean doctors and nurses became a highly visible component of New York's private and municipal health system. There were more Korean doctors in New York than in rural Korea. Korean accountants, chemists, engineers, and technicians signed on with American corporations.

While the medical professionals thrived, it gradually dawned on the other Korean professionals that advancement was slow or nonexistent.

Ambitious New York Koreans took their green cards and futures in their own hands. Relying on capital amassed before emigrating or the earnings of two jobs or a lump sum from an informal Korean credit association, a *gye,* they opened small businesses.

These aspiring Korean entrepreneurs were also helped by business classes which were held by their consulate. In the early stages of the Korean success story, the Korean Consul acted as a liaison between Korean-American businesspeople and Korean wholesalers. Later when the profit margins became too small, Korean New Yorkers started their own wholesale businesses and became their own suppliers.

Some Koreans started their business life peddling made-in-Korea wigs, handbags, and sweatshirts in black and Puerto Rican areas deserted by Jewish and Italian retailers. They peddled these items on the street purchased with a line of credit from an overseas Korean company.

In time they were able to open fruit and vegetable stores and discount clothing and bag stores in transitional neighborhoods. Whether welcomed or resented, crime and racial tension were part of the cost of doing business. While many Koreans soon outgrew marginal neighborhoods and made it to the fleshpots of Manhattan's Upper East Side, other Koreans replaced them and their businesses still thrive in the high-crime areas of the outer boroughs.

Koreans concentrated on fruit and vegetable selling because it was labor intensive and didn't require a large outlay to start. In the early days, five thousand dollars was the start-up cost. Their profit margin came from working around the clock and employing only members of their family. They also weren't hampered by any shortcomings in English. These Korean businesses caught on with innovations like salad bars. In 1971 the first Korean opened his store and by 1980 they controlled the majority of produce stores.

They formed their own organization, the Korean Produce Retailers Association (KPRA), for mutual assistance and to deal with problems in the produce business. Soon, determined Koreans were hiring the latest immigrants from South and Central America and moving on to other businesses like liquor stores and cleaning shops, which required higher capitalization.

The success of Koreans also inspired resentments. There was friction in minority neighborhoods and even demonstrations and boycotts. Local groups in Harlem demanded that Koreans hire black employees. There was a whisper campaign that associated Korean business success with the Unification Church and the high-living Reverend Sung Yung Moon. Koreans were even the objects of racial attacks.

In 1977 the Koreans at the Hunt's Point produce market had enough of the racial slurs and the shabby offhanded treatment. Reacting to a racist incident at the market, the low-profile Korean community went uncharacteristically public and picketed. In short order they made their point and collected three thousand dollars from the wholesalers for the KPRA, and a public apology.

New York's Korean community is growing. In 1980 it numbered twenty-two thousand; a decade later it had climbed to close to three hundred thousand. The community, which has its own enclaves throughout the city, has also kept its cohesion though organizations and associations.

Korean groups form around different businesses, like the community's one thousand dry cleaners or three hundred fifty fishmongers, or the most recent Korean phenomenon, "manicurists." In the tradition of old ethnic fraternities and social clubs, they provide the members with health insurance and other benefits. There are also Korean "prosperity associations," where Korean Horatio Algers pool ideas about business and sponsor community programs. Local Korean Protestant churches are also sources of group solidarity.

The new Koreans are mainly middle class and urban from South Korea's capital Seoul and from Pusan. They have brought their cosmopolitan culture to the city. The latest Korean best-sellers, magazines, videos, and cassettes are readily available. Cable television shows recent Korean programs. There are two New York Korean dailies and four imported South Korean newspapers. Even the Korean-style modern bar/restaurants with hostesses have made their appearance in New York.

Though many Koreans opened businesses in ghetto neighborhoods vacated by earlier ethnic businesspeople, they tended to settle in white lower-middle-class and middle-class neighborhoods concentrated in northern Queens. They have made homes in Sunnyside, Woodside, Elmhurst, and Flushing. They have arrived!

The 1980s were a boom time for New York's high-visibility Korean grocers, but the recession of the 1990s cut heavily into their profit margins. Korean grocers talk about business declining from ten to forty percent. Business has slowed down and some have even failed. Some Koreans have even returned to their homeland, where a strong economy has helped to lower the rate of Korean emigration. Despite this downturn, Koreans still control thirty-five hundred groceries, delis, and supermarkets in New York City, or fifteen percent of the total.

Though relatively new to New York, Koreans are a high-profile group with a presence in practically every area of the city. Koreans are an essential element of the city's day-to-day existence in hospitals, pharmacies, and the ubiquitous fruit and vegetable market. Though sometimes misunderstood, they have earned the city's respect and regard.

Empire State's Koreatown

Directions: Subway 6 To 34th Street/Lexington Avenue.

New York's wealthy classes retreated to Fifth Avenue and the thirties to escape the immigrant advance in the nineteenth century. There were mansions and luxury hotels. The first Waldorf was built on 34th Street and Fifth Avenue for the then-amazing figure of thirteen million dollars to attract the swells who ate off silver plates. By the time the area was mainly big department stores in 1929, the Waldorf was superseded by the biggest building in the world, the Empire State Building.

Manhattan's Koreatown is known by Koreans as *Sam Ship Iga,* literally 32nd Street, this commercial quarter's main drag. Though it is in the shadow of Manhattan's number-one tourist attraction, the Empire State Building, it doesn't attract anything like the crowds that visit the Chinese enclave downtown. Despite a continuing effort by the Korean-American Small Business Service Center to attract tourists and local Occidentals, mainly Koreans patronize the restaurants, bars, gift shops, grocery stores, and pharmacies at the bustling heart of Koreatown, between Fifth Avenue and Broadway on 32nd and 33rd Streets.

Koreatown proper is a purely commercial strip on Broadway between 23rd and 34th Streets. While there are other ethnics in the area, it is the center for Korean wholesalers in the city, and Korean retailers buy here regularly. The buyers and sellers deal in electronics, inexpensive clothing, handbags and luggage, cosmetics, and jewelry. There are 350 Korean wholesalers, importers, and corporations, as well as branches of the important Korean banks and the offices of three Korean newspapers. They even have their own hotel. The Hotel Stanford at 43 West 32nd Street attracts a primarily Korean clientele from all around the United States and the world.

Korean Place Marks

Korea Gallery, *The Consulate General of the Republic of Korea, 460 Park Avenue (212-759-9550). Monday–Friday 10 A.M.–5 P.M.; Saturday noon–6 P.M.*

While not exactly in Koreatown, it is nearby, and a cultural focal point for the whole Korean community. The exhibition openings are important events for the Korean diplomatic and resident community. The showings seem to alternate between traditional and modern works.

The Korean Table—24 Hour Kimchi and Barbecue

Korean cooking is the hearty eating of Asia. The Koreans have adapted the cuisines of the Chinese and Japanese to their own taste. The flavors are direct and uncomplicated. The food is barbecued steak and short ribs and rich soups with dumplings. There are Korean stuffed peppers filled with pork and fried chicken bits (*la joki*). The Koreans take meat eating seriously; they eat it raw in their own versions of steak tartar and liver tartar. They also like their fish raw in Japanese sushi. The Korean national dish is *kimchi*, pickled cabbage laced with hot peppers. It keeps everyone warm during the long Korean winters. *Kimchi* is served as a side dish or in *pan chon*. Another popular Korean *pan chon* is spinach with garlic and hot peppers.

The Korean restaurants in Manhattan are mostly all-night nonstop affairs. The Koreans are a people who never seem to sleep and these round-the-clock workers need twenty-four-hour restaurants. The restaurants come out of the same mold whether they are two-floor-high football fields or four tables and a sushi bar. The tables and chairs are of light wood and simple and the rooms are Oriental screens and rice-paper paneling. In the better restaurants there are ceiling beams and photographic blowups of Pusan or the New York skyline.

Kang Suh Restaurant, *1250 Broadway at the corner of 32nd Street (212-564-6845). Daily 24 hours.*

Kang Suh is giant sized and spread out, with three men manning the sushi bar downstairs and six waitresses in white in the upstairs dining room. During the day Korean business executives and their Occidental counterparts in pin stripes come here to dine on prime beef and a wide variety of *pan cho,* while in the wee hours of the morning it's constant motion, with Korean greengrocers popping in for barbecue or sushi before or after the Hunts Point Market.

Gam Mee Ok, *43 West 32nd Street (212-695-4113) Daily 24 hours.*

Gam Mee Ok is a late-night hang-out, with natural brick and wood banquettes. The service is careful and caring and there are even menus supplied in English for the occasional tourist or local. Koreans come in for the renowned bone soup (a beef broth cooked for hours) or other simple peasant dishes on a menu that just includes six items.

New York Kom Tang Soot Bul House, *32 West 32nd Street (212-947-8482). Daily 24 hours.*

Kom Tang is open twenty-four hours a day and 365 days a year. They open their back room for private parties and do a lot of business with Korean and Japanese business travelers. They make a legendary bone soup, served in combination with ox tongue, ox tripe, and ox knuckles. The inexpensive luncheon specials include popular dishes like prime short ribs, a pork and *kimchi* casserole, and pan-fried beef.

C'est si bon, *30 West 32nd Street (212-564-8411). Daily 8 A.M.– 5 A.M.*

This cafe combines a bakery, tea house, and music studio. The green tea or ginseng tea go great with custard or butter cream buns as you watch a Korean music video on the cafe's TV.

Ham II Kwan, *28 West 33rd Street (212-563-3695). Daily 24 hours.*

The staff are obliging even in the wee hours of the morning. They are specialists in steak and barbecued short ribs (*kalbi*), prepared at the table, which their hardworking, mostly male clientele enjoys with Korean OB beer or shots of *sojo* (a strong liquor made from yams).

Myung Dong Kai Gunk Soo, *43 West 33rd Street (212-629-5599). Daily 10:30 A.M.–10 P.M.*

The restaurant is spacious and Korean functional; the menu is brief and very basic. The chicken broth is sweet as sugar and the Korean pancake (filled with *kimchi,* pork, and scallions) is served in its own frying pan. The Myung Dong has a reputation for its "handmade" noodles.

Dou Rei Buffet, *306 Fifth Avenue between 31st and 32nd Streets (212-564-9898). Daily 11 A.M.–10 P.M.*

This is a regular stop for Korean tourist groups visiting Koreatown and the Empire State Building. The buffet-style all-you-can-eat restaurant provides an opportunity for those less familiar with Korean food to sample a wide variety of Korean tastes and flavors.

Korean Supermarkets

In the Korean supermarkets the aisles are so crowded with delicious things to eat that you sometimes have to get through the store sideways. Utensils, pots, pans, and plates are sold along with the food.

Han Ah Rheum, *25 West 32nd Street (212-695-3283). Daily 8* A.M.*–9:00* P.M.

Near the entrance, past the twenty-five-pound bags of rice, there is a wonderful selection of Korean cold delicacies. The meat section has the most popular Korean cuts like short ribs and ox feet. There are a wide variety of hot pepper pastes for the most incendiary *kimchi.* The wait at the cashier counter can be diabolically long.

The Korean Protestant Ethic

Koreans are the city's only Protestant Asians. The majority are Protestant Christians, who take the Protestant ethic seriously. They are success-oriented believers in self-sacrifice. In every Korean neighborhood, commercial or residential, there are Protestant gift shops that look like Hallmark Card stores. Korean churches often dominate the social lives of New York's Koreans and are a source of important business contacts.

Koryo Books, *35 West 32nd Street (212-564-1844). Monday–Saturday 10* A.M.*–9* P.M.

The store cards have quotes from the Bible and a complete selection of religious books. There are also cassettes of Korean and classical music and Korean greeting cards. The selection of books about Korea in English are excellent.

Korean Roots

Korea has its own tradition of natural medicine, with folk doctors prescribing herbs and roots. Its miracle drug is the ginseng root, not exactly a cure, but a source of energy and virility.

Natural Oriental Herbs, *2 West 32nd Street (212-594-6929). Monday–Saturday 10* A.M.*–7* P.M.

The ginseng comes in many different forms, from teas to soft drinks, to invigorate the Korean energies, which never seem to flag. There are also deer extracts for lagging libidos and teas for dieting. The helpful proprietor will ask the right questions and study your tongue to make the appropriate recommendations.

Korean Day Parade

The Korean Day Parade is timed to coincide with the Korean Moon Festival, which is the Korean holiday of thanksgiving. It annually takes place on the third Saturday in October. The Parade makes its way from the Avenue of the Americas and 44th Street down Broadway to 23rd Street.

Korean Day is part marching bands and part Korean folkloric groups, the drums and brass contrasting with singing strings, the drill team following Korean country maids in flowing silks. Young men in martial arts uniforms bounce down the Avenue to the hammering beat of an Oriental drum.

There are the flags of South Korea and official Korean delegations leading the way for American-Korean Associations. The greengrocers march and the dry cleaners march and the fishmongers march. The Korean churches and Buddhist temples float down the Avenue on floats along with TV stations and beauty queens.

Koreatown in Flushing

Directions: Subway 7 to Main Street.

The Dutch dubbed it Vlissingen after a Dutch town in 1643, but it was settled by English dissenters. The English Anglicized Vlissingen to Flushing. It was the garden spot of colonial Queens, with the nation's first large-scale nursery. Even George Washington admired William Prince's botanic gardens.

In the middle of the nineteenth century Flushing was a popular resort for wealthy Manhattanites. It was elegant summer-house country along the Flushing River. In 1910 Flushing, which was now incorporated into New York, took its first tentative steps toward development, and by the opening of the 1939 World's Fair in Flushing Meadow it had two hundred small apartment houses.

The theme of the World's Fair in 1939 and the later Flushing Fair from 1964 to 1965 was the world of the future. The future for Flushing turned out to be, to a large extent, Korean. The Koreans among others have added the energy of the East to historic Flushing.

In the years before the Koreans came, Flushing was losing steam. Main Street couldn't compete with the suburban malls and the housing was showing its age. Landmarks from the colonial times and the Gilded Age were allowed to decay.

The new immigrants turned Main Street around and picked up the pulse of the city. They opened new businesses and started families. The older residents, who remembered a greener, more rural Flushing, couldn't help but approve.

Koreans may do business in Manhattan, but Flushing is home. Hardworking Korean families occupy cozy brick houses and high-rise luxury apartments in the vicinity of Union Street, Main Street, and Northern Boulevard. It is second in Korean population only to Koreatown in Los Angeles.

The Koreans of Flushing are a tight-knit immigrant community. They have extended the fine art of organization from their businesses to their local institutions. Korean parents have fought for high-quality education for their children through the Korean Parents Association and even succeeded in establishing an Asian Children's Day in Flushing.

Flushing's Korean-American Business Association has worked to defend the interests of local Korean businesses. It has mediated disputes between Korean businesses and other ethnics and encouraged policies such as the posting of signs in English in Korean stores, which helps increase harmony and understanding between groups. In cooperation with Chinese Flushing, the Association helped direct an annual cleanup campaign of downtown Flushing, which included the first subway station beautification program.

On the cultural front, Flushing Koreans have formed groups to preserve their culture and teach the next generation—the born-in-America generation—the Korean language, history, and music. The Korean businesses on Union Street in their own way have promoted things Korean from ginseng elixirs to Seoul music to Korean fashions.

Korean Culture Clubs

Queens Korean Culture Society, *37-17 Union Street (718-961-8801).*

This society promotes and preserves Korea's five-thousand-year-old culture through educational programs and the sponsorship of special exhibits and events.

Korean Performing Arts Center, *41-25 Kissena Boulevard (718-321-1773).*

The Korean Performing Arts Center keeps alive Korean dance and music by sponsoring programs and performances for adults and children. It is the major sponsor of Flushing's East–West ballet company, which performs Korean traditional folk dances as well as classical ballet.

Flushing Foods

The small round-the-clock Korean restaurants in and around Union Street are informal social clubs where Koreans, who have a scrupulous code of public behavior, can for the moment be themselves and let down their guard. It is a place to celebrate life, as they do in their one-year-old and sixty-one-year-old milestone birthday *chanch'i* (parties).

Cosy House, *36-26 A Union Street (718-762-0167). Daily noon–1 A.M.*

Don't look for the name, it's nowhere to be found (in English) outside this closet-sized restaurant. The restaurant may be plastic tablecloths and mismatched silver, but it is thoroughly Korean. It will take a while for the surprised Korean waitress to find the English menu. The Korean dumplings in broth and the Korean barbecue beef are good choices for people who don't like their food red hot.

Ko Hyang Restaurant, *42-96 Main Street (718-463-3837). Daily 11 A.M.–3 A.M.*

Ko Hyang is the place to relax after an eighteen-hour day of hosing and pruning and sorting fruits and vegetables. The lights are dimmed and the dark-wood room and leatherette booths spell comfort. It's late, but a cold beer and *koo-chul-pan* Korean pancakes filled with shredded beef and black mushrooms will help in the unwinding process.

South River, *45-05 Main Street (718-762-7214). Daily 24 hours.*

South River is the restaurant in the Korean community to see and be seen. The parking lot is the image of the crowd, bumper-to-bumper Mercedes and BMWs. The host is brash and fast-talking in English or Korean. The Japanese sushi is limp and the monkfish is hot and the decor is Japanese rock-garden modern.

Kum Gang San, *138-28 Northern Boulevard (718-461-0909).
Daily 24 hours.*

Kum Gang San is the kind of restaurant that is popular in Seoul, with a
waterfall and wooden bridge in front for tradition, and a Western-style
cocktail piano playing a medley of songs from *A Chorus Line.* There is a
great selection of *pan chon,* and the short ribs and steak are grilled at the
table.

Bakeries

Les Bonnes Cafe, *36-12 Union Street (718-939-3040). Daily
9 A.M.–9 P.M.*

Les Bonnes Cafe is a bakery and cafe, a place for a casual sit-down with
green tea and a sweet bun stuffed with cream or custard. Just pick your
own Korean version of sponge cake, donut, or a pastry in front and the
beverage will follow. Les Bonnes also sells fresh Korean breads.

Canaan Bakery, *36-40 Union Street (718-460-6094). Daily 8 A.M.–
9 P.M.*

The Canaan Bakery is patisserie cream cakes and Korean sweet rolls with
or without sweet fillings, American sandwiches, and soft drinks. They are
specialists in multilayer cakes for special occasions.

Greengrocers to the City

The Koreans gained high visibility in New York City when they became
the local fruit and vegetable store owners, and New Yorkers deserted the
supermarkets for Korean high quality. New Yorkers were also impressed
by the care Koreans took in preparing and displaying their produce. They
liked the fact that they were open around the clock. The high prices came
later, along with the salad bars and the Chinese buffets. In Flushing they
have the greengrocers' greengrocer.

Green Farm, *42-01 Main Street (718-961-6179). Daily 24 hours.*

Green Farm has Korean delicacies like singo pear, which is used to make
their raw liver specialty. It also has the cheapest, if not the best, produce
in Flushing.

Koreans have their own supermarkets in Flushing, which also carry products for the Chinese and Japanese communities. They are streamlined affairs no different from an American chain supermarket, except for the products lining the shelves.

Han Ah Reum Market, *29-02 Union Street (718-445-5656). Daily 9:30 A.M.–9:30 P.M.*

The market in the heart of the Korean residential district is an interesting Korean cross section. You will find a smartly dressed young women from a manicure salon going through the prepared *kimchi* and a greengrocer with five o'clock shadow and a permanent yawn stocking up on fish sauce and a Korean real estate man eager to pay and leave.

Sam Bok, *42-21 Main Street (718-359-7345). Monday–Saturday 10:30 A.M.–8:30 P.M.; Sunday 10 A.M.–7 P.M.*

Sam Bok has all the Korean brands in canned and frozen foods. There are taro roots for Korean soup and frozen Korean dumplings. The seafood counter specializes in Korean seafood salads like squid in pepper sauce.

Kuh Wah Oriental Food, *142-06 41st Avenue near Union Street (718-961-0999). Daily 9 A.M.–9 P.M.*

Kuh Wah is one of Flushing's original Oriental food markets. The emphasis here is on food, both Korean and Japanese. There is a varied selection of freshly prepared Korean cold appetizers, hot and pickled, vegetarian and seafood. It has all the right fixings for creating your own Korean dinner with standout fresh and frozen meat and fish departments.

Korean Curiosities

Korean handicrafts are embroidery and cabinet making, and they have a tradition of lacquer work and inlaid boxes. Korean crafts decorate the living rooms of Union Street.

G. Youn and Company, *36-14 Union Street (718-359-1187). Monday–Saturday 9:30 A.M.–8 P.M.*

G. Youn is Korean gifts: gaudy ceramics and mother-of-pearl boxes that practically glow in the dark. The furniture is also heavy on the decoration, and even the slippers are embroidered with iridescent colors.

Korean Harvest Festival

On the third Sunday in September, from 10 A.M. to 6 P.M., Flushing Meadow becomes the scene of a full-scale celebration of Korean culture and the Korean thanksgiving. Korean shamans perform a ritual blessing. There are traditional dances with fans and masks, and shamans in traditional costumes of swirling silk. The drum and the gong are played like lightning and thunder by leaping musicians. Taekwondo martial arts experts kick and thrust in a graceful sort of warfare. In between the entertainment, ceremonies, and exhibitions, Koreans and other spectators browse around the Korean arts and crafts displays of scrolls, ceramics, and even contemporary paintings with Korean themes. Korean foods are served from fiery *kimchi* to warm reassuring buckwheat noodles.

Japanese Manhattan

The Japanese in Manhattan and upscale Riverdale are multinational corporation New Yorkers. They are here on assignment for one of the hundreds of Japanese companies headquartered in the city. They are New Yorkers for only a short duration and not about to go native, and that gives their local cultural institutions added vitality.

In recent years the corporate Japanese have been joined by Japanese students and creative artists, who have gravitated to the East Village instead of the Upper East Side. According to the latest City Planning Department statistics, the East Village currently has one of the largest concentrations of Japanese in the City.

New Yorkers are also intrigued and attracted by Japanese culture. There is a vogue in things Japanese, from fashions to cosmetics to Wall Street takeovers. Japanese black on black is the look and Japanese high-tech is the substance. The city has taken to Japanese religion and meditation and made a religion out of Japanese sushi.

The Japanese themselves are now part of the landscape, as they move conservatively suited in groups through Manhattan's board rooms and financial centers. The Japanese, though numbering in the tens of thousands, are not that high profile; they entertain themselves in Japanese bars and restaurants and edify themselves in Japanese museums. They have their own organizations and even their own hotel.

Culture Clubs

The Japanese are not all business. In Japan, the arts are avocations for both the person in the boardroom and the person on the assembly line. Things the West takes for granted, like kite making and flower arrangements, are art and matters of exacting technique. The Japanese also have their own forms of Western arts, like Kabuki, a kind of Japanese ballet where dance becomes total theater. Japanese following their tradition pursue these arts collectively.

The Japan Society, *333 East 47th Street (212-832-1155).* *Monday–Saturday 11* A.M.*–5* P.M.

The stated purpose of the Japan Society is to provide Americans with information about Japanese arts, literature, and culture. It presents traditional Japanese music and dance and past and current Japanese films. There is a library and a gallery, where there are exhibits from Japanese scroll painting to contemporary abstractions. Demonstrations of crafts like paper cutting are also given. New York's Japanese community takes full advantage of its attractive Japanese-style facilities.

Nippon Club, *145 West 57th Street (212-581-2223).*

The Nippon Club promotes Japanese-American friendships while it promotes Japanese arts. It has a wide variety of lectures and exhibits in Japanese and English. There are concerts and dance recitals and classes in the art of flower arrangement, the Japanese thirteen-string Koto, the tea ceremony, and brush painting.

Buddhism and Zen

In some Buddhist sects religion consists of long mystical explanations and abstract reasoning. There are complex rites and rituals with sutras and mandalas. Zen Buddhism is a way to awareness, a meditation and a paradox. The Zen Koan is an unanswerable question and a self-contradictory statement that the master places before the initiate. Both ways are embraced by the Japanese and by New Yorkers looking for meaning.

Japanese Buddhist Church, *332 Riverside Drive (212-678-9214).*

The Japanese Buddhist Church, which is attended by corporate Japanese, Japanese Americans, and American converts, is a house of worship for the *Jodo Shinshu* sect, the largest Buddhist group in Japan. This is traditional

Japanese Buddhism, with chanting and gongs and kneeling. This landmark religious institution has expanded into the adjacent Beaux Art Buddhist Academy to create a Buddhist Community Center with a library, a community space, and rooms for priests and visitors.

All the Zen institutions offer training and "meditation time" for a fee.

The First Zen Institute of America, *113 East 30th Street (212-684-9487).*

New York Zen Center, *440 West End Avenue (212-724-4172).*

Zen Studies Center, *223 East 67th Street (212-861-3333).*

Japanese Books and Galleries

For the Japanese the art of the word and the visual arts are not that far apart. Chinese calligraphy was an integral part of literary forms like *Haaku* (poems) and it was the precursor of the *sumi-e* brush and ink painting. In New York, Japanese bookstores sell prints and curios, and galleries show Japanese wood-block prints.

Zen Oriental Book Store, *521 Fifth Avenue (212-697-0840). Monday–Saturday 10* A.M.–7 P.M.

The bookstore draws the Japanese crowds, but there is a lot of room for non-Japanese browsing. Besides the Japanese books, cards, and magazines, there are books in English about Japanese literature and arts, including the martial and Zen. There are also dolls, ceramics, Japanese fans, lacquer boxes, and calligraphy.

Ronin Gallery, *605 Madison Avenue (212-688-0188). Daily 10* A.M.–6 P.M.

The Ronin is a landmark gallery that shows antique jade jewelry with seventeenth-century wood-block prints, and even examples of the bamboo basketmaker's art or the swordmaker's skill.

Japan Gallery, *1210 Lexington Avenue (212-288-2241). Hours vary, call in advance.*

The Japan Gallery is chrysanthemum Japan with delicate Japanese watercolors and fine examples of *sumi-e* brush and ink blossoms and bamboo reeds.

Bonsai and Other Japanese Gardens

Bonsai trees are exquisite Japanese miniatures of cherry, pomegranate, buttonwood, plum, and jasmine. They are formed by painstaking pruning and pinching. The bonsai have to be mother-henned like delicate children. They cannot be placed in direct sunlight or exposed to extremes of temperature and must be root-pruned and repotted every few years. In Japan and Japanese New York there are bonsai masters who look upon bonsai as a mystical mission.

Bonsai Dynasty, *851 Avenue of the Americas (212-947-6953). Daily Monday–Saturday 7:30 A.M.–6 P.M.*

Bonsai Dynasty has all the tools, plants, and books to become a bonsai master. They have rare nursery stocks for the bonsai gardener.

Bonsai Garden, *135 West 28th Street (212-947-6953). Monday– Saturday 7:30 A.M.–5:30 P.M.*

The Bonsai Garden is a tranquil museum of every variety of dwarf tree. The staff are interested and friendly and will explain the ins and outs of things like drainage and fertilizing.

The Japanese garden is a state of mind, calm and meditative. It is gravel and rocks, or a hill and a pond, or waterfalls set off by shrubs. It is the perspective of the observer and the shrine in the distance from a summer-house. The Japanese garden is a vast park or the corner of a courtyard or a room.

Brooklyn Botanic Gardens, *1000 Washington Avenue (718-622-4433). November–March: Tuesday–Friday 8 A.M.–4:30 P.M.; Satur-day–Monday 10 A.M.–6 P.M. April–October: Tuesday–Friday 8 A.M.–6 P.M.; Saturday–Monday 10 A.M.–6 P.M.*

Directions: Subway 3 to Brooklyn Eastern Parkway/Museum.

The Japanese garden is by a Japanese master, Takeo Shiota. There is a pavilion and a pond, and within the pond the gateway to a shrine. The hill opposite is five small falls splashing over the shrubs. The Ryoanji Garden is raked gravel cut off by a wall, a temple wall. It is a place for meditation.

The Asia Society, *725 Park Avenue (212-288-6400). Tuesday, Wednesday, Friday, and Saturday 11 A.M.–6 P.M.; Thursday 11 A.M.–8 P.M.; Sunday noon–5 P.M.*

The Japanese garden is framed by a trellis and surrounded by red granite. It is a moment of silence in the center of the city.

The Japan Society Gallery, *333 East 47th Street (212-832-1155). Monday–Saturday 11 A.M.–5 P.M.*

The Japanese garden is an interior garden with a skylight softening the hard edges, adding depth to the rock and spaces.

Sushi Bars and Tatami Rooms

Japanese cuisine is simple and severe, like Japanese design or the lines of a Japanese flower arrangement. The fish delicacy is raw *sashimi* or with vinegar rice, sushi. The Japanese catch includes tuna, yellow tail, and fluke set off with shaved ginger and radish. The Japanese also lightly batter-fry shrimp with vegetables in a tempura. When it comes to meat it is a straightforward barbecue teriyaki, on or off skewers, and *sukiyaki* thinly sliced with vegetables and cellophane noodles cooked at the table. Noodles, the wheat kind, are a Japanese obsession.

Japanese restaurants in the early days, before they discovered that New Yorkers didn't necessarily know the difference, had across-the-board quality, very small portions, and very limited menus. The sushi was an afterthought. Today only the restaurants that are expensive or have a regular Japanese clientele walk the extra mile.

The Japanese in Japanese restaurants are out for a good time. The dinner is their entertainment, with scotch and saki. The Japanese haven't had a Puritan revival, so they are able to drink, smoke, and laugh with impunity until the hostess diplomatically tells them it is time to close. In some restaurants the Japanese can do this in the privacy of a *tatami* room, eating Japanese style, shoes off, from mats.

Sushi Hatsu, *1143 First Avenue near 62nd Street (212-371-0238). Daily 5:30 P.M.–3:30 A.M.*

Located far away from the maddening restaurant crowds, Sushi Hatsu attracts Japanese big sushi spenders. All the action takes place around the crowded but congenial central sushi bar, where the chef carves and sculpts the raw fish and rice. One of the very best.

Mitsukoshi, *461 Park Avenue at 57th Street (212-935-6444). Monday–Saturday noon–10 P.M.*

Mitsukoshi is high-flyer expense-account dining below the Park Avenue premises of New York's most elegant Japanese boutique. Japanese agree it has the freshest, firmest, and shapeliest sushi in the city. The surgeon/chefs at the sushi bar are artists. Reserve a *tatami* room in advance.

Menchanko-tei Restaurant, *39 West 55th Street between Fifth Avenue and Avenue of the Americas (212-247-1585). Monday–Saturday 11:30 A.M.–12:30 A.M.; Sunday 11:30 A.M.–11:30 P.M.*

The wonderful appetizers are the best prelude to the steaming cauldrons of noodles and broth. Enjoy them with refreshing Japanese beer or unusual hot saki. A Japanese breakfast including miso, sticky rice, grilled salmon, scrambled eggs, and green tea is a great way to start the day.

Hatsuhana, *17 East 48th Street between Fifth and Madison Avenues (212-333-3345). Monday–Friday 11:30 A.M.–9:30 P.M.*

Hatsuhana is upstairs/downstairs with a Sushi bar on each level. The sushi is excellent, from the dark tuna to the orange roe. But sushi is just the beginning of the Japanese big tastes in small packages. There are fried tiny crabs and fried chicken bits, morsels of boiled beef, and slices of broiled duck.

Hakubai, *66 Park Avenue at 37th Street (212-686-3770). Daily 7:30 A.M.–10 P.M.*

Hakubai is eating in Japan, or at least that portion of Japan that is New York's Japanese Hotel Kitano. The food from *miso* (clear soup) to *suki-yaki* is exceptional. There are *tatami* rooms and also tea ceremonies for the Japanese and American visiting fire fighter. It is expensive, but a one-of-a-kind experience.

Sharaku, *14 Stuyvesant Street corner of Ninth Street and Third Avenue (212-598-0403). Sunday–Thursday noon–11:30 P.M.; Friday and Saturday noon–2:30 A.M.*

Sharaku attracts East Village students and artists, Japanese and Occidental, with their inexpensive sushi samplers and authentic hot and cold Japanese noodles. The setting is attractive and uncluttered, with Japanese prints on the walls and Oriental screens for privacy.

Toraya, *17 East 71st Street (212-861-1700). Monday–Saturday 11 A.M.–5:30 P.M.*

Toraya is a New York first, a traditional Japanese teahouse in an Upper East Side townhouse, both austere and elegant. The teas are exotic and come with Japanese sugar and bean paste confections with Eastern flavors like ginger and green tea.

Japanese Festivals

Sakura Matsura—The Cherry Blossom Festival

April is when the cherry blossoms are in full bloom at the Brooklyn Botanical Gardens. Spectators of this special spring happening gather in the Garden's Cherry Esplanade—the site of seventy-six exquisite examples of Kwanzan cherry trees—to be moved and amazed by their delicate beauty. Besides the natural spectacle, every year Japanese cultural groups provide entertaining and informative exhibitions and displays which may include everything from tea ceremonies to martial arts.

Obon Festival

In Riverside Park near the New York Buddhist Church, on the Saturday nearest to June 15, Japanese Buddhists celebrate the *Obon*. The *Obon* was the selfless act of a disciple of Buddha from the sixth century, who freed his mother who was suffering in the land of death for her greed on earth. The daughters of the church dance in modest kimonos with small mincing steps.

Filipinos

History

The Filipinos populate 7,100 islands about five hundred miles from the coast of Southeast Asia. The two largest in the group are Luzon in the north, which contains the capital of Manila, and Mindinao in the south.

The specific identity of individual Filipinos is derived from the language they speak and their island of origin. The Visayans are primarily from the central Philippines, the Tagalogs inhabit Luzon mainly around Manila, and the Iloconos reside in northwest Luzon. Most Filipinos share a Malay ethnic identity and more than eighty percent adopted the Catholic religion during Spain's three-hundred-year colonial occupation of the country.

During the first half of the nineteenth century the Philippines was a land of great inequalities. It was dominated by a Spanish social and ecclesiastical hierarchy and a small mestizo aristocracy. Most Filipinos were poor agricultural laborers whose lives were rigidly controlled by large land-holders.

Finally, a naval attack by the American forces in concert with continual fighting by indigenous rebel armies led to a defeat of Spain. Although the Filipinos had been promised freedom, in an international atmosphere that proclaimed American manifest destiny, American troops ruled and local revolutionary leaders were arrested or killed.

The first generation of Filipinos to enter the United States were known as the *pensiados.* They were the first beneficiaries of the American educational system established in the Philippines after the American victory over the Spanish in 1898. They were an educated elite who were handpicked by the Americans to become the country's future leaders. They were the beneficiaries of a special educational bill signed by President Taft.

These *pensiados,* after their secondary schooling in English, were sent to America for an advanced education, primarily in the professions. They were sent to forty of America's finest universities, and boarded with the families of educators and missionaries. There were four hundred *pensiados* from a pool of twenty thousand applicants.

This pattern of Filipino students coming to America to attend American universities continued, peaking in 1938 before the war, with fourteen thousand Filipinos enrolled in graduate and undergraduate schools. Many students who came to America were forced by financial circumstances to drop out of college and join the majority of Filipino immigrants struggling to make a living in low-level agricultural and manufacturing jobs.

The America that these newcomers sometimes encountered on the mainland did not always agree with the images from their civics books. Prejudice and discrimination were an integral part of their American experience. In Los Angeles County, a Filipino was denied the right to marry a white woman on the basis of a local miscegenation statute. Racist vigilantes attacked and terrorized Filipinos from Washington's Yakima Valley to California's San Joaquin Valley.

By 1935 nativist sentiment throughout the nation resulted in the passage of a repatriation bill. Under the terms of this law Filipinos were to be provided with free passage to their homeland without any special rights of American repatriation. Only 7,400 Filipinos took up the government's offer.

With the outbreak of World War II and the occupation of the Philippines, the patriotic Filipino community campaigned for the right to serve in the American military. As a result of their efforts, they were granted American citizenship, superseding an eighteenth-century law that in effect barred naturalization to all Asians.

After the war a new more affluent, educated, and sophisticated Filipino began to make the journey to America. Many were destined for New York and the opportunities that beckoned to the bright and ambitious. They were not interested in earning money to invest in land back home or the vagaries of minimum wage employment. They were drawn by the American dream.

This newest group of Filipino immigrants gravitated to urban areas and represented the country's professional and technical elite. They were doctors, teachers, nurses, pharmacists, and engineers, and were in great demand in an expanding economy.

By the terms of the Immigration Act of 1965, they were granted relatively easy access to America's economic "promised land." Though many had to seek additional education in the states to meet rigorous licensing requirements, they were grateful for a chance to practice an occupation for which opportunities were limited in their own country.

In contrast to past Filipino immigrant generations, who were overwhelmingly single and male, the new immigration arrivals were divided between men and women. They had stable families and had usually been educated in English and were fluent in the language. They were career oriented and eager to have a secure life in the USA. Today, sixty percent become citizens five to eight years after their arrival.

The transition of Filipino professionals from the Philippines to America was eased by the similarities in American and Philippine educational systems. Philippine nursing and medical schools were modeled on the best American institutions.

In the 1960s and 1970s, in contrast to the restrictive laws of the 1930s, legislation was created to smooth the entry of foreign physicians into the United States to cope with a new Medicaid demand. By 1976 nine thousand Filipino physicians were practicing in America, many of them in New York. Many nurses from the Philippines also immigrated to New York to meet the nurse shortage. Today, about one-fifth of all New York nurses are Filipino!

Between 1972 and 1986, when the Marcos regime declared martial law and suspended the Philippine constitution, many upscale political refugees also came to the United States. Some had been financial rivals of the Marcos family and their allies, others were the victims of human rights violations. Benigno Aquino, the leader of the political opposition, was among this group. His wife, Corazon Aquino, would restore democracy to the Philippines on February 25, 1986. In one of life's reversals of fortunes, Ferdinand Marcos and his followers became New York exiles.

While Filipinos are proud of their own culture and history, they also take pride in their ability to assimilate and become a part of a new homeland. They are wary of cultural confrontation and do not desire high visibility as a group. Filipinos only want to be rewarded for their own individual accomplishments.

The New Neighborhood

Filipinos have been a vital part of the Manhattan community east of Gramercy Park and north of 14th Street for a couple of decades. In an area with a large share of the city's hospitals, including the NYU Medical Center, Bellevue Hospital, and Beth Israel Medical Center, Filipino doctors, nurses, and physical therapists play an important part in keeping the hospitals functioning.

In fact, a special law in 1989 was passed to make it possible for even more Filipino health professionals to become legal residents of New York. Under the 1989 Nurses Relief Act, Filipinos could not only become permanent residents in their own right, but also were permitted to bring in close relations. This started a "chain migration" that has visibly increased Filipino numbers on the East Side hospital row.

In this small corner of Manhattan, Philippine food shops, groceries, and restaurants are multiplying and cultural and spiritual centers are expanding. The Filipinos have a community life that is increasingly visible and involved.

Though Filipinos are proud of their image as successful medical professionals, they believe there can be too much of a good thing; sometimes image becomes stereotyped and caricature. High-profile Filipino New Yorkers also represent a wide variety of callings and interests.

New York Filipinos are a part of the New York theater scene. Cely Carillo starred in the *Flower Drum Song* and more recently, in 1993, Lea Salonge won a Tony for her performance in *Miss Saigon*. Some are financial managers, like Wall Street wizard Lilia Clemente, who is playing an important part in developing the first stock exchange in China. Josefina Natori is a well-known designer of lingerie and heads her own garment industry firm. Loida Lewis is a former civil rights lawyer and currently chairperson of the board of a billion-dollar food corporation.

Philippine Place Marks

The Philippine Center, *556 Fifth Avenue (212-575-7920).*

The Philippine Center is unique; the only building on Fifth Avenue without windows. It also is faced with adobe blocks imported from the Philippines and has a mock bamboo roof (inspired by Muslim designs) that give it character. On the ground floor there is a picture gallery for showing Filipino art, past and present, and tourism and trade exhibits. The center houses official Philippine government offices from the Department of Tourism to the Presidential Commission on Good Government (which functions to recover the hidden assets of the Marcos family). Kalayaan Hall is located on the second floor and it is an auditorium for concerts, recitals, dance programs, fashion shows, and even religious ceremonies.

The Philippine Table

Philippine cuisine is an odd combination of tastes, part Malay, part Spanish, and part Chinese. The appetizer is a deep-fried diminutive eggroll called *lumpia,* which is long and thin, shaped almost like a cigarette. The savor of stews called *adobo* (chicken, pork, or octopus) are Pacific fresh, with the odd kick provided by vinegar, chilies, soy, and garlic. *Pancit* (noodles) is a staple of the table, with many varieties, from rice to egg. When Filipinos celebrate, they pull out all stops with a whole spit-turned suckling pig with all the trimmings. The *lechon* is sometimes slathered with a thick liver sauce. Later, it is all washed down with *halo-halo,* the Pacific Islander malted, combining preserved fruit, sweet beans, evaporated milk, and crushed ice.

Elvie's Turo-Turo, *214 First Avenue between 12th and 13th Streets (212-473-7785). Monday–Saturday 11 A.M.–9 P.M.; Sunday 11 A.M.–8 P.M.*

Elvie's is a popular place for take-out or a quick bite with Filipino medical personnel from Beth Israel and Bellevue. It is fast-food-style Filipino with a steam table, a counter, and several tables and chairs. If you are in an adventurous mood, just point to what looks good on the steam table. The *kare-kare* (stewed oxtail in peanut gravy), *ukoy* (mixed vegetable fritters), and the chicken *adobo* are the local Filipinos' favorites.

Metro Manila Restaurant, *188 First Avenue between 11th and 12th Streets (212-477-8339). Daily 6 A.M.–11 P.M.*

Metro Manila has a Pacific Island feeling, very relaxed and amiable. It also is the only restaurant in Manhattan serving Filipino breakfasts, and its luncheon buffet has outstanding *adobos.* Many Filipinos keep the restaurant busy with *lechon* banquets.

Manila Garden Restaurant, *325 East 14th Street between First and Second Avenues (212-777-6314). Daily 11 A.M.–11 P.M.*

The Manila Gardens, with tinkling cocktail piano, is for nights out. The food attracts a loyal following of local Filipinos. Start with the tasty

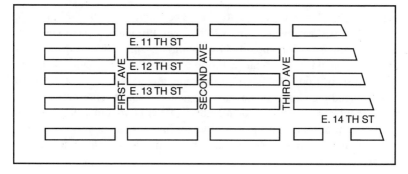

Manhattan/Little Manila

steamed dumplings (*somai*). If you are of a mind for meat, try the typical Philippine specialty *paksiw na lechon* (roasted pork with spiced liver sauce). If you have a taste for vegetables, the *pinakbet,* which includes bitter melon, okra, and string beans in a sauce including shrimp paste, is different and delicious.

New Manila Food Market, *351 East 14th Street (212-420-8182). Daily 8 A.M.–9 P.M.*

Along with the Philippine staples like rice flour, noodles, canned tropical fruits, and fresh root vegetables, New Manila sells Philippine kitsch like embroidered pillows and handmade flowers. It has a nice selection of extremely sweet Philippine cakes, rolls, and puddings.

Snow Queen, *231 First Avenue at 14th Street (212-673-9365). Daily 8 A.M.–8:30 P.M.*

Snow Queen is small shop (neatly) stacked to the rafters with a full range of Filipino and other Oriental food products. Prepared foods include vegetable and meat stews, Filipino egg rolls, and Filipino barbecue for take-out, and a wider selection of Filipino delicacies in a display case to reheat at home.

Philippine Independence Day

For two weeks prior to the independence day celebration, there are special events, concerts, and exhibits at the Filipino Center.

On the first Sunday in June, Filipinos have a full-fledged independence day festival. It is a day of national celebration, when Filipinos recall the heroism of great national figures from the rebel leader Aquinaldo to the recent political martyr, Pinoy Aquino. The line of march starts on 41st Street and works its way down to 26th Street. Filipino dancers in brilliant bird-of-paradise colors dip and bow, with fans spread like fragile wings from each hand. On a float, a Filipino troubadour serenades a beauty queen tossing tropical flowers to the crowd. Very serious and dignified middle-aged men and women carry flags and banners representing clubs and organizations. The senior members of the community and Filipino government officials have places of honor in the reviewing stand. A food fair, a musical variety show, a craft show, and an art exhibit are among the special events.

chapter fourteen

The East Indians

In the early years of the twentieth century, when India was still a colony of Great Britain, the first Indians migrated to New York. They came to enter institutions of higher learning and introduced their own systems of philosophy and spiritual discipline. Though they encountered prejudice and obstacles to becoming citizens, they continued to pursue the American dream. Today, immigrants from the Indian subcontinent represent the nations of India, Pakistan, and Bangladesh. They play important roles in the city as engineers, doctors, businesspeople, and academics. They run the retail newsstands, drive the cabs and limousines, and operate popular restaurant rows.

History

The first East Indians entered New York in the early part of the twentieth century, between 1904 and 1914. They were a very small group composed of political refugees, educators, and artists. They were joined by Punjabi agricultural laborers from California who were looking for work in the city after the failure of the West Coast harvest.

In 1917 court rulings barred immigrants from Asiatic countries. The only East Indians who were able to enter were from the the West Indies; once these Indians gained resident status, they had difficulty getting naturalized. The courts were arbitrary, classifying some Indians as white and eligible for naturalization and others as nonwhite and ineligible.

A ruling by the Naturalization and Immigration Authority in 1926 revoked the citizenship of forty-six Indians. Prafulla C. Mukerjii, a New York Bengali, demanded his day in court and even protested to the U.S. Senate. He testified before Congress for a bill to reinstate all forty-six but it was killed in committee. He finally was able to regain his own citizenship on a legal technicality.

Mr. Mukerjii, who was one of New York's leading Indian citizens and the president of the prestigious Tagore Foundation, was not satisfied with the ruling on the case and the response of the government. He was determined to win equal rights for the Indians and formed the Hindu Citizenship Committee to fight the injustice.

New York's Indian community celebrated in 1946 when the law was rescinded and Indians could become citizens and enter the country on a limited quota. There was a slight setback in 1952 when the McCarran-Walter Act, with its rigid immigration ceiling, based quotas on racial characteristics rather than country of origin, and Western Hemisphere Indians and East African Indians were included in the same small quota.

The Hart-Celler Immigration Act, which went into effect in 1965, finally dispensed with the racial and country-of-origin quotas. Visas were awarded on the basis of familial relationships or scarce occupational skills, and Indians were now able to enter New York in substantial numbers.

The Indian newcomers were English speaking, highly educated, and familiar with Western-style American customs. The new immigrants were skilled professionals and mainly male: engineers, scientists, and doctors. While Indian physicians readily found positions in New York's health system, Indian engineers who were trained abroad did not always have the requirements desired by New York firms.

The Indians who had problems being placed started their own businesses or took jobs selling insurance or real estate to their own upscale community. As Indian New Yorkers became more settled, they left the bachelor apartments they usually shared with other Indians and began bringing over their families, which received special preference under the Hart-Celler Act.

The Indian immigrants who settled in New York were diverse. They represented the countries of India and Pakistan and later Bangladesh. They were Hindus, Muslims, Sikhs, Christians, Jains, and Parsis. They identified strongly with their native Indian states and native languages and viewed themselves and one another as "Northerners" and "Southerners."

They had a wide range of habits and customs. There were meat-eaters, fish-eaters, and strict vegetarians who would not touch milk or eggs. While caste was less important than in the past, it played a part in differentiating Indian New Yorkers. There were fair-skinned Aryan Indians and the darker Dravidians

Pakistanis had a strong proud sense of their special identity. They were Muslims—Sunni and Shiite—and speakers of Urdu and Punjabi. They represented the urban educated elites from the cities of Karachi, Derabad, and Lahore.

New York's Indians formed their own societies and fraternal groups. They had over forty-four associations and organizations. The purpose of these groups, from the northern Cultural Association of Bengal to the southern Kerala Samaj of New York, was primarily social.

In 1971 New York's Indians incorporated the Association of Indians in America (AIA) to confront issues that affected the whole Indian community and to deal directly with American society. AIA formed a tier of professional organizations to defend Indian physicians and engineers, who were sometimes characterized as poorly trained and culturally maladjusted. AIA organized an "honor banquet" recognizing the accomplishments of Indians and Indian Americans to improve the image of the community.

In the 1990s AIA has been joined in its efforts to defend Indian interests by the Federation of Indian Associations. The new group also represents Indian commerce and issues an annual community directory. The new Indian merchants have a higher profile than the earlier generation of professionals.

New York's Indians have bought up the newsstands and candy and stationery stores that sell the city's newspapers. They have even purchased the *Union News,* which controls many of New York's most important magazine and newspaper franchises. By the nature of the business they control they have become a neighbor to most New Yorkers and are no longer exotic. In the 1990s fifty percent of the 275 licensed newsstands are owned by Indian or Pakistani vendors, and they run many of the others.

===== Little India on Lexington Avenue =====

The first Indian New Yorkers congregated uptown around Columbia University; though many lived together in dormitory-type arrangements, they did not have the numbers to form a neighborhood. They did their shopping on Lexington Avenue, where an Armenian named Kalyustan supplied them with Indian spices and grains. When it came time for the Indians to open their own shops and restaurants in the city, they located them in the same area, between Park and Lexington Avenues, from about 27th to 30th Streets.

A few families even occupied apartments above the shops, but the area never became more than an Indian commercial strip. New York's affluent Indians headed for the suburban borough of Queens: Flushing, Rego Park, Elmhurst, and Forest Hills. They could afford to live among New York's successful second- and third-generation ethnics and didn't need the security of their own separate neighborhood. A later, less affluent generation of Indian, Pakistani, and Bangladeshi immigrants would establish their own safe enclaves, more isolated from an alien Western culture, where they could cultivate a deepening sense of ethnic identity and consciousness.

The Indian Table—Tandoori and Curry

Indian cuisine is not all hot curries and sweet chutneys. Although the combination of spices in curry may be its core, Indian cooking has as many variations as the regional checkerboard of the Indian subcontinent. In the North wheat is king and breads are the staple of the table, while in the South rice is the staff of life. Southerners tend to be vegetarians while Bengalis are fish fanatics. The northern Bengalis also break the north–south divide by preferring rice. The Indian shortening *ghee* lends body to their cooking, especially the vegetarian dishes.

Indian flat breads are more than the staff of life. There are light puffs of deep fried *poori,* a baked leavened bread stuffed with potato (*aloo paratha*), and *papadam,* a circular spicy crisp that is the king of crackers. There are clay-oven kebabs and chicken tandoori. The curries are hot and spicy and reach the peak of heat in the *vindaloo. Raita* (yogurt and cucumber), chutney (sweet pickle), and *dal* (yellow lentils) are the relishes which neutralize the chilies. The Bengalis make *biryanis,* a flavored rice made with nuts and saffron.

Kenara Restaurant, *99 Lexington Avenue (212-684-6568). Daily 24 hours.*

Kenara is fast-food Indian, steam-table style, with the richest Indian sweets. The atmosphere is casual, cafeteria-style eating and Indians relaxing, being themselves. The curry makes no allowances for American tastes but there are refreshing mango shakes to cool down the incendiary spices. Kenara is open around the clock to satisfy the appetites of New York's cabbies.

Madras Palace, *104 Lexington Avenue between 27th and 28th Streets (212-532-3314). Monday–Saturday 11:30* A.M.*–3* P.M.*, 5:30* P.M.*–10* P.M.

The food is Madras vegetarian and the atmosphere is subdued, but not the cooking, which is hot and spicy. The *chola batura* (bread baked with chick peas) and the *bonda* (dumplings filled with vegetables) are a good way to start the meal. Madras is the only Indian restaurant in the city certified to be strictly kosher by a rabbi.

Annapurna Restaurant, *108 Lexington Avenue between 27th and 28th Streets (212-679-1284). Daily 11:30* A.M.*–3* P.M.*, 5* P.M.*–11* P.M.

The new owners haven't missed a beat; Annapurna maintains a high standard of Kerala Southern cuisine. The waiters are anxious to please and tend to hover. The decor is early maharajah. The Indian Emperor Shahjahani had his sauces flavored with almond paste, which go well with Annapurna's lamb. The Southern-style *dosa* (crepes filled with vegetables) are very good dipped in coconut chutney.

Gaylord, *102 Lexington Avenue between 27th and 28th streets (212-686-1422). Daily 11:30* A.M.*–3* P.M.*; 5* P.M.*–11:30* P.M.

Gaylord, in its latest incarnation, offers interesting variations on Indian regional cuisine. Tandoori clay-pot cooking does wonderful things to chicken, meat, and fish. Though not as luxurious as the original Gaylord, the service is first rate.

Curry in a Hurry, *119 Lexington Avenue at 28th Street (212-683-0904). Daily 10* A.M.*–4* A.M.

Curry in a Hurry used to be a hole-in-the-wall cafeteria with tasteless steam-table curry and dried out *samosa*. It is still a cafeteria, but it occupies two glittering floors with Tiffany-style globe lights and beautiful pictorial views of India and a panorama of Little India. The tandoori, vegetarian, and combination platters are a great value.

Maurya, *129 East 27th Street off Lexington Avenue (212-689-7925). Daily noon–3* P.M.*, 5* P.M.*–11* P.M.

Maurya is traditional tandoori clay-pot cooking in a sleek cosmopolitan setting. More than chicken, the tandoori surprises include *shahi paneer* (cheese with herbs) and fish *tikka* (fish marinated with spices and herbs). The inexpensive luncheon buffet is all-you-can-eat.

Shopping on the Avenue

The Lexington Avenue Indian Bazaar is best seen on weekends, when Indians arrive en masse to stock up on short-grain Indian rice and yellow lentils, shop for saris, or bargain for an appliance. It's a real family outing with Dad searching for a parking space, while the wife and kids start their circuit of the stores, sometimes with an autocratic mother-in-law in tow. The kids keep their restlessness in check, while the grown-ups look at the saris one after another, third-degree a merchant over a sewing machine, or pick through the fresh produce. They know at the end of the day they will be rewarded with an ultra-rich sweet or even a curry chow-out.

Food Markets

Indian food shops have the sweet spicy aroma of the East; plastic envelopes of spices from coriander to cumin line the shelves along with sticks of incense. There are burlap bags of basmati rice—short-grain brown and long-grain white—large enough to feed an army, and an exotic assortment of dried beans and grains, including three varieties of lentils (*malka masoor*). The produce counter looks alien to the American eye with its ginger roots, giant kaunda squashes, hot chilies, and Chinese radishes.

The stores stock a wide variety of prepared and canned Indian foods and Indian and English cleaning products with an overwhelming odor of disinfectant. Though the clientele is mostly Indian and Pakistani, there are also West Indians who cook with Indian "heat" and amateur chefs from Murray Hill. At the counter in front, by the tapes of Indian music and magazines, the Indian proprietor chatters with cronies, never missing a beat on the register as he rings up sales.

Kalustyan's, *123 Lexington Avenue between 27th and 28th streets (212-685-3451). Monday–Saturday 10 A.M.–7:30 P.M.; Sunday 11 A.M.–6 P.M.*

Kalustyan's is a holdover from the old Armenian neighborhood, but deserves a mention since it was the first to import Indian food and spices into the city. Despite the competition from Indian retailers, it holds onto its trade with exceptional products like its own spice mix for *garam masala*. It also has a full line of Middle Eastern foods, exotic coffees, and teas.

India Spice World, *126 Lexington Avenue between 28th and 29th Streets (212-686-2727). Daily 10 A.M.–7:30 P.M.*

India Spice World is neatly arranged, with a long wall of shelves like a library of Indian foods. The prices are clearly marked, which is a problem in some other stores. India has a large following from the West Indies and Guyana, where they cook with Indian spices.

Saris

Though most Indian men have opted for Western-style dress, Indian women still favor the sari and wear it with considerable flair. The sari is six yards of cloth that makes an elegant cultural statement. The draping of the sari is second nature to Indian women—with one expert motion wound around the body and flung over a shoulder. The traditional sari fabric reflects regional designs and colors, but nowadays bright Benares embroidered silks have been replaced by inexpensive Japanese and Hong Kong synthetics. A tight blouse called a *choli* and a half slip are worn under the sari.

Women from the northern and central part of India wear pastel saris, while Southern women prefer dark colors with gold brocaded edges. Generally the upper part of the sari, the *palau,* is worn over the left shoulder, but Gujarati women drape it over the right shoulder. In Madras the sari is composed of nine yards of material. Punjabi women entirely forsake the sari, favoring a tunic called the *kurta* worn over tight trousers, set off by a diaphanous scarf over the shoulders. Rajasthani women replace the sari with long printed skirts decorated like Indian figurines with mirrors and a form-fitting short-sleeved jacket.

Little India Emporium, *128 East 28th Street (212-481-0325). Monday–Saturday 10 A.M.–7:30 P.M.; Sunday noon–7 P.M.*

Indian women survey the sari collections in this second-floor establishment with a gimlet eye. The saleswomen stand diplomatically aside. The customers try one and another, and the bargaining begins. The Emporium also sells trimmings, bangles, cologne, and blouses to be worn under saris.

Sapna Sari Palace, *116 East 28th Street (212-689-6182). Monday–Saturday 10 A.M.–7 P.M.; Sunday 1 P.M.–6 P.M.*

Sapna has been around forever. The customers are familiar faces and their needs are anticipated. The fabrics and styles are classics. Weekends it's a wait to try on the saris and suitings.

Fine Arts

The art of India is a display that dazzles: radiant rainbow embroidery and bronze and brass deities in motion, carved panels too intricate to be entangled, and fabulous inlaid boxes. The arts and crafts of the nation are inextricably connected with the spiritual; the subject is the eternal, the Godhead in its many incarnations.

Annapurna Fine Arts, *120 Lexington Avenue (212-696-0229). Daily 10 A.M.–7 P.M.*

The people working in this fine arts—and crafts—shop have a passion for the arts of India, whether it's a brass of a dancing Shiva symbolizing the world's cycles or a carved panel of the regal elephant god Ganesh in all his glory. Though the Annapurna deals with the new and the "semi-antique," it has the feel of a small museum.

═══ Little India in the East Village ═══

In the days of the hippie East Village, enterprising Indians sold the counterculture Indian blouses and love beads along with the Eastern philosophy, followed by Indian meals even a hippie could afford. The fad for Indian clothes subsided in the seventies but the Indian restaurants that satisfied Bohemian appetites remained and prospered. This Indian restaurant row covers the south side of Sixth Street with tributaries on First and Second Avenues. At the latest count, there are thirty restaurants and most of them are Bangladeshi owned.

Sonali Restaurant, *326 East Sixth Street between First and Second Avenues (212-505-7517). Daily noon–1 A.M.*

Come dinner time, Sonali resembles the rush-hour IRT. People are lined up at the door, squeezed between the narrow lane of tables. The rush-hour mood extends to the service, though to be fair, the staff are ever cheerful and obliging. But the food is worth the bother, from the lighter-than-air *paratha* to the richly satisfying lamb masala. The Indian dinners, the vegetable and meat *thalis,* are a real bargain with soup, *nan* (Indian bread), a main dish, and dessert for the price of a single entree uptown.

Prince of India, *342 East Sixth Street (212-228-0388). Daily noon– midnight.*

The decoration awkwardly contrasts natural hanging plants and plastic roses. The food also has a split personality, with curries neutralized for Western tastes and shrimp tandooris that could charm a maharajah.

Windows on India, *344 Sixth Street corner of First Avenue (212-477-5956). Daily noon–midnight.*

Windows on India is Sixth Street prices with roomy, gracious dining ambience. Along with outstanding, economical meat and vegetable *thalis,* there are exciting selections, including tandoori salmon steaks and Southern Indian rice lentil crepes—*dosa.*

Mitali, *334 East Sixth Street between First and Second Avenues (212-533-5208). Daily noon–midnight.*

Mitali is spacious seating and obliging service. They don't try to hustle you out the door when they really get busy. Come with a big group and eat family style with plenty of *pakora* (cheese and vegetable fritters) and *samosa* (deep-fried pastry filled with vegetable or meat) appetizers and a variety of curries.

Haveli, *100 Second Avenue between Fifth and Sixth Streets (212-982-0533). Daily noon–midnight.*

Since Gaylord's went to restaurant heaven, Haveli is the class restaurant act in the East Village. The restaurant is designed to resemble an elegant old-fashioned Indian mansion with a balcony, the *haveli.* The menu is Indian eclectic, calculated to appeal to the most benighted tourist.

Festivals

India Day Parade

The India Day Parade celebrates Indian Independence on August 21, an Indian national holiday. The parade is organized and sponsored by the Federation of Indian Associations. The marchers are members of Indian organizations representing all the regions of India and all its language groups. The feeling is more solemn than the Fourth of July.

In its first years it went along Lexington Avenue, passing Little India, but today the parade is a Madison Avenue march from 34th Street to 21st Street. Indian dignitaries in limousines and open cars lead the line of march followed by the leaders of the Indian Federation.

The parade is Indian dance troops in gold lamé, American marching bands in high-collar uniforms and caps, and Indian raga players in white. There are floats representing the moment Indian won its freedom with gentleman in cutaway coats and floats with Indian beauties in evening gowns throwing flowers. The crowd is small but enthusiastic, waving flags with Brahman dignity. Later the marchers and the spectators join together for independence celebrations in Lexington Avenue restaurants.

India Festival

The Federation of Indian Associations takes over the Central Park Mall in the last week of May or the first week of June to celebrate the Indian Festival. It is an affirmation of the Indian identity, transcending religion and geography. There are the haunting rhythms of the sarod and sitar and dancers in extravagant costumes. Indian crafts are on display and voluptuous Indian women put on a sari fashion show. Home-cooked Indian food—breads, curries, rice *pulao,* and kebabs—are served out by members of participating organizations. There are smiles all around, and not just from the politicians, as long-lost friends and relatives exchange greetings and children play on the grass. The festival originated in 1974 with the support of Indian community leaders from around the country.

Sikh Day Parade

On the first Saturday in May Sikhs from across the nation gather in Manhattan to celebrate the *Vaisaki,* the founding of their faith and their religious and cultural identity. It is the birthday of *Khalsa,* an affirmation of a new moral code, customs, and set of beliefs that were handed down in 1699 by Guru Gobind Singh. According to the Sikh faith, at this moment in time caste and ritual were replaced by brotherhood and a doctrine of love.

The turbaned and bearded Sikhs and their wives and daughters in saris parade on Madison Avenue from 42nd Street to 23rd Street with a sense of martial dignity (they are noted soldiers in their country). The floats depict important events in Sikh history: great battles, moments of spiritual transcendence, and even tragic attacks. The recent desecration of their holy of holies, the Golden Temple, is solemnly recalled. There are also lighthearted moments, as Sikhs on parade share handfuls of nuts and currants with the spectators.

Divali

In November all Hindus observe Divali, the Indian New Year and the festival of lights. The celebrants light lamps to guide the departed souls back to earth. It is the Indian thanksgiving, though no one eats turkey. There are processions resembling the Macy's parade, with floats that are massive painted shrines with a whole range of Hindu deities, accompanied by the beating of drums and the whining of Indian woodwinds. In the spirit of other New York holidays the Indian merchants hold sales.

Little India in Flushing

Directions: Subway 7 to Main Street/Roosevelt Avenue.

During the week Indian Flushing is women and children; it is as if the men went off to war, though they are only away at work. The Indian grocery and sari shops are on Main Street, concentrated mainly, though not exclusively, between Franklin and Holly Streets. The scene in Flushing is less sophisticated than Manhattan; these are the later arrivals who don't necessarily speak English. The Indians in Flushing still keep to the extended family; there are usually three generations who wield authority. People seem to express themselves more freely in the battle between proprietors and shoppers, though the women have a modesty and shyness that hasn't been worn down by New York directness. The professional long-time resident Indians are already in Long Island and the New Jersey suburbs.

Hindu Place Mark—The Temple of Flushing

Hindu Temple of North America, *45-57 Bowne Street between Holly Avenue and 45th Avenue (718-539-1587).*

The Hindu Temple is a place of prayer and offerings (*puja*) where the priest (*pundit*), a high-caste Brahmin, leads the praises to the Indian pantheon.

Flushing's Hindu Temple of North America is the real thing; its gray pagoda tower ornamented with Indian gods and its solid walls were the work of one hundred skilled craftsman from the southern state of Andra Pradesh. In 1976 this twenty-ton granite structure was reassembled by twenty-five of these workmen.

Statues of the god Shiva, the six faces of Shanmuga, and the goddess of wealth, Lakshmi, have places of honor, but Ganesh, the elephant God, is at the center. Ganesh is wisdom, he solves problems; but he is also the god of gluttons.

On weekends and Hindu holidays the rituals are more elaborate, with the congregation sitting cross-legged, chanting, and the *pundit* in his white dhoti regaling the gods with milk and rose petals and tropical fruits while perfumed incense fills the sanctuary.

Neighborhood Restaurants

The Indians of Flushing are getting more cosmopolitan in the nineties, and even have their first local restaurant, but local Indians are still rather tentative when it comes to dining outside the home.

Shere Punjab Restaurant, *42-87 Main Street (718-358-1999). Daily 11 A.M.–11 P.M.*

The restaurant is cheerful; even empty it seems welcoming. The food of this Punjabi restaurant is rich regional cooking that luxuriates in heavy cream and butter. The afternoon buffet is a good way to get acquainted.

Shumiana, *42–47 Main Street (718-445-2262). Daily 9 A.M.–11 P.M.*

Shumiana is one of a handful of Indian restaurants that prepare only Gujarati vegetarian cuisine. They also make great sweets and a variety of exotic ice cream flavors.

Neighborhood Shopping

Indian shops in Flushing are all in a row and nondescript; if it weren't for the Indian script on the signs advertising specials you wouldn't know one from the next. The prices are lower than in Manhattan and people buy in larger quantities, but the stock is identical. The area in front of the stores is paved with asphalt and people are always milling around, with women wheeling baby carriages and men working on their cars. After school the children rush in for *julabi* pretzels (a rich sweet made with chick pea flour) and *ras gola* (cream cheese balls in syrup). On weekends the crowds can block the street. There is a sense of real community and activity around the stores, like it is the center of the Indian village.

Ganesh Grocery, *42-45 Main Street (718-461-2314). Daily 10 A.M.–10 P.M.*

Ganesh Grocery keeps a wide range of Indian publications along with an image of Lord Ganesh, an Indian god. It has a nice selection of Indian preserved fruits, nuts, and grains. In fact, it has all the staples of the Indian grocery without the clutter and disarray. It is a comfortable place to become familiar with the ingredients of the Indian table.

Indian Bazaar, *42-67 Main Street (718-358-5252). Daily 10 A.M.–8 P.M.*

The Indian Bazaar is a typical Indian market with giant cans of *ghee,* twenty-five-pound sacks of basmati rice, and spices to the ceiling, plus a very large selection of music and videos. The owners are Muslim and have announcements and fliers for events involving the Muslim community.

Japan Sari House, *42-73 Main Street (718-886-0457). Daily 10 A.M.–8:15 P.M.*

The fabrics come from Japan and the rest of the Orient; some, at least on the hangers, don't look very appropriate. This is the K-Mart of saris. The women shop here for everyday wear but go to Jackson Heights Little India to buy apparel for special occasions.

The Festival of Ganesh

In September the Hindus of the south visit Flushing's Hindu Temple on Bowne Street to celebrate Ganapathy, when Ganesh rises from the underworld. On this day women adorn Ganesh with flowers and spread before him a banquet of coconuts, bananas, oranges, and avocados. The floor of the altar is covered with flower petals. Worshipers bow to the image while throwing handfuls of rice, and periodically put their fingers on a flame carried on a silver tray and touch their foreheads.

After a vegetarian feast, the worshipers drive to the Flushing Meadow lake and put a replica of Ganesh in the water to return to the land of the dead.

═══════ Little India on 74th Street ═══════

Directions: Subway 7 or N to 74th Street/Roosevelt Avenue.

Only twenty years ago 74th Street was the usual main street mix of candy store, deli, dry cleaner's, and hardware store. It was dull but utilitarian, casual and friendly. The "Avenue" was the place to go for the essentials, when you did not feel like exerting the effort to get over to the mall.

Change came to 74th Street in 1973, as the first Indian merchants lent a hint of the exotic to the block. Subhash Kapadia and Nitin Vora opened an electronics shop that catered to overseas Indian shoppers who needed appliances with 220 current. The merchants were attracted by the convenient location, near both the subway and buses at Roosevelt and Broadway, the Queens Indian neighborhood in Flushing, and Kennedy Airport. Their success inspired other Indians to open businesses on this block.

Gradually the mom and pop stores of yesteryear yielded ground to big, bold Indian specialty stores. The shops were grand and gaudy, with an excess of mirror and chandelier. The displays were exuberant and brightly colored and the inventory, from diaphanous saris to gold filigree necklaces, was endless. The area became a veritable bazaar.

The street scene on 74th Street, Jackson Heights, is straight out of Bombay: groups of women in saris browsing for saris, extended families double-parked while stocking up on sacks of rice and cans of *ghee,* and a couple celebrating an anniversary by buying an Indian bauble, bigger than a cut diamond or a 24-carat gold necklace, and unashamedly extravagant. They all parade back and forth in a very purposeful shopping cavalcade, not even noticing the awkward and awestruck tourists coming around the corner staring into shop windows.

English may be the second language on this street, but the people, even the most self-involved shoppers, are open and friendly. The merchants are gracious and if they have the time are only too eager to discuss what's on sale, and may even give you a "special price." There is no need for any sightseer to feel self-conscious in Little India on 74th Street.

This neighborhood draws Indian, Pakistani, and Bangledeshi shoppers from all over the Eastern seaboard. They come for the familiar sights, sounds, and smells of another continent! They come for the infectious vitality and brisk tempo of life, even if it only lasts for a shopping expedition.

Eighty-two Indian retail businesses line this Indian boulevard. They include twelve restaurants, twelve groceries, seventeen jewelry stores, and twenty clothing stores specializing in saris. Although this is the largest Indian shopping area in the city, this neighborhood is purely commercial. Most of Queens' fifty-six thousand Indians live in Flushing.

The merchants who constitute Little India on 74th Street are not just about money and business, they have a strong sense of ethnic solidarity. During the devastating earthquake in 1993, which killed twenty thousand Indians, they banded together to raise thousands of dollars for relief.

Little India Bargains

Restaurants

The restaurants on 74th Street are places for a bite between buying, not for gracious dining with bowing servers and elaborate presentation. Every

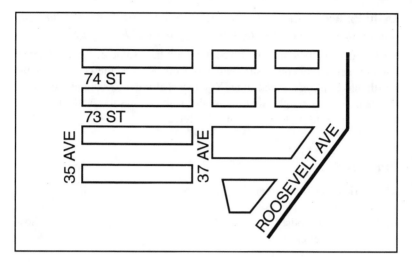

Jackson Heights/Little India

afternoon Indian eating is one endless buffet, as Asians and Occidentals see how much *dosa* (Indian vegetarian crepes), meat and vegetable curry, and tandoori chicken and kebabs they can consume in one sitting. Though at night most restaurants revert to a conventional menu with conventional waiters, the breathless rush continues as if everyone were double parked.

Jackson Heights Diner, *37-03 74th Street (718-672-1232). Daily 11:30 A.M.–10 P.M.*

The Jackson Heights Diner doesn't have the rotating stools, comfortable booths, or refrigerated cases with mile-high meringues. The restaurant is simple and sort of bare, but it does serve up inexpensive and tasty Indian food (from the gourmet South) at old-fashioned diner prices. It drew enough Manhattan "swells" for its *iddly* (lentil cakes), *dosa* (lentil and rice crepes), and incendiary vegetable curries that it decided to open a high-price Upper East Side branch.

Kwality, *37-17 74th Street (718-779-1513). Daily noon–10 P.M.*

Kwality is the name of an Indian mainstream restaurant chain. This one is more upmarket than most of the local competition. The light *poori* almost floats. The goat (very young) curry is special, a strong taste that is never gamy and still very tender. The sweets are rich and syrupy, with the almond milk fudge a standout. At the Kwality sweet shop next door Indian candy is available for enjoying at home.

Delhi Palace, *37-33 74th Street (718-507-0666). Sunday–Thursday noon–10:30 P.M.; Friday and Saturday noon–11 P.M.*

Delhi Palace is the class of 74th Street, with handsome decor and relaxed friendly service. Though the owner is from Kerala, the cuisines of the North and South get equal time. You can really get to sample the Indian kitchen, from the light *samosa* to the smooth masalas and distinctive tandoori at its 11 A.M.–4 P.M. lunch buffet.

Markets

The markets on 74th Street are bigger and more spread out than the usual Indian emporium. They sell in even bigger bulk and at lower prices than in the neighborhoods. During the Divali sales the crowds resemble those on a Delhi street corner.

Aisha Spices, *37-66 74th Street (718-458-0300). Daily 9 A.M.– 8 P.M.*

Aisha is more than just spices and the more exotic the better. It has a large produce section for fruits and vegetables that complement a curry. There are wide varieties of grains and beans (all neatly ziplocked in plastic bags), including six kinds of lentils for *dal* and other things. The rice bags are piled up like they were protecting a questionable levee.

Patel Brothers, *37-46 74th Street (718-898-3445). Daily 9:30 A.M.– 8 P.M.*

Patel may be the most common name in the Indian lexicon, but the bargains this grocery chain offers in Indian delicacies and staples are unique (though not everybody is interested in forty-five-pound bags of Indus Valley basmati). The Brothers supply Queens and Long Island with fine prepared chutneys, pickles, curry, mango pulp, cashews, and their own brand of *chappati* flour.

Saris with Style

In this Little India the shops are more contemporary and upbeat, and even the mannequins look like they are having a good time. The stores are more department store style than boutique. They do their best to highlight the designs and fabrics, hanging them from on high or neatly stacking them in rows. If there is space left over, they'll squeeze in fabrics for men's suits, cut-rate perfumes, 220-current appliances, or 22-carat gold necklaces.

ISP, *37-07 74th Street (718-426-2700). Daily 10:30 A.M.–7:30 P.M.*

Of course the initials stand for Indian Sari Palace; almost all the sari shops are called some variation of sari palace. The store is vast and the salesmen are tireless, racing around with yardstick in hand to cut fabrics for their very demanding clientele. Throughout the day the same men do battle with discounters from the Manhattan garment center peddling their "goods." ISP also retails ties, perfumes, and fabrics for men's apparel.

Indian Gold

The United States may have gone off the gold standard, but that glittering commodity has lost none of its luster for the Indians. They are the original gold bugs and hoarding this metal is practically a national obsession. Diamonds may be a Western woman's best friend, but for an Indian it's bound to be gold, the basic ingredient of any respectable dowry. While the West is content with 14 and 18 carat, Indian jewelry is gold at its purest, 22 and 24 carat. The jewelry is classical, the image of the ornaments worn by gods and demigods carved on temple walls. Don't expect spare delicacy.

Bhindi Jewelers USA, *37-30 74th Street (718-505-1555). Wednesday–Monday 11 A.M.–7 P.M.*

Bhindi is Indian contemporary with recessed lighting and jewelry displayed like pictures at an exhibition, in stylish frames or in sleek display cases. The necklaces, earrings, bracelets, bangles, and *karas* (for the men) are Indian elaborate without going over the top. The sales help are helpful and won't inquire at every pause in the conversation if the customer is ready to buy.

Sona Chaandi, *37-14 74th Street (718-429-4653). Daily 11 A.M.– 7 P.M.*

Sona Chaandi is a Queens single-family house done up to resemble a jewelry store straight out of Vegas, Atlantic City, or Dehli. Crystal chandeliers and great expanses of mirrors are everywhere, and the letters of the store name above the plate glass and on the stairs are brilliant scarlet. Behind the glass next to all the gold that glitters, including coins and bars, there is a mechanical mannequin compulsively trying on a necklace. Worth a visit for the curiosity value.

Index

A

A & B Trading (food store), 244
A & N Food Market, 439–40
A La Vieille Russie Gift Shop, 284
A. W. Kaufman Clothing Store, 196
Abbey Tavern, 111
Abyssinian Baptist Church, 320
Ach Tov Restaurant, 210
Adam Clayton Powell, Jr., Gallery, 321
Adnan Restaurant, 296
African-American Day Parade, 327–28
African Americans
    arts, 323–24, 332
    associations and cultural centers,
        310–13, 328, 331, 332–33
    bakeries, 325
    broadcasting, 315, 328
    celebrations, 327–29, 334
    history and settlement, 4, 99, 104,
        308–18, 329–32
    museums and archives, 321–23
    music, 326–27
    nightclubs, 326–27
    places of worship, 320–21
    publications, 310, 314
    restaurants
        in Brooklyn, 333
        in Harlem, 324–26
    See also Cubans; Dominicans; Haitians;
        West Indians
African Street Festival, 334
Aigner's Chocolates of Distinction,
    57
Aisha Spices, 484
Al-Ajami Restaurant, 305
Al-Ghadeer Restaurant, 303
Al-Sharequi Groceries, 300
Alba Bakery, 171
Albany Bake Shop, 216

Alku Toinen Finnish Cooperative
    Apartments, 94
Allan's Quality Bakery, 342
Alleva Dairy, 141
Al Noor Halal Meat, 303–304
Alnoor Clothing Store, 299
American Cut Flowers, 247
American Ethnic Parade, 18, 286
American Federation of Labor, 100
American Hungarian Library, 64
American Irish Historical Society, 108
American Museum of Immigration, 10
American Scandinavian Society of New
    York, 86
American-Scandinavian Foundation, 86
Americas Society, 402
Amici's Restaurant, 161
Ana's Bakery, 373
Ancient Order of Hibernians, 125, 126
Andrusha Cafe, 284
Andy's Tavern, 150–51
Angel's Flake Patties, 347
Angelos Food Emporium, 244
Annapurna Fine Arts Store, 476
Annapurna Restaurant, 473
antiforeign attitudes, 4
Apollo Theater, 324
Aquascutum (clothing store), 39
Aquavit Restaurant, 87
Arab Mosque (in Brooklyn), 294
Arab Party (*Mahrajan*), 300–301
Arabs
    associations and cultural centers, 302,
        304–305
    bakeries, 297–98, 303
    belly dancing, 306–307
    broadcasting, 300
    clothing and cosmetics, 299–300
    festivals and observances, 300–301, 307

Arabs *(continued)*
  food stores, 298–99, 303
  history and settlement, 286–93
  music, 300, 306
  places of worship, 294–95, 304–305
  restaurants
    Atlantic Avenue neighborhood (Brooklyn), 295–97
    in Bay Ridge (Brooklyn), 302–303
    in Manhattan, 305–306
Arbeely, Joseph, 289
Arbeely, Najib, 287
Arion singing group, 45
Arthur Avenue neighborhood, Italian culture in, 159–60
Arthur Avenue Poultry Market, 164
Arthur Avenue Retail Market, 159
Artuso's Cafe and Bakery, 162
Asia de Cuba Restaurant, 379–80
Asia Society Garden, 459
Asian Children's Day celebration, 452
Asian-American Dance Theater, 418
Asians. *See* East Indians; Far East Asians.
    See also under specific nationalities
Asprey and Company (clothing store), 40
associations and cultural centers
    for city founders' history, 21–24, 35–36
    for general ethnic history, 13–16
    See also under specific cultural groups
Astor, John Jacob, 43, 50, 238
Astoria, Greek culture in, 234, 237–39
Astron Gift Shop, 245
Atlantic Avenue neighborhood, Arab culture in, 292–93
Audubon, James, 348, 370
Audubon Terrace, 318
Auggie's Brownstone Inn, 333
Aunt Len's Doll and Toy Museum, 322
Austrian Cultural Institute, 51–52
Austrians, history and settlement, 4
Avegerinos Restaurant, 249
Avery Fisher Hall, 51
Ayrassi Pastry, 303
Azteca Deli Grocery, 384

B
Badoo's International Restaurant, 347
Bahamas (nightclub), 374

Bainbridge, Irish culture in, 113–18
Balanchine, George, 281
Balducci's (food store), 156
Bally Bunion Pub, 124
Bangladeshis. *See* East Indians
Barbados Bakery, 342
Barbisio & Cellini Hat Shop, 222
Bari Pork Store, 171
Barney Greengrass Delicatessen, 205
Bartholdi, Frederic Auguste, 9
Bartok, Bela, 61
Baryshnikov, Mikhail, 281
Batista, Fulgencio, 376
Battery Park, 154
Bay Palace Seafood Restaurant, 433–34
Bay Ridge
    Arab culture in, 301–302
    Irish culture in, 122–25
    Norwegian culture in, 80–81
Bedford-Stuyvesant, African American culture in, 329–32
Bedford-Stuyvesant Restoration Center, 332
Bedloes Island, 9, 10
Beirut Makolate (food store), 232–33
Belvedere Bakery, 171
Bella's Mini Market, 279
Belmont neighborhood, Italian culture in, 157–59
Benin Gallery, 322
Benito's The Original Restaurant, 138
Benito's II Restaurant, 138
Bennett house, 34
Bensonhurst, Italian culture in, 166–67
Berk of Burlington Arcade (clothing store), 39
Bernadette Ryan's Irish Shop, 112
Beth Hamedrash Hagodol Synagogue, 190
Bhindi Jewelers USA, 485
Bialystoker Synagogue, 190
Biancardi's Butcher Shop, 164
Bicentennial Bakery and Restaurant, 354
Big Paddy's, 116
Bill's Flower Market, 247, 248
Billie Holiday Theater, 332
Birdland, 326–27
Black Fashion Museum, 322
Black Sea Bookstore, 228
Black Thorn Pub, 116
Bleecker Street Pastry, 146

Blessing of the Waters, 251–52
Bliss Tavern, 121
Block, Adriaen, 21
Block Island, 73
Bobover Hasidic Synagogue, 209
Body Shop, The, 13
Bohemian Hall, 71
Bois Verna, 350
Bonsai Dynasty, 459
Bonsai Garden, 459
Borgatti's Ravioli & Noodle Company, 163
Borough Park, Jewish culture in, 207–13
boroughs, characteristics of, vi
Boswyk, 329
Botánica Reyes, 375
botánicas, 355, 366–67, 374–75
Bowling Green, The, 25–26
Bowne House, 32
Brasilia Restaurant, 398
Brazilian Independence Day Festival,
    399–400
Brazilians
    festivals, 399–400
    history and settlement, 397
    music, 399
    restaurants, 398–99
    shopping, 399
Bright Bakery, 434
Brighton Beach, Jewish culture in, 223–28
British
    clothing and furnishings, 38–41
    food stores, 38
    founding role of, 23–24
    restaurants, 13, 36–38
British Open Pub, 38
broadcasting
    African American, 315, 328
    Arab, 300
    Cuban, 376
    ethnic variety programming, 17
    Haitian, 350
    Korean, 446
Bronck, Jonas, 28, 74
Bronx
    Irish culture in, 113–20
    Italian culture in, 151, 157–59
    founders' place marks in, 28–30
Bronx County Historical Society, 15
Brooklyn
    Arab culture in, 292–93

ethnic shifts in, 6
German culture in, 45, 57–58
Haitian culture in, 352–53
Irish culture in, 122–25
Italian culture in, 136, 166–67,
    173–74
Jewish culture in, 207–13
Polish culture in, 259–60, 264–65
Brooklyn Battery Tunnel, 292
Brooklyn Botanic Gardens, 459, 462
Brooklyn Bridge, 57–58, 123, 213
Brooklyn Ethnic Music and Dance Folk
    Festival, 19
Brooklyn Historical Society, 15
Budapest Pastry, 65
Buddhist places of worship, 415, 437,
    457–58
Burberrys, Ltd. (clothing store), 39
Burlingham Slip, 12
Bushwick, 55, 329
Byblos Restaurant, 305

C

C'est si bon Restaurant, 449
Cabana Carioca Restaurant, 398
Cabrini, Francesca, 144
Cafe Al Mercato, 159
Cafe Arbat, 226
Cafe Biondo, 140
Cafe Cappuccino, 225
Cafe Edelweiss, 242
Cafe Fledermaus, 13
Cafe Giardino, 169
Caffe Carciofo, 175
Caffe Mille Luci, 170
Caffe Roma, 140–41
Calabria Pork Store, 164
Calandra Cheese Shop, 164
Cali Viejo Restaurant, 394
Cali Viejo II Restaurant, 394
Canaan Bakery, 454
Canaan Baptist Church, 321
Canal Food Corp, 428
Candy Man (sweet shop), 212
Canton Gourmet Restaurant, 439
Capri Bakery, 365
Caputo's Bakery, 176
Caribbean All-Stars Festival, 344
Caribbean Studies Institute, 339

Caribbeans. *See under specific nationalities*
Carl Schurz Park, 50
Carnegie Deli, 205
Carosello Penagramma Italiano (gift shop), 142
Carroll Gardens, 173–74
Casa Del Mar Restaurant, 394–95
Casa Italiana, 153
Casa Rosa Restaurant, 174
Casa Victoria Cafe, 147
Casablanca Ritz Cafe, 307
Casimir, John, 254
Castle Clinton, 8–9
Castle Garden Immigration Station, 44, 99
Castle Garden Landing Depot, 3
Cedars of Lebanon Restaurant, 306–307
Celtic Connection Gift Shop, 118
Central Park, 213
Central Synagogue, 201
Centro Español, 401
Centrum Ksiask Polskiej (Polish Book Center), 267
Cerini Coffee & Gifts, 165
Chao Fu Lau Restaurant, 425
Charles Weiss Clothing Store, 196
Chassidic Art Institute, 216
Chatham Square Chapel, 311
Chavez, Cesar, 381
Cheffy's Jamaican Restaurant, 341
Chelsea, Spanish culture in, 400–401
Cherry Blossom Festival (*Sakura Matsura*), 462
Chez Price & Jean Restaurant, 353
Chicanos. *See* Hispanics
China Buddhist Association, 437
China Glatt Restaurant, 210
Chinatown, 410–18
Chinatown (Flushing/Queens), 436–37
Chinatown (Sunset Park/Brooklyn), 432–33
Chinatown Cultural Festival, 432
Chinatown History Museum, 416
Chinatown Summer Outdoor Festival, 415
Chinese
  associations and cultural centers, 407, 408, 411, 414, 415–16, 433, 437–38
  bakeries, 425–26, 434–35, 439–40
  banquet halls (Chinatown), 418–25
  festivals, 407, 415, 430–32
  food stores, 427–29, 436, 439–40
  gift shops, 430
  herbalists, 429, 436, 440
  history and settlement, 4, 5, 6, 379, 405–409, 432–33
  monuments, 414
  museums and galleries, 415–16
  music, 438
  places of worship, 415
  publications, 412
  restaurants
    in Flushing (Queens), 438–39
    in Sunset Park (Brooklyn), 433–34
    in Chinatown, 418–25
  teahouses and ceremonies, 426–27
  theater and dance, 416–18
Chinese Consolidated Benevolent Association, 414
Chinese Country Kitchen, 423
Chinese Cubans
  history and settlement, 379
  restaurants, 379–80
Chinese Dance Company of New York, 417
Chinese Independence Day(s) Parade(s), 432
Chinese Merchants' Association, 414
Chinese New Year, 407, 430–31
Chinese-American Arts Council, 415–16
Chisolm, Shirley, 314, 331
Christatos & Koster Flower Shop, 248
Christina's Restaurant, 263
Christine's Restaurant, 270–71
Church of the Most Precious Blood (Catholic), 137
Church of the Transfiguration (Chinese), 415
City Lore—New York Center for Urban Folk Culture, 15–16
Civic Center, 103–105
Clan Na Gael, 120
Clemente, Lilia, 465
Club Broadway, 385
Cobble Hill, 173–74, 292
Cock's Bajan Restaurant, 342
Cocles Town, 33
Coco Pazzo Restaurant, 156
Coisa Nossa (newsstand/music store), 399
Coleman, John, 96
Collect, The, 129
Colombians
  food stores, 395

history and settlement, 391–93
publications, 392
restaurants, 393–95
Colored Orphan's Asylum, 100
Columbia University, 36
Columbus Day Parade, 177–78
comogie (women's hurling), 119
Confucius Plaza and monument, 414
Cong Ly Restaurant, 443
Congregation Shearith-Israel, 201
Congregation Yetev Lev D'Satmar,
    220–21
Congregational Church of the Pilgrims, 294
Continental Restaurant, 264
Copeland's Restaurant, 325
Corfu Center (gift shop/newsstand), 245
Costanza's Gifts, 165
Costello's Bar, 110, 112
Cosy House Restaurant, 453
Cotton Club, 316, 323, 326, 327
Court Pastry, 177
Court Street neighborhood, Italian culture
    in, 173–74
Crazy Chicken Restaurant, 394
Cream Puff bakery, 54
creole restaurants, 350–51
criolla restaurants, 363–64, 366, 372–73
Criminal Courts Building and Prison (The
    Tombs), 104
Cristoforo Colombo Bakery, 170
Crow Hill, 213, 337
Crown Bagel, 216
Crown Deli, 209
Crown Heights
    Jewish culture in, 213–18
    West Indian culture in, 337–39
Crown Palace Hotel, 215
Cruz, Celia, 368
Cuban Day Parade, 378–79
Cubans
    arts, 376
    broadcasting, 376
    festivals, 378–79
    history and settlement, 5, 6, 375–77, 379
    publications, 376
    restaurants, 377–78
Cucina Regionale Restaurant, 145
Curry in a Hurry, 473
Cypriot Emigrant Cultural Organization
    (CYPRECO), 240

Czech Festival, 72
Czechs
    associations and cultural centers, 67–68,
        69, 70, 71
    festivals, 72
    history and settlement, 66–71
    places of worship, 71
    restaurants, 72

D
D'Amico Foods, 175
D & A Merchandise (women's clothing
    store), 196
Da Nico Restaurant, 138
da Ponte, Lorenzo, 128
da Verrazano, Giovanni, 127
Dai Thanh Food Market, 443
Dairy Farm Food Product 428
Dalmazio Imports, 173
Damascus Bakery, 298
Dance Theater of Harlem, 324
Danes
    associations and cultural centers, 74–75
    history and settlement, 73–75
    publications, 75
Dante Alighieri monument, 154
Danza's Restaurant, 168
David's Restaurant, 231
De Lillo Pastries, 161
Del Pueblo Restaurant, 364
DeLancey mansion, 26
Delhi Palace Restaurant, 484
Derby Pub, 117
Deutsch-Amerikanische Scheuetzen
    Gesellschaft, 47
Deutsches Haus, 51
Dewar's Restaurant, 341
Di Paolo's Dairy, 141
Diamond District, 201
Din Lay Company (gift shop), 430
Dionysos Taverna, 241
Divali (Indian New Year) celebration,
    478–79
Doctor's Row, 149
Dominican Day Parade, 375
Dominican Record Shop, 374
Dominican Studies Institute, 371–72
Dominicans
    archives, 371–72

Dominicans *(continued)*
 bakeries, 373
 botanicas, 374–75
 festivals, 375
 history and settlement, 368–70
 music, 374
 publications, 372
 restaurants, 372–73
Dominick's Restaurant, 160–61
Don Enterprises Gift Shop, 430
Don Paco Lopez Bakery, 389
Donna's Jerk Chicken, 347
Dou Rei Buffet, 449
Douglass, Frederick, 311
Dutch
 founders organizations and archives,
  34–36
 founding role of, 21–23, 32–33, 34–36
 terms and place names, 34
Dutch Hill, 45
Dutch West India Company, 22, 23, 32
Dvorak, Antonin, 68
Dyckman House, 28
Dynasty Supermarket, 428

E
E. Rossi & Co. (gift shop), 142
Eamon Doran Restaurant, 111
East Broadway Gourmet Restaurant, 422
East Flatbush neighborhood, 345–46
East Harlem, Italian culture in, 148–50
East Harlem Music School, 367
East Indians
 associations and cultural centers, 470,
  471, 478
 festivals, 477–79, 481
 clothing and furnishings, 484–85
 food stores, 474–75, 480–81, 484
 gift shops, 475–76
 history and settlement, 469–72, 481–82
 jewelry stores, 485
 publications, 471
 restaurants
  in East Village, 476–77
  in Flushing (Queens), 480–81
  in Jackson Heights (Queens), 482–84
  Lexington Avenue (Manhattan),
   472–73
 sari stores, 475, 481, 484–85

shopping, 474
East Lake Restaurant, 438
East Village
 East Indian culture in, 476–77
 Ukrainian culture in, 275–78
Eastern States Buddhist Temple of
  America, 415
Ebbets Field, 213
Eddie's Delicatessen, 117
Educational Alliance, 190–91
Egidio Cafe and Bakery, 162
Eichler's Judaica store, 212
Eiffel, Alexandre Gustave, 9
18th Avenue Bakery, 170
El Barrio, 360–61
El Barrio Center (music store), 367–68
El Barrio Steak House, 364
El Buen Gusto Restaurant, 388
El Congo Botánica, 366–67
El Conquistador Restaurant, 389
El Meson Colombiano, 395
El Pollo Dorado Restaurant, 373
El Ranchito Restaurant, 384
El Sitio Restaurant, 395
El-Asmar International Delights (food
  store), 299
Eldridge Jobbing House (linens store),
  198
Elias Corner Restaurant, 241
Ellis, Samuel, 11
Ellis Island, 3, 9, 10–12, 33, 37
Elvie's Turo-Turo Restaurant, 466
Emilia's Restaurant, 160
Empire State Building, 77
Emporium Brazil, 399
English
 founders' organizations and archives,
  35–36
 history and settlement, 2
 restaurants, 19
 See also British
English Harbor Fish & Chips, 37
English-Speaking Union of the United
  States, 36
Enrico Fermi Cultural Center, 159–60
Ericson, John, 76, 85
Ericson, Leif, 77, 85
Esposito Pork Store, 175–76
Espresso bars, 169–71
Estia Restaurant, 249

Ethnic Folk Arts Center, 16
ethnic history
    museums and archives, 13–15
    organizations, 15–16
    See also under specific nationalities
European Bridal Favors, 172
Excellent Dumpling Noodle Shop, 425
    exploring, guidelines for, v–vi
Ezra Cohen Linens Store, 198

F

F & S Meat Market, 272
Faicco Pork Stores, 147
Family Store, 303
Fang Yang Old House, 439
Far East Asians, 405–468
Farel O'Toole's Pub, 121
Farrel House, 123
Fashion Avenue, 201
Fatoosh Barbecue, 295–96
Fatoosh Pitza, 298
Feast of Our Lady of Mt. Carmel
    (Belmont/Bronx), 165
Feast of Sacrifice (*Id-al-Adha*), 307
Feast of St. Anthony of Padua
    Belmont/Bronx, 166
    South Village, 148
Feast of St. Rosalia (Bensonhurst), 173
Felafel 'N' Stuff Restaurant, 306
Ferrara's Bakery, 141
Ferraro, Geraldine, 134
Festa Italiana, 145, 148
Festa of Our Lady of Mount Carmel, 149,
    150, 151, 159
Festa of San Gennaro, 136, 137, 143
Festival of Ganesh, 481
Festival of Simchas Torah, 222–223
Festival of the Arts (Jewish), 207
festivals
    African American, 334
    Arab, 300–301
    Brazilian, 399–400
    Chinese, 430–32
    Cuban, 378–79
    Czech, 72
    Dominican, 375
    East Indian, 477–79, 481
    of ethnic diversity, 18–20
    Filipino, 467–68

    Hispanic, 404
    Hungarian, 66
    Irish, 125–26
    Italian, 136, 142–43, 148–50, 151, 158,
        165–66, 173, 177–78
    Jewish, 199, 205–206
    Korean, 451, 452, 456
    Norwegian, 84–85
    Polish, 272–73
    Puerto Rican, 368
    Spanish, 404
    Swedes, 89–90
    Ukrainian, 280–81
    Vietnamese, 443–44
    West Indian, 339, 344–45
FFA Gallery, 261
Fiesta de Santiago Apostole, 404
Filipinos
    associations and cultural centers, 465–66
    festivals, 467–68
    food stores, 467
    history and settlement, 462–65
    restaurants, 466–67
Fine & Klein (leather goods store), 197
Fine & Shapiro Restaurant, 204
Finns
    associations, 91, 94
    history and settlement, 90–92
    place marks in Sunset Park, 92–95
    publications, 94
    sauna tradition, 95
Fiona's, 119
Fire Department Museum, 106
First Avenue Meat Products, 272
First Zen Institute of America, 458
Fishkin's Clothing Store, 195
Five Corners neighborhood, 103
Five Points, 310
Flannery's Bar, 111
Flatbush
    Jewish culture in, 229–30
    West Indian culture in, 345–46
Flaum Appetizers, 221
Floridita Restaurant, 378
Floris Toiletries Store, 40
Flushing
    Chinese culture in, 436–37
    East Indian culture in, 479
    Korean culture in, 451–52
    founders place marks in, 30–32

Flushing Chinatown Planning Council, 437
Flushing Remonstrance, 30, 32
Flushing Town Hall, 31–32
Foley Square, 104
Folksbeine Theater, 203
Fordham Manor neighborhood, 157
Forman's Clothing Store, 196
Fort George, 25
Forzano Italian Imports, 142
founders of New York, 21–24
  organizations and archives, 34–36
  place marks
    in Flushing, 30–32
    in Harlem, 27–28
    in Lower Manhattan, 24–34
    in the Bronx, 28–30
    in Washington Heights, 27
    on Staten Island, 32–34
Fountain Cafe, 296–97
Four Seasons Players, 417
Fox Oaks Rock, 32
Francisco Verrazano monument, 154
Frank Randazzo's Sons Fish Market, 165
Fratelli Raviolli, 177
Fraunces Tavern, 26
Freie Bibliotek und Lesehalle, 47
French and Indian War, 24
Friend's Meeting House, 31
Friml, Rudolph, 68
Fulton Farmer's Market, 12, 13
Fulton Fish Market, 12

G

G & G Projections (clothing store), 197
G & M Kosher Caterers, 193
G. Youn and Company Gift Store, 455
Gaelic football, 119–20
Gaelic Park, 103, 115
  Sports Center, 120
Galaxy Cafe, 242
Gallery Nillson, 89
Gam Mee Ok Restaurant, 448–49
Gambero & Rosso Restaurant, 168
Ganesh, Festival of, 481
Ganesh Grocery, 480
Garden of Fragrances and Aromas, 300
Garibaldi, Giuseppe, monument, 128, 154
Garibaldi-Meucci Museum, 137–38

Garment Center, 200–201
Garvey, Marcus, 335
Gaylord, 473
Gebhardt's Restaurant, 56
General Slocum, sinking of, 45, 47, 48
George's Kreopoleion (butcher shop), 245
German Cathedral, 48
German Dispensary, 48
German Jews. *See* Jews
Germania Orchestra, 50
Germans
  associations and cultural centers, 2, 44, 47, 56
  bakeries, 53–54
  in Brooklyn, 57–58
  delicatessens, 54, 57
  in the East Village, 47–48
  exhibits and archives, 51–52
  festivals, 49, 58–59
  food stores and butchers, 57
  history and settlement, 2, 42–49, 50
  music, 50–51
  publications, 49
  restaurants, 52–54, 56
  in Ridgewood, 55–57
  in Yorkville, 48–49, 50
Gertel's Bakery, 193
Gianni's Restaurant, 13
Gibran, Kahlil, 289
Gig Young Bakery, 343
Gino's Foccaceria, 168
Gino's Pastry Shop, 161
Glaser's Bakery, 54
Glatt Dynasty, 203
Glocca Morra Pub, 110
Gloria's In and Out Restaurant, 341
Goatville, 360
Goethe House, 51
Golden Key Food Store, 228
Golden Malaysian Restaurant, 423–24
Golden Monkey, 438
Golden Unicorn Banquet Hall, 420
Gran Cafe Italia, 170
Grand Central Station, 75
Grand Deli, 194
Grand Ticino Restaurant, 145
Great Irish Fair, 126
Grecian Cave (nightclub), 243
Greek Independence Day, 250–51

Greeks
  associations and cultural centers,
    236–37, 240, 245, 251
  bakeries, 242, 250
  festivals, 245, 247, 250–52
  flower markets, 247–48
  food stores, 244–45, 250
  gift shops, 243–44, 245
  history and settlement, 234–52
  music and dance, 240, 242
  nightclubs, 242–43
  publications, 236, 245
  restaurants/tavernas
    in Astoria (Long Island), 240–41, 243
    in Manhattan, 248–50
Green Farm (food store), 454
Greenpoint, Polish culture in, 259–60,
    264–65
Greenwich Village
  East Indian culture in, 476–77
  Italian culture in, 143–48
  Ukrainian culture in, 275–78
  See also East Village
Grinnell Gallery, 323
Guang Ming Herbal Store, 429
Guss's Pickles, 193
Gustavus Adolphus Lutheran Church, 53
Guttman's Restaurant, 211
Guv'nors, 37
Guyana Roti House, 347
Guyon-Lake-Tysen house, 34

H
H & M Simcha Center (gift shop), 213
Habana San Juan Restaurant, 388
Haiti Art D'Inc., 351
Haitians
  art, 351
  associations and cultural centers, 349,
    352
  bakeries, 354
  botanicas, 355
  broadcasting, 350
  history and settlement, 5, 348–50
  music, 354–55
  publications, 349, 350
  restaurants (Brooklyn), 353–54
  restaurants (Manhattan), 350–51
  Voudou rites, 355

Hakubai Restaurant, 461
Hallet's Cove, 238
Ham II Kwan Restaurant, 449
Hamafitz Stam Judaica shop, 217
Hamilton Heights, 318
Han Ah Rheum Food Store
    (Koreatown/Manhattan), 450
Han Ah Reum Market (Flushing/Queens),
    455
Hans's Gasthaus, 56
Happy Dumpling Restaurant, 438
Harlem
  African American culture in, 315–19
  founders' place marks in, 27–28
  Italian culture in, 148–50
  Puerto Rican culture in, 360–62
Harlem Week, 328
Harmony Palace, 421
Harris Levy Linens Store, 198
Hatsuhana Restaurant, 461
Havel, Vaclav, 69, 72
Haveli Restaurant, 477
Hee Seung Fung Teahouse, 421
Heidelberg Restaurant, 52
Hell's Kitchen neighborhood, 18–19, 45,
    101
Henderson Place, 50
Henry Street Settlement, 191
Hessians. See Germans
Hindu Temple of North America, 479, 481
Hispanic Society of America Museum, 402
Hispanic-American Day Celebration, 404
Hispanics
  bakeries, 389–90
  festivals, 404
  food stores, 396
  history and settlement, 390–91
  in Williamsburg/Brooklyn, 220
  museums and archives, 402
  music, 397
  restaurants
    in Jackson Heights (Queens), 395–96
    in Sunset Park (Brooklyn), 388–89
  theater, 403
  See also specific nationalities
Ho's Ginseng & Company, 429
Hodgson, Robert, 30
Holland Society of New York, 35
Honcharenko, Ahapius, 273
Hong Fat Restaurant, 423

Hong Kong immigrants. *See* Chinese
Hotel Theresa, 320
Hudson, Henry, 21
Hughes, John (Catholic Archbishop), 106
Hughes, Langston, 335
Hunan House Restaurant, 422
Hungarian House (cultural center), 64
Hungarian Independence Day celebration,
   66
Hungarians
   associations and cultural centers, 60,
      64
   bakeries, 65
   bookstores and libraries, 63
   festivals, 66
   food shops, 64–66
   history and settlement, 5, 59–66
   publications, 59, 60, 63
   restaurants, 64–66
Hunt, Richard M., 9
Hunterfly Houses, 332
Hunts Point Market, 448
hurling and *comogie,* 119
Hus, Jan, 67
Hyatt Homestead, 119
Hyde Park Antiques Store, 41

I

Ice Cream Center, 212
Id-al-Adha (Feast of Sacrifice), 307
Ideal, 53
Il Bocconcino Restaurant, 146
Il Colloseo Restaurant, 167
Il Cortile Restaurant, 139
Il Nido Restaurant, 155
Il Vigneto Restaurant, 156
illegal aliens, policy toward, 6
Imatra Hall, 92, 93–94, 95
immigration
   historical events influencing. *See
     historical sections in each chapter*
   places connected with, 8–16
   quotas and policy changes. *See
     historical sections in each chapter*
Immigration and Naturalization Service
   (INS), 13
Independent Kletzker Brotherly Aid
   Society, 189

India Day Parade, 477–78
India Festival, 478
India Spice World, 474–75
Indian Bazaar, 480
Indian New Year. *See Divali*
Indians. *See* East Indians; Native
   Americans
Indo-Chinatown, 440–41
International Grocery, 250
International Home, The, 88
International *Moshiach* Center, 218
International Restaurant, 389
Ipanema Restaurant, 398–99
Irish
   associations and cultural centers, 2, 97,
     99, 106, 107–108, 115
   bakeries, 118, 119
   festivals, 99, 120, 125–26
   clothing and crafts, 112
   delicatessens, 117–18, 119
   firehouse companies, 105–106
   gift and craft shops, 112, 118, 122, 124
   history and settlement, 2, 6, 96–103
   in Bainbridge, 113–18
   in Bay Ridge (Brooklyn), 122–25
   in the Bronx, 113–20
   in Manhattan, 103–12
   in Woodlawn, 118–19
   in Woodside (Queens), 120–22
   music. *See* restaurants and pubs
   publications, 16–17, 97, 108
   restaurants and pubs (Bainbridge), 115–17
   restaurants and pubs (Bay Ridge), 124
   restaurants and pubs (Manhattan),
     109–12
   restaurants and pubs (Woodside), 121–22
   sports, 119–20
Irish American Cultural Center of New
   York, 108
Irish Arts Center, 108
Irish Books and Graphics store, 108
Irish Imports, 122
Irish Pub East, 111
Irish Secret (clothing store), 112
Islamic Center, 304
Islamic Cultural Center, 305
Islamic Society of Bay Ridge, 302
ISP (Indian Sari Palace), 485
Israel Folk Dance Festival, 207

Israel Gift Center, 198
Issawi Halal Meat and Groceries, 304
Ital Delight Restaurant, 341
Italian Consulate, 153
Italian Cultural Institute, 153
Italian Food Center, 141
Italian Historical Society of America, 153
Italian Opera House, 128
Italian Village, 143–48
Italians, 177–78
    associations and cultural centers,
        130–31, 133, 153 158, 159–60, 178
    cafes and bakeries
        in the Bronx, 161–63
        in Brooklyn, 169–71, 175, 176–77
        in Manhattan, 140–41
        in South Village, 146–47
    festivals, 136, 177–78
        in the Bronx, 158
        in Brooklyn, 165–66, 173
        in Manhattan, 142–43
        in South Village, 148–50
    delicatessens, 163, 164
    food stores, 141–42, 147–48, 156–57,
        163–65, 171–72, 175–77
    gift shops, 142, 165, 172–73
    history and settlement, 127–34, 134–57,
        166–67
    in East Harlem, 148–50
    in Greenwich Village, 143–48
    in the Mulberry Street neighborhood,
        134–38
    in the Uptown neighborhood, 151–54
    monuments, 153–54
    museums and archives, 137–38, 153
    music, 169–71, 173
    places of worship, 137, 144–45, 150
    publications, 129, 133
    restaurants
        in Belmont (the Bronx), 160–61
        in Bensonhurst, 167–69
        in the Court Street neighborhood,
            174–75
        in East Harlem, 150–51
        in South Village, 145–46
        in Uptown (Manhattan), 154–55
        in the Mulberry Street neighborhood,
            138–40
Itzu's Restaurant, 221

J
Jackson Heights
    East Indian culture in, 481–82
    Hispanic culture in, 390–91
Jackson Heights Diner, 483
Jade Palace Sea Food Restaurant, 439
Jaeger Clothing Store, 39
Jagiellonia Restaurant, 263
Jamaicans. *See* West Indians
Jan Hus Presbyterian Church, 71
Japan Gallery, 458
Japan Sari House, 481
Japan Society, 457, 460
Japanese
    associations and cultural centers, 457
    festivals, 462
    gardens, 459–60
    history and settlement, 456
    museums and galleries, 458
    music, 457
    places of worship, 457–58
    publications, 458
    restaurants and sushi bars, 460–62
Japanese Buddhist Church, 457–58
Jeweler's National Exchange, 201
Jewish Daily Forward, 189
Jewish Museum, 202
Jewish Repertory Theater, 203
Jewish Theological Seminary, 202
Jews
    appetizer shops, 204–205, 221
    associations and cultural centers, 183,
        185, 189, 190–91, 199–200, 207, 208,
        224
    bakeries, 193–94, 211–12, 216–17, 228,
        232–33
    caterers, 193
    festivals and observances, 199, 206–207,
        222–23
    clothing and furnishings, 194–98, 222
    delicatessens, 13, 192, 193–94, 205–206,
        209–10, 221–22, 227–28
    food stores, 193–94, 211, 227–28, 232–33
    gift shops, 198–99, 212–13, 217–18,
        220, 233
    history and settlement, 4, 5, 114,
        179–86, 186–89, 223–24, 229–30
    museums and archives, 190–91, 202,
        215–16

Jews *(continued)*
  nightclubs, 225–27
  publications, 189, 228
  restaurants
    in Borough Park (Brooklyn), 209–11,
      212
    in Brighton Beach (Brooklyn), 224–27
    in Crown Heights (Brooklyn), 216–17
    in Flatbush (Brooklyn), 230–32
    on the Lower East Side, 191–92
    in Manhattan, 203–206
    in Williamsburg (Brooklyn), 220–22
  synagogues, 190, 201–202, 209, 220
  theater, 203
Jimmy's Lechonería, 364
Jing Fong Banquet Hall, 420
Jobst & Ebbinghaus Butcher Shop, 57
Jodamo International Clothing Store, 197
Jodo Shinshu Buddhist sect, 457
Joe's Italian Deli, 163
Johnson, James Weldon, 335
Judaica stores, 198–99, 212–13, 217–18,
  222, 233
Jumel Terrace, 318

K

K & K Restaurant, 271
Kalustyan's (food store), 474
Kam Kuo Food Inc., 428
Kam Wan Restaurant, 13
Kang Suh Restaurant, 448
Karam Restaurant, 302
Karl Ehmer Delicatessen, 57
Katz's Delicatessen, 192
Kavkaz Restaurant, 225
Kee, Wo, 410
Kelly, John, 100
Kelly, Paul (Paolo Vaccareli), 136
Kenara, 472
Kentrikon Astorias Gift Shop, 245
Kentshire Antiques Store, 41
Kerensky, Alexander, 281
Kiev Restaurant, 279
Kim Lau Memorial, 41
King Felafel Restaurant, 302
Kings College, 36
Kingsland Homestead, 32
Kingston Pizza, 216
Kinsale Tavern, 110

Kiryakos Grocery, 244
Kismet Records, 285
Klein's of Monticello (women's clothing
  store), 196
Kleine Deutschland, 45, 47–48, 62
Kleine Konditorei (restaurant), 52
Know Nothings, 99
Ko Hyang Retaurant, 453
Kodesh Religious Articles, 212
Kom Tang Soot Bul House Restaurant, 449
Konijn Eisland (Rabitt Island), 223
Korea Gallery, 447–48
Korean Day Parade, 451
Korean Harvest Festival, 456
Korean Performing Arts Center, 453
Korean Thanksgiving celebration, 451,
  456
Koreans
  associations and cultural centers, 445,
    447, 452–53
  bakeries, 454
  broadcasting, 446
  festivals and observances, 451, 452, 456
  food stores, 450, 454–55
  gift shops, 455
  herbalists, 450–51
  history and settlement, 444–47
  museums and galleries, 447–48
  publications, 446, 450
  restaurants
    in Flushing (Queens), 453
    in Manhattan, 448–49
Koryo Books, 450
Kosciuszko, Thaddeus, 254
Kosciuszko Foundation, 269–70
Kosher Candy (sweet shop), 217
Kosher Castle, 209
Kosher Delight Restaurant, 210
kosher eating. *See* Jews, restaurants and
  food stores
Kosher Korner, 232
Kossar's Bialystoker Kuchen Bakery, 194
Kramer's Pastries, 54
Kryzanowski, Wladimir, 255
Kuh Wah Oriental Food Store, 455
Kum Gang San Restaurant, 454
Kurikka, Matti, 945
Kurowycky Meats, 280
Kwality Restaurant, 483
Kwong Wah Company (bakery), 426

L

La Cabana Argentina Restaurant, 396
La Colombianita (food store), 395
La Famille Restaurant, 325
La Fe Restaurant, 388
La Gran Vía Bakery, 390
La Guardia, Fiorello H., 131, 149, 159
La Kasbah Restaurant, 204
La Marketa Records, 367
La Marquetta, 361–62
La Nosheria Restaurant, 210
La Nueva Bakery, 365
La Nueva Cabana Restaurant, 373
La Pequeña Colombia Restaurant, 394
La Poblanita (food store), 396
La Saline, 352–53
La Selecta Musical (music store), 397
La Victoria China Restaurant, 380
Labelle Capoise Restaurant, 351
Lace-Up Shoe Shop, 197
Landau's Glatt Kosher Deli, 222
Lantern Festival, 431
Latinos. *See* Hispanics
Laura Ashley (clothing store), 40
Laura Ashley Home (furnishings store), 40
Lazarus, Emma, 8–9, 183
Le Madri Restaurant, 155
Le Rendez-Vous Restaurant, 353
Le Soleil Restaurant, 350–51
Lebanese
   associations and cultural centers, 289
   history and settlement, 286–93
   publications, 289
   See also Arabs
Lectorum Libria, 402
Lee Avenue Kosher Bakery, 221
Lee Avenue Kosher Pizza, 221
Lee Avenue Sforim, 220
Lefebvre de Laboulaye, Eduard-Rene, 9
Lefkos Pyrgos Cafe, 242
Leibel Bistritzkys' food store, 193
Leif Ericson Park, 83
L'Ermitage, 284
Les Bonnes Cafe, 454
Leske's Bakery, 83
Leslie Bootery, 197
Levana Restaurant, 204
Levy, Asser, 180
Levy, Moses, 180
Lewis, Francis, 30

Lexington Avenue neighborhood, East
   Indian culture in, 471–72
Lexington Restaurant, 366
Liberty Island. *See* Bedloes Island
Lickety Split (nightclub), 327
Liederkranz singing group, 45
Lillehammer Restaurant, 82
Lincoln Center, 152–53
Litscho, Daniel, 253–54
Little Bohemia, 69–71
"Little Flower." *See* La Guardia, Fiorello
   H.
Little India Emporium, 475
Little Poland Restaurant, 271
Little Shanghai Restaurant, 434
Lolita Clothing Store, 196
Long Island, Greek culture in, 234–40
Los Arrieros Restaurant, 394
Lou S. Siegel's Restaurant, 203
Louis Chock Clothing Store, 197
Lower East Side Festival, 199–200
Lower East Side neighborhood
   German culture in, 47
   Jews in, 186–89
Lower East Side Tenement Museum, 191
Lubavitchers, 213–16, 337
Lucky China Lui Bakery, 426
Luna Restaurant, 139
Lunch Restaurant, 297
Lung Fong Chinese Bakery, 426
Lye Yan Inc. (food store), 428

M

M & I International Foods, 227–28
M. Friedlich Clothing Store, 196
MacMeanin's Restaurant, 13
Madona Bakery, 163
Madras Palace Restaurant, 473
Maggio, Antonio (James March), 136
Magnolia Tree Earth Center Grandiflora,
   333
Mahrajan (Arab Party), 300–301
Main Street 28 Food, Inc., 440
Mambi Restaurants, 372–73
Manchester New York Restaurant, 37
Mandarin Court Restaurant, 422
Manganaro's Groceria, 157
Manhattan
   Arabs in, 304

Manhattan *(continued)*
  East Indians in, 188
  Filipinos in, 465–66
  founders' place marks in, 24–27
  Greeks in, 246–47
  Haitians in, 350
  Irish in, 103–12
  Italians in, 151–54
  Japanese in, 456
  Jews in, 186–89, 199–206
  Koreans in, 188
  Polish in, 268
  Puerto Ricans in, 362
  Scandinavians in, 85–90
Manhattan tribe, 25
Manila Garden Restaurant, 466–67
Manoir Restaurant Banquet, 354–55
Mansoura Pastry, 232
March, James (Antonio Maggio), 136
Marchese Grocery, 164
Marco Polo Restaurant, 174–75
Maria's Bakery, 426
Marimekko Clothing Store, 87–88
Mario's Restaurant, 160
Marti, José, 376
Martin Luther King, Jr., Day Parade, 328
Masaryk, Thomas, 72
Masjid Al Farouq Mosque 294–95
Masjid Malcolm Shabbazz Mosque, 321
Mastellone's Market, 175
Mattie Haskin's Shamrock Imports, 112
Maurya Restaurant, 473
Maxine's Bakery, 354
Mazel Pizza, 210
Mazzei, Filippo, 128
McDaniels Restaurant, 231
McDonald's Dining Room, 333–34
McGuire, Peter J., 100
McMahon's Pub, 116
McSorley's Old Ale House, 110
Medgar Evers College, 339–40
Medici 56, 204
Mehadrin Supermarket, 211
Mehu Gallery, 351–52
Meisner's Glatt Kosher Restaurant, 211
Mejlander & Mulgannon Delicatessen, 84
melting pot, New York as, 1–7, 34
Memories, 284
Menchanko-tei Restaurant, 461
Merkaz Stam Judaica Shop, 218

Mermelstein's Restaurant, 216
Merryland Restaurant, 302
Meson Toledo Restaurant, 403
Metro Manila Restaurant, 466
Metropolitan Opera House, 152–53
Mexicans
  bakeries, 384
  food stores, 384
  history and settlement, 380–82
  music, 384–85
  restaurants, 383–84
Mexico Lindo Bakery, 384
Middle Eastern restaurants, 19
Mideast Bakery, 303
Midwood (Midwout), 229–30
Mike's Delicatessen, 83
Milano Restaurant, 168
Miller's Cheese Store, 193
Minuit, Peter, 22, 25
Mitali Restaurant, 477
Mitsukoshi Restaurant, 460–61
Mittel Europa, settlers from, 42–47
Mocca Restaurant, 64
Moishe's Homemade Kosher Bakery, 194
Molfetas Restaurant, 249
Molnar, Ferenc, 61
Mon Jardin Restaurant, 232
Monitor (warship), 76, 85, 259
Monte Leone's Bakery, 176
Moon Festival
  Chinese, 407, 431
  Korean, 451
Moroccan Star Restaurant, 297
Morris-Jumel Mansion, 27–28
Mos Deli, 228
mosques, 294–95, 302, 304, 305, 321
Most Holy Redeemer Church, 48
Mount Carmelo. *See* Our Lady of Mount Carmel Church
Mount Morris, 370
Mrs. Stahl's Delicious Knishes, 225
Mukerjii, Prafulla C., 470
Mulberry Bend neighborhood, 129
Mulberry Street neighborhood, Italians in, 134–38
Muñoz Marín, Luis, 358
Murphy, Charles Francis, 100–101
Murray Hill, 32
Museum of the City of New York, 14–15

museums and archives showing ethnic history, 13–15. *See also under specific nationalities*
Mussolini, Benito, 132
Mutual Cut Flowers, 247
Myers of Keswick food shop, 38
Myung Dong Kai Gunk Soo Restaurant, 449

N

N. Peal Clothing Store, 40
N. Y. Noodle Town, 425
Nassau Meat Market, 267
National (restaurant/nightclub), 227
National Black Theater, 324
National Cafe, 377
National Greek Heritage Folklore Festival, 245
National Museum of the American Indian, 25
Native Americans
  during early European settlement, 21, 22, 32–34, 74
  in Civil War draft protests, 99
  National Museum of the American Indian, 25
Natural Oriental Herb Store, 450–51
Near East Bakery, 298
Near East Restaurant, 297
neighborhoods, guidelines for exploring, v–vi
Netherlands Benevolent Society, 35
Netherlands Memorial Monument, 25
Netherlands-America Community Association, 35
Netherlands-America Foundation, 35
New Acropolis Restaurant, 249
New Amsterdam colony, 22–23, 42
New Chao Chow Restaurant, 423
New Manila Food Market, 467
New Netherlands, 22–23
New Orange, 23
New School of Social Research, 185
New Utrecht. *See* Brooklyn
New Viet Huong Restaurant, 442
New Vietnam Restaurant, 442
New York Aquarium, 8
New York Kom Tang Soot Bul House Restaurant, 449

New York Zen Center, 458
New-York Historical Society, 14
Nick's Bakery, 347
Nieue Harlem, 315
Ninth Avenue Fair, 18–19
Nippon Club, 457
Nitin Bakery, 373
Nom Wah Tea House, 427
Nordic Delicacies Delicatessen, 84
Nordisk Tidende (newspaper), 81
Norsemen's Federation, New York Chapter, 81
North Carolina Country Kitchen Restaurant, 334
North Star Pub, 13, 37
Norwegian Seamen's Church, 85–86
Norwegians
  associations and cultural centers, 79
  festivals and observances, 78–78, 79, 84–85
  gift shops, 84
  history and settlement, 77–80
  in Bay Ridge, 80–81
  places of worship, 85–86
  publications, 79, 81
Nosh World Ice Cream Store, 217
Nureyev, Rudolph, 281
NW3, 37
Nyborg and Nelson Restaurant, 87

O

O'Flannagan's Bar, 111–12
Obon Festival, 462
occupations and businesses, immigrant clustering in, 7
Ocean Palace Seafood Restaurant, 434
Ocean Star Seafood Corp., 429
Odessa (nightclub), 226
Odessa Coffee Shop, 279
Old Poland Bakery, 265
Old Poland Restaurant, 263–64
Olsen's Bakery, 83
Oriental Gallery, 416
Oriental Garden Seafood Restaurant, 423
Oriental Palace Chinese Seafood Restaurant, 434
Oriental Pearl Banquet Hall, 420–21
Original Vincent's Restaurant, 140

Orwasher's Appetizer Shop, 205
Ossie's Table, 210
Otto Chicas Rendon Botánica, 366
Ottomanelli's Meat Market, 147
Our Lady of Guadalupe Church (Spanish),
    401, 404
Our Lady of Lebanon Church (Maronite),
    294, 301
Our Lady of Mount Carmel Church, 150,
    157, 159
Our Lady of Pompeii Church, 144–45, 148
Oval Park Delicatessen, 117–18
Owls Head Park, 123

P

Paco's Botánica, 367
Paddy's Field, 103
Paddy's Market, 18–19
Pakistanis. *See* East Indians
Palantine Germans, 1, 43. *See also*
    Germans
Pan Am Men's Wear, 197
Pan-Asian Repertory Theater, 417
Panacea Herb Shop, 267
Paola's Restaurant, 156
Paolucci's Restaurant, 139
Paprika Weiss, Importers, 65
Park Heights Records, 344
Pasta Factory, 163
Pasta Fresca, 172
Pastosa Ravioli Company, 177
Pastrami Factory (delicatessen), 13
Patel Brothers (food store), 484
Patrissy's Restaurant, 140
Patsy's Pizza, 151
Peck Slip, 12
Pedro Paramo Restaurant, 383
Peggy O'Neill's Pub, 124
Pei, I. M., 409
Peking Duck House, 422
Pennsylvania Station, 75
People's Flower Corp., 247, 248
People's Hall of Fame, 15
Periyali Restaurant, 249
Philippine Center, 465–66
Philippine Independence Day celebration,
    467–68
Phillip Colleck of London Ltd. (antiques
    store), 41

Pho Bang Restaurant, 442–43
Pho Tu Do Restaurant, 443
Piccolo Mondelo Pescheria, 172
Pie Restaurant, 283
Piemonte Homemade Ravioli Company,
    142
Pier 17, 13
Pietersen, Mons, 75
Pilgrims of the United States, 36
Pizza Margherita Caffe, 162
Pleasant Grove Kitchen, 333
Plow and Harrow District, 410
Pod Strechna Restaurant, 263
Poles
    associations and cultural centers,
        257–58, 259, 261, 269–70
    bakeries, 265–66
    festivals and observances, 272–73
    delicatessens, 266–67
    food stores, 267, 271–72
    gift shops, 267–68
    history and settlement, 253–58
    museums and galleries, 261–62, 269–70
    music, 261–62, 267–68, 270
    natural products stores, 267
    publications, 255, 257, 267–68, 270
    restaurants
        in Greenpoint (Brooklyn), 262–64
        in Manhattan, 270–71
Police Academy Museum, 105
Police Headquarters, 104–105
Polish American Bookstore (*Polska
    Ksiegarnia*), 268
Polish and Slavic Credit Union, 262, 264
Polish Artists' Gallery, 269
Polish Book Center, 262
Polish Book Center (*Centrum Ksiask
    Polskiej*), 267
Polish Institute of Arts and Sciences, 269
Polish National Alliance of Brooklyn,
    U.S.A. (PNA), 261
Polonia Restaurant, 271
Polska Ksiegarnia (Polish American
    Bookstore), 268
Polska Restaurant, 264
Pope John Paul II Square, 261
Popieluszko, Jerzy, monument, 261
Portal Norteño Restaurant, 396
Porto Rico Importing Company, 147
Poseidon Bakery, 250

potato famines, as influence on immigration, 2, 44, 98
Poznanski's Bakery, 266
Primavera Restaurant, 155
Primorski Restaurant, 225
Prince of India Restaurant, 476
publications, ethnic, 16–17. *See also under specific nationalities*
Puerto Rican Day Parade, 368
Puerto Ricans
  arts, 362–63, 364
  associations and cultural centers, 363
  bakeries, 364–65
  botánicas, 366–67
  festivals and observances, 368
  history and settlement, 4, 5, 356–62
  museums, 362
  music, 367–68
  publications, 357, 360
  restaurants, 363–64
Puglia of Little Italy Restaurant, 139–40
Pulaski, Casimir, 254
Pulaski Day Parade, 254, 272–73
Pulitzer, Joseph, 9, 60
Puski-Corvin Bookstore, 63

Q
Quakers, history and settlement of, 30, 31, 32
Queen's Head Tavern, 26
Queen Ann Ravioli & Macaroni Inc., 172
Queens
  ethnic shifts in, 6
  Irish culture in, 120–22
Queens Korean Culture Society, 452
Quong Yuen Shin & Company (gift shop), 430

R
Rabbi Eisenbach Judaica Store, 198
Rabbit Island (*Konijn Eisland*), 223
Raffetto Ravioli Store, 148
Rafi Food Store, 233
Ramadan observance, 307
Randazzo's Steak House and Restaurant, 168
Rao's Restaurant, 150
Rashid Sales (music store), 300

Rasputin (restaurant/nightclub), 227
Rastafarians, 340
Ratner's Dairy Restaurant and Bakery, 192
Raven Chanticleer's African American Wax Museum of Harlem, 322–23
Rebbe's House, 215
Red Hook, 136, 173–74
Red Tulip Restaurant, 64
Remnant of Israel (*Shearith Israel*), 180
Remsen House, 238
Restaurant Caridad, 372
restaurants. *See listings for specific ethnic groups*
Restauration, celebration of landing of, 77–78, 79
Reyniers, Griet, 309
Rhinelander Sugar House Prison Window Monument, 105
Riazor Restaurant, 403
Richmond Restoration, 33–34
Richmond. *See* Staten Island
Ridgewood, German culture in, 55–57
Rigo Hungarian Viennese Pastry, 65
Riverdale neighborhood, 456
Roaring Twenties Pub, 116
Rocco Restaurant, 145
Rocco's Cafe & Bakery, 146
Rolf's German-American Restaurant, 53
Roma Luncheonette, 161
Ronin Gallery, 458
Ronnie's Bakery, 342
Rosa Mexicano Restaurant, 383–84
Rose Restaurant, 353
Roumeli Taverna, 241
Royal Copenhagen Porcelain, 88
Rudy's Bakery, 57
Rugby neighborhood, 345
Ruppert, Jacob, 44
Russ & Daughters Bakery, 194
Russian House Gift Shop & Bookstore, 284
Russian Jews. *See* Jews
Russian Nobility Association in America, 282
Russian Orthodox Church Synod of Bishops Outside Russia, 282
Russian Samovar Restaurant, 283
Russian Tea Room, 283
Russian World, 285
Russians
  associations and cultural centers, 282

Russians *(continued)*
  catering, 284
  gift shops, 284–85
  history and settlement, 281–82
  music, 283, 284, 285
  restaurants, 283–84
Ryan's Ale House, 124
Ryan's Irish Pub, 111
Rzeszowska Bakery, 265
Rzeszowska Restaurant, 262

S

S. J. Shrubsole Antiques Store, 41
S.A.S. Italian Records, 173
Sabor Restaurant, 377
Sahadi Importing Company (food store),
  299
Sahara East Restaurant, 305
Saigon Restaurant, 442
Saint Jacques Majeure & Sainte Viergo
  Botanica, 355
Sakura Matsura (Cherry Blossom
  Festival), 462
Sally O'Brien's Pub, 122
Salonge, Lea, 465
Salute to Israel Parade, 206–207
Sam's Restaurant, 175
Sam Bok Food Store, 455
Sam Ship Iga (Koreatown), 447–48
Sambuca (restaurant/nightclub), 374
Sammy's Rumanian Jewish Restaurant, 192
San Domingue, 348
Sander's Kosher Bakery Shop, 221
Sandy's Lechonería, 364
Sapna Sari Palace, 475
sari stores, 475, 481, 484–85
Satmar sect, 218–20
Savoy, 435
Sbarro's Salumeria, 171
Scandinavian Design (furniture store), 88
Scandinavians
  associations and cultural centers, 86–87
  bakeries, 82–83
  clothing and furnishings, 87–89
  delicatessens, 83–84
  gift shops, 88
  history and settlement, 73–80
  in Manhattan, 85–90
  organizations and culture clubs, 81
  restaurants, 81–82, 86–87

Schaller & Weber Delicatessen, 54
Schapiro's House of Kosher and
  Sacramental Wines, 194
Schermerhorn Row, 13
Schomburg Center for Research in Black
  Culture, 323
Scotch. *See* British
Sea King Sea Food & Meat Market, 436
Sea Lane Bakery, 228
Second Avenue Deli, 206
Secrets of Beauty (cosmetics shop), 267
Seligman, Joseph, 182
Serengetti Craft Shop, 344
Sette Mezzo Restaurant, 155
74th Street neighborhood, East Indian
  culture in, 481–82
Shaarey Shimoyim Synagogue, 190
Shabbos Fish Market, 217
Shapiro's House of Kosher & Sacramental
  Wines, 194
Sharaku Restaurant, 461
Shearith Israel (Remnant of Israel), 180
Shere Punjab Restaurant, 480
Shneerson, Rabbi Menachem M., 213, 214
Showman's Lounge, 327
Shrine of Our Lady of Mount Carmel,
  150
Shulie's Clothing Store, 196
Shumiana, 480
Shun An Tong (herbalist), 440
Sido, 306
Signes Imports (gift shop), 84
Sikh Day Parade, 478
Silver Palace Banquet Hall, 420
Silver Swan Restaurant, 53
Simchas Torah Festival (Willliamsburg),
  222–223
Singh's Hot Roti, 342
Sisu Curio Shop, 233
slavery, in early New York, 309–10
Slavs. *See under specific nationalities*
Snaps Restaurant, 87
Snooky's, 326
Snow Queen Food Store, 467
Sobor Icons, 285
Somalis, immigration of, 293
Sona Chaandi Jewelers, 485
Sonali Restaurant, 476
South River Restaurant, 453
South Street Seaport, 12–13
South Village, Italians in, 146–50

Southeast Asia Food Trading Company, 443

Southern Deli, 227

Soviet Four Continents Bookstore, 284

Soviet Jews. *See* Jews

Spain Restaurant, 403

Spaniards
  associations and cultural centers, 401, 404
  festivals and observances, 404
  history and settlement, 400–401
  museums and archives, 402
  publications, 402
  restaurants, 403
  theater, 403

Spanish Harlem, 360–61

Spanish Institute, 402

Sporting Club Gjoa, 81

SPQR (restaurant), 139

St. Anthony's Catholic Church, 144

St. Anthony's Festa, 148, 158, 159

St. Demetrios Greek Orthodox Church, 238, 239

St. George's Church (Melkite), 304

St. George's Episcopal Church, 30–31

St. George's Society of New York, 36

St. George's Ukrainian Catholic Church, 275, 277, 281

St. Irene of Chrysovalantou Greek Orthodox Church, 239–40

St. Jacques Botanica, 355

St. John Nepomucene Catholic Church, 71

St. Joseph's Church (Maronite), 304

St. Lucia Day celebrations, 89–90

St. Marc Boulangerie, 354

St. Mark's-in-the-Bouwerie, 27

St. Mark Records, 354

St. Martin's Episcopal Church, 321

St. Nicholas Greek Orthodox Church, 251–52

St. Nicholas Patriarchal Cathedral (Russian Orthodox), 282

St. Patrick's Cathedral (old and new), 99, 107

St. Patrick's Cathedral Rectory, 107

St. Patrick's Day Parade, 99
  in Bay Ridge, 125

St. Paul's Chapel, 26–27

St. Phillips Protestant Episcopal Church, 320

St. Rosalia Society, 173

St. Stan's neighborhood, 260

St. Stanislaus Catholic Church (Manhattan), 269

St. Stanislaus Kostka Catholic Church (Greenpoint), 259, 260–61

St. Stephen's Day (Hungarian) celebration, 66

St. Stephen's of Hungary Catholic Church, 62, 63

Stage Deli, 206

Stani Restaurant, 243

Starpolski Delicatessen, 266

Starting Gate Pub, 122

State Office Building 319–20, 321

Staten Island, founders' place marks on, 32–34

Statue of Liberty, 8–10, 33

Steeple Chase Park, 126

Steve's Delicatessen, 266–67

Stodyce Wedel Candy Shop, 266

Straker's Caribbean Record World, 343–44

Strauss Bakery, 211

Stravinsky, Igor, 281

Striver's Row neighborhood, 318–19

Studio Museum, 322, 328

Stuyvesant, Peter (colonial governor), 1, 22, 24, 27, 30, 55, 180, 309

Stuyvesant Clinic, 48

Stylowa Restaurant, 263

Sudanese, immigration of, 293

Sugar Hill neighborhood, 318

Sun Golden Island Restaurant, 423

Sun Hop Shing Tea House, 427

Sun Say Gay Restaurant, 424

Sunset Park neighborhood, 91
  Chinese culture in, 432–33
  Finnish culture in, 92–93
  Hispanic culture in, 385–88

Sunshine Restaurant, 424

Surma (The Ukrainian Shop), 280

sushi bars, 460–62

Sushi Hatsu, 460

Swedes
  associations and cultural centers, 75, 76, 77
  festivals and observances, 89–90
  history and settlement, 75–77
  places of worship, 86
  publications, 75, 76

Swedish Seamen's Church, 86

Sybil's Bakery, 347–48
Sylvia's Restaurant, 325
synagogues, 190, 201–202, 209, 220–21
Synod of Bishops of the Russian Orthodox
    Church Outside Russia, 282
Syrians
    Christians, history and settlement of,
      286–93. *See also* Arabs
    Jews, history and settlement of, 229–30
Sziliard, Leo, 61

T

Tacos Mexico Restaurant, 396
Tai Hong Lau Restaurant, 421
Tai Tung Rice Shop, 424
Taipan Bakery, 439
Taiwan Center, 437
Taiwanese. *See* Chinese
Take-Out Shop, 440
Taller Boriqua, 363
Tamarind Tree Restaurant, 346–47
Tammany Hall, 97, 131, 186, 293, 336
Taverna Vraka, 243
Tea and Sympathy Restaurant, 38
Teitelbaum, Rabbi Joel, 219
Teller, Edward, 61
Telly's Taverna, 241
Temple Emanu-El, 183
Temple Emmanuel-El, 201
Temple Shearith Israel, 180
Ten Ren Tea & Ginseng Company, 427
Tequalita's Restaurant, 389
Teresa's Restaurant, 271
Terranova Bakery, 162
Terranova Pasta. *See* Pasta Factory
Tet New Year, 443–44
Theresa Towers, 320
Tibor Meat Specialties, 65
Tino's Salumeria, 163
Titanic Memorial Lighthouse, 13
Todaro Brothers food store, 157
Tombs, The, 104
Tommaso's Restaurant, 168
Tommy Makem's Irish Pavillion (pub), 110
Tompkins Square Park, 47, 48, 279
Toraya Restaurant, 461–62
Tota's West Indian Bakery, 343
Traditional Irish Bakery, 118, 119
transportation, ix–x

Trastevere Restaurant, 204
Trattoria Pesce Pasta, 146
Trattoria Spagetto, 146
Tri-Eddy's Deli, 119
Trinity Church and Churchyard, 26
Triple Eight Palace Banquet Hall, 420
Tripoli Restaurant, 296
Trotsky, Leon, 281
Trunzo Brothers Meat Market, 171–72
Tsai, Gerald, 409
Tsakonas, Chriastos, 235
Turkish restaurants, 19
Tweed, William Marcy ("Boss"), 100
22 West Restaurant, 325
Tzivos Hashem Toy Store, 218

U

U.S. Custom House, 25
Ukrainian East Village Restaurant, 279
Ukrainian Institute of America, 277
Ukrainian Museum, 277
Ukrainian National Home, 279
Ukrainian Shop (Surma), 280
Ukrainians
    associations and cultural centers, 274,
      275–76
    bakeries, 279
    festivals and observances, 280–81
    food stores, 279
    gift shops, 280
    history and settlement, 273–75
    museums, 277
    music, 275, 277–78
    restaurants, 278–79
Umberto's Clam House, 139
Uncle George's Diner, 241
Uncle Nick's Restaurant, 249
Uncle Vanya Restaurant, 283
Union Franco-Americaine, 9
Upper East Side neighborhood, Italians in,
    151–54
Uptown neighborhood, Italians in, 151–54

V

Vaccareli, Paolo (Paul Kelly), 136
Valencia Bakery, 365
Valentine-Varian House, 29–30, 115
Van Cortlandt Mansion, 29

Van Cortlandt Park, 118
Van Salee, Jansz, 309
Varians, 29
Vasata Restaurant, 72
Verdi, Giuseppe, monument, 154
Verrazano, Francisco, monument, 154
Verrazano Bridge, 33
Veselka Restaurant, 278
Via Brazil Restaurant, 399
Victor's Cafe 54, 378
Viennese restaurants, 13
Vietnamese
  festivals, 443–44
  food stores, 443
  history and settlement, 5, 440
  restaurants, 441–43
Villabate Bakery, 171
Village Irish Imports Plus, 124
Vincent's The Original Restaurant, 140
Vincent's Meat Market, 164
Vinegar Hill neighborhood, 123
Viva Mexicano Restaurant, 395–96
Vlissinge. See Flushing
Von Steuben Day Parade, 49, 58–59
Voudou rites, 355

W

Wald, Lillian, 183, 191
Waldman's Dry Goods, 222
Wall Street Stockade, 24
Wallabout Bay, 122
Wang, An, 409
Wang, Wayne, 409
Ward, Samuel Ringold, 311
Wardard China and Porcelain, Inc., 430
Washington, George, 26, 29, 66, 123, 310, 370
Washington Heights
  Cuban culture in, 371
  Dominican culture in, 370–71
  founders' place marks in, 27–28
Wax Museum, 322–23
Wayt House, 238
Wedding Coach Bridal Shop, 172
Weeksville Society, 332–33
Weeksville-Carrsville, 329
Weinfeld's Skull Caps, 199
Weiss Bakery, 211
Well's (nightclub), 327

Welsh. See British
West Battery. See Castle Clinton
West Indian Carnival, 215, 344–45
West Indian Day Parade, 339
West Indians
  associations and cultural centers, 336
  bakeries, 342–43, 347–48
  festivals, 339, 344, 345
  clothing and crafts stores, 344
  in Crown Heights, 214–15
  history and settlement, 4, 5, 334–37, 345–46
  music, 343–44
  restaurants
    in Crown Heights, 340–42
    in Flatbush, 346–47
White Eagle Bakery, 266
Wicked Monk Pub, 124
Wigner, Eugene, 61
Williamsburg
  Hispanic culture in, 219
  Jewish culture in, 218–23
Williamsburg Bridge, 136
Williamson's Irish Imports, 13
Wilson's Bakery & Restaurant, 325
Wim and Karen's Scandinavian Furniture, 88
Windows on India, 477
Wo, Kee, 410
Won Ton Garden Noodle Shop, 425
Woodlawn, Irish in, 118–19
Woodlawn Cemetery, 118
Woodside, Irish in, 120–22
Works Progress Administration (WPA) art, 11
Wui Chuen Company, 429

Y

Yah Hong Chinese Herbs, 436
Yankee Stadium, 44
Yao Han Restaurant, 438
Yarmulowsky's Bank, 189
Ye Mei Fung Bakery, 439
Yellow Hook. See Bay Ridge
Yemeni Cafe, 296
Yeshiva University Museum, 202
Yivo Institute for Jewish Study, 202
Yonah Schimmel Knishes Bakery, 194
Yorkville
  Czechs in, 68–69

Yorkville *(continued)*
  Germans in, 45, 48–49, 50
  Hungarians in, 61, 62–66
Yorkville Casino, 49
Yorkville Packing House, 66
Young Israel Beth El Synagogue, 209
Ypsilanti, Alexander, 250

Z

Zabar's Appetizer Shop, 205
zacharoplasteia. See Greeks, bakeries

Zakopane Gift Shop, 268
Zakrzewska, Marie, 255
Zaro's Restaurant, 13
Zelig Blumenthal Judaica store, 199
Zen Buddhist centers, 415, 437, 457–58
Zen Oriental Book Store, 458
Zen Studies Center, 458
Ziegfield, Florenz, 46, 323
Zito & Sons Bakery, 147
Zolotoy Kluchnik (food store), 228
Zygos Taverna, 241